STAR SONGS AND
WATER SPIRITS

STAR SONGS AND

WATER SPIRITS

A GREAT LAKES NATIVE READER

Edited by Victoria Brehm

Ladyslipper Press
Tustin, Michigan

Star Songs and Water Spirits: A Great Lakes Native Reader
First edition, ©Victoria Brehm, 2011
All rights reserved
Introductions, notes, index, and chronology copyright Victoria Brehm, 2011

Library of Congress Cataloging-in-Publication Data
Brehm, Victoria
Star Songs and Water Spirits: A Great Lakes Native Reader
1. Indians—Great Lakes Region—literature
2. Indians—Great Lakes Region—social life and customs
3. Indians—Great Lakes Region—history
Includes index, bibliography, and chronology

ISBN 978-0-9843340-0-1
Printed in the United States of America
Design and production: Boreal Press
Cover: Clarity

Ladyslipper Press
15075 County Line Road
Tustin, Michigan 49688

Dedicated to those Great Lakes Native artists
who have been willing to share their stories with the world.

Approximate locations of major and (removed) Great Lakes nations

Haundosaunee refers to the Six Nations of the Iroquois Confederacy: Mohawk, Cayuga, Onondaga, Oneida, Seneca, and Tuscarora.

Huron-Wendat refers to the original Wendat who migrated to Quebec; Wyandot refers to the Wendat who migrated to the USA.

Ojibwe and Chippewa are the same linguistic group divided by Lake Superior.

Ho-Chunk and Winnebago are the same nation, split between Wisconsin and Nebraska.

CONTENTS
▼▼▼▼▼▼▼▼▼▼

The Diaspora

I come back from the diaspora,
I have walked and walked
thinking that somewhere
I would find a piece of land
like the one I had before
with those beautiful valleys
those geese and this immense blue sky.
I come back from the diaspora,
I have walked and walked
thinking that somewhere
I would find my brothers,
Are they still my brothers?
Do we still pray the same god?
Do we still sing the same songs?
Do we still look the same?
I come back from the diaspora,
Would you still offer me a meal?
Would you still tell me one of your stories?
I come back from the diaspora,
my ancestors haven't left a thing,
haven't left a written history about them,
I saw the photos of my family on a wall somewhere,
I saw the pipe of my grandfather in a museum somewhere,
I saw my culture being told by strangers.
I come back from the diaspora,
Is it really the end of the one way?
Is it really the end of the brutality?

Claudine Sioui, Huron-Wendat, 2004

Claudine Sioui (1957-   ) lives in Quebec City, where she teaches Spanish. She was inspired to write "The Diaspora" after a friend told her he had seen his grandfather's pipe in a museum. She then remembered "the sad, mixed emotion that many Native people share in silence: even as they are kept apart from what is theirs, there is a choked joy to reconnect with their identity. Is it possible to put all the broken pieces together again?"

STAR SONGS AND
WATER SPIRITS

❖ GREAT LAKES NATIVE LITERATURES ❖

The Song of the Stars

We are the stars which sing,	Nilun pesazmuk elintakquik,
We sing with our light.	Nt'lintotebin k'pesaukhenmâgonok,
We are the birds of fire	Nilun sipsizuk squ´tek;
We fly across the heaven,	K'p'mitoiapon pissokiqs
Our light is a star.	K'pesaukhenmagon pesazum.
We make a road for Spirits,	K't'lintoanen âût niwesquok;
A road for the Great Spirit.	Otâût K'chî-Niwesq.
Among us are three hunters	Koitchimkononnoak nohowok katonkewinoak,
Who chase a bear:	Nosokoat moinial
There never was a time	Nit mesq tepnaskwiewis
When they were not hunting;	Mesqkatonketitiq
We look down on the mountains.	Ketlapinen pemtenikek
This is the Song of the Stars.	Yot lintoak'n [pesazmuk].[1]

From *Kalóskap the Master, and Other Algonkin Poems*,
Charles Godfrey Leland and John Dyneley Prince, 1902

Ten thousand years ago when the glacier retreated growling to the north, a freshwater world was born. The stars were radiant then, and their brightness filled the night. Before industry lit the ceaseless, smoking fires that transformed the land, waters, and sky, the stars that rose and set over the waves of the Great Lakes sang to the humans who watched them, sometimes enviously, from below. They sent messengers to guard their sacred chestnut trees, and they drew humans to them with their power and their beauty. Together with the Great Spirit, they dispatched the sky warriors—the thunderbirds—to battle the spirits of the underwater deeps—the serpents and lynxes—so the world might be restored to balance and humans live in peace and plenty. The peoples who watched the stars arc above their campsites, who traveled the unpredictable waters first in skin boats and then in bark canoes buoyant as leaves, knew creatures who came in dreams with lessons from a world alive in all directions. Humans did not rule this world, but they could learn to survive in it, and telling the stories that came from the messengers was one way to ensure their hard-won knowledge would live on. Although they could scarce have imagined how the stars would grow dim and the world would be transformed, their stories have endured.

A fluted spear point, dropped or lost in the hunt, may endure for ten thousand years, and a number of them in the Great Lakes region have. But what of the stories the hunter who lost that point listened to around the campfire as he made more points for tomorrow? Knapping, or flaking, a point for a spear, or later an arrow, is a tedious business. A good craftsman can turn one out in about a half-hour, faster if he's experienced and in a hurry, but stone points, especially flint, which is thirty times sharper than steel, are also fragile. It took hundreds of points a year to kill the game necessary to live, and that meant much time spent in a boring, repetitive task. Weaving mats and bags and tanning skins—women's work—was no less humdrum. Stories have always been a way to pass the time, to entertain and to teach as well, because they make sense of experience, explaining the world and commenting on its problems. That the world of the first storytellers who lived by the lakes was different in climate, landscape, and culture, that their stories were not written down, does not mean important ones were lost. Oral literatures are remarkably resilient. Flood stories, like Noah and his ark, were told for millennia before one ended up as a moral in the Old Testament. The tales Homer told about Troy were recited for centuries before a scribe transcribed them; even then they were precise enough that nineteenth-century archaeologists used them to locate and excavate the ruins. The poem that begins this introduction is a story about the northern lights (birds of fire), the Milky Way (road of the spirits), and the origin of the constellation Ursa Major that has been told by Natives in the northern reaches around the world for thousands of years.Cultures that don't need writing train storytellers whose task is to remember and recount ritual and history as accurately as possible, so nothing important will be lost.

The key word is "important." What is important to a culture changes over time, so some stories disappear, replaced by others that are more relevant to new leaders or new ceremonies. Older stories may be retold, but the details change to reflect a transformed reality, for example, the introduction of Christian elements in a sacred Great Lakes creation story that appears to be far older than the coming of black-robed priests in the 1600s, or the disappearance of star stories when they were no longer needed to predict planting and harvesting times. One scholar has written sensitively of the connections between history and story:

> The historical past was real, but the evidence that survives of it can be distorted and disconnected, like a shadow cast on a field of rocks. The evidence includes traditions often imperfectly transmitted between generations; ceremonies whose symbolism has changed to become supportive of new values; origin myths naturalized to new locations; ceremonial objects whose full significance was known only to elders who have died; the bones of Indians whose deaths silenced personal stories that still await telling; buried artifacts that speak of technologies long forgotten; and earth constructions that speak of rituals long abandoned.[2]

Stories, unlike bones or fire pits, can't be radiocarbon dated. They are not fossils. They are living things that are changed and adapted by their tellers for their own purposes, but this does not mean that the creatures of the oldest Great Lakes stories no longer exist. They are caught in a web of ancient time that knows no calendar but its own.

When Beaver Was Very Great

Anne M. Dunn, Anishinâbe

IT HAPPENED IN THE LONG, LONG AGO THAT BEAVER WAS VERY GREAT. He walked upright and stood as tall as the tallest man. Furthermore, Beaver was highly intelligent and deeply spiritual. Beaver had the ability to improve his environment and make it more hospitable for many other animals, too.

Beaver established communities of families that worked together to build great earthen lodges. The lodges were so well constructed that Beaver did not have to gather wood for fires to heat the lodges. Beaver did not have to make robes or clothing of any kind because they were blessed with fur-covered bodies.

Beaver had wonderful long sharp teeth which allowed them to fell large trees with ease. Beaver often cut trees for their human neighbors whom Beaver had grown to pity. In exchange, Beaver asked only for the tender bark and twigs to store for winter food. During warm weather, Beaver probed the bottom of lakes and rivers for roots and relished many kinds of greens. Beaver made long canals and built fine roads throughout their territory which made transport and travel easier. They shared the canals and roadways with their neighbors.

The Anishinabe learned many good things by observing Beaver. Beaver bathed several times a day. Soon, people adopted these habits of cleanliness and good grooming practices.

Beaver were excellent parents and raised respectful, industrious children. So the Anishinabe imitated Beaver's parenting skills. Beaver worked hard to accomplish good deeds that would benefit the entire community. They did not quarrel and fight among themselves and did not make enemies of their neighbors. They experienced no jealousy when others excelled.

Therefore, as time went on, Beaver prospered more than people. So a delegation of men went to Creator and reminded him that he had promised that they would be the greatest of all created beings. Then they pointed out that Beaver had surpassed people in many things. The people demanded that Creator do something to restore their original role and reduce the status and power of Beaver.

Creator said, "If people need an advantage over Beaver in order to surpass him, I will limit Beaver's stature and cause him to desire to live only in and on the water."

The delegates were satisfied and returned to their lodges.

Beaver did not diminish all at once, but each generation became smaller than the one before, and after many years they have become the Beaver we know today. But Creator allowed Beaver to retain all of their previous skills. They are still intelligent, industrious, and generous. They still work together to modify their habitat and build secure lodges which they share with extended families. They are still affectionate, considerate, and kind. They do not fight and quarrel among themselves and have only a few enemies. Beaver's greatest enemy is Man. Man, who learned so many things from our little brother, but failed to learn the important lesson of building inclusive communities.

Because of Beaver's character and former greatness, the Anishinabe believe that they are still worthy of great respect. Therefore, it is dishonorable to allow a dog to eat Beaver flesh, for the dog has never been as great as Beaver, nor can it ever be.

1995

Judging from many traditional Great Lakes Native stories that were first written down in the nineteenth century, some of them may be old indeed: giant beavers became extinct in the lakes region about nine thousand years ago. The lakes as we know them now seem eternal, but they are comparatively young; their shorelines and water levels are only about two thousand years old. Before that, for ten thousand years, shorelines changed as the waters rose or fell, the climate warmed or cooled, rivers appeared or vanished, and cultures came or left. Do the many flood narratives told by lakes nations date from the Middle Archaic period when melting glaciers raised lake levels by hundreds of feet, sometimes catastrophically, drowning forests, islands, and lakeside hunting camps? Melting ice water bursting from behind a glacial ice dam released one hundred trillion cubic meters of cold, fresh water—more than the current volume of the Great Lakes—into the Labrador Sea about eight thousand years ago, affecting climate around the world for two centuries and bringing on a much colder period than before. The most severe cold spell in the last ten thousand years, it would be odd if this deluge hadn't affected literature, but did those stories, or parts of them, survive? Lake levels could drop just as precipitously, miraculously it would seem to peoples who were not conversant in glacial geology. There are stories of gigantic man-swallowing fish that may have been based on the sturgeon, which can grow to

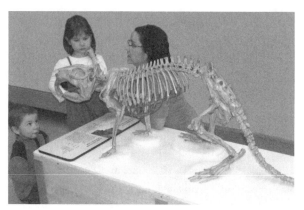

Giant beaver skeleton, 10,000-8000 BC, with Bernard Dufour, Gaïa Dufour, and Kathleen Brosseau

nine feet, weigh three hundred pounds, and live more than a century. In the 1700s an aged Lake Superior chief told of mastodons, animals that became extinct during the Paleoindian period thousands of years ago. Did he know of them because the chain of Native cultures on the Great Lakes is still unbroken so a story can endure, passed from storyteller to storyteller, for uncounted generations? Or did someone, perhaps generations before him and in a different place, dream a story after seeing a skeleton leached out of a riverbank in spring?

Scholars maintain that narratives about floods and gigantic creatures are archetypal—that is, they are prevalent all over the world in all cultures—and are imaginary, told to make sense of universal fears and cultural change. Although stories may incorporate historical information, it is frequently transformed, so that the point is not the flood or the creature that inspired the plot, but how spirits and humans reacted—the moral lesson—because in order to remain relevant, traditional knowledge must adjust to change. The first story told about a giant beaver may have been quite different from the one reprinted here; it may or may not have been passed down, changing in the process, for nine millennia. But the existence of this story in the present is a link to that past, however tenuous, and so it is with the past that we must begin.

6

The Great Lakes Before Contact

In the beginning, everyone was a hunter. The glacier that had locked the land in ice for more than a million years had begun to retreat a bit, to present-day Port Huron, Michigan, and northern Wisconsin, allowing the soft, dark trees and elusive animals of the spruce and fir-clad boreal forest to begin to flourish south of the tundra that met the rivers and glacial lakes of the ice front. The climate was wetter and colder than it would be later, but the hunting was good. Paleoindian peoples, nomadic big game hunters who lived ten to fourteen thousand years before the present, followed the mastodon, giant beavers, deer, elk, and barren-ground caribou north into the new Great Lakes country.

Archaeologists refer to these hunters as Paleoindians because no one knows what they called themselves, and they ranged across much of the continent, hunting wherever the land was glacier-free. They were nomadic by necessity, following the game herds and hunting cooperatively in small groups. The techniques they used for bringing down a mastodon can only be guessed. Their sharp, fluted, flint points were attached to a detachable bone spear shaft mounted on a handle. This technology allowed each hunter to thrust several foreshafts into the animal until a vital organ was struck. Perhaps the large animals were also driven into a deadfall or swamp or hamstrung in some way. Smaller animals would have been dispatched quickly by a well-aimed foreshaft with its razor-sharp point. When the mastodons disappeared and other big game moved north, some of these hunters may have followed to become the ancestors of the Cree and Ojibwe. Some stayed in the ice-free portions of the Great Lakes basin and developed new hunting techniques and different points for the game that had remained or had begun migrating into the area as the climate warmed.

Paleoindian points from Michigan and Ohio

The archaeological record is not complete, but it does suggest that everywhere across North America Paleoindian hunters were gradually replaced by or changed into three cultures termed Early, Middle, and Late Archaic, which lasted from about eight thousand years ago until the beginning of the Woodland cultures about three thousand years ago. In the Great Lakes region, Archaic peoples hunted and gathered wild foods; they also fished and traveled in small boats from mainland camps to offshore islands for the summer. Rather than follow large, migratory game animals, they capitalized on the diverse local foods that became available as the climate grew much warmer than contemporary peoples have ever known it. They became adept at using locally available minerals for tools, including copper, along with the flint of earlier eras that, in many regions, meant traveling long distances to obtain. They buried their dead ceremoniously, with red ochre coloring (powdered hematite) that they found close to home, with precious shells obtained in trade from far away, and with spear points and polishing stones for the hunts that came after death.

In the western Lake Superior region, one Archaic culture specialized in using copper to supplement bone tools and ornaments such as beads. The Old Copper Complex of cultures apparently began using float copper from streams and nuggets found in glacial drift to cold hammer into tools. As they invented mining techniques to separate copper from the veins and bedrock on Isle Royale and the Keweenaw Peninsula and then processed that ore into tools, weapons, and ornaments, they became the first metallurgists in the world. Their technology linked

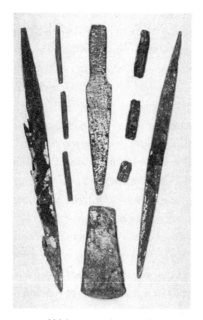

them to other cultures through trading networks, and so their copper is still unearthed south into the Appalachians, while marine shells and minerals from other regions are found in the Great Lakes.[3] Where there is trade in objects, there is also trade in stories, rituals, and people, who bring more stories with them. Was it during this time that copper began to be considered a powerful spirit, the role it plays in so many lakes stories?

The Archaic period slowly ends and the Woodland period begins with improved technology: the introduction of ceramics, the beginnings of farming, and later, the building of mounds, some of which, like the Serpent Effigy Mound in Ohio, are spectacular constructions hundreds of feet long that were used to track the stars and planets. This period, from about three thousand years ago until the beginnings of Contact with Europeans about four hundred years ago, marks a gradual change from the world of hunting and gathering to one of agriculture, as farmers developed varieties of corn, beans, and squash adapted to northern climates, even though many still continued the seasonal

Old Copper Culture tools

round between winter hunting camps and warm weather villages. The invention of the bow and arrow replaced spears and made hunting and warfare more efficient; pottery made life easier for the cook. Because of agriculture, life became more assured, so populations increased until, shortly before the first Europeans came to the lakes in the 1600s, the land was as densely populated as its resources could support, especially for those who lived beyond the range of agriculture in the North. The Great Lakes region was not an "empty wilderness"; it wasn't even wild, but a settled place, a landscape that had been divided into hunting territories and semipermanent farming settlements, burned to preserve prairie for game, and cut by mazes of trails in every direction.[4]

From beyond the inferno of cultural destruction that accompanied the coming of the Europeans and the industrialized fur trade, the centuries just before Contact appear to have been eras of relative plenty and pleasantness, aside from fickle weather and sometimes deadly skirmishes between competing neighbors. Religious and political rituals, such as the Feast of the Dead and the *Midéwiwin,* involved hundreds of people in elaborate ceremonies to link communities and kin. But even though religion and rituals, politics and power—and the literatures and languages that reflected them—had become more complex and sophisticated than Paleoindian ancestors might have imagined, the legacy of thousands of years of hunting and gathering in bands where sharing and cooperation were essential to survival still marked the values—and the literature—people carried forward. They told their stories in a landscape we would find surpassingly beautiful, but frightening as well, and in which few of us would survive a week alone. But to them, that landscape was as familiar as the insides of their lodges, although not without danger and hardship. What we call the "natural" world, to distinguish it from a world changed by industrialization, was to them the universe.

HAUDENOSAUNEE - IROQUOIS

The Great Lakes After Contact

MÉTIS → MIXED ONES / GREAT LAKES RACE

When the French came to the lakes seeking a passage to the Orient and found furs instead, the Huron controlled the fur business, acting as middlemen between the hunting cultures of the Lake Superior regions and merchants farther east. They made a rich living by doing so. The Haudenosaunee (Iroquois), who had already hunted out their fur-bearing animals to trade with other Europeans, had little else to barter. What the Huron were disinclined to share, the Haudenosaunee took by force, massacring the Huron and scattering the survivors and their allies from western Lake Superior to Quebec. In time, the French began a more organized trade centered at military posts, and bands were encouraged to move nearby, forsaking their traditional territories at least part of the year. French traders married Native women, known as "daughters of the country" for their rich trade connections, and a new Great Lakes race, the *Métis* (/may-TEE/: mixed ones), was born. These multitalented, multilingual, mixed-race peoples ran the fur trade, first with Europeans and then with North Americans, until it disappeared in the 1840s; then they ran territorial governments and logging camps and fisheries until the end of the century when the US government gave them the choice of being classified as "Indian" and taking up a personal piece of land on a reservation—an allotment—or giving up any claims to reservation land and, theoretically, assimilating into white culture. In Canada, which was sometimes more tolerant, they were able to continue their own separate culture.

The movements of peoples, bands, and nations across the lakes region were exacerbated by European wars for power fought on North American battlefields, beginning with King William's War in 1689 and continuing through the War of 1812. Natives and their allies usually lost, but while the Europeans could retreat to their fatherlands, the Natives' mother earth disappeared on the treaty tables. The problems brought by whites' wars were exacerbated by the fur trade, a multinational economic engine that drove the North American continent for three centuries and shaped the lives of everyone involved. Although it allowed several generations of lower-class whites from Europe to earn decent livings, the effects of the trade on Natives reach from the past into the present through treaties, displacements, and two governments' control of Native lives.[5]

Romanticized history depicts fur-laden Natives clamoring for copper kettles, knives, and guns, but they went without these when necessary. The most coveted goods were beads and cloth, which were beautiful, and alcohol, which made visionary trances less work than self-inflicted starvation by fasting. In the highly competitive market of the fur business, traders frequently used liquor to encourage Natives' loyalty or to pay them, even though every government and most companies forbade it. Trappers who had promised furs to one trader might give their furs to another who supplied them with whiskey, thus bankrupting the trader who had extended credit. The fur companies did nothing, since the "whiskey trade" was theoretically illegal, but it flourished when competition was intense and the authorities looked away. Whether or not they used whiskey, traders tried to get as many furs as possible for the least amount of goods; Natives, not surprisingly, attempted the opposite. Traders cheated each other, Natives changed traders in the midst of the season without repaying loans, companies squeezed out independent traders, Natives got credits from more than one trader at once, and companies undercut each other across the USA-Canadian border.

The beginning of the federal treaty eras in the United States and Canada ended this mayhem, since fur companies discovered they could require treaties to include provisions for repayment of Native debts, and they could preside over the negotiations as well, effectively forestalling oversight. Since in some areas fifty percent of the goods given Natives were never paid for with furs in the spring, these debts could be considerable. Traders might write off the debts from year to year, especially Métis ones who were related to the trappers, but the national and international companies kept finer books. The debts of individual traders eventually devolved upon the bands, which had no way to pay except by selling land. By the 1840s and 1850s, the USA had assumed debts worth hundreds of thousands of dollars and paid the sums to fur-trading companies. These debts were then used to compel the bands to sell their land when whites wanted it. The process was hardly fair, especially since companies often inflated the debts owed them, using a category called "depredations," which supposedly meant destruction of posts and goods but functioned like expense-account padding. In the end, much of the money paid to Natives by national governments for land cessions went directly into the coffers of the fur companies.

And they weren't paid much. It was cheaper for the fledgling United States to buy lands than to fight wars for them (the Indian Wars in the US West after the Civil War cost about one million dollars per Native killed), but a moral justification was still needed. For this the Enlightenment concept of cultural evolution worked nicely, suggesting that "savages" could be educated into "civilization" and thus become self-sufficient farmers in the white tradition. Once Natives were Christianized, clothed, and consigned to the field with a hoe, they would need less land, of course, which was the entire idea. Since the USA and Canada had no reason to pay a fair price if they could avoid it, when bands and nations didn't negotiate toughly, they were not well paid. An Indian agent at La Pointe, Wisconsin, once calculated that the nations there had sold eleven million acres in the 1837 treaty for less than eight cents an acre. The 1842 Copper Treaty paid the same Northwest Territory Chippewa seven cents an acre for twelve million acres. Worse, the government had been able to extinguish Native titles by paying only about two-thirds of what the land was worth to the Chippewa when engaged in their traditional subsistence occupations. The land's value to lumber, mining, and mineral companies was incalculably high. The agent brought this unfairness to the attention of the Michigan Indian superintendent, who had once run the American Fur Company, who fired him.

After land was sold and the annuity process begun, former traders rushed in to supply Natives with goods whenever a payout was held. Annuities varied from ten to twenty thousand dollars per band or nation per year and were paid for twenty to thirty years, usually funded by the sale of government bonds. Acquiring annuity money was a good deal easier than acquiring furs and many traders simply switched their businesses to the annuity payment grounds. Again, profit mattered most, so most annuity goods were overpriced and shoddy.

Even as treaties and removal impoverished Native nations, they enriched state, province, and federal treasuries beyond measure. Once white governments assumed control of the land, they resold it to settlers to finance roads, bridges, and canals and to pay politically well-connected officials to supervise removing bands west. Treaty payments were used to support teachers, carpenters, blacksmiths, and missionaries who were hired to coerce assimilation, thus making the Natives pay for their own cultural transformations. For example, Notre Dame University, in South Bend, Indiana, was founded on illegally seized Potawatomi land and paid for by Potawatomi treaty payments. In the end, the Natives received only a small fraction of the money paid for each acre sold, if they could collect even that without years of petitioning Washington. It would get worse.

In 1887 the US General Allotment Act (Dawes Act) required persons who considered themselves "Indian" to be enrolled by the US government and to select a sixty-acre parcel of land on their band's or nation's reservation where they could become farmers, owning their land individually instead of jointly as in the past. The allotment owners would keep all the profits they derived from their parcels, but they would also be responsible for taxes. Those who did not register did not receive land and frequently ceased to be considered Native. Land that was not allotted, or that allotment owners could not pay taxes on, was sold to anyone who bid on it, usually the timber, mining, and mineral companies. In addition, monies from the sales of resources and land did not go directly to the allotment owners or the band or nation. Instead it was placed it in a trust fund, administered by the federal government, which seldom agreed to spend it. Not surprisingly, it was so irresponsibly mismanaged that a class-action lawsuit, *Cobell v. Salazar*, faces the USA. Attorneys proved that Native peoples were cheated of $137 billion dollars in oil, gas, timber, and other royalties since 1887. They have offered to settle the claims for $27.5 billion. In 2010 the government offered $3.4 billion, which Natives will probably accept.

Once settled on allotments, many bands began a decades-long process of slow starvation and cultural disintegration because much reservation land near the Great Lakes is useless for anything but timber harvesting and subsistence farming. It is no accident that there are no large reservations south of where the last glacier stopped, since the topsoil it removed from the north was deposited below that line. This land in the southern regions of the lakes—some of the richest farmland in the world—was sold to whites, often illegally. The allotment system, like the treaty process, once again enriched everyone but Natives. When the vast, old-growth forests that covered the entire Great Lakes region had been shaved flat by clear-cutting and the slashings burned, when the northern landscape had become a desolate, smoking ruin and the southern one was fenced or studded with factories, the companies who had profited turned themselves into banks and moved to the cities, while governments congratulated themselves on the progress of ethnic cleansing by describing it as Manifest Destiny and erecting statues to homesteaders.[6]

It is impossible to imagine the pristine lakes Natives knew before this devastation because there is no longer a body of water in the post-industrial world that clean. The Great Lakes that are now polluted with chemicals, foreign species, sewage, and agricultural runoff were once so transparent that explorers wrote of seeing clearly sixty feet down. The air was, except for the occasional forest fire, clean and fresh. And without electric lighting or airplane contrails, the sky was alive with stars. Those who were forced to witness the destruction during the nineteenth and early twentieth centuries were appalled. Chief Mac-ke-te-pe-nas-sy (Andrew Jackson Blackbird, *c.*1815-1908) of the Michigan Odawa wrote,

> "How sinks my heart, as I behold my inheritance all in ruins and desolation. Our forests are
> gone and our game is destroyed . . . . The beautiful old basswood tree stood there, bending so
> gracefully, and the brown thrush sang with her musical voice. That tree was planted there by the
> great Creator—the Great Spirit—for me to sport under, when I could scarcely bend my little bow.
> I watched that tree from childhood to manhood and it was the dearest spot on earth to me in this
> wide world. Many happy youthful days have I spent under that beautiful, shady tree, free and in
> peace. But, alas, alas! The white man's ax has been there. . . . "[7]

After the allotment acts, the governments of Canada and the USA then began the next steps to acquire the remaining Native lands by encouraging those still living on reserves and reservations to move to the cities to look for work. Governments could then end all their remaining responsibilities with a policy of Termination, which forced reservations and reserves to assume complete responsibility for education, welfare, and incomes. The predictable result was more forced land sales to raise cash. The last land holdings would have been lost except for the determination of one Menominee woman, Ada Deer, who pressured the US Congress to end Termination and to restore treaty relationships. Canadian legislators soon followed. Those who had left reservations and moved to cities on the promises of government programs that never materialized frequently encountered only prejudice.

The first half of the twentieth century was the darkest period for Natives in the Great Lakes region. Reservations, or what remained of them, were frequently landscapes of poverty and disease, the children forcibly removed to boarding schools where they were stripped of their languages and cultures. Urban Natives, living in wretched conditions and working for discriminatory wages, found solace where they could, often in alcohol and its seductive relief from pain. Many faced the stark choice offered repeatedly before: assimilate or die.

During the 1960s, however, Natives from different nations who lived together in urban areas began pan-Indian organizations to fight against abuses, aided by more enlightened governmental and social attitudes. Educational assimilation and the losses of language it had caused had created an unexpected benefit: the first large generation of English-speaking Native leaders, many of them attorneys, who fought to enforce treaty rights—including legalized gaming. Although casinos can cause moral anguish, the profits have, for the first time since the early 1800s, begun to reverse the losses of lands and peoples that seemed permanent. Populations have rebounded, urban dwellers can sometimes move home to reserves or reservations and know there will be work, and language schools are flourishing, although few nations near the Great Lakes remain fluent. The past cannot be restored, but this book gives ample evidence that Native conversations with it in contemporary arts grow more vibrant each year.

The World of Native Stories: Nature

Observing the sky, land, and waters is critical for understanding Native literatures because the natural world is the source of all life, beginning in the earliest stories where Sky Woman requires a few grains of soil with which to recreate the world. The settings of the traditional literatures have always been hunting/gathering/agricultural landscapes that concentrate on activities, not on the contemporary aesthetics of appreciation. Looking at a landscape as "beautiful," or as a subject for painting or photography, is a result of urbanization, where most people do not live in direct contact with the natural world. In contrast, traditional Native literatures are frequently concerned with the difficulties of traversing the landscape, sometimes because of someone's magic or evil intent. If a landscape is described as pleasant, it is usually because it is safe from conflict and provides food and shelter. It is not an aesthetic object of reverence that has been split off from daily life by central heating and automobiles; it is not separate from the sky or the underworld. The stars and planets were not the subject of romantic songs, but a calendar of living spirits who signaled when planting should begin or ceremonies be held. And the waters were inhabited by creatures who must be placated because even though they could end life in an instant, they could also give great gifts to those who were brave enough to communicate with them.

One great constant in the three-leveled universe of sky, land, and water is the ability of things to change into something else, to metamorphose. Anything that is animate, or alive, can change, including particular

[Handwritten annotation at top: WINDIGOG → Hungry people, DESPERATE FOR FOOD IN WINTER CHANGING INTO HUGE CANNIBAL MONSTERS WITH hearts TURNED TO ICE, who TERRORIZED WINTER camps WITH THEIR greed FOR FAT]

rocks, trees, and stars. Flint, for example, had once been a first-born twin deity, killed and scattered over the world as rocks by his brother who, in some versions of the origin stories, became the human-like shape-shifter, transformer, and trickster character known to all the lakes' nations. Copper is not a deity, but it is still animate and had great power, particularly for success in hunting. Humans could become trees, animals, and spirits—a thunderbird or bear. Some rocks and landforms, such as the Sleeping Giant of Thunder Cape in Lake Superior, are animate because a deity once resided there and may still. Corn, which came to the Great Lakes around AD 800, had once been a person, cut and scattered over the land, only to return as food for the people. Since it is animate, corn can weep, even as humans do. Hungry people, starving and desperate for food in winter, could metamorphose into *windigog*,[8] huge cannibal monsters with hearts turned to ice, who terrorized winter encampments with their insatiable greed for fat. So deeply embedded is the idea of animate and inanimate that the languages of Great Lakes peoples are organized on that principle. The gender of something does not always matter; whether it is animate or inanimate does.

Although this may sound like a fairy-tale world of changeable creatures and monsters now, to Natives, who had no such category as contemporary fiction, it was reality. They navigated their way through this world by having respect for all things, since one never knew what or who might have power, and by spirituality, which was woven into the fabric of their lives in a way that only the most devout can now understand. Spirit helpers, who were usually animals but sometimes stars, took pity on those who fasted and begged for help and also came to supplicants in dreams, which could predict the future and give guidance as well. Fasting for visions of spirit helpers began as children's play and evolved at puberty into a several days-long fast in isolation from the community that marked the change from child to adult. The personal visions one had then and the spirit helpers met during those visions endured through life to give help in times of need.

Characters in traditional stories are often hunters, asking their elder animal brothers to give their lives so that the people may eat and be clothed against the cold. Animals, who were superior to people and had their own societies, consented because they pitied humans. They were thanked with apologies, respect, and gratitude, since arrogance and thoughtlessness would mean they would refuse to come forward to be killed and starvation would result. If the hunter set out with a prayer of supplication and treated the bones with respect, the animals would not really die forever, but be reanimated in another realm, much like people. Bears were especially sacred, and their skulls were carefully cleaned, decorated with ribbons, and hung on posts as a gesture of respect and admiration.[9]

Sometimes though, no matter how careful the hunters were or how industrious the people had been in caching wild foods or planting and harvesting crops, a summer drought followed by a long winter exhausted supplies and windigog stalked the snow-buried camps. Food and hunger are frequent elements in the traditional stories because they were ever-present concerns in the lives of storytellers, especially in winter, and that was the time for story-telling. Summers were filled with work and festivities, for this was when the bands that had split apart and moved to isolated winter hunting camps came back together to collect maple sap, to fish, to plant crops where that was possible, and to enjoy each other's society. There would always be stories at these times, since stories carried all the information that the cultures deemed important—religion, science, philosophy, psychology, history—but certain stories belonged to certain seasons. Narratives that used animals from the sacred origin stories, such as the snake, were not told during warm weather when they were about or when the constellations that mirrored them, such as Scorpius, known to Natives as the Great Snake, were abroad in the night sky. Those stories must wait for winter when the orbit of those stars kept them below the horizon and the animals were hibernating.[10]

The entire universe was a community where everyone had to cooperate; if they didn't, creatures died. In many stories, the wolf helps the hunter, but only if he promises to leave the occasional carcass in the woods to help the wolves in turn. Stories like this reflect a world where it took a partnership of male and female, plus an extended family and small community, to survive. There were no idlers except for the very old and the very young. Hunting especially, which was usually a male job, took endless days and was physically exhausting. Chopping wood, gathering food, preparing clothing and shelter, and planting crops were tasks for women and children because they were somewhat easier. Most Great Lakes bands had no beasts of burden except a dog *travois* to transport goods over miles of snow and swamp that white nineteenth-century surveyors complained were impassable. Farming in the southerly regions of the lakes was no less labor intensive. Agriculture, as anyone who has grown up on a farm will attest, is back-breakingly hard work, even with modern machinery. The seven thousand acres of corn that stretched out from the Huron villages in what is now southern Ontario did not know John Deere and did not tend themselves. They were not only subsistence, but a cash crop as well, since when traded to the peoples from the north for furs and meat, the surplus from those fields provided what the farmers could not. The early Jesuits, who came to Huronia in the 1600s expecting the forests of an "untracked wilderness," got lost in the corn fields instead.[11]

Despite this history of sharing and community, stories of forsaken, abandoned children forced to survive in a hostile world are unusually frequent in Great Lakes literatures. Stories, no matter how important or how beautiful, change to reflect events, and after Contact the Great Lakes became a war zone with a diaspora of displaced peoples. European demands for trade and territories ushered in centuries of ethnic cleansing, first by Natives and then by whites, a long battle that is still being fought. European aggression began a slowly unwinding catastrophe of Native nations pushed west across the lakes ahead of military posts and settlers until, despite the best efforts of war leaders like Little Turtle, Pontiac, and Tecumseh, many bands and nations were reduced to circumscribed reservations, sometimes beyond the Mississippi River.

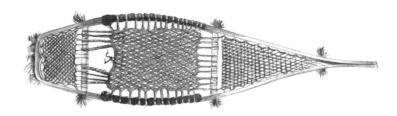

Snowshoe, 1826. Thomas McKenney

Nor did the climate help. After a warming period drexw to a close about AD 1250, the climate deteriorated until 1850, with the years between 1550 and 1800 encompassing the most severe winter weather. This is the Little Ice Age, which drove the Norse from Greenland, changed the hunting culture of the Inuit when the bowhead whales no longer came, and, later, inspired Charles Dickens with the image of a snowy Christmas. The windigo may be a creation of northern nations during these centuries, a response to the starvation of the displaced in the winter camps, especially during the *onabani-gîsiss*, the "crust on the snow" or "broken

14

→ page 13

snowshoe moon," a time when even the best hunters could not supply food for their families. How, they must have asked, could a once-pleasant life in a landscape that had provided everything for everyone for so long have become so hard?

When an entire people is exiled from its garden, stories of abandoned children who make their way alone not only reflect a history of far-scattered hunting groups isolated from each other in the bitter snow, but also a new reality of war, dislocation, disease, and the collapse of culture. The forsaken child is the forsaken band or nation, driven to the four directions to escape death. Much of the literature crafted after Contact is one of trauma, as surely as that of the European Holocaust. It is not the charming children's stories endlessly retold by white writers, but allegories of survival in landscapes made harsh and unforgiving by both climate and politics. And survival is key. As Mark Anthony Rolo writes in "We Are Still Here" (p. 471), survival was by no means assured. It was accomplished only by a stubborn intelligence and a steadfast devotion to place that few non-Natives can imagine.

That the forsaken child appears in contemporary Native literature as well as in older stories underscores the long continuum of characters, plots, and themes that have endured from unknown beginnings into the present. Great Lakes Natives have adapted in response to climate, wars, industrialization, and ethnic cleansing, but they retain their own cultures still. Rooted in unwritten history, they have survived past trauma into contemporary art. Native literatures were saved, not because nineteenth-century ethnologists wrote them down, but because they are weightless and portable and could be carried into exile. Once a comfort of the endless winters around the Great Lakes, stories were always told to amuse, to instruct, to distract from the cold, hunger, and threats outside the warm circle of family, band, and culture. Stories explained how the world had been created and how to behave in it. They explained the ways of creatures in the sky, earth, or waters. They were history, literature, and religion with no distinctions made among them. Listeners waited for the best parts, which a gifted storyteller could postpone for hours, if not days, by adding incidents like an on-going soap opera. Genius among Native peoples has always resided in words, and the ability to speak to persuade others commands utmost respect. No one can become a leader without a talent for stringing words together in a compelling narrative, and storytellers have always been the most gifted of all. Stories are the library of culture, ethics, and religion. If they are sometimes funny as well, remember that it's easier to recall something humorous rather than a sad or scary sermon, especially when you're hungry or afraid.

The World of Native Stories: Language

To read a translation of a traditional oral story is to be allowed a small and shadowed glimpse into a past far different from the most foreign contemporary culture. There is no airplane that will take us as far away as a campfire near Lake Huron a thousand years ago. Only by reading can we become travelers through culture, space, and time. Still, despite the best intentions of all involved—storytellers, recorders, translators, and ourselves as sympathetic and imaginative readers—we are forced to remain tourists. The cultures reflected in the firelight that flickers through the early texts reprinted here are eternally separated from us by technology and time, and we must accept that we may never understand these stories completely. That does not diminish their beauty, their fascination, or their importance for writers and readers now.

The problem for us, reading translations of the traditional stories decades after they were first recorded and perhaps centuries after they were first told, is that so much is missing. We're not taking part in a performance of a familiar story in the language we normally speak that reflects the concerns of our lives, no matter what our ethnicity. Few of us hunt in order to eat, live in lodges made of natural materials, move from place to place according to the seasons, or even farm for a living. Because of urbanization and technology, we have often lost not only the music of Native languages, but also the experience of being part of a group gathered around the fire with the snowy stars and dark outside and the chance to be part of a performance by interacting with a storyteller who is someone we have always known.

Through language we understand the world. If the language we speak divides the world into animate and inanimate, we will learn to perceive the world that way. If our language is Ojibwe, which has more than a dozen words for "snow," we will recognize and differentiate between all the varieties, whereas a language like English, which has only one word for "snow," will tend to make us less observant or use more adjectives. For example:

sôgipo	it snows
biwipo	snow begins to cover the ground
bissipo	it snows small flakes
mângadepo	it snows large flakes
jakipo	soft watery snow is falling
zhakipon	heavy, wet snow
bimipo	snow storm
ishpagonaga	deep snow
jakâgonaga	soft snow
magwagoneshin	settling snow
assanâgonaga	hard, settled snow
gawâgonaga	frozen snow
onâbanad	hard, crusty snow
missanwimagad	snow falling from trees
gônika	there is snow

There are dozens more words for other snowy concepts in other dialects of Ojibwe, such as *nimaagnagiid*, which means "to head off through deep snow," perhaps implying difficulty or danger. Because language enables as well as restricts how we think, it is impossible to understand completely literatures created in a language not our own unless we become bilingual. What we really get with a translation is a picture of a story, rather than the story itself. Even the best translations can only approximate, and sometimes mental concepts that occur in one language but not in another cannot be translated at all. In addition, because of the possibilities for adding syllables to words, many Native languages are quite precise. Each word may contain many possible images, so sentences can seem like small poems.

Peoples who have lived around the Great Lakes for the last four hundred years or longer have spoken languages that were later classified as belonging to one of three great language families: Algonquian, Iroquoian, and Siouan. The terms used to refer to them by government agents, such as "Chippewa," were often translations of the names they used to describe themselves. Sometimes the government nickname had nothing to do with the nation's real name and may have been highly derogatory. For example, "Fox" became the nickname for the Meskwaki ("red-earth") when the French and their Native allies failed to exterminate them because they were too clever to be caught. Carl Masthay of St. Louis, Missouri, a linguist who has studied Native languages, provided the following etymologies:

Algonquian: Anishinâbe (/uh-NEE-shee-NAW-BAY/: Indian, ordinary person): Ojibwe/Chippewa (unknown meaning; "puckered up," a common translation, is linguistically impossible); Odawa/Ottawa (to trade); Mississauga (river with many outlets); Nipissing (at the little waters); Potawatomi (unanalyzable); Kickapoo (he has almost cut it, filed it in making a notch); Meskwaki (red-earth people); Sauk (outlet, or river's mouth); Illinois (he [who] speaks the regular way); Miami (no etymon available); Shawnee (person of the south); Menominee (wild rice people).

Iroquoian: Haudenosaunee (/hah-dee-noh-SAW-nee/: they [who] are of the extended lodge): Huron (boar's head, bristly head, from the hairstyle); Wéndat/Wyandot (a shortening from "[those who speak] one language" or "the same language"; Mohawk (*kanyę'kehá·ka'*: flint-place people); Oneida (*onęyote'a·kâ·*: people of the standing stone); Onondaga (*onǫntá'ke·kà'*: hill-place people); Cayuga (*kayohkhó·nǫn'*: people of Oiogouen, a town name with an unknown etymology); Seneca (*onǫntowá'ka·'*: people of the big hill; the translation into Mahican as *ahsinni-ika* "stone-place" produced the Dutch and English Seneca); Tuscarora (*taskarú·de·*: dry-salt eater, from the Catawba language).

Siouan: Chiwere (belonging to this place, the home people) and Ho-Chunk/Winnebago (Hochungara, *ho·-čǫk*: fish-big or voice-big [people of the parent speech or great voice] or the preferred "big fish," implying the sturgeon; Winnebago is from Algonquian meaning "people of the dirty or muddy water"); Lakota/Dakota (allies).

Anishinâbe (*Nishnabe;* plural *Anishinâbeg;* or the slang term Shinnob) is the name by which most Great Lakes peoples refer to themselves. It means "human being" or "original man, spontaneously created man" with at least six other attempted translations. Early ethnologists referred to these peoples as Algonquin (a language in southern Ontario) and termed the closely related languages they spoke as variants of a larger, widespread language family that is now called Algonquian, composed of just over 50 languages. The term Algonquin is from Maliseet *elakómkwik,* meaning "they are our relatives or allies." Speakers of the different languages of the inclusive term Anishinâbe can usually understand each other without great difficulty. Indeed, during some periods of the fur trade, dialects of Algonquin were a *lingua franca* (common language) that could take a trader across most of the northern regions of North America from the Atlantic westward. Earlier, in the sixteenth century, when the Huron in Ontario controlled the trade around the Great Lakes, many groups spoke both some form of Algonquin and the Iroquoian Huron language.

We are reading many traditional stories in translation, and no translation, however sensitive, can ever replicate the original. Consider the following story of the formation of the Sleeping Bear sand dunes in northwest Lower Michigan, now a national park. This is Odawa Chief Fred Ettawageshik's (Both-Day) 1940s retelling of this very old story, given here in a close translation. He called it "The Legend of The Manitou Islands and Sleeping Bear Point," and it concerned a place his ancestors had lived near for centuries:

Agoding kitchi jajigo   iiaing   agaming   Wisconsin aki   nongo ejnika-demigog
Once   long time ago   out where   across the sea   Wisconsin land   now   it is called,

baka dewin gidago, apitchigo   gisnagad gibati-nad gaie nibowin   Makwa miniwa nij
hunger   existed very much   difficult   plentiful   and death.   Bear   also   two

makonsag, tibeiw,   nibina so-gwan gib-mosewag. Manpi   agaming
little bears   on the beach   many   days   they walked.   Over here   across the sea

bagosend-mowad wibi-jawad.   Mawipi   nises-sesnand-monid
they were wishing   to come here they.   After a while   whimpering with hunger they

makonsan. Miiwi   gi-gijen-dang   makwa, ji-manen-dong jidka-mada-gawad.
little cubs. So then   made up her mind   bear,   to attempt   they to swim across.

Mi-gibko-biwad,   eadowi-ing   bi-ianid   makonsman. Madja-wad! kitchi-wasa
They waded into water   on either side   they came   her little cubs. Going away!   very far

wi-ija-wag.   Mawipi   mi biiek-sinid   makonsag. Keta-nam-sig
they are going.   After a while   so   they become tired   cubs.   "Try hard they,"

ajinad   makwa. Kago aniwi   wasa geiabe.   Mijigo bedebam-damwad
she says to them   bear,   "Not very   far   yet."   Soon   they come within sight

aki   Apitchi-dash-go gaiewi   eshkam   ninin-wiswag   makonsag.
land.   Much   but   so   they also   gradually   become weaker   they cubs.

Gonama-dash-go midasswe ta-bagano-wang gaiabe wida-goshnowad, mi
Perhaps but just   ten   miles away   still   for them to arrive,   so

gi-ano-wited   bejig makons gig-osa-bid! Wiba   dashgo miiwi
became exhausted they   one   cub   so he sank!   Very soon   but   so then

gaiewe wi   bejig giano-witod,   gig-osa-bid gaiewi. Apitchigo ish-ken-dam
he also that one   he became exhausted   so he sank   also.   Very much heart broken

makwa. Kadash-go gego   gaiewi wajitch-ked. Ga-gawa-dagad dash makwa.
bear.   But nothing something   she also   could do she.   She waded ashore   thus   the bear.

Miiw tibeiw   gija-gish-ing ajinabidq wod   abing   gadpine-nid
So   on the shore   she lay down   looking   out there   on water   where they died

nidjan-sesan. Bisaga-bim-gadni,   nij minic sesan. Mi-dash-go gaiabe
her children. They come to surface   two little islands. So thus   still

wendjish-gishing igwe nongo awi makwa,   akewabimad niwi nidjan sesan.
wherefore she   lies there   now that bear,   guarding   those her children.

This story may be nearly as old as the giant beavers. The great sand dunes now called Sleeping Bear after the Odawa story were created between three thousand five hundred and five thousand years ago when Native people were living near Lake Michigan. One clue to the age of the story is its concern with hunger, a feared problem for hunting and gathering cultures in a land reforesting itself after the last glacier, or for agricul-

Sleeping Bear Dunes

tural peoples enduring climatic shifts. The dozens of whites who have rewritten this story have used fire, not hunger, as the reason for the Mother Bear's flight, perhaps because of the horrifying firestorms caused by nineteenth- and early twentieth-century white clear-cutting of the old-growth forest that covered the northern Great Lakes country. Fire was used as a tool by Native peoples to keep land open for agriculture and to clear out underbrush for game habitat. It was seldom fear-inducing and usually could be avoided. Only hunger would compel the bear, a sacred animal and the symbol of culture, to hazard a long lake crossing that would endanger her cubs, the future of her kind. This is a scenario Natives in the lakes region must have faced more than once: stay and starve, or risk moving and losing the children to cold and exhaustion. It is hardly the stuff of sentimental children's stories, yet that is exactly what it has become as white culture has exploited a Native story without regard for history, accuracy, or respect.

In addition, many of the traditional literatures reprinted here were collected near the turn of the twentieth century by ethnologists engaged in what is called "salvage ethnology." Since, as they then believed, Native peoples were doomed to disappear or become completely acculturated into western culture, it was critical to collect as many stories as possible as fast as possible, preferably from bands and nations as remote from the influence of whites as could be found, so the literature, and particularly the language, would be "pure"—whatever "pure" meant. Acculturated Natives, such as the Potawatomi or Odawa, who had adapted to white ways with success, were less interesting and so their traditional literatures were often slighted.

Many of these same ethnologists were not particularly interested in how a story was told, or when, or under what conditions, but in what it said and how the language worked so that when all the Native speakers were gone, as it was assumed they soon would be, a scholar could still replicate the language as a historical artifact. Demonstrating the artistry of the original language use or the charm of the performance, if there was a performance, was not often a concern. Stories were considered data about culture and language, not necessarily art, so translations were crafted to be as accurate and close to the original language as possible.

The resulting transcriptions can be opaque and awkward to read, since explanatory gestures, shadings of tone or voice, animation, and artistry must be guessed. Even Native scholars who spoke both English and their own languages had trouble translating. One wrote: "A sad thing in recording these animal stories is the loss of spirit—the fascination furnished by the peculiar Indian vocal tradition for humor. Indians are better storytellers than whites. When I read my story mechanically I find only the cold corpse."[12]

Nor do we know if the text the ethnologist painstakingly copied down, frequently stopping the informant and asking her or him to repeat a phrase or sentence, is the same story that would have been told to an audience of contemporaries around the lodge fire or later, the kitchen table. The differences may be subtle or great, and some stories may have been invented just for the ethnologist. Chief Elias Johnson, Tuscarora, writing in *Legends, Traditions, and Laws of the Six Nations* in 1881, described how

> It is very difficult for a stranger to rightly understand the morals of their stories, though it is said by those who know them best that the story was always an illustration of some moral principle.
>
> To strangers they offer all the rites of hospitality, but do not open their hearts. If you ask them, they will tell you a story, but it will not be such a story as they tell when alone. They will fear our ridicule and suppress their humor and pathos; so thoroughly have they learned to distrust pale faces that when they know that he who is present is a friend, they will still shrink from admitting him within the secret portals of their heart.
>
> And when you have learned all that language can convey, there are still a thousand images, suggestions and associations recurring to the Indian, which can strike no chord in your heart. The myriad voices of nature are dumb to you, but to them they are full of life and power.

Stories are living things that change from performance to performance according to the will of the teller and the audience. A translation is a dead thing, a snapshot of one version told at one particular time by one person who may have been telling an abbreviated version to please a paying white person with a pen and paper and subsequently, a recording machine. The same storyteller might have told a different version to grandchildren to highlight a problem they were facing.

More recent ethnologists have tried to remedy this by retranslating the earlier texts, breaking up the paragraphs into lines that might replicate the pauses in oral delivery, using capital letters or different typefaces to suggest changes in emphasis, and generally forcing modern readers to slow down and pay attention as if it were an oral performance. But, once again, the result can be difficult to read and distancing: capital letters SHOUT, italics *whisper*, and broken   lines

                    interrupt

                                   the flow of the narrative. All translations, early or late, are influenced by the cultures of the translators, so contemporary retranslations say as much about how this era views the role of ethnology and translation as they do about the traditional texts. There are no perfect answers. All readers can do is understand that no translated story from any era is free from the biases of the translator and read warily but sympathetically, grateful for what has endured and for the intelligence it sheds on contemporary Native arts.

The Plan of This Book

Star Songs and Water Spirits is structured by the seasons and their moons, reflecting the thousands of years of Great Lakes life before Contact. It begins with winter, not only because that is the beginning of the ceremonial year, but because it is also the traditional time for telling sacred stories, the bedrock layer of literature. Basil Johnston, an interpreter of traditional Anishinâbe religion and ceremonies, explains that

> If the Native Peoples and their heritage are to be understood, it is their beliefs, insights, concepts, ideals, values, attitudes, and codes that must be studied. And there is, I submit, no better way of gaining that understanding than by examining Native ceremonies, rituals, songs, dances, prayers, and stories. For it is in ceremony, ritual song, dance, and prayer that the sum total of what people believe about life, being, existence, and relationships are symbolically expressed and articulated; as it is in story, fable, legend, and myth that fundamental understandings, insights, and attitudes toward life and human conduct, character, and quality in their diverse forms are embodied and passed on.
>
> 1976

These stories are communal in a way we can scarcely understand, trained as we are to read in silence and isolation—behavior the first lakes peoples would have found bizarre, or worse, a symptom of madness or sorcery. Stories came to storytellers from dreams or from the deities—one didn't create them as we think of artists writing a novel—and the storyteller passed on in performance what he or she had heard as a child, had been given in a dream or vision, or had been trained to recite. Since stories were history and practical information, it was important to remember them correctly and to pass them on with care and, ideally, with artistry, which also allowed for some creative reinterpretation to comment on current events and to force hearers to think about the implications of social problems. Stories encompassed all cultural understanding: philosophy, religion, psychology, science, and the laws, disciplines that are now separate and kept in books.

This bedrock layer of story, like the glacier-scarred bedrock Precambrian Shield that outcrops near the Great Lakes, has been changed by the passage of time and the stresses of wars, but it is the foundation for all that has followed. Twenty-first-century lakes' Native literatures may be different in form and content, but like a palimpsest—a piece of vellum or manuscript that has been scraped and reused but on which the earlier writing still appears, ghostlike—contemporary stories are written anew on an old page. Sometimes the links to oral literatures may be obvious; sometimes they are subtle and pass unrecognized by those who do not know traditional stories. But on rocks, palimpsests, and literatures the past can still be seen, however faintly, and stories must be read down through the layers before the most recent can be understood.

The stories, poetry, and autobiography collected here have been created by Natives and persons of Native descent, either written by themselves or recorded by ethnologists and translators fluent in the languages of the nations they studied and who also used translators. There are myriads of "Indian stories" written by whites who were acquainted with Natives: captives, missionaries, government agents, teachers, travelers, and summer residents in the "wilderness." Many of these collections recreate Native life from a white perspective, bowdlerize

21

stories so they are acceptable for children, add Western religious moralizing, or truncate plots to make them conform to Western literary conventions: Henry Wadsworth Longfellow's *Hiawatha,* the most famous Great Lakes pseudo-Native story, is a good example. Few of these narratives describe concerns Natives had, such as star lore, which is often a component of Native stories, or deal intelligently with spiritual practices. The storytellers of traditional tales were nearly all leaders, chiefs or holy women and men willing to risk transferring their art into that new technology, printed English. Contemporary writers are no less distinguished. Read together as they have been printed here, they replicate a conversation that has been going on since the stars were bright.

Star Songs and Water Spirits is as comprehensive as feasible, including most types and themes of Great Lakes Native literatures, drawn from as many different nations as possible. Sadly, some nations disappeared into the maelstrom of war before their stories were written down, although their literatures may have survived under other names. The literature in each seasonal section is organized thematically, an attempt to create some coherence from the thousands of published Great Lakes texts available, and to highlight the links between traditional and contemporary arts. Each season begins with its calendar moons, which reflect the harvests and ceremonies, and with an introduction to the themes of the literature appropriate to the time of year: sacred origin stories in winter, family relationships in spring, creatures and spirituality in summer, the arts of war and hunting in fall. Since scholars of ethnoastronomy are now beginning to understand that there may have been a large, complex, philosophical, and spiritual compendium of star lore in North America before Contact,[13] there are star stories in each section that reflect seasonal events, such as solstices. Because oral literature is as complex and artistic as any printed text, many stories are introduced as art as well as a reflection of culture. Background information on cultural practices and identifications of many plants and animals emphasize how precisely traditional artists incorporated the natural world. This information suggests connections between texts and what might have inspired them, and it emphasizes that some stories, particularly sacred ones, should be told only in particular seasons. Information makes ancient texts more accessible to contemporary readers who may not be able to identify plants or constellations or understand older cultural practices that have not persisted into the present.

Earlier, old-fashioned ethnographical and anthropological collections left traditional stories to stand by themselves without explanation and frequently without naming the artist. Even if the reader has a Ph.D. or was raised in the culture, understanding stories presented this way—particularly star stories—is a gamble at best. Recently, neo-conservative Native scholars have suggested that any explanatory editing, theorizing, or arranging of texts replicates the domination of Native cultures by European-American ones, or that these practices create an idealized Native image that serves non-Natives' nostalgia. Although this argument deserves respect, it ignores two realities: all literatures are cultural creations enmeshed in and arising from everyday practices, some of which may not have survived, and Native literatures are highly complex and sophisticated works of art that cannot always be understood without background knowledge. As "The Legend of The Manitou Islands and Sleeping Bear Point" suggests, failure to understand the cultural contexts of Native stories contributes to the misappropriation of texts as sentimental children's literature and to the very nostalgia about Native lives that the critics deplore. One function of knowledge, after all, is to make our ignorance more precise.

With great regret, some texts were shortened. Oral stories are repetitious by design; frequently events are repeated four or more times to ensure retention and to replicate the four directions plus the upper, middle, and lower worlds. In order to include as many different types of texts as possible, sacrifices were necessary. Giving only part of a text is also an old practice to safeguard knowledge, and readers who are interested in learning more should seek a Native elder for training. Some texts have been paired to illustrate how different tellers used the same or similar material, since sacred stories frequently exist in many versions, all authentic. The equivalent would be pairing sections of the Old Testament and the Torah by different translators in a Judeo-Christian anthology: parts of the story are necessarily missing, but no disrespect is intended.

Stories like "The Women of the Eastern Sky" or "A Moose and His Offspring" remind us that traditional North American Native literatures are as complex and carefully wrought as any in Greek or Latin, and that they may well be older than any European literature: older than the *Nibelungenlied* of the Germanic tribes that so bedeviled a collapsing Rome, older than the *Cid* of what would become Spain, older than the *Beowulf* of English legend. This North American literature is equal to the tales Homer recited, not only in age but in beauty, and like the landscape and the peoples it portrays, it belongs to North America in ways Homer never can. Despite the length of this book, a dozen others, longer and filled with different texts, would not exhaust the riches created by the Native peoples of this place.

This is the literature of frequently displaced and dispossessed peoples and their cultures, peoples shoved aside by recent immigrants who were sometimes technologically but never intellectually superior. The names Natives gave to places around the Great Lakes still define them hundreds of years later, even though most of the current inhabitants do not recognize the complex allusions suggested by Michigan, Erie, Wisconsin, Penetanguishene, Ottawa, Toronto, or Keweenaw. Yet these names are like an unseen web over the land on which North Americans have built young skyscrapers and office buildings, appropriating place names as they forgot or dismissed what those names originally signified: a persistence and understanding of place by cultures that knew this landscape—lakes, portages, passages, hills and streams—for thousands of years before Europeans arrived. Michilimackinac was old and historic when Chaucer told ribald tales in that new, vernacular language called English to amuse the aristocrats at his slightly second-class court. His counterparts on the Great Lakes—diplomats who also knew a few good stories—told equally amusing and ribald tales about a trickster character to the same sorts of leaders. But students in universities today are far more apt to study so-called classic literatures, as if they were the only classics, rather than North American Native literatures, and not only because Native languages are harder to master. Once a colonizing culture has spent several centuries convincing itself the Native nations are so inferior they do not deserve to keep their own lands and languages, treating Native literatures as worthy of universal study is unlikely. Education is not only about knowledge, but socialization and power as well. For Canada and the United States to respect Native literatures as classics equally with Greek and Latin would require a realignment of values and a recognition of past brutalities that few are prepared to make. Yet Native stories are as important to the residents of North America as Chaucer, Shakespeare, or Homer. Of all the miracles North America has been granted—a richly endowed continent, technological prowess, and political stability—the endurance of this literature must be ranked as one of the most fortunate.

WINTER

Winter/Spring Moons
January, February, March[14]

Miami
ayaapia kiilhswa	buck moon	Bucks drop their horns.
mahkwa kiilhswa	bear moon	Bear have their young.
mahkoonsa kiilhswa	cub moon	Time of bear cubs.

Shawnee
haatee-kiishthwa	crow moon	Crows come back.
shkipiye-kiishthwa	maple sugar moon	Maple sugar sap begins to run.
haatawi-kiishthwa	the pass-over moon	Bridge of the seasons.

Mohawk (old | modern)
*gahyadahgowah	tsyothorkó:wa'*	body great with young	great cold	Deer visibly pregnant
*gonh rahdagah	enníhska'*	outer scales of tree buds fall	?	Birch bud scales scatter.
*ganusgwouhgah	ennihskó:wa'*	first frogs sing	great February	Spring peepers chorus.

Ho-Chunk in Wisconsin
hųųčwíčonįwii	first bear moon	Bears begin giving birth.
hųųčwiroágnį	last bear moon	Young bears give birth.
wakéhikirúxewii	raccoon-mating moon	Raccoons breed now.

Meskwaki
TcAgimAʻ kwikīceswA	little bear moon	She bear makes young stay in the cold.
TAgwanī'A	cold moon	Snow is frozen enough for walking.
Pāpōʻkwī'A	ice-breaking moon	Warm mornings, cold afternoons; ice breaks up.

Ojibwe/Odawa/Potawatomi
kitchi-manito-gisiss	Great Spirit moon	
namebini-gisiss	sucker fish moon	Suckers come to shallow water
onabani-gisiss	broken snowshoe moon	Snow crust makes hunting hard.

Potawatomi
Mukő kíses	(little) bear moon	Young bears give birth.
Tikőninì kises	dark and cold moon	Coldest time of year.
Tchītchắk kises	crane moon	Cranes are seen flying over.

Memonimee
mätchäwätûk keso'	Great God moon	
nomäpin keso'	sucker fish moon	Suckers come to shallow water.
mwunäo keso'	snow crust moon	Crust forms on snow.

·❖· WINTER ·❖·

Long Trail to the East
John Isaac, Anishinâbe

Cold winds blowing, blowing,
Ice sheets gather, thicken,
   Alas! Alas!
Caribou southward, far southward,
Great ice, wider, wider.
   Alas! Alas!
Cold winds, cold west winds,
Wigwams eastward, onward, eastward.
   Alas! Alas!
Over waters, black waters, stone waters,
Cold winds blowing, blowing!
   Alas! Alas!
Women sleep death sleep,
Children sleep long sleep.
   Alas! Alas!
Long moons, snow moons,
Chouqua winds blowing, blowing
   Heigh! Heigh!
White bear, food and blanket,
Wigwam, fire, sea chief barking.
   Heigh! Heigh!

                             1919[15]

When the nights are long and the fire is warm, then comes the time for stories. There is time to listen, to learn how the world came to be and how to live in it. Most important, the sacred animals are hibernating and can't hear, so they won't be offended if they are gossiped about. Rather than princesses and castles, Native peoples tell about someone marrying an animal or falling in love with a star, a boy who kills monsters, or how certain constellations came to be. Some stories describe the sacred, such as the beginning of a world, a nation, a clan, or a religion. The heroes of sacred stories usually act in traditional ways: they are miraculously conceived or born, overcome evil, embark on a quest that requires great courage, and return triumphantly with valuable knowledge. Jesus and Hayẹhwatha' (Hiawatha) are heroes of this classic type. They are frequently male, and scholars believe they are the creations of hunting cultures that used the idea of the hunt or quest as a metaphor for the development of self-awareness from birth through old age. Sacred female heroines such as Sky Woman are usually created by agricultural peoples where women supervised the raising of crops and the preparation of food.

Culture heroes appear in creation stories and Native peoples in North America tell eight different types, two of which are told near the Great Lakes. Earth-Diver stories incorporate a flood and an animal—often the least respected—who dives to find earth with which to recreate the world. Emergence stories describe how the people came out from underground. Scholars believe Earth-Diver stories are among the oldest in the world, originally coming from Asia with migrating hunters, and are a mark of semino-madic cultures. Emergence stories are thought to be told by agricultural peoples and to symbolize the growth of crops.

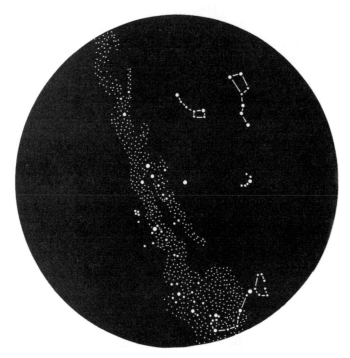

Great Serpent and Milky Way

All origin stories attempt to answer profound questions. Who made the world? How was it created? Where did we come from? Natives stress the unbreakable bond between people and the universe, including plants, animals, the sky, land, and waters. The creation of the world is not static, an event concluded long ago, but a living power that imbues all life with the sacred now, dissolving the boundaries between spiritual concerns and ordinary life. The creatures, plants, stars, and landforms in stories are not haphazard choices, but highlight precise characteristics the audience should understand immediately. Specific plants are given by the spirits for food and medicine and so retain a special life force from their origins. The characteristics of animals are also important. Wolves, the most widely distributed species after humans, are better hunters and more faithful family members than people. When one is killed by the great Underwater Beings, and so brings death into the world, it is the worst loss possible.

The Underwater Beings—the Great Snake and, in the Great Lakes region, the underwater panther or Micipijiu (Missipeshu: Great Lynx)—are some of the most powerful deities in the universe. For an ordinary person to look upon the Great Serpent was to die instantly; only those who had special powers could approach and kill the serpent and so obtain miraculous medicine from the red mark on his forehead. Serpents controlled knowledge of healing rites and success in war; they were the most powerful spirits in Native religions across North America, especially the Midéwiwin, or Grand Medicine Society of the lakes region, where the Great Serpent, one of the founders of the society, met the souls after death.

Native sky lore tells how the dead enter the Path of Souls, the Milky Way, via a portal known as the Hand, part of the constellation known as Orion. They travel from north to south on the Path to reach the eternal village of souls, but laying across the southern reaches of the Path is the Great Serpent, who will determine whether the dead can continue or will be lost forever. The constellation Natives called the Great Serpent (Scorpius) lies directly across the Milky Way in the southern reaches of the sky during the summer months, with the large red star Antares at its head, shining in the west. This celestial phenomenon may explain the near-universal Native reluctance to tell stories involving the sacred creatures during the summer months: the Great Snake is abroad overhead to hear and take revenge. Only when the Great Serpent constellation drops below the horizon or is blotted out by the sun, during fall and early winter, is it safe to talk of the creatures who hold so much power in the sky, on land, and in the waters.[16]

Creation stories are living entities recrafted daily, not just by oral storytellers, which few of us will ever have the privilege of hearing, but by contemporary Native artists. They allude to sacred characters to comment on them, or they retell part of a story to stress the links or ruptures between past and the present. Artists now may do in many forms—music, short story, dance, painting, cinema—what storytellers still do orally: subtly rearrange the elements of a traditional story to encourage observers to think about cultural threats, changes, and adaptations. This allows everyone to participate in making meaning, in making sense of the universe.

And then, Trickster comes walking around.

His name comes from a free translation of the Cree Wissaketjak (Wīsahkītsāhk), which means "the trickster or deceiver."[17] He is known by many names in North America: Wakdjunkaga (the Tricking One in Ho-Chunk), Nanabushu (probably Great Hare), Manabush, Manabozo, Old Man, Mischief Maker, Blue Jay, Coyote, Raven, Winabojo (Rabbit) or Missapos (Great Hare). The term "Trickster" is a creation of white scholars, who have wasted a century trying to figure out how a sacred, god-like world creator can also be a cheat, liar, glutton, prankster, and idiot. Their failure to understand how the Tricking One can be a culture hero as well as a buffoon points up the problems of trying to establish strict story categories that Native storytellers don't have.

Early white writers copied the idea and the animal, and so the Trickster of the Cherokee, Rabbit, became Br'er Rabbit, and in the hands of Walt Disney, Bugs Bunny. The Coyote of western nations became Road Runner, beloved character of the Saturday morning cartoons. Although whites made the Tricking One into a joke, in Native art Trickster is a far more complex figure: he is a sacred clown. He is at once a world creator and a world destroyer, a god and a fool. Even as stories of his pratfalls teach humans how not to behave, from his mistakes come wonderful gifts for the people. Not surprisingly, Trickster is anathema to organized religion—or organized anything else—because he represents the forces of creativity that undermine accepted categories, polite behavior, social power structures, logic, government, and whatever else cultural leaders decide people "should" do. Trickster is always "walking around," as if in a genial dream world where there are no requirements and no rules. No wonder we love him.

Trickster exists to destabilize our most cherished beliefs while, at the same time, making us laugh at ourselves for being so rigid. But because his bad behavior is transient—he is always chasing inanely toward the next disaster—we can laugh at his mistakes and learn from them without becoming rigidly moralistic. He teaches how difficult it is to live up to the values all humans cherish, and so he serves as a mediator between the ideal and the reality. For example, humans are by nature greedy and vulgar, as is Trickster, but through his messes, we can see where lack of restraint leads. Rather than listening to a pious sermon, we are delighted by Trickster's discomfiture and disasters, a far more pleasurable way to learn.

Trickster narratives are made up of smaller units of story, and a gifted artist can arrange these units in creative ways that intrigue the audience without violating the basic principle of the narrative. The possibilities are endless and, to the uninitiated, can seem chaotic, as when Trickster, formerly seen behaving stupidly, appears in sacred stories as a hero. And that is exactly the point. Acknowledging that events sometimes spiral out of our control, that we are not always responsible for everything that happens to us, and that the world may not always be completely understandable according to Western logic can be comforting and liberating. That is one function of Trickster, in whatever guise, animal or human, he appears. Trickster is always comic rather than tragic. This means that there is no final episode, but a continued movement forward. "Trickster was walking around," exactly as we all must.

This section begins with the sacred origin story of Sky Woman, in different versions by different Haudenosaunee tellers. It then moves west to other nations' origin stories, which incorporate the birth of Trickster and a cycle of flood stories that describes the recreation of the world. Almost all cultures tell stories about a great flood; these may be the result of rising sea levels at the end of the last ice age. In the Great Lakes stories, the flood is precipitated when *manidog* kill Trickster's nephew, a wolf who hunts for him. To revenge his nephew, Trickster must kill Toad Woman, who helped create the world in the first place, and the great underwater serpents. This is the agricultural origin story of Sky Woman retold by a hunting culture that valued wolves as expert hunters more than it valued toads as guardians of crops. Next are a few of the hundreds of humorous Trickster tales, followed by tales about Turtle who, after he helped form the world, got overconfident. The last ancient story in the Winter section is about the Ho-Chunk hero Red Horn, perhaps the planet Mars in human form, who has wonderful, epic adventures as he makes the world safe for the people who will come after him.

When the gods and spirits leave, the challenges begin. How will people live peaceably? What is a good life? Who shall determine what is right? When the Haudenosaunee became so warlike that they risked destroying each other, they created a unique and powerful idea for a confederacy. The formation of the League of the Iroquois, or the Iroquois Confederacy, is a story of nation building that illustrates how story, politics, religion, and national identity intertwine. The narrative tells how a fatherless boy transforms individuals and societies through compromise, so that local villages can combine to form a state with central authority that can be passed down through the generations to ensure the safety of the people.

The league describes a way to control change, but that is not always possible. When seemingly uncontrolled change occurs, revitalization movements—attempts to rework existing beliefs—arise to explain the inexplicable and give comfort. From darkness of the nineteenth century came several Native revitalization movements: the Ghost Dance of the Plains, parts of the Midéwiwin of the Ojibwe, the Seventh Fire, and the Handsome Lake religion of the Haudenosaunee. The concept of the Seven Fires is a different type of revitalization philosophy, one based on ancient tradition transformed for the post-industrial era that looks critically at the influence of technology. Basil Johnston does the same with his updating of the ancient story of the *windigo* to include timber companies.

Johnston's monster is a reminder that despite the entertainment of stories, the climate of the lakes is uncompromising. Winter in the Great Lakes has always caused death and suffering to people and animals alike. Yet to read Johnston's reinterpretation side-by-side with his telling of the traditional tale is to witness how a gifted storyteller can transform a story to address current events. Other contemporary writers in this winter section do the same. Interspersed with ancient stories are recent poems that recall the incidents and characters of the texts they accompany. These poems close the circle between the deep past, where the stories began, and the present, where they still live.

❖ THE ORIGIN OF THE WORLD ❖

The story of Great Lakes peoples begins in sky world, one like our own except that the inhabitants have great powers and are immortal. Their rituals, and the objects, plants, beings, and animals they encounter are the basis for life on earth. They do not understand sickness and death until a woman, known as Aataentsic[18] by the Huron-Wendat, is cast into the darkness of the waters below to begin the world as we know it. She is Sky Woman and will become mother of the earth and its people.

The language of the origin stories is frequently formal and traditional, the tellers refer to ancestors as a mark of authenticity, and they themselves were usually prominent, respected individuals. There are dozens of versions of the following Onondaga story of Haon hwendja wa khon', the Earthgrasper; the earliest fragment was recorded in 1623. All the versions included here were told to ethnologists who spoke speakers' languages and who also used interpreters. Some like William Jones (1871-1909), were also bilingual. John Buck (Skanáwà·ti, Across the Swamp), bore one of fifty names from the time of Hayęhwatha'. As chief and fire-keeper of the Grand River Onondaga, he was the official keeper of records for the Iroquois Confederacy and a man of great eloquence. He related his version of the origin story in 1889, shortly before his death. B. N. O. Walker (Hen´toh, He Leads, 1870-1927) was a member of the Big Turtle clan who taught and worked in the Indian service in Kansas, California, Arizona, and Indian Territory. During the last twenty years of his life, he became a writer and published two books: *Tales of the Bark Lodges* and *Yondooshahweah*. He told his version in 1911 and it is filled with his trademark humor. George Wright (Häh-shēh´träh, Footprint of the Wolf) was a Wendat by adoption whose father was French and St. Regis Seneca and whose mother was Delaware and African. Wright worked as an interpreter most of his life. He came to Wendat (Wyandot) lands in Indian Territory in the 1850s, and told his version in 1899, not long before he died. John Armstrong related his creation story at the Cattaraugus, New York, Reservation in 1896, a few years before his death. Näkuti (Sunfish) was 84 when he dictated his version of the beginnings of the Menominee people about 1913.

Onondaga, Skanáwà·ti (John Buck)

He who was my grandfather was wont to relate that, verily, he had heard the legend as it was customarily told by five generations of grandsires, and this is what he himself was in the habit of telling. He customarily said: Man-beings dwell in the sky, on the farther side of the visible sky. . . . The lodges they severally possess are customarily long. In the end of the lodges there are spread out strips of rough bark whereon lie the several mats.

Skanáwà·ti

Seneca *ho-de-no-sote*

Early in the morning the warriors are in the habit of going to hunt and, as is their custom, they return every evening.

In that place there lived two persons, both down-fended[19] and both persons of worth. Verily, one of these persons was a woman-being, a person of worth, and down-fended. Besides her there was a man-being, a person of worth, and down-fended.

In this end of the lodge there was a doorway. On the one side of it the woman-being abode, and on the other side of it the man-being abode.

Sometime afterward, then, this came to pass. As soon as all the man-beings had severally departed this woman-being came forth and went thither and, moreover, arrived at the place where the man-being abode, and she carried a comb with her. She said: "Do thou arise. Let me disentangle thy hair." Now, ver-ily, he arose, and then, moreover, she disentangled his hair, and straightened it out. It continued in this manner day after day.

Sometime afterward her kindred were surprised. It seems that the life of the maiden was now changed. Day after day it became more and more manifest that now she would give birth to a child. Now, moreover, her mother, the Ancient One, became aware of it. Then, verily, she questioned her, saying to the maiden: "Moreover, what manner of person is to be joint parent with thee?" The maiden said nothing in reply. So now,

Indian graves at the mouth of the St. Peters, 1857. Seth Eastman

at that time, the man-being noticed that he began to be ill. For some time it continued thus, when, verily, his mother came to the place where he lay. She said: "Where is the place wherein thou art ill?" Then the man-being said in reply: "Oh, my mother! I will now tell thee that I, alas, am about to die. . . ."

Sometime after they had laid the burial-case in the high place, the maiden, now a woman-being, gave birth to a child, which was a female, a woman-being. . . .[20] The girl child grew rapidly in size. It was not long after this that the girl child was running about. Suddenly, it seems, the girl child began to weep. It was impossible to stop her. Five are the number of days, it is said, that the girl child continued to weep. Then the elder one (her grandmother) said: "Do ye show her the burial-case lying there in the high place." Now, verily, they carried her person, and caused her to stand up high there. Then the girl child looked at it (the corpse), and then she ceased weeping, and also she looked pleased. It was a long time before they withdrew her, and it was not a long time before she began to weep. Now, verily they again carried her person and, moreover, they caused her to stand there again. So it continued thus, that, day after day, they were in the habit of carrying her and causing her to stand there on the high place. It was not long before she by her own efforts was able to climb up to the place where lay the dead man-being. Thus it continued to be that she at all times went to view it.

> The girl grows up meeting regularly with her father at this grave. He then instructs her that she must travel on a dangerous journey to marry the creator, Te hara Liawago (He Holds the Earth, Sky-Holder or Earthgrasper), the most powerful being in the universe.

Now, at that time he told her, saying; "Do thou have courage. Thy pathway throughout its course is terrifying, and the reason that it is so is that many man-beings are traveling to and fro along this pathway. Do not, moreover, speak in reply if some person, whoever he may be, addresses words to thee. And when thou hast gone one-half of thy journey, thou wilt come to a river there and, moreover, the floating log whereon persons cross is maple. When thou dost arrive there, then thou wilt know that thou art half-way on thy journey. Then thou wilt cross the river, and also pass on. Thou must continue to travel without interruption. And thou wilt have traveled some time before thou arrivest at the place where thou wilt see a large field. Thou wilt see there, moreover, a lodge standing not far away. And there beside the lodge stands the tree that is called Tooth.[21] Moreover, the blossoms this standing tree bears cause that world to be light, making it light for the man-beings dwelling there. . . .

There then she placed her basket of bread on her back by means of the forehead strap.[22] It was early in the morning when she departed. She had been traveling some time when she was surprised to hear a man-being speak to her, saying; "Do thou stand, verily." She did not stop. Aurora Borealis it was who was talking. She had passed on some distance when she heard another man-being talking to her, saying; "I am thankful that thou has now again returned home, my child. I am hungry, desiring to eat food." She did not stop. It was Fire Dragon of the Storm who was speaking to her.[23] Sometime after she was again at the place where people customarily crossed the river. Now, at that place, he, the chief himself, stood, desiring to try her mind, saying; "Verily, thou shouldst stop here; verily thou shouldst rest thyself." She did not stop. She only kept right on and, moreover, she at once crossed the river there.

She traveled on for some time, and when the sun was at yonder height she was surprised that there was spread out there a large field. At that time, verily, she stopped beside the field. Now she looked and there in the distance she saw a lodge—the lodge of the chief. Verily she went thither. When she arrived there, she looked and saw that it was true that beside the lodge stood the tree Tooth, whose flowers were the sources of the light of the earth there present, and also of the man-beings dwelling there. Verily, she then entered the lodge. Then she looked and saw that in the middle of the lodge a mat was spread, and that theron, moreover, lay the chief. Now, at that time, she removed her pack-strap burden, and then she also set the basket before him, and then, moreover, she said: "Thou and I marry. . . ."

She sleeps at the foot of Earthgrasper's mat, then the next day she soaks corn, washes it, pounds it into meal, and makes mush. When the hot mush splatters on her, she does not shrink away, even though she has had to remove her clothes and is badly burned. The chief has his two pure white dogs lick her body where it was burned, which makes it bleed. The chief then takes up sunflower oil and anoints her body. She spends two more nights with the chief, sleeping at the foot of his mat, and returns to her father, passing the same temptations from Aurora Borealis and White Fire Dragon on her way. Earthgrasper sends corn to her people, which rains through the roofs of the lodges, and the woman discovers she has been made pregnant by the chief's breath. She has a little girl, named after the spring winds. Earthgrasper, however, becomes sick.

His suffering became more and more severe. All the persons dwelling in the village came to visit him. There he lay and sang, saying, "Ye must pull up this standing tree that is called Tooth. The earth will be torn open, and there beside the abyss ye must lay me down. And moreover, there where my head lies, there must sit my spouse." That is what he, the Ancient One, sang. . . .

Verily, it did thus come to pass that they did uproot the standing tree . . . that grew beside the lodge of the chief. And all the inhabitants of that place came thither with the intention of looking into the abyss. It did thus come to pass that everyone that dwelt there did look therein. At that time, the chief then said, addressing his spouse: "Now, too, let us two look into the abyss. Thou must bear her, [thy child], on thy back. Thou must wrap thyself with care." Now moreover, he gave to her three ears of corn and, next in order, the dried meat of the spotted fawn, and now, moreover, he said: "This ye two will have for provision." Now he also broke off three fagots of wood which, moreover, he gave to her. She put them into her bosom, under her garments. Then verily, they went thither to the place. They arrived at the spot where the earth was torn up, and then he said: "Do thou sit there." There, verily, she sat where the earth was broken off. There she hung both legs severally into the abyss. Now, insofar as he was concerned, he, the chief, was looking into the abyss, and there his spouse sat. Now at that time he upraised himself and said: "Do thou look hence into the abyss." Then she did in this manner, holding with her teeth her robe with its burden. Moreover, there along the edge of the abyss she seized with her hands and, now, moreover, she bent over to look. He said: "Do thou bend much and plainly over." So she did do thus.

As soon as she bent forward very much he seized the nape of her neck and pushed her into the abyss. Verily, now at that time she fell down thence. Now, verily the man-being child and the man-being mother of it became one again. When she arrived on earth, the child was again born. At that time the chief himself arose and said, moreover; "Now, verily, I have become myself again. I am well again. Now, moreover, do ye again set up the tree."

Wendat, Hen´toh (B. N. O. Walker)

The world underneath was a vast sheet of water. No land was anywhere in sight. A pair of large white birds with long crooked necks—Swans we are told—was swimming about on the waters.[24] They heard a peal of thunder, the first ever heard in this world. They glanced upwards. They saw the tree and the woman as they fell from the sky. One of them exclaimed, "What a strange creature it is that is coming down from above!" And he added, "I know that she cannot be borne up by the waters. Let us swim close together and hold her upon our backs." They swam close together and the woman fell lightly upon their backs and rested.

Hen´toh

While swimming along, the swans bent their long necks and looked at their burden. They said to each other, "What a beautiful creature it is! But what shall we do with it? We cannot always swim like this and hold her up. What shall we do?" The other replied, "The only way is to go and see the Big Turtle. He will call a council of the animals to decide as to what shall be done."[25]

They swam until they had found the Big Turtle. They showed him the strange creature, told him all they knew about her, and asked whether he intended to call a council of all the animals to decide her fate.

A *moccasin* [a runner], sent by the Big Turtle, went around and called all the animals to a council. They came at once, and for a long time remained looking at her in great wonder. The Big Turtle then warned them of what they had to do; for they had to decide upon what was to happen. They should not even think of dropping her into the waters and leaving her to die. Since she had been sent to them in that way, it must be for their own good and, indeed, they had to find a place for her to rest upon.

Whistling swan

Now, they were all greatly concerned with the matter. A tree had fallen from above, they had been told by the Swans. Someone stood up and suggested that if the Swans could show the place wherein the tree had disappeared, the divers might go down and perhaps get just a little bit of the earth clinging to its roots. The Big Turtle added, in support of this idea, that if the Swans could show the place wherein the tree had fallen, a little bit of the dirt clinging to its roots might be gotten and an island be made for the woman to live upon. He offered, moreover, to hold the island upon his back.

The Swans then turned around and, with the woman resting upon their backs, they swam ahead of all the animals until they had reached the spot where the tree had disappeared. There they stood still.

The Turtle then summoned the best of the divers, the Otter, to go deep down into the waters, in search of some dirt clinging to the roots of the tree. The Otter at once went down out of sight. The animals were beginning to think that he would never come back when, after a while, they saw him coming back through the clear waters. So exhausted was he that, reaching the surface, he opened his mouth, gasped, and down again he went dead. The Muskrat was summoned next. He dived down and remained still longer out of sight. He failed in the same way. The Beaver was then called, being the next among the best divers. He met with the same fate as the Otter and the Muskrat.

A number of other divers were, in turn, sent down, until so many had lost their lives to no avail that the Big Turtle declined to summon any other but welcomed anyone who would volunteer and dive in quest of the tree.

There was no one to offer himself for a long time. Now then, an old Toad, grandmother, lost in the crowd, spoke up and said that she would try. The animals all looked at each other and, with much laughter, jeered at the small and ugly old Toad, so futile was she vainly in attempting what so many well-known divers had failed to accomplish. The Big Turtle, on his part, agreed that she did well to try and that, perhaps, she would be more lucky than the others.

Silhouettes of Great Lakes turtles

Then the Toad took a deep breath and down she went. The animals gathered close together and kept gazing at her, until she had dropped out of sight. They watched and waited for so long that they began to say to each other that it was done with her, that she would never come back. They kept waiting ever so long, for they had not yet given up all hope. They could not see a thing, however. A bubble of air came up through the waters and, by and by, burst at the surface. Yet they could not see her coming. The Big Turtle thought that she was likely soon to appear and said, "Let us swim right to the place where the bubble has burst and, if Toad comes back, we shall hold her up for fear that she may fall back." So it was done. Just then, some of them could see her rising from the deep. Some others said, "She must have some earth, for she has been away so much longer that the others." Very soon she glided upon the waters, to one side of the Big Turtle, opened her mouth and spat out just a few grains of earth (*oehda*) that fell on the edge of the Big Turtle's shell. And she gasped before falling back without life. The Toad is held in reverence by the Wyandots, and none of them will harm her, to this day.[26]

The Little Turtle at once began rubbing and spreading the dirt around the edge of the Big Turtle's shell. It began to grow into an island. The animals were looking on as it grew. The island soon became large enough for the woman to live upon. The two white birds swam to its edge and the woman stepped off on to it. The island grew larger and larger until it had become our island [Turtle Island, the world], as we know it.

Wendat-Adopted Seneca, Häh-shĕh´träh (George Wright)

This is why the Toad has always been called Mahshoohtahah, Our Grandmother, by the Wyandots.

The Island grew to be a Great Land—all of North America, which to the Wyandot was all the land of the earth. The Wyandot name for the Great Island means, literally, "The land which stands up from the Great Water," but it is correctly rendered "The Great Island." It rests yet on the back of the Big Turtle. He stands deep down in the Great Water, in which the Swans were swimming when they saw the Woman fall from heaven. Sometimes he becomes weary of remaining so long in one position. Then he shifts his weight and moves (changes) his feet and then the Great Island trembles, and the Wyandot cry out, "He moves the earth! He moves the earth!" Thus do the Wyandot account for the earthquake.

Seneca, John Armstrong

So now, verily, it was [Aataentsic's, Sky-Woman's] custom to travel about from place to place continually. She knew, verily, that when she traveled to and fro the earth increased in size. So now it was not long, verily, before the various kinds of shrubs grew up and also every kind of grass and reeds. In a short time she saw there entwined a vine of the wild potato.[27]

There out-of-doors the woman-being stood up and said: "Now, seemingly, will be present the orb of light which shall be called the diurnal one" [the sun]. Truly now, early in the morning, the orb of light arose and now, moreover, it started and went thither toward the place where the orb of light goes down. Verily, when the orb of light went down, it then became night, or dark. Now again, there out-of-doors she stood up, and she said, moreover: "Now, seemingly next in order, there will be a star present here and there in many places where the sky is present." Now, truly, it thus came to pass. So now there out-of-doors where she stood she there pointed and told, moreover, what kind of thing those stars would be called.

Toward the north there are certain stars, severally present there, of which she said: "Nia´gwai' ha-/dishe'' (They Are Pursuing The Bear), they will be called." So now, next in order, she said another thing: "There will be a large star in existence, and it will rise customarily just before it becomes day, and it will be called, Tgĕñdĕñ´withä' (It Brings The Day)." Now again she pointed, and again she said: "That cluster of stars yonder will be called Gatgwä´´dä (Its Cluster Is Present), and they, verily will know the time of the year at all times. And that is called De'hoñnoñt´gwĕn' (They Are Dancing). Next in order is Ieniu''ciot (She Is Sitting). Verily, this one will accompany them as soon as they start to travel: Nanganiă´´gon Ga'sä´don' (Beaver Its Skin Is Spread Out) is what these shall be called."[28]

Wendat-Adopted Seneca, Häh-shĕh´träh (George Wright)

Another council was called. The Little Turtle came in the Cloud. At this council it was determined to give the Sun life and a spirit, so that it could "run about the sky." The Mud Turtle[29] was directed to dig a hole clear through the earth (the Great Island), so that the Sun could go through the sky by day and then, through the hole in the earth, back to the East by night. This the Mud Turtle successfully did. But it seems that the Sun often loitered in this subterranean passage-way and remained there for long periods. The world was left in total darkness at these times. It was resolved to call a third great council to deliberate upon the matter and to chide the Sun.

To this third council came the Sun, the Little Turtle, and the other animals. The council decreed that the Little Turtle should make the Sun a wife, and that she should shine while he was going back to the East through the subterranean passage-way made by the Mud Turtle. The Little Turtle made the Moon for a wife for the Sun. Many children were born to them, and these are the Stars that "run about the sky," as the Wyandot call the stars that move like the sun and moon.

After a time the Sun was displeased with his wife, the Moon, because she ran into the underground passage earlier than she ought to have done and before the Sun had passed through. So offended was the Sun that he abused her most harshly and almost killed her and would have destroyed her if the Little Turtle had not come and rescued her. Sun robbed her of all her heat and much of her light and so maimed her that she could not keep pace with him in the sky. The New Moon represents all that was left of the Sun's wife when the Little Turtle rescued her from her husband's wrath. The Little Turtle cured her to that degree that she regained gradually her original form; when, however, she had attained this, she immediately sickened from grief because of her husband's inattention and neglect and pined away, diminishing daily until she altogether disappeared. When next seen she was again of the same size and form as when rescued by the Little Turtle; then she increased gradually, animated with the hope that when she had reached her former fullness she could recover her husband's favor. Failing in this, she again wasted away; and this has been repeated over and over to this day; and it always will be until the end of time. To assist her in lighting the earth at night the Little Turtle made many lights and fastened them to the sky; these are the fixed stars that have no course and which do not run about the sky. Sometimes they fall off the sky; thus do the Wyandot account for the meteors or shooting stars.

From her labors in the heavens and the important functions which the Little Turtle exercised, she was called Wahtrohnohnohneh, "The Keeper of the Heavens," or "She Who Takes Care of the Sky." The Wyandot believe the comet is the cloud in which the Little Turtle went up to the sky, burnished and brightened by the Little Turtle with rays taken from the midday sun. In this she rides through the heavens to perform her duties.

Wendat, Hen´toh (B. N. O. Walker)

The woman, during all this time, was living with her grandmother, an old woman whom she had found on the island. Soon after her fall from the sky, the woman felt that she was with child. Twin boys, in truth, were to be born to her. One of them said to the other, "I shall not be born in the manner of other children. Indeed, I shall kick my way out through her side."

His brother remonstrated with him and said, "It should not be so! For this would injure, or even kill, our mother." The other one retorted that it made no difference to him, having well nigh made up his mind to do just as he pleased. While the Good One then came to this island in the manner of other children, the Evil One kicked and tore his way through his mother's armpit and became the cause of her instant death.

From the very first it thus became known to the grandmother that one of the twins was good and the other bad. Their grandmother took charge of them and trained them from their earliest childhood in what their work was going to be, that is, making the island ready for the coming of the People. While the Good One was ever kind, thoughtful, unselfish, and helpful to his grandmother, the other was always willful and bad, ugly towards his brother, and disrespectful to his grandmother. As they grew in size, the good nature of one of the boys developed more and more, and the other's wickedness day by day became still more marked. Tsesta was the name of the Good One and Taweskare that of the Evil One.[30]

They were educated by their grandmother in the usual way as if they had been human children. When the time for their work had come, it was understood that Tsesta enjoyed greater powers than his mean brother; therefore, he was the first to take up work. Tsesta then began to prepare the island for the coming of the People and made everything in such a way that—if left undisturbed—hunger, work, and pain would have been unknown to the People. His brother Taweskare, however, would always disturb and upset what Tsesta had done, saying that the People should not find life so easy on the island. It seems that the Good One had to work first and, after a while, stop and allow his brother to have his turn. Thus Taweskare had a chance, from time to time, to undo or spoil Tsesta's work. As time went on, Tawaskare's wickedness grew even more emphatic and, when his brother's turn would come, it was not possible to restore things as they had been in the first place.

Thus Tsesta made smooth or slightly rolling plains and clear forests, with flat ground everywhere; and Taweskare came and pulled out steep hills and mountains here and there, piling up huge rocks in places, scattering pebbles and boulders all over the land, and obstructing the forests with swamp brambles, briars, and thickets. Every stream or river running one way was coupled by Tsesta with another running the opposite way side by side, so that the people might travel up and down stream without labour and paddling. Taweskare found out that traveling would thus be made far too easy; he, therefore, pulled out one of every second river, leaving the other running in various directions at random. The Good One, resuming his work, made all kinds of trees covered with savory fruits, just within one's hand's reach; the blackberries, strawberries, and raspberries he brought forth on high bushes, scattered about in vast clusters, in such a way that it were mere pleasure to gather them up. The maple was made so that syrup would just drip out when the tree was tapped. Then came the Evil One. Finding the bushes too luxuriant and the fruits too sweet and juicy, he spoiled them and tore them apart very sadly, making them small and thorny; and the fruits, thereafter, grew small, bitter, and full of hard seeds. Into the maple tree he poured some water and in that way thinned the syrup into sap, which could not be reduced into syrup without exacting labour and trouble. Among very many other things, Tsesta had made fishes without scales, but the other coated them over with large flinty scales, such as could hardly be scraped off.

It was fortunate, however, that Tsesta could always partly undo the evil effects of his brother's work, for life would have proved intolerable, indeed, to the People.

The Twins continued their work on the island for a long time, until it became what we know it to be. In the long run, however, strife arose between them. It is still remembered that the Bad One once took his flight westwards, there to have his own way, unhampered. To his great enjoyment, he made huge mountains out west, and barren wastes. Tsesta enjoyed the privilege of going out once and improving things. He went all over that rough country, boring springs here and there, and placing rivers and vegetation in the valleys and forests alongside.

Strife was growing ever more bitter between the Twins and became such that there was no telling as to what was about to happen. Tsesta soon found out, by chance, that Taweskare entertained the utmost dread of the deer's horns. He, therefore, gathered a vast number of deer's horns, strewed them along a trail, and then chased his brother ahead of him. Taweskare, unaware of his doom, soon found himself engaged along the path strewn with the dreaded deer's horns.

Entangled in these sharp horns, he fell to the ground and, while struggling for escape, met with a speedy death.

After Taweskare's death, the island was not yet ready for the people. Tsesta improved it and tried his best to stamp out the many evils brought forth by his brother. Most of his memorable deeds have now been forgotten. Last of all, he made the People, the Wyandots.

Sometime later, the People were all assembled in the underground world, far in the North somewhere. Their head chief led them to the opening of the great cavern into this island. From the cave's entrance they had their first view of the world. As they were all gazing at it, a terrific storm cloud rose into the sky, followed by most vivid flashes of lightning. The People were frightened. Someone then appeared to them and spoke to their chief, saying that they had nothing whatever to fear, for lightning and thunder never would strike a Wyandot.

The storm passed away and, still beholding in wonder the beautiful world, the People passed out of the cavern's opening. They divided themselves into bands that traveled in all directions and thereafter established villages, now scattered about the land.

Menominee, Näkuti

In the beginning, the Menominee came into existence near the mouth of the Menominee River. First of all, a bear came forth from under the earth and became a man. Then another followed him and became a woman and they existed there. The name of the man was Sekätcok' mau (Chief of chiefs), and he sprang from the great underground bear or the turtle.[31]

As soon as the man and woman saw each other they were pleased and recognized that they were to be mates. The man realized that they would need shelter. He built the first mat wigwam for their home and then made a canoe in order that he might go out on the waters and catch sturgeon, which were very abundant at the foot of a nearby cataract, where they had been created for the use of man. Sekätcok'mau was very successful in taking sturgeon. He brought home a large quantity which his wife prepared. First she split them from the head down and drew them; then she hung them over a frame to dry. When they were sufficiently cured she cut them into flakes and made the first sacrifice and feast to all the powers.

The Significance of a Water Animal

Ray A. Young Bear, Meskwaki

Since then I was
the North.
Since then I was
the Northwind.
Since then I was nobody.
Since then I was alone.

The color of my black eyes
inside the color of King-
fisher's hunting eye
weakens me, but sunlight
glancing off the rocks
and vegetation strengthens me.
As my hands and fingertips
extend and meet,
they frame the serene
beauty of bubbles and grain—
once a summer rainpool.

A certain voice of *Reassurance*
tells me a story of a water animal
diving to make land available.
Next, from the Creator's
own heart and flesh
O ki ma was made:
the progeny of divine
leaders. And then
from the Red Earth
came the rest of us.

"To believe otherwise,"
as my grandmother tells me,
"or to simply be ignorant,
Belief and what we were given
to take care of,
is on the verge
of ending . . ."

1991

Young Bear (1950-   ), whose first language is Meskwaki, is a poet and novelist who blends an ancient-sounding poetic voice with modern technique. In his novel, *Black Eagle Child*, he wrote, "To be ignorant, uninformed, and oblivious to one's origins was to openly defy 'the one who created you' and invite adversity." He strives to "maintain a delicate equilibrium with my tribal homeland's history and geographic surrounding and the world that changes its face along the borders."

❖ SACRED HEROES ❖

THE TRICKING ONE

The origin of the Great Lakes peoples is frequently combined with Trickster, particularly by nations living near the western and northern lakes. What is a sometime clown doing in sacred stories that tell of the birth of people and animals, the coming of death, the right of revenge, and the recreation of the world after the great flood? Remember that Trickster does travel around, and in the process he became a culture hero to several Great Lakes nations, slyly infiltrating their origin stories. While many Trickster stories, such as the theft of fire or the host who cannot provide food, are common around the world, most have regionally specific animals, plants, and landscapes to demonstrate what the Tricking One has given to the people. The death of Wîsa'kä's brother and Nanabushu's wolf nephew, which bring death into the world, are examples, while the virgin miraculously made pregnant by the wind is another. In Southwestern versions a virgin is impregnated by the sun, but the climate of the lakes is windy and, on the eastern side of the lakes, as cloudy as the Pacific Northwest. Anyone who has lived through a Great Lakes winter will testify that even glimpsing the sun is miracle enough.

The Ojibwe stories reprinted here were collected from Wâsägunäckang (He Who Leaves the Imprint of His Foot Shining in the Snow) near Lake Superior between 1903-1905 by William Jones, an ethnologist of Ojibwe-Meskwaki ancestry. Jones also collected the episodes of Wîsa'kä, although he never names his Meskwaki informants. The Menominee sections were recorded in the 1920s by Leonard Bloomfield from a traditional storyteller, Charles Dutchman (Nehtsī´wihtuk, He Who Storms at It), a shaman Bloomfield described as a man of "abounding vitality and humor." An unnamed source told Trickster tales to Hágaga (Third Born Son, Big Winnebago, Sam Blowsnake/Carley), who wrote them down in the Winnebago syllabary that was translated by Oliver Lamere for *The Winnebago Trickster Cycle* in the 1920s.

Readers will notice that some writing here seems stilted. Jones, Bloomfield, and others were translating as closely as possible to the original language while still remaining understandable in English. Since the original texts were spoken in ceremonial rhetoric that was sometimes filled with ancient words, a close translation may seem awkward and repetitious, but it does give a taste of the original.

The Birth of Menapus

Menominee, Nehtsī´wihtuk (Charles Dutchman)

He who created all things, having completed this island, then created man. When he had completed him, he gave him Indian corn and squash and beans; these things he doled out to his human creature. Then he took thought, who had created all things. "Now then, let this one, too, have life," he thought, "this Earth, and let her arise together with a girl, so that she may have a child."

At this the Earth arose from there to live in human shape. In her arms she held a child; it was a girl. She built herself a house, a round lodge. Then, with whatever thing there was, she made a thatching.

When, having now a house, the little old woman dwelt there, bringing up her little daughter. The time came when the girl began to walk about; then, at last, she could give her daughter chores to do. Finally came a time when she used to gather firewood, going about piling up faggots and large dry sticks. Then came the time when the Creator of all things intended to create game animals. At once the little old woman knew what that Creator of all things intended to do, for she was concerned for her daughter, whom she had been at such pains to raise. Too well the little old woman knew that her daughter would come to naught. Nevertheless then, she told her what to do:

"Now then, my daughter, there is great danger for your fate. Something is going to happen to you. Be on your guard. This which I shall tell you, try, as well as may be, to keep in mind," she said to her daughter. "When out-of-doors here you are going about, working at this and that, do not ever pick up kindling when facing toward the North, when you go about piling them. Always you are to stand with your face to the South, like this, when you pick things up." So spoke the little old woman to her daughter. Of course, the girl accordingly did as she was told. "Why, what is this thing that is to happen to me?" thought the girl as she went about her task.

Things went well enough with her after her mother had told her this; but then at one time, why, the girl simply made a slip. As she went about outdoors there, working at this thing and that, gathering firewood, she forgot herself. She stood facing the north while she leaned over to pick up sticks. Then the wind came rushing on. The girl did not remember at all; unheeding she kept on at her firewood. On came the wind, blowing with violence. Whatever sort of thing she may have had for a dress, up over her back it was blown, her skirt, opening in the wind. Now, of course, the girl did feel the wind and tried to fling her skirt, poor thing, down over her legs. In the end she did manage to get her dress down straight. Then she remembered what her mother had told her. "Oh dear, now my mother will surely scold me!" thought the girl. Not at all was she able any more to gather firewood; truly now she felt oppressed in her mind. So then she went home; she remained standing outside the door there, fearing the scolding her mother would give her. There she kept standing, in the doorway. At once the little old woman knew about her.

"Oh dear, Daughter, come inside! We are in a sorry plight! Did I not tell you, 'Keep it well in mind.' Whatever is to become of you now?" said the little old woman to her daughter. So then, at any rate, the poor girl came in and went and took her seat within the lodge. "Alas, Daughter, be on your guard! But there is no escape! It will happen anyway, that which is to happen to you," she said to her daughter.

After a little while, the girl knew that she was carrying children. "Oh, so this is what my mother bade me fear!" thought the girl as she sat there. Then, in time, the girl fell sick. Then indeed was the little old woman frightened, when her daughter fell ill. And then at one time, her children came into the world, the girl's children fell forth, one after the other. The entire extent of the earth roared loud, as Menapus with loud noise struck the ground. So then, it was a boy; truly glad then was the little old woman that she was to have a grandson. The little old woman took up the boy; she placed him by her hearth; she took her bowl and with it covered her grandson.

Then these large spirit animals came forth into life. As fast as they did so, they went from there, one after the other. Where this sky hangs over the world, in that direction went this creature which is called the Southern Eagle.[32] Then another spirit animal was born; toward the place where the sun sets in this direction went this one. Then another was born; toward the place whence the cold blows, this was the direction in which it went. Then another, in turn, was born; as soon as it was born it rose to its feet, and thither whence comes the dawn, this way it went from there. Then these game animals of all kinds were born in succession. Oh, truly it was beautiful, as the game animals were born; all of them even then started away in single file. Then all kinds of flying fowl and the small animals, all these then were born.

But then, at the very last, this Flint Rock[33] came into the world. When it was born, then truly with its body it entirely cut apart that mother of theirs. Oh, how the blood did flow! So then the girl bled to death; after a time she had ceased to live. Alas, the little old woman laid her poor daughter to rest; she laid her away in the ground. When she had laid her away, poor thing, there dwelt the little old woman. But what had become of her fire? Their fire had been entirely put out by the flow.

But as for the boy, when he placed himself to sit up, at once the earth would roar, so great was his mystic power. The poor little old woman straightened out her house and sat there. After a time, it occurred to her to lift up the bowl. Why, the boy straightened up and sat there, looking round. "Mm, my darling little grandson!" said the little old woman to her grandchild as she took him up into her hands. Attentively the boy gazed at this grandmother, who was holding him in her arms. So then she kept and reared her grandson. Whatever poor stuff the little old woman was in the way of eating, she tried to get her grandchild to eat. The boy up and reached for what his grandmother gave, and ate it. In due time the boy was walking; then truly he ran all over the place. At last the boy grew large, and also he truly was well able to speak, so that the little old woman now conversed with her grandson. Then once, by chance as it were, he questioned his grandmother, "Now, Grandmother, how does it happen, this thing, that there is no fire?" he asked his grandmother.

"Oh, Grandchild, Grandchild, what a pitiful question! Your mother, when all of you were born, that was when our fire was flushed out with the flow."

"So that is it!" Menapus answered his grandmother. "In that case, Grandmother, I shall look for it, to see if somewhere or other there be not fire," he told his grandmother.

"Oh, Grandchild, on the other shore of this great sea [Lake Michigan] there is a land. There dwell some people; they possess fire," his grandmother told him. "You cannot possibly get there."

"So that is it! Why, Grandmother, it is not far. I shall go fetch it. It is I, Menapus I am called, Grandmother. There is nothing I cannot do. I shall bring it," he said to his grandmother.

"Well, Grandson, it will be well enough, if you bring it!" the little old woman answered her grandson.

"Oh, but Grandmother, how will my uncles continue to fare as long as the earth shall endure, if through the course of time there is to be no fire?"

As a matter of fact, the Creator of all things had planned all this, and that Menapus should continue to set things right, being his firstborn child. So then the boy set out. When he reached the sea, why, off without end it extended beyond the reach of sight. "Now then, how am I to do this thing?" reflected the lad. Then he saw some of those things on little oak trees they hang; round things as big as this; oak galls they are called.[34] Little Menapus broke one off; he hollowed it out. When he had entirely hollowed it out, "Now then. Let me be small!" he said. Lo, a tiny little boy, as big as this, he was! Then he went inside the oak gall. After going inside, he closed up the place by which he had entered. "Now then, from the west let the wind blow, and let there be a mighty wind!" said little Menapus. At the edge of the water lay the oak gall. In a little while the breeze came blowing. Truly then that oak gall simply bounded along over the water. "Now then, at the landing place of him who possesses the fire let me be blown ashore!" said little Menapus.

Oh, how the wind sped! In very short order he was blown ashore on the other side of the water, where that great land must be. Then, in due time, "There, it really seems that this thing in which I am is no longer moving," he thought. He made a little hole in it and, when he looked out from there, why, he saw sky. So now he made larger the hole in his oak gall. Sure enough, he beheld land. Then little Menapus crawled out. When he looked upshore, lo, there stood a large house. "Well, so this is that place for which I am bound," thought Menapus. "Very well, let me be a rabbit. I shall be small," he said. Why, there sat a little rabbit.[35]

He who dwelt there had daughters. Two daughters had he, young girls. At this time they came to fetch water. When they came there and drew the water, why, all at once there at the edge of the water sat quivering a tiny rabbit. "Oh, Sister, do look at this creature! Really, he is pretty!"

"Yes, Sister, let's catch him; we'll take him along home. He must be cold. I tell you, when he is warmed up he will be lovely. We shall have him for a pet," said those girls to each other.

So then they caught him. Oh, when they had caught him, they held him by turns and thought him so dear. "Now, don't tell Father about it; he will scold us," said one to the other.

"No, indeed," answered the other.

Now the old man, their father, was blind; he could not see at all. When they came to the house and entered, they set it down by the fireside to warm it. Oh, when Menapus saw the fire, he trembled and trembled where he sat. But he was only doing this in pretense; he was not really suffering from the cold at all. Oh, those girls laughed over him and thought him cunning. But the old man lay at the far side of the lodge; he was blind; he did not see it. Then suddenly he called from there, "Dear me, children, what is that you are giggling over?" One would think you had brought something in here to play with! You know, it has been said, 'A god has been born in a land over yonder across the sea, a being of great power is he.' One would almost fear you had come upon him," said the old man.

"Why, Father, it is only we who are playing our games here," they said to their father.

So then the old man ceased talking. But in due time, having thought over what he would do, Menapus made a jump for one of the glowing logs. Then the girls did tell their father about it. "Oh dear, Father, this creature wants to carry off the fire!"

"There! Didn't I tell you?"

Out ran Menapus, and at once the old man leaped up and ran, pursuing him. Truly, the old man pressed close upon Menapus as he fled this way and that up the slope of the shore. Why, even though the other was blind, he could not run fast enough to lose him. Every time he took a look behind him, there was the other running right close.

Then, at one stage, truly he sprinted at a great rate: now was the time when he ran down the slope of the shore. When he had come in sight of the water, "Heigh, Younger Brother, wherever you are, come get me! I want to cross. I want to get to the other shore," cried Menapus. As for the Great Hairy Fish, as it was lying at rest, suddenly it heard its older brother. To the shore it went and beached itself. Dear me, Menapus did surely go fast, running to his younger brother, the Great Hairy Fish.[36]

"There, hold on to my horns here," it told Menapus, as without stopping his course, he flung himself on its head. He took hold of its horns; he pushed off with his foot, and at once he was speeding along far out from shore. Oh my, oh my, the old man just barely failed to reach the Hairy Fish as he snatched at it. Straight for his grandmother's house, truly Menapus's hair blew in the wind; splendidly he darted along. Very soon he reached his grandmother. "There, Grandmother, I bring you fire; set your hearth agoing!" he said to his grandmother.

The little old woman set about building the fire. And thus it was that fire came to be even here, on this island. Thus it was, then, that at this one time Menapus fared when he had been born, by this earth. That is all.[37]

The Coming of Death

Meskwaki, Unidentified

Once on a time the *manitous* dwelt upon this earth. They also dwelt beneath the earth, and far away where the stars are now. They were like people, marrying and rearing children just as people do now, and they were tall and big and mighty. Over them ruled Gīshä Mŭ´nĕtōa, the greatest manitou of them all. He, too, had taken to himself a wife and, of the four sons who were born to him, two were destined to become great manitous.

Now the elder of the two sons was Wīsa'kä, the younger, Kīyāpā'tä. They were different from all other children before them for, even when very young and small, they were mightier manitous than those who were older than they. And the older they grew, the stronger they walked in their might as manitous. The manitous beheld the growing might of the two boys and became jealous. And then drawing apart, they made talk one with another about it. At last the youths became equal in power with their father and, on seeing it, the father was greatly angered. Then he, too, became jealous.

Gīshä Mŭ´nĕtōa then called a council of all the chiefs and foremost manitous upon earth and when they were gathered together within his lodge, this was what he said:

"Oh, my kindred, I have called you together to tell you of my trouble. I have long kept it to myself, but I cannot any longer. You know well my two elder sons, Wīsa'kä and Kīyāpā'tä. You have seen them grow up, till now they are full-grown boys. Alas, you have also seen how they have grown in their might as manitous. And now you see how they surpass the greatest of you and are even equal with me. It will not go well with us if these youths continue in their might, the older they grow. By and by they will drive us away from the places where we now dwell. Then Wīsa'kä will create people. These he will put to live in the places where we now live and, then he, and not I, will be Gīshä Mŭ´nĕtōa. So for the welfare of me and of you and of us all these two boys of mine must die."

Thereupon the manitous burst forth, talking angrily one with another. And the din of their voices was like the growl of the Thunderers in their wrath. And the whole earth trembled. The manitous agreed that Wīsa'kä and Kīyāpā'tä should live no longer; and when they had hushed, Gīshä Mŭ´nĕtōa spoke to them again.

"My kindred, go to Hŭʻkī's[38] lodge, for it is there the youths dwell. She loves them, and she uses every effort to keep them always with her. Go to the lodge when the boys are away. Tell Hŭʻkī all that I have told you, and persuade her to be on our side; for without her help we shall not succeed."

Up then rose the manitous, all of them together and, rushing out of the lodge, they hurried to the place where Hŭʻkī dwelt. And the tramp of their feet, as they went, was so heavy that the whole earth shook beneath them. On coming to the lodge, they found that the boys were away; and so they entered, and beheld the aged woman seated upon the *otasani* (raised platform).

Straightway they told Hŭʻkī all that their chief had commanded them. She at first tried to put them off, and have them talk of other things. But the manitous would listen to nothing. Then Hŭʻkī pleaded for her grandsons, beseeching that their lives be saved. But the manitous would not hearken to her prayers in behalf of Wīsaʻkä and Kīyāpāʻtä.

Then the aged woman was sad. She bowed her head, bent far forward, and hid her face in the palms of her hands. And there she sat in silence and in thought. By and by she lifted her head, lifted it slowly; and as she looked at the manitous, this is what she told them:

"You may kill Kīyāpāʻtä, but I give you this warning. You will gain nothing by slaying him. He is now great and, if you slay him, it will be the means of his becoming even a greater manitou. He will live forever. And as for Wīsaʻkä, he is a mightier manitou than his younger brother. You will never be able to slay him, however much you may try. And if you make the attempt, it will be the fiercest fight ever fought by manitous. But you will not listen to me. You persist in demanding the death of Wīsaʻkä and Kīyāpāʻtä on the ground that it will be for the welfare of us all. Very well, have your own way. If you demand that I must be on your side in this fight, I suppose I must do what you say. But this much I will not do: I will take no active part in this war against my own grandsons."

Then the manitous rushed joyfully out of the lodge, joyfully because they could tell Gīshä Mŭ´nĕtōa that Hŭʻkī had yielded to their demands. They doubted much the things she said about the might of her grandsons. They had made up their minds to slay the boys, and at once set to work to accomplish their purpose.

The manitous called a council to which came all the manitous, old and young, and they invited Wīsaʻkä and Kīyāpāʻtä to be present. When the two boys came and entered the gathering, this is what the manitous told them:

"All of us are going on a journey. It is over the beautiful country which belongs to Gīshä Mŭ´nĕtōa and we ask you boys, his sons, to come with us. There are two parties of us. One is of the old, the other of the young. We should like you, Wīsaʻkä, to accompany the older manitous and you, Kīyāpāʻtä, to go along with the younger ones."

The youths consented and joined each his own party. Thereupon the manitous departed from the gathering, the older ones with Wīsaʻkä going one way, and the younger ones with Kīyāpāʻtä the other. In a little while the two parties were out of sight of each other. On coming into the beautiful country, Wīsaʻkä noticed that the manitous, one after another, kept dropping out along the way. By and by the company dwindled down to a few very old manitous. These few chose Wīsaʻkä their leader and, pushing him ahead, bade him to lead. On nearing a cluster of hills, Wīsaʻkä stopped and glanced over his shoulder. And as he looked, he beheld only one manitou behind him, one very aged manitou, who was in the act of stooping.

"Go on, do not stop for me," said the old manitou. "I shall be up and following you as soon as I shall have tied my moccasin string."

Wīsaʻkä continued on, making no reply. On coming into a hollow between the hills, he looked again over his shoulder and this time he found he was alone. Straightway he hurried to the top of a hill ahead of him but, before reaching it, he suddenly felt a twitch through his body and then heard a cry from afar, "Oh, Wīsaʻkä, my elder brother, I am dying!"

Wīsaʻkä listened and heard the cry repeated. Then he looked everywhere round about him and, while he did so, he heard the voice calling to him as before. But he was unable to find whence it came, no, not even after he had heard the cry calling to him a fourth time.

Then Wīsaʻkä ran from crest to crest, hoping to catch sight of his younger brother. But, alas! Nowhere could he see even a single manitou. He then returned home, but even there Wīsaʻkä was unable to find Kīyāpāʻtä. Then it was he began to suspect that some harm had befallen his younger brother at the hands of the manitous.

Wīsaʻkä set out to search for Kīyāpāʻtä, going from lodge to lodge, but from each he was turned away with the answer, "I went with such and such a party, and how can I know where your younger brother has gone or what has become of him?"

Wīsaʻkä searched for Kīyāpāʻtä in every lodge of the manitous and did not leave off asking for him until night. Failing to find a sign of him, Wīsaʻkä returned home. He was sorely grieved, because he was now sure that the manitous had harmed his younger brother.

Wīsaʻkä went out the next day to weep. He wept for four days and, on the evening of the fourth day, he returned to his lodge. There, in the middle of the lodge, he sat himself down on a mat and wept more bitterly than ever. And, lo, while he wept for his younger brother, he heard a footstep approaching without. At that Wīsaʻkä hushed and hearkened at the tread of the step, which grew softer the nearer it approached.

The footstep stopped at the entrance-way. A tap sounded on the wood and a voice in an undertone called, "Open to me, my elder brother; I would come in."

It was the ghost of Kīyāpāʻtä!

"Do not rap, my younger brother," whispered Wīsaʻkä, "and do not ask to come in. I must not let you enter. I have a better place than this where you may dwell. It is in the West, beyond the place where Sun goes down. Thither you shall go and you shall not be alone. I will create a people after the race of our mother, and they shall follow you, and live with you there forever. And there they shall call you Chĭbĭabōsă—because you shall watch over them in the spirit world. The manitous have already heard me weep for you. So now you must leave this place and, as you go, take with you this drum and this fife and this gourd-rattle and this fire. You will need these things when you welcome our nephews and our nieces into the world of spirits."[39]

Thereupon the ghost reached its hand through the crack in the entrance-way and received the drum and the fife and the gourd rattle and the fire. And as the ghost started to go, it blew upon the fife, beat upon the drum, and whooped. And there straightway sprang from the ground a vast throng of ghosts, whooping as they rose, and accompanied the ghost of Kīyāpāʻtä on its way to the land beyond the place where Sun goes down.

Nanabushu and the Wolves

Ojibwe, Wâsăgunăckang (He Who Leaves the Imprint of His Foot Shining in the Snow)

Thereupon he [Trickster] started away. The first time that night came on, there he stopped to camp; he slept. And then in the morning he started on; straight towards the region of the north wind he went. In the morning, before it was noon, he came out upon a lake. He saw three Wolves running along; he gazed at them. Oh, then out cried Nanabushu [Nänabushu], "Hey, hold on, my friends! Wait for me!"

The Wolves spoke one to another, saying, "Why, that is Nanabushu!" One was an old Wolf and two other Wolves were his sons. "Don't, don't you speak to him! Keep on going, keep on going!"[40]

Oh, with what great speed then ran Nanabushu! Once more he cried aloud, "Hold on, hold on, my friends! Wait for me a while, I wish to speak with you!"

Finally the old Wolf stopped and stood.

So Nanabushu arrived over there. "Well, halloo, halloo, my friends!" And of his nephews Nanabushu inquired, "Where are you going?"

"Oh, far away towards the dawn."

"What is the name of the place?"

"Place of Cedar Knots."[41]

"Oh!" Nanabushu said, "That is the very place where I too am going."

The Wolf asked Nanabushu, "What are you carrying on your back?"

"My bag with personal belongings is what I have on my back. Why," Nanabushu said, "I will go along with you. What are you looking for? I, too, am bound for that place."

"Last summer on a hunt were your nephews. Much game they killed and a good deal of dry meat and grease was what they cached; that is what we are going there for. Furthermore, on another hunt your nephews wish to go." Thus spoke the old Wolf.

"Oh," Nanabushu said, "I am going along with you."

"Oh, no!" said the old Wolf. "You cannot keep pace with your nephews."

"Ha, ha! Never mind! I myself will run too."

"Very well, just as you please."

Then off started the Wolves running. As they went their way up from the shore, he picked up his pack and flung it upon a log. "*Pinus resinosa* shall it be called till the end of the world."[42]

Thereupon they started off. Always running were the Wolves, and Nanabushu himself ran with great speed.

Out upon another lake they came, straight across the ice they made their way. Some people were abiding at the place: they saw the Wolves. "Halloo, see the Wolves that are running by! They are four, four is their number!"

And Nanabushu was using his hand as he went running by.

Again yelled the people, "Like what is the look of one of the Wolves? He is entirely without tail!" Oh, how the people laughed! "It must be Nanabushu!"

Straight on they kept going. Oh, but how tired now was Nanabushu becoming! When it was evening, they made camp. Where it was exceedingly cold by the shore of a lake was the place where they camped.

There was no fire. A shallow place in the snow they dug, and that was where they lay down to sleep. Likewise Nanabushu dug a shallow place in the snow, and there he lay down to sleep. Very tired he was, and very much was he sweating, for hard had he been running. He was not able to sleep. Now was he becoming chilled, ever so cold was he.

The old Wolf spoke to his little son, saying, "I say, lend him one of our blankets."

The little Wolf threw his tail over where Nanabushu lay asleep. Ah! But Nanabushu then became exceedingly warm. Upon that he went to sleep. And when he awoke, he was in a very heavy sweat. Whereupon he said, as he flung aside the wolf tail, "Good gracious! Certainly a great producer of sweat is the dog tail." Once more to sleep went Nanabushu. Again he awoke, so very cold was he again. The little Wolf over there was asleep. Thereupon once more Nanabushu pulled on the wolf tail to cover himself.

The little Wolf then drew away his tail. "It was but a moment ago that you called it a dog tail."

Ah! Then once more Nanabushu became cold.

And as soon as the dawn was appearing, then began the sound of them getting up; they could be heard shaking themselves. And while they could be heard starting away, the old Wolf said, "Come, Nanabushu, get up from bed! Already have your nephews started away."

Well, once more started Nanabushu, together with them. Again with great speed ran Nanabushu all the day long. And on the next evening said the old Wolf, he spoke to his sons, saying, "It is your uncle's turn to look for a place where we shall camp."

Thereupon the young Wolf said, "Go look for a place where we are to camp."

And so Nanabushu went to find a place where it was very calm, where there was a very dense growth of balsam trees. "Therefore here is a place where we will camp."[43]

Then there was where they slept. In the middle of the night there arose a shout of the young Wolves getting up, for they were cold. They could be heard starting away. And in the morning up spoke the old Wolf, "Come, Nanabushu! We have now been left behind. Now far away must be your nephews."

Whereupon then off started the elders. They found the others at the shore of a lake in a cold part of the place. And then once more they started on their way all together. Ah! With great speed went running Nanabushu. Sometimes afar he was left behind, and so continually was he waited for by his companions. "Walk fast, walk fast, Nanabushu!"

Thereupon on the next evening they went into camp. And then spoke the old Wolf. He addressed Nanabushu, saying, "Now, tomorrow is when we shall arrive at the place whither we are bound."

In the morning they set out together. Ah! Once more on the run started Nanabushu. When it was noon, they came out upon a lake. They beheld someone seated far out on the ice. Up spoke the old Wolf, "Look, Nanabushu! Maybe your nephews have shot and hit something." Thereupon they kept on till they reached the place where the being was sitting. The old Wolf had his head up, looking about, for he scented a moose. And Nanabushu himself did the same. So he was addressed by his companion saying, "Do you smell a moose?"

"Yes," he said.

"How many are they?" said the old Wolf.

"They are three," said Nanabushu. "One cow and two calves."

"No," said the old Wolf, "there is but one moose."

Thereupon off running started the youths, likewise the old Wolf and Nanabushu too. Ahead went the youths. In the meantime away had gone the moose, so after the moose ran the youths. To Nanabushu then said the Wolf, "As you go, keep a careful look." Once as they were going along they saw a wolf tooth sticking from a tree. Whereupon said the old Wolf, "I say, take up your nephew's pointed arrow!"

And Nanabushu said, "What am I to do with a dogtooth?"

The old Wolf then pulled it out. And so, after he had shaken the pointed arrow, very nice was the arrow. When he saw it, then Nanabushu said, "I say, let me carry my nephew's arrow as we go along!"

The old man then said, "Only a moment ago you called it a dog tooth. Do go on!"

Whereupon they started on their way. And then on another occasion they saw where a wolf had eased himself as he went along. Thereupon said the old Wolf, "Come, Nanabushu! As you go along, pick up what your nephew has killed."

And then said Nanabushu, "What have I to do with dog dung?"

Thereupon the old Wolf picked it up. And then he shook it, whereupon the flesh of slain game he obtained from it. And when Nanabushu saw the flesh of slain game, he said, "I say, do let me carry along the game killed by my nephew!"

Whereupon said the old man, "Only a moment ago you called it dog dung. Keep on going."

Now, by and by as they went along, said the old Wolf, "Ah! A moose have your nephews killed." Very hungry was Nanabushu, and he was tired. And when he saw the Wolves as they were lying down, very full were they from eating. Nothing he saw, and no moose he saw, only the blood on the snow. Thereupon said the old Wolf, "Let us make a camp!"

Oh, but Nanabushu was lazy! Much against his will he helped the Wolves make the camp. After they had finished the camp, then up rose all the young Wolves. Thereupon then vomited the youths; exactly like meat that has newly been cut up, such was the appearance of the moose meat. Whereupon Nanabushu was greatly delighted with the thought of eating. Ha! And then they started cooking. Ha, but Nanabushu truly ate a great deal!

Now, there in that place they made their home, and often on a hunt went the youths. Many moose they killed, and deer, and various kinds of game they slew. Never was Nanabushu hungry; often meat that was nice he had for his food. . . .

Now, once the old Wolf spoke to Nanabushu, saying, "It is now about time that we should be moving. One of your nephews will I give to you, and he will be the one for you to accompany when he goes to hunt. One, too, will I accompany. I will give you fire." Thereupon the old Wolf broke wind. "Now, that is a flint." Again the old Wolf broke wind. "Now, that is the punk."[44] Again he broke wind. "That is kindling." Again he broke wind. "That is birch bark. After a while, when you go into camp and have gathered the firewood, then shall you leap over the place where the wood is, whereupon up will start the blaze. Do not try to do it merely for the sake of doing it."

The Death of Nanabushu's Nephew

Thereupon they started away; into different lands they went. Now, ahead went his nephew, and Nanabushu himself traveled behind. And before they arrived where they were to camp, Nanabushu thought, "Now, I shall try to make a fire." Whereupon, after he had gathered the wood together at a place, he then leaped over it, upon which up blazed the fire. Ah! Verily, much pleased was Nanabushu.

Thereupon they set out. And when he arrived at the place where the youth had put down his pack, then there he made the camp, for the youth himself was away on a hunt for game. Now, when Nanabushu desired to make the fire, he put on the wood and so again he leaped over it. For all that, it barely caught fire. Once again he leaped over it, and even less was the fire there. Again he leaped over, and no fire at all did he see. At last night came on. Now, when back came the youth, he heard the sound of somebody thumping on the ground. It turned out to be Nanabushu leaping over and over. Whereupon said the youth, "What, Nanabushu, are you doing? Perhaps you have been kindling fires without any reason."

"No," said Nanabushu.

And so, after the youth himself had leaped over, then the fire blazed up.

And very cold was Nanabushu at the time.

And then he said to him, "Don't ever do it again, not till you go into camp. Then may you do it." And so truly that was what Nanabushu did. Not till he had put on the wood did he then leap over, whereupon the fire blazed up.

Now, continually were they traveling about, and often did the youth slay the game; ever so frequently Nanabushu had good food to eat. Very fond was he of his nephew. Now, once Nanabushu had a dream that his nephew fell into a river. Whereupon he then said to his nephew, "I wish that you would be careful when you are following after game. And when you see a river, just fling a stick ahead of you, for that is where you shall step. Even though it be a very small brook, do throw a stick ahead of you, and there you shall step, even though there be only the dry bed of a stream. Don't ever forget what I am telling you."

So for a long time they went traveling about. Once upon a time his nephew did not return home. Whereupon thought Nanabushu, "Therefore my dream must have perhaps come true."

But in the meanwhile the youth was in pursuit of some game. Almost was he about to overtake the game when he saw the dry bed of a stream. Although he was mindful of what he had been told by his uncle, yet there he fell into a great river. He remained there.

Now, Nanabushu himself on the morrow set out to look for his nephew and, when he found a great river, then at once he lost track of his nephew. Hereupon he greatly wept, and then he started off down the stream. Once as he went down to the river, very anxious was he to drink; and so, as he lay down to drink, then he beheld some berries under the water, whereupon he wanted to get them, but he could not get hold of them. For a long while he tried in vain to get them. Finally, as up this way he looked, there he beheld the berries hanging. They were the things that cast the reflection in the water. And when he saw it, he said, "This is what they shall be called till the end of the world, high-bush cranberries."[45]

Thereupon he continued his way. Another time, when he came down to the river, he saw a White Loon and a Kingfisher; in the water they were looking. Nanabushu then asked of them, "What are you watching for?"

Thereupon they said, "Manitous dwell in this place. It is they who took Nanabushu's nephew. Now, the skin of that Wolf, which they use for a flap over the doorway, is the thing for which we were watching."

Truly, indeed, was Nanabushu angered. Thereupon he inquired of them, "Where do they live? Rightly declare it to me."

Whereupon they said, "This is the place where dwell the manitous who seized your nephew."

"Be sure to relate it truthfully." And then he asked Kingfisher to come. Thereupon Nanabushu painted the Kingfisher and the Loon.

Ah! Truly they were pleased. Thereupon they said, "If it becomes very hot, then all will come forth. It is upon this island that they usually sleep."

And all the while was Nanabushu angry. And when he let them go, he nearly killed the Kingfisher for, as he was going to seize him, he missed catching him. Thereupon off started Nanabushu into the forest; he went to make a bow and some arrows. And then said Nanabushu, "I will that it be very warm tomorrow." And so truly there was a very clear sky on the morrow. Thereupon Nanabushu went over to a place opposite the island, and there on the bank of the river he stood. "Like a tree I will look, like a stump that is exceeding strong." And so there upon his arm he put his bow. And when the sun was rising, it grew very warm. And when it was nearly noon, then out began coming the manitous.

And then said the manitous, "Did you yourselves ever see that stump before?"

"No," said some of them.

But some of them said, "Yes, we ourselves are accustomed to seeing it."

Some of them said, "Woe to us should Nanabushu take on such a form!"

All sorts of manitous came forth. And now they said to the White Bear, "I wish you would go wrestle with that stump."[46]

Thereupon truly thither went the White Bear and he tried shaking it, but not a whit did he move it. Thereupon said the White Bear, "It is not Nanabushu, it is wood!"

Ah! But yet some of them feared it. And the Otter too came forth. Whereupon he said, "Ha, ha, ha, ha!" as he began laughing. "Never before have I seen it."

And then again they said, "Let us see you, Big Serpent, go try it!"[47]

Whereupon truly thither he went. Whereupon he twined round Nanabushu's neck. And then tight coiled the Serpent. Well, far on its way had gone the sun. When almost out of breath was Nanabushu, then was he let go by the Big Serpent. Thereupon said the Serpent, "Why, that is not Nanabushu; it is wood!" Whereupon they felt at ease. And then at the last out came two manitous; they were the chiefs. Thereupon they went to sleep where it was warm.

Accordingly Nanabushu went after his bow and arrows that he might go shoot them. Now, there were two red-burned Turtles, and now they were going to tell. Whereupon to them said Nanabushu, "Hush, hush! Don't you tell! In return I will adorn you in gay color." Accordingly Nanabushu took them up, and then painted them. Ah! They were greatly pleased. Thereupon he said to them, "Red-burned creatures you will be called till the end of the world."[48] Whereupon he was told by the red-burned Turtles, "Do not shoot straight at them. Where they cast a shadow is the place to shoot at them."

And so Nanabushu went to where the manitous were. And when he got to where they were, then he shot at them, right at their bodies, but he did not hit them. Now, another arrow he fixed upon his bow, whereupon he shot at the shadows they cast, and then he hit them. And so quickly another he shot at the chief.

Now, then was the time they knew it was Nanabushu. "Oh, Nanabushu is killing the chief!" Accordingly Nanabushu started to flee. Ah! And then by the Water was he pursued. Now once, when nearly overtaken by the Water, he then saw a Woodchuck sitting up. Whereupon he said to him, "Alas! My little brother, by a manitou am I pursued."

"Well, where is the manitou about whom you are talking? Pray, come into this little hole of mine!"

Nanabushu Slays Toadwoman, the Healer of the Manitous

So Nanabushu came into the Woodchuck's hole. So after Nanabushu had gone inside, then the Woodchuck went in too, whereupon he closed the entrance of his hole. And not till the water had flowed past, then again out went Nanabushu. Now once, as he went walking along, he heard somebody singing:

"From the ends of the world do I come with the sound of my rattles."

After that he sought, listening for the singer, whereupon he saw an old woman, a toad. Some linden bark she carried upon her back, and rattles too were hanging from the old woman's girdle. Thereupon Nanabushu inquired of the old woman, "What, my grandmother, do you intend doing with that linden bark?"[49]

Whereupon said the old woman, "Why, Nanabushu indeed has shot the manitous, and I am going to heal the manitous. And for Nanabushu will be set a snare made from this linden bark. All over the earth will twine be laid. And if it pulls when he steps into it, then will it be known where Nanabushu is. Are you not yourself Nanabushu?"

"No," said Nanabushu. "Do you suppose that you would be permitted to live if you should see Nanabushu?" And then he said to her, "Where do you abide?"

"Yonder, near by where the chiefs are. On this evening is truly when I will do some wonderful healing, whereupon the upper arm of Nanabushu's nephew shall I be given to eat this evening."

So then to her said Nanabushu, "What is the nature of your song when you sing?"

Whereupon the old woman revealed it, saying, "This is the way I usually sing when I sing, 'From the ends of the world do I come with the sound of my rattles.'"

Now, after he had been told everything, then he slew her. And after he had flayed her and put on her skin, he then took up the linden bark and put it upon his back, and the rattles, too, were hanging at his belt. And then he went in the same direction whither the old woman intended going. He, too, went singing along the way, "From the ends of the world do I come with the sound of my rattles."

And when he arrived at the home of the chiefs, then he beheld his nephew's skin used as a flap over the entryway. Nanabushu beheld it move with a quiver. Whereupon he said, "Ah, me! My grandson, will you lead me to the place where I am to sit?"

Now, truly was he led to the place where the old woman would have sat. And then he saw a kettle with food cooking in it. It was the upper arm of Nanabushu's nephew that was cooking. It was usual for the old woman first to eat before she began with the work of healing. And so Nanabushu said, "I am not going to eat, not till after I have finished, then will I eat." And this said Nanabushu, "All of you go out-of-doors, I only here will remain." And after all of them had gone out, then yonder, where lay the chiefs, he beheld his arrows that were sticking out from the bodies of the chiefs. Thereupon he shoved them in

55

farther, working them back and forth, whereupon he truly killed them. So now they were dead. Accordingly he said, "Therefore now dead are the manitous."

And then they cried aloud, "Alas! Now dead are the manitous. Now, then, take you the linden bark twine everywhere over the earth, and string it around. For then it will be known where Nanabushu is, should he happen to step into it and be caught." Thereupon they all started away, laying the linden bark twine.

And when all had started away, Nanabushu cut the manitous into pieces and made a great cooking of the manitou flesh. And when he had finished cooking, he invited the children, and then fed them. Now, by one of the children that was peeping in was Nanabushu recognized to be who he was. Thereupon he said to it, "Hold on, my little brother, don't you tell!" And when Nanabushu sliced off some manitou grease, he then gave it to the small boy. Whereupon he said to him, "Fond-of-Raw-Fat[50] shall you be called till the end of the world." Then, after Nanabushu had taken up the manitou skins and the skin of his nephew, he then started off running and, as much of the linden bark he saw stringing about, all of it he touched as he went along.

Thereupon said all who were then living, "Halloo! Nanabushu is now touching against the snare."

Thereupon the water now began to come forth, and a mighty rain began to pour, and also the rocks from above began to fall, to the end that Nanabushu be crushed. Many were killed by the rocks and the water. Now, Nanabushu tried in vain to flee to a mountain. Right when he saw that the earth was overflowing with water, then he gathered together some logs and made a raft. Seven[51] only embarked upon that raft when the earth was flooded over with water. And so they remained there on the raft. Some gamefolk, too, he put aboard, birds, and all the various creatures that fly about in the air.

And after they had been a long while on the raft, he spoke to them that were good at diving. "Can you procure a little earth? If you fetch it to me I would create an earth." Now, he first employed a kind of duck, but the bird was not able to come within reach of the earth; it was drowned before it got there.[52] He had it tied with linden bark twine, for that was what he did to them all—the Ducks and the Loon and the Beaver.

Muskrat

And when it came floating up to the surface, then another Duck, and also the Loon, had the same thing happen to them. They were not able to fetch any earth. And next he had the Beaver dive, but it also met the same fate: it drowned before it reached the bottom. Every time that one came up, he looked to see if it had hold of any earth, but nothing of earth he found. So next he had the Muskrat dive; also he had it tied with linden bark twine.

So then into the water dived the Muskrat. Much farther down he pulled on the linden bark cord. At last he felt the Muskrat pulling at the cord, and that was when it was drowning. Thereupon Nanabushu pulled it up.

When he examined the Muskrat, he found that it was holding a little earth in both its paws, and a little earth it also had in the mouth, and there was a little in each armpit too. Thereupon, after Nanabushu took

56

the Muskrat up in his hands, he breathed upon it, whereupon he revived it. Now, that was what he had done to them all. Now, when Nanabushu had dried the earth in his hands, he then rolled it into a ball. So then next he had the Raven go find if the earth could be seen anywhere out of the water, but the Raven did not return. Then next the White Pigeon[53] he employed, whereupon a tiny twig did the Pigeon fetch. And after Nanabushu had stuck it into the earth which he had there in his hand, he then tossed it into the water. At the same time he said, "I will that an island come into existence here." And at the same time he breathed upon it.

Trailing You

Kimberly Blaeser, Anishinâbe

For Ike

Trailing you in stories
and then in the dreams
that come just before morning
so that I wake listening for you to finish
what you were saying
or I sit up, swinging my legs to the side of the bed
rushing until my feet feel the carpet
and the rest of what I was expecting
becomes a dream too.
Those mornings I won't talk until
I go over it all the way I can remember it
waking up because my nose is so cold
and the fire has gone out in the bedroom stove
lying under the crazy quilt
peeking out of the blankets that cover the window to see
who is out in the yard
what kind of day it is
what's hanging on the clothesline
feeling the last warmth of the flannel sheets
before I swing my legs out and my bare feet touch
no carpet
but ice-cold linoleum covered with bits of gritty sand
that stick to my feet
as I run into the kitchen
where a fire is going in the cook stove
where you have been sitting drinking coffee.
Sometimes I see your face when you turn.
Other times it won't come clear
but I refuse to look at the pictures.
I want you more real than that
not to cry over as if you aren't still here.

If I could tell you the things I'm doing
bring them to you over smoked fish and coffee
you'd make them over for me with your talk and teasing
link with your eyes my past and present.
So I trail you waking and sleeping
hear you laughing as you splash cold water on my face
when I've slept too long
see your hands and hear the water
trickle into the wash basin as you pour for me
smell the side pork and hot biscuits
listen to you call "Kim-a-dill, Kim-a-dill"
as if I were a bird
and in these memories and dreams and stories of you
I find the places you sat and rested while cutting wood
I see the hole you broke the ice when you fell through
and the path of broken ice as you kept heaving yourself up
over and over with your gun ahead of you all the way to shore
and I wonder if these poems are the path I make and I wonder
how far it is
to shore.

1992

Kimberly Blaeser (1955-   ), who grew up on White Earth Reservation in northwestern Minnesota, is a professor of English at the University of Wisconsin-Madison. *Trailing You*, a collection of poems, won the 1993 Diane Decorah First Book Award from the Native Writer's Circle of the Americas.

From *The Trickster*

Ho-Chunk, Hágaga (Third-Born Son, Sam Blowsnake/Carley, 1875-†)

Hágaga

As he was walking along suddenly he came to a lake, and there in the lake he saw numerous ducks. Immediately he ran back quietly before they could see him and sought out a spot where there was a swamp. From it he gathered a large quantity of reed-grass and made himself a big pack. This he put on his back and carried it to the lake. He walked along the shore of the lake carrying it ostentatiously.

Soon the ducks saw him and said, "Look, that is Trickster walking over there. I wonder what he is doing? Let us call and ask him." So they called to him, "Trickster, what are you carrying?" Thus they shouted at him, but he did not answer. Then, again they called to him.

But it was only after the fourth call that he replied and said, "Well, are you calling me?"

"What are you carrying on your back?" they asked.

"My younger brothers, surely you do not know what it is you are asking. What am I carrying? Why, I am carrying songs. My stomach is full of bad songs. Some of these my stomach could not hold and that is why I am carrying them on my back. It is a long time since I sang any of them. Just now there are a large number in me. I have met no people on my journey who would dance for me and let me sing some for them. And I have, in consequence, not sung any for a long time."[54]

Then the ducks spoke to each other and said, "Come, what if we ask him to sing? Then we could dance, couldn't we?" So one of them called out, "Well, let it be so. I enjoy dancing very much and it has been a very long time since I last danced." So they spoke to Trickster, "Older brother, yes, if you will sing to us we will dance. We have been yearning to dance for some time but could not do so because we had no songs." Thus spoke the ducks.

"My younger brothers," replied Trickster, "you have spoken well and you shall have your desire granted. First, however, I will erect a dancing-lodge." In this they helped him and soon they had put up a dancing-lodge, a grass-lodge.[55] Then they made a drum. When this was finished he invited them all to come in and they did so. When he was ready to sing he said, "My younger brothers, this is the way in which you must act. When I sing, when I have people dance for me, the dancers must, from the very beginning, never open their eyes."

"Good," they answered.

Then when he began to sing, he said, "Now remember, younger brothers, you are not to open your eyes. If you do they will become red."

So, as soon as he began to sing, the ducks closed their eyes and danced.

After a while one of the ducks was heard to flap his wings as he came back to the entrance of the lodge and cry, "Quack!" Again and again this happened. Sometimes it sounded as if the particular duck had somehow tightened its throat. Whenever any of the ducks cried out, then Trickster would tell the other ducks to dance faster and faster. Finally a duck whose name was Little Red Eyed Duck[56] secretly opened its eyes, just the least little bit it opened them. To its surprise, Trickster was wringing the necks of his fellow ducks. He would also bite them as he twisted their necks. It was while he was doing this that the noise which sounded like the tightening of the throat was heard. In this fashion Trickster killed as many as he could reach.

Little Red Eyed Duck shouted, "Alas! He is killing us! Let those who can save themselves." He himself flew out quickly through the opening above. All the others likewise crowded toward this opening. They struck Trickster with their wings and scratched him with their feet. He went among them with his eyes closed and stuck out his hands to grab them. He grabbed one in each hand and choked them to death. His eyes were closed tightly. Then suddenly all of them escaped except the two he had in his grasp. When he looked at these, to his annoyance, he was holding in each hand a scabby-mouthed duck. In no way perturbed, however, he shouted, "Ha, ha, this is the way a man acts! Indeed these ducks will make fine soup to drink!"[57]

Then he made a fire and cut some sharp-pointed sticks with which to roast them. Some he roasted in this manner, while others he roasted by covering them with ashes. "I will wait for them to be cooked," he said to himself. "I had, however, better go to sleep now. By the time I awake they will unquestionably be thoroughly done. Now you, my younger brother, must keep watch for me while I go to sleep. If you notice any people, drive them off." He was talking to his anus. Then turning his anus toward the fire, he went to sleep.

When he was sleeping some small foxes approached and, as they ran along, they scented something that seemed like fire. "Well, there must be something around here," they said. So they turned their noses toward the wind and looked and, after a while, truly enough, they saw the smoke of a fire. So they peered around carefully and soon noticed many sharp-pointed sticks arranged around a fire with meat on them. Stealthily they approached nearer and nearer and, scrutinizing everything carefully, they noticed someone asleep there. "It is Trickster and he is asleep! Let us eat this meat. But we must be very careful not to wake him up. Come, let us eat," they said to one another.

When they came close, much to their surprise, however, gas was expelled from somewhere. "Pooh!" such was the sound made.

"Be careful! He must be awake." So they ran back. After a while one of them said, "Well, I guess he is asleep now. That was only a bluff. He is always up to some tricks." So again they approached the fire. Again gas was expelled and again they ran back. Three times this happened. When they approached the fourth time gas was again expelled. However, they did not run away. So Trickster's anus, in rapid succession, began to expel more and more gas. Still they did not run away. Once, twice, three times, it expelled gas in rapid succession. "Pooh! Pooh!" Such was the sound it made. Yet they did not run away. Then louder, still louder, was the sound of the gas expelled. "Pooh! Pooh! Pooh!" Yet they did not run away. On the contrary, they now began to eat the roasted pieces of duck. As they were eating, the Trickster's anus continued its "Pooh" incessantly. There the foxes stayed until they had eaten up all the pieces of duck roasted on sticks. Then they came to those pieces that were being roasted under ashes and, in spite of the fact that the anus was expelling gas "Pooh! Pooh! Pooh! Pooh!" continuously, they ate these all up too. Then they replaced the pieces with the meat eaten off, nicely under the ashes. Only after that did they go away.

After a while Trickster awoke, "My, O my!" he exclaimed joyfully, "The things I had put on to roast must be cooked crisp by now." So he went over, felt around, and pulled out a leg. To his dismay it was but a bare bone, completely devoid of meat. "How terrible! But this is the way they generally are when they are cooked too much!" So he felt around again and pulled out another one. But this leg also had nothing on it. "How terrible! These, likewise, must have been roasted too much! However, I told my younger brother, anus, to watch the meat roasting. He is a good cook indeed!" He pulled out one piece after the other. They were all the same. Finally he sat up and looked around. To his astonishment, the pieces of meat on the roasting sticks were gone! "Ah, ha, now I understand! It must have been those covetous friends of mine who have done me this injury!" he exclaimed. Then he poked around the fire again and again but found only bones. "Alas! Alas! They have caused my appetite to be disappointed, those covetous fellows! And you, too, you despicable object, what about your behavior? Did I not tell you to watch this fire? You shall remember this! As a punishment for your remissness, I will burn your mouth so that you will not be able to use it!"

Thereupon he took a burning piece of wood and burnt the mouth of his anus. He was, of course, burning himself and, as he applied the fire, he exclaimed, "Ouch! Ouch! This is too much. I have made my skin smart. Is it not for such things that they call me Trickster? They have indeed talked me into doing this just as if I had been doing something wrong!" Trickster had burnt his anus. He had applied a burning piece of wood to it. Then he went away.

As he walked along the road he felt certain that someone must have passed along it before for he was on what appeared to be a trail. Indeed, suddenly, he came upon a piece of fat that must have come from someone's body. "Someone has been packing an animal he had killed," he thought to himself. Then he picked up a piece of fat and ate it. It had a delicious taste. "My, my, how delicious it is to eat this!" As he proceeded however, much to his surprise, he discovered that it was a part of himself, part of his own intestines, that he was eating. After burning his anus, his intestines had contracted and fallen off, piece by piece, and these pieces were the things he was picking up. "My, my! Correctly, indeed, am I named Foolish One, Trickster! By their calling me thus, they have at last actually turned me into a Foolish One, a Trickster!" Then he tied his intestines together. A large part, however, had been lost. In tying it, he pulled it together so that wrinkles and ridges were formed. That is the reason why the anus of human beings has its present shape.[58]

After that he walked down a slope and finally came to a lake. On the opposite side he saw a number of women swimming, the chief's daughter and her friends. "Now," exclaimed Trickster, "is the opportune time: now I am going to have intercourse." Thereupon he took his penis out of the box[59] and addressed it, "My younger brother, you are going after the chief's daughter. Pass her friends, but see that you lodge squarely in her, the chief's daughter." Thus speaking he dispatched it. It went sliding on the surface of the water. "Younger brother, come back, come back! You will scare them away if you approach in that manner!" So he pulled the penis back, tied a stone around its neck, and sent it out again. This time it dropped to the bottom of the lake. Again he pulled it back, took another stone, smaller in size, and attached it to its neck. Soon he sent it forth again. It slid along the water, creating waves as it passed along. "Brother, come back, come back! You will drive the women away if you create waves like that!" So he tried a fourth time. This time he got a stone, just the right size and just the right weight, and attached it to its neck. When he dispatched it, this time it went directly towards the designated place. It passed and just barely touched the friends of the chief's daughter. They saw it and cried out, "Come out of the water, quick!" The chief's daughter was the last one on the bank and could not get away, so the penis lodged squarely in her. Her friends came back and tried to pull it out, but all to no avail. They could do absolutely nothing. Then the men who had the reputation for being strong were called and tried it but they, too, could not move it. Finally they all gave up. Then one of them said, "There is an old woman around here who knows many things. Let us go and get her." So they went and got her and brought her to the place where this was happening.

When she came there she recognized immediately what was taking place. "Why, this is First-born, Trickster. The chief's daughter is having intercourse and you are all just annoying her." Thereupon she went out, got an awl and, straddling the penis, worked the awl into it a number of times, singing as she did so: "First-born, if it is you, pull it out. Pull it out!" Thus she sang. Suddenly, in the midst of her singing, the penis was jerked out and the old woman was thrown a great distance. As she stood there bewildered, Trickster, from across the lake, laughed loudly at her. "That old naughty woman. Why is she doing this when I am trying to have intercourse? Now, she has spoiled all the pleasure."

As he went wandering around aimlessly he suddenly heard someone speaking. He listened very carefully and it seemed to say, "He who chews me will defecate; he will defecate!" That was what it was saying. "Well, why is this person talking in this manner?" said Trickster. So he walked in the direction from which he had heard the speaking and again he heard, quite near him, someone saying: "He who chews me, he will defecate; he will defecate!" This is what was said. "Well, why does this person talk in such fashion?" said Trickster. Then he walked to the other side. So he continued walking along. Then right at his very side, a voice seemed to say, "He who chews me, he will defecate; he will defecate!" "Well, I wonder who it is who is speaking. I know very well that if I chew it, I will not defecate." But he kept looking around for the speaker and finally discovered, much to his astonishment, that it was a bulb on a bush.[60] The bulb it was that was speaking. So he seized it, put it in his mouth, chewed it, and then swallowed it. He did just this and then went on.

"Well, where is the bulb gone that talked so much? Why, indeed, should I defecate? When I feel like defecating, then I shall defecate, no sooner. How could such an object make me defecate!" Thus spoke Trickster. Even as he spoke, however, he began to break wind. "Well this, I suppose, is what it meant. Yet the bulb said I would defecate, and I am merely expelling gas. In any case I am a great man even if I do expel a little gas!" Thus he spoke. As he was talking he again broke wind. This time it was really quite strong. "Well, what a foolish one I am. This is why I am called Foolish One, Trickster." Now he began to break wind again and again. "So this is why the bulb spoke as it did, I suppose." Once more he broke wind. This time it was very loud and his rectum began to smart. "Well, it surely is a great thing!" Then he broke wind again, this time with so much force that he was propelled forward. "Well, well, it may even make me give another push, but it won't make me defecate," so he exclaimed defiantly.

The next time he broke wind, the hind part of his body was raised up by the force of the explosion and he landed on his knees and hands. "Well, go ahead and do it again. Go ahead and do it again!" Then, again, he broke wind. This time the force of the expulsion sent him far up in the air and he landed on the ground, on his stomach. The next time he broke wind, he had to hang on to a log, so high was he thrown. However, he raised himself up and, after a while, landed on the ground, the log on top of him. He was almost killed by the fall. The next time he broke wind, he had to hold on to a tree that stood near by. It was a poplar and he held on with all his might yet, nevertheless, even then, his feet flopped up in the air. Again, and for the second time, he held on to it when he broke wind and yet he pulled the tree up by the roots. To protect himself, the next time, he went on until he came to a large tree, a large oak tree. Around this he put both his arms. Yet, when he broke wind, he was swung up and his toes struck against the tree. However, he held on.

After that he ran to a place where people were living. When he got there, he shouted, "Say, hurry up and take your lodge down, for a big war party is upon you and you will surely be killed. Come let us get away." He scared them all so much that they quickly took down their lodge, piled it on Trickster, and then got on him themselves.[61] They likewise placed all the little dogs they had on top of Trickster. Just then he began to break wind again and the force of the expulsion scattered the things on top of him in all directions. They fell far apart from one another. Separated, the people were standing about and shouting to one another, and the dogs, scattered here and there, howled at one another. There stood Trickster laughing at them till he ached.

Now he proceeded onward. He seemed to have gotten over his troubles. "Well, this bulb did a lot of talking," he said to himself, "yet it could not make me defecate." But even as he spoke he began to have the desire to defecate, just a very little. "Well, I suppose this is what it meant. It certainly bragged a good deal, however." As he spoke he defecated again. "Well, what a braggart it was! I suppose this is why it said this." As he spoke these last words, he began to defecate a good deal. After a while, as he was sitting down, his body would touch the excrement. Thereupon he got on top of a log and sat down there but, even then, he touched the excrement. Finally, he climbed up a log that was leaning against a tree. However, his body still touched the excrement, so he went up higher. Even then, however, he touched it so he climbed still higher up. Higher and higher he had to go. Nor was he able to stop defecating. Now he was on top of the tree. It was small and quite uncomfortable. Moreover, the excrement began to come up to him.

Even on the limb on which he was sitting he began to defecate. So he tried a different position. Since the limb, however, was very slippery, he fell right down into the excrement. Down he fell, down into the dung. In fact he disappeared in it, and it was only with very great difficulty that he was able to get out of it. His raccoon-skin blanket was covered with filth, and he came out dragging it after him. The pack he was carrying on his back was covered with dung, as was also the box containing his penis. The box he emptied and then placed it on his back again.

Then, still blinded by the filth, he started to run. He could not see anything. As he ran he knocked against a tree. The old man [Trickster] cried out in pain. He reached out and felt the tree and sang: "Tree, what kind of a tree are you? Tell me something about yourself!"

And the tree answered, "What kind of a tree do you think I am? I am an oak tree. I am the forked oak tree that used to stand in the middle of the valley. I am that one," it said.

"Oh, my, is it possible that there might be some water around here?" Trickster asked.

The tree answered, "Go straight on." This is what it told him.

As he went along he bumped up against another tree. He was knocked backwards by the collision. Again he sang: "Tree, what kind of a tree are you? Tell me something about yourself!"

"What kind of a tree do you think I am? The red oak tree that used to stand at the edge of the valley, I am that one."

"Oh, my, is it possible that there is water around here?" asked Trickster.

Then the tree answered and said, "Keep straight on," and so he went again.

Soon he knocked against another tree. He spoke to the tree and sang: "Tree, what kind of a tree are you? Tell me something about yourself!"

"What kind of a tree do you think I am? The slippery elm tree that used to stand in the midst of the others, I am that one."

Then Trickster asked, "Oh, my, is it possible that there would be some water near here?" And the tree answered and said, "Keep right on."

On he went and soon he bumped into another tree and he touched it and sang: "Tree, what kind of a tree are you? Tell me something about yourself."

"What kind of a tree do you think I am? I am the basswood tree that used to stand on the edge of the water. That is the one I am."[62]

"Oh, my, it is good," said Trickster. So there in the water he jumped and lay. He washed himself thoroughly.

It is said that the old man almost died that time, for it was only with the greatest difficulty that he found the water. If the trees had not spoken to him he certainly would have died. Finally, after a long time and only after great exertions, did he clean himself, for the dung had been on him a long time and had dried. After he had cleansed himself he washed his raccoon-skin blanket and his [penis] box.

As he was running along, he came to a valley. There he heard someone beating a drum, the drumming followed by many war whoops. Somebody there was making a great noise. So loud was this noise that it seemed to reach the skies. "Well, I wonder what these people are up to? I guess I will go over and see for I have not had any fun for a long time. Whatever they are doing, I will join them. If they are going to dance, why I will dance too. I used to be a fine dancer." Thus Trickster spoke. Then, as he walked across the valley, again and again he heard that noise.

Everyone was shouting with joy. It was wonderful! "Ah! There must be many people over there," he was thinking to himself. Again he heard them shout and, once again, when the drum was beaten, it seemed as if the heavens would burst asunder. Then again the people gave a tremendous shout. Now he became so anxious to join them that he began to run. The shouting was now quite close to him. Yet he could see no one anywhere. Again he heard the shouting. It was very loud. It sounded as if the sky would burst asunder.

To him it seemed as if, even at that moment, he was walking in the midst of people shouting. Yet he did not see anything. Not far away, however, he saw, lying around, the bones of an animal and, farther still, he saw an object that turned out, on closer inspection, to be an elk's skull. It had many horns branching in every direction. He watched this head quite carefully and then he saw where the noise had come from and where the celebration was taking place. It was in the elk's skull. The head was filled with many flies. They would go inside and then, when they rushed out, they made the noise that he had heard and which he had taken to be shouting. He looked at the flies and he saw that they were enjoying themselves greatly and he envied them.[63]

"Well, I said that I would join in whatever they were doing and I am going to. I wonder what I would have to do in order to join them?" Thus pondered Trickster. Then he said, "Younger brothers, you are certainly having a lot of fun. You surely are doing an important thing. I would very much like to be like one of you. How can I do it? Do show me how I can do it so that I, too, can join you." Thus he spoke.

Then they answered him, "Well, there is no difficulty involved. We enter through the neck as you must have seen by this time." Thus they spoke.

Then Trickster tried to enter but failed. He wanted very much to enter but he was unable. "How do you manage to get in, my younger brothers?" he asked. Great man that he was, he could not accomplish it, much as he wished to!

Then they said to him, "If you wish to come in just say, 'Neck, become large!' and it will become large. In that way you can enter. That is the way we do it." Thus they told him.

So he sat down and said, "Neck, become large!" and the hole in the neck became large. Then he put his head in and entered. He put his head in up to his neck. All the flies ran away and the opening into which he had thrust his head became small again. Thus he was held fast. He tried to free himself exerting all his power, but it was of no avail. He could do absolutely nothing. He was unable to free his head from the skull of the elk.

When he realized that nothing could be done, he went down to the stream wearing the skull. He had long branching antlers, for he was wearing an elk's skull. When he came to the river he walked along the edge, and as he went along he came to a place inhabited by human beings. There he waited until night. The next morning he did the following. As soon as the people came to get water from the river, he stretched himself out and lay there with his raccoon-skin blanket, quite a fear-inspiring object to look upon. His whole body was covered with the raccoon-skin blanket and he had long branching horns on his head.

Early in the morning a woman came for water and saw him. She started to run back but he said to her, "Turn back; I will bless you!" So she turned back and when she got there, he said to her, "Now, go home. Get an axe and bring it over here. Then use all the offerings that are customary, of which your relations will tell you. If you strike the top of my head with the axe, you will be able to use what you find therein as medicine and obtain anything that you wish. I am an elk-spirit. I am blessing this village." Thus he spoke to her. Then he continued, "I am one of the great spirits living in these waters."[64]

So the woman went home and when she got there she told all the people what had happened. "There is a water spirit at the place where we dip for water who blessed me. He told me that he had a medicine-chest in the box that he carried and that if we brought an axe and suitable offerings, placed them there, and then split his head open, what we found within his skull we could use for making various medicines." Thus she spoke.

Thereupon the people went to the river with their various offerings and, sure enough, there they found him, quite fear-inspiring to look upon. The offerings—red feathers, white deer skin, and red-yarn belts—they brought in great quantities. After they had placed all these things before him, they selected a man who was to take the axe. He struck the skull and split it open and behold! there they found Trickster laughing at them. He arose and said, "A nice head-dress I have been wearing but now you have spoiled it!" Then he laughed uproariously.

When he got up the people said, "It is Trickster!"

However he spoke to them and said, "Inasmuch as you have made these offerings to me they will not be lost. For whatsoever be the purpose for which you use this head, that purpose will be accomplished." So then they made themselves various medicinal instruments and afterwards found that they were efficacious. Then Trickster left and continued wandering.

Suddenly he heard something singing: "Trickster, what is it you are packing? Your penis it is you are packing!"

"My, what an awful thing he is saying, that contemptible person." He seems really to know what I am carrying." On he went. Shortly after this, and from a definite direction, he again heard singing. It was as if it was just at his side:

"Trickster, what is it you are carrying? Your testicles, these you are carrying."

"My, who is this that is mentioning these things? He must indeed have been watching me. Well, now I will carry these things correctly." Thereupon he emptied his box and threw everything out. Then he placed his testicles underneath next to his back. As he was doing this again, suddenly, he heard someone singing right at his side:

"Trickster, what is it you are packing? What is it you are packing? Your testicles underneath, your testicles underneath!"

"My, what a contemptible person it is who is thus teasing me. He must have been watching my pack." So again he rearranged his pack. He now put the head of his penis on top. Then he went on but soon, unexpectedly, he heard the singing at his side again:

"Trickster, what is it you are packing? Your penis you are packing! The head of your penis you have placed on top, the head of your penis you have placed on top!"

"My, what an evil one it is who is saying this," and he jumped towards him.

But the one who had been singing ran away, exclaiming, "*Tigi! Tigi! Tigi!*" It ran into a hollow tree. It was a chipmunk.

"I will kill you for this, you contemptible thing," said Trickster. Thereupon he spoke to his penis, "Now then, my younger brother, you may go after him for he has been annoying you for a long time."

So he took out his penis and probed the hollow tree with it. He could not, however, reach the end of the hole. So he took some more of his penis and probed again, but again he was unable to reach the end of the hole. So he unwound more and more of his penis and probed still deeper, yet all to no avail. Finally he took what still remained, emptying the entire box, and probed and probed but still he could

Eastern chipmunk

not reach the end of the hole. At last he sat up on a log and probed as far as he could, but still he was unable to reach the end. "Ho!" said he impatiently, and suddenly withdrew his penis. Much to his horror, only a small piece of it was left. "My, what a great injury he has done to me! You contemptible thing I will repay you for this!"

Then he kicked the log to pieces. There he found the chipmunk and flattened him out, and there, too, to his horror he discovered his penis all gnawed up. "Oh, my, of what a wonderful organ he has deprived me! But why do I speak thus? I will make objects out of the pieces for human beings to use." Then he took the end of his penis, the part that has no foreskin, and declared, "This is what human beings will call the lily-of-the-lake." This he threw in a lake near by. Then he took the other pieces, declaring in turn: "This the people will call potatoes; this the people will call turnips; this the people will call artichokes; this the people will call ground-beans; this the people will call dog-teeth; this the people will call sharp-claws; this the people will call rice." All these pieces he threw into the water. Finally he took the end of his penis and declared, "This the people will call the pond-lily."[65] He was referring to the square part of the end of his penis. What was left of his penis was not very long. When, at last, he started off again, he left behind him the box in which he had until then kept his penis coiled up.

And this is the reason our penis has its present shape. It is because of these happenings that the penis is short. Had the chipmunk not gnawed off Trickster's penis, our penis would have the appearance that Trickster's had first had. It was so large that he had to carry it on his back. Now it would not have been good had our penis remained like that and the chipmunk was created for the precise purpose of performing this particular act. Thus it is said.

1956

TURTLE

Turtle had some problems after his brush with fame when he offered Sky Woman a place on his back. His worst was that he adored women, and that led him into all kinds of other trouble. Non-Natives seldom understand what genius it takes to create a laugh-out-loud-funny cycle of stories about one of the greatest manidog in the universe, one that some nations believe was the second creature Earthmaker brought to life. The Judeo-Christian equivalent would be skits about King David, who also had a weakness for women, as a bad stand-up comic in a strip club. The many tales about Turtle illustrate that although Native people may fear and respect the manidog, they also imagine them much like ourselves: struggling with temptation, greed, fear, lust, and every evil that people are capable of creating. In this story, Turtle's lust leads him to grave mistakes. Wīsa'kä, one of the sons of Gīshä Mü'nĕtōa, or the Great Spirit, punished Turtle by making him live in water. He does, however, give him great power in return: Turtle will know how to preserve life.

How Turtle Lost His Place Among the Great Manitous
Meskwaki, Unidentified

One day when Wīsa'kä was walking alone, he saw Turtle coming toward him. "There comes that creature! Going to see another woman, I suppose," said Wīsa'kä to himself smilingly. Then he sat down on the grass to await Turtle.

Turtle was walking along with his head down, seeming to be in deep thought. When Wīsa'kä called, "Hello, Turtle! Going to see another woman I suppose?" Turtle threw his head up and stopped.

"Hello, elder brother. What are you doing here?" said Turtle, very much amazed to see Wīsa'kä.

"Nothing," replied Wīsa'kä. "I saw you coming toward me, so I sat here to wait for you. I thought perhaps you would tell me who this woman is you are going to see."

"Don't speak about that," said Turtle, looking very serious. "I am going to see no woman. I am out walking as you are." Then looking at Wīsa'kä he asked, "Would you do something if I asked you?"

"I don't know," replied Wīsa'kä. "Tell me what it is and I will see."

"It is to join me in a shooting contest," replied Turtle. "See that tree far off yonder?"

"Yes," replied Wīsa'kä, perceiving Turtle's object in proposing the contest.

"Well," said Turtle, "we will shoot at that to see who is the better shot."

"All right," said Wīsa'kä. "You shoot first."

Turtle's arrow only grazed the bark on one side of the tree. Then Wīsa'kä shot, hitting the tree in the center and splitting it. And, as usual after he has shot his arrow, and it has struck, there followed a heavy rumbling and the world shook.

"You have beaten me this time," said Turtle, starting to go, adding as he walked off, "I would shoot again with you, but I must go over here to a dwelling."

Wīsa'kä started off in the opposite direction, but stopped when he was out of Turtle's view. Then taking a roundabout way so Turtle could not see him, Wīsa'kä arrived at the dwelling before him. When Turtle came he pulled away very gently the curtain over the entrance, and popped in. He saw a beautiful young woman seated by the fire, busy at her needlework. "That is the prettiest woman I have ever seen!" thought Turtle to himself. He withdrew his head, pulled the curtain back over its place, and hurried over to the lodge of his brother.

When the brother came in he noticed that Turtle had on his most beautiful clothes. He was painting his face when his brother said, "She must be a very pretty woman you are going to see. I never saw you dress so carefully as this. Who is she? What is her name?"

"Hush your mouth," replied Turtle. "Everyone who meets me asks me what woman I am going to see, who she is, and what her name is, as though I spent all my time with women. I am dressing up because I wish to appear well."

The brother made no reply. When Turtle got ready to go he asked, "Brother, may I take the medicine bag out with me for a little while?"

"What for?" asked the brother.

"If I tell you will you let me take it?" begged Turtle.

"That is a hard question to answer, my brother," replied the brother.

"Then I will tell you why I want the medicine bag," said Turtle, who was now becoming impatient. "Over in that lodge is the most beautiful woman I ever saw. I don't know who she is, nor her name. I am going to woo her, and the only possible way for me to win her is to have this medicine bag with me."

Otter skin medicine bag

"Oh no!" said the brother. "You can't use this medicine bag for that purpose. Wīsa'kä gave us these medicine bags to hang in our lodges to drive away Pänäni (death and evil). They are to hang in our lodge until we move. No, you must not take this medicine bag."[66]

The brother then went out of the lodge. Turtle watched him until he had disappeared from view. Then he put the medicine bag under his robe and stole out of the lodge.

Arriving at the lodge where the beautiful woman was, Turtle stopped at the entrance to pull the robe over his head. Then he pulled the blanket aside gently and walked in. He went by her without saying anything to her, and sat down in a place where he could look into her face. She went on with her sewing without looking up or taking the least notice of Turtle.

By and by, when he had stared into her face for some time, he coughed very gently. She raised her eyes and smiled softly. Turtle was happy, and at once began to talk and ask questions. At first the young woman only smiled, but after a while became bolder and so replied to his questions. Turtle stayed in the lodge a long time and would not leave when the young woman told him. It was beginning to be dark when Turtle, thinking that the young woman liked him very much, asked her, "You and I are going to marry each other, are we not?"[67]

"No," she replied. "I am not going to marry you. I am young yet, and I am not prepared. Are you not going home?"

Turtle sat there, believing yet that the young woman liked him. Seeing that he was not preparing to leave, she rose, put down her sewing, and said, "I am going home now, before it gets too dark." Then she lifted the curtain and went out of the lodge.

After a while Turtle followed after her and overtook her. He put one arm around her waist, and they walked side by side until the young woman said, "I am tired and sleepy; I will lie down here to rest."

Turtle was very happy to hear the young woman say she wished to lie down. He hurried around to find a place for her to rest. He found an anthill but did not know at the time it was one, because the night was so dark.

As the young woman lay down, Turtle put the medicine bag underneath her head, then lay beside her. By and by Turtle put one of his arms under her head for the young woman to rest on, then placed the other hand on the lower part of her body. In that position Turtle [rolled] into a deep sleep. The young woman then quietly rose and Wīsa'kä resumed his own form again. He took up the medicine bag and started for his home in the North, leaving Turtle sound asleep.

Turtle slept until the Sun began to show himself, when the ants began to come out of the hill and sting him. Turtle smiled with his eyes yet closed, embraced the anthill, and whispered, "Don't tickle me that way, because you wake me." The ants ran all over Turtle and bit him so much and in so many places that he opened his eyes. When he saw what he had been embracing and what awoke him, he jumped to his feet. The young woman was gone—so was the medicine bag. Nowhere could he find her tracks, to find which way she had gone. Then Turtle was very much alarmed because he thought that she must be a manitou.

Turtle became very sad. He did not mind so much being fooled by a woman as he did to lose the medicine bag on account of a woman. He went to his brother's lodge, told him everything that had happened, and showed him how badly he felt because he had taken the medicine bag without his consent. Turtle then set out in search of the lost medicine bag. He went everywhere in this world but could not find it anywhere. He went to the East, where Sun lives. It was not there. Then he went to the South, where Cāwano and the Thunderers live.[68] It was not to be found there. He went to the West, where Tcīpaiyāpōswa lives.[69] He did not find it there. Then he visited the places under the earth where manitous live. He could not find it there. Then he went up to the White River where the Great Manitou and other manitous live, but he did not find the medicine bag there.[70] Then Turtle felt very sad. He was tired traveling so long and so far. He sat down and thought to himself thus: "There is just one place where I have not gone—that is where Wīsa'kä lives, and that will be the hardest journey. I wonder if he could have been that young woman! He was the last one I saw before I saw her the first time. I will go to his lodge. If I don't find the medicine bag there, then I don't know where else to go to find it."

Then Turtle rose and started toward the north where Wīsa'kä lives. The journey was so long and hard that when Turtle arrived at Wīsa'kä's lodge he was so weary that he could scarcely walk any farther. He entered the lodge and found Wīsa'kä seated by the fire and Grandmother Earth seated upon the raised platform.

"Hello, my younger brother!" said Wīsa'kä, welcoming Turtle. "Come sit down here by me. You look tired."

Turtle did as Wīsa'kä told him. Wīsa'kä then rose and fetched food and placed it upon a mat before Turtle. Turtle ate until he could eat no more. Then while he was admiring the beautiful things in the lodge from the place where he sat, Wīsaʻkä asked, "My younger brother, why have you come to my lodge? I never asked you to come."

Turtle replied, "My elder brother, I lost my brother's medicine bag. I have been everywhere in the world and everywhere else where the manitous live, and I can't find it. This is the only place where I have not gone to, and that is why I came here, so as to find my brother's medicine bag."

"It is here," replied Wīsaʻkä. "Come, and I will show it to you." Turtle followed Wīsaʻkä out of the lodge. They went into another lodge where there were ever so many medicine bags. In among these was the one belonging to Turtle's brother. Wīsaʻkä returned it to him and Turtle set out for home with it. When he arrived there, he gave it to his brother.

It happened one day when Turtle was walking alone along the bank of a river that he met Wīsaʻkä. "You are just the one I wish to see," said Wīsaʻkä to Turtle. "You took your brother's medicine bag one day from his lodge when he told you not to do it. Then you went to woo a young woman and lost the medicine bag. You came to my lodge to find it, and I returned it. Now listen to what I tell you. You can no longer be a great manitou because of what you have done. Hereafter your home will be in the water. But I give this one great power: You will know the medicine that can head off Nokanowa (breath of life, spirit) before it crosses the river [of death].[71] When men come to you and ask you for this medicine, tell them where to find it."

Then Wīsaʻkä threw Turtle into the water of the river. There Turtle lives to this day. He is yet a manitou, but not the great manitou he used to be.

1890s

RED HORN

Some scholars believe this epic to be among the most ancient stories of the Siouan peoples, as old as or older than Trickster, and the world here is quite different from his. The role of women is greater, perhaps because women had more power among the agricultural Ho-Chunk and because this story may be old enough to reflect a time when the Ho-Chunk reckoned descent in the female line, as more western Siouan tribes do today. The name "Red Horn" is believed to be a recent adoption from nations farther west, but the character of He Who Wears Human Heads As Earrings or Stcohordcika is ancient, the incarnation of Wīragō´cge xetera, the Morning Star [Venus] or Great Star [possibly Mars or Sirius] and a god of war, whose world is an archaic one of great epic heroes who battle evil forces, here giants, to make the world safe for the people. Kunu, or oldest brother or First Born male, as he is also known, was a creation of Maona, the Creator, and his eight brothers are known as Haynu, Haga, Nagi, Little Kunu, Little Haynu, Little Haga, and Little Nagi. They are the ancestors of the eight clans of the Ho-Chunk. Kunu's arena is the rim of the world; he chases the sun and the planets. He is helped by Storms As He Walks, who is a Thunderbird. As with all serious, religious texts, the activities of the gods are meant to be examples for the humans who will come after them, particularly the rituals involving war, marriage, and games. Hágaga (Third Born Son) wrote the story in Ho-Chunk syllabary, and Oliver Lamere translated it.

Hágaga (Third-Born Son, Sam Blowsnake/Carley), Ho-Chunk

Long ago ten brothers lived together in a lodge. Of these ten the youngest one always stayed at home. His older brothers loved him very much. While he stayed at home, they went hunting bear and deer. They would always return about sundown. One morning, when the older brothers were still at home, a person entered the lodge. He had a gourd hanging from his belt which rattled as he walked. "Kunu (Oldest Brother)," he said, "at last I have come upon you. The chief's daughter is going to be married and whoever wins the race shall marry her."

Kunu answered, "All right."

When they were ready to start, the brothers said, "Younger brother, you must stay at home."

And so they set off. When they approached the place where they were to race, they were greeted with whoops of welcome and they answered with whoops. The people were saying, "Kunu has come and the one at whom Kunu used to throw deer lungs, his youngest brother, he has also come along." So Kunu looked behind him and, sure enough, there was his little brother following, wearing an untanned deerskin blanket turned inside out. The fur was on the outside.[72]

"See here," Kunu said to his youngest brother, "I told you not to come." He was ashamed of him for he, Kunu, was proud of his success with women.

But the other brothers said, "That's all right. He can look after our things."

When they got to the appointed place, the people said, "Ho! Kunu, it is only for you they are still waiting." The chief's daughter, for whom the race was to be run, was sitting on the platform. All those properly called spirits were present: the Thunderbirds, the Night-Spirits,[73] the Deer, the Bears, and all the birds of the air.

Turtle was now seen moving across the valley. "Come," they said, "Let us go after Turtle. He is just across the valley and he usually makes trouble and causes scandal." So away they ran in pursuit of him. Thus the race started. When they came to the top of the hill, there he was on the next hill shaking his sacred pipe. When they arrived at the hill on which he had first been seen, he was just going over the next one. When they got there he was going over the third hill, and when they got there he was nearing the fourth hill. Then said the runners, "Turtle is very tricky. Someone had better go over there and watch him." When they got there they found a small red turtle hiding.[74] They stamped upon him and thrust him into the earth and went on.

They saw the youngest brother running after them and taking part in the race. "He Who Gets Hit With Deer Lungs is about to do something. Look at him," the spectators called out and all laughed at him.

But on he went. First he passed Kunu, his oldest brother and, as he passed him, the latter exclaimed, "Little brother, I am no good. If you are good, try with all your strength to win." So on the youngest brother went and he came to the second oldest brother who repeated what Kunu had said. Thus he kept on passing them, one after the other. They were running around the rim of the world. Their goal was the place where the sun sets, the West. To that place the youngest brother was pointing.

On he went till he came in sight of another group of runners. They were Black Hawk, Hummingbird, Eagle, and two of his other brothers. When he saw that he could not get any closer to them, he took one of his arrows and shot in their direction. It alit beside the runners. He had turned himself into the arrow. His brothers said, "Little brother, try with all your strength!" Again, he shot one of his arrows and he went way past Black Hawk and his group. From there on he ran as hard as he could, leaving them farther and farther behind. When he came in sight of the goal, he saw Turtle walking in the middle of the valley.

The spectators all shouted, "He Who Gets Hit With Deer Lungs is coming! He must have turned back!"

Then he passed Turtle. Finally he passed the last group of runners.

"Who won the race?" everyone asked.

"Well, the one who won the race has just come in," was the answer.

Then Turtle said, "Kunu's little brother followed me in pretty close. I am getting old, I fear."

"Say, Turtle, you always cause disputes. Kunu's brother won the race," shouted the spectators.

Turtle, however, did not listen and, addressing one of his brothers, said, "Bring down your sister-in-law," the chief's daughter, for whose hand the race was run.

So Oval-Turtle climbed the platform and said, "Sister-in-law, come down." But she refused.

Thereupon Turtle himself went up, took her by the wrist, dragged her down, and took her home. The sister of the chief's wife cried, but it was of no avail. Just then, however, Kunu returned and the people said to him, "Kunu, your little brother won the race, but Turtle has taken the chief's daughter home by force."

Kunu answered, "All right. I always longed to get hold of that man!" Thus he spoke and took hold of his bald-headed war club. "Where does he live?" he asked. They showed him and he set off.

When he came in, Turtle was still holding the chief's daughter by the wrist. She was crying. "Turtle," said Kunu, "I have heard a good deal about you and I just long to see you. My little brother won the race but yet, it is you took the chief's daughter. So I have come after her."

Then Turtle said, "It is true that your brother followed me in very close."

Kunu took hold of the chief's daughter by the other wrist, but Turtle would not let her go. Then he struck him with his war club which made a tremendous noise. There, on his four legs, Turtle stood wheezing.

When Kunu finally got outside, Turtle called out, "I want to make friends with your brother who won the race and that is why I am giving you this woman, not because I am afraid of you."

Kunu returned home with the chief's daughter. However his little brother said, "I am not old enough to marry. You had better marry her." Then he offered her to the next youngest brother. But this one too said, "I am not old enough to marry." So he offered her to the brother next to him. Thus they passed her on until she was finally offered to Kunu. And he said "All right," thanked them, and married her.

Now, the next morning, the older brothers all went out hunting. Kunu was the first one to return home with a deer on his back. He put his bow and arrows next to the lodge and laid a furless skin in the middle of the lodge. He put his deer-pack down and dressed it. The lungs he laid aside and went on with his task. Then his wife picked them up and threw them at Kunu's little brother, striking him in the breast. She laughed. But Kunu got angry and said, "Why did you do that?"

"Well," she answered, "I understand that this is what they always do to him and that is the reason why they called him by that name. That is why I am doing it."

"No one ever did that to him before," said Kunu. "Once I told him to fast and he refused so I threw a deer lung at him and that is the reason why they called him by that name, but no one ever hit him with a deer lung."

By this time the other brothers had returned and the youngest brother told them, "My sister-in-law hit me with a deer lung."

And they said to her "How did it happen? Did you not see him?"

"No, I did not," said the woman.

Now the little brother stood up and said, "Those in the heavens who created me did not call me by this name, He Who Is Hit With Deer Lungs. They called me He Who Wears Human Heads As Earrings." With that he spat upon his hands and began fingering his ears. And as he did this, little faces appeared on his ears, laughing, winking, and sticking out their tongues. Then he spoke again, "Those on earth, when they speak of me, call me Red Horn." With this he spat upon his hands and drew them over his hair which became very long and red. Now his brothers became fonder than ever of him and gathered around him laughing.

The next oldest brother said to him "What a wonderful thing you possess."

"Come sit next to me," the little brother said to him. Then he spat upon his hands again and passed them over the head of his older brother and the latter's hair became yellow on one side. Then the third brother told his little brother how much he admired him and the latter said, "Come sit next to me." Then he again spat upon his hands and passed them over his brother's head and his hair became very long. Then the little brother said, "This is no ordinary power and I will use no more of it for you."

The next morning, very early, someone came running, shouting, "Ho! Ho! He Who Wears Human Heads As Earrings, Red Horn, you and your brother Kunu are invited to go on a warpath."

"All right." Then Red horn said, "Hand me a dish." As soon as one had been given him, he stood with his legs spread out and holding the dish in his hands said, "Dish, enlarge yourself!" Then he threw it between his feet and it became larger. Again he said "Dish, enlarge yourself!" Four times he said this and, holding it on its edge, he threw it between his legs. Each time it became larger. After the fourth time it just fitted in between his legs, spread out at their farthest.

Then said Kunu, "Oh, what a nice dish you have, little brother! Would it be possible for you to enlarge mine?"

But the little brother said, "You saw me do it. Why don't you do it for yourself?"

Then Kunu said, "Very well, give me a dish," and one was given to him. He spread his legs even farther apart than his brother had done and holding it in both hands said four times, "Dish, enlarge yourself!" However he struck a stone that happened to be there and he broke the dish in two. "Oh my!" he exclaimed, "I have spoiled my dish."

"Hand it here, I will fix it for you," said Red Horn.

"Take another plate," said Kunu.

But the little brother said, "No, I will fix it for you as it is." Holding the broken pieces together, he spread out his legs and threw them on the ground between his legs, saying four times, "Dish, enlarge yourself!" and the dish became larger. Four times he did this and finally he had a dish nearly as large as that which he had made for himself.

Then Kunu said, "Little brother, let me carry the dishes." So with Kunu carrying the dishes they started out, the two younger brothers next to Red Horn, following. Kunu said, "You two had better not go. You were not invited."

"We do not have to go to the place where you are having a feast. We just want to go and see the people," they replied, and so they were allowed to come along. When they arrived at the appointed meeting place, they heard someone singing in the lodge and they went in. The lodge was already full of guests. "Ho! He Who Wears Human Heads As Earrings has come. Clear a place for him in the center of the lodge," they said.

Having made a place in the center of the lodge, the host began talking, saying, "Warriors, I know that I am raising unjustifiable expectations in your minds, but I am going on a hunt and therefore have had my nephews get me a few squirrels for a feast. They have just put them on to cook. I wish the choicest pieces to be given to He Who Wears Human Heads As Earrings, Red Horn."

"Very well," Red Horn said.

Then the host repeated the same to Otter and to Turtle. The others were all given ordinary portions of the food.[75]

Then the host said, "Sons of warriors, I greet you. When you are ready, may all begin the fast-eating contest to see who can finish first." Saying he blew his flute as the signal for them to start. Red Horn finished first, Wolf second, Otter third, and Turtle last. Turtle said, "I thought you were going to do this, so I took my time and ate it all. You have allowed one man to escape."[76]

Then the host rose and spoke again. "Now this is all. Doubtless some of you are very busy just now. However, in four days, I intend to go on the warpath or go hunting. If any of you wish to go along, you have plenty of time to make moccasins for yourselves." So he spoke and departed.

In four days they started on the warpath. The first night they camped outside the village. The leader called for someone to go and obtain food. The first one he thus called upon was He Who Wears Human Heads As Earrings.

"It is good," said the latter.

Then the leader called upon Wolf and said, "Otter will start from one side and Turtle from the other." They both said, "Very well."

Now Turtle, not being very good at hunting, demurred and said, "I shall send the small turtle in my place. He always kills large bears." So off went small turtle.

Very soon they heard someone from the other side of the camp saying, "There! There! Go over there, and I will give you a smoke." Whoever it was seemed to be saying this as he was walking along.

Then the war-leader said, "Go there and shoot the one talking." So they went over and killed it. It was a bear. From the other side of the camp someone approached again saying the same thing. Again the leader said, "Go and shoot it." And they did. Then from the third side of the camp Otter came saying he heard the same thing. The leader spoke again, "Go over there and shoot it." And they did. During all this time Turtle was absent. Finally they heard him shout. The war-leader said, "Turtle, go over there and shoot it." But when they got there, they met Turtle returning all alone. "Well?" they said to him, and Turtle replied, "There is someone in the cave." So they went over to see and, sure enough, they found a very large bear, larger than those that had been killed by the others.

The next morning they again started out and about evening they camped. Once more the leader called for someone to obtain food for them and once again Turtle told one of the small turtles to go in his place. All four did the same thing they had done the evening before. The next morning they went on their way again and when evening overtook them they camped and the same thing happened as on the previous night. The fourth night when they were camping, the leader called for some scalps and said he wished to obtain four people, that is, two specific couples. These couples were newly married and so fond of one another that they left the village in order to be alone. "I am going to call on Storms As He Walks, a thunderbird, and He Who Wears Human Heads As Earrings, or Red Horn, to go and see where they are. These two are to go together."

"Very well," they said and they went. Storms As He Walks was a nephew of the leader, both having come from the home of the Thunderbirds.

On the way, Storms As He Walks said, "My friend, if you were like me, we could travel in the clouds."

"But, my friend," answered Red Horn, "we can do it anyway even if I am not a thunderbird."

"Very well," said the other, "it is good." Thereupon they both traveled in the clouds. As they walked, a drizzling rain began to fall all around them.

"Come, let us camp," said those that were being hunted, "it is raining."

The scouts alighted on the earth just beyond them and then returned to their own lodge. There they told the leader that those whom they were to kill had been seen and that they did not seem to be expecting any harm.

Then the leader replied, "All right; that is good. As soon as dawn approaches, we shall make ready for the attack," said the leader, "but be on guard against Turtle, for he is very tricky."

At dawn they started. Once more they were warned, "Keep close watch on Turtle because he is very tricky."

As expected, very soon after, Turtle said, "Boys, I want very badly to go out.[77] I shall turn aside here."

Thus he spoke and they replied, "Very well, go on." Not long after they said, "Where is Turtle?" But he was nowhere to be found so they said, "Let us make the rush." Then the war whoop was given and they made the rush. Very soon after, Storms As He Walks gave the first victory cry and shouted, "Sons of war!"[78] Then He Who Wears Human Heads As Earrings gave the second victory cry, Wolf gave the third, and Otter the fourth. The others were then permitted to strike the dead one, so they came along until all had done so.

When it was all over, along came Turtle. "I wish those cowards had defended themselves," he said, "so that I might have reached here in time."

The victors went home and, when they came near the village, they chose one of their number to break the news to their relatives and to make preparations for the Victory Dance. So the one chosen went on home crying, "Storms As He Walks is killed! Red Horn is killed! Wolf is killed! Otter is killed!" All the old men of the village looked ashamed and despondent and said, "The ones we depended upon are lost!" Just then the warriors gave the victory war whoop and began to circle around the village. Those who had been reported dead were in the lead, and the whole village began circling around them in joyfulness.[79] The war-party finally came to the place prepared for the Victory Dance and began to dance. Many times did they dance. During the dancing the girls nudged Red Horn and all seemed very much smitten with him, but he refused to pay any attention to them at all. For four days they danced and then they went home . . . .

Now in this village there lived an old woman with her granddaughter. Their lodge was on the outskirts. One day the old woman said to her granddaughter, "You must court Red Horn." But the granddaughter refused. The grandmother, however, insisted, saying, "He likes you." Finally the girl consented. She teased him, and behold! he turned about and smiled at her. The other girls then became jealous of her, hooted at her, and shoved her about. The girl cried bitterly and told her grandmother about it but the old woman said, "Oh, they are only jealous of you. Remember that Red Horn is your husband, so stop crying." The young girl wore a white beaver-skin as a wrap.

Then the men went on the warpath for the fourth time. This time they camped ten nights. They were after ten scalps. They camped the first night just outside the village. The other young women used to take moccasins to the camp and offer them to Red Horn but he would refuse them. Finally the girl with the beaver wrap gave him a pair of moccasins and he accepted them.[80] Again the other girls said, "She does not know how to do anything," and shoved her about.

Finally the war party returned and this time Turtle was one of the victors. When they were near the village a messenger was sent forward and the voices of the victors were audible in the distance. They were saying, "Storms As He Walks was killed first, Red Horn was killed second." When the old woman heard this she called her granddaughter aside and said, "Your husband is killed," and she began to cut off the girl's hair.

The granddaughter cried bitterly while she was cutting her hair. "Why are you doing this?" said the girl.

Then the old woman said again, "It is said that your husband has been killed." Just then the victory war whoop was given and Red Horn was the first in the line of victors. "Oh!" said the old woman, "I have spoiled my granddaughter's hair."

Then the warriors all came to the dancing place and again they danced four days. Many of the young men were very friendly with Red Horn. They wanted him to court their sisters but he refused. They would tell him of the nice girls in the village and tell him to go after them, but he would not go. Instead, he asked them, "Where does the girl who wears the white beaver skin as a wrap live?"

But they said, "We told you to court nice girls and you refused. What do you want with this one?" They then said, "She lives just outside the village near the dump-pile." Some of the young men, however, said, "Why do you say such things to him? Perhaps he likes her." So they told him where the girl really lived.

Before he got there the old woman said to her granddaughter, "Granddaughter, if Red Horn comes, you must not drive him away." The old woman knew that he would be there. Just then someone lit a light and went to the place where the young girl was lying. The old woman rose from her bed and said, "I am afraid this orphan will not keep him very warm." Then she took a robe and covered them. And so Red Horn was married.

Now the people said, "We have been helped by these warriors. Let us make them our chiefs."

Shortly after, the war-leader again went on the warpath. Four more times he went and then, when all the dances were over, he said, "We must now return."

Then said Storms As He Walks, "Uncle, I have grown used to my friend and I like the human beings very much, so I am going to remain here. The human beings are going to have very hard times." With these he went to his lodge, taking his war-bundle along with him.

In this way did the actors of this story become the chiefs of the people. Kunu, the brother of Red Horn, was made head-chief.

Then, in the course of time, a man came to the chief's lodge carrying a pipe. This he turned towards Red Horn's mouth. It was to signify that a man had been shot and that the arrow was still in him. When Red Horn got to the place specified, the man lay there with the arrow still in him. First, Hawk went towards him, breathed upon him, took hold of the arrow and pulled it out about half-way. "Ouch!" said the man. Then Wolf tried it, but he could only move it a very little. Then Turtle tried it and pulled very hard but, instead of pulling it out, he almost killed the man. "Heigh!" exclaimed the man.

Finally Red Horn tried it, taking hold of the arrow and shaking it. At last he pulled it out. Then spitting into his hand he rubbed the sputum over the wound, healing him. He took home with him a young woman who had been given to him as a present in payment for his doctoring. This woman he gave to one of his older brothers. He doctored four more times and each time he was presented with a woman and, each time, he gave the women to one of his brothers until they were all married.

Now, once again, the people cried, "Here are some men coming this way who are weeping." So all went to the edge of the village to see them. The latter got nearer and nearer, carrying a sacred pipe ahead of them.

When the men got very near they asked, "Where does the chief live?"

"In the middle of the village, in that long lodge there, that is where he lives," said the people. "This is one of the chief's friends," they said, pointing to Turtle.

Then the suppliants went toward Turtle and directed the stem of the pipe towards his mouth. "Ho!" said he. They told him that giants had come upon them and that they were coming to him for assistance to help them against these giants. Then Turtle went home and constructed a drum and all night they heard him drumming.

His friends, however, said, "We need not go there until he calls." So they stayed away. But he did not call them. In the morning, he went out, but his friends did not go along, and so very few indeed followed. What could he do with these few followers? The result was that those who had asked for help were beaten again.[81]

Some evenings afterwards it was said, "They are coming again." One of the villagers, however, asked the newcomers why they didn't call upon the chief who lived at the end of the village beyond. So they went there and found Turtle in the chief's house. They suspected, however, that Turtle was there on purpose, so they directed the pipe toward Red Horn.

But the latter said, "My friend, you smoked it for them before, you may smoke it again."

"Ho!" said Turtle, and the pipe was stuck into his mouth. Turtle made a drum again and danced that night. In the morning they went to encounter the giants. The one who was helping the giants most was a giantess with red hair, just like Red Horn's hair. Turtle said to Red Horn, "My friend, the giantess has hair just like yours and she is the one that is securing victory for her people because she is a very fast runner. When they play ball she does all the work. Coyote and the Martin are also married to giantesses and these also greatly aid them."[82]

On this occasion the chiefs had come along so most of the people accompanied them and, consequently, they had many good runners.

Then said Turtle to Wolf, "My friend, let us go and match the ball-sticks." This they accordingly did, placing Red Horn's ball-stick together with that of the giantess so that he might play against her. Storms As He Walks' stick was matched against that of a giant, Wolf's stick against that of Coyote, and Otter's against that of Martin.

Just then, the giant chieftainess said, "When shall we be ready to play ball? I am getting rather anxious."

To which Turtle replied, "Just as soon as my friend comes we shall start."

Then the chieftainess said, "Who is your friend that it takes him so long to come?"

"Wait till he comes! You certainly will laugh when you see him."

"Why, what is there funny about him that I should laugh?" said the giantess.

"Just wait till he comes," said Turtle, "just wait till he comes, and then you will see."

Soon after that he came and Turtle said to him, "My friend, let us go over there and look at the sticks of the ball players."

"Very well," said he. They went and found the giantess there and, when she saw him, she most certainly laughed and bowed her head.

"There you are," said Turtle. "I thought you said you would not laugh?"

"Yes," said the giantess, "but I did not laugh at him."

"Well," said Turtle, "look at him again."

The giantess looked again and the small heads he was wearing in his ears stuck their tongues out at her. Again she laughed and bowed her head. Then Turtle made fun of her.

Soon after the people said, "Now, come, start the game."

Then said Turtle to He Who Wears Human Heads As Earrings, "My friend, let us, you and I, start the game." So they gave a war whoop and tossed the ball to the giants while the others stood guard. Coyote was placed opposite Wolf. Then Turtle said to Red Horn, "As soon as the ball comes near, hit the giants' sticks."

"Ho!" said Red Horn.

The ball was tossed up and when it came near the ground, Red Horn stuck his stick out, keeping the others away from Turtle. Turtle caught the ball. Then he ran among the giants swinging his stick. "Big black cowards," he said, "stand back or I will knock some of you down!" The giants' sticks rattled about him but he came out with the ball. He threw the ball low, making it rise higher and higher. It lit just beyond where Wolf and Coyote were standing. Coyote seized it and started to run around the others.

Turtle stood in distance saying, "My friend is going to do something, my friend is going to do something!" He meant Wolf. Wolf watched Coyote very carefully and struck him in the flank with his shoulders. Up in the air he sent him flying. Turtle gave a whoop as he saw this, for it was just what he wanted Wolf to do when he said, "My friend is going to do something." Turtle then got the ball again and sent it through the goal into the very midst of the giants. Thus they won the first point. Turtle shouted, "Come on! Come on! It is such fun to play ball!"

Again they played. This time Otter and Martin were guardians of the goal. The ball was tossed up and again Turtle got the ball and whirled it in the midst of the giants. Getting clear, he threw the ball but it rose gradually as it went farther and lit just beyond the place where Otter and Martin were standing. Martin seized it and ran, but again Turtle shouted, "My friend is going to do something." Otter headed Martin off and, watching carefully, hit him in the flank with his shoulder, sending him into the air.

"Oh dear, our son-in-law," said the giants.

Then Otter put the ball through the goal.

After this, Martin began to move about and got up, using his ball-stick as cane.

"Come! Come! It is such fun to play ball!" they said, and the game was started again. Storms As He Walks and the giant chieftainess were together at the goal as before.

Turtle caught the ball and whirled it into the midst of the giants. "You women, you big black cowards, stand back or I will knock some of you down," he said and he whirled about. When he got clear he threw the ball low and let it rise as it went farther and farther. Just where the giantess and Storms As He Walks stood, there it lit. Storms As He Walks got the ball and ran with it, the chieftainess after him. When she caught up with him, he ran harder and caused it to thunder. The chieftainess got frightened and jumped aside. Then Turtle gave a whoop in the distance and began poking all sorts of fun at the giantess.

The mother of the latter said, "You good-for-nothing woman, hit him!"

Again the giantess came nearer to him, but as he ran all the harder and thundered, she screamed and jumped back. Turtle, all this time, was having his usual fun on the side, shouting at her and poking fun at her. Finally, Storms As He Walks ran through the goal, winning the point.

"Come on! Come on! It is such fun to play ball! Let us start again!"

They gave a whoop and started again. Kunu and Turtle were at the throwing-off place. Turtle said, "My friend usually swings his stick pretty wide." And sure enough Kunu swung his stick in such a way as to interfere with the giant's stick, giving Turtle a chance to catch the ball, which he did. And then, clear of the giants, Turtle threw the ball to the place where Red Horn and the giantess were standing. Red Horn got the ball and ran with it, the giantess after him.

Turtle, as usual, began poking fun at her and shouting. Just as she caught up to Red Horn, the latter turned about and the little faces in his ears stuck out their tongues at her and the eyes winked at her. She was running with upraised stick but, when she saw the faces, she laughed and let down her stick.

This made Turtle shout all the more. "My friend, look back at her. My friend, look back at her!" Then he gave whoops.

The mother of the giantess was talking very excitedly, "That good-for-nothing woman, she is smitten with him! She will make the whole village suffer on her account!"

And so Red Horn ran through the goal, winning the point. The giants were thus beaten in all four points. The giant chieftainess was whipped by her people because she lost the game on account of her falling in love with Red Horn.

The giants wanted to try again and the chieftainess said, "I will match myself against Red Horn no matter what happens to me." Then the other chiefs, his friends, also matched themselves with the giant chiefs. The only giants not included in these were some of the very old people. Almost the whole village of giants was included. The game, however, again resulted in victory for Red Horn and his friends, with the giants losing all the four points.

Then said Turtle, "My friends, something just occurred to me."

"What is it?" they said.

Then he said, "This giantess has the same color hair as my friend Red Horn and I think that we ought to spare her life and let my friend here marry her."

"Ho!" they exclaimed, "if that is your desire, then let it be as you wish." Thereupon they gathered together all the giants and placed them in four circles. Then they told the giantess that they had decided to spare her life. She was very grateful.

Turtle then said, "If we kill all these one at a time we would never get through, there are so many of them. So I think that we had better leave this to our friend Storms As He Walks." Thus spoke Turtle.

So Storms As He Walks went towards them with his club and struck the first circle. Then it thundered and the Thunderbirds above said, "Storms As He Walks is shooting. What can he be shooting at? He said that he liked the human beings." Then again for the second time it thundered. "Ho-o-o! What can Storms As He Walks be shooting at?" they said again. Then a third and fourth time it thundered. The Thunderbirds said, "Surely he has shot something."

As soon as the giants had been killed, the people left the place where the game had been played. They were living in the first village that had been attacked by the giants. "We are not being treated very well here, so let us go with you and live in your village," they said. So they went home with the victors.

> The giants return for more games: who can shoot the farthest, who can stay under water the longest, and dice, all of which they lose. Finally, they ask to wrestle.

Then the giants had another council and they decided to have a wrestling match. So the gourd-carrier went to the people and said, "They wish to play a game with you again."

"What do they wish to play?" the people asked.

The gourd-carrier answered, "They wish to wrestle."

"Friends," some of the people said, "we shall not be any good at this game."[83] In the morning, however, they went over to the giants anyway.

Turtle, Storms As He Walks, and Red Horn were to take part in the wrestling. About noon Storms As He Walks was getting rather tired, and as he got very tired, he thundered. His uncle up above in the sky heard it, but he said to the other Thunderbirds, "Don't go over there because he said he preferred the human beings."

In thundering, Storms As He Walks was calling upon his fellow Thunderbirds. That is why his uncle spoke in this fashion to the others, for he knew that if they came to his aid he would be able to throw his opponent. Because his uncle said this, Storms As He Walks could not get any of the Thunderbirds to come down. Finally his feet swung from under him and he was thrown. Turtle cried, "Ho—Ho!"

Not long after that Red Horn began to get tired. Finally he also was thrown. Again Turtle said, "Ho—Ho! My friends." Then Turtle said, "The one I am wrestling with has been a long time trying to fall down but I am holding him up." Saying this he lifted the giant up and holding his head downward he bunted him on the ground breaking his neck. Turtle, however, as well as his friends, lost the game and they were all killed.

Up to this time they had been the only ones to play successfully. When they were killed, all those remaining in the village were also killed.

At this time, Red Horn's first wife was pregnant and, finally, the old woman's granddaughter gave birth to a male child who was the very likeness of his father, Red Horn, having long red hair and having human heads hanging from his ears. Not long after this, the giantess also gave birth to a male child whose hair was likewise just like his father's. Instead of having human heads from his ears, he had them attached to his nipples. As these two had been spared by the giants, very good care was taken of them. The best of food was always brought them to eat. Finally they grew to be quite large boys. The oldest one called the giantess "mother," and the son of the giantess called the Woman With the White Beaver Skin as a Wrap, "mother." Every day the older son went out somewhere. The old people took great care of him and his brother. They were always preparing arrows to bring to them. Thus the children always had plenty of arrows. One day the younger one said, "Where is it that you go every day when you are away from us? You make me very lonesome."

Then the older one said, "I fast and utter my cry in order to be blest by the Thunderbirds."[84]

"When you go again, let me know so that I may go along and utter my cry for a similar blessing," said the younger one.

"Well, then, have your mother tan two deerskins for you and I will tell my mother to tan two for me." The mothers then tanned two deerskins apiece for each. These they took and went away.

After walking for some time they came to a pleasant, level country in which a large village was situated. Then the older brother said, "These are the people that killed our father." In the middle of the village, in the chief's lodge, the scalps of their fathers were tied to poles and used as flags. They were very much faded and Red Horn's hair had turned white. Then said the older one, "Brother, I hope that you are like me when you cry, for all who hear me must die." So saying, he sang wailing songs and the giants in the village began to move about.

"Ho, hark! Somebody is singing something." Even as they spoke they jumped, head first, into the fire.

When he got through, the older brother said, "Now when I sing, all those of the same size as myself who hear me, they also shall die." So saying, he sang wailing songs and all the young people in the village who heard him jumped into the fire head first.[85]

Then the old men of the village began to foretell what was likely to happen, saying, "Some of you must remember that Red Horn had two wives. Now, if these two wives gave birth to children, they must certainly be grown up by this time. Perhaps they are the ones who are causing all these things. Let someone therefore watch the scalps." So they put four guards at the foot of the poles and these were told to look upward all the time.

"Come," said older brother, "let us try to take our fathers' scalps away from these people." So they painted two of their arrows red and two black. Then, taking two quivers, each one started for the poles to which their fathers' scalps were attached. Every now and then they stopped and rested their quivers. Finally the brothers turned themselves into light feathers and let themselves float upward. They alit on the scalps, the younger on Turtle's scalp. Then taking the arrows that they had painted, they shot them into the throats of the guards who were looking upwards. The guards had had their bodies painted, two of them being black and two of them red. That is why the boys painted their arrows in the same fashion. When those who had been painted black were shot by the black arrows, they coughed up black blood until they died. The other two did the same when they were shot, except that their blood was red.

Then the boys took the scalps and ran.

"They have taken the scalps!" shouted the giants and gave chase to them.

The boys fought as they ran. Whenever they shot one of their arrows off, it would mow down the giants as far as it sped. When the arrows were about spent, the boys would reach for one of their quivers and thus, freshly supplied, they fought on. When their arrows were again spent, they would reach for the other quiver. When, finally, all their arrows were gone, they said, "Now is the time to stop running and to fight in the same manner in which the giants fight." So they turned and gave chase to the latter. Loosening their bowstrings and using their bows as clubs, they struck right and left, killing all the giants except a few who succeeded in taking flight. The boys would run down one group of giants and, when they had killed these, they returned and chased another. They had fled in all directions. Finally they came upon a little girl who was carrying her little brother on her back. These were the last left. Then said the older brother,

"I thought I would destroy all of you but if I did that, whom will the people be able to call giants in the future? Because Earthmaker has created you, I will spare you, but you can no longer stay on this earth." So saying, he threw them across the seas.

This done, the boys returned to the giants' village. There they built a big fire and threw all the bodies of the dead giants into it. It made a big blaze for the giants were very fat. When they were through, they took all the bones out and said, "Let us look for a grinder." They searched about the village and found one. Then they put the bones into the grinder and pounded them fine. When they thought they had enough, they filled their tanned buckskins with them.

These they took back with them and returned to the place where they left the scalps. These they now carried in their hands and continued home. The younger one carried Turtle's head and the older one Thunderbird's and Red Horn's head. When they got home it was late at night. They went to the center of their village and there the older one said to his brother, "Take your bones, then go over half the village, throw some in each lodge and some around the lodges. Try to put bones in every place in your half of the village. I will go over the other half and do the same." After they had gone around for some time, each one in his direction, they met at the place from which they had started. "Did you have enough?" the older one asked and the younger said, "Yes." "Well, then, let us go to our own lodges."

When they got there the older one took Red Horn's head and handed it to his little brother and said, "Take it to your mother, and tell her to lie in bed with it."

So he went to his mother and woke her up. She said, "Oh, my son, you have returned?" "Yes, mother," said he, "Won't you lie with father?"

"Oh my son, your father has been dead a long time," she said.

"But nevertheless here he is," he said.

"Why that is only a skull. How can I lie with that?" retorted the woman.

Then, when he met his brother, he said, "My mother also refuses."

"It is strange that they won't lie with father now. However, tell them to make a bed in the center of the lodge anyhow," the older brother said. So they made a bed and upon it they placed the heads in a row.

Early in the morning, the older brother said to the younger one, "Go look at them." As there was a partition there, he went in and looked and he beheld their father and his friends, all alive, sleeping and snoring.

Then he went outside and saw people fast asleep scattered here and the village. "And so it should be," one of the brothers said, "so it should be. Our fathers are alive again, sleeping in the center of the lodge while people are sleeping outside, scattered throughout the village." Thus did the older brother speak from inside the lodge. Then he addressed his younger brother again saying, "Wake up one of our mothers and tell her to get breakfast for these people."

So the other brother went and woke one of the mothers and said, "Mother, get up and make breakfast for our fathers."

"But your fathers died a long time ago."

"Yet in spite of that they are here, asleep in the center of our lodge," the brother said.

So she looked up and, sure enough, there they were! Crying with surprise she went and woke the other mother and they all said, "Oh-o-o! Our sons have brought our husband back to life again!"

Then one of the boys said, "Wake up the wives of our other fathers and tell them to get breakfast for their husbands." So one of the mothers went and, behold! Outside of the lodge, all over the village, the people were sleeping. Then she went out and woke the other wives so that they might get breakfast for their husbands.

Kunu's brother and all who had been killed by the giants had now come to life again. In the morning the whole village began to stir. All these men had loved the boys very much before but now, indeed, they loved them even more. When they awoke, they picked them up and carried them in their arms, each in turn although they were grownup men. The boys were very much handsomer than their fathers, although their fathers were themselves handsome men

Then the older boy said, "Fathers, you must have been very weak indeed for, look, this is what we did to them," and he showed them how they had battled with the giants. And then he added, "My little brother carried you and I carried the other two."

Then said Turtle to the younger brother, "You have made me very happy because I was in a shameful condition. I therefore give you my war weapons with which I never failed to conquer."

Then said Storms As He Walks to the older brother, "My son, I also give you my weapon, one of the best that exists." The boy rose and thanked him.

Then Red Horn said, "My sons, I have nothing to give you, for I am not your equal and, besides, you are already just like me." And indeed they were.

Red Horn's sons have many adventures; they marry, but the older one does not have children because he is holy. Then Wolf and others must leave.

After a while Wolf said, "My friend, I cannot remain this way always. Earthmaker created me differently from you and I cannot live forever like a human being. I shall now leave and roam over the earth and seek my food."[86]

"My friend," said Red Horn, "I shall get lonesome without you for I have grown very used to you."

Then Otter spoke, "I, too, shall have to leave, my friend, although I, likewise, have grown used to you. However, I shall always be near enough so that we may be able to see one another whenever we like." Storms As He Walks had already left with the Thunderbirds, returning with them after they brought the war-bundle to the earth. The different beings that had come from various places were now all returning to their homes and to their natural condition.

The war-bundle received from the Thunderbirds was kept on earth by the people and that is how we now have a thunderbird war bundle. It was always used in war and it is still used for that purpose to the present day.

This is the origin of the war weapons of Red Horn.

1908-1913

▲▲▲
▼▼▼

Lacrosse

Lacrosse is an ancient game invented by Native people. Some say Nanabush invented it to avenge the death of his brother, Wolf. He invited the Thunderers to play against and defeat the underground manidog who killed his brother, then gave the game to the Thunderers, who also directed the rackets be shaped like war clubs. Depending on the nation, lacrosse was used for many different purposes: it could be a war game, healing rites, spiritual worship of the Creator, reinactment of a sacred story, and entertainment. Goals could be as much as a mile apart and sometimes there were hundreds of players. Lacrosse was coached by religious leaders and the players wore red, as if readying themselves for war, but there were few firm rules. Games could last for days and injuries—sometimes crippling—were common. Gambling was common as well, and frequently large sums were wagered. Women had their own form of the game, called *shinny*, which used twin balls tied to a stick and a goal that was a line drawn between the two teams. The team that hit the balls over the goal four times won. In 1913 Alanson Skinner recorded this description of the game among the Menominee:

The game of lacrosse is not played for amusement alone, but often for a religious or war-like motive. Given once a year by a man who has thunder power, several days before the game bits of tobacco are sent out to those whom he desires as guests. The messengers who carry the tobacco state the day and hour of the game, departing at once without further ceremony.

In the meanwhile, the person giving the game prepares a feast, the ingredients of which are carried to the nearest lacrosse ground. On the morning appointed, the host and his relatives arrive first, carrying goods of all sorts, usually mats, calicos, and beaded belts, as presents to the winners among the guests. These are hung on cross bars upheld by two upright poles which are a permanent fixture at one side of every lacrosse ground. The host then spreads out a mat and lays his sacred war club, pipe, and thunder charms on it. He never takes part in his own game.

The number of guests is of no consequence as long as there are enough to make two equal parties. The sides are chosen by the men delegated as leaders who collect all the lacrosse bats from the players, shuffle them together, and then spread them out in two parallel rows of equal number, the men going on whichever side the Thunderers have decreed that their bats shall fall.

At a given signal they pick up their clubs and gather around an old man or chief who has been led to address them. He speaks to them for a few minutes, telling them why and for whom the game is being played, and exhorting them to play roughly or gently, as dictated in the host's original dream. Then the men on one side usually mark one cheek with red paint, so that they may be distinguished from their opponents. They now gather in the center of the field, the ball is tossed among them, and the struggle is on.

The object of each is to get the ball to their opponent's goal, high poles stuck at the opposite ends of the field. Sometimes these goals could be a mile or more apart. In order to do this, the greatest speed and skill in dodging is required. The ball is usually thrown against the post from a short distance, so that part of each party usually stays behind the rest as a goal guard. The side scoring the first four goals wins the game.

Ball play on the ice, 1853. Seth Eastman

Usually two men combine and have their games played off on the same day by the same set of men, one in the morning and one in the afternoon. The host never takes part in his own game but sits idly by. At the conclusion of the game, the prizes brought by the host are distributed among the winners.

There are special medicines for success in lacrosse and most champions attribute their skill to the use of these. In some cases, games are given for the sake of a person who recently died, if the deceased was a thunder man. It is said that anciently the players wore "tails," presumably those of the deer, tied to their backs during the game.

❖ PROPHETS OF RENEWAL ❖

HAYĘHWATHA' (HIAWATHA)[87]

There is no perfect version of the story of Hayęhwatha' and the founding of the League of the Iroquois, or the Iroquois Confederacy, but the selections reprinted here come from the version considered to be the most complete: Chief John Gibson's 1912 recital of the story in Onondaga. Ganiódaíio' (Skanyátaí·yo': Handsome Lake, Gibson) was born in 1849, the son of a Seneca mother and an Onondaga chief who held the title of Thatótáho'. Blinded at 31 by a lacrosse injury, Gibson subsequently became one of the greatest interpreters of the culture of the Haudenosaunee.[88] Because he was also a preacher in the Handsome Lake doctrine, there are Christian-influenced elements in his retelling of the story of Hayęhwatha' that may not have been in the original. Gibson died in 1912, shortly after completing his recital.

The hero in this version is Tekánawíta' (Deganawideh: Determined Man[89]), born of a virgin into poverty and exile in the Huron country. He is aided by Hayęhwatha', who lost his family and then became a peacemaker. In this version Hayęhwatha' was once a cannibal; in others he and Tekánawíta' are twins. Here their task is to convince the Mohawk, Oneida, Cayuga, Seneca, and Onondaga nations to lay down their weapons and stop the cycle of revenge and war, to accept the doctrine of the Power and the Good Message and Great Peace. To do so they create the idea of a confederacy of nations led by chiefs appointed by the clan mothers, symbolized by a longhouse. Each nation is represented by a council fire in the longhouse, with the Seneca as Keepers of the Western Door and the Mohawk as Keepers of the Eastern Door. The Confederacy rests upon shared power, structured with complex rituals for solving disputes and replacing leaders, so that it can be perpetuated when the first chiefs are gone.

Tekánawíta' and Hayęhwatha' are successful until they encounter the Onondaga Thatótáho', snake-ridden and insane, who refuses to give up evil. In exchange for accepting the message, Tekánawíta' and Hayęhwatha' promise to make him Fire Keeper, the main chief of the League whose duty is to call the nations together to settle their differences. They also give him complete veto power. Once he agrees to this compromise, they "comb the snakes from his hair," an image that echoes in art to the present, and he regains his sanity. Tekánawíta' and Hayęhwatha' create the complex rituals that will support the Great Peace, including the creation and naming of fifty permanent chiefs selected by the clan mothers, the Ritual of Condolence for replacing a chief who dies, and the use of *wampum,* which has metaphysical and supernatural properties to heal the sick, convey history, and codify law. Tekánawíta' also establishes the symbols of the rising smoke of the council fire signaling the Confederacy is meeting, and the great tree, under whose roots the nations discard their weapons of war, never to be seen or used again.

Concerning the League

Skanyátaí·yo' (Handsome Lake, John Gibson, Seneca-Onondaga, 1849-1912)

Skanyátaí·yo'

This is what happened when it originated, the Great Law. This is what happened in ancient times. There was warfare, and they habitually killed each other, the Indians of the several nations. This is what was going on. They scalped one another at the various settlements; that is, the warriors were roaming about across the bush, scalping the inhabitants. Moreover, this was happening where the Mohawks resided at the lakeshore, on the northerly side of the lake, Lake Ontario, which is where a mother lived with her daughter. The old woman was called Kahẹto'ktha' (Kahẹ·tó'ktha': End of the Field); her daughter, as to her, she was named Kahẹtehsụk (Kahẹ·téhsụk: She Walks Ahead). These two left the place where they lived, going far away into the bush, where they set up camp and lit a fire, at a place where no one travels, a place where the river forks called Kahanayẹ'.[90] They lived there for a long time, and for several years never did any man come to visit them.

Just about then it started. She noticed, the old woman, that it was evident her daughter was going to have a child. Then the old woman was surprised at how it could be possible that her daughter was going to have a child; she was surprised at where, in fact, she might have gotten it, since she had never seen a man. Thereupon she questioned her daughter, saying, "Who then is the father of the child you two are going to have?"

Then Kahẹtehsụk said, "Mother, I do not know what happened nor how it is."

But the old woman did not believe what she said, her daughter. Thereupon the old woman began to get angry and said, "Probably it is not true what she said, Kahẹtehsụk." That is how it was, every day and every night the old woman got angry, it seems, when she questioned her daughter, saying, "Now I will question you. Moreover, now you will tell me the truth, the real truth and nothing else, only this very true matter, that is, who is the father of the child you two are going to have? Now you shall tell the truth."

Thereupon Kahẹtehsụk said, "Mother, I will tell you that actually I do not know."

Thereafter Kahẹto'ktha' became depressed and she got angry, saying, "It's not true what she said, Kahẹtehsụk." Thereafter the old woman, getting angry, said, "Surely you must know who is the father of the child you two are going to have." Then her daughter became unhappy and cried, and that is the way it was for quite some time: both the old woman and her daughter were unhappy.

This, then, is what happened when it was night and they were asleep. The old woman dreamed and she saw a man[91] arrive where they had their house and he said, "I have a message along which I shall tell you: you should stop the kinds of thoughts you are having. Indeed, your thinking is that probably it is not true what she says, your daughter. This, indeed, is the reason why it is not wholesome, your preoccupation with her confinement and her saying, 'Indeed, I don't know where it came from nor how it is.' Now I will tell you what happened to your daughter's life, for it is true that she does not know what happened. This is the reason why you should now stop. Don't cause your daughter to worry. Moreover, you should ease her mind by apologizing to her. Actually a great thing has happened, for he is appointing your daughter to be the instrument of a male child's birth. He is sending him, the one you all believe is the Ruler [Hawẹní·yo'],[92] and he is coming from the sky above the earth; and he will be born of Kahẹtehsụk herself.

"Moreover, when he is born, the boy, I will give him a name; you will say Tekánawíta'. And when you see him, the two of you will be kind to him, and don't bother him when, in the course of time, he becomes a man. In fact, he is going to be working here beneath and on the other side of the sun. Moreover, once he is born, Tekánawí·ta', he will grow rapidly, and it will not be long before you two will see many unusual things: he will reveal his powers, and all of the people will acknowledge them when they see Tekánawíta'. Actually, he will travel to different villages all over the bush, to small settlements of families, and there he is going to work to stop what is going on and, indeed, what is going on is that they are killing one another, specifically they are scalping one another. In fact, they are shedding each other's blood, people of their own kind, living here on earth. That is why he decided it, the Maker, as you say, the Ruler who has created the world and the sun which gives light all over the earth and the islands, also the moon which gives light at night, also the rivers which keep flowing, also the lakes and the great bodies of water, and he also has planted the many kinds of vegetation, also the shrubs and the forests. And there, moreover, he created them; that is, he gave life to people of their kind so that they might continue to dwell there. As to that, indeed, what happened here on earth is extremely sinful, that is their shedding each other's blood, just pools and flowing streams of people's blood. This is why Hawę́ní·yo' decided to send Tekánawíta' here, and his mission will be to end their killing one another."

As to the old woman, Kahęto'ktha', and her daughter, Kahętehsųk, now another day has dawned for them. Then the old woman said, "My daughter, I understand now that it is true; indeed, you don't know where you got the child you are about to have, for a man I saw when I dreamed last night told me everything, everything about where it comes from, the child you are about to have. And indeed this: it is you, especially, whom he chose and it is there from your person that Tekánawíta' will be born."

That, then is how it was and in a short time a boy was born. Thereupon the old woman said, "Now, indeed, Tekánawíta' has arrived." And it was evident that he was very healthy. Every day he grew, and in a short while he began to walk around, and when, quite soon, he started to talk, this is what he began to speak about: "It is not good for people to be unkind to one another." Every day it was evident that he was growing rapidly.

Eventually it came about that the old woman said, "This is what I think: it is time to go to the village of our relatives."

Thereupon Kahętehsųk said to her son, Tekánawíta', "My son, what will you say to your grandmother, who wants us to go to the village now?"

Thereupon Tekánawíta' said, "That is what I want, to see people of our own kind."

Thereupon the old woman said, "In three days' time we will depart."

Then Tekánawíta' said, "This is what will happen when I see our people: we shall converse, and I will tell them that they are now arriving, the Power and the Good Message and Peace."

Thereupon they went home, returning to where the women had come from. When they got back to the village, one of them sent a message notifying the leading chief of the village. When he was notified, the leader, then he circulated the news and everybody gathered. Then the chief spoke, thanking them and greeting the old woman and also her daughter and also their child, and when he had completed his welcome he said, "Now then, we will listen well to the message you two have brought along."

Thereupon Kahęto'ktha' said, "The truth is that it is of great importance, the message we all are bringing along. This, as a matter of fact, is it: for many winters we have been gone, I and my daughter, Kahętehsųk, and the reason we went away from here was that, indeed, it was too dangerous because of their killing one another. So I began to think, 'It might be possible for me and my daughter to survive somewhere by kindling a fire at a place where no one roams about.' At the place where the river forks we erected our shelter. There, moreover, an important event occurred concerning my daughter, Kahętehsųk, for when she had grown up, it was not long before it came to be evident that she was going to have a child. I had not seen any man and this was the reason that I questioned her, saying, 'Who is the father of the child you two are going to have?' Then she spoke, saying, 'I do not know what happened.' Thereupon I, an old woman, became angry, and my mind was troubled, and I was disappointed, thinking, 'It is not true what my daughter is telling me about how, then, it happened.' A few times I asked her the same question about her doings, but she kept saying, 'I don't know what happened.' This, then, is what happened: when night approached us, I dreamt I saw a man entering the place where we have our shelter. This is what he said: 'I have come to tell you to stop it, that is, indeed, your anger, your uneasiness, and your disappoint-ment at what it is like, your daughter's life, the fact that she is going to have a child; it is true that she does not know where it came from and what it is that happened. This, then, is what I came to tell you: you should repent; more specifically, you should apologize to your daughter. Actually what is happening is that a great event is taking place in that Tehaęhyawaki,[93] as you call the Ruler, chose your daughter, Kahętehsųk. It is there, of her body, that he will be born, the one he sent, the one you will all see here on earth. Moreover, when he is born, you will call him Tekánawíta', and he is going to work beneath the sun where the earth is located, and it will stop, the persistent matter of their slaughtering one another, their own people.' So therefore you are now seeing this one, our child, Tekánawíta', and this is the reason we came back home. We thought that you ought to hear the wonderful and important message, the message that came to us. In relation to that, you will all now see Tekánawíta'. "

"Truly, all of us together have heard it, every one living here. This, certainly, is true: an amazing event has taken place. It is a long time that mother and daughter have been gone, Kahęto'ktha' that is, and her daughter, Kahętehsųk. Moreover, today, they have returned home; they have come back with our child. Indeed, we have been notified about how everything came about. It is from the sky that he came with his mission, an important one, for he came to work for peace to come about among the people living here on earth and for it to let up, the mutual slaughter, for it to end among us who dwell here. Now this is what will happen: we will greet them, shaking hands with Kahęto'ktha' and Kahętehsųk and also their son, Tekánawíta'—welcoming him back—which means we will thank him for visiting us and for seeking out our village first, so that we can hear the message with which he will travel to other places and different groups of people. Now then we who live here are gathered with the one who has great power, Tekánawíta', and shortly after he has grown to manhood here on earth, we will observe his work. So, I beseech all of you to be kind to Tekánawíta'. Now, therefore, you will stand up, now all of us living here will stand up, and furthermore, they will be first to welcome him, the children, shaking hands with Tekánawíta' and also with his mother and also with his grandmother. Thereupon the whole group of old people and young people, now we will all welcome him by shaking hands with Tekánawíta' and also with his mother and grandmother." Thereupon they all stood up, and as to Tekánawíta', all of the children welcomed him, shaking his hand and greeting him. Then the whole crowd came to welcome him, shaking his hand and greeting him. . . .

Thereupon Tekánawíta' said, "Indeed, so be it, you shall hear about what you must do. As to that, first as to the duties of our mothers, that is to say, the women, these will bake bread, corn bread, which they will collect. Thereupon as to you, you people, you will collect the flesh of game animals. These, then, will supply provisions of bread and meat. Then they should assemble, everyone, at the place provided. The inhabitants, all of them, will gather in the same place, and everyone will hear me tell about the matter you wish to know about."

The older women spread the news, and everyone at the village was notified of the specific day they had chosen for them to assemble. Thereupon the inhabitants collected the corn bread and also the meat of game animals, and then they assembled. Then he joined them, Tekánawíta', who by now was a young man. Then the older people said, "Now, then, we will ask questions about what it means for you to say 'Now it is arriving, the good Message' and this, specifically, 'Power' and this, specifically, 'Peace,' so that now they will hear it, the entire crowd, when you explain what you mean."

Thereupon Tekánawíta' stood up in the center of the gathering place and then he said, "First I will answer what it means to say 'Now it is arriving, the Good Message.' This indeed is what it means: when it stops, the slaughter of your own people who live here on earth, then everywhere peace will come about, by day and also by night, and it will come about that as one travels around, everyone will be related. Then indeed, in the future days to come.

"Now again, secondly, I say, 'Now it is arriving, the Power,' and this means that the different nations, all of the nations, will become just as a single one, and the Great Law will come into being, so that now all will be related to each other, and there will come to be just a single family, and in the future, in days to come, this family will continue on.

"Now in turn, the other, my third saying 'Now it is arriving, the Peace.' This means that everyone will become related, men and also women, and also the young people and the children, and when all are relatives, every nation, then there will be peace as they roam about by day and also by night. Now, also, it will become possible for them to assemble in meetings. Then there will be truthfulness, and they will uphold hope and charity, so that it is peace that will unite all of the people. Indeed, it will be as though they have but one mind, and they are a single person with only one body and one head and one life, which means that there will be unity. Moreover, and most importantly, one is going to assemble in meetings where it will be announced that all of mankind will repent of their sins, even evil people, and in the future, they will be kind to one another, one and all. When they are functioning, the Good Message and also the Power and the Peace, moreover, these will be the principal things everybody will live by; these will be the great values among the people." Then Tekánawíta' said, "Now that I have finished my task, I will depart. . . ."[94]

Thereafter Kahętehsųk and her mother, Kahęto'ktha', and their child, Tekánawíta', returned home. When they arrived back there, Tekánawíta' said, "Now I will get going and start to build myself a boat. Furthermore, when I have finished my boat, I will depart, and it is towards the east that I will go. Moreover, I want you not to become unhappy when the time comes for me to get ready to leave."

Thereupon Tekánawíta' went away all day long. When it got dark, he returned home not carrying anything with him, nor did he say anything, and then they went to sleep until dawn. Thereupon he departed again, returning home carrying nothing with him, nor saying anything, and then they slept until dawn. Thereupon he departed again, returning at dusk, and again he had nothing with him. That is how it goes: every day he departs, and he always returns when it gets dark. For a long time that is what it is like, and never does he say anything, and it is the same with his grandmother and also his mother: they never say anything when he arrives at night.

After a time Tekánawíta' said, "Now then, I can tell you, grandmother, and mother too, that I have now finished it. Therefore, at dawn, we will leave. Moreover, first we will go to the top of a hill, where I will show you a certain tree, a pine tree, growing on top of the hill. This will be able to tell my fortune when I am gone.[95] Now that I have finished my boat, I will launch it. Furthermore, you two will help me when we launch the boat. Moreover, you will observe what kind of boat it is that I made here on earth. I alone will use the boat for the length of time that I will travel about where there are lakes and also where there are rivers. After my task is completed, my work, then no one may use my boat, for as to that, I shall take it back when I return from the earth.

Thereupon Kahęto'ktha' and Kahętehsųk understood that now, indeed, the time had come for it to happen as foretold in his grandmother's dream. At dawn the two women prepared a meal. When they were finished the grandmother, Kahęto'ktha', said, "Now, indeed, we have finished, and we will all eat. Truly, we do not know whether this is the last time all of us will eat together." Now, indeed, the time had come that the man told about and that was revealed from within his dream. Thereupon they ate.

When they finished the meal, Kahętehsųk said, "I love you my child, Tekánawíta'. Now indeed, the time has come for us to part. As to that, we do not know whether in the future, in days to come, we will ever see each other again."

Thereupon Tekánawíta' said, "Now, moreover, we will leave to go to the top of the hill, where the living tree stands, the great pine." Then they departed.

When they arrived there, they ascended to the top of the hill. When they got to the top of the hill, they stopped. Thereupon Tekánawíta' said, "This living tree is able to tell our fortune. Now, indeed, the time has come for my work to begin. So now I will leave, going towards the east. Moreover, once I have departed, you should notch this living tree. Thereupon sweet sap will appear, and you two will eat it, and this is what you will think: 'We are in luck,' for all is peaceful as I pass through the long road of my work. Moreover, this is what will happen if you notch it and blood begins to spill. Thereupon you will know at once that something has spoiled our good fortune. If just so it should happen, that blood should begin to spill from this living tree, that is, if something should spoil my good fortune and my blood should begin to spill, then here on earth we may not see each other again . . . ."

Thereupon he said, "I myself, will be the first to notch it, and you two will watch to see what is to happen, what kind of luck is to be mine." When he notched it, sap flowed, and he said, "I will have good luck when I travel." Thereafter they ate the sweet sap which resembled honey. Thereupon Tekánawíta' said, "Now you two saw that it is able to tell what kind of luck is mine." Now after Tekánawíta' hit the growing tree with his stone ax, sap flowed from it. And they, eating it, found that it was sweet, like honey.

Thereupon Tekánawíta' said, "Now you are looking at how it is to be in the future, for a number of days to come, for it is able to inform you about the state of my affairs, however many times you look at it. So now we will depart, going to the place where the boat I have completed lies. This, presently, is what you will see: the kind of boat I will launch when I take off for the other side of the lake."

Thereafter Tekánawíta' said, "Now, indeed, we'll depart," and they left, Tekánawíta' walking in front of them and they following him, his grandmother and his mother. They followed a path until, it seems suddenly, they saw a rock ledge at the top of the hill where they arrived. Thereupon he showed it to them, and they saw a stone boat and paddles of stone. Thereupon Tekánawíta' turned it right side up, the boat. Thereupon he said, "Examine it, and you will know what kind of a boat I have made here on earth."

Thereupon Kahęto'ktha' and Kahętehsųk examined it and, surprised at the kind of boat it was, thereupon Kahętehsųk said, "I love you, my child, but what are you doing in launching a stone boat, for surely, indeed, it will sink beneath the water's surface, the boat?"

Thereupon Tekánawíta' said, "If it is true that it will sink, my boat, then I also may not survive nor can my work go forward here on earth."[96] Thereupon Tekánawíta' said, "Now, indeed, you two will help me as we drag the boat, then into the water we will launch it, and you will watch as I get in. You, moreover, will be the first to see this surprising accomplishment, and it is you who are to be witnesses as I take this step." Thereupon he said, "Now, then, let's pull the boat."

Thereupon his grandmother and his mother and Tekánawíta' pulled the boat, and then they launched it on the water. Thereupon he shook hands with his grandmother and his mother and said, "Don't become unhappy now that we are separating. Furthermore, don't ever forget how it began, this matter, and also what happened concerning my mission, for it is you who witnessed my departure today." Thereupon he got into the boat and disconnected it. Thereupon his grandmother and his mother watched it depart, Tekánawíta' 's boat, with him in it. He was in the boat, paddling swiftly when it left, and in a short time he actually disappeared as he was paddling along, Tekánawíta' . . . .

This, moreover, is what happened when he crossed over, Tekánawíta'. There was a man's camp near the lake where resided a husband and wife and their family who had come from Kanyę'ke[97] and the reason for their departure had been their killing one another by scalping, which was why they had left that vicinity, moving their camp a distance towards the west into the bush near a lake where they had erected their shelter and where they had settled down with their family. Shortly thereafter, the man went out to dip water at the lakeshore. This one, when he had dipped, climbed back up the bank, rested, and then, looking in the direction of the lake, he saw something coming in the direction of and proceeding towards the lakeshore to the place where he stood. It came along swiftly and soon he realized that it was a man coming along propelling a boat. In a very short while after landing, the man disembarked, pulled the boat out of the water, and then the man who had been standing there looked at him, the man pulling his boat out of the water, and the man who had been standing there saw the stone canoe, which was the boat he had propelled, that one, the man who was arriving.

Then he came to the place where he was standing, the one who had been resting, the one who had gone to dip water. They gave thanks and greeted each other, and then he began speaking as soon as he arrived, saying, "Now we are seeing each other, we who are strangers, just now being the first time I am seeing you." Thereupon the one who had been resting there said, "It is true, this is the first time we are meeting, we who are strangers, this is the first time I have seen you, and I don't know you. Where, then, did you come from, and what is your name?"

Thereupon he began to speak, he who had just arrived, saying, "I have come from kindred people and my name is Tekánawíta'. Now, then, I will ask you where, in fact, you have come from and what you name is?"

Thereupon the man said, "Indeed, it is Kanyę'ke we came from, my family and I, we having just now fled our shelter at the village because too much warfare was going on. This, in particular: they have been scalping one another by day and by night, and they are in the process of massacring one another, and the reason I am here is for us to survive, my family and I. As for me, indeed, my name is Thoihwayei.

Thereupon Tekánawíta' said, "Now I understand who you are. Now, moreover, I tell you that it is you I chose, for you to be the first person I meet. So now I will tell you what you should do. As to that, you should now return home at once, and without delay go back to the settlement. And this, when you arrive back there, go straightway to the place where he has his house, the leading man of the village, or I should say the chief, and this is what you will tell him, indeed, you will say, 'It is arriving, the Good Message, and next this, the Power, and next this, the Peace.' Moreover, what will happen is that he will ask you, 'Who is it, then, who has told you about this?' And you will say, 'Tekánawíta'.' If he says, 'Where did you see him?' You will say, 'At the lake shore and, in fact, he is coming and will be arriving soon in the village. Thereupon you [all] will hear everything, that is, he himself will reply to everything.'

"Now you shall hear what you should do when you go to tell the chief. As to that, in this direction, here, there are located two groups. These are dangerous, so I will first halt their evil and sinful activities which go on by day and by night to the extent that both are dangerous, and I will end it as soon as possible. Thereupon peace will take hold among the inhabitants. Moreover, when I have completed this task, then I will go to Kanyę'ke." Thereupon Tekánawíta' said, "Now, then, you go back, go straight to the village."

After Tekánawíta' had departed in that direction he came to a house belonging to a cannibal who had his house there.[98] Then Tekánawíta' went close to the house. Then, when he saw the man coming out, departing, sliding down the hill to the river, and dipping water, thereupon Tekánawíta' hurriedly climbed onto the house to the place where there was a chimney for the smoke to escape. He lay down on his stomach and, looking into the house, he saw that the task of breaking up meat and piling it up had been completed.

Then the man returned, and he was carrying a drum with water in it. Thereupon he poured it into a vessel, put meat into the liquid, and hung the vessel up over the fire until it boiled. Moreover, the man watched it and, when it was done, he took down the vessel, placing it near the embers. Thereupon he said,

"Now indeed it is done. Moreover, now I will eat." Thereupon he set up a seat, a bench, thinking that he will put it on there where he eats. Thereupon he went to where the vessel sat, intending to take the meat out of the liquid, when he saw, from inside the vessel, a man looking out. Thereupon he moved away without removing the meat and sat down again on the long bench, for it was a surprise to him, seeing the man in the vessel. Thereupon he thought, "Let me look again."

Thereupon he, Tekánawíta', looked again from above where the smoke hole was, again causing a reflection in the vessel, and then the man, standing up again, went to where the vessel sat, looked into the vessel again, saw the man looking out, and he was handsome, he having a nice face. Thereupon the man moved away again, and he sat down again on the long bench, and then he bowed his head, pondering and thinking, "I am exceedingly handsome and I have a nice face. It is probably not right, my habit of eating humans. So I will now stop, from now on I ought not to kill humans anymore." Thereupon he stood up again, went to where the vessel sat, picked up the vessel with the meat in it, and then he went out, sliding straight down the slope beside the river and near an uprooted tree he poured out the vessel full of meat.[99] Meanwhile Tekánawíta' hurriedly climbed down again from on top of the house and went to where he had gone, the man carrying the vessel containing human flesh. Just then, he having ascended the top of the hill, the one holding the vessel, the two met.

Thereupon they both stopped, and the man said, "We two are meeting; where do you come from? We are strangers; what is your name?"

Thereupon he began to speak, saying, "Really, it is true, we are strangers; it is the first time we have met. Now, moreover, I will tell you that the place I came from is the other side of the lake and, as to me, my name, indeed, is Tekánawíta' . . . ."

Thereupon Tekánawíta' said, "Now I understand everything. So now you will return, going to the village to tell your people, 'Now it is arriving, the Good Message, also the Power, and also the Peace.' Now, indeed, you have ended your killing of humans. That, moreover, is how it will happen: kindred people will stop massacring and scalping one another. As to that, it will stop now. From now on it will come about that everyone will be related, members of all of the different nations. So go back now, take note of these matters, and accept the Good Message, and the Power, and the Peace. I also will depart now. I will go to the place where it crosses over the water, the warpath, from west to east, the path that leads to settlements of all the nations whose people, for a long time, have slaughtered one another. Moreover, that will now stop."

Then Tekánawíta' said, "Now, then, I will pass on, going to Kanyę'ke where they are expecting my arrival." Thereupon Tekánawíta' left, getting back to where he had his boat next to the lake. Then he departed. Moreover, when he got to the vicinity of the village, there, near the river, he kindled a fire. Thus at dawn they saw smoke rising near the river. Thereupon the chief said, "You two investigate who kindled the fire, causing smoke to rise near the river, and if you see the man, bring him back, saying, 'The chief commissioned us to summon you to come back with us.' Indeed, now he is arriving, the one who sent word that he is coming. Maybe this time it is that man who is arriving."

Thereupon the two departed, going to where the smoke had risen near the river. Arriving there they saw the man sitting next to the fire and they said, "He sent us along, the chief, we have come to fetch you and take you back to where he has his house, the chief, there where the village lies."

Thereupon Tekánawíta' said, "That is how it shall happen. Very well, let's go."

Thereupon that is where they went, to the place where the chief had his house, and they arrived there. Thereupon the chief said, "It was I who sent them there to summon you, thinking perhaps this time it is you, whom we have been expecting, Tekánawíta', who has sent a message that he is coming. For a long time we have been expecting you."

Thereupon Tekánawíta' said, "Indeed, it is I. I have now arrived."

Then the chief said, "I will notify the Great Warrior and his deputy. We will all assemble as a group, we will have a meeting, and you will wait until we are ready."

Then Tekánawíta' said, "I accept the way in which you are planning it. I will wait until you are ready."

Thereupon the chief sent his message to them, the Great Warrior and his deputy, for the two of them at once to spread the news among all of the people, to come together at the chief's house, for now he has arrived, the man whose name is Tekánawíta'. Thereupon they were informed, and immediately the two spread the news among all of the people to assemble at the chief's house, and the news spread immediately that now he had arrived, Tekánawíta', and all of the people wanted to see the man, the one who had sent a message that he was coming. Then everybody, men and women and infants and children, they all assembled at the chosen place. And this: when all were ready the chief stood up, saying, "Now we are ready. So now we'll proceed with the matter. Now you will reveal the matter you have along."

Then Tekánawíta' stood up, saying, "I, indeed, am arriving with the Good Message and the Power and the Peace. Now it will cease, the warfare and the scalping and the shedding of human blood. This, actually, is how it is on earth: there are pools and streams of human blood. And this will now cease. This too: you are the first whose village I am visiting with this message you are hearing now."

Thereupon the chief and the Great Warrior and his deputy conversed in whispers, deciding that they would ask what was the meaning of the three words. Thereupon he stood up, the chief, saying, "We have heard you report the message you are bringing, and we want to ask you about the three words. First, what does 'Good Message' mean, secondly what is 'Power,' and thirdly, what does it mean that 'Peace is now arriving?'"

Then Tekánawíta' stood up in front of the whole group and said, "You shall listen well, for you wanted to ask questions so as to understand what it means, 'Good Message.' This is what it means: people respect each other as though they are one person. Also everybody is related among the various nations, so that now they will stop, the sins and activities of evil people. Now everyone will repent, the old people and the young people. Now everyone will respect one another among all of the nations. And just this is what will operate again—the good—and that is what the 'Good Message' means.

"Secondly, this is what 'Power' means. All of the Nations will unite all their affairs, and the group of several nations will become just a single one, and their power is that they shall join hands. This, moreover, will be the basis upon which they will survive as a group, forming a single family, similar to being one person having one head and one life, surrounded by the Good Message. This is how peace will now come about among all of the nations, and power will arise for families to continue on from here on in.

"Thirdly, this is what 'Peace' means. Now it will stop, the massacre of humans and the scalping and bloodletting among themselves, specifically among the people of the various nations. Now as to that, it will end, the human slaughter, because the Great Spirit never planned for humans to hurt one another nor to slaughter one another. So now it will end, the warpath, and everywhere it will become peaceful. The different nations' villages are as neighbors and as to the localized families and their children, what will happen is that they all will be very close relatives, and it will come to pass that they will become just like one family which will encompass every nation and every language. And this: when everyone can travel from village to village, then it will end, the danger and terror, and then everything will be peaceful and they will rejoice by day and by night as the family continues on, there being no end to peace. That is what it means, the Great Law of Peace, that everyone will be united. Now I am finished."

Thereupon the Great Warrior stood up, saying, "Now we have heard Tekánawíta' explain to us the three words he mentioned. As to me, this is what I personally am questioning: what will happen if we accept the Good Message and the Power and the Peace, and the other tribes do not accept it? Subsequently this could happen: perhaps they will come to massacre us. Hence this is what I personally would say to this man who has arrived, Tekánawíta', whatever the message he has along which now he has finished delivering to us, moreover, this is it. I might believe it, if he were able to climb that tree growing over there beside the river, on the high bank, and if when he sits on the top of the tree, subsequently we were to cut down the tree, which would get knocked down in the direction of the river. Now if this man who has arrived, Tekánawíta', were to pass the test, surviving until dawn tomorrow, then I will immediately accept whatever message he has along."[100]

Thereupon the deputy to the Great Warrior stood up saying, "I will tell you this: I affirm what he said, the Great Warrior, to the full extent. If he is able, this man, to climb up and perch on top of the tree, and then we cut the tree which will topple into the river, and if this man will pass this test, if we see him the next morning, then I will accept and believe the message he has brought along. . . .'

Thereafter Tekánawíta' stood up and said, "First I will respond to the questions of the chief, to what he said, for now it is beginning, that is the action of the Good Message because indeed, [the chief I am now naming] Hayęhwatha' is accepting it. This, moreover, is how it is happening: because it kept you awake as it was arriving, the Good Message, and this especially, the Power and the Peace, consequently this is now your name and they will use it to address you: Hayęhwatha'. And all of the people will live by it, your name, and it will help them in succeeding generations to say, 'Hayęhwatha.' '"

Thereupon Tekánawíta' said, "Now then, I will respond to all of the words spoken by the Great Warrior and his deputy for they want for me to climb the tree growing at the top of the bank beside the river. Thereupon they will cut the tree so that it will go down into the river and, if I pass the test and survive until tomorrow, then they will accept the Good Message, the Great Warriors. Moreover, I agree to it, that this is how it shall happen."

Thereupon the whole group said, "That is just what we want, for the truth to emerge."

Thereupon Tekánawíta' said, "Now just that is what I also am prepared for, that I should climb the tree growing there, I sitting down on the top of the tree, and then everyone will observe what is to happen."

Thereupon the Great Warrior said, "Now we are ready to go to where the tree is growing . . . ."

Thereupon Tekánawíta' said, "Now then, I will climb up." Thereupon he went towards the growing tree. Thereupon he climbed it, sitting down there on the top of the tree while a large crowd watched as witnesses as they chopped into it, the growing tree, cutting the tree which went down towards the river, and into the water's depth went the branches. He disappeared underneath the water's surface, Tekánawíta' did, and nowhere did they see him again. Thereupon the Great Warrior said, "Now, indeed, it is coming to pass that we do not see Tekánawíta' anywhere. So now we will go home to wait until tomorrow, just in case, indeed, he should reappear."

Thereupon the crowd went back home and, next day, early in the morning before sunrise, a young man got up and went to the river bank where he saw smoke rising near the corn field. Then the young man went to the place where the smoke was rising and saw him, the man did, Tekánawíta'. Thereupon he ran quickly, going to the place where Hayęhwatha' had his house, and when he arrived he said, "I saw Tekánawíta'." Thereupon Hayęhwatha' said, "At which place?" and the young man said, "Next to the river, on the flats, beside the corn field, where smoke was rising, and when I got there I saw him sitting next to the fire, and I recognized Tekánawíta' who yesterday got submerged in the river. . . ."

Thereupon Tekánawíta' stood up and said, "Now it is done, everyone has become united. Moreover, as to you Great Warrior, this, indeed, is what happened: you were of two minds, with one you were thinking that it is not true what you have heard about the Good Message, and with the second you were thinking that to the extent that you will see an affirmation, it might be true. So now you accept the Good Message and the Power and the Peace. Now, moreover, I will tell you that this is your name, they will say Tekaihokę, and the people of all of the nations will be sustained by your name in future days and nights as the families continue on."[101]

Thereupon he said, "You next, you who are deputy to the Great Warrior, now I will tell you this: indeed, when you confirmed it, you accepted the entire Good Message. Moreover, as to your name, this is what they will be saying: Tsha'tekaihwate', and this is what the people will live by, your title name, as long as the families continue on, and thus it will go. Moreover, now the task is done, and you will cooperate, you chiefs, Tekaihokę and Hayęhwatha' and Tsha'tekaihwate'. And this: now you will all work for the Good Message, and the Power and the Peace.

Moreover, at present it [the Great Law] is young as the day is when the sun is rising and lights up the earth. Just as it causes warmth all over the earth and for all people, we will help the people of every nation. And just as all of the many things grow on earth and sustain the people, the newly arriving Great Law will come to shed light on the minds of the people, the elders and the younger people, everybody, even the children, and this is what you will work at: everyone shall become related to one another, so that it will become a single family consisting of every tribe. And they will be kind to one another, all of the people, and this is what will unite them: the Good Message, and the Power, and the Peace. Now, moreover, you will all begin to work . . . ."

Thereupon Hayẹhwatha''s daughter, the eldest, became ill and shortly she died. Thereupon Hayẹhwatha' became mournful at the loss of one of his daughters, two of whom survived, he having three children. But not long after that the next one, in turn, became ill. Then Tekaihokẹ and Tsha'tekaihwate' decided they were able,[102] but in a short time, then, she died. Now, then, as to the chief, Hayẹhwatha', it broke his heart, and then Tekaihokẹ and Tsha'tekaihwate' began to raise his spirits, trying to console him. Thereupon they decided, the young warriors, that they should divert Hayẹhwatha'. They decided to play lacrosse in order to divert him. Thereupon when the warriors played on the flats, Hayẹhwatha' and Tekaihokẹ and Tsha'tekaihwate' sat down on top of the hill, and the crowd sat down there too as they began to play lacrosse. While they were playing, Hayẹhwatha''s young daughter, she was his last remaining daughter and she was pregnant, now she left, taking a barrel along to go dipping water in the river. Arriving at the river, she dipped the water, turned back, and returned, going back towards the house. But when she was half-way home, they hollered loudly, saying, "Look at the animal that is flying," as they saw it coming down steadily from on high. Then in a little while it was flying on high. Then in a little while it was flying very low. Thereupon the players and the crowd said, "It is beautiful, indeed let us catch it." Thereupon they ran, chasing it, and it went just where Hayẹhwatha''s daughter stood. They ran there, chasing the bird, and they smashed into Hayẹhwatha''s daughter, injuring her. In a very short time, she died, this, the last of Hayẹhwatha''s three children. Thereupon Hayẹhwatha' cried, saying, "Now they are all gone, my children. So now I will leave, I will split the sky, going in an easterly direction, [I am deeply disturbed at] what happened to me."[103]

Thereupon Hayẹhwatha' departed, going in an easterly direction, and he arrived at a place where he saw in a corn field a lean-to. When he got there he lit a fire. Thereupon he cut off a sumac branch, cored it, cut it into short lengths, and then he strung up the sticks making several short strings. Thereupon he sat down next to the embers with his head bowed and gazed in front of him at the suspended rod, there where the short strands were strung up.[104]

Thereafter a man who was guarding the corn field sat down near the field by a log and, when he saw smoke rising from the lean-to, the man stood up, left, going slowly to the lean-to, and thought, "I will see who kindled a fire, causing smoke to rise." When he got near the house, he looked and saw a man inside the house; he was sitting near the fireplace, and in front of him was a suspended rod with short strands hanging down, and he was gazing at the hanging objects. Then the man moved away very slowly. Thereupon he returned, going straight to the place where the chief had his house. . . .

Thereupon the chief said, "I know now what is needed, what it is that man is announcing with the short strands that are strung up. Now, I also will make them." Thereupon the chief cut off the tips of feathers and strung them up into short strands and said, "Now I am finished, the short strands are my words, and these will lead the man. This, moreover, is what you will take along, this. Thereupon you will hand him the short strands," he said, "and as you get there you will say to him, 'We have arrived with a message we have along inviting you to go to the chief's house, and this will lead you there, this short strand.' Thereupon you will hand it to him."

When he handed it to him, the short strand, the man immediately looked at it and began to speak, saying, "This is what is right and I accept it. Therefore I shall arrive at the chief's house, and he will ready himself. . . ."[105]

Then they assembled immediately and, when they were ready and saw the man coming, the chief said, "Be prepared with a place for him to sit." Thereupon they made space, and when he arrived they showed him the seat that was ready and there he sat down. Thereupon the chief stood up and said, "It is a wonderful thing that has happened, you arriving at the place where we live. Perhaps you have a message along; so that is what you will reveal, the kind of message you have, bestowing it unto us. So now we will listen well."

Thereupon Hayęhwatha' stood up, holding a short strand that was strung up, and said, "Now today is when we are meeting. So now you will all listen well to the kind of message I have along. This, indeed, is it: "Kanyę'ke Mohawk, our village, is where I come from; there the following amazing events took place.

> Hayęhwatha' now recounts all that has happened to Tekánawíta' and to himself up to this point.

Thereupon the chief said, "This is it, then: we will keep you here; you will stay together with us until Tekánawíta' arrives." Thereafter the chief said, "You will stay here; we will be together at my house." Thereupon the crowd departed in various directions and when it was almost dark the chief said, "In that direction is the place where you will spend the night." Thereupon Hayęhwatha' got there, and they lay down; in the middle of the night Hayęhwatha' heard a man speaking up outdoors, saying, "Are you here? Are you asleep?" Thereupon Hayęhwatha' said, "I am here and I am not asleep." Thereupon the one outside answered saying, "Now, indeed I have arrived as I promised that we would all meet here, I, that is, Tekánawíta', so now come out," and then Hayęhwatha' said, "So be it."

> Tekánawíta' now relates to Hayęhwatha' what success he has achieved so far. He is gathering together the nations who have accepted his message at Onondaga where the Great Sorcerer resides. Eventually the nations assemble on the lakeshore and Tekánawíta' gives them their names: Mohawk, Oneida, Cayuga, and Seneca, and asks them to use a "single mind" to attempt to change the habits of Thatótáho', the Sorcerer. When they hear a shout that sounds like a clap of thunder, one chief from each nation embarks with Tekánawíta' in the stone canoe to cross the lake to the Sorcerer.

So then this: when it was nearly in the middle of the lake, the boat in which they were moving along, [the Sorcerer] shouted, saying, "Is it time yet?" and immediately a wind arose, a strong one, accompanied by large waves, and they got frightened, they riding in the boat. Thereupon Tekánawíta' said, "Rest, wind!" and at once it stopped, where it was blowing. It wasn't long before he hollered again in their direction, saying, "Is it time yet?" and at once it started up, the whirlwind. When the boat was about to turn over, Tekánawíta' said, "Stop, wind!" and it stopped at once.

Then they landed, they disembarked, and then they went along, circling around at his back, and arrived at the place where he sat, the man—on top of the hill is where he sat, high up—and then they separated. Tekánawíta' stood in front; towards his right, in turn were Hayęhwatha' and Hotatshehte'; and Hakaęyųk was on the other side with Skanyataiyo' (Handsome Lake). Thereupon Tekánawíta' said, "Now we have arrived; the chiefs have come with me, I having promised that we will come, so now we will all

Thatótáho', 1980. Cleveland Sandy, Cayuga

cooperate. Now this is what we will change: the fact that indeed, it is dangerous by day and by night." Thereupon the one sitting there looked at Tekánawíta' and also at Skanyataiyo', and Hayęhwatha' said, "You see at your left, there they stand, the ones who will cooperate with you, so that it will function, the Great Law; now indeed, it is arriving, the Good Message and the Power and the Peace." Then the man looked at Hayęhwatha' and Hotatshehte' and Hakaęyųk, and they observed that all over his head beings were writhing—it was like snakes, his hair, and his fingers were gnarled—all over they were writhing, nor was he about to talk. Thereupon they saw something hanging on him.

Thereupon Tekánawíta' said, "Indeed, this is what has been accomplished: a single mind they have used, the several tribes, the ones indeed, of whom yet more are coming."

Thereupon Tekánawíta' said, "Now, indeed, all of them have arrived, they of the four nations, that is the Mohawks and the Oneidas and the Cayugas and the Senecas; they are the ones who have accepted the Good Message and the Power and the Peace, that which will now function: the Great Law. Moreover, everything reposes there, the minds of the several nations, and as to you, they place before you their proposition that it is you who are to be the title bearer[106] and Great Chief, and you also are to be Fire Keeper at the place where we will kindle the fire, whose rising smoke will pierce the sky. Then one will see it in all of the settlements on earth.[107] Now, moreover, it is accomplished, now she has arrived, our mother, the great Matron whose name is Tsikųhsahsę' (Fat Face); now she has accepted the Good Message, and this, moreover, is what you should confirm and adopt, the Great Law, so that she may place antlers on you, our mother, and they shall together form a circle, standing alongside your body."[108]

. . . Thereupon the man bowed his head. Thereupon his hair stopped writhing and all of his fingers became quiet. Thereupon Tekánawíta' said, "Now, indeed, it is functioning, the Peace."

Thereupon the man spoke up saying, "Now I confirm this matter, I accept the Good Message and the Power and the Peace."

Thereupon Hayęhwatha' said, "So now indeed we will arrange his body, and that is how it will be righted; thus, it will happen that he will become human. Thereupon when Tekánawíta' put his hand on the sitting man's head and stroked his head, it subsided, his hair. Thereupon Hotatshehte' and Tekaihokę disentangled the objects hanging from his shoulder. Then Tekánawíta' straightened out his fingers.

Thereupon his face, and he said, "Now as to this, it has been righted; your body is that of a human being."

Thereupon Tekánawíta' said, "Now indeed, is the time that we will mark; indeed, from this time on it will change, the way in which things proceed on earth: the slaughtering, scalping, and bloodletting among their own people as well as their enemies in various other tribes. So now it is stopping on this very day, now this is how it will be: they will survive, the people, that is the elders and the young people and the children, and those still in the ground, the unborn who will be our grandchildren, those comprising families continuing on in generations to come. Moreover, as to that which sustains our lives, the wild deer, we will remove from their heads their antlers, and this will become a symbol, for we will place these antlers on the Great Chief."

"So now we are instituting this rule of the Confederacy Council and this is what they will live by, all of the people, the ones with families to come, as the generations of our grandchildren continue on. They are the ones for whom we have undertaken the task. So now it will ease their minds when peace emerges, and it will condition good thoughts as all become aware of it in their crowd, the group of League nations, and this is what will guide them all: the Good Message and the Power and the Peace and the Great Law of the League. So now we are completing the tasks concerning all of the rules of the principal place. Moreover, you chiefs, it is your work."

Thereupon Tekánawíta' said, "So now you shall consider this: what will you do when they relinquish their power to you, the warriors? Indeed, as they say, the war clubs, the killers of humans, and the tomahawks and other weapons, as to these, it will be better for us to hide them from them, so that they cannot see them again, our grandchildren."

Thereupon Tekánawíta' said, "There is only one way for it to get done, for us to be able to hide the weapons from them: we will pull up our tree, Great Tall Tree, Great Long Leaf,[109] and it will pass right through, making a hole through the earth. Thereupon we will pick up everything and throw it down where the earth is opened up, all of the war clubs, and the strong current in the earth will carry these away. Thereupon we will replant the tree, and they will never see the war clubs again, our grandchildren. Thereupon all will continue to think peacefully by day and by night as the families continue on."

1912

HANDSOME LAKE

Nineteenth-century New England saw the beginning of several religions. Ralph Waldo Emerson invented Transcendentalism, Joseph Smith revealed Mormonism, William Miller began the Seventh Day Adventist denomination, the Shaker movement was at its height, and utopian communities sprang up in several places. New religions were everywhere and the Haudenosaunee were no exception. Their prophet, Handsome Lake (Skanyátaí·yo', Ganiódaíío', 1735-1815), was born in the Seneca village of Conawaugas[110] on the Genesee River in New York. Although he was Chief Cornplanter's half-brother and a member of a noble family entrusted with leadership, until he had his vision of the New Religion, Handsome Lake was an alcoholic and an invalid. He was dying, and his culture was dying as well, destroyed by loss of land, broken treaties, poverty, and white hostility. The rituals of the League had been forgotten and the old cycles of violence had begun anew.

The New Religion of Gaíwiio`[111] is a conservative code, recalling traditional Haudenosaunee belief. However, Handsome Lake also sought to repress certain behaviors from the past: acting out dreams, sexual freedoms, and the powerful role of women. With the culture of the Longhouse fractured and the reservation system in place, Handsome Lake made it possible for men to work in the fields without loss of face, and he stopped the power of women to control the behavior of men, a doctrine he may have adopted from Christian missionaries influenced by St. Paul.

The stated times for the proclaiming of the Gaíwiio` are at the Six Nations' meeting in September and at the Midwinter Thanksgiving in the moon *niskowukni* between January 15 and February 15. The time consumed in reciting the Gaíwiio` is always three days. At noon each day the expositor stops, for the sun is in midheaven and ready to descend. All sacred things must be done early in the morning. The following selections from the first day of the Gaíwiio` are taken from the version by Sosondowa (Great Night, Chief Edward Cornplanter, 1851-1918) written in the present tense in 1903 as if Handsome Lake were narrating, and transcribed by Seneca ethnologist Arthur C. Parker 1913. The notes throughout are by Parker.

The Code of Handsome Lake (Gaíwiio`)

The beginning was in *yaíkni* (May), early in the moon, in the year 1800.

It commences now.

A Time of Trouble
The place is Ohio [on the Allegheny River], in Dionosadégî [Cornplanter Village].
Now it is the harvest time, so he [Handsome Lake] said.
Now a party of people move. They go down in canoes the Allegheny river. They plan to hunt throughout the autumn and the winter seasons.

Sosondowa

Now they land at Ganowoñ´gon (Warren, Pennsylvania) and set up camp.

The weather changes and they move again. They go farther down the river. The ice melts, opening up the stream, and so they go still farther down. They land at Dione:gâ (our younger brethren, Pittsburgh, Pennsylvania). It is a little village of white people. Here they barter their skins, dried meat, and fresh game for strong drink. They put a barrel of it in their canoes. Now all the canoes are lashed together like a raft.

Now all the men become filled with strong drink (gonigä´nongi). They yell and sing like demented people. Those who are in the middle canoes do this.[112]

Now they are homeward bound.

Now when they come to where they had left their wives and children these embark to return home. They go up Cornplanter creek, Awégäon.

Now that the party is home the men revel in strong drink and are very quarrelsome. Because of this the families become frightened and move away for safety. So from many places in the bushlands campfires send up their smoke.

Now the drunken men run yelling through the village and there is no one there except the drunken men. Now they are beastlike and run about without clothing and all have weapons to injure those whom they meet.

Now there are no doors left in the houses for they have all been kicked off. So, also, there are no fires in the village and have not been for many days. Now the men full of strong drink have trodden in the fireplaces. They alone track there and there are no fires and their footprints are in all the fireplaces.

Now the dogs yelp and cry in all the houses for they are hungry.

So this is what happens.

The Sick Man

And now furthermore a man becomes sick. Some strong power holds him.

Now as he lies in sickness he meditates and longs that he might rise again and walk upon the earth. So he implores the Great Ruler to give him strength that he may walk upon this earth again. And then he thinks how evil and loathsome he is before the Great Ruler. He thinks how he has been evil ever since he had strength in this world and had done evil ever since he had been able to walk. But notwithstanding, he asks that he may again walk.

So now this is what he sang: Ogíwe (Seneca ohki·we·h: Death Chant), Yéondâ´thâ (Women's Song), and Gonéowon (Harvest Song). Now while he sings he has strong drink with him.

Now it comes to his mind that perchance evil has arisen because of strong drink and he resolves to use it nevermore. Now he continually thinks of this every day and every hour. Yea, he continually thinks of this. Then a time comes and he craves drink again for he thinks that he cannot recover his strength without it.

Now two ways he thinks: what once he did and whether he will ever recover.

The Two Ways He Thinks

Now he thinks of the things he sees in the daylight.

The sunlight comes in and he sees it and he says, "The Creator made this sunshine." So he thinks. Now when he thinks of the sunshine and of the Creator who made it, he feels a new hope within him and he feels that he may again be on his feet in this world.

Now he had previously given up hope of life but now he begs to see the light of another day. He thinks thus for night is coming.

So now he makes an invocation that he may be able to endure the night.

Now he lives through the night and sees another day. So then he prays that he may see the night and it is so. Because of these things he now believes that the Great Ruler has heard him and he gives him thanks.

Now the sick man's bed is beside the fire. At night he looks up through the chimney hole and sees the stars and he thanks the Great Ruler that he can see them for he knows that he, the Creator, has made them.

Now it comes to him that because of these new thoughts he may obtain help to arise from his bed and walk again in this world. Then again he despairs that he will ever see the new day because of his great weakness. Then again he has confidence that he will see the new day, and so he lives and sees it.

For everything he sees he is thankful. He thinks of the Creator and thanks him for the things he sees. Now he hears the birds singing and he thanks the Great Ruler for their music.

So then he thinks that a thankful heart will help him.

Now this man has been sick four years but he feels that he will now recover.

And the name of the sick man is Ganiódaíio,[113] a council chief (Hoyáne, Perfect One).

The Strange Death of the Sick Man

Now at this time the daughter of the sick man and her husband are sitting outside the house in the shed and the sick man is within alone. The door is ajar. Now the daughter and her husband are cleaning beans for the planting. Suddenly they hear the sick man exclaim, *"Niio?!"* (So be it.) Then they hear him rising in his bed and they think how he is but yellow skin and dried bones from four years of sickness in bed. Now they hear him walking over the floor toward the door. Then the daughter looks up and sees her father coming out of doors. He totters and she rises quickly to catch him but he falls dying. Now they lift him up and carry him back within the house and dress him for burial.

Now he is dead.

The People Gather about the Dead Man

Then the daughter says to her husband, "Run quickly and notify his nephew, Tääwônyâs,[114] that he who has lain so many years in bed has gone. Bid him come immediately."

So the husband runs to carry the message to Tääwônyâs. And Tääwônyâs says, "Truly so. Now hasten to Gaiänt´wakâ,[115] the brother of the dead man, and say that he who lay sick for so many years is dead. So now go and say this."

So the husband goes alone to where Gaiänt´wakâ lives, and when he has spoken the wife says, "Gaiänt´wakâ is at the island planting." So he goes there and says, "Gaiänt´wakâ, your brother is dead. He who was sick for so many years is dead. Go at once to his bed."

Then Gaiänt´wakâ answers, "Truly, but first I must finish covering this small patch of seed. Then when I hoe it over I will come."

Now he who notifies is Hâtgwíyot, the husband of the daughter of Ganiódaíio². So now he returns home.

Now everyone hearing of the death of the sick man goes to where he lies.

Now first comes Tääwônyâs. He touches the dead man on every part of his body. Now he feels a warm spot on his chest and then Tääwônyâs says, "Hold back your sadness, friends," for he had discovered the warm spot and because of this he tells the people that perhaps the dead man may revive. Now many people are weeping and the speaker sits down by his head.

Now after some time Gaiänt´wakâ comes in and feels over the body of the dead, and he too discovers the warm spot but says nothing, but sits silently down at the feet of the dead man.

And for many hours no one speaks.

Now it is the early morning and the dew is drying. This is a time of trouble for he lies dead.

Now continually Tääwônyâs feels over the body of the dead man. He notices that the warm spot is spreading. Now the time is noon and he feels the warm blood pulsing in his veins. Now his breath comes and now he opens his eyes.

The Dead Man Revives

Now Tääwônyâs is speaking. "Are you well? What think you?" (*isegen onênt´ayei` hênesni´goê*).

Now the people notice that the man is moving his lips as if speaking but no words come. Now this is near the noon hour. Now all are silent while Tääwônyâs asks again, "My uncle, are you feeling well?" (*onigênt´gaiye`*).

Then comes the answer, "Yes I believe myself well." So these are the first words Ganiódaíio' spoke (*iwi!´naí ónê´t gaíye hê´neknígoên*).

Now then he speaks again saying, "Never have I seen such wondrous visions! Now at first I heard some one speaking. Some one spoke and said, 'Come out a while' and said this three times. Now since I saw no one speaking I thought that in my sickness I myself was speaking, but I thought again and found that it was not my voice. So I called out boldly, 'Niio?!' and arose and went out and there standing in the clear-swept space I saw three men clothed in fine, clean raiment. Their cheeks were painted red and it seemed that they had been painted the day before. Only a few feathers were in their bonnets. All three were alike and all seemed middle-aged. Never before have I seen such handsome, commanding men and they had in one hand bows and arrows as canes. Now in their other hands were huckleberry bushes and the berries were of every color.

"Then said the beings, addressing me, 'He who created the world at the beginning employed us to come to earth. Our visit now is not the only one we have made. He commanded us saying, "Go once more down upon the earth and (this time) visit him who thinks of me. He is grateful for my creations, moreover he wishes to rise from sickness and walk (in health) upon the earth. Go you and help him to recover." Then said the messengers, 'Take these berries and eat of every color. They will give you strength and your people with us will help you rise.' So I took and ate the berries. Then said the beings, 'On the morrow we will have it that a fire will be in the bushes and a medicine steeped to give you strength. We will appoint Odjis′kwâthên (Dry Pudding) and Gayänt′gogwûs (Dipped Tobacco), a man and his wife, to make the medicine. Now they are the best of all the medicine people. Early in the morning we will see them and at that time you will have the medicine for your use, and before noon the unused medicine will be cast away because you will have recovered. Now moreover before noon many people will gather at the council house. These people will be your relatives and will see you. They will have gathered the early strawberries[116] and made a strawberry feast and moreover will have strawberry wine sweetened with sugar. Then will all drink the juice of the berry and thank the Creator for your recovery and moreover they severally will call upon you by your name as a relative according as you are.'

"Now when the day came I went as appointed and all the people saw me coming and it was as predicted.

The Message of the Four Beings

"Now the messengers spoke to me and said that they would now tell me how things ought to be upon the earth. They said: 'Do not allow anyone to say that you have had great fortune in being able to rise again. The favor of the four beings is not alone for you and the Creator is willing to help all mankind.'

"Now on that same day the Great Feather[117] and the Harvest dances were to be celebrated and at this time the beings told me that my relatives would restore me. 'Your feelings and spirits are low,' they said, 'and must be aroused. Then will you obtain power to recover.' Verily the servants of the Creator [Hadionyâ′geonon] said this. Now moreover they commanded that henceforth dances of this same kind should be held and thanksgiving offered whenever the strawberries were ripe. Furthermore they said that the juice of the berry must be drunk by the children and the aged and all the people. Truly all must drink of the berry juice, for they said that the sweet water of the berries was a medicine and that the early strawberries were a great medicine. So they bade me tell this story to my people when I move upon the earth again. Now they said, 'We shall continually reveal things unto you. We, the servants of him who made us, say that as he employed us to cure unto you to reveal his will, so you must carry it to your people. Now we are they whom he created when he made the world and our duty is to watch over and care for mankind. Now there are four of us but the fourth is not here present. When we called you by name and you heard, he returned to tell the news.

"This will bring joy into the heaven-world of our Creator. So it is that the fourth is not with us but you shall see him at another time and when that time is at hand you shall know. Now furthermore we must remind you of the evil things that you have done and you must repent of all things that you believe to have been evil. You think that you have done wrong because of Ogíwe, Yéondâ′thâ, and Gonéowon and because you partook of strong drink. Verily you must do as you think for whatsoever you think is evil is evil.

Ganiódaíio' Commanded to Proclaim the Gaíwiio`

"'And now behold! Look through the valley between two hills. Look between the sunrise and the noon!'

"So I looked, and in the valley there was a deeper hollow from which smoke was arising and steam as if a hot place were beneath.

"Then spoke the messengers saying, 'What do you see?'

"I answered, 'I see a place in the valley from which smoke is arising and it is also steaming as a hot place were beneath.'

"Then said the beings, 'Truly you have spoken. It is the truth. In that place a man is buried. He lies between the two hills in the hollow in the valley and a great message is buried with him. Once we commanded that man to proclaim that message to the world but he refused to obey. So now he will never rise from that spot for he refused to obey. So now to you, therefore, we say, proclaim the message that we give you and tell it truly before all people.

'Now the first thing has been finished and it remains for us to uncover all wickedness before you.' So they said."

The Great Message of the Four Beings

1

"Now the beings spoke saying, 'We must now relate our message. We will uncover the evil upon the earth and show how men spoil the laws the Great Ruler has made and thereby make him angry.

"'The Creator made man a living creature.

"'Four words tell a great story of wrong and the Creator is sad because of the trouble they bring, so go and tell your people.

"'The first word is *onéga* (*uneka*: strong drink, whisky or rum). It seems that you never have known that this word stands for a great and monstrous evil and has reared a high mound of bones. Gánigoêntdontha, you lose your minds and onéga causes it all. Alas, many are fond of it and are too fond of it. So now all must now say, "I will use it nevermore. As long as I live, as long as the number of my days is I will never use it again. I now stop." So must all say when they hear this message.' Now the beings, the servants of the Great Ruler, the messengers of him who created us, said this. Furthermore they said that the Creator made onéga and gave it to our younger brethren, the white man, as a medicine but they use it for evil for they drink it for other purposes than medicine and drink instead of work and idlers drink onéga. No, the Creator did not make it for you.'

So they said and he said. *Eniá:iehûk!* (It was that way.)

2

"Now spoke the beings and said, 'We now speak of the second word. This makes the Creator angry. The word is *got´go* (witchcraft).

"'Witches are people without their right minds. They make disease and spread sickness to make the living die. They cut short the numbered days, for the Creator has given each person a certain number of days in which to live in this world.

"'Now this must you do: When you have told this message and the witches hear it they will confess before all the people and will say, "I am doing this evil thing but now I cease it. forever, as long as I live." Some witches are more evil and cannot speak in public so these must come privately and confess to you, Handsome Lake, or a preacher of this Gaíwiio`! Now some are most evil and they must go far out upon an abandoned trail and there they must confess before the Creator alone. This course may be taken by witches of whom no one knows.

"'Now when they go they must say:

"I think that way
So now I cease.
Now this is appointed
For all of my days,
As long as I live here
In this earth-world.
I have spoken."

"'In this manner all must say and say truly, then the prayer will be sufficient.'"

So they said and he said. Eniá:iehûk.

3

"'Now the beings spoke again saying, 'This is the third word. It is a sad one and the Creator is very sad because of this third word. It seems that you have never known that a great pile of human bodies lies dead because of this word, *Onóityíyende*, the *nigâ´hos´sää*, the secret poisons in little bundles named *gawênnodûs´hä* [compelling charms, superstition]. Now the Creator who made us commands that they who do this evil, when they hear this message, must stop it immediately and do it nevermore while they live upon this earth-world. It matters not how much destruction they have wrought—let them repent and not fail for fear the Creator will not accept them as his own.'"

So they said and he said. Eniá:iehûk.

4

"'Now another word. It is sad. It is the fourth word. It is the way *yondwínias swáyas* [she cuts off by abortion].

"'Now the Creator ordained that women should bear children.

"'Now a certain young married woman had children and suffered much. Now she is with child again and her mother, wishing to prevent further sufferings, designs to administer a medicine to cut off the child and to prevent forever other children from coming. So the mother makes the medicine and gives it. Now when she does this she forever cuts away her daughter's string of children.[118] Now it is because of such things that the Creator is sad. He created life to live and he wishes such evils to cease. He wishes those who employ such medicines to cease such practices forevermore. Now they must stop when they hear this message. Go and tell your people.'"

So they said and he said. Eniá:iehûk.

6

"'Now another message.

"'Go tell your people that the Great Ruler is sad because of what people do.

"The Creator has made it so that the married should live together and that children should grow from them.

"Now it often happens that it is only a little while when people are married that the husband speaks evil of his wife because he does not wish to care for her children. Now a man who does that stirs up trouble with his wife and soon deserts her and his children. Then he searches for another woman and when he has found her he marries her. Then when he finds her with child he goes away from her and leaves her alone. Again he looks for another woman and when he has lived with her for a time and sees her growing large, he deserts her, the third woman.

"'Now this is true. We, the messengers, saw him leave the two women and the Creator himself saw him desert the third and punished him. Now a sure torment in the after life is for him who leaves two women with child, but the Creator alone knows what the punishment is for the man who leaves the third.'"

So they said and he said. Eniá:iehûk.

10

"'Now another message to tell your people.

"'The married often live well together for a while. Then a man becomes ugly in temper and abuses his wife. It seems to afford him pleasure. Now because of such things the Creator is very sad. So he bids us to tell you that such evils must stop. Neither man nor woman must strike each other.' So they said.

"Now furthermore they said, 'We will tell you what people must do. It is the way he calls best. Love one another and do not strive for another's undoing. Even as you desire good treatment, so render it. Treat your wife well and she will treat you well.'"

So they said and he said. Eniá:iehûk.

14

"'Now another message.

"'This is what your people do.

"'An old woman punished her children unjustly. The Creator is sad because of such things and bids us tell you that such practices must cease.' So they said.

"Now this is the way ordained by the Creator: Talk slowly and kindly to children and never punish them unjustly. When a child will not obey let the mother say, 'Come to the water and I will immerse you.' If after this warning the child is still obstinate she must take it to the water's edge and say, 'Do you now obey?' and she must say so again and if at the third time there is no obedience then the child must be thrust in the water. But if the child cries for mercy it must have it and the woman must not throw it into the water. If she does, she does evil."

So they said and he said. Eniá:iehûk.

15

"'Now another message of things not right.

"'Parents disregard the warnings of their children. When a child says, "Mother, I want you to stop wrong-
doing," the child speaks straight words and the Creator says that the child speaks right and the
mother must obey. Furthermore the Creator proclaims that such words from a child are wonderful and that the mother who disregards then takes the wicked part. The mother may reply,
"Daughter, stop your noise. I know better than you. I am the older and you are but a child. Think
not that you can influence me by your speaking." Now when you tell this message to your people
say that it is wrong to speak to children in such words.'"

So they said and he said. Eniá:iehûk.

16

"'Now another message.

"'Tell your people that the Creator is sad because of what they are doing.

"'Some people live together well as man and wife and family, but the man of the family uses strong drink.
Then when he comes home he lifts up his child to fondle it and he is drunk. Now we, the messengers of the Creator, say that this is not right, for if a man filled with strong drink touches his child
he burns its blood. Tell your people to heed this warning.'"

So they said and he said. Eniá:iehûk.

19

"'Now another message.

"'Now the Creator of mankind ordained that people should live to an old age. He appointed that when a
woman becomes old she should be without strength and unable to work. Now the Creator says
that it is a great wrong to be unkind to our grandmothers. The Creator forbids unkindness to the
old. We, the messengers, say it. The Creator appointed this way: he designed that an old woman
should be as a child again and when she becomes so the Creator wishes the grandchildren to help
her, for only because she is, they are. Whosoever does right to the aged does right in the sight of
the Creator.'"

So they said and he said. Eniá:iehûk.

1903

THE SEVENTH FIRE

The ideas of the Seven Fires are founded on traditions such as the creation and recreation of the world on the back of a turtle, and they also suggest that if people believe and behave in certain ways, the future will be a return to the better values and practices of the past. The Seven Fires update earlier, nineteenth-century Native religious revivals to include avoiding contemporary technology, but the basic ideas are the same: a return to the values of a pre-Contact world.

Lone Wolf, Odawa

Let me tell you about our vision of the Seventh Fire. Our prophets said that the world was created with seven ways of being, each with its own fire that lights up and contributes to the specific lifestyle of that level, giving it power. Each fire represents a world and a people.

Kije Manido made the First World in the East and the First Couple, and he gave them everything they needed to exist. We were all related back then. But as the First People multiplied, they began to be tempted by Moje Manido, the Great Snake and Panther.[119] Moje Manido lured them away from the Red Path, the Path of Life that Kije Manido had made for them to follow—they no longer worked to live a good life. Things got out of hand, so he had to do something. He called on Animiki (Thunder) and asked him to make a great rain. Animiki agreed and began to rumble. Soon the world was flooded, everything was destroyed. Then Kije Manido felt bad. So he asked Nanabozho to help recreate a new world. Nanabozho remade all things—plants, animals, and people—and he made a paradise in the West for people to go when they die.

Nanabozho asked Muskrat to dive to the bottom of Kije Gan, the Great Waters, and bring up a piece of the earth. Muskrat tried many, many times. Finally, exhausted, Muskrat succeeded and from this Nanabozho made Makinaak (Turtle) Island. Everything was very beautiful. Kije Manido asked Nanabozho to be the master of all animals and the teacher of man. Nanabozho taught our ancestors how to live: how to use, to respect, and to take care of all the plants and animals. Nanabozho taught all things how to deceive their enemies. He taught us about the ways to be Odawa and the dangers of straying from that path, the Path of Life, about how to use *mashkiki* (medicine), and about how to show respect for that power by always placing a dish of food or tobacco plus mashkiki in our medicine bags. It's also Nanabozho who taught us that on earth there is a right path that some follow but also many side paths leading to deserts, about how we must help our dead travel the Path of Souls, and about our responsibility to always stay in touch with our ancestors.

Kije Manido and Nanabozho gave us another chance to prove ourselves. All this happened during the Second and Third Fires. Then our prophets taught that the Fourth Fire would be the time when white faces would appear and that they would either be friends or bring death. It was death that came—physical and spiritual—to the Anishinâbeg. But Kije Manido promised that by returning to the Red Path, the Path of Life—the traditional ways—that the life of the Seventh Fire will come and we will return to the ways things were in the beginning. We will again have *pimadaziwin*.[120] With the Seventh Fire, the circle will be

114

mended, the Old Ways will return, and my people will return to the good life. Kije Manido once more will destroy the imperfect world, including all people not following the traditional ways: those who stubbornly insist on following the path of technology, the ways of non-Indians that make people selfish and threaten existence. Those of us following the Red Path will return to perfection and be reunited with our ancestors.

Our great hope is that the community currently living—tomorrow's ancestors—will be wise enough to hear Kije Manido and follow the right path leading to this unity: the Red Path and not the path of technology. Our prophets also have taught that the worlds of the Fifth and Sixth Fires are to prepare and strengthen us.

No one knows when the Seventh Fire will happen. It's part of the Great Mystery. It may be in my generation. Things are very powerful now. It may be that we are just fanning the embers of it, and it will be for my children or for my grandchildren.

The world and people of the Seventh Fire only will happen when all Anishinâbeg have faithfully returned to the Red Path, destroying all non-Indian values and all people who follow them, as these create imbalance. We will know of the Seventh Fire when a young man, actually Nanabozho, appears who will show us where to find the ancient birch bark scrolls of our origins that were buried during our long migration from the east. Then our spiritual and physical illness once again will be overcome.

1998

❖ WINTER STARS ❖

To Natives of an earlier time, stars were a living calendar of spirits, complete with stories about the characters. Together with the moons and planets, the stars and constellations that moved about the sky during the year were also a way of measuring time and the seasons, of knowing when the weather might change or when a ceremony should be held. The Native year opens with the new moon of midwinter. At dawn of the fifth day after this moon, the Haudenosaunee Midwinter Ceremony begins, the most important of the year for this nation. A nine-day thanksgiving festival, special days are set aside to name children born during the past year; to guess what dreams mean; to heal the sick; and to dance in honor of the Three Sisters (corn, squash, and beans), secret medicine societies, and bears. Participants wearing False Face masks and Husk Face masks (p. 131) help lead the festivities.

Men out hunting needed a way to know when this moon would occur so they could be home, and their marker was a constellation Europeans had named the Pleiades, but which Native nations named according to their cultures. In Huron they are known as Hutiwatsija, or the Cluster, from their tight group of seven to ten stars in the sky; in Seneca as De'hoñnoñt´gwĕn' (They are dancing); and in Onondaga as Ootkwatah, which means "There they dwell in peace." These cold weather stars were used to mark the limits of the agricultural year across North America, setting in the west just past dark after the last frosts of spring when the planting season could begin without fear of frosts, and rising in the east just before dawn after the first frosts of fall when the harvest should be complete. When the Ootkwatah are directly overhead at nightfall, Haudenosaunee hunters knew it was time to begin the trek home for the Midwinter Thanksgiving ceremonies where the stars would dance over the council house at the zenith of their yearly orbit. Northern nations without agriculture often saw the stars as the head of a bear and used the constellation's movements to mark when they could begin leaving winter hunting camps to gather at the maple sugaring woods.

The idea of this constellation as star dancers is ancient and widespread, from South America to Canada,

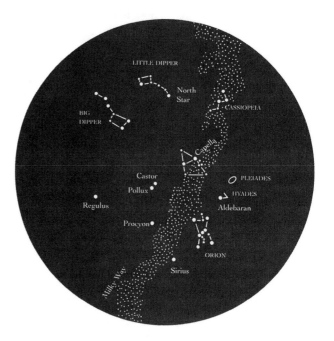

Winter star map

and here are two versions.[121] The first has an oft-repeated plot involving food and mothering, while the second combines the Seven Sisters with another widespread story plot, a human who marries a star woman who descends in a basket. Marriages between humans and stars, known as star husband or star woman stories, nearly always have problems—Where will the couple live? What about the children?—and often end in divorce or death. Here the ending accounts for the faintness of one of the stars in the constellation.

The Dancing Stars

Dawendine (The Dawn, Bernice Loft Winslow, 1902-†), Mohawk

The daughter of a distinguished chief and elder of Mohawks at the Six Nations Reserve near Brantford, Ontario, Dawendine collected stories from her family and from elders. Before her marriage to an American and an urban life outside Boston, she developed a successful public speaking career. She then worked at compiling her writings until her husband's death in 1962, when she began lecturing again about the crucial role Native peoples had played in the creation of Canada. Her typescripts and manuscripts were discovered and published in 1995 as *Iroquois Fires* when she was ninety-two.

It was the month of January, Gah-yah-dah-go-wah, on the Six Nations Reserve. Although outside the log cabins and homes the cold was very concentrated, the skies were brilliantly clear, and overhead the great vault was studded with stars and groups of stars. On the morrow the great Festival, Gaih-wah-nus-gwah-go-wah (Kaihwanǫ·ska'kó·wa·h: very precious matter), of the Cayuga Longhouse, was to begin at dawn.

Curious as to how the nation knew the exact time to begin the rite every year, I asked the Keeper of the Faith, Ho-drih-hont of the Cayuga tribe.[122] He, Jacob Hess, had stopped in that evening, and so it was that I heard anew the complete story of the origin of the Pleiades, although it had been told to me by my father, the Chief, as well as by my grandmother Loft, under the title Deh-ho-dee-denh (They Flew Over).

The Keeper of the Faith began by telling us that this time of the year received its name from the fact that the doe was very heavy with young. Later on, the young fawns would be born. For this reason the selected group of hunters who went out to secure the venison for the feast that was part of the Festival were instructed not to kill the does. The following month, February, was known as Gonh-ra-da-gah, meaning "when the outer scales of buds of trees fall." This time of year was like a pivot, indicating a swing of the year from winter months to returning life and spring.

The Keeper suggested that we step outside the lodge to locate, directly overhead, a small, compact group of stars, one of which was dimmer than the rest. He told us to observe the position of the young moon riding up the Trail.[123] On the morrow, he said, the new moon would be five sleeps, or five nights old, and that was when the ancient ceremony was designated to begin. Once more, with all seated within the lodge, he began his story.

For many many years, ages in fact, people have observed and wondered, just as you probably have, how these stars came to be, and how they came to be grouped in this fashion. In Cayuga we call the formation the O-ganh-yah. Many stories have been told about their mystery and beauty.

Our people have many thanksgiving rites, with accompanying dances, when we gather together around fires in our different tribes and thank the Great Spirit for all that he has given.

Before the white man or any other nations came to this continent, the ceremonies were held in the woods around a fire. At that time, only the older people attended the ceremonies, while the children remained in the lodges.

It was back in the dim past that this strange thing happened.

As usual, the elders had gone to the thanksgiving gathering and the children had been left in the tee-pees. Since it was too early to retire, the older boys, after playing for some time, had tired of their games and decided to call a councilor meeting of their own. They wanted very much to see what was being done at the elders' ceremonies, so a scouting party was formed. The young son of the chief was made the leader of the group.

Leading the way, he brought them to a deep part of the wood where they could easily watch the older people and the meeting without being detected themselves. Eagerly they watched the ceremony begin. The head faith-keeper rose, welcomed the people, and placed the sacred tobacco in the fire. As the smoke ascended, he addressed his words to the Great Spirit, first giving thanks for all mankind; then, in proper order, for the Earth, our Mother, for streams, grass, herbs, trees, seeds, corn, and berries; for small and great animals of the woods, for birds, for the winds; for the Moon, our grandmother, who gave us life and light by night, and for the Sun, our brother, who lighted the earth for us by day and gave us warmth.

When he had finished, others spoke and gave thanks in their own way. Then a dance followed, after which the sharing of the food—the feast—completed the ceremony.

All this time the boys had watched and listened well. Then they stole back to the lodges and decided, since they were not included in this interesting ceremony, that they would hold one of their own.

Next day, they were up very early and went to the woods, looking for a suitable place to conduct their dance and feast. One path they followed brought them to a high hill, on the top of which there was an open space that suited their purpose. Here they planned to meet when the dark cloud-blanket of night appeared.

Different tasks fell to each boy. One was appointed to bring meat, another corn or hominy, another a vessel in which to cook the food, and still another the tobacco. Also, a fire must be prepared. But the only lad who was able to fulfill his mission was the one who was to procure the tobacco.

When the camp was stilled in slumber that night, the boys crept away from the lodges and followed their hilltop trail. The young son of the chief soon had a fire burning and, although they were all disappointed to hear there was to be no food, they agreed to hold their ceremony without it.

Just as the faith-keeper had done, the chief's son placed the sacred tobacco on the fire and began to give thanks in the same order as they had been offered by the older men. The boys then joined in the dance, with one beating the water drum or the tom-tom. Round and round they whirled. After a while the chief's son said, "Since we have no food, let us have one more dance."

Eagerly they began their dance again. The singing grew louder and the drum-beats quickened. Their feet scarcely seemed to touch the earth. Faster and faster danced the boys around the fire. Soon their feet left the ground and they were heading skyward. Higher and higher rose the dancing figures.

As the group left the earth, the mother of the young chief awoke. Sensing something wrong, she found her boy was not in the lodge. She went to the next teepee to see if he was there. Here the mother of the boy who had been asked to bring corn called to her son but received no reply either.[124]

The two mothers went outside and listened. Far away the singing voices and the drum-beats could be heard. Other lodges were awakened and found other boys missing. Now, alarmed, they began a search by following the singing, and found their way to the hilltop. There they saw the strange scene of wild glee about a fire that was steadily rising into the air. The people could see them plainly in the firelight as they danced skyward. The parents called and shouted to the boys, begging them to return. But only one heard and looked back. The others continued their dance upward into the sky. It was the chief's son who looked down at his mother, and at once he fell to earth and disappeared into the ground. Sadly the people stood and watched the boys dance onward to the sky.

Then a voice was heard saying, "Do not grieve too much. We are on an endless journey, a trail of dance and song. In summer watch us coming by way of the south to the setting sun. In the winter you will see us coming by way of the north toward the rising sun. When we are directly overhead, observe the ceremonies."

On and on the dancers whirled until they appeared but a ring of fire. Higher still they rose until the ring seemed a small ball or circle of light. Still the people gazed skyward and remained watching until the circle broke and the dancers took their places as a star-formation among the other star people.

Ever since that time, when these stars are at a certain place overhead in their dance across the sky, the Iroquois observe the New Year Festival. Then, too, the mid-winter moon, Nis-go-wa-geh-neh, is five sleeps old, riding onward up the Trail.

Origin of the Pine Tree (O-nenh-dah)

That winter was so long to the mother of the chief's son who fell to earth. She mourned for him, and often was found at the place where he had fallen.

Spring came, and in the spot a small green shoot began to grow. Many winters and springs passed, and the shoot grew into a beautiful pine tree, which the Iroquois called O-nenh-dah (*onehta'*).

One day the bark of the tree became bruised. The people noticed red blood issuing from the wound. And so they knew this was the spirit of the young chief who had fallen to earth. The blood began to pale and grow whiter and clearer in color.

Then the spirit of the pine tree, the young chief, was heard speaking to them in low, murmuring tones, "This is my blood. Take it and use it for my people. It will help cure many diseases and heal wounds. Take my life-blood and with it caulk the seams of your canoes, so they may be safe and swift on the waters. I am O-nenh-dah, the Pine, your guide in the forest. My topmost branches point east and west. Use me, my bark, for healing, my wood for your fires, my needles for your medicine. Grow tall as I, in summer and winter, ever the same. Ever look upwards, reaching to the sky."

So it is in the undertones of the Pine that we hear the young chief's voice. Tall and straight the Pine tree grows, ever seeking the sun and sighing for his brothers in the star world.

c.1940s

The Seven Star Dancers

Gawasowaneh (Big Snowsnake,[125] Arthur C. Parker, 1881-1955), Seneca

Now this even happened a long time ago in the days when the whole world was new. Our Creator it was, S'hoñgwadiĕnnu'k´dăon (Shŭkwatyĕnukta'ŭ'), had finished his work. One of the first men beings lived with his nephew in a lodge near a river. The river was broad and had a wide sandy shore. The nephew received the name Djinaĕñ´dă' (Elk) and his uncle sent him away to dream on the shore of the river, there to stay and dream until his dream-helpers appeared. For a long time he did not eat, but drank water and sweat himself in a sweat lodge.

One night he thought that he saw a light upon the water and he looked and saw lights moving toward him. Hiding in the reeds on the shore he watched. Soon he saw seven shining young women dancing in the water against the shore, and they made no splashing but went up and down. He heard them speak but could not understand what they said. He observed them all intently, for all were without clothing and were very beautiful of body. The youngest appeared the most beautiful of all. The young man watched her and thought that she would do for a wife.

Hoping to catch her he rushed out from his hiding place, but the maidens were alarmed and leaped into a great corn basket and were drawn rapidly up into the sky, and he looked and said, "They are dancing" (De'hoñnoñt´gwên').

Djinaĕñ´dă' continued his vigil and the next night he saw the dancers swing back over the water in their basket. Soon they came to the shore and alighted. Again he heard their voices and again they began their bewitching dance. Djinaĕñ´dă''s eyes were upon the youngest dancer and she appeared more beautiful than ever. He waited until she danced very near to him and away from the basket, then he rushed out from his hiding-place and pursued the maidens, at length grasping the youngest before she touched the basket. But she gave a leap, and the youth holding to her was drawn upward as she fell into the basket. She looked to see who held her so tightly and immediately both fell to the earth.

The maiden gazed upon Djinaĕñ´dă' and asked him what he wanted. "I want to marry you," he said. "You have caused me to love you."

"Then we shall be married," said the maiden, "but we must return to the sky and prepare for living upon the earth." So the basket came down and drew them into the sky.

Djinaĕñ´dă' was taken to the lodge of the dancing sisters and then led to the lodge of a great chief who caused him to recline upon the ground. The chief then took him apart, joint by joint, and removed all his organs. After cleansing them, he replaced them and Djinaĕñ´dă' was regenerated. He now felt very strong and able to do mighty things.

His bride now came to him and said that she would now return to the earth with him and live as his wife. The sisters then placed the couple in the basket and lowered them to the earth. They came down on the beach of the river but it was changed and there was a great village of men beings there.

Djinaĕñ´dă' inquired where his uncle lived but no one knew. Finally an old man said, "An old man such as you describe lived in the woods with his nephew near this place more than a hundred years ago."

The couple now tried to live contentedly but could not understand the ways of the people, and so, in time, the two returned to the sky. The wife rejoined her sisters but she had lost her brightness, and Djinaĕñ´dă' roamed the sky world hunting game which he captured by running it down.[126]

My grandmother told me that they are up there yet.

1923

Danse Sacrée
Linda Sioui, Huron-Wendat

Vision solaire
Âme tremblotante
Gavée de déceptions
Fatiguée d'avoir vomi
Une pluie de déchets
Âme pourtant imprégnée
De beauté et de justice

Guerrière de l'Arc-en-ciel
Ivre de lumière
Elle danse, danse et virevolte
Avec les Ancêtres
À l'intérieur du Cercle sacré

Scintillement lunaire
Poussière d'étoile
Elle illumine la nuit sombre
De blancheur argentée
Et s'élève, s'élève et s'envole
Pour s'unir aux Pléiades.

2005

Sacred Dance
Carl Masthay, translator

A solar sight
A trembling soul
Filled with deceptions
Tired of having vomited
A rain of lost matter
But still pregnant
With beauty and justice

Warrior of the Rainbow
Drunk from light
She dances, dances, quickly turning
With the Ancestors
Within the sacred Circle

Lunar sparkling
Star dust
She brightens up the gloomy night
With silvery whiteness
And rises, rises, and flies away
To unite with the Pleiades.

2010

Linda Sioui (1960-   ) is a member of the Huron-Wendat Nation who lives in Wendake, the historic Huron homeland outside Quebec City. A graduate student of anthropology, her best memory is the summer she spent in the ancestral homeland in Huronia, on the shores of Georgian Bay.

·◈· WINTER CREATURES ·◈·

Weendigo

Here is a dreaded monster of the Native universe, the scourge of winter that stalked the hungry camps when no game could be found. Weendigo may have appeared during the terrible winters of the Little Ice Age, when cannibalism in isolated camps was a real possibility. Psychologists call it "windigo psychosis," and suggest that creating a character to assume the guilt of cannibalism allows the culture to function without incapacitating guilt when food is again available. The Weendigo is not limited to starvation in winter, Johnston teaches, but comes from the worst impulses of humans that are with us still: the greed and excess that risk destruction to all. Basil Johnston has worked to preserve Anishinâbe language and culture all his life, recording stories, traditions, and ceremonies so that they would not be lost.

Basil Johnston (1929-   ), Anishinâbe

Of the evil beings who dwelt on the periphery of the world of the Anishinaubae peoples, none was more terrifying than the Weendigo. It was a creature loathsome to behold and as loathsome in its habits, conduct, and manners.[127]

The Weendigo was a giant manitou in the form of a man or a woman who towered five to eight times above the height of a tall man. But the Weendigo was a giant in height only; in girth and strength, it was not. Because it was afflicted with never-ending hunger and could never get enough to eat, it was always on the verge of starvation. The Weendigo was gaunt to the point of emaciation, its desiccated skin pulled tautly over its bones. With its bones pushing out against its skin, its complexion the ash gray of death, and its eyes pushed back deep into their sockets, the Weendigo looked like a gaunt skeleton recently disinterred from the grave. What lips it had were tattered and bloody from its constant chewing with jagged teeth. Unclean and suffering from suppurations of the flesh, the Weendigo gave off a strange and eerie odor of decay and decomposition, of death and corruption.

When the Weendigo set to attack a human being, a dark snow cloud would shroud its upper body from the waist up. The air would turn cold, so the trees crackled. Then a wind would rise, no more than a breath at first, but in moments whining and driving, transformed into a blizzard. Behind the odor and chill of death and the killing blizzard came the Weendigo.

Even before the Weendigo laid hands on them, many people died in their tracks from fright; just to see the Weendigo's sepulchral face was enough to induce heart failure and death. For others, the monster's shriek was more than they could bear. Those who died of fright were lucky; their death was merciful and painless. But for those who had the misfortune to live through their terror, death was slow and agonizing.

The Weendigo seized its victim and tore him or her limb from limb with its hands and teeth, eating the flesh and bones and drinking the blood while its victim screamed and struggled. The pain of others meant nothing to the Weendigo; all that mattered was its survival. The Weendigo gorged itself and glutted its belly as if it would never eat again. But a remarkable thing always occurred. As the Weendigo ate, it grew, and as it grew so did its hunger, so that no matter how much it ate, its hunger always remained in proportion to its size. The Weendigo could never requite either its unnatural lust for human flesh or its unnatural appetite. It could never stop as animals do when bloated, unable to ingest another morsel, or sense as humans sense that enough is enough for the present. For the unfortunate Weendigo, the more it ate, the bigger it grew; and the bigger it grew, the more it wanted and needed.

The Anishinaubae people had every reason to fear and abhor the Weendigo. It was a giant cannibal that fed only on human flesh, bones, blood. But the Weendigo represented not only the worst that a human can do to another human being and ultimately to himself or herself, but exemplified other despicable traits. Even the term "Weendigo" evokes images of offensive traits. It may be derived from *ween dacaoh*, which means "solely for self," or from *weenin n'd'igooh*, which means "fat" or excess.

The Weendigo inspired fear. There was no human sanction or punishment to compare to death at the hands of the Weendigo, no threats more certain to bring about the exercise of moderation. The old people repeatedly warned, "Not too much. Think of tomorrow, next winter. *Kegoh zaum! Baenuk!*" (Think of others! Balance, moderation, self-control.) As long as men and women put the well being of their families and communities ahead of their own self-interests by respecting the rights of animals who dwelt as their cotenants on Mother Earth, offering tobacco and chants to Mother Earth and Kitchi-Manitou as signs of gratitude and goodwill, and attempting to fulfill and live out their dreams and visions, they would instinctively know how to live in harmony and balance and have nothing to fear of the Weendigo. If all men and women lived in moderation, the Weendigo and his brothers and sisters would starve and die out.

But such is not the case. Human beings are just a little too inclined to self-indulgence, at times a shade too intemperate, for even the specter of the Weendigo to frighten them into deference. At root is selfishness, regarded by the Anishinaubae peoples as the worst human shortcoming.

In the meantime, the Weendigo waited in the shadows, hungry to the point of collapse and tormented by an unrelenting ache that was worse than any ache known to humans. Sooner or later a man or woman would have to leave his or her camp or village and come within reach. Of this the Weendigo was certain, given the weakness and unchangeableness of human nature. But to suspend one's labor to rest and renew oneself or to take up another interest for self-growth is not in and of itself bad. As Western Europeans say, "All work and no play make Jack or Jill dull." There is nothing harmful in humankind's inclination to rest, play, celebrate, feast, and pursue hobbies. The trouble is that some people don't know when to stop and appear not to care, because nature, or Kitchi Manitou, has endowed them with slightly more than is good for them: appetites, passions, and desires that dilute their talents, common sense, and judgment. It doesn't take much. A fraction too much or too little of anger, envy, or lust is enough to create an imbalance in a person's character to impair his or her judgment and weaken his or her resolution. Is it any wonder, then, given humankind's inherent selfishness and imbalance, that men and women, when put to the test, would prefer safety to risk, ease to toil, and certainty to uncertainty, which makes them so conservative that when the opportunity arises they tend to indulge their self-interests?

In this and other respects, the Weendigoes are men and women except on a grander, exaggerated scale. Nature has done them a disservice by endowing them with an abnormal craving, creating an internal imbalance to such a degree as to create a physical disorder. The Weendigo has no other object in life but to satisfy this lust and hunger, expending all its energy on this one purpose. As long as its lust and hunger are satisfied, nothing else matters—not compassion, sorrow, reason, or judgment. Although the Weendigo is an exaggeration, it exemplifies human nature's tendency to indulge its self-interests, which, once indulged, demand even greater indulgence and ultimately result in the extreme—the erosion of principles and values.

It is ironic that the Weendigo preys upon and can only overcome ordinary human beings who, like itself, have indulged themselves to excess and hence illustrates the lesson that excess preys and thrives on excess.

The Weendigo was born out of human susceptibility. It was also born out of the conditions that men and women had to live through in winter when it was sometimes doubtful that the little food they had would carry them through until spring. From the moment their supplies began to thin, the people faced starvation and death . . . and the Weendigo. What they feared most in their desperation and the delirium induced by famine and freezing to death was to kill and eat human flesh to survive. Nothing was more reprehensible than cannibalism.

In the following stories, humans must kill the Weendigo to betoken that they must put an end to certain self-serving indulgences or be destroyed. Every community had its catalog of stories of Weendigoes, of men and women becoming Weendigoes, of the carnage perpetrated by these giant cannibals that ends in the people's destruction. In the end, David slays Goliath; moderation triumphs over excess. The Nipissing Weendigo story exemplifies this moral.

There was once a man, as reasonably successful as any other hunter, whose family fell upon hard times during an unusually hot and dry summer, when the berries burned before they ripened. The birds and animals had enough sense to leave to find some other place, but the humans didn't have such an instinct to let them know what was forthcoming and to take measures to protect themselves. All the humans had was a kind of optimism, a conviction and hope that conditions could not long remain the way they were. And so, men and women remained anchored where they were, hoping for a change in the weather.

That winter the man and his family, like their neighbors, were reduced to eating roots and bark and snowbirds before the winter was half over. Everyone was desperate, but only this one man went to a sorcerer for a talisman that would enable him to find food and allay his hunger. The sorcerer gave him a powder made of roots, with instructions for him to brew it and drink it as a tea in the morning.

In the morning, before anyone was awake, the man woke up and made a tea, which he drank. Almost at once he began to grow in height until he was six times the height of an ordinary man. For the moment the man was so absorbed by his growth and height that he forgot his hunger and his family's situation. He went forward to try his pace and the length of his stride. The pace of his motion pleased and excited him. He could go faster and cover greater distances than any human being alive. He would be able to outrun most large animals. In his flush of ecstasy, with the advantages and benefits now available to him, the man overlooked the disadvantages and forgot other things. He ran until he was gasping for breath and tired; then he sat down to rest. It was only then that he became conscious of his hunger, a reality that he had temporarily forgotten. His hunger was now greater than before, and having had little sustenance before his hard run, the man weakened himself to the point of shaking. He thought of food, but the thought of animal flesh sickened him. Yet he was still hungry. He needed food to allay not only his hunger but his peculiar indescribable craving. He needed something at once, or he would collapse and waste away, providing fodder for the ravens, lynxes, and wolves. After a short rest the giant wobbled to his feet and went on.

Soon, from atop a hill, the giant saw a village in the distance. It was such a welcome sight. He put his hands to his mouth and hailed the residents before he waved at them in greeting. His voice so boomed and crackled like thunder that it startled him and so frightened the people in the camp that many dropped in their tracks and died. The giant had meant no harm. All he meant to do was to let them know that he was in their land and was there on friendly business. But he had killed many of them, though he didn't know it then, without even laying a hand on them. The rest fled.

The giant did not break his stride as he went forward. He forgot his hunger for a few moments as he listened to the echoes of his thunderous voice and saw the stricken human beings keel over. But his hunger restored him to reality, the reality made sensible by the aroma of human flesh. In a few moments the giant was in the encampment. He took a corpse and ate it whole. He grew, but he didn't know it. He ate another corpse. He grew some more. His hunger should have diminished, but it didn't. Instead, it was as demanding as before. And he ate until he had eaten all the inhabitants who had died of fright. And he was no less hungry—no better satisfied at the end of his ravenous meal, despite all he had eaten. Without so much as touching any of the meat that had been stored by his victims for their future needs, the giant, formerly a man, now became a Weendigo.

A man of the village survived the carnage only because he had been away when the Weendigo attacked his people and their homes. Without family or home, the man now had only one thing to live for: revenge. He set out at once, following the trail left by the Weendigo. Toward the end of winter, hundreds of miles away, the man overtook the Weendigo, now shrunk in size to the normal stature of an ordinary Weendigo. The man slew the Weendigo in the same way the monster killed his victims—unmercifully. With utter indifference to his cries for mercy or of fear and pain, he clubbed the Weendigo to death, leaving its remains to the ravens or whoever craved even the flesh of a cannibal.

A human being could become a Weendigo by his or her own excesses. That was the usual way. But one human being could also transform another into a Weendigo.

One man asked another man and wife for the hand of their daughter in marriage. The father refused, pointing out that the petitioner had already had several wives, more wives than most men, and should not take on yet another lest one of the wives be neglected. The father suggested that the man should think of other men who did not yet have wives.

The man took the refusal as an insult, as humiliating as a slap in the face in public. He didn't say anything to the father, but he was cut to the quick. As soon as he got home, he made an effigy of the girl with snow and then immersed it in water before setting it outside in the cold, where it froze solid. Afterward he buried the effigy in ashes, performing a ritual and chanting arcane psalms as he did so.

Around the same time, while the girl and her family were camped on their trap line some distance from the main village, she complained of being cold, although she did not have a fever and was not shivering. She was cold within and without. It was more than a physical cold that chilled the flesh; this cold chilled the blood, the spirit, and the soul as well. It was a chill that numbed her entire being and made her unbelievably hungry, which was strange because she and her family had just eaten a short time earlier. The family made her a hot broth and a hot meal and wrapped her in blankets, but the girl didn't even touch the food, complaining that the smell alone made her ill and that the extra blankets and heat added to her discomfort. She was hungry and wanted food, but not the kind that she had been accustomed to eating . . . something different.

At last, unable to stand her hunger, she turned on her own family and, with great strength born of desperation, overcame and bludgeoned her family and then ate them.

When the family was overdue to return to the village by several days, the suitor-sorcerer volunteered to go in search of them. He found what he had hoped to find. As the creator of the "new" girl and her rescuer, custom allowed that he could claim the girl as his wife if he wanted to. The girl was in a daze, unable to recall what had become of her family, of whom other than their few possessions there was no trace. But her hunger had subsided, and she went meekly with her rescuer.

Her introduction into the family, not only as one of the wives but as the favorite, caused a great deal more friction and unhappiness in the household than already existed. The other women resented the girl and wouldn't talk to her, but they talked about her, about her survival while her family had died. The only one who seemed to be happy with the arrangement was the sorcerer, certain that the women in the household would eventually come to terms with the situation and that their lives would become stabilized.

But the relationships in the household did not warm up as the sorcerer had hoped, and he blamed his newest wife for not making enough of an effort to fit in. The accusation only made matters worse, hurting the girl even more than she was already hurt and intensifying her loneliness and sense of isolation, even in the company of people. The other women had families to visit and talk with, but she had none, not even the remembrance of a single one. She had only this vague sense that there was a family, that she must have had someone to love and someone to love her in return. She longed for affection and to care for someone, to belong some place where she wanted to be. Every chance she had, whenever they were alone, she asked her husband who she was, where she came from, and whether she had kin, but all he would tell her was that he had come upon her in the woods and that she was probably abandoned.

Finally, she overcame her fear and asked one of the other women in the sorcerer's household if the woman knew who she was or if she knew how she might find out. The other woman didn't know what to make of such a question—didn't know if the younger woman was putting her on or actually had lost her senses. She retorted sarcastically, "Why ask me! Why don't you ask him? What's the matter with you? Don't you know that he'd do anything for you?" The other woman hissed, "ASK HIM!"

The young woman persisted, explaining that she had already asked and had not received any satisfactory answer. Now she pleaded for help. But the older woman remained adamant. "Ask him again!" she barked, intimating in her tone that their husband knew more about her than he let on.

Following the older woman's advice, the younger woman badgered their husband to tell her what she wanted to know. She asked him several times a day until her questions drove him to such exasperation that he told her that she had murdered and then eaten her own family. He said he had kept this fact from her to save her from guilt and that if it wasn't for his care and protection, other Weendigoes and manitous would have killed her by now.

The girl was horrified, but she didn't believe the sorcerer's story. She went to the oldest woman in the household and told her what their husband had said. The older woman explained that someone had indeed killed her family and that people suspected she had done it. People were afraid of her.

The younger woman went into a depression. She had killed the people who had loved her and whom she had loved. She no longer had anything, no memories or hopes, nothing but guilt and remorse, loneliness, and self-revulsion. Then an awful hunger settled on her, making her feel as if she had not eaten in several days and that if she did not eat she would collapse and die that night. And as the hunger mounted, she forgot everything else. There was nothing else, only hunger. She thought of food, meat, but such thoughts made her nauseated. She wanted nourishment, not ordinary food but human flesh. Along with this hunger, she was enveloped by a chill akin to one brought on by fear and the onslaught of a sickness. As it settled in, the cold went deep into her soul and spirit, hard and brittle as flint. She had to get warm or else turn into ice and die. She bundled up and gathered wood with which she made a fire and then continued to cast firewood into the blaze until it was an inferno. She stood near the blaze, but it didn't do her any good, and her hunger grew sharper. Finally, she hurled herself into the flames.

Those present were horrified. They screamed; they tried to remove her body from the flames, but the heat drove them back and they were driven away from the crematorium by the sight and stench of death. There was no outcry from the girl as she was consumed by the fire, only a hiss and vapor of steam issuing from her body as it was transformed into carbon, black.

In the morning, when the sorcerer and his wives sifted through the cold ashes in search of the girl's remains so they could give her a proper funeral, they uncovered a figurine of a woman in ice and next to it a figurine of an infant, the unborn child that she had been carrying. In the end the girl had her revenge. . . .

The Modern Weendigoes

Once woods and forests mantled most of the North American continent. It was the home of the Anishinaubaek (Ojibway, Ottawa, Pottawatomi, and Algonquin), their kin, and their neighbors; it was also the home of all the animals of the land, water, and air. Furthermore, this land was the wellspring from which all drew their sustenance, medicine, and knowledge.

Also dwelling in the woods and forests were Weendigoes that stalked villages and camps, waiting for foolish humans to venture alone beyond the environs of their homes in winter. Even though a Weendigo is a mythical figure, it represents real human cupidity. However, as time went by, more and more learned people declared that such monsters were a product of superstitious minds and imaginations.

As a result, the Weendigoes were driven from their place in Anishinaubae traditions and culture and ostracized by disbelief and skepticism. It was assumed, and indeed it appeared, as if the Weendigoes had passed into the Great Beyond, like many North American Indian beliefs and practices and traditions.

Actually, the Weendigoes did not die out or disappear; they have only been assimilated and reincarnated as corporations, conglomerates, and multinationals. They've even taken on new names, acquired polished manners, and renounced their cravings for raw human flesh in return for more refined viands. But their cupidity is no less insatiable than that of their ancestors.

One breed subsists entirely on forests. When this particular breed beheld forests, its collective cupidity was bestirred as it looked on an endless, boundless sea of green These modern Weendigoes looked into the future and saw money accounts, interest from investments, profits, in short, wealth beyond belief. Never again would they be in need.

They recruited woodsmen with axes, cross-cut saws, chains, and ropes and sent them into the forests to fell the trees. The forests resounded with the clash of axes and the whine of saws as blades bit into the flesh of spruce, pine, and cedar to fulfill the demands of the Weendigoes in Toronto, Montreal, New York, Chicago, Boston, and wherever else they now dwelt. Cries of "Timber!" echoed and reechoed across the treetops, followed by the rip and tear of splintering trees. Then, finally, the crashes thundered throughout the bush. As fast as woodsmen felled the trees, teamsters delivered sleighload after sleighload to railway sidings and to riverbanks. Train after train, shipload after shipload of timber, logs, and pulp were delivered to mills. Yet, as fast as they cut and as much as they hewed, it was never enough; quantities always fell short of the demands of the Weendigoes.

"Is that all? Should there not be more? We demand a bigger return for our risks and our investments."

The demands for more speed and more pulp, more timber and more logs were met. Axes, saws, and woodsmen, sleighs, horses, and teamsters were replaced, and their calls no longer rang in the forest. Instead, chain saws whined, and Caterpillar tractors with jagged blades bulled and battered their way through the forest, uprooting trees to clear the way for automatic shearers that topped limbs and sheared the trunks. These mechanical Weendigoes gutted and desolated the forest, leaving death, destruction, and ugliness where once there was life, abundance, and beauty. Trucks and transports, faster and bigger than horses and sleds, operated day and night delivering quantities of cargoes that their predecessors, horses and sleighs, could never match.

Still, the Weendigoes wanted more. It didn't matter if their policies of clear-cutting to harvest timber and pulp resulted in violations of the rights of North American Indians or in the further impairment of their lives—just as it didn't matter to them that their modus operandi resulted in the permanent defilement of hillside and mountainside by erosion. They are indifferent to the carnage inflicted on bears, wolves, rabbits, and warblers. Who cares if they are displaced? What possible harm has been done? Nor does it seem as if these modern Weendigoes have any regard for the rights of future generations to the yield of Mother Earth.

Profit, wealth, and power are the ends of business. Anything that detracts from or diminishes the anticipated return, whether it is taking pains not to violate the rights of others or taking measures to ensure that the land remains fertile and productive for future generations, must, it seems, be circumvented.

And what has been the result of this self-serving, gluttonous disposition? In ten short decades these modern Weendigoes have accomplished what once seemed impossible. They have laid waste to immense tracts of forest that were seen as beyond limit as well as self-propagating, ample enough to serve this generation and many more to come. Now, as the forests are in decline, the Weendigoes are looking at a future that offers scarcity, while many people are assessing the damage done, not in terms of dollars, but in terms of the damage inflicted on the environment, the climate, and botanical and zoological life.

These new Weendigoes are no different from their forebears. In fact, they are even more omnivorous than their old ancestors. The only difference is that the modern Weendigoes wear elegant clothes and comport themselves with an air of cultured and dignified respectability. But still the Weendigoes bring disaster, fueled by the unquenchable greed inherent in human nature. Perhaps, as in the past, some champion, some manitou, will fell them....

1995

The Stone Giants

The Haudenosaunee equivalent of the Anishinâbeg Weendigoes is the Gĕnon'´sgwa' or Jokao, the Stone Coats or Stone Giants. These are male or female cannibal monsters from the far north who have a special finger than can locate people who are hiding. Some storytellers link them to Bad-Mind, or Flint; others see them as the offspring of winter, again linked to flint because the word for ice and for flint, used for projectile points and arrow heads, is derived from the same root, which means "glaring," or "ice-like."

Aurelia Jones Miller, Seneca

There were different things in the olden days, strange happenings, strange animals and birds, and strange people. It seems that they do not live any more, so men only half-believe the tales of them now.

The stone giants are a kind of men-being that are now gone. What we have heard about them I will tell.

There was once a far north country where a race of giants dwelt. They were very tall and bony. It was cold in that north country and the giants lived on fish and raw flesh. When the summer came to that region there was dry sand upon the ground and the giants, it is supposed, taught their children to rub it on their bodies every day until the blood came out where the skin was worn through. After a while the skin became hard and calloused, like a woman's hand when the harvest is over. Each year the

Stonish giants, 1827. David Cusick, Tuscarora

young rubbed their bodies with the sand, until, when they had grown to be men, it was hard like rawhide and the sand stuck in and made them look like men of stone. This is what some wise men thought, but others said stone giants were born that way.

As time went on these giants grew more ferocious and warlike. They became tired of the flesh of beasts and fish and yearned for the flesh of men. Then they sallied forth to the lands south of them and captured Indians and devoured their flesh, tearing it from their living bodies. All the nations and tribes of Indians feared them, for no arrow would pierce their hard stony coats. Thus, secure in their armors of callus and sand, no season was too cold for them, no journey too long, and no tribe strong enough to overwhelm them. They became more and more boastful and arrogant until they even laughed at the warnings of the Great Ruler, the Good-Minded, and hallooed up to the skies mocking words. "We are as great as the Great Ruler," they said. "We have created ourselves!"

When the Confederacy of the five brother nations was young, these terrible stone giants crossed the river of rapids and swept down upon the scattered settlements of the Five Nations. By day they hid in caves and at night they came forth in the darkness and captured men, women and children, rending their bodies apart and chewing up their flesh and bones. When they pointed their fingers at men, the men fell down dead.

The medicine men cried to the Good-Minded Spirit until it seemed that prayer was only like hollow talking in one's throat. The giants kept on with their raids and feasted undisturbed. No dark place was secure from their eyes; they penetrated the deepest shadows and found the hiding places of those who fled from them. Villages were destroyed and abandoned; councils were not held, for sachems and chieftains were the victims for the flesh-of-men feasts of the giants. The boldest warriors shot their strongest arrows from their strongest bows upon these invaders, but though the arrow shafts were strong and tipped with the toughest of flint, when they struck the stone-coated giants, the arrows broke and the flints snapped and the giants gathered up the warriors and shredded their meat from their bones with their sharp teeth.

At last the Good Ruler saw that men would become exterminated unless he intervened. Thus he commanded the Holder of the Heavens to descend from the sky and use his strategy to destroy the entire race of stone giants. Accordingly, the Holder of the Heavens dropped from the place above the clouds and, hiding in a deep forest, took the form of a stone giant and went among the band. Awed by his display of power, his wonderful feats, and his marvelous strength, they proclaimed the newcomer the great chief of all the stone giants. In honor of his installation, the Holder of the Heavens swung his huge war club high over his head and roared ferociously, "Now is the time to destroy these puny men and have a great feast such as never before!"

Leading forth the mighty tribe, he planned to attack the stronghold of the Onondagas. Arriving at the foot of the great hill on whose summit was the stockade where the Onondagas had assembled, he bade the giants hide in the caves in the hills or make burrows and there hide. They were to await the dawn when they would commence the assault. Having instructed them, the Holder of the Heavens went up the fort hill on a pretense and then gave the whole earth a mighty shake. So mighty was the shaking that the rocks broke from their beds and fell in masses over one another and the earth slid down making new hills and valleys. The caves all collapsed and the crouching stone giants were crushed to bits. You could see bones once in caves among the Onondagas. All but one was killed and he, with a terrible yell, rushed forth and fled with the speed of a being impelled by the Evil-Minded to the Allegheny Mountains where, finding a cave, he hid so long in the darkness that he became the Gĕnon´´sgwa.'

1905

The False Face Society

After the giant disappeared into the mountain and became a Gĕnon'´sgwa', a hunter lost in the woods near his cave dreamed of him. Gĕnon'´sgwa' directed the hunter to create masks from the basswood tree, and this was the beginning of the False Face Society. The False Faces, along with the Husk Faces, whose masks are made from corn husks and who represent agricultural spirits, and the Hadidos or Society of Animals, compose the three Haudenosaunee healing societies. During the Midwinter Rites, the False Faces leave the longhouse in the Traveling Rite to blow ashes on the sick to heal them. Different masks have different powers. Haduigona (The Great Humpbacked One), controls high winds and disease; Hanogagh (He is whistling) has a puckered mouth; Hayondiha masks have a smile. The Green Corn Dance renews the power of the masks. Edward Cornplanter, who dictated "The False Face Society" to the Seneca ethnologist Arthur C. Parker in the early twentieth century, was an expert on Haudenosaunee story and law, as well as being a preacher of the Handsome Lake doctrines.

Sosondowa (Great Night, Edward Cornplanter, 1851-1918), Seneca

The society, known as the False Face Company, was to be a most secret one and only for a qualified number. Its object was to benefit, protect, and help all living things of the earth. Its meetings were to be held only when the moon was away and when there was no light in the night. The hunter taught the chosen band a new dance and a new song and beat time with a large turtle shell as he sang. He explained the meanings of the masks and distributed them among the band, telling each person his special duty to the new society. He explained the relation of mankind to the rest of nature, and enjoined all to use every influence to protect all living nature. In return for this kindness, he promised that a great power should come upon them, the power of the spirits of the Gĕnon'´sgwa' and how they should become great medicine men, whose power should be over the spirits of the elements. He unfolded and conducted the band through all the elaborate ceremonies that had been taught him in the forest by the animals and trees and spirits of the Gĕnon'´sgwa'. The Company was to have no outward sign and members were to recognize one another only by having sat together in a ceremony.

False Face and Husk Face masks

So deeply was the assembled company impressed by the hunter's words that the new society at once became a strong and well united organization and other lodges spread rapidly through all the nations of the Iroquois, and the False Face Company became one of the greatest factors for good that the people had ever known. They drove all the witches away and cured all the sickness of the people.

The masks are carved from living basswood trees and are thereby supposed to contain a portion of the life or spirit of the tree. In making these masks the Iroquois select the basswood not alone for its absorbent quality which is supposed to draw out disease, but for remedial values as well. In solution a tea of its bark will cure a cold and relieve spasmodic afflictions. Its astringent sap is applied to relieve wounds and bruises, while the mask itself is supposed to be of signal importance in the relief of corruptive diseases.

In the ceremonies attending the making of a living mask, the tree is visited for three days. At the dawn of the first day the leaders of the False Face Society gather around the tree and smoke the sacred tobacco into the roots and throughout the branches to their topmost. As the smoke "lifts to the sunrise," songs of incantation are sung and the tree is asked to consent to share its heart with whomsoever the sacred gift is to be sent. At sunrise the ceremony is repeated and the next day continued in the same manner until the three days' propitiation chant is completed, and then the axe is lifted to the tree. If at the first stroke of the axe the tree remains firm and unbending, it has consented to lend its heart. An outline of the face is then drawn on the bark and cut into the tree to a depth of about six inches.

After thanking the tree, this block is gouged out to be carved into the desired shape during a final song and dance that concluded the ceremony.

1923

The Sick Child

Famous for her artwork in *The Indians' Book* (1907), Angel DeCora was born in 1871, the daughter of the fourth son of the hereditary chief of the Ho-Chunk and a Métis mother. She was tricked into going to the Hampton Institute boarding school by hearing it described as an exciting trip on the train, although her parents may have consented. When she returned home three years later, many of her family were dead, her mother had remarried, and the life DeCora had known was shattered. She returned to the East, graduating from Smith College and studying at the Drexel Institute and the Boston Museum School. She then earned her living as a commercial artist and as a teacher at the Carlisle Indian School in Pennsylvania. She died during the influenza epidemic in 1918. In "The Sick Child," she recalls her fear as a young child who is sent on a difficult task in winter. Her original illustrations are included.

Hinook Mahiwi Kilinaka

Hinook Mahiwi Kilinaka (Woman Cloud Floating, Angel DeCora), Ho-Chunk

It was about sunset when I, a little child, was sent with a handful of powdered tobacco leaves and red feathers to make an offering to the spirit who had caused the sickness of my little sister. It had been a long, hard winter, and the snow lay deep on the prairie as far as the eye could reach. The medicine-woman's directions had been that the offering must be laid upon the naked earth and that to find it I must face toward the setting sun.

Girl facing hills

I was taught the prayer: "Spirit grandfather, I offer this to thee. I pray thee restore my little sister to health." Full of reverence and a strong faith that I could appease the anger of the spirit, I started out to plead for the life of our little one.

But now where was a spot of earth to be found in all that white monotony? They had talked of death at the house. I hoped that my little sister would live, but I was afraid of nature.

I reached a little spring. I looked down to its pebbly bottom, wondering whether I should leave my offering there or keep on in search of a spot of earth. If I put my offering in the water, would it reach the bottom and touch the earth, or would it float away, as it had always done when I made my offering to the water spirit?

Once more I started on in my search of the bare ground.

The surface was crusted in some places, and walking was easy; in other places I would wade through a foot or more of snow. Often I paused, thinking to clear the snow away in some place and there lay my offering. But no, my faith must be in nature, and I must trust to it to lay bare the earth.

It was a hard struggle for so small a child.

I went on and on; the reeds were waving their tasseled ends in the wind. I stopped and looked at them. A reed, whirling in the wind, had formed a space round its stem, making a loose socket. I stood looking into the opening. The reed must be rooted in the ground, and the hole must follow the stem to the earth. If I poured my offerings into the hole, surely they must reach the ground; so I said the prayer I had been taught and dropped my tobacco and red feathers into the opening that nature itself had created.

No sooner was the sacrifice accomplished than a feeling of doubt and fear thrilled me. What if my offering should never reach the earth? Would my little sister die?

Not till I turned homeward did I realize how cold I was. When at last I reached the house they took me in and warmed me but did not question me, and I said nothing. Everyone was sad, for the little one had grown worse.

The next day the medicine-woman said my little sister was beyond hope; she could not live. Then bitter remorse was mine, for I thought I had been unfaithful, and therefore my little sister was to be called to the spirit-land. I was a silent child and did not utter my feelings; my remorse was intense.

My parents would not listen to what the medicine-woman had said but clung to hope. As soon as she had gone, they sent for a medicine-man who lived many miles away.

He arrived about dark. He was a large man, with a sad, gentle face. His presence had always filled me with awe, and that night it was especially so, for he was coming as a holy man. He entered the room where

133

the baby lay and took a seat, hardly noticing anyone. There was silence save only for the tinkling of the little tin ornaments on his medicine-bag. He began to speak: "A soul has departed from this house, gone to the spirit-land. As I came I saw luminous vapor above the house. It ascended, it grew less, it was gone on its way to the spirit-land. It was the spirit of the little child who is sick; she still breathes, but her spirit is beyond our reach. If medicine will ease her pain, I will do what I can."

He stood up and blessed the four corners of the earth with song. Then, according to the usual custom of medicine-doctors, he began reciting the vision that had given him the right to be a medicine-man. The ruling force of the vision had been in the form of a bear. To it he addressed his prayer, saying: "Inasmuch as thou hast given me power to cure the sick, and in one case allowing me to unite spirit and body again,

Family with sick baby

if thou seest fit, allow me to recall the spirit of this child to its body once more." He asked that the coverings be taken off the baby and that it be brought into the middle of the room. Then, as he sang, he danced slowly around the little form.

When the song was finished, he blessed the child and then prepared the medicine, stirring into water some ground herbs. This he took into his mouth and sprinkled it over the little body. Another mixture he gave her to drink.

Almost instantly there was a change; the little one began to breathe more easily, and as the night wore on she seemed to suffer less. Finally she opened her eyes, looked into mother's face, and smiled. The medicine-man, seeing it, said that the end was near, and though he gave her more medicine, the spirit, he said, would never return.

After saying words of comfort, he took his departure, refusing to take a pony and some blankets that were offered him, saying that he had been unable to hold the spirit back and had no right to accept the gifts.

The next morning I found the room all cleared away, and my mother sat sewing on a little white gown. The bright red trimming caught my eye. I came to her and asked, "Please mother, tell me for whom is that, and why do you make it so pretty?" She made no answer but bent over her work. I leaned forward that I might look into her face and repeat my question. I bent down and, oh! the tears were falling fast down her cheeks. Then we were told that our little sister was gone to the spirit-land, and we must not talk about her. They made us look upon her. We felt of her and kissed her, but she made no response. Then I realized what death meant. Remorse again seized me, but I was silent.

1899

The Coming of Spring

Aurelia Jones Miller, Seneca

This allegory of the end of winter is told by all the nations of the Great Lakes region; the details, however, vary according to location and language. The Haudenosaunee describe winter as Hotho or Ha'´t'howā´ne' (He who is clad in ice) or Tawiskaron (flint, because the words for ice and flint come from a common stem that means "ice-like" or "glaring"). Winter's cold is then turned into walls of ice by Old Man Winter, while the North Wind uses weapons "like flints" to torture people.

In the ancient times when this world was new, an old man wandered over the land in search of a suitable camping spot. He was a fierce old man and had long white flowing hair. The ground grew hard like flint where his footsteps fell, and when he breathed the leaves and grasses dropped and dried up red and fell. When he splashed through the rivers the water stopped running and stood solid.

On and on the old man journeyed until at last on the shores of a great lake by a high mountain he halted. He gathered the trees that had been uprooted by hurricanes and made a framework for a dwelling. He built the walls of ice and plastered the crevices with branches and snow. Then, to guard his lodge against the intruder, he placed up-rooted stumps about on every side. Not even bad animals cared to enter this house. Everything living passed by it at a distance. It was like a magician's house.

The old man had but one friend. It was North Wind, and it was he alone who might enter the door of the stronghold and sit by the fire. Very wonderful was this fire and it gave flames and light but no heat! But even North Wind found little time to enter and smoke with the old man, for he took greater pleasure in piling high the snow and driving hail, like flints, against the shivering deer or hungry, storm-bound hunter. He liked to kill them. There came times, however, when North Wind needed new tricks and so he sought the advice of the old man—how he might pile up the snow banks higher, how he might cause famine or make great snow-slides to bury Indian villages.

One very dismal night both North Wind and the old man sat smoking, half-awake and half-dreaming. North Wind could think of nothing new and the old man could give no more advice. So, sitting before the fire, both fell asleep. Towards morning each sprang to his feet with a cry. Not their usual cries, either, were their startled yells, for instead of a shrill *"Agēē! Agēē! Agēē!"* the North Wind only gasped hoarsely and the old man's jaw opened with a smack and his tongue, thick and swollen rolled out on his chin.

Then spoke the North Wind: "What warm thing has bewitched me? The drifts are sinking, the rivers breaking, the ice is steaming, the snow is smoking!"

The old man was silent, too sleepy to speak. He only thought, "My house is strong, very strong."

Still the North Wind called loudly: "See, the rivers are swelling full, the drifts are getting smaller." Then he rushed from the lodge, and he flew to the mountain top where snow made him brave again. So he was happy and sang a war song as he danced on snow crust.

At the lodge of the old man a stranger struck the door-post. The old man did not move but, dozing, thought, "Oh some prank of North Wind." The knocking continued and the old man grew more sleepy. The door rattled on its fastenings, but the old man's head did not rise to listen but dropped on his chest and his pipe fell down to his feet.

The logs of the lodge frame shook—one fell from the roof. The old man jumped to his feet with a war yell. "Who is it that dares come to my house in this way? Only my friend North Wind enters here. Go away; no loafers here!"

In answer the door fell down and a stranger stood in the opening. He entered and hung the door upright again. His face was smiling and, as he stirred the fire, it grew warmer inside. The old man looked at the stranger but did not answer his pleasant words; his heart was very angry. Finally when he could no longer keep silent, he burst forth: "You are a stranger to me and have entered my lodge, breaking down my door. Why have you broken down my door? Why have your eyes a fire? Why does light shine from your skin? Why do you go about without skins when the wind is sharp? Why do you stir up my fire when you are young and need no warmth? Why do you not fall on my wolf skins and sleep? Did not North Wind blow the sun far away? Go away now before he returns and blows you against the mountains. I do not know you. You do not belong in my lodge!"

The young stranger laughed and said, "Oh why not let me stay a little longer and smoke my pipe?"

"Then listen to me," yelled the old man in anger. "I am mighty! All snows and ice and frosts are my making. I tell the North Wind to cut the skins of men to let the blood through to make war paint on the drifts. I tell him to freeze things that are food. Birds and animals run away from the North Wind. I pile the drifts on the rocks on the mountains and when it gets very high the North Wind knocks it off to crush the villages beneath."

Listlessly the stranger viewed the raving old man and only smiled and said, "I like to be sociable. Let me stay a little longer and we will smoke together."

So, shaking with fear, the old man took the pipe and drew a breath of smoke and then the warrior sang, "Continue to smoke for me, I am young and warm, I am not afraid of boasting, I am young and strong. Better wrap up, you are old. I am here. I am here, keep on smoking. I am Dedio's'nwineq'don, the Spring. Look at your hair. It is falling out. Look at the drifts, they are melting. My hair is long and glossy, see—the grasses are sprouting! I want to smoke with you. I like smoking. See—the ground is smoking! My friend Dăgă'ĕn'dă, the South Wind, is coming. I guess your friend is dead. You better wrap up and go away. There is a place. You cannot own all things always. See—the sun is shining. Look out now!"

As the young warrior sang the old man shrank very small and shriveled up smaller until his voice only whispered, "I don't know you!"

And so the young warrior sang, "I am the Spring, I am the chief now. The South Wind is coming. Don't be late. You can go yet while I sing."

A rushing wind made the lodge tremble, the door fell in and an eagle swooped down and carried Ha''t'howā'ne' away toward the North.

The lodge fire was out and where it had burned, a plant was growing, and where the provisions were buried in a hole, a tree was starting to have buds. The sun was shining and it was warm. The swollen rivers carried away the ice. So the winter went away and in the morning it was spring time.

1905

SPRING

Spring/Summer Moons

April, May, June[128]

Miami

aanteekwa kiilhswa	crow moon	Crows are numerous.
čéčaahkwa kiilhswa	crane moon	Cranes are seen flying over.
oohkoowia kiilhswa	whippoorwill moon	Whippoorwills are heard.

Shawnee

pooshkwi-kiishthwa	halfway moon	Halfway to summer.
hotehimini-kiishthwa	strawberry moon	Wild strawberries are ripe.
mshkati-kiishthwa	raspberry moon	Wild raspberries are ripe.

Mohawk (old | modern)

*ganusgwouhtagowah	onerahtókha'*	more frogs singing	leaves time? Spring begins.
*ganagaht	onerahtokkó:wa'*	hills/indentations	great leaves time? Planting begins.
*oyaghneh	ohyaríha'*	berry moon	Wild strawberries are ripe.

Ho-Chunk in Wisconsin

horóhiginįnįwíi	fish moon	Fish are active; easily caught.
mą́įtawúšiwíi	earth-drying moon	Ground is too wet for planting.
mą́įra'ų́wii	digging moon	Planting begins.

Meskwaki

PāpaʿkwáʾA	Ice breaks moon	Time when ice breaks loose.
ĀpāmineʿkäʾA	fish(?) time	Fish are active; easily caught.
AʿkiʿkäwikīceswA	planting moon	Planting begins.

Ojibwe/Odawa

sisibâkwat-gisiss	maple sugar moon	Maple sap runs now.
wâbigoni-gisiss	flower moon	Flowers bloom.
ode'imin-gisiss	heart berry moon	Wild strawberries are ripe.

Potawatomi

Pikòn kises	bark moon	Birchbark is easily stripped.
Otéwomin kises	strawberry moon	Wild strawberries are ripe.
Miskő́minè kises	raspberry moon	Raspberries are ripe.

Menominee

sopomakwin keso'	sugar-making moon	Maple sap runs now.
pakuen keso'	loose bark moon	Birchbark is easily stripped.
otahamin keso'	heart berry moon	Wild strawberries are ripe.

❖ SPRING ❖

Song for Securing a Good Supply of Maple Sugar

Widjigawiwinaha	(Untranslatable/obsolete)
Hindiyane	(Untranslatable/obsolete)
Mitigon	From the trees
Giongigog	The sap is freely flowing

Kítcimákwa, Ojibwe, 1920s

Although spring technically begins with the vernal equinox in March, when the sun rises and sets exactly east and west and day and night are of equal length, in the Great Lakes spring really starts when the maple sap begins to run. For people without other sweets, maple sap and sugar (*sisibâkwat*) were a gift from the Great Spirit. Traders' copper kettles may have made the rendering of syrup easier, but the tradition of collecting and reducing tree sap, both maple and birch, predates Contact. The love of maple syrup continues undiminished, and this section begins with song and story about maple sugaring. For Mountain Wolf Woman and others who lived traditionally, the year revolved through food gathering, preparation, and storage. In her description of gathering lily roots and berries, two things stand out: there were no grocery stores or electricity, and food gathering was communal recreation as well as work, a great difference from a woman shopping alone in a sterile grocery store to buy strawberries in January. Traditional stories about food signaled the beginning of the gathering seasons—spring, summer, and fall—and reaffirmed everyone's place in a balanced world.

Narratives of other spring gathering activities follow, including one about that cherished Great Lakes delicacy, the whitefish, a bountiful species that once swarmed the rivers and lakes so thickly it could be scooped up with dip nets. Such a treasure could not escape being the subject of a sacred story, and this one also describes the founding of a clan. Indigenous nations are usually divided into clans (dodems/totems. Ojibwe *ototeman, od-ode-m-an*: his brother-sister kin). This identifies group members to outsiders and to other members of the same dodem who might live far away. Certain dodems, represented by their clan origin story animal symbols, might have specific responsibilities to the band, such as policing campsites (bear) or, as in the whitefish story, leadership from a crane who solves a problem. Dodems regulated marriage—persons could not marry others from the same dodem—and integrated neighboring bands into larger groups. Over the course of the eighteenth century many bands of Ojibwe (or Chippewa) combined to form one large nation of many clans, which the governments of the USA and Canada referred to as a "tribe" for the purposes of treaty negotiation but which leaders did not always recognize as a legal entity.

Even more sacred than fish, tobacco is another gift of the Great Spirit for the people. Ely S. Parker (1828-1895), a Seneca who was a brigadier general and aide to Ulysses Simpson Grant during the US Civil War and after, noted that during the Seneca Maple Thanksgiving, "Every spring, at the foot of the largest maple tree in each village, a ceremonial fire was built and a prayer chanted by the Keeper of the Maple Thanksgiving ceremony, as he threw upon the embers pinches of the sacred incense tobacco. The maple tree started the year. Its returning and rising sap, to the Indian, was the sign of the Creator's renewed covenant."[129] Stories of tobacco—a sacred pathway to the spirits that was first given as seeds to be planted when the soil warmed—are included here, though the soft, sacred smoke beloved by the spirits rises through stories in all seasons.

Another ceremony held in spring is the Midéwewin, or Grand Medicine Society, a rite created by the Ojibwe that was adapted by other Great Lakes nations and may be the most enduring religious belief of the lakes. French priests and traders described similar shamanistic healing rituals when they first met Natives in the 1600s, and there is no reason to believe those ceremonies, which apparently became known as the Midé, were new in the seventeenth century. As indigenous cultures experienced increasing physical and philosophical pressures, the Midé became part of a revitalization movement that included Christian elements, and the rituals increased in sophistication, eventually becoming complex works of art.

Historically Midé celebrations were usually held twice a year, in spring and fall, though the ritual can be held at any time to give thanks or to ask for healing. There was no age or gender requirement for admission; young children who need the rite could be admitted by parents with the understanding that they would learn the required lore at a later time. In the past, dancing, singing, drumming, and feasting ceremonies took place over four days in a specially built lodge, sometimes over a hundred feet long, usually oriented east and west and surrounded by animal deities. Inside were the sacred Midé trees and rocks. Initially there were four stages of instruction and initiation, called degrees: *ocgemidéwid* (*oshkimidéwid*: first, young), [*n*]*i*[*zh*]*omidéwid* (second), [*n*]*issomidéwid* (third), [*n*]*iomidéwid* (fourth). The point of all is to increase health and length of life so that the initiate might achieve everlasting life through reincarnation. A person who attains the fourth degree is considered to have mastered the entire doctrine of the Midé, known as *atisokan* (*aadizookaan*), and can then become a Midé leader in turn.

Individuals who are being initiated into one of the degrees fast, purify themselves in a sweat lodge, and are accompanied into the Midé lodge during a complicated ritual that involves being "shot" with small, white *megis* (*miigis*: wampum) shells by the Midé priests. The candidate falls unconscious, mimicking death; when revived, the shell is spit out, and health is restored. Each degree is accompanied by particular facial markings and decorated paraphernalia including rattles, animal skins, and personal songs inscribed on birchbark. All those who wish to join the Grand Medicine Society to receive the gift of health and eternal life are required to master at least the rudiments of traditional Midé lore. From the first degree through the fourth degree and sometimes beyond, all candidates for all degrees learn ritual procedures, herbal medical training, and the traditions of the Midé origin story.

In the past, individuals who could afford the time to master the material and to pay the fees, which doubled with each stage, went on to a fifth stage, *nonomidéwid*, and to *kabemidéwid* (whole), the sixth [whole] stage. But the higher degrees, especially five and six, were frequently associated with evil shamanism and lucrative sorcery for private clients. By the first half of the twentieth century these practices had so perverted the Midé that practitioners became feared and the rite lapsed. It was revived several decades later, with free instruction and an emphasis on humility, and continues to be practiced today. At present, the Midéwewin encourages holistic, traditional approaches to healing physical and psychological illnesses by developing the attributes of generosity, love, respect, honor, humility, obedience, and hope. The goal of practitioners is to find the center of the self in harmony with the powers of the universe and to develop a way of life that embodies respect for all living things. One contemporary form of the medicine lodge practiced in the Great Lakes region is known as the Three Fires Society, which offers ceremonies with English interpretation. Traditional Midé ceremonies are conducted in the traditional language.

Maple sugaring and Midé ceremonies were not just for sweets and salvation, however. They were also a way for families to arrange marriages between their children who otherwise would spend long months confined to the band or family group or who were separated by mission or government schools. Love belongs to spring as do the flowers, and for Great Lakes peoples before recorded music, warm weather and the sound of the courting flute were linked. Many love songs were sad or filled with longing, though they were often played in a major key on what the Ojibwe called a *bibi´gwûn* (*bibigwan*), a flageolet. Love and marriage, particularly respect and proper behavior between men and women, are the focus of stories as well as music. Beginning with "The Tempest," a cautionary tale about a mother's arrogance, the narratives reflect the tangled problems of love and culture over time, including relations between humans and animals.

Once one is past the enchanting world of seasonal rituals and traditional tales, the reality that cultural disruptions, old and new, always fall the hardest on children becomes inescapable. Because the Great Lakes region was a diaspora of war-torn peoples for centuries, forsaken children frequent the literatures. In addition, because Native cultures usually cherished children above all else, describing evil and derelict parents created great shock value and sympathy. The stories here begin with one of the earliest recorded: the Shawnee Prophet's story about an abandoned child, where one point is to remind white allies that what began as a rhetorical conceit of fathers and children between equals eventually became all too real, with the children abandoned. In this Tenskwatawa was prescient, since the abandonment of Natives to starve on reservations eventually led to their abandonment in urban areas, with the sundering of family ties sometimes the result. From this continuing diaspora, however, nations that otherwise might have been isolated on reservations came together to form pan-Indian movements such as the National Congress of American Indians (NCAI), the Native American Rights Fund (NARF) and, most dramatically, the American Indian Movement (AIM). These were attempts to unite nations on a national scale the same way Pontiac and Tecumseh had once tried to organize on a regional one. Although the narratives reprinted here are but a small sample of the many stories of abandoned children in the literature, it is important to notice that these children almost always survive victoriously. Sometimes they reject humans altogether to become animals, a highly negative comment on human culture. More commonly, they triumph over the elders who sought to harm them. Forsaken children who grow into skill and eventually mastery testify to a culture's strength and endurance.

⋅❖⋅ SPRING HARVESTS ⋅❖⋅

MAPLE SUGAR AND PLANTS

The Origin of Maple Sap

Chief Shunien Josette (Silver Money, 1827-†), Menominee
Chief Niopet Oshkosh (Four in a Den, 1829-†), Menominee

When Manabush returned empty-handed from his hunting trip, he and his grandmother, Nokomis (*nookomis*: my grandmother), gathered together all their effects, moved away from the place where they had dwelt, and built a new wigwam among the trees in a new locality.

These trees were maples, and the grandmother of Manabush said to him, "Now my grandson, you go into the woods and gather for me some pieces of birchbark; I am going to make sugar." So Manabush went into the woods and gathered some strips of birchbark, which he took back to the wigwam, where his grandmother had cut some pieces of bark to make thread for sewing together pieces of birchbark to make vessels to contain the sugar.

The grandmother of Manabush then went from tree to tree, cutting a small hole into the bark of each and inserting into each cut a small piece of wood over which the sap ran into the vessels placed beneath. Manabush followed his grandmother from tree to tree, watching her and looking for the sap to drop into the vessels, but none was to be seen. When she had gone around among the trees and cut holes for as many vessels as she had made, Manabush went back and looking into the vessels saw that all of them had suddenly become half-full of thick sirup.

Manabush dipped his finger into the sirup and tasted it. Finding it sweet, he said, "My grandmother, this is all very good, but it will not do to have these trees produce sirup in this manner. The people will not have any work if they make sugar so easily; they must cut wood to boil the sirup for several nights, to keep them occupied that they may not get into bad habits. I will change all this."

So Manabush climbed to the very top of one of the trees, when he took his hand and scattered water (urine) all over the maples, like rain, so that the sugar should dissolve and flow from the trees in the form of sap. This is why the uncles of Manabush and their descendants always have to work hard when they want to make sugar. Wood must be cut, vessels must he made, and the sap that is collected must be boiled for a long time; otherwise the people would spend too much time in idleness.

1890s

▲▲
▼▼

Indian Sugar Camp (1853). Seth Eastman

Making Maple Sugar

Frances Densmore

Many Great Lakes nations considered maple sugar one of their most important foods. It was used to season vegetables, fruits, fish, and cereals such as wild rice, a type of grass. It could be dissolved in water to make a summer drink or syrup with herbal medicine for children. Granulated sugar cakes in the shapes of animals, people, moons, and stars were commonly used as gifts. Strings of small birchbark cones of sugar, like clusters of grapes, were a children's delicacy.

The yearly round began in the "sugar bush," or maple grove, about mid-March. It was a happy time when groups of two or three families, who may have shared a sugar camp for many seasons, would return to the woods, bringing their kettles, supplies, rolls of birchbark, and any small children or invalids on sleds pulled by dogs. Two structures were generally left in the sugar camp from year to year: a large frame of poles that when recovered with bark or matting would be the lodge, and a smaller bark-covered structure that housed the bark and wood utensils for making sugar.

Sap was collected by using a hand axe to make a three-inch diagonal cut in a tree about three feet above the ground. Below the lower end of this cut, the bark was removed in a four-inch line perpendicular to the ground; then a wooden spile, usually made of slippery elm, was inserted into a cut in the tree. Birchbark dishes were placed on the snow below the taps to collect the sap that ran during the day when the weather warmed. The size of the sugar bush was measured in these "taps," since each tree could have several. Nine hundred was average.

The collected sap was hauled back to camp in bark containers, pails, or barrels, and then poured into kettles and boiled over an open fire in the lodge or outside until enough evaporation had taken place. Thickened syrup was filtered using a basswood mat or clean cloth and then held until "sugaring off," a day when the weather was bad or sap collecting had stopped. At this time, the kettles were cleaned and scoured with stiff rushes, the thickened sap was poured back into them with a small piece of deer tallow to keep the sugar soft, and a maple-wood paddle was used to stir the boiling syrup until it had thickened enough to be "grained." This syrup was poured into wooden trays and worked rapidly with a granulating ladle until it formed sugar crystals. The finished sugar was stored in birchbark containers called *makuk*s, some of which could hold a hundred pounds or more. The finest sugar, usually from the first run of sap, was pressed into molds or wrapped as cakes in birchbark tied with basswood strings. Gum sugar, which everyone loved, was made by taking syrup from the kettle just before it was ready to grain and pouring it on the snow until it thickened and then wrapping it in bark.

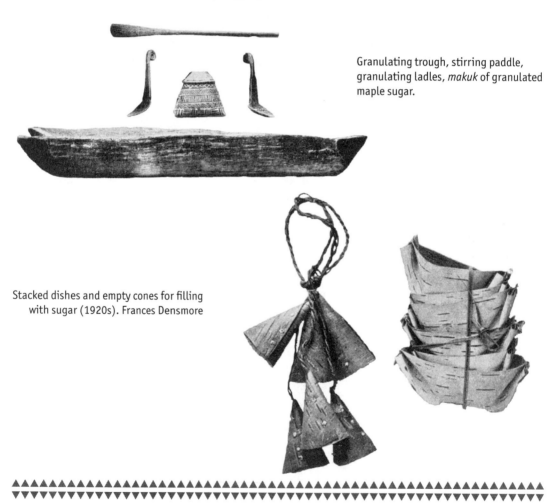

Granulating trough, stirring paddle, granulating ladles, *makuk* of granulated maple sugar.

Stacked dishes and empty cones for filling with sugar (1920s). Frances Densmore

Livelihood: Spring (from *Mountain Wolf Woman*)

Kéhachiwinga (Mountain Wolf Woman), Ho-Chunk

Kéhachiwinga

orn in 1884 into the Thunder Clan at the East Fork River, Wisconsin, Kéhachiwinga (Wolf's Mountain Home Maker) dictated her auto-biography in the 1950s. Kéhachiwinga is a compelling narrator, much like her brothers Sam and Jasper Blowsnake whose narratives are also included in this collection. She was Christian during her youth but eventually joined the Native American Church, staying with the peyote group for the rest of her life. Here she describes the spring activities of the traditional yearly round of Great Lakes Natives at the turn of the twentieth century.

In March we usually traveled to the Mississippi River close to La Crosse, sometimes even across the river, and then we returned again in the last part of May. We used to live at a place on the edge of the Mississippi called Caved In Breast's Grave. My father, brother-in-law, and brothers used to trap there for muskrats. When they killed the muskrats, my mother used to save the bodies and hang them up there in great numbers. When there were a lot of muskrats, then they used to roast them on a rack. They prepared a lot of wood and built a big fire. They stuck four crotched posts into the ground around the fire and placed poles across the crotches. Then they removed the burning wood and left the embers. They put a lot of fine wood crisscross and very dense on the frame. On this the muskrats were roasted, placed all above the fireplace. As the muskrats began roasting, the grease dripped off nice and brown, and then the women used long pointed sticks to turn them over and over. The muskrat meat made a lot of noise as it cooked. When these were cooked, the women put them aside and placed some more on the rack. They cooked a great amount of muskrats. When they were cooled, the women packed them together and stored them for summer.

In the spring when my father went trapping on the Mississippi and the weather became very pleasant, my sister once said, "It is here that they dig yellow water lily roots."[130] So, we all went out, my mother and sisters and everybody. When we got to a slough where the water lilies were very dense, they took off their shoes, put on old dresses, and went wading into the water. They used their feet to hunt for the roots. They dug them out with their feet, and then the roots floated up to the surface. Eventually, my second oldest sister happened upon one. My sister took one of the floating roots, wrapped it about with the edge of her blouse and tucked it into her belt. I thought she did this because it was the usual thing to do. I saw her doing this, and when I happened upon a root, I took it and did the same thing. I put it in my belt too. And then everybody laughed at me! "Oh, Little Siga is doing something! She has a water lily root in her belt!" Everybody laughed at me and yelled at me. My sister had done that because she was pregnant. I suppose she did that to ward off something because she was pregnant. Thus she would not affect the baby and would have good luck finding the roots. Because I saw her do that, I did the same thing, and so they teased me.

When they dug up a lot of roots in this fashion, they put them in a gunny sack, filling it half-full and even more. Then we carried them back to camp, and my mother and all my sisters scraped them. The roots have an outside covering, and they scraped that off and sliced them. They look something like a banana. The women then strung the slices and hung them up to dry in order to store them. They dried a great amount, flour sacks full. During the summer they sometimes cooked them with meat, and they were really delicious.

Upon returning home, mother and father planted a garden in front of the log house where we usually lived. Nearby stood the well that my father had made. When people leaned over the edge to peer in, they could just barely see the water shimmering at the bottom. There were four posts going all the way down to the bottom, and these were nailed about with boards which lined the length of the shaft and extended above the ground around the well. A shelf was built around the top of the well, and over this was a little house which contained a pulley wheel. To this a bucket was attached by a long rope. It was a long cylindrical bucket with a hole and stopper on the bottom. This they sent down to the water. When the filled bucket was pulled up, it was rested on the shelf that went around the well, and this released the stopper so the water ran out. The water was icy cold. The Indians used to come there for water. It was very good water that we had.

At the time we were there when mother and father planted a garden, the blueberries ripened, and we picked blueberries. There were pine trees all around where we lived, the kind of pine trees that are very tall and look as if they had been trimmed all up the trunk almost to the top. That is the way it used to be around our home. The pine trees were very dense, and there was no underbrush. Under the trees the blueberries grew in profusion. All the Indians picked blueberries. They came carrying boxes on their backs, and when they filled the boxes, they left. At that time they used to come to our house for water, and when they brought the water up, the turning wheel would say, "gink, gink, gink, gink."

All the berry pickers carried boxes on their backs. The boxes were square and were divided into four square compartments. There were two holes on opposite sides of the box, and cords were strung across these holes. They called these boxes *wankšíkwak'in*, that is, carry on a person's back. They used to carry them by horseback too, a pair slung in front and in back of the person riding the horse. This is the way they went to town to sell the berries. There they bought food for themselves, bringing the berry boxes back full of groceries. This is the way that they earned money.

They were paid a good price; fifty cents a quart is the price they used to get toward the beginning of the season, and as the season wore on, toward the end, they got a quarter. They saved their money, and they even bought horses. Some of the Indians had no wagons, and that is why they let the horses carry the berries, but some of them had wagons. Thus the Indians came through history. That is the way they procured food for themselves. They saved food and they saved money.

1958

FISH

Addik Kum Maig, or the Origin of the Whitefish

Chief Nabinoi, Ojibwe

Demonic skulls appear in folktales the world over, but thanks to a wise bird, this one's mischief leads to enormous benefit. From it comes whitefish, the particular delicacy of the Great Lakes, and the founding of the Crane clan. This makes the story sacred. Schoolcraft translates Addik Kum Maig (*adik-ameg*) as reindeer, or deer, of the waters, and graceful and once plentiful, whitefish are that. George Johnston, Jane Johnston Schoolcraft's brother, collected this story from someone he described as "aged" in the 1830s.

A long time ago there lived a famous hunter[131] in a remote part of the north. He had a handsome wife and two sons, who were left in the lodge every day while he went out in quest of the animals upon whose flesh they subsisted. Game was very abundant in those days, and his exertions in the chase were well rewarded. The skins of animals furnished them with clothing and their flesh with food. They lived a long

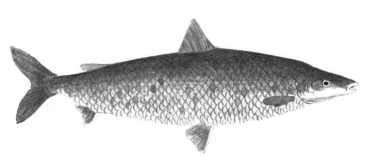

Whitefish (1826). Thomas McKenney

distance from any other lodge, and very seldom saw anyone. The two sons were still too young to follow their father to the chase and usually diverted themselves within a short distance of the lodge. They noticed that a young man visited the lodge during their father's absence, and these visits were frequently repeated. At length the elder of the two said to his mother, "My mother, who is this tall young man that comes here so often during our father's absence? Does he wish to see him? Shall I tell him when he comes back this evening?"

"Bad boy," said the mother, pettishly, "mind your bow and arrows, and do not be afraid to enter the forest in search of birds and squirrels with your little brother. It is not manly to be ever about the lodge. Nor will you become a warrior if you tell all the little things you see and hear to your father. Say not a word to him on the subject."

The boys obeyed, but as they grew older and still saw the visits of this mysterious stranger, they resolved to speak again to their mother and told her that they meant to inform their father of all they had observed, for they frequently saw this young man passing through the woods, and he did not walk in the path nor did he carry anything to eat. If he had any message to deliver, they had observed that messages were always addressed to the men and not to the women.

At this, the mother flew into a rage. "I will kill you," said she, "if you speak of it."

They were again intimidated to hold their peace. But observing the continuance of an improper intercourse, kept up by stealth as it were, they resolved at last to disclose the whole matter to their father. They did so. The result was such as might have been anticipated. The father, being satisfied of the infidelity of his wife, watched a suitable occasion when she was separated from the children that they might not have their feelings excited and, with a single blow of his war club, dispatched her. He then buried her under the ashes of his fire, took down the lodge, and removed, with his two sons, to a distant position.

But the spirit of the woman haunted the children, who were now grown up to the estate of young men. She appeared to them as they returned from hunting in the evening. They were also terrified in their dreams, which they attributed to her. She harassed their imaginations wherever they went. Life became a scene of perpetual terrors. They resolved, together with their father, to leave the country and commenced a journey toward the south.

After traveling many days along the shores of Lake Superior, they passed around a high promontory

Sandhill crane

of rock where a large river issued out of the lake and soon after came to a place called Pauwateeg.[132] They had no sooner come in sight of these falls, than they beheld the skull of the woman rolling along the beach. They were in the utmost fear and knew not how to elude her. At this moment one of them looked out and saw a stately crane sitting on a rock in the middle of the rapids.[133] They called out to the bird. "See, grandfather, we are persecuted by a spirit. Come and take us across the falls, so that we may escape her."

This crane was a bird of extraordinary size and great age. When first descried by the two sons, he sat in a state of stupor in the midst of the most violent eddies. When he heard himself addressed, he stretched forth his neck with great deliberation and, lifting himself by his wings, flew across to their assistance. "Be careful," said the crane, "that you do not touch the back part of my head. It is sore, and should you press against it, I shall not be able to avoid throwing you both into the rapids." They were, however, attentive on this point, and were safely landed on the south shore of the river. The crane then resumed his former position in the rapids.

But the skull now cried out. "Come, my grandfather, and carry me over, for I have lost my children and am sorely distressed."

The aged bird flew to her assistance. He carefully repeated the injunction that she must by no means touch the back part of his head, which had been hurt, and was not yet healed. She promised to obey but soon felt a curiosity to know where the head of her carrier had been hurt and how so aged a bird could have received so bad a wound. She thought it strange and, before they were halfway over the rapids, could not resist the inclination she felt to touch the affected part. Instantly the crane threw her into the rapids.

"There," said he, "you have been of no use during your life. You shall now be changed into something for the benefit of your people, and it shall be called Addik Kum Maig."

As the skull floated from rock to rock, the brains were strewed in the water in a form resembling roes, which soon assumed the shape of a new species of fish, possessing a whiteness of color and peculiar flavor, which have caused it, ever since, to be in great repute with the Indians. The family of this man, in gratitude for their deliverance, adopted the crane as their totem, or mark; and this continues to be the distinguishing tribal sign of the band to this day.[134]

1839

From *Walking the Rez Road*
Jim Northrup (1943-   ), Anishinâbe

Few problems have sparked more gunshots and court cases since the nineteenth century than indigenous fishing rights. Beginning in 1837 with the first treaty in present-day Wisconsin, Natives ceded land but never ceded hunting and gathering rights. Whites conveniently forgot this, despite writing additional treaties with the same provision. In 1889, the state of Wisconsin began heightened enforcement of state fish and game laws on ceded territories, even though these laws didn't apply to Natives. This was followed by threats and acrimony until a court decision in 1983, *Lac Courte Oreilles Band of Lake Superior Chippewa Indians v. Lester P. Voigt*, enforced the former treaties by allowing Natives access to recreational and subsistence hunting, fishing, and gathering on public lands in their former ceded territories. As Northrup points out with his trademark dry humor, it's only gotten more complicated since then.

Named Writer of the Year in Syndicated Columns for 2001 by the Wordcraft Circle of Native Writers and Storytellers for his column "The Fond du Lac Follies," Northrup was also honored as writer of the Best Feature Story in 1987 by the Native American Press Association. The film, *Jim Northrup: With Reservations*, received an award at the Dreamspeakers Native Film Festival 1997, was named Best of Show at Red Earth in 1997, and was chosen Best Short Film at the Native American Voices Showcase 2002 at the Fargo Film Festival.

Barbed Thoughts

I am Anishinaabe,
in the spring we spear fish
rez government wishes we wouldn't
it makes some white people mad.
That's par for the course
in the spring we spear fish
they've been mad at us
since they got here,
rednecks try to stop us
with threats, gunfire, and bombs.

The state attempts a buyout
thinking cash can do anything.
We're valuable to the media
we fill their columns and empty air
good people witness for us.
We thank Munido for fish, for life,
as we praise our grandfathers
and their generational wisdom.
Spearing is more than a treaty
right—it's an eating right.
We do what has been done since
there have been Anishinaabe.
I am one of them.
I spear fish.

Jabbing and Jabbering

"They said we'd get arrested if we go spearing off the rez," said Tuna Charlie.

"Who is going to arrest us for using our treaty rights?" asked Luke.

"Either the rez game wardens or those from the state," answered Sonny Sky.

The three Shinnobs were sitting in Luke Warmwater's back yard, carving knockers for next fall's wild rice harvest. It was a good five months before ricing, but they wanted to be ready.[135] Mostly, they wanted to be outside, enjoying the spring weather on the Fond du Lac Reservation in northern Minnesota.

"Tribal government is supposed to protect our treaty," said Tuna.

"Yah, they're supposed to, but the state is offering them two million dollars if we don't use our treaty rights," said Luke.

"What a power trip, just think, being able to decide where to spend two million," said Sonny as he stood up. "I'd bet a million bucks none of that two million will reach the people." No one wanted to take his bet.

He folded up his knife as the curls of cedar fell from his lap. Sonny looked down the length of the knockers, checking them for a warp. He made a couple of practice ricing strokes. The faint smell of cedar came from the pile of shavings at his feet.

"I'm ready for ricing now. Are we gonna go spearing tonight or not?" asked Sonny.

"Yah, let's go, I'm not afraid of jail," bragged Tuna.

"I don't think we have to sweat jail, we just have to worry about getting our stuff taken away, you know, spears, canoes, lights, batteries, and maybe the cars," said Luke. "After that we'll have to show up for court."

"They can't catch us, we'll be using the treaty rights our elders gave us," said Sonny as he walked to his mostly primer-gray truck.

"Meet you at Tuna's house just before dark," yelled Luke.

Sonny agreed by giving out two brief beeps of his truck horn. He threw them a Sawyer wave as he left the driveway.

Tuna and Luke continued working on the knockers. Tuna used an axe to split the cedar log into quarters. Luke was roughing out the shape of the knockers with a hatchet. He was using an Atlanta Braves kind of a stroke. Luke sat back down and took out his knife to carve the cedar.

"How many of these are we making?" asked Luke.

"My ma needs a pair, and my cousin said he'd pay money for some."

"Two pair done, two more to go, then."

The warm southerly breeze was shrinking the remaining snow. The crows were back; they could hear them cawing in the distance. It felt good to be sitting in the warm sun after the usual long, cold winter. Sugarbush was over so they were getting ready for ricing. There is always something to do to prepare for the next season, Tuna thought.

Ten miles east of the carvers, five other Shinnobs were sitting at a shiny conference table. It was the regular Tuesday morning meeting of the Reservation Business Committee. The Chairman was sitting at the head of the table. He was sipping hot coffee.

"Let's get this over with, I have to be somewhere in an hour," said the Chair, looking at his watch. The thick turquoise chunks on the watch band caught the morning sun.

"The state of Minnesota is going to give us two million dollars to forego our rights to hunt, fish, and gather in the ceded territory. They also said they'd give us all the walleye we want," reported the District One representative.

"That won't satisfy those dissidents from Sawyer, they're dead set against selling or leasing treaty rights. They say the rights belong to future generations," said District Two, as he spread butter on his sweet roll.

"What's wrong with those people, we're not living in the 1800s. We have to be pragmatic and try to get along with the state," said District Three, biting into his sweet roll.

"What are we going to do with the money?" asked the Secretary Treasurer.

"We sure can't give out a per-capita payment, we have to pay off that loan for the factory," said the Chair. "We'll tell the people that we're using the money to build a war chest to protect treaty rights—call it research or something."

"I still don't understand why the factory went belly up," said District One.

"You were the one who wanted to hire his white friend from high school," accused District Two, reaching in front of District One to get the last sweet roll.

"I never would have guessed he would turn out to be a thief," muttered District One defensively.

"How long did he get away with it before we found out from the bank?" asked the Chair.

"According to the auditors, about two and one-half years," replied the Secretary-Treasurer, looking through his cigarette smoke.

"The manager we had before that wasn't too good either," said District One.

"At least he wasn't a thief—kind of stupid, but not a thief," said District Two. "He would overbid on some projects so we didn't get them and underbid on the ones we did get. That guy must have cost us a couple hundred thousand dollars."

"No sense living in the past. How do we get out of this current mess?" asked District Three.

"The only way I can see is to lease the treaty rights to the state. Besides, there are not many that use them anyway," claimed District One.

"Sure, you know why? The state has been arresting them for over sixty years. They call it poaching," said District Three.

"The Shinnobs from Wisconsin have been using their rights to hunt, fish, and gather off the reservation for a couple of years now," advised the Chair. "It's the same treaty."

"Look what has happened. Did you see the protests on TV at the boat landings? I saw some angry white people swearing, throwing rocks at the spearers. I read one newspaper report about gunfire on the lakes," said District Two.

"Well, we sure don't want to get the white people mad, either at the boat landings, or at the state capitol," said the Secretary-Treasurer.

Five heads bobbed in agreement around the table.

"Notify the state we're willing to lease our rights for a year. We can even give a little per-capita payment just before the next election. But first, we have to get the bank off our back," said the Chair. "We can lease the treaty year after year."

"Okay, I'll call the bank; you have our attorney draw up the agreement. Maybe we can sign it before the dissidents find out," said the Secretary-Treasurer.

"Henry Buffalowind is already down in St. Paul. I think he has that tentative agreement with him. He's our lawyer, he'll keep it quiet," reported District Three.

"Don't let the media get a hold of this, you know how those bleeding heart liberals are," warned District Two.

"I hate those media bastards," growled the Chair.

"Does anybody think we're taking on too much without letting the people know?" wondered District One.

Districts Two and Three glared at him. He took a drink of coffee to hide behind his cup.

"Nah, they elected us to make these decisions for them. They don't know half of the problems we face every day," said the Chair, again looking at his watch. "Okay, it's decided then; we lease our rights to the state for one year. Let's see if we can find a make-work project to keep the renegades busy."

"We got that grant for fire protection. Let's hire the trouble-makers to cut fire breaks around the houses," suggested District Three.

"Good idea. They'll be too tired from cutting wood to spend any time on the lakes," crowed District Two.

"Okay, meeting adjourned. I'm going fishing. I've got to pick up my new three-hundred-dollar graphite rod from the sports shop. The guy there said I could catch fish in heavy dew with that rod. I'll be gone for a couple of days," said the Chair.

The five RBC members split up like they were accused of committing a great crime. Their work day was over at 9:30 A.M.

Ten miles west of the meeting site, Luke and Tuna were done making knockers. They began to get ready for spearing. Luke had three spearheads, he just had to attach them to the spruce poles. His canoe was loaded on the car already. He had to rig up a light.

"I can use this spotlight. I'll take off the case and duct tape the bulb to my old motorcycle helmet," said Luke. "I've got enough wire to reach the battery."

"Okay, I'll fix the spears while you do that," said Tuna. He carved the spruce poles so they would fit the steel spearheads. Tuna sharpened the spears with a whetstone.

Later that afternoon they were ready to go. They drove to Tuna's house to meet Sonny and his partner Asibun (raccoon).

Sonny's canoe was sticking out the back of his truck as he pulled up.

The powwow tape could be heard before he shut the truck off. He had a thermos of coffee, some bologna sandwiches, and two extra car batteries.

"I've been charging these all day," said Sonny, pointing at his batteries. "We should have enough light."

"Where are we going?" asked Tuna. He gave Asibun a nod of hello.

"Take your pick, we have over three hundred lakes to choose from. I don't think we should go to a lake that has cabins," said Luke, as he gave Sonny a spear to use.

"Let's just make this a short trip—see how the fish are running," said Sonny.

"Who all is going?" asked Asibun.

"Just us so far. I bet a lot of others will try it once they hear about us," Sonny said.

"Where are the game wardens?" Tuna asked.

"According to my police-band monitor, they are on routine patrol looking for deer shiners," answered Asibun.[136]

"Let's go to Hook Lake," suggested Tuna.

"Where's that? I never heard of Hook Lake," said Asibun.

"A little farther down the line," laughed Sonny.

They all joined in the laughter as they saw Asibun had fallen for one of the oldest jokes on the rez. The Kingbird Singers could be heard as Sonny started up his truck. They convoyed off after picking a lake south of the rez in the ceded territory. The daylight was used up as they drove down the back roads. They doubled back a few times to make sure they weren't being followed. It sure is hard to sneak around with a canoe on top of the car, Luke thought.

The boat landing was deserted when they got there. The smell of thawing lake met them. It was ice-covered except for a collar of open water fifty feet out from the shore. They hid the vehicles down an old logging road after dropping off the gear at the landing.

The Shinnobs offered tobacco to the Creator after getting in the canoes. Tuna was going to spear first while Luke paddled. Sonny was spearing while Asibun was acting as the motor. The canoes separated, Luke going one way around the lake, Asibun going the other. The paddlers stayed close to the shallows where the walleye nests were located. They could see the male walleyes circling the nests, trying to fertilize the eggs. The battery-powered lights lit up the lake bottom. Some of the light reflected off the surface and bounced into the trees. They could see birds sleeping on some of the branches.

Sonny tensed when he saw something reflecting his light. He moved his spear over to jab at it. Asibun moved the canoe over closer to where the light was pointing.

"It's just a Budweiser walleye," said Sonny. "Keep paddling."

"Sure are a lot of beer cans down there," said Asibun.

Tuna was getting good at picking out the fish eyes from the beer cans that were cluttering the lake bottom. He usually speared the fish right behind the head. Tuna would then carefully bring the fish up and drop them down into the canoe. The splash of the fish when they came to the surface was the only

Fishing by Torchlight (1848-56). Paul Kane

noise they heard on the lake. They could hear the loons singing, but that didn't count as noise.

The Shinnobs changed places in the canoe, and the motor became the spearer. The canoes came together on the other side of the lake from the landing. The Shinnobs decided to call it a night when they got back to the landing.

At the landing they counted their catch. Sonny's canoe held thirteen walleye and a large mouth bass. Luke's canoe held eleven walleye and three bass. One of the walleyes in Luke's canoe looked small compared to the others.

Sonny and Asibun teased Luke and Tuna about the small fish. They compared it to a minnow and called them baby killers.

"Anybody can spear those great big fish, it takes real skill to hit those small ones," explained Luke.

They laughed and loaded up the canoes and the rest of the gear. They drove straight home because the police band monitor told them the game wardens had gone home for the night. Both vehicles were full of spear-fishing stories. They ate the bologna sandwiches and drank coffee while driving home. The heaters were blowing hot to knock the chill off the spearers. The four Shinnobs cleaned fish in Luke's backyard. It took less than a half-hour to finish up. Luke took the pile of fish guts out to where the ravens would find them. The four agreed to deliver the night's catch to the Elderly Nutrition Program. The fish sticks on the menu were crossed off and walleye fillets were added instead. The elders of the community were going to eat fresh fish because of the spearers.

During the next two weeks, the spearers had several confrontations with the RBC and the game wardens. Shinnobs from all over the rez were going spearing. Threats and promises didn't stop them. Neither did the offer of free walleye from the state. The Reservation Business Committee realized they couldn't stop the people from getting fresh fish. They quit trying and called off the game wardens. The RBC got special permission from the state to allow Shinnobs to keep spearing.

There was no way to stop the treaty lease however. The RBC began getting heat from the people for leasing their treaty. Other bands of the Lake Superior Chippewa were calling and faxing the RBC. Most of the messages were negative about the treaty lease. There was talk of a recall election. The RBC were called sellouts. In the midst of the troubles, Henry Buffalowind quit and went to work for another tribe on the other side of the state. The RBC was going to great lengths to avoid the media. Phone calls were not returned to anyone.

The RBC called a special meeting to decide what to do. It was held one evening in the Chairman's garage.

"We got the bank off our back, but the people are mad as hell about the treaty," said the Secretary-Treasurer.

"Is there any way we can get out of it?" asked the Chair.

"Nope, Buffalowind told me before he left that we're committed for a year," said District One.

"Notify the state we can't lease the treaty anymore. The state is already asking about next year's lease. We have to give them formal notice that we're not going to lease after this year," ordered the Chair.

"I wonder how this will affect the next election?" wondered District One.

No one had an answer for him. The Chair adjourned the meeting, and they went their separate ways. Three of them were thinking of updating their resumes.

In an effort to save face, the Chair asked Luke and Tuna if he could go spearing with them some night. Luke agreed; Tuna didn't say anything.

Luke told the Chair he would have to provide his own canoe, light, battery, spear, and partner. The Chair decided on District Two as his partner. He hired Luke to make him some spearing equipment.

That night they all met at a landing north of the reservation. Earlier Luke had called some friends from the media. The newspaper and TV people were waiting at the landing when the Shinnobs arrived. The Chair and District Two brushed off requests for an interview. They quickly launched their canoe onto the dark lake. They left so fast they forgot to offer tobacco. The Chair was spearing and District Two was the motor. The TV cameras taped them as they were going out.

Luke and Tuna quietly followed fifty feet behind the first canoe. They didn't forget to offer tobacco. Luke was going after fish the first canoe missed. Tuna and Luke also wanted to keep an eye on their leaders.

Luke heard a short, sharp cry of surprise. He looked up, and his light showed the Chair with his neck caught in a Y-shaped tree branch. The Chair was pushed past the point of balance by the tree and District Two's paddling. He dropped his spear, which hit District Two a glancing blow.

The Chair jumped into the lake to keep the canoe from turning over. Luke and Tuna saw and heard the splash as their leader hit the icy water. District Two, with thoughts of gunfire on the lakes, saw the Chair leave the canoe. When the falling spear hit him, he thought he was shot.

The inside of his mouth tasted like copper. He rolled out the side of the canoe into the cold water. The canoe turned over when he left it. The cold water made him give out a small yell. The frigid water started both of them shivering immediately.

Luke and Tuna paddled up to help them. The Chair and District Two were standing in water that came to the tops of their shirt pockets. Luke helped them right their canoe and helped them find their paddle and spear. The light and battery couldn't be found. Tuna could see their lunch floating away. They held the canoe steady while their leaders climbed back inside.

The Chair and District Two decided to quit. When they headed towards the landing, Luke and Tuna glided off, still looking for fish. Luke could see the fish as their eyes reflected the light. He turned and looked back at the boat landing to check on their leaders.

The Chair and District Two were surrounded by the media people. Their wet, cold clothes were steaming in the hot TV lights.

Luke flipped another fish in the canoe. Tuna loafed along and let out a small chuckle. He could feel the canoe shaking as Luke laughed. The two Shinnobs continued looking for fish.

1993

TOBACCO

Tobacco is one of the most precious crops Natives grow, since it is involved in nearly all the rituals of traditional religious practices, and those are deeply intertwined with daily life. Few areas in the Great Lakes region, however, are suitable for growing the heat-loving *Nicotiana tabacum,* a tropical crop native to the Americas, and so more southerly bands and nations were able to develop an extensive trade with peoples farther north to replace a less palatable mixture made of sumac bark and dried red osier leaves known as *kinnikinnick.* Because tobacco is so central to culture and has been grown in North America for at least 6000 years, all nations have stories about its origin. The first is a Wendat story collected in Kansas in the 1880s that would have had its origin, long before Contact, in present-day Ontario where Wendat tobacco fields once covered hundreds of acres. In this story, tobacco comes from a sacred clan animal that becomes a woman, and women did much of the farming. "Wassamo," from the Odawa, is a wonderful story, filled with magic and descriptions of the underwater beings: white snakes and a malevolent spirit of Great Lakes islands. Chief Chusko's story is not about the origin of tobacco but about its pleasurable—and addictive—qualities that ensnared both spirits and people.

How the Wyandot Obtained the Tobacco Plant
Unidentified Wendat

The village stood by the lake. Clear streams flowed into the lake from the hills. On the hills were large trees. The Hawk Clan lived in this village. In the village lived an old man of the Bear Clan. He had a young wife of the Hawk Clan. Two daughters were born to them. When she was twelve years old, the first daughter died. Much grief did her death bring to the Old Man and his young wife. When the second daughter reached the age of twelve, she, too, was seized with a fatal sickness and soon died also. And the mother soon died of grief. The Old Man was left alone in the lodge, in deep sorrow. But he went about to do good. He was held in much esteem by all the village of the Hawk people.

One day when the Old Man and others of the village were standing by the lake, a large flock of immense Hawks, half-a-tree tall, came flying over the blue hills and the lake. They wheeled and circled about the lake and its shores. One of their number fell to the ground. It lay on the lake shore with its wings thrown above its back like a dove shot with an arrow. The other Hawks flew about for a short time. They screamed and called to each other. Then they flew back over the blue hills from whence they came.

The visit of the Great Hawks to the lake terrified the people in the village, and those standing on the bank of the lake by the Old Man ran about and called aloud from fright. The Old Man was not frightened by the Great Hawks. He said, "I will go and see the stricken Hawk that fell down."

The people said, "Do not go to the Hawk."

But the Old Man replied, "I am old. Life is almost done. The heavens are black. I am full of sorrow. I am alone. It can matter little if I die. And I am not afraid of death. I will see the stricken Hawk."

He went on. The way grew dark. But the Hawk lying on the ground remained before him. As he advanced, a great flame swept down and consumed the Hawk. When he came to where it had lain, ashes were all about. Lying in these was a living coal of fire in which he saw his firstborn daughter. He stooped to look. He saw it was indeed his daughter. He took her up. She spoke to him. Then the other people of the village came also.

The child spoke to them. She said, "I have returned with a precious gift for the Wyandot. I am sent with it to my own clan, the Hawk people."

Then she opened her hands. They were full of very small seeds. These she planted in the ashes of the fire from which she had risen. Soon a large field of Tobacco grew from the little seeds.

The Girl lived with her people. She taught them how to cultivate and cure the Tobacco. She taught them to make offerings of it and to smoke it in pipes.

And the Wyandot were thus more fortunate than any other people. They alone had Tobacco.

1880s

Wassamo, or the Fire Plume
Chief Chusko, Odawa

Wassamo was living with his parents on the shores of a large bay on the east coast of Lake Michigan. It was at a period when nature spontaneously furnished everything that was wanted, when the Indian used skins for clothing and flints for arrowheads. It was long before the time that the flag of the white man had been first seen in these lakes or the sound of an iron axe had been heard. The skill of our people supplied them with weapons to kill game and instruments to procure bark for their canoes and to dress and cook their victuals.

One day, when the season had commenced for fish to be plenty near the shore of the lake, Wassamo's mother said to him, "My son, I wish you would go to yonder point, and see if you cannot procure me some fish, and ask your cousin to accompany you." He did so.

They set out and in the course of the afternoon arrived at the fishing ground. His cousin attended to the nets, for he was grown up to manhood, but Wassamo had not quite reached that age. They put their nets in the water and encamped near them, using only a few pieces of birchbark for a lodge to shelter them at night. They lit up a fire, and while they sat conversing with each other, the moon arose. Not a breath of wind disturbed the smooth and bright surface of the lake. Not a cloud was seen. Wassamo looked out on the water toward their nets and saw that almost all the floats had disappeared. "Cousin," he said, let us visit our nets, perhaps we are fortunate."

They did so and were rejoiced as they drew them up to see the meshes white, here and there, with fish. They landed in fine spirits and put away their canoe in safety from the winds. "Wassamo," said his cousin, "you cook, that we may eat." He set about it immediately and soon got his kettle on the fire, while his cousin was lying at his ease on the opposite side of the fire.

"Cousin," said Wassamo, "tell me stories or sing me some love songs." The other obeyed and sung his plaintive songs. He would frequently break off and tell parts of stories and then sing again, as suited his feelings or fancy. While thus employed, he unconsciously fell asleep. Wassamo had scarcely noticed it in his care to watch the kettle and, when the fish were done, he took the kettle off. He spoke to his cousin but received no answer.

He took the wooden ladle and skimmed off the oil, for the fish were very fat. He had a flambeau of twisted bark in one hand to give light, but when he came to take out the fish, he did not know how to manage to hold the light. He took off his garters and tied them around his head and then placed the lighted flambeau above his forehead so that it was firmly held by the bandage and threw its light brilliantly around him. Having both hands thus at liberty, he began to take out the fish, every now and then moving his head as he blew off the oil from the broth. He again spoke to his cousin, but he now perceived by his breathing that he was asleep. He hastened to finish the removal of the fish and, while he blew over the broth repeatedly, the plume of fire over his forehead waved brilliantly in the air.

Suddenly he heard a laugh. There appeared to be one or two persons, at no great distance. "Cousin," he said to the sleeping boy, "some person is near us. I hear a laugh; awake and let us look out." But his cousin was in a profound sleep. Again he heard the laughing. Looking out as far as the reflection of the fire threw light, he beheld two beautiful young females smiling on him. Their countenance appeared to be perfectly white, and they were exceedingly beautiful.[137]

He crouched down and pushed his cousin, saying, in a low voice, "Awake! Awake! Here are two young women." But he received no answer. His cousin seemed locked up in one of the deepest slumbers. He started up alone and went toward the females. He was charmed with their looks, but just as he was about to speak to them, he suddenly fell senseless, and both he and they vanished together.

Some short time afterward the cousin awoke. He saw the kettle near him. Some of the fish were in the bowl. The fire still cast its glare faintly around, but he could discover no person. He waited and waited, but Wassamo did not appear. Perhaps, thought he, he is gone out again to visit the nets. He looked, but the canoe was still in the place where it had been left. He searched and found his footsteps on the ashes. He became uneasy "Netawis! Netawis!" (Cousin! Cousin!), he cried out, but there was no answer. He cried out louder and louder, "Netawis! Netawis, where are you gone?" but still no answer. He started for the edge of the woods, crying "Netawis! Netawis!" He ran in various directions repeating the same words. The dark woods echoed "Netawis! Netawis!" He burst into tears and sobbed aloud.

He returned to the fire and sat down, but he had no heart to eat. Various conjectures passed in his mind respecting his cousin. He thought, he may have been playing me a trick. No, impossible! Or he may have become deranged and run into the woods. He hoped the morning would bring with it some discovery. But he was oppressed by the thought that the Indians would consider him the murderer of the lost man. "Although," reasoned he, "his parents are my relations and they know that we are inseparable friends; they will not believe me if I go home with a report that he is lost. They will say I killed him and will require blood for blood."

These thoughts weighed upon his mind. He could not sleep. Early in the morning he got up and took in the nets and set out on foot for the village, running all the way. When they saw him coming, they said,

"Some accident has happened." When he got in, he told them how his cousin had disappeared. He stated all the circumstances. He kept back nothing. He declared all he knew. Some said, "He has killed him treacherously." Others said, "It is impossible, they were like brothers; sooner than do that they would have given up their lives for each other."

He asserted his innocence and asked them to go and look at the spot of their encampment. Many of the men accordingly went and found all as he had stated. No footsteps showed that a scuffle had taken place. There were no signs of blood. They came to the conclusion that the young man had got deranged and strayed away and was lost. With this belief they returned to the village. But the parents still waited and hoped he would return. Spring came on, and the Indians assembled from various quarters. Among them was Wassamo's cousin. He continued to say that he had done nothing to hurt his friend. Anxiety and fear had, however, produced a visible change in his features. He was pale and emaciated. The idea of the blood of his friend and relation being laid to his charge caused a continual pain of mind.

The parents of Wassamo now demanded the life of Netawis. The village was in an uproar. Some sided with the parents, some with the young man. All showed anxiety in the affair. They at last, however, decided to give the life to the parents. They said they had waited long enough for their son. A day was appointed on which the young man should give his life for his friend's. He still went at large. He said he was not afraid to die, for he had never committed what they laid to his charge. A day or two before the time set to take his life, he wandered in a melancholy mood from the village, following the beach. His feelings were wrought to such pitch that he thought once or twice to throw himself into the lake. But, he reflected, they will say I was guilty, or I would not have done so. I would prefer dying under their hands. He walked on, thinking of his coming fate, till he reached the sand banks, a short distance from the village. Here we will dismiss him for the present.

When Wassamo fell senseless before the two young women, it must have been some minutes before he recovered, for when he came to himself, he did not know where he was and had been removed to a distant scene. On recovering his senses he heard persons conversing. One spoke in a tone of authority saying, "You foolish girls, is this the way you go about at nights, without our knowing it? Put that person you brought on that bed of yours, and let him lie not on the ground." After this Wassamo felt himself moved to a bed. Sometime after he opened his eyes fully and was surprised to find himself in a spacious and superb lodge, extending as far the eye could reach.

One spoke to him, saying, "Stranger, awake, and take something to eat." He arose and sat up. On each side of the lodge he beheld rows of people sitting in regular order. At a distance he could see two prominent persons who looked rather older than the rest and who appeared to command obedience from all around them. One of them, the Old Spirit Man, addressed him.

"My son," said he, "those foolish girls brought you here. They saw you at the fishing ground. When you attempted to approach them, you fell senseless, and they conveyed you underground to this place. But be satisfied. We will make your stay with us pleasant. I am the guardian spirit of Nagow Wudjoo (sand mountain: Grand Sables on the south shore of Lake Superior). I have wished frequently to get one of your race to intermarry with us. If you can make up your mind to remain, I will give you one of my

160

daughters—the one who brought you away from your parents and friends." The young man dropped his head and made no answer. His silence they construed into an assent to their wishes.

"Your wants," continued the Old Spirit, "will all be supplied, only be careful not to stray away far from this. I am afraid of that Spirit who rules all islands lying in the Lakes. For he demanded my daughter in marriage, and I refused him; when he hears that you are my guest, it may be an inducement for him to harm you. There is my daughter. Take her; she shall be your wife." And forthwith they sat near each other in the lodge and were considered as married.

"Son-in-law," said the Old Spirit, "I am in want of tobacco. You shall return to visit your parents and can make known my wishes. For it is very seldom that those few who pass these Sand Hills offer a piece of tobacco. When they do it, it immediately comes to me. Just so," he added, putting his hand out of the side of the lodge and drawing in several pieces of tobacco, which someone at that moment happened to offer to the Spirit for a smooth lake and prosperous voyage. "You see," he said, "everything offered me on earth comes immediately to the side of my lodge." Wassamo saw the women also putting their hands to the side of the lodge and then handing something around, of which all partook. This he found to be offerings of food made by mortals on earth.

"Daughter," said the Old Spirit Woman, "Nauonguisk (*na'ângish*: son-in-law) cannot eat what we eat, so you can procure him what he is accustomed to." "Yes," she replied and immediately pushed her hand through the side of the lodge and took a whitefish out of the lake, which she prepared for him. She daily followed the same practice, giving every variety of fish he expressed a wish for. Sometimes it was trout, pike, sturgeon, or any other fish the lake furnished. She did the same with regard to meats or the flesh of any animal or fowl he asked for. For the animals walked over the roof of the lodge, the birds sat upon its poles, and the waters came so near to its side that the Spirits had only to extend their hands to the outside to procure whatever they wanted.

One day the Old Spirit said, "Son-in-law, you must not be surprised at what you will see, for since you have been with us, you have never seen us go to sleep. It was on account of its being summer, which is constant daylight with us. But now what you call winter is approaching. It is six months night with us, you will soon see us lie down, and we shall not get up, but for a moment, throughout the whole winter. Take my advice. Leave not the lodge, but try and amuse yourself. You will find all you wish there," raising his arm slowly and pointing. Wassamo said he would obey and act as he recommended.

On another occasion a thunderstorm came on, when every spirit instantly disappeared. When the storm was over, they all again re-entered the lodge. This scene was repeated during every tempest. "You are surprised," said the Old Spirit, "to see us disappear whenever it thunders. The reason is this: A greater Spirit, who lives above, makes those thunders sound and sends his fire. We are afraid and hide ourselves."

The season of sleep approached, and they, one after another, laid themselves down to their long sleep. In the meantime Wassamo amused himself in the best way he could. His relations got up but once during the whole winter, and they then said it was midnight and laid down again.

"Son-in-law," said the Old Spirit, "you can now, in a few days, start with your wife to visit your relations. You can be absent one year, but after that time you must return. When you get to the village, you must first go in alone. Leave your wife a short distance from the lodge and, when you are welcome, then send for her. When there, do not be surprised at her disappearance whenever you hear it thunder. You will also prosper in all things, for she is very industrious. All the time that you pass in sleep she will be at work. The distance is short to your village. A road leads directly to it, and when you get there, do not forget my wants, as I stated to you before."

Wassamo promised obedience to their directions and then set out in company with his wife. They traveled in a good road, his wife leading the way, till they got to a rising ground. At the highest point of this, she said, "We will soon get to your country." After reaching the summit, they passed, for a short distance, under the lake and emerged from the water at certain sand banks on the bay of Wekuadong (Wîkwedong: bay-at, Little Traverse Bay on Lake Michigan).

Wassamo left his wife concealed in a thicket, while he went toward the village alone. On turning the first point of land, who should he meet but his cousin. "Oh, Netawis, Netawis," said his cousin, "you have just come in time to save me. They accuse me of having killed you." Words cannot express their joy. The cousin ran off in haste for the village and entered the lodge where Wassamo's mother was. "Hear me," he said, "I have seen him whom you accuse me of having killed. He will be here in a few moments." The village was in instant commotion. All were anxious to see him whom they had thought dead. While the excitement was at its height Wassamo entered the lodge of his parents. All was joy at the happy meeting. He related all that had happened to him from the moment of his leaving their temporary night lodge with the flame on his head. He told them where he had been and that he was married.

As soon as the excitement of his reception had abated, he told his mother that he had left his wife a short distance from the village. She went immediately in search of her and soon found her. All the women of the village conducted her to the lodge of her relations. They were astonished at her beauty, at the whiteness of her skin, and more so at her being able to converse with them in their own language. All was joy in the village; nothing but feasting could be seen while they had the means of doing so. The Indians came from different quarters to offer them welcome and to present their tobacco to the Spirit's daughter.

Thus passed the summer and the fall, and Wassamo's parents and relations and the Indians around were prospered in all things. But his cousin would never leave him; he was constantly near him and asking him questions. They took notice that at every thunderstorm his wife disappeared and that at night as well as during the day she was never idle. Winter was drawing on, and she told her husband to prepare a lodge for her to pass the season in and to inform the Indians beforehand of her father's request. He did so, and all now began to move off to their winter quarters. Wassamo also prepared for the season. He gave one half of his lodge to his wife. Before lying down, she said, "No one but yourself must pass on the side of the lodge I am on."

Winter passed slowly away and, when the sap of the maple began to run, she awoke and commenced her duties as before. She also helped to make sugar. It was never known before or since that so much sugar was made during the season. As soon as the Indians had finished their sugar-making, they left the woods and encamped at their village. They offered tobacco profusely at the lodge of Wassamo, asking for the usual length of life, for success as hunters, and for a plentiful supply of food. Wassamo replied that he would mention each of their requests to his father-in-law. So much tobacco had been offered that they were obliged to procure two sacks made of dressed moose skin to hold it. On the outside of these skins the different totems of the Indians who had given the tobacco were painted and marked and also those of all persons who had made any request.

When the time arrived for their departure, they told their relatives not to follow them or see how they disappeared. They then took the two sacks of moose skin filled with tobacco and bade adieu to all but Netawis. He insisted on going with them a distance and, when they got to the sand banks, he expressed the strongest wish to proceed with them on their journey. Wassamo told him it was impossible, that it was only spirits who could exert the necessary power. They then took an affectionate leave of each other. The young man saw them go into the water and disappear. He returned home and told his friends that he had witnessed their disappearance.

Wassamo and his wife soon reached their home at the grand sand hills. The Old Spirit was delighted to see them and hailed their return with open arms. They presented him with the tobacco and told him all the requests of the people above. He replied that he would attend to all, but he must first invite his friends to smoke with him. He then sent his *mezhinauwa* (*mîzhinawe*: official messenger) to invite his friends the spirits and named the time for their reception. Before the time arrived, he spoke to his son-in-law. "My son," said he, "some of those manitous I have invited are very wicked, and I warn you particularly of the one who wished to marry my daughter. Some of them you will, however, find to be friendly. Take my advice and, when they come in, sit close to your wife—so close you must touch her. If you do not, you will be lost, for those who are expected to come in are so powerful that they will draw you from your seat. You have only to observe my words closely, and all will be well." Wassamo said he would obey.

About midday they commenced coming in. There were spirits from all parts of the country. One entered who smiled on him. He was the guardian Spirit of the Ottowas [Odawas], and he lived near the present Gitchy Wekuadong (Grand Traverse Bay). Soon after, he heard the sounds of the roaring and foaming of waters. Presently they rushed in and passed through the lodge like a raging tempest. Tremendous pieces of rocks, whole trees, logs, and stumps rolled past and were borne away by the strong current with the noise and foaming of some mighty cataract in the spring. It was the guardian spirit of waterfalls. Again, they heard the roaring of waves, as if beating against a rocky shore. The sounds came rapidly on. In a few moments in rolled the waves of Lake Superior. They were mountain high and covered with silver-sparkling foam. Wassamo felt their pressure and with difficulty clung to his seat, for they were of frightful appearance and each one seemed as if it would overwhelm them. This was the last spirit who entered. It was the Guardian of Islands in the surrounding lake.

Soon after, the Old Spirit arose and addressed the assembly. "Brothers," he said, "I have invited you to partake with me of the offerings made by the mortals on earth, which have been brought by our relative. Brothers, you see their wishes and desires. Brothers, the offering is worthy of our consideration. Brothers, I see nothing on my part to prevent our granting their requests; they do not appear to be unreasonable. Brothers, the offering is gratifying. Our wants for this article are urgent. Shall we grant their requests? One thing more I would say—Brothers, it is this. There is my son-in-law; he is a mortal. I wish to detain him with me and it is with us jointly to make him one of us."

"Hoke! Hoke!" (Yes! Yes!) ran through the whole company of Spirits.

The tobacco was then divided equally among them all. They decided to grant the requests of the people on earth and also respecting the Old Spirit's son-in-law.

When the Spirit of Islands passed Wassamo, he looked angrily at him. The guardian spirit of the Ottowa bands said, "It is very strange that he can never appear anywhere without showing his bad disposition."

When the company was dispersed, the Old Spirit told Wassamo that he should once more visit his parents and relatives and then it should be only for a short time. "It is merely to go and tell them that their wishes are granted and then to bid them farewell forever." Sometime after, Wassamo and his wife made this visit. Having delivered his message, he said, "I must now bid you all farewell forever." His parents and friends raised their voices in loud lamentation. They accompanied him to the Sand Banks, where they all seated themselves to see them make their final departure.

The day was mild; the sky clear; not a cloud appeared, nor a breath of wind to disturb the bright surface of the water. The most perfect silence reigned throughout the company. They gazed intently on Wassamo and his wife as they waded out into the water, waving their hands. They saw them go into deeper and deeper water. They saw the waves close over their heads. All at once they raised a loud and piercing wail. They looked again. A red flame, as if the sun had glanced on a billow, marked the spot for an instant, but the Feather of Flames and his wife had disappeared forever.

*c.*1830s

❖ SPRING STARS ❖

In the early 1600s a writer observing Haudenosaunee women, who did most of the farming, noted that "The women are the most experienced star gazers; there is scarcely one of them but can name all the stars; their rising and setting. The position of [Ursa Major] is as well known to them as to us, and they name [other constellations] by other names." Stars in the head of the constellation Taurus [Aldebaran and the Pleiades] were their signal to begin planting. They called these stars "a horned head of a big, wild animal which inhabits the distant country, not their's, and when it rises in a certain part of the heavens, at a time known to them, then is the season for planting."[138] Northern nations saw this constellation as the head of a great bear, whose den was the Northern Crown. When the bear came from her den, it was time to leave the winter hunting camps and gather again in villages.[139] These beliefs illustrate that the stars or planets often used in stories are ones that can be related to activities—hunting, traveling, religion, and agriculture—and have movements that are somewhat predictable, and so they

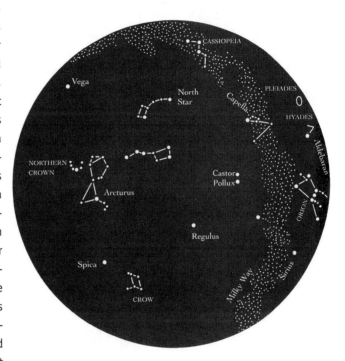

Spring Star Map

can be observed over a lifetime, rather than centuries, without the aid of instruments.[140] This made them critical to agriculture, since farmers need accurate weather information that transcends any individual season. Plant too soon during an early warm spell and the crops will be lost if a late-season frost occurs. If there are no seeds left to replant, famine threatens. This is one reason the Seven Sisters (the Pleiades) are so beloved: their disappearance in spring signals predictably warm weather for planting, and their reappearance in autumn signals the last days to harvest before killing frosts.

The great constellation in this and all seasons, however, is Ursa Major, more prosaically known as the Big Dipper, which rides directly overhead in the spring sky. It is the most dramatic constellation, a large group of stars that "runs about the sky" during the year, from overhead in spring, to the northwest in summer, the north in autumn, and the northeast in winter. Because Ursa Major can be used to determine the season, the passage of time during the night, and the location of other stars, it became a catalyst for stories. There is no better time to tell star tales than when the constellation is directly overhead, and so the two included here were most likely told to mark the spring (vernal) equinox, which occurs around March 21, when the sun is halfway between the winter solstice (literally 'sun-stopping'), the shortest day of the year, and the summer solstice, the longest. During the equinox, day and night are both twelve hours long, and the sun rises and sets exactly east and west, and so observers can know easily when it occurs.

Winter lingers long in the Great Lakes, however, and usually thick, crusted snow still covers the ground at the vernal equinox; thus it can seem as if spring has been locked up by someone evil, the situation of the "Star of the Fisher." To the Ojibwe and to some nations farther north, the constellation *odjiganang* (/o-JE-guh-nung/: fisher-star) not only resembled a bear, but also one of the most valuable furbearers of the far northern forests: the fisher (*odjiig*), a type of marten. Fishers are about three feet long and are solitary and elusive, except during their breeding season from February through April, the time around the equinox; therefore the position of the constellation, and perhaps the story, may have served to remind hunters, as well as to encourage listeners with hope that warmer weather would soon arrive. If the wording of this story seems awkward, remember that the language is sacred and highly formal. In addition, the translator was attempting to keep as much of the original word order as possible while rendering the text in readable English.

"The Origin of the Dipper," from the Menominee, combines the Ojibwe story of the Fisher Stars with a story type from western nations in which a woman becomes an animal, usually a bear, to wreak revenge on those who have harmed her. Here the wronged wife becomes a fisher and then a god. Since knowledge of the changing of the seasons was directly related to agricultural activities and women did many of those, having the Fisher Stars represented by a woman in a story told by a part-agricultural nation is logical. In addition, a woman as a fisher signals great power, since female fishers controlled mating and reproduction.

Star of the Fisher

Wâsägunäckang (He Who Leaves the Imprint of His Foot Shining in the Snow), Ojibwe

Now, in a town did the people live; in a really large town they dwelt. Now, it happened to be in the winter-time. And so, while they were in winter camp, a certain man got to turning matters over in his mind. It was not getting summer; when the time was at hand for the summer to be, why, there was no summer. And so with an uncertain feeling they waited for the coming of summer.

"Wonder what could have happened!" said the people. Now, it so happened that in time they came to realize how far the winter had gone. "It may be well for us to hold a smoker," said a certain one. Thereupon the man made ready for holding the smoker. And so in a while they were gathered together for a smoke.

Now, all were in the relation of sons-in-law to them.[141] Now, they knew that the knowledge of one of their sons-in-law was not wanting in anything. And so then did they come filling up the place in the wigwam, smoking together in assembly. Thereupon these men held forth in talk upon various things, there where they were sons-in-law. And this to them said the Fisher: "Yea, I myself know who it is causing this. I am not at a loss to know the one that is doing this. There is, to be sure, a certain one doing it; he is holding back the summer; he is not willing to let the summer come hither to this place," to them said the Fisher. "There will be, perforce, no coming of the summer; and that is a truth which I now impart to you," they were told by the Fisher.

Naturally, of course, they knew that he correctly spoke the truth in what he said. Thereupon they spoke to him, saying: "How shall we bring it about for the summer to come?" they asked of him.

"Yea, I know what we might do."

"Very well," he was told. "Therefore will we do whatsoever you shall say. For it will not be summer soon, however long we may continue to wait for the coming of the summer. There is really one that has shut up the birds of summer."

"Well, now" they said to him, "pray, who may he be that will be willing to go seek for the being?"

"Yea, this is the only way we shall succeed in having the summer come; not so very many times should we sleep to get to where the summer is. This is the number of times we should sleep, ten times we should sleep; that is how far away it is to where the summer is. Pray, be careful to do what you can! For it is on the morrow that we shall depart. Well, I shall have charge of the undertaking," they were told by the Fisher.

So then it was that the Fisher desired to lead the expedition, for it chanced that as many as were sons-in-law there wished to go. So by them all he met with approval. Now, all who therefore then came to agreement among themselves were they that were sons-in-law. Even so was Caribou then son-in-law there where the people were; even so was Fox then son-in-law where the people lived in a town; even so was Beaver then son-in-law at the place where the people dwelt in a town; even so was Muskrat then a son-in-law at the place where the people lived in a town; even so was Otter then a son-in-law at the place where the people dwelt in a town; and so on, for every creature of all these small animal-folk then spending the winter there was a son-in-law at the time.

"Now, it is on the morrow that we depart," to them said the Fisher. And this he said to them: "Pray, do you be zealous!" he said to as many as were in his company.

"Truly, now, that is the way we shall be," he was told.

And so then they departed. "Now, truly difficult is it over there to where we are going, and on that account I feel uncertain about your support. If only you be good at doing things, then shall we arrive at the place for which we are bound," he said to them.

And so now were they off. They went till night overtook them, so thereupon they went into camp. When the morrow was come again, they continued on their way. By the time they had camped five times, then did they grow hungry; nothing did they have to eat at the places where they slept. Truly did they crave to eat. Then they were told by their leader: "Yea, I know a certain one, without mentioning the name, who is abundantly supplied with the food we want. Therefore on the morrow let some of us visit the being, but do not by any means let us all go," he said to his companions. Indeed, concerning a certain one they felt some doubts, and that was Otter.

"By the way, perhaps you had better not go," they said to him, "for you might laugh. It is likely that if you laugh at the being, we shall not be given food. And in a comic way will it act when the being is about to give us food. And so on account it is feared that you may not contain yourself, Otter. We beg of you, therefore, do you remain here," they said to him.

But unwilling to do that was Otter. "In spite of your wish, I too will go along," he said to them.

"Do you take pains, then, that you do not laugh, lest by doing so you cause distress to your belly. An old woman it is whom we are going to visit. Now, this is the way she will act when we have entered into where she dwells. 'Pray, what shall we give these visitors to eat?' she will say. Now, this is the way she will behave, for, as often as she exerts a strain upon her body, she will break wind. And now on account of that are you all not to laugh at her. In case you laugh at her, why, she then will cease from what she is doing; we shall not be given any food."

In a while they were on their way; presently, indeed, they came within sight of where she lived. Now, in front went he who was their leader. So then at last they went into where she was. Sure enough, when Otter looked, he beheld an old woman seated there. Barely in the doorway was he permitted to enter.

When they looked, they saw that the place was thoroughly full of birch-bark boxes; behold, it was bear-tallow that she had for food in them. Presently, turning about in her seat, she then drew one of the birch-bark boxes towards her, when she broke wind. Thereupon was Otter possessed of an uncontrolled desire to laugh. So, when pulling the birch-bark box again towards her, she broke wind with a loud report. Thereupon, as if he were being tickled, Otter clapped his hands in laughter. "Who in the world could keep from laughing at that?" and so he then laughed aloud at her.

At this she ceased from her work in vainly trying to feed them.

And so in consequence out of doors they went; it was then that Otter was given a scolding. He was on the point of receiving a flogging by his companions, so deep was the disappointment he caused them.

So then, "I beg of you, let us go over there again!" he said to his companions.

"Oh, don't you go, Otter!" he was told. "You are too much given to laughing," they said to Otter.

Thereupon truly was he left behind. In a different way they dressed themselves when they planned to make another visit with her. And this to them then said Otter from yonder place where he was left behind. He spoke to them as they were leaving, saying: "I beg of you, as far as my arm is to the elbow is the amount of bear-tallow you shall fetch to me," he said to his companions.

"Yes, we will fetch it to you," he was told. Thereupon they departed.

In a while they entered again into where she was. Well, she acted in the same way as before, she broke wind. It was all the while that she broke wind when preparing food for them. To be sure, nobody laughed. And so presently they were fed. And then later, when they had finished eating, she made ready some food which they could carry away with them on their backs. Therefore then were they successful in obtaining what they were to eat after they had been fed by Red-Net.[142] It was then that pleased was Otter. Now, sure enough, they fetched to him that amount of the bear-tallow; as far as his arm measured to the elbow was how much they fetched to him.

Well, thereupon then again they continued on their way. Then again they slept. Truly were they amazed at the way the snow was sinking. So now for the seventh time they slept. By this time were they again growing hungry by reason of their supply of food running short. "Verily do I know of a place from whence we may obtain some food to eat," said the Fisher.

"Very well, let us go over there!" he was told.

Thereupon truly on their way they went. Presently, indeed, they fell into the path of another, in that path the ten followed. As farther on they continued, more frequent grew the number of paths running into the one they were on, paths that were used when coming home with game. As soon as into view appeared the home of him dwelling there, with much greater frequency came other paths into the one they were on, that were used in fetching home game. Only a little while before someone had dragged a bear along. In a while they went into where he was.

Full as can be was the dwelling of the man. They marveled at the strange appearance of him. Truly small was his mouth, up and down was the way his mouth was opened. And so in another respect did they regard him with wonder, really did he scarcely have a neck, a red ribbon did he wear for a necklace. Presently they were spoken to by him saying: "Pray, what shall I give them to eat?" And then they heard him utter with his voice, this he uttered when he said: "What shall I give them to eat? Isp!"[143] he uttered. And already then was there a beginning of their being fed. And so all the while that was his exclamation whenever he had something to say, that "Isp!" was what he uttered.

Now, the one that was there was Big-Penis;[144] so it was a chief that they had visited. And so later they were fed again, whereupon again they carried away what had been given them by Big-Penis. So the Fisher said to them: "Now shall we reach the place for which we are bound."

In time they slept again. "It is on the day after tomorrow that we shall get to the place for which we are bound," the Fisher said. Now, by this time there was scarcely any snow on the ground. Presently they continued on their way. And then truly during the day, while traveling across the country, they did not see any more snow; and it was also growing warmer. "Now, therefore, on the morrow shall we arrive at where we are going," said the Fisher.

Then they slept again. When the morrow came again, then on their way they went. And so there was now no more snow. In time it was evening. "It is straight over yonder way where dwells he whom we have come to seek," to them said the Fisher. "I beg of you," he said to them, "do you but only look, by a lake dwell the people. And in the very center of the town is where he dwells who rules the town. It is he who holds the summer in his keeping," he said to his companions.

Presently he spoke to Caribou, saying: "I beg of you, as soon as the dawn of day begins to break,"—he looked over toward the narrows of the lake—"it is over there that I would have you cross. And you, Fox, you are to bark at him. And so that is as much as I am going to instruct you," he said to him. "And you, Muskrat, you shall go among the canoes, gnawing holes in them, which is the work for you to do tonight. And you, Beaver, you shall go about gnawing the paddles, and so that is what you shall do tonight." Beaver then had received an order from their leader. "And that is truly what we shall do, while I myself will go against the wigwam," he said.

In a while was the night coming on, whereupon then departed his comrades. And so then he waited for the coming of the morning. Now, he had told Fox to go barking at them as they went. "It is along this very shore that you shall bark at them as they go, Fox," he said to him. Well, it was now growing day, when, sure enough, he heard Fox going along barking. So presently up the people quickly woke on hearing the noise. "Harken to the sound! A dog comes barking along by yonder shore!"

"What is it?" said the people.

"It may be at a caribou that it is barking," said the people. "It may be that the dog is driving it into the water over there at the narrows. Already now, in fact, is it leaping into the water!"

When the people saw it, "Hey, look yonder! A caribou goes swimming along! Now, indeed the dog is driving it into the lake. Come on!" said the people. And so truly then they scrambled wildly into their canoes, all rushed madly to get into their canoes.

And so, when all had scrambled into their canoes, then against the town did the big Fisher make an attack. When he rushed into a wigwam, he saw his cousin seated there. He beheld him feathering his arrows with sturgeon-glue. "Well, my cousin!" he said to him. "Therefore now have I come to where this bird of summer is. Why," he said to him," for no particular object do I come to visit you," he said to him.

"Really!" he was told.

"By the way, O my cousin!" he said to him, "is that the way you generally do when feathering your arrows?"

"Oh, nonsense!" he was told.

"Nay, I am serious," he said to him. "Now, this is the way I generally do when feathering my arrows. Just you let me show you," he said to him. Then he picked up the stick that he used when rubbing the glue upon the arrows. Now, close beside him was he seated; when the Fisher rubbed the sturgeon-glue over his cousin's mouth, then was the cousin unable to get his mouth open, however much he tried!

The Fisher leaped to his feet. Now, all the space the whole way round was a mass of birch-bark boxes. When he poked a hole into one, out burst forth some birds of summer. And when he set to work poking holes into box after box of birch-bark, he found them one after another filled with all kinds of ducks and all kinds of other creatures. And by and by out of a certain box burst forth the mosquitoes.

Now, as for the people yonder, they were busily engaged trying to keep on the trail of Caribou. And so at a loss to know what to do was he whose mouth had been closed with glue. After a long while had passed, he found an awl with a short handle; forcing it through a corner of his mouth, he then called aloud, and this he said: "Oh, the big Fisher has come after the birds of summer!" thus was what he cried aloud.

Presently him the people heard. "What is the sound of what he says?" On looking hitherward, everywhere did there seem to hang a smoky haze. "Listen and hear!" they said. "The birds of summer has the big Fisher come and got!" was what, indeed, he was heard saying in a loud voice. At that they truly whirled their canoes about.

Whereupon some broke their paddles when whirling about, and the canoes of some began to leak rapidly; some failed in trying to get back home by canoe. And so out there they broke their paddles, and as they went, some sank to the bottom before they were able to get back to land.

In a while the big Fisher had cut up the entire dwelling of his cousin. Then his cousin grabbed for a bow, for by him was he now about to be shot. Now, his cousin had a tree standing there, then up the tree he hastened. And so from up there he looked down at him, he kept watch of his cousin, who intended to shoot at him. Well, now was he on the point of being shot at; at the moment that his cousin aimed with the bow was when he dodged round to the other side of the tree. And then off this way[145] into the sky he whirled.

Thereupon his cousin shot him at the end of his tail, whereupon the tail was broken.[146] So it was from yonder place in the sky that he spoke to his comrades, saying: "I beg of you, do all that is within you," he said to his comrades. "I may not be able to come to yonder place where you dwell. It is here that I shall always be, however long the world may last, so that my grandchildren may behold me," he said to them.

So it was in a while that he addressed them again, saying: "When you have arrived at yonder place from whence you came, then shall you decree how long the winter should be. Do you take pains to see that you bring things favorably to pass," he said to them.

Thereupon truly on their homeward way they went. At no place anywhere did they catch up to the boundaries of the summer. At last they reached the place from whence they had gone away. In course of time they said, on coming together in assembly: "How shall we bring to pass that which we had been told? The time is now come for us to decree that which we had been commanded." Then truly, coming together, they sat down, then did they decree. Now they were told: "Do you give name to the moons."

And this was what Caribou said: "I myself will count the number of moons," he said.

"Very well," he was told.

Thereupon truly did he speak: "As many as the hairs on my body, so may the number of moons before it shall then be summer," he said. And so, when he had finished, then was he addressed: "It might then happen that you would be an easy prey for one to lay you low with a blow.[147] There would be too much snow if such were the number of moons. Not even would you be visible from under the snow."

"Then accordingly, there shall not be so many moons."

"They would really be too many," he was told.

So then presently, "Pray, let me count the number of winter moons there shall be," so said Chipmunk. "As many as the number of stripes upon my back, so shall the number of moons in winter be. Behold, six is the number of stripes upon my back," so he said.

"Now, that truly is just about the proper number for the winter moons to be," thus they said. "Very well, that truly is what the number of moons shall be."

Accordingly then did they act upon his work. "Now, that will be just the right number of moons," so they said. And so they then fulfilled the decree.

And that is all, the buttocks of the ruffed grouse now hang aloft.[148]

*c.*1905

Ruffed grouse

Origin of the Dipper
Unidentified Menominee

This is a sacred story concerning the power given through fasting to a young man who was clean, and pure, and free from sin, and whose name was Wânasâtakiu. No one can ever bear this name again because he was so powerful.

This young man said to his mother: "Make me a pair of moccasins, for I am going to travel to yonder village. I start tomorrow." In the morning he took his blanket, bow and arrows, and his magic flute and passed out through the village.[149] As he went by, a few young men came out and called to him, "Hay! Wânasâtakiu, where are you going?"

"Oh, only to those Indians at their village!"

So he passed by and took a big road over which he journeyed. He stopped overnight at a point halfway, and in the morning he arrived quite early at the Indian town, where there were many large bark wigwams. When he drew near one of these lodges, he stopped and stood outside a little way off until the mistress of the house came out and saw him. She went inside again directly and said to her son. "There is a young man standing outside there. Go and see him."

So the youth went out and invited the stranger in. "Where do you come from?" asked his host.

"Why, from the Indian village nearby," answered the visitor.

Dacota Village (1853). Seth Eastman

"Why are you standing out here then? Come in." So they both entered together, and the host said to his mother. "Cook something and give this one a meal, so that we can eat together."

When they had finished eating, the host said, "Come out with me, and we will sit on the scaffold that has been erected for the purpose." When they were seated on the platform, the host spoke again, "My friend what did you come here for?"

"I came here purposely," returned the stranger.

"Then I must tell you," said his host, "there are lots of young men in this world, and over yonder in that village there are many that are pure, innocent, and clean. Over there is our great chief's house, and he has some daughters. That is why all the young men in this world come here, to be near his house. That is why they gather here. These girls hate all the youths who come, and they send them away, but tonight we will both go over to look at the other young men who flock there."

"All right," said the guest to his friend, "I will go over with you."

Sure enough, that evening they went over, the guest carrying his magic flute.[149] When they arrived, they saw a crowd of young men standing there, coaxing and courting. They entered in turn to speak to the girls, but though the maidens heard their words, they would not answer or speak to them, except to order them off, so that the youths came out one by one and went away.

When the first youth saw and heard all this, he said to his friend and host, "When it is my turn, I shall

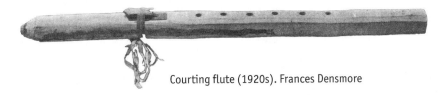

Courting flute (1920s). Frances Densmore

173

get that girl and take her away with me. That is what I came here for in the first place, but this time I only came to see the other youths. Now we will go home, but tomorrow night we shall come again, and then I will go in and see those girls."

So they went home and, when they arrived there, he and his chum sat on the scaffold, and he blew on his magic flute, so that the girls could hear his songs and sacred music. Indeed, the girls did hear the songs and music, as did the other suitors who were standing outside. All said in wonder: "Who can that be playing? Who is he?"

"Why it is Wânasâtakiu!" said someone.

"Oh yes, it is he!" cried another.

"Oh my," said others, "Maybe he will get these girls, or at least receive answers from them!"

The next night Wânasâtakiu came and entered the lodge. He found the girls to be the handsomest in the whole world, pure, honest, and good, and that was why all the young men were trying so hard to marry them. When it was his turn, he went in and sat down beside one girl who was lying down, and she, knowing that it was someone who was mysterious, inquired: "Who are you?"

The young man answered: "Well, it is me. Well, it is me. Well, it is only me." Then he lay down beside her.

The girl thought she knew who it was, so she said, "Is it you, Wânasâtakiu?"

"Yes, it's me, but what do you want to know for?"

"Why I only wanted to know if it was really you, for I have been waiting for you for a long time. I heard about you quite a while ago. All these young men that you see standing outside are strangers, and somebody else."

Then Wânasâtakiu took the girl to be his wife, according to their custom, for she accepted him when he lay down with her. Then, as Wânasâtakiu was a famous hunter and great in power, he lived with his new wife for a year, killing everything that he desired, for nothing was hard to him. After this time had passed, he said to his wife: "We will now go over to my house and live with my parents for a while." On their way to his parent's lodge, Wânasâtakiu said, "We will go through the Indian village." When they were seen coming, the unsuccessful suitors called out, "Oh, here comes Wânasâtakiu on his way home with his bride!"

The new wife lived with her mother-in-law for a time. Whenever a feast occurred, her husband would attend. One time he met another nice girl whom he married and lived with as his wife, while his first spouse knew nothing of it. When the feast was over, he returned to his home and said to his wife, "Make me a pair of moccasins, I am going to join a war party."

This was only a lie, his scheme to make an opportunity to live with his paramour. There was indeed a war party about to set out, but the youth went over to dwell with the other woman. He then sent over his paramour's parents to tell his father and mother that he had been killed, and they and his wife believed it.

Every night for four nights Wânasâtakiu went out to the foot of the hill and played on his flute, and each night his discarded wife heard it and recognized the song. She knew well enough that he was not killed and was playing the flute to spite her. Every day the poor woman cut wood as usual and carried it home, until one day she went in the direction from which she heard the flute. There she saw a dead tree and chopped it down, thinking it would give a lot of wood and last a long time. When the tree fell, it broke into pieces, and out ran a mouse. The woman snatched up her ax to kill the animal, but it stopped and spoke to her.

"Don't kill me! I was going to tell you something, but now I won't tell you because you want to slay me!"

"Oh then tell me!" cried the deserted wife. "If you do, I will pay you well. I will give you some of my hair oil to eat, it is sweet, come, tell me, and you may have it tonight."

Then the mouse answered, "Do you hear a flute song evenings at the top of yonder hill?"

"Yes," replied the woman, "I do."

"Well then," returned the mouse, "That is your husband. It is he that plays there. The others told you a lie; he is not dead, he is alive, and he is staying with another woman."

When the wife heard this, she was so angry she went right home without cutting any more wood. The mouse had said to her, "On your shelf you will see a bundle. Open it, and you will find it to be a bunch of dried bones which represent your man's death." When she arrived at her lodge, she opened the bundle, and the bones all fell to pieces.

The mouse had also said, "You go over this evening near that hill and watch for your husband there. You will see him playing. You can see his tracks." The woman went there and found all these things were true. So she said to herself, "Well now, my man Wânasâtakiu, where in the world can you ever escape me? When you come here again, you will get it, and you will know it comes from me!"

Then she sat down right there, in sight of the whole great village, and began to sing her magic song, directing it against her husband, for she also had great power. Her song meant that she was offended and would not have the man live with her again, and her song told that she was a god. She sang it loud enough for all the villagers to hear. They listened and were frightened, for they heard her say that her name was Ut′cikasikäo, really a God Woman.

The deserted wife sang this song four days at this place, and all the people heard and were frightened, knowing her to be a great-powered god woman. On the fourth and last day, in the morning, she threw herself on the ground and rolled over and over like a horse, and when she had finished, she had become a small animal, a fisher. Then she went into the village, and at her approach the people, knowing her, ran away into this world to hide. The fisher went directly to the place where her husband was cohabiting with his paramour and killed both of them with all their relatives. She chased them all over this earth before she caught them and bit them to death. Then she cried, "I am now so mad nothing can ever pacify me. I will never go home again, but as I am really possessed of power I will make a sign for those who are to people the world in the future, and they will say of me that I did right."

So she jumped up and ascended into the northern heavens. She is now there as a female and is called Ut′cikanäo, the "Fisher Star," meaning the Dipper.

This is a real, true, sacred living-powered story, pertaining to the nature of all females, as the female is the mother of mankind. It is said of the Dipper that any girl who was pure and fasting may receive some of her power and it shall be known as long as this world shall stand.

1915

❖ SPRING CEREMONY AND BELIEF ❖

THE MIDÉWIWIN

Awinegicig Agode Naawind (Beautiful as a star hanging in the sky is our Midé lodge).[150] The Midéwiwin, or Grand Medicine Society, of the Ojibwe may have antecedents in some of the oldest religious practices in North America. Although the rite began with the Ojibwe in the Great Lakes region, it soon spread to many lakes nations and beyond, accruing ritual and story and incorporating elements of other religions such as Christianity as it was adopted and adapted. The primary focus of the oral traditions of the Midéwiwin is the origin of the world and of the Ojibwe and the gift of the Midéwiwin to the people to help them overcome death. The Shell-Covered One, or Shell, sent Bear to Gitci Manido with the idea of the Midé. The spirits agree to let Bear lead from the depths of the earth to the surface of the water, from the east to Lake Superior, bringing his medicine bundle for the people.

Because Midé priests were the custodians of knowledge about death and resurrection, some stories were associated with the stars, particularly the Milky Way, known to many nations as the route souls take after death. Appearing as a path that whirls in the night sky, it is known to the Haudenosaunee as Dja-swĕn-doʻ, the belt of a great hunter named Ga-do-wǎǎs, and to the Cree as the Tchipaï meskenau, the Path of Souls. The Meskwaki call it Wâpisīpow (the White River) and see the stars as manidog who live along the banks of a river where ordinary people never go. The bridge to the road is guarded by a huge serpent in some versions (see star map, p. 28) and by the spirits of dogs in others. The dogs, which may be the stars Castor and Pollux or Sirius and Antares, allow only the good to pass (see "The Dogs of the Chief's Son," p. 365). Some scholars believe that the stories of the Sky Road as a path for souls are thousands of years old, associated with mortuary ceremonies that predated Midéwiwin and with the archetypal stories of a person who travels to the land of the dead to retrieve a loved one.[151]

Eshkwaykeezhik (James Red Sky), who narrates "The Creation of the World" and whose scrolls accompany this section, was an elder in the Presbyterian church and a fourth-degree Midé from Ontario who interpreted the birchbark scrolls where Midé masters kept mnemonics of the origin stories and migration charts. Here he gives his version of the first part of the Midé origin story, describing the four bears' breakthrough. The next version is by Náwajíbigókwe (Woman Dwelling Among the Rocks), who was a prominent member of the Midéwiwin on the White Earth reservation in Minnesota. She gives a Lake Superior version of the history of the Midé. Asked by the ethnomusician Frances Densmore to describe the founding of the rite, Mrs. Mary Warren English, sister of William Warren, the author of *History of the Ojibway People,* interpreted Náwajíbigókwe's words. Náwajíbigókwe told Densmore that she had taken four degrees in the society and received four great instructions, and she tried to live according to them. She stated that she "could blow on her medicine bag and produce evil results upon those who displeased her, provided they were not of the Midé," but she "would be powerless against a member of the Midéwiwin." She "would not, however, exert this evil power, for it would displease the Midé manido. Some do this, and it always reacts in evil upon themselves."

The Creation of the World

Eshkwaykeezhik (Last Sky, James Red Sky, Jr.), Ojibwe

When God first made this world, he didn't think or work anything to make this world. He just said this and that, and it happened—just by the word of God. What he wanted [for] this world, he took it. So he thought that nobody could live on this world, because nothing went right. There was too much ice. There was too much water. Nobody could live on this earth. Well, he said, he'd try a second time . . . and he tried and he knew he was going to make it. So after the second time there was still too much ice—too much ice and too much water. Nobody can live like that. It didn't take him one day or one week or one month. I was told that it took him probably 2000 years—maybe 4000 years.

Eshkwaykeezhik

Well, he was trying, but it didn't look very good. Nobody can live on this earth that way. Too much water, too much ice. He knew he was going to make it—make this world all right. So he tried it a third time. He tried it, and he made it go. And he was convinced he was going to make it. The earth looked pretty good. Not so much water, not so much ice. So he tried again. That was the third earth. After trying the third time, he tried the fourth time.

When he tried it the fourth time, everything went nice. The hills were green, the water was nice, and the streams were running. The trees grew—the leaves on the trees—everything was beautiful. When he looked among the hills, everything was very nice; well, he thought, it was going to be perfect—perfect to live on. It looked very nice that anybody could live on it.

So he thought he'd make a man. So he spat on the ground. And afterwards he picked the ground up, moistened it, and he held it in his hand. After he held it in his hand for a long time until it was warm, when he opened his hand there stood a man. And he laid his hand on it and breathed on it. So he laid it down on the ground. Then that man stood on the ground. Then he said . . . he spoke to him, and he spoke back to him. When the man spoke, there was flames coming out of his mouth. And when he looked, his eyes glistened. Lights came out of his eyes. Flames came out of his mouth. He says, "Well, that's not very good, because he'll be the same as I am if he breathes like that all the time—God's way. He would be able to do anything: soften rocks, tear trees into shreds—pull them all out like hair. That wouldn't be very good if he was like that." So he put his hand on him, to cut him down a little bit—there was too much high pressure in him of the godliness he had in him.

Red Sky describes how God lets man walk around, then he creates woman. Eventually the world fills up, and the people need dodems (clans) to prevent incest.

When this world was full of human beings, it got so all the people were dying off—dying off like that, and God didn't know what to do about it. So he thought he'd teach them some way to worship him. So

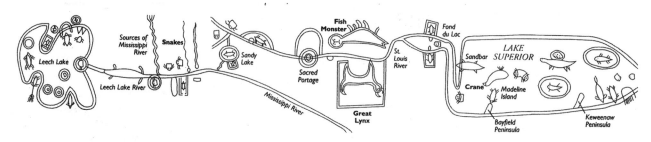

Eshkwaykeezhik's Migration Chart (c.1960s)

later, when he got this all organized, he said, "I'll have them meeting at the centre of a . . . different conti-nent across the water. That's where I'll have this meeting. So where I think God took it was in Palestine. And so when God got this organized, he brought all these birds and animals—all the living creatures in the world—to this one place. So then they had a meeting.

So God thought, "Well, I want these people to worship me. I don't know how to get them to worship me." So he called a meeting of all the birds—all the birds and all the creatures. And so they had a meeting

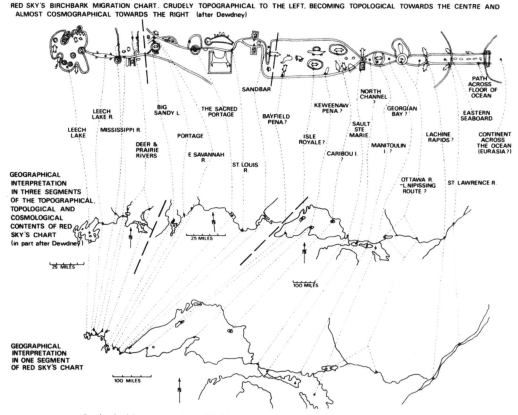

Geological Interpretation of Eshkwaykeezhik's Chart (1979). G. Malcolm Lewis

178

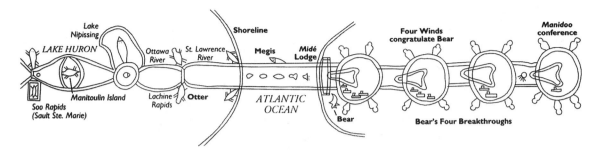

to talk about it—somewhere across the Big Water, where this Manito was. So he said to this meeting, "Now who's going to take it? Who's going to take it across to the people?" Well, the Bear was there. He says, "I'll take it across to the people."

So when he went out, this Everlasting Life that he was carrying was very heavy—very heavy. He could hardly walk. When he put his arms out, he stuck his arms up to the elbows. Same with his hind feet; he stuck them right to his knees.

After walking a little ways he came to a wall. He couldn't go anywhere. He didn't know what to do. So he stuck his tongue out. Then his tongue went through as if it were a bullet shot out of a rifle. It went right through to the other side. He went right through the little hole and then came out on the other side and took this Life—Everlasting Life that he was carrying. After looking around he didn't see no earth—nothing. So he got out, he found another wall. He did the same thing—stuck his tongue out, and it went right through as if were a bullet shot out of a rifle. And in the hole he went through with this Pack he had—heavy Everlasting Life. And when these people saw this, the manito at the East, the manito at the South, manito at the West, and manito at the North, they thanked him for the work he did.

Well, that wasn't the end. That was the second time. Well, he started out . . . and found another wall. That was the third time. And he did the same thing. He stuck out his tongue, and it went through as if shot out of a gun. Then he went through here. And when he got on the other side, it happened the same thing. When he went through he did the same thing. That was the fourth time he did the same thing.

After he was there—when he got out—he seen this little place. He thought he'd go into this little place, what we call today Midéwegun (*midewigaan*: Midé lodge). So towards the east there was a little door, and a little door to the West. After he got in, he took eight steps. Then he took out a little tree, and he planted it. He stuck the little tree into the middle of the Midéwegun. After a while, a Thunderbird came and landed on this tree.

"This is where I'm going to listen to the Indian whenever he calls upon God. When anything—some kind of sickness or some kind of bad luck happens—he'll have God. I'll listen to everything right from here."

This is what we see on this tree. There's a bird on the tree. And a little later there came a great big Rock. God said, "This is the foundation of this Midéwegun. This is the foundation. I'll uphold this as long as the earth lasts. It won't fall down. Nobody will turn it over, can't take it down. If the Indian fights for it, I'll still be here to protect it."

And after he came out, he came down; he came to the shore of a Big Water. After a little while, while he was walking back and forth there, he didn't know what to do. So finally he heard someone talking to him.

"What have you got there?"

"Oh, I've got something I've got to take to the Indians, across this Big Water."

"Well," he said, "I'm the one that can do it." This is Megis (miigis), the Shell—seashell.

So they started unloading and reloading. They tell me it looked as if a white man was loading a great big ship. That's what it looked like when they transferred what he was carrying.

So he went out—the Megis—he came out of the water. He had followed the bottom of the ocean. And after a little while he came up. When he came up, he looked around. He seen this great big hill. After he looked around, there was a small narrows where he went through. On the right hand side he seen this great big hill—high . . . high. So he thought he'd go up and look around. So he found another manito there, and he left word with him that [whoever] wants help—that has sickness or disease or misfortune—is unlucky—he'll go to him. He'll fix him up.

Well, after a bit he came up, looked around. He didn't see nothing. No land anywhere—couldn't see no land. And he went down again and followed along the bottom of the ocean and came up again. Still he didn't see nothing—no land in sight nowhere. So, after a while he went down again. He did the same thing—followed along the bottom of the ocean, came up again, went along there. So he'd come up again. Looking around, he seen land just as if it was a little string going along there. That was land.

"Well," he said, "I'm glad." He was glad he found land. Well, he didn't go down this time. He just went along, and he seen this river coming down into the ocean. Well, he thought he'd stop there and look around. Well, he seen a little wigwam. . . .

c.1960s

The Origin of the Midé

Náwajíbigókwe (Woman Dwelling Among the Rocks), Ojibwe

The Chippewa believe in many manido, or spirits. The highest of them all is called Kijie Manido, literally translated, "Uncreated Spirit." Those connected with the Midé are: Midé Manido, the Midé spirit, and four manido, one at each point of the compass. These are called: Wabunukdaci manido, the East Spirit; Cawanunkdaci manido, the South Spirit; Ningabianunkdaci manido, the West Spirit; and Kiwedinunkdaci manido, the North Spirit [c = /sh/]. In the Midé it is also the belief that there are four layers beneath the earth and four above the earth. These layers, or planes, are distinct from each other.

Originally all the inhabitants of the earth (Chippewa Indians) who were to learn the Midé lived on Madeline Island, in Lake Superior, and in that portion of the country. They were selected by the Midé manido to be taught the Midé religion.

There was first a consultation among the four manido (East, South, West, and North). This took place at the center of the earth, not under the earth, but at some place far away. There they sat together and talked and decided to teach the Midé to these particular Indians. So the East manido was selected to go among these Indians and teach them. Before he left the others, he told them that they must get everything ready and decide exactly how the Midé should be taught to the Indians. Of course the East manido could not approach the Indians in his spirit form, so he was born of an old woman who had lived with her husband all her life but had had no children. This old couple lived on Madeline Island.

The people were astonished and said, "He must be a wonderful person to be born in this way," so both mother and child were treated with great respect.

He was indeed a wonderful child. Whatever he said came true. He would say to his father, "Go and get a bear," and his father would find one without any difficulty. It was no effort at all for the family to get enough food. The child grew up rapidly, and when he was a young man, he had as his friend and companion one who was his mother's brother's son—his cousin.

When he grew up, he began to consider, "I must begin to instruct these Indians in the Midé; that is the purpose for which I came."

After thinking this over, he said to the old man, his father, "We will go on a journey to the end of the lake"; his mother went with them. The point to which they went was not where Duluth now stands but was where Superior is located. This was the location of the old town of Fond du Lac.

They reached this place and stayed four days. On the fourth day a terrible storm came from the northeast, sweeping across the lake. During the storm the East manido said to his father and mother, "My cousin at Madeline Island is very ill; we must go back."

His father said, "It is impossible to even put the canoe on the water in such a storm."

Then the East manido said, "Put the canoe on the water, and the waves will at once subside."

As soon as his father put the canoe on the water, the storm subsided.

It was about noon when this happened, and the distance to Madeline Island was about eighty miles, but they paddled so fast that they reached there before sundown. When they arrived, they found that the cousin had been dead four days, but the body had been kept so that they could see him.

The East manido told his father and mother and their friends not to weep for the young man. Then the next morning he told the people to make a long lodge extending east and west, such as is now used for the Midé. He showed them how to make it with the top open and the sides of birchbark and leaves, and he said that they must all bring tobacco and cooked food. In the center of the lodge he placed a Midé pole and told the Indians to sit in rows around the lodge; he also made a Midé drum and rattles, such as are still used.

West of the pole and a few feet away he placed the hewn coffin of the dead man; on the south side of the lodge he seated the relatives and friends. Then he told his father to take the Midé drum and sing.

The old man said, "I do not know how to sing."

His son said, "Just try; make the effort, and you will be able to sing."

Then the East manido spoke to the parents of the dead man and to his own parents, saying, "I am about to leave you. I will be absent four days. You must stay here continuously and do every day as I have told you to do today." The old man promised to sing the Midé songs and do everything as he had been told to do.

Then the East manido took vermilion paint and also blue paint and made marks across the faces of the parents of the man and also his own parents—streaks across their foreheads, the lowest red, then blue and red alternately. Then he started away and said he would return on the morning of the fourth day. He went through the air toward the eastern sky. They could see him go.

After he had disappeared, the old man took the Midé drum and sang more and more Midé songs. They came to him one after another. He was assisted by his son. Even while his son was absent, he directed him spiritually. During the four days that the East manido was absent the sun shone constantly. There was not a cloud, and the wind did not blow.

On the morning of the fourth day they looked toward the east and saw the sky streaked with colors like those he had painted on their foreheads. The Indians all looked in that direction with expectation. All this time the old man had been drumming and singing. A little before noon they heard a peculiar sound

Medicine Dance in the Midé Lodge (1853). Seth Eastman.

in the sky. It was from the East. Some one was calling "*Wa, hi, hi, hi,*" as they call in the Midé ceremony. They watched the sky and saw four Indians walking toward them in the sky, giving this call. Each Indian had a living otter in his hand.

The East manido came down to the Midé enclosure, lifted the drapery, and allowed the others to pass in. The four manido[g] came in and took their stand at the east end of the lodge. A little beyond the center was the coffin of hewn logs in which lay the body of the young man, who had now been dead eight days. The four manido[g] held the otters with the right hand near the head and the left hand below. These otters were their medicine bags.

The East manido stood first in the line. He began to sing, went halfway to the coffin, blew on his medicine bag, and shot from there toward the coffin. Then the top of the coffin burst open, and the East manido marched around the lodge and took his place at the end of the line. Then the next one, the South manido, did exactly as the East manido had done. When he had shot, the young man opened his eyes and breathed. Then the South manido took his position at the end of the line. Next came the West manido. When he had shot, the young man raised up and looked at the manido. Last came the North manido, and when he had shot, the young man rose up entirely well in every respect.

Then these four manido[g] began to talk to the Indians and to tell them that this was the method by which they were to treat the sick and the dead and that the East manido would instruct them in all they were to do.

Then these manido[g] told the Indians that they would never see them again. The manido[g] would never come to earth again, but the Indians must offer them gifts and sacrifices, which would be spiritually received. They must always remember that the Midé was given to them by the manido[g]. The last manido taught them the religion of the Midé and put souls in their bodies and arranged how these souls should live in the next world.

A great many times some of these Midé people have a trance in which they follow the spirit path and see their dead friends. They also receive messages in dreams. They are especially liable to do this when sorrowing for their friends.

It is told to Midé members that about halfway to the Spirit Land there is a punishment place where fire burns out all that is evil in them. Sometimes there is so little left of the person that he turns into a frog. There are many little frogs in that place, but the good pass through it unharmed. This is the only phase of punishment taught, except that if a person dies while drunk he will remain drunken forever and his punishment will be an eternal and unquenchable thirst.

Those initiated into the Midé are instructed how to lead a good life. These instructions are given only to the members. Less heed is paid to the instructions than in the old days, but very sick people are still restored by means of the Midé.

1905

Kegĕt′	Verily
Mijakwat′	The sky clears
Nimitĭg′wakĭk′	When my Midé drum
Medwe′undjĭn	Sounds
Nin′a	For me
Kegĕt′	Verily
A′nâtĭn	The waters are smooth
Nimitig′wakĭk	When my Midé drum
Medwe′undjĭn	Sounds
Nin′a	For me

Gegwédjiwébĭnûñ, *c.*1909

183

❖ LOVE AND MARRIAGE ❖

There are few happy, romantic love stories in traditional indigenous literatures. Partly this is because romantic love is the invention of the last few centuries after the troubadors, and most traditional stories are older than that. Marriage was about the power of the families involved and what each could gain from the mating of their children. Another reason there is a lack of Harlequin-romance Hollywoodized star-crossing is that these artists are better than that. They are interested in love not as romantic fulfillment, but as part of a complex web of relations to others and to the natural world. They are even more inspired when there is a problem because of some flaw in the lover or the lover's family: selfishness, greed, pride, lust. And they seldom indulge themselves with happy endings. Remember that many versions of the original story begin with a young woman kicked out of the upper world for having annoyed her powerful husband. Traditional Native literatures are folk literatures, and although the stories and music that arise from a culture may be beautiful, they are also frequently dark. In addition, because indigenous cultures were once inextricably interwoven with the natural world, there are numerous stories of humans mating with animals, with stars, and with powerful spirits, all of which convey lessons about what is possible and what should never be wished for lest it actually happen. The stories that follow will frustrate those who want to read about the further adventures of Hiawatha as a dashing hero with Minehaha as his doe-eyed, submissive Indian princess, but these are more interesting, as well as authentic. This is not to suggest Natives were not romantic. They developed a wooden flageolet used only for courting and were known for playing this flute and singing mournful love songs in a nasal drawl, sometimes an entire day. Young men tossed the spring wildflower now known as Dutchman's Breeches at young women or chewed the roots as a love charm, believing that women would be attracted by the scent. They did not, however, necessarily expect love to lead to marriage unless both sets of parents, and sometimes elders as well, consented. Frances Densmore, who noted that most love songs were plaintive, expressing sadness and disappointment, collected the following song from Mec´kawigábau (Stands Firmly) at Lac du Flambeau Reservation in Wisconsin at the turn of the twentieth century.

He is Gone

❖ ❖ ❖

Peeta Kway (Biiteikwe: Foam-woman) (The Tempest)
Unidentified Odawa

The point this storyteller makes is that arrogance of power about choosing a mate for a child will return to haunt even a sorceress. Indeed, the only control exerted in this story is by the spirits of Lake Michigan, presumably the underwater beings and perhaps the spirit of the islands who came growling through "Wassamo." A beautiful young woman imprisoned is a common folktale motif, but in European fairy tales she is usually a princess in a tower, not one on a raft that travels the lakes. It is no surprise that this story, which involves lake travel and storms, would be told by the Odawa, who were traders throughout the Great Lakes and beyond. They understood the capriciousness of the lake spirits, and they would have experienced weather so terrible that it inspired them to sing their war songs preparatory to drowning.

There once lived a woman called Monedo Kway[152] on the sand mountains called the Sleeping Bear of Lake Michigan, who had a daughter as beautiful as she was modest and discreet. Everybody spoke of the beauty of this daughter. She was so handsome that her mother feared she would be carried off, and to prevent it she put her in a box on the lake, which was tied by a long string to a stake on the shore. Every morning the mother pulled the box ashore and combed her daughter's long, shining hair, gave her food, and then put her out again on the lake.

One day a handsome young man chanced to come to the spot at the moment she was receiving her morning's attentions from her mother. He was struck with her beauty and immediately went home and told his feelings to his uncle, who was a great chief and a powerful magician. "My nephew," replied the old man, "go to the mother's lodge, and sit down in a modest manner, without saying a word. You need not ask her the question. But whatever you think she will understand, and what she thinks in answer you will also understand." The young man did so. He sat down, with his head dropped in a thoughtful manner, without uttering a word. He then thought, "I wish she would give me her daughter." Very soon he understood the mother's thoughts in reply.

"Give you my daughter?" thought she, "You! No, indeed, my daughter shall never marry you."

The young man went away and reported the result to his uncle. "Woman without good sense," said he, "who is she keeping her daughter for? Does she think she will marry the Mudjikewis?[153] Proud heart! We will try her magic skill, and see whether she can withstand our power."

The pride and haughtiness of the mother was talked of by the spirits living on that part of the lake. They met together and determined to exert their power in humbling her. For this purpose they resolved to raise a great storm on the lake. The water began to toss and roar, and the tempest became so severe that the string broke and the box floated off through the straits down Lake Huron and struck against the sandy shores at its outlet. The place where it struck was near the lodge of a superannuated old spirit called Ishkwon Daimeka Daimeka (Ishkwândemika: door-keeper), or the Keeper of the Gate of the Lakes. He opened the box and let out the beautiful daughter, took her into his lodge, and married her.

When the mother found that her daughter had been blown off by the storm, she raised very loud

185

cries and lamented exceedingly. This she continued to do for a long time and would not be comforted. At length, after two or three years, the spirits had pity on her and determined to raise another storm and bring her back. It was even a greater storm than the first, and when it began to wash away the ground and encroach on the lodge of Ishkwon Daimeka, she leaped into the box, and the waves carried her back to the very spot of her mother's lodge on the shore. Monedo Kway was overjoyed, but when she opened the box, she found that her daughter's beauty had almost all departed. However, she loved her still because she was her daughter and now thought of the young man who had made her the offer of marriage. She sent a formal message to him, but he had altered his mind for he knew that she had been the wife of another.

"I marry your daughter?" said he. "Your daughter? No, indeed! I shall never marry her."

The storm that brought her back was so strong and powerful that it tore away a large part of the shore of the lake and swept off Ishkwon Daimeka's lodge, the fragments of which, lodging in the straights, formed those beautiful islands which are scattered in the St. Clair and Detroit rivers. The old man himself was drowned, and his bones are buried under them. They heard him singing as he was driven off on a portion of his lodge, as if he had been called to testify his bravery and sing his war song at the stake.

1830s

Moowis, the Indian Coquette

Bame-wa-wa-ge-zhik-a-quay (Woman of Stars Rushing Through Sky, Jane Johnston Schoolcraft, 1800-1842), Chippewa

Bame-wa-wa-ge-zhik-a-quay

"Moowis" first appeared in *The Literary Voyageur* or *Muzzeniegun* (*mazina'igan*: book, paper, letter, magazine), a small, hand-written literary magazine the Schoolcrafts composed at Sault Ste. Marie during the winter of 1826-1827 and circulated to friends in Detroit and the East. The story is reprinted here in its earliest version, perhaps straight from the teller, who was probably O-shau-gusged-awayqua (The Woman of the Green Valley), Jane Johnston Schoolcraft's mother. According to many Native cultures, the woman who spurns her lover in this story is behaving badly, since her handsome beau would have never paid court to her if she had not encouraged him. She has led him to believe she will accept him; thus he comes to the family lodge at night and, as the custom, lifts the side and crawls in beside her. Normally, if a couple were still together in the morning, a marriage would be planned. This time, however, the flirting woman has evidently changed her mind and caused great embarrassment to her suitor, a loss of face he is not about to forgive. Schoolcraft described the name "Moowis," derived from the Ojibwe noun *mo,* meaning 'filth or excrement', as being one of the most derogative and offensive possible.

There was a village full of Indians, and a noted belle or *muhmuhdawgoqua* (*mamandaagokwe*: lady, well-groomed woman) was living there. A noted beau or muhmuhdawgoninnie (*mamandaaginini*: gentleman, well-groomed man) was there also. He and another young man went to court this young woman and laid down beside her, when she scratched the face of the handsome beau. He went home and would not rise till the family prepared to depart, and he would not then arise. They then left him, as he felt ashamed to be seen even by his own relations. It was winter, and the young man, his rival, who was his cousin, tried all he could to persuade him to go with the family, for it was now winter, but to no purpose, till the whole village had decamped and had gone away. He then rose and gathered all the bits of clothing and ornaments of beads and other things that had been left. He then made a coat and leggings of the same, nicely trimmed with the beads, and the suit was fine and complete. After making a pair of moccasins, nicely trimmed, he also made a bow and arrows. He then collected the dirt[154] of the village and filled the garments he had made, so as to appear as a man, and put the bow and arrows in its hands, and it came to life.

He then desired the dirt image to follow him to the camp of those who had left him, who thinking him dead by this time, were surprised to see him. One of the neighbors took in the dirt-man and entertained him. The belle saw them come and immediately fell in love with him. The family that took him in made a large fire to warm him, as it was winter. The image said to one of the children, "Sit between me and the fire; it is too hot," and the child did so, but all smelt the dirt. Some said, "Some one has trod on and brought in dirt." The master of the family said to the child sitting in front of the guest, "Get away from before our guest; you keep the heat from him." The boy answered saying, "He told me to sit between him and the fire." In the meantime, the belle wished the stranger would visit her.

The image went to his master, and they went out to different lodges, the image going as directed to the belle's. Towards morning, the image said to the young woman (as he had succeeded), "I must now go away," but she said, "I will go with you."

He said, "It is too far."

She answered, "It is not so far but that I can go with you."

He first went to the lodge where he was entertained and then to his master and told him of all that had happened and that he was going off with her. The young man thought it a pity she had treated him so and how sadly she would be punished. They went off, she following behind. He left her a great way behind, but she continued to follow him. When the sun rose high, she found one of his mittens and picked it up but, to her astonishment, found it full of dirt. She, however, took it and wiped it, and going on further, she found the other mitten in the same condition. She thought, "Fie!! Why does he do so?" thinking he dirtied in them. She kept finding different articles of his dress on the way all day in the same condition. He kept ahead of her till towards evening when the snow was like water, having melted by the heat of the day. No signs of her husband appearing, after having collected all the cloths that held him together, she began to cry, not knowing where to go as their track was lost on account of the snow's melting. She kept crying "Moowis has led me astray," and she kept singing and crying, *"Moowis nin ge won e win ig, ne won i win ig."*[155]

1826

Meskwaunkwāātar (The Red Head)

Tenskwatawa (One With Open Mouth, The Prophet, 1775-1836), Shawnee

Tenskwatawa (1830). George Catlin

This tale is fascinating and not only because of the magical elements. Since Natives do not normally have red hair, is this a magical element that confers power? Is this story related to the Red Horn hero cycle (p. 73) or to stories about one of the stars that shines red, such as Antares or Mercury? Is it related to the story of Mashkawshakwong (n. 131) and so part of another cycle of stories about heroes having red hair that is now lost? Does it imply European ancestry: for example, Thomas Jefferson, who had red hair and who initiated the policy of removal? Why does Meskwaunkwāātar consider himself too good for any woman, no matter how beautiful? Why does he reject his son, only to have second thoughts when it is too late?

If this tale refers to mixed-race culture, the elements would make historical sense. Native women who married white traders were often considered more privileged than women who married Natives—until the traders returned to their previous lives in Quebec or Europe and abandoned the women and their mixed-race children to "the country"—their relatives, who might not be able to take them in, or the officials at the fur trade post. Does Meskwaunkwāātar's change of heart at the end suggest that whites and traders would someday mourn what they had abandoned?

When C. C. Trowbridge gave his manuscript of eleven stories to the Wisconsin Historical Society in 1874, fifty years after the tales had been recorded, his letter noted that: "Through the aid of a chief, one of these old 'story tellers' would come with the Interpreter to the Indian office, and . . . announce his story and relate it with all the accompanying signs and gesticulations which one might expect to see on the stage. I stood at a desk and took down the words as the Interpreter uttered them. . . . There was never any subsequent copying or rewriting." The translator and Trowbridge also retained the songs that accompanied the story, a rare occurrence.

The narrator here is Tecumseh's brother, who told his stories long after his brother's death, but before he was removed to Kansas with his nation. He undoubtedly needed money, and the white people who had seized his country would pay. Given Tenskwatawa's imagination and flair for drama—two qualities that led to the destruction of his brother's carefully constructed alliance—it is not surprising that his stories are so good, incorporating archetypal traditional elements, such as an ugly woman winning a handsome husband by devious means, and innovative ones, such as the method by which the Itch Woman becomes pregnant. But like all of Tenskwatawa's stories, the ending is one of melancholy loss. It may be that Tenskwatawa was, once again, creating a parable of Native-white relations, where everyone would lose.

Kautaupee (Attention!)

There was a large town whose chief had a wife, a son, and four daughters. The chief himself and each of these relatives had red hair. The son of this chief (who was the youngest child) was a paragon of beauty. In those days the Indians erected a kind of scaffold in the wigwam, and this young man never suffered himself to be seen, except by his own family, but kept secreted upon this scaffold. The young maidens of the village had a strong curiosity to see him, which was increased by his efforts to prevent the gratification of their wishes. They often went to the wigwam in considerable numbers and begged the intervention of the mother's authority. But the young man would not be entreated or commanded, though in all other things he was a pattern of obedience. It was customary for the young females, when they had been foiled in an attempt to see this youth, to withdraw to the house of a poor woman who lived at some distance and who was sorely afflicted with a hereditary complaint like the itch. They called her Oamaak Oakwaa, or Itch Woman. Their object in visiting her was to obtain a little amusement after their defeat, and this consisted in teasing her. "Why don't you go and try to see this young man?" said they. "He will not see us, but perhaps he may exhibit himself to you."

The sisters of this young man were desirous that he should suffer himself to be seen by the young women and that he should form a matrimonial connection with one of them. The eldest sister went up to his scaffold one day and said to him, "Brother, now you have grown up and are of a proper age to marry, and I have come to talk with you. Your other sisters and myself are anxious that you should get a wife among these pretty girls who come daily to visit you. We are very lonely, because you never associate with us, and we should be happy if you would get a wife, so that we might have a brother and a sister-in-law to live with us." The young man did not answer his sister, and she descended. After this the young females began to come singly, and at each visit this elder sister would go up to the young man tell him that a young woman, naming her, had come to see him, and was in love with him. But he always answered, "You had better drive her away," and the sister was obliged to retire.

At length the time arrived when each of the women of the village had made the attempt and had been driven away. They met one day by common consent to relate to each other the events of their visit, and finding that every one had been treated like the others, they began to despair. "But," said one, "we have been unsuccessful, and now let us go to Oamaak Oakwaa. We are young and handsome, she ugly and diseased. But never mind that. We will persuade her to go and try her fortune, and we will have some fun of it."

So they went to the house of Oamaak Oakwaa. "Well," said one to her, "we have all been defeated in our attempts see young Meskwaunkwāātar, and we think that you may be successful if you should try."

"Oh no," said the other, "if you who are so young and beautiful have been rejected, how certain shall I be to meet the same fate?"

"But," returned the girl, "nothing is effected without some exertion. You but make the attempt and, if you fail, you will not be the only one."

In the night, after the departure of her visitors, Oamaak Oakwaa thought she would gratify her desire to see the fellow at least, though she could not hope for his affection. As the young man never descended from his scaffold unless when he could do it undiscovered, he kept a piece of cane, extending from the scaffold almost to ground, for urinating. Under this Oamaak Oakwaa reposed herself, and in the night she heard a noise.

It was Meskwaunkwāātar, who was about to urinate. She placed herself exactly under the cane—and when he was done, "Now," said she, "I know him, and I will go home."

In the morning the young women met and proceeded to the wigwam of the Itch Woman to learn how she had succeeded. "Well," said they, "did you go to try your fortune last night?"

"My friends," replied Oamaak Oakwaa, "you have kept me for a long time as the butt of your wit, and my infirmities and disease, so far from exciting your pity, have only been a source of amusement to you. I neither went to the young man's house, nor do I desire to go, for I am certain that his sisters would start at the sight of me and would drive me away. In mercy to me, do not speak on this subject again, for I have been a laughing stock for you long enough." The young women, touched with pity, engaged not to tease her any more.

Some time after this Oamaak Oakwaa discovered that she was pregnant. "Aha!" said she to herself, "now these young tormentors will have a new subject to tease me about. They will ask me who will be the father of my child. I certainly will be ashamed to confess that I slept under the reed, and I therefore must only acknowledge that a man will be his father."

One day, one of the young women resolved to go and see Oamaak Oakwaa, and when she arrived there, she discovered the change in her appearance. She said nothing until her return when she acquainted her young friend with the fact. The next day they all went to pay a visit. "Why, how you have grown!" said one to her. "What is the reason of this? You are certainly very fleshy." "Oh," said another, "I can guess the reason. You will have a little one, will you not?"

"Perhaps so," replied the other.

"By whom?" said the first.

"By a man, of course," answered Oamaak Oakwaa.

"What man?"

"That you are not to know now," said she, "but when the child is born, I will inform you. Until that time let me rest in peace, for no endeavours of yours will be able to attain your present object."

The visitors departed, and sometime after they went again to see the Itch woman. "Why," said they, "you have grown small since we saw you before. Have you had a child?"

"Yes, some months since."

"Where is he?"

"Dead."

"Where buried?"

"In the woods."

"How did he look?"

"Exactly like his father."

"Are you grieved for the loss of the child?"

"Sincerely grieved."

After offering some consolation to the mother, the young women departed. In a short time they repeated their visit, and they found Oamaak Oakwaa employed in husking corn. "Why," said they, "are your breasts so large? Certainly you must have deceived us about the death of your child or you would not now bear so much the appearance of a nurse."

"No," said the other, "though it is unaccountable, my breasts have been full of milk ever since his death."

Entertaining strong suspicions, the young women resolved to withdraw and hide themselves for the purpose of watching. They did so and, soon after they had gone, the mother arose and, having looked around to see that no one was near, she removed some corn leaves from the body of her infant who lay hid and took him up. At this the young females rushed suddenly upon her and reproached her with her deception. They saw that the child had red hair and knew he must be the issue of the father or son of the family of red heads. They demanded of the mother whether the young man who kept himself invisible was the father, and she answered in the affirmative.

Astonished at what they saw, they proceeded to the house of this young man and related to the sisters the circumstances of their visit. These communicated the information to their parents, who dispatched the eldest to see if the news were true. She returned with a confirmation of the report, and they sent her then to bring the mother to live with them. Oamaak Oakwaa set out, and the sister carried the child. Upon approaching house she ran with it to her sisters and then to her father and mother. They were convinced, and they embraced the child and its mother with affection. Then the elder sister took the child in her arms and went up to see her brother. "Look here!" said she. "I have a little nephew. Do you know him?"

"Know him! No."

"Why," replied she, "he is certainly your child. Every feature in your face is copied in his."

"He is not mine," said the young man. "Take him away. I have been imposed upon. I now recollect the circumstance of having used the reed, without hearing the usual noise. Take him away, I say."

She descended and, having told her sisters the result of her interviews, they wept profusely. At length they advised their sister to try once more, and if their brother did not acknowledge the child, they would adopt it and raise it. So she returned and entreated her brother to confess the fact, for that his sisters had determined to adopt the child if he rejected it.

"The child is not mine, and I repeat to you, send it away, and send away too his guilty mother. For my part I am so grieved at this circumstance that I am determined to leave my father's house and never be seen here again."

The young woman related to the mother of the child what she had heard, and Oamaak Oakwaa departed with a sorrowful heart. "Ah my dear infant," said she, "your father has determined to leave us, but we will follow him closely."

On the following day the young man prepared his pack and set out toward the east, but discovering soon that the object of his hate lived in that direction, he turned about and proceeded westward.[156] As soon as Oamaak Oakwaa heard of his departure she took her infant and followed him. In the evening he encamped, and not long after his encampment, Oamaak Oakwaa came up. "What do you want here?" said he. "Cannot I get rid of you in any way?"

"Alas! no, Meskwaunkwāātar," said she. "Your little child cried so much at your departure that I was compelled to follow you."

"Well," replied he, "you will not have that excuse again." At this he struck them on the head with his tomahawk and killed them. In the morning he rose and left his encampment in high spirits. About an hour after his departure Oamaak Okwaa and her little boy came to life, and she was surprised to see that she had not any appearance of the disease which had troubled her so much, but that she was fair, beautiful, and that her little child had grown very much. She thought this a precursor of good fortune and, having dressed herself and boy very neatly, she proceeded in quest of his father. At night she arrived at his camp.

"Are you here again," said he, "to trouble me?"

"How can it be otherwise," answered Oamaak Oakwaa. "Your boy looked so sweetly when I awoke in the morning that I thought his tears might now have some effect upon your hard heart."

"To convince you that they have not," said he, "take that!" And he struck her again with his tomahawk and killed her. Some time after he killed the boy and, putting the bodies together, he built a fire and burned them. In the morning he was pleased to see that all was burned except a few bones. He thought he had taken a course which could not fail to rid him of his troubles.

But after he had been gone some time, the mother and her son rose like a phoenix from the ashes, more beautiful than ever. Oamaak Oakwaa combed the boy's beautiful long hair and, having washed herself, she commenced the pursuit. "Now," she [said] to her son, "your father will reach a village today, and there he will marry two wives. As we pass that village it will be necessary for you to present some wampum to your grandfathers and also some pigeons for a feast of soup."

Presently, Oamaak Oakwaa called upon Metholetshaakēē (Thunderbird), and they spread their blankets upon his back, got upon him, and continued their route. When the bird had risen into the air, the mother said to the son that she would begin to sing as soon as they arrived in the village and that they would pass directly by the wigwam in which his father would be. When they arrived there, they would not soar in the air but would go near the earth that they might be seen, and when directly opposite the wigwam of his father, he must spit upon the ground, and his spittle would drop down in wampum. Then he must blow with his breath four times, and flocks of pigeons would fall for grandfather in the village.

Meskwaunkwāātar made the best of his way to the village, where he married two wives as Oamaak Oakwaa had predicted. He was seated between them, and they were employed in combing his long beautiful hair, which was parted and divided to their hands, when Oamaak Oakwaa and her son arrived on the back of Metholetshaakēē.

She commenced her song:

Meskwaunkwāātar	Red Head
Meskwaunkwāātar	Red Head
Meskwaunkwāātar	Red Head
Nau wāū tshee,	He is going to
au pōā shee waa	a present
tar kōā lee—,	give—,
Meskwaunkwāātar	Red Head
Meskwaunkwāātar	Red Head
Nau wāū tshee	He is going to
au pōā shee waa,	a present

tar kōā lee—,	give—,
Meskwaunkwāātar	Red Head
Meskwaunkwāātar	Red Head

Meskwaunkwāātar heard the singing and told his wives to stop, for somebody called him, but they saw he was mistaken and kept hold of his hair, fearing to have him go. He listened again, and the singer approached. Certain that he was called, he pushed his wives away and rushed out of the wigwam. He saw Oamaak Oakwaa and her son passing along just far enough from the earth to admit of his reaching the feathers of the bird. He ran to meet them. "Oh my dear wife and my dear son, how glad I am to see you. I knew you were coming! Oh my dear wife, permit me to take my son and talk to him."

But they passed on without heeding him and, when they arrived at the middle of the village, the boy spit to the ground, and the earth was covered with wampum for some distance around. The villagers scrambled about to collect it. In a short time they saw large flocks of pigeons flying close to them, and they set themselves about killing them with clubs.

Then the travelers changed their song, repeating:

Meskwaunkwāātar	Red Head
Meskwaunkwāātar	Red Head
Meskwaunkwāātar	Red Head
Me shāū,	He has
au pōā shee waa	a present
tar kōā lee—,	given—,
Meskwaunkwāātar	Red Head
Meskwaunkwāātar	Red Head
Meskwaunkwāātar	Red Head
Me shāū,	He has
au pōā shee waa	a present
tar kōā lee—,	given—,
Meskwaunkwāātar	Red Head
Meskwaunkwāātar	Red Head
Meskwaunkwāātar	Red Head
Me shāū,	He has
au pōā shee waa	a present
tar kōā lee—,	given—

All this time Meskwaunkwāātar was following the mother and her son and entreating them to stop a moment, only one moment, to speak to him. But they did not regard him. The woman proceeded, singing, "When Meskwaunkwāātar left his village, he said he would not come back."

"No, my dear wife," said he, "I only came to make a visit. Do stop for me!"

But she continued on, and at length arrived at a large lake. Her bird flew across, and Meskwaunkwäätar turned into a Bluejay and followed her. She sank in the middle of the lake with her little son and turned into a shell. Meskwaunkwäätar turned back at this and with the greatest difficulty reached the shore whence he started. There he remained, looking at the lake and weeping. At length he concluded to have a dance, and he danced some time and then flew away into the air.

The tears of Meskwaunkwäätar are still to be seen under the eyes of the blue jay, in little black marks.

1820s

Ogimawkwe Mitigwäki (Queen of the Woods)

Simon Pokagon (Pakâkwaan, His Rib,[157] c.1830-1899), Potawatomi

Simon Pokagon

By the time Simon Pokagon wrote the first novel by a Native, the Pokagon band had forsaken traditional governance and become citizens, owning their lands individually in southwest Michigan. Their former chief, Leopold, Simon's father, had managed his band's relationship with the USA with skill and cunning, as their patrimony, which included the southwestern part of Michigan and Chicago, was taken away by treaties. From the old Pokagon village near South Bend, Indiana, he took his band to Michigan, and taught them how to be Catholic, Christianized farmers, thus managing to escape relocation west.

Simon was educated at Notre Dame, Oberlin, and Twinsburg, Ohio. He read Greek and was a trained musician, but he spent most of his life attempting to get the USA to pay the three cents per acre it had agreed upon when it took the Pokagon lands. He was finally successful shortly before the Chicago World's Fair of 1893, where he was able to give a formal deed, a bit ironically, to the mayor of Chicago. Pokagon, like his Odawa contemporary and schoolmate, Andrew Blackbird, had grown up in a still-pristine world and lived to see it despoiled by unrestrained white settlement and industrialization after the Civil War.

When a newspaper editor urged him to write, Pokagon began *Queen of the Woods,* a semiautobiographical novel about a summer in the woods. With it he attempted to preserve the language he had grown up speaking, teach some episodes of his nation's history, and campaign against alcohol use. *Queen* combines the format of a classic, nineteenth-century temperance novel with a Native romance set in a pristine forest, concluded by several chapters of direct address to the reader about the evils of drink. Although the novel avoids the painful truth, Pokagon's beloved first wife, the heroine Lonidaw of *Queen of the Woods,* died from alcoholism at thirty-five. He did not live to see his novel published, but it was brought out in several editions after his death in 1899.[158]

On my return home from Twinsburg, Ohio, where I had attended the white man's school for several years, I had an innate desire to retire into the wild woods, far from the haunts of civilization, and there enjoy myself with bow and arrow, hook and line, as I had done before going to school. Judging from my returning love of the chase and from various conversations with educated people of the white race, I have come to the conclusion that there is a charm about hunting and fishing, planted deep in the human heart by nature's own hand, that requires but little cultivation to lead the best educated of even the most civilized races to engage heartily in the sport. Hence I have been forced to the conclusion that when our children are educated and return from school to live among their own people, unless places can be secured for them away from the influences that cluster about them, the result of their education must necessarily in some cases prove disappointing to those who have labored so ardently in their behalf. In fact I have personal knowledge of a few cases where educated children of our race, instead of influencing their own people to a higher standard of civilization, have themselves fallen back into the ancient customs of their own people. This, however, should in no wise discourage our educators, or be regarded by them as an impeachment of the possibilities of our children; for I believe with all my heart that if white children were placed under like conditions and circumstances, the result would be similar.

I knew no other language but my mother tongue until past twelve years of age. In those days I took great pleasure in hunting, fishing, and trapping with an old man by the name of Bertrand.[159] There are many white men yet living who were personally acquainted with that remarkable man. He was a person well calculated to please and instruct a boy in his knowledge of the habits of animals and of places and things with which he was personally acquainted. He was of medium height, uncommonly broad shouldered, and well developed in body and limb.

When laughing, or excited in talking, he opened his mouth so wide that his great double teeth could be plainly seen. He always appeared in the best of spirits, having the most hearty laugh of any man I ever knew. As old as I now am, I would walk twenty miles to hear such a laugh. His skin was dark for an Indian, notwithstanding he claimed to be one-quarter French. When speaking of himself, he always talked as if he was a white man. On public occasions among our people, owing to his strength and courage, he was regarded as a sort of police force. I recollect one day during a feast some *au-qua[-wog]* (women) came running to him in great excitement, telling him some half-breeds had brought *awsh-kon-tay-ne-besh* (firewater) with them, and were giving some to little boys. He started for them on the double-quick, and before they realized what he was doing, he seized all their bottles and broke them against a rock. There were three in the party, and they all rushed for him with sticks and clubs. He knocked each one down in turn with a single blow of his fist. As they lay on the ground, a white man present said, "Bertrand, you struck those Indians awful blows." The old man straightened himself up, saying, *"Ae* (Yes) me tells you me did. *Au-nish-naw-be-og* (Indians) hab no idea how hard a white man can strike." For that timely reproof he was given a place at the head of the feast. He prided himself in speaking English, which he always tried to do if any were present who he thought understood the language. Among his white neighbors, he was always referred to as "the 'Injun' who murders the English language."

A short time after my return from school I called on the old man. I told him that I had just returned from three years' hard study and would like to have him take mother and me to some wild retreat where I might spend my vacation in hunting and fishing. He seemed highly pleased with the idea and told me that he knew of a place up the big "Sebe" (river) that could be reached by boat in less than one day's sail, where there was an old abandoned wigwam.[160] It was the wildest place that could be found within fifty miles, and there was an abundance of game and fish. Arrangements were made at once, whereby mother and I were to bring our goods to the river on the following day, where he would meet us with his big dugout canoe.

As agreed, we all met on the banks of the beautiful "Sebe," loaded our goods into the boat, and pushed off from shore, he at the paddle and I at the helm, with mother and Maw-kaw (Maw-kwa: Bear?), our family dog, as passengers. About noon, as we were quietly making our way up the stream, we caught sight of *mi-tchi-sib-wan* (an osprey), with folded wings plunging headlong with the roar of a rocket into the water a short distance from *o-tchi-mân* (our boat), and while yet the water surged and foamed where she went down, she arose to the surface and tried to rise in air but could not, floundering about in a zigzag course toward the shore. We gave chase with the boat, and as we overhauled the struggling bird we saw, to our surprise, that she had clutched her claws into the back and near the head of *ogaw* (a pickerel), so large that she could not raise it above the surface of the water and was trying in vain to loosen her hold. The old man seized his dipnet, scooped up both osprey and fish, and dropped them into the bottom of the boat. He then grasped with all his might into the gills of the fish, while I seized the osprey with both hands about the wings. We then pulled the unhappy pair apart, while the old dog continued to whine as if a tom-tom was being beaten in his ears.

"Vell, vell," exclaimed the old man, "I kakkalate dat meby dis chase, and the funny catch, do make you feel gooder than to be at school good many years." He then dropped the fish into the bottom of the boat and asked, "Sime, what one of these two do you feel badest for and villing to let go—dat bud or de vish?" I replied, "The bird" of course." He then asked *nin-gaw* (my mother) the same question, who replied likewise. He then said, "Dat be right; it's not in human nature to veel bad for vishes, so we will keep de vish and eat 'im tonight, and let de bud go."

I then asked, "Can you explain why we feel more sorrow *for bin-es-si* (the bird), when in fact she got fast in trying to kill the innocent *gi-go* (fish)?"

He replied, "I tink meby I can. You know, Sime, dat de vish hab no love at all; da eat urn up one an uder—eat urn their own shilren—and we like to eat urn vish, but no like urn osprey." He then grasped hold of the bird's tail-feathers and pulled them out, saying, "Now let 'im go; des quills am good for your cap like um *mi-gi-si mig-wan* (eagle quills). The old man now became much excited and, as we rode along, he would point to where he had trapped *jang-we-she* (mink), *wa-jask* (muskrat), and *a-se-pan* (coon). At times he would laugh out most heartily in telling how some animals had outwitted him, springing and upsetting his traps, and then, in telling how he had finally succeeded in catching them, would again laugh more heartily than before.

Just as *gi-siss* (the sun) was going down, we reached our landing place. The shore on either side was fringed with rushes, flags, and goldenrod, and grasses tall between; and scattered here and there wild roses breathed their rich perfume, scenting the evening air. Leaving *tchi-mân* (the boat), we ascended the banks of the stream and went some distance round an abrupt headland, beyond which lay *o-ga-be-shi-win-aki* (our camping ground).

It was indeed a strange, romantic place. A great wigwam there stood. Apparently it had been located so as not to be seen by any that might pass up and down *se-bin* (*sípe*: the stream). It was built of logs of giant size and, one might well conclude, was intended for wigwam and *wa-ka-i-gan* (fort) as well. The grounds about were carpeted with *mash-kos-su* (grass). The underbrush had been cleared off years before, leaving the towering trees, which hung their archways of green high above the lawn. As we opened the door of the deserted wigwam, it creaked on its hinges like the cry of murder which *pas-we-we* (echo) repeated in one continuous wailing through *mi-tig[-og]* (the woods). Old dog Maw-kaw, startled at the sound, bellowed out a howl-like cry which, intermixed with the shrieking roar, died away, leaving a strange impress on the soul! Slowly we entered in. Birds flew all about the spacious room, chirping a wild alarm and brushing our heads with their wings to frighten us away. *O-was-is-swan* (their nests) hung from roof and wall throughout the room. Soon they quieted down, taking to their nests again, but watched us with suspicious eyes. In one corner of the room, was *mi-chi bo-daw-wan* (a huge fireplace) with chimney built of *mit-i-gons* (sticks) and *wa-bi-gan* (clay) in it; we built a hasty *ish-ko´-te* (fire).

Unlike most men of our race, the old man would dress *gi-go* (the fish) and cook it, too. This, with *maw-da-min* (corn cakes) and salt, furnished a splendid meal of which we ate, thanking the Great Spirit, the cook, and the bird that caught the fish. As night came on, with our blankets wrapped about us, we all lay down to sleep. By the embers' red light, bats were seen flitting about the spacious room, dodging here and there and then out of sight, while with a soft, whizzing sound, *ja-gash-[k]ân-dawe* (flying squirrels) passed and repassed above us in curved lines from wall to wall.

It was indeed an ancient, novel place. Long before the break of day, *ak-i-we-si* (the old man) rose and started homeward, as he had promised his family he would be home at noon. I seized my bow and arrows, telling mother I might not be in until after sunrise. "Go on," she said, "only leave Maw-kaw with me." After seeing the old man safely off *pin-dig-ki tchi-mân* (in his boat), I carefully climbed to the top of the high headland we had passed around the night before, which like a sentinel for untold centuries had guarded the river's valley deep below. I there found an open field, which, from all appearance, had been used during the Indian wars as a lookout for enemies. Here by the faint light of the moon and the glimmering of the stars I dimly surveyed the wild region about me.

It was a beautiful, quiet morning. All nature slept, until the morning feathered bells rang out: "Whippoorwill! Whippoorwill! Whippoorwill!" Slowly, but surely, the curtain of night was lifted from the stage of the woodland theater; above me, one by one the stars hid themselves, the moon grew pale, while all the warblers of the woods opened their matinee, free to all, chanting from unnumbered throats, "Rejoice and praise Him! Rejoice and be glad! Rejoice! Rejoice!" Just as the sun tinged the topmost branches of the highland trees, a white fog-cloud appeared above the winding river as far as eye could reach. It looked as though the stream had risen from its ancient bed and was floating in midair. As in wonder and admiration I gazed upon it, a gentle breeze bore it away far beyond the valley from which it arose; and yet it still retained all the curves and angles of the stream until it passed beyond my sight.

While enraptured, there I stood, beholding the beautiful scenery hung by Nature's hand and listening to the woodland choir, loud the alarm birds (blue jays) screamed out their hawklike cries. Abruptly the concert closed, and all was still. Looking up, I saw advancing toward me across the open field a herd of deer, feeding as they came. Quietly stepping behind a bush, I selected the patriarch of the flock and, as he passed broadside before me, in three heartbeats of time, I three successive arrows sent into his side. He ran one breath and, headlong, dying fell. Quickly bleeding and disemboweling him, I carried him across my shoulders down a trail through the woods toward the old wigwam. Coming to *mi-tig* (a fallen tree) of monstrous size, I laid the deer thereon; and while resting there, I heard the sweet voice of my mother, singing in her native tongue:

> From Greenland's icy mountains,
> From India's coral strand,
> Where Afric's sunny fountains,
> Roll down their golden sand,
> From many an ancient river,
> From many a palmy plain,
> They call us to deliver
> Their land from error's chain.[161]

I had heard her sing it many times before, but never did it reach my soul so touchingly as then. Stooping low so as to get a view below the branches of the trees, I could plainly see the old log cabin, and my mother in front of it. I listened until she sang the whole of that beautiful hymn. It so filled my heart with love divine that in my soul I saw Jesus standing with one hand on the sinner's head and the other resting on the throne of the Great Spirit, saying, "Come unto me."

After singing each stanza, and sometimes when half-finished, she would pause and listen, as if she loved to hear the echoing angel of the woods join in the refrain. As she closed the sacred song, I approached cautiously behind her and threw my burden down. She screamed aloud and, turning quickly around, gazed a moment in silence, then laughed until all the woods replied. She took hold of the arrows, still fast in his side; praised me for my unforgotten skill; would feel his newly grown, soft, and velvet horns, exclaiming, "*Kwaw-notch, kwaw-notch maw-mawsh-kay-she* (*gwanâtch wâwâshkeshi*: beautiful, beautiful deer!) How could you have *o-daw* (the heart) to take *nin bim-á-dis-win* (*obimádiswin*: his life)? After breakfast she skinned the deer and prepared the meat for jerked venison for future use, according to our ancient custom.

While living in that secluded place, I felt a freedom and independence unknown to civilization. There, undisturbed, I could hunt and fish, contemplating the romantic beauties and wonderful grandeur of the forests about me. While in communion with the Great Spirit, I could feel, as my fathers had before me, that I was chief of all I surveyed.

Late in summer, he meets Lonidaw and her white deer on the shore of the river, then finds their camp and meets her mother, who agrees to accompany them back to his camp. The albino deer—which is very rare—is always sacred. They are called *Manito sucsee wabe* (Minéto wâbisúkisì: the sacred white deer). This deer is sacred not only because of his color,

198

but also because of his devoted attention to Lonidaw, symbolizing her association with everything that is pure about unspoiled nature.

On reaching the boat, launched by the river's shore, Lonidaw handed her mother the ball of twine which she had brought. She quickly tied the cord to the bow of the boat, carefully got in and, while Lonidaw held the ball, she pushed out into the stream. I now first knew why the twine was brought. The maid I now left alone. With none to hear except the deer, our words were very few and simple, but our thoughts were many and filled in eloquence. Soon the mother reached the other shore, and with her hand a motion made for Lonidaw to wind up the cord. In her nimble hands the ball spun like a top; the boat returning, as if impelled by some unseen power divine, soon reached our landing place. I now reached for the maiden's hand to help her into the boat. The watchful deer sprang forward, as if to help her too; but quick as *she-gos-see* (the weasel) she bounded in herself, handed me the ball, grasped the oar, and like *wâ-bi-si* (the swan) pushed out into the stream.

The deer gave one whistling, snorting snuff, then bounded twenty feet or more into the stream, swimming close behind the boat until it reached the other shore. Pulling back the boat with the cord, soon I crossed and joined them on the other side. As we neared our wigwam summer home, our dog, old Maw-kaw, met us on the trail, with hair along his back upturned and threatening growl, came near the maid, and nosed her hand. The mother stopped, and standing still she asked, *"Ne-daw-yo-em-e-waw-au-nish?"* (Is that your dog?) *"Ae,"* I replied. She then said, "I fear *msaw-mawsh-kay-she saw au-ni-moosh"* (The deer will kill him).[162] *"Yaw-kaw"* (O no), I said, "He is *maw-in-gawn au-ni-moosh* (a wolf dog) and has killed many a deer and wolf." While yet I spoke, the deer sprang at the dog as fiercely as the mountain *pe-zhen* (*bizhiw*: lynx) that guards her young, striking him with his three-pronged antlers square in the breast; and as he turned to run, gave him another cruel punch full in the rear, which sent him yelping into the house. My mother heard the fearful yells and thought perhaps *me-she-be-she* (*mishibizhiw*: a panther) had pounced upon the dog and quickly shut to the door. I opened it, and we three, without a word, walked into the room. She gazed at them in wonder and surprise, thinking perhaps it might be that I had caught the maiden mocking spirit of the woods beyond the river, with some other being of her kind, together with the sacred deer of white, which now stood just outside the open door with head drooped low, as if expecting to give the skulking dog another punch.

Fearing the deer might venture in, quickly I shut to the door, saying, *"O-gaw-she-maw me-de-mo-gay?"* (Do you know this old lady?)

She gazed at her with the most inquiring look I ever saw, then rushed into her arms, exclaiming, "My dear Ko-bun-da!" while the stranger answered back, "My dear Ka-law-na! My dear Ka-law-na, are we dreaming or are we both awake?" Unclasping their embrace, my mother threw her arms about the daughter's neck, while her mother threw hers around mine, *o-dgin-di-win* (kissing) us as if we were but little children. Then both sat down and wept with joy together.

Lonidaw and I also wept, to see them weep. At last, looking upward through her tears, my mother said, "Ko-bun-da, do tell me where you have been and all about it; for I was told time and time again that you perished in *mit-a-gog* (the woods) near Ni-jo-de sa-ga-ig-an-og (Twin Lake[s]) near Menominee village in trying to hide from the United States troops the time they so shamefully captured the most of our people, forcing them toward the setting gesis (sun) beyond the great river."

We all reclined on our blankets to listen to her story. She began: "On the morning of that sad day at Twin Lakes, of which you speak, Sin-a-gaw my husband, told me that a stranger had been around, informing all the *Au-nish-naw-bay-og* (Indians) that our Christian priest wished all the tribe to meet him at *Au-naw-ma-we-gaw-ming* (praying house: wigwam church) and desired me to go with him. But being *au-kee-zee* (sick), I remained at home. He faithfully promised me he would be back by the middle of the afternoon, but night came on, and neither he nor any of those I had seen going to church in the morning had yet returned. I felt impressed, deep down in my heart, that something awful had happened. As I was sadly brooding over my thoughts, the door was wide upon flung, and in came a little boy of the white race, who was a playmate of *au-nish-naw-be o-nid-[j]an-is[-og]* (Indian children) and who loved Sin-a-gaw, my husband, and me. As he rushed into our wigwam, all out of breath, he was crying, 'Murder! Murder! Murder! O dear, dear!' He could say no more, falling exhausted on the floor. In a few moments he raised up and stammered out, 'O dear, dear! Lots and lots of white men I never seed before, all dressed in blue, have got all the Injuns in the church tied together with big strings, like ponies, and are going to kill all of urn. O dear, dear! Do run quick and hide!' I said, 'Hold on, Skiney. Do tell me if you saw Sin-a-gaw among them?' He replied, 'O dear! Yes, me did; and me hear somebody say, "Skiney, come here," and it was Sin-a-gaw. And he talk low and say to tell you to hide in the big woods a few days, then go to the old Ottawa trapper's wigwam, and if he not get killed, meby he get loose and find you. Do run quick! Dear, dear, they will get us! Me do wish I could kill urn all.'"

I gathered up what few clothes I had and left our home, never to return. I ran across the great trail to your wigwam; no one was there. I heard several going past on the run. I heard someone speak in a heavy voice. It was Go-bo. I never heard him talk excited before. He said the whole country was alive with white warriors catching *Au-nish-naw-bay-og*, to kill or drive them toward the setting sun. All doubts of Skiney's story were now removed. I ran north into a desolate swamp, which I had been taught from infancy was the home of *jin-awe* (rattlesnakes) and *maw-in-gwan-og* (wolves), and there hid myself in the hollow of a fallen sycamore tree. It was an awful *ne-tchi-wad te-be-kut* (stormy night); wolves howled in the distance, as if following on my track; *me-she-be-she* (a panther) near by me screamed like a woman in dire distress. In the morning Loda, that girl, was born! I there remained one week, keeping *aw-be-non-tchi* (the infant) wrapped up as best I could. On the morning of the seventh sun I started northward to find the old trapper. I was weak and hungry, as all I had eaten while there was a small piece of jerked venison not larger than my hand and a few beechnuts; but, thanks to the Great Spirit, I found in my journey an *o-me-me* (a young pigeon) so fat it could not fly. I sat down on a log and ate it raw. It tasted good and gave me strength. In four days I reached the old trapper's wigwam, where myself and child were kindly cared for. I there first learned the fate of my people and was told *tchi ki das-sos* (that you were trapped) in the church with many others and driven far westward.

THE TRAIL OF DEATH

Removal of the Indiana Pottawatomi in 1838, drawn by George Winter, an eyewitness.

By the 1830s, the Potawatomi had signed several treaties with the USA, and some had already begun the process of removal to the West. The Prairie Potawatomi from Wisconsin and Illinois were moved to western Iowa. A large tract in Kansas near the Osage River was assigned to the others, but there were already problems with white squatters there. Several bands had remained in southern Michigan and northern Indiana, unwilling to surrender their lands, livelihood, and the graves of their ancestors.

One of these bands was led by [one called] Menominee, who was a Christian and encouraged his people to follow the leadership of the young Catholic priest, Benjamin Marie Petit, who served at Chichipe Outipe [Duck Head], the Menominee Mission chapel. By 1838 there was a sizable settlement around the chapel at Twin Lakes, near present-day Plymouth, Indiana, and Father Petit reported nearly a thousand Natives who looked to the mission for guidance.

But even though Menominee had refused to sign away his people's lands, drunken younger band leaders did it for him, ceding the last twenty-two sections to the United States. On August 5, the Indian agent came to try to coerce Menominee to remove by order of the president of the United States. Menominee replied that:

> He, like me, has been imposed upon. He does not know that you made my young chiefs drunk
> and got their consent and pretended to get mine. He does not know that I refused to sell my lands
> and still refuse. He would not by force drive me from my home, the graves of my tribe, and my

children who have gone to the Great Spirit, nor allow you to tell me that your braves will take me tied like a dog, if he knew the truth. My brothers, the President is just, but he listens to the word of young chiefs who have lied. When he knows the truth, he will leave me to my own. I have not sold my lands. I will not sell them. I have not signed any treaty and will not sign any. I am not going to leave my lands, and I do not want to hear any more about it.

On September 4, 1838, the Indian agent came back with the militia. Father Petit was allowed to hold a final service in the chapel; the worshipers made a last visit to their cemetery. Then, while the band watched, the Indian agent torched their homes and crops. After packing sixty wagons with children and the infirm, they started the 660-mile march to Kansas. Menominee, after trying to hold off the troops with a dagger, was indeed tied like a dog, bound hand and foot, and tossed in a wagon. Their route led through the Wabash valley, a country denuded by drought. There was little water, and most of it was contaminated, leading to typhoid fever. As more and more Natives became sick and could no longer walk, they were left behind, since there were no more wagons. Progress was painfully slow, and there were burials at every stop.

Father Petit was finally released from church business and able to join them near present-day Danville, Illinois, fifteen days after the march began. He wrote: "Early the next morning they heaped the Indians into the baggage wagons, and everybody mounted. At our departure, Judge Polke, chief conductor, came to present me with a horse which the government had procured from an Indian for my use along the way. At the same time, the Indian approached me and said, "My father, I give it to you, saddled and bridled." The sad procession moved on across Illinois, past Springfield and Jacksonville, crossed the Mississippi at Alton, crossed the Missouri at Independence, and finally reached the Osage River in eastern Kansas sixty days after they began. Only about 650 had survived, to reach Kansas without shelter or food at the beginning of winter. Father Petit, never physically strong, collapsed, and Abram Burnett, one of the band, carried him in his arms to the Jesuits in St. Louis, where he died. Menominee went with his people into captivity and left no further record.[163]

▲▲
▼▼

"Late in wintertime my husband returned and found me and our little one. He had traveled on foot and alone across the great plains from far beyond the 'father of waters' and was so broken down in health and spirits that he seemed all unlike himself. He sought to gain new life by drinking 'firewater' more and more; but alas, in a few years it consumed him, and he faded and fell, as fall the leaves in autumn time. I have lived since then among the Ottawas up the great Sebe. I learned of them to do all kinds of bark and braid work, by which Loda and I have supported ourselves. Although she came to me in the most desolate wilderness of sorrow, yet she has been my only joy and hope. I often think the circumstances under which she was born in the swamp, amid the screams of birds of prey and the cries of beasts and songs of singing birds, had much to do with her wonderful gifts. She can imitate all creatures from the mouse to the elk, from the bee to the swan."

As she said these last words, Lonidaw smiled on me and, placing one hand over *nin o-daw* (her heart) said, *"E-we-nin"* (That's me). We two listened until after midnight to their strange stories of sunshine and of storm. I then engaged the attention of the beautiful girl, as I was indeed anxious to have many things explained that were hidden in mystery. I inquired for what reason she and her mother were camping across the Sebe? She replied, "We are making mats and rugs to sell to white people. The finest flags and rushes we have ever found grow on *wau-bawsh-k[e]-ke an-a[w]-kan-nash* (a marsh of rushes) close by." I then inquired why it was she always went up and never down the stream. "Well," said she, "in gathering flags and rushes for our work, I went up Sebe on account of the beautiful scenery along the shore and also that my deer might have good feeding grounds; but on returning home with my flags and rushes I always take another course along the old trail, which is much nearer.

I now inquired where she got the snow-white deer. "I will tell you all about that," she replied. "Some four years ago, while I was passing through the woods, I affrighted *ki nin-ge suc-see* (the mother deer)[164] by the trail side, which ran away and left *o-kit-a-ga-kons[-i-ma]* (her fawn) when first born. It mistook me for its mother. I tried to drive it back; still it continued to follow me. I then tried to run away from it but could not, and it followed me home. We raised it on pony's milk," said she, "and you may think it strange, but if I pet *aw-es-si* (any animal) or human kind in the presence of that deer, he will pitch at them with all his might. In fact, he drove from our camp the pony that had nursed him because I sometimes petted her. "

I said, "He must love you."

"Yes," she said, "I think he does; and although he has never told *ki-sa-gi[-i-]a* (his love, he loves you) in words, yet by his acts he has shown the secret of his heart; and if you had taken my hand last night, as you attempted to do, to help me into *tchi-mân* (the boat), I believe, as I live, he would have served you as he did *ki[t-]an-i-mos* (your dog) a short time after.

I then asked, "What did your mother and you think yesterday, when I came to your wigwam and through mistake let broad daylight in upon you?"

She answered, "We were surprised but felt quite safe from the fact that the deer followed you in, taking his place by my side. We well knew if you undertook to do us harm, you would encounter *ki[t]-esh-ka-nog* (*odeshkanog*: his antlers) in a manner you did not expect." She further said, "When you met me at *se-bin[g]* (the river) the morning before, for the first time, I felt mistrustful of you and would have left at once, only I expected my deer every moment, as he was feeding just below; but as he did not come on as I expected, I hastened away; but he overtook me before I reached the marsh."

With some reluctance I now asked, "What did you tell your mother about me on your return home?"

"Ek-waw, ek-waw!" (Well, well!) said she, with a curious smile, "I told her I met *osh-ki-naw-we* (a young man) *a-gam-ing Se-be* (near the river's shore) *a-gwi-win-on do-wan o-gi-maw* (dressed like a chief), *gi-git mo-ja-gis-sin-on i-go* (and he spoke kindly to me),[165] *ma-kaw tchi min-bim ib-a-to* (*tchi dash nin-gimi nagana*: but that I ran away and left him), and after I had gotten away, I began to wish I had stayed longer and learned more about him, for he could speak the Ottawa and Pottawattami *o-daw-naw-naw* (*o-de-naw-ne-waw*: tongue)."

"Well, what did *ki[t-]o-gaw[-]sha-maw ik-kit* (*kinga-shi-maw iwa*: your mother say)?"

She said, "You did *kit-chi* (right), Loda, *mis-so-ke pa-was* (keep away) from such *nidg au-nish-nobe-og* (widj-au-nish-no-be-og: fellows); *ne-sa-ge-ze ke-te-mesh-ke mau-tchi osh-kee-[n]aw-waw* (no doubt he is a drinking, lazy, bad young man)."

We all talked on and on, regardless of night or time, until interrupted by harsh gratings on the door, which, with its squeaking wail, wide open flung, followed by the deer, which put his fore feet just inside the door, and there stood still. Fearing his jealous heart, I quickly left Lonidaw's side, while she sprang to his head. Pressing her hands against his face, she said, "*I-ja-pik-wan, i-ja-pik-wan* (Go back, go back)[166] *mau-tchi maw-mawsh-ka-she* (*mau-tchi wâwâshkeshi*: bad deer); *i-ja-pik-wan, i-ja-pik-wan* (*ajeshkâ, ajeshkâ*: go back, go back)."

He backed outside the open door and she, too, went out. Her mother said, "Step to the door, and see them play," and we did so. The deer would run in circles swift about her, then turning square about, rush straight toward her, dropping on his knees in front of her and rubbing his chin on the ground by a rolling motion to and fro with his neck and head; then, like a purring cat, roll over and, springing to his feet, like a young dog would run round and round the old wigwam, stopping just in sight now and then, as if trying to play hide-and-seek with her. At last he walked boldly up to her, and she placed her arm over his neck and shoulders, patting him under the neck and chin, which he seemed to enjoy, with eyes half-closed as if almost asleep. I will not admit that I was jealous of the deer, but most humbly confess that I did covet the attention he received.

> Pokagon and Lonidaw marry, but the deer becomes emaciated and runs away, never to be found. They retire to the wilderness and have two children, but their son dies of alcoholism when barely a teen-ager, and their daughter is killed when two drunken fishermen ram her canoe on the lake outside their wigwam and she drowns. Lonidaw dies of grief. After her funeral, Pokagon returns to their home and spends an agonized night communing with the Great Spirit, during which he has a vision.

I fell *ni-baw* (asleep) while on *nin[-]gi-dig[-og]* (my knees) in prayer; and in the *[n]a-gwi-i-dis te-be-cut* (the visions of the night) I was lifted high above the *au-kee* (ground), and there on steady *nin-gwi-gan* (wing), like *tchi-tchi-gig-waw-ne* (the osprey) watching for some victim of the deep, so I, balancing in mid-air, watched unnumbered multitudes of the palefaced race, which filled the wide, extended *taw-awd-ino* (plain, valley) beneath. While wondering there, I gazed. I beheld marching among the mighty throng the most vicious-looking creature my eyes ever beheld; no brush of *mau-tchi manito* (the devil) could paint his wicked *[osh-]kin-jig* (face); no language of Ki-tchi-isk-u-to (hell or big-fire) could describe it. About his form was wrapped *wa-be-yon* (a blanket) with *an-ong-og* (the stars) and stripes thereon, among which was outlined an American *mi-gi-si* (eagle) with wings half-spread, while across *ni-kat-i-gwan* (*o-kat-i-gwan*: his forehead) deeply impressed, I read "United States and City Seals." Under *nin[-]ki-tchi-nik* (*o-kitchi-ni-ka-ma*: his right arm), half-concealed, he held a bundle of poisonous *gin-e-big-og* (serpents) which writhed, convulsed, and hissing, snapped *wi-bi[d]-og* (their teeth), and escaping in great numbers, they ran like *ni-ki-bi-win* (a flood) in all directions, still the numbers held grew nonetheless. In *ki[-]tchi-nig* (*o-kitchi-nindji-ma*: his right hand) he held a scorpion whip, which he wielded with such skilled force that it sounded more like the report of a gun than the snap of a lash. Thus clothed with civic and national emblems, the despot marched forth on *ki-mi-gan* (*o-mi-gan*: his trail), defiantly treading, with feet of steel, upon beating human hearts that were yet struggling in *mis-kwi* (their own blood). *Nin-o-daw* (my heart)[167] almost ceased to beat as I saw the defiant despot marching toward beautiful homes, drawing his mantle closer about him so as to conceal the snakes and scorpions hidden there, as if k*awin a-ga[w]-tchi-win* (no shame) *nin[-]in-en-o-win* (*od-ini-gaw-a-gen-da-mowin*: his conscience) stung, with brazen face he boldly entered in the homes of sunshine and of smiles. Some, when they met him, grasped *o-nindg* (*o-nin-dji-ma*: his hand), as though he were a friend, or brother, or some benefactor of their race. Others, when they saw him, closed their doors against him, saying to the monster man, "If thou will keep aloof from us, we will not disturb thee"; but regardless of their wishes, he forced his way into many homes, blighting the fairest of the household. . . .

1899

❖ CHILDREN AND FAMILIES ❖

S tories of abandoned children, known the world over, are unusually frequent in Great Lakes Native litera-tures. The reason may be simple: when war and disease made the peoples of the lakes a diaspora without par on the continent, artists responded with stories of lost or abandoned children. The abandonment can occur without reason, by mistake, as punishment, or as an evasion of responsibility. The abandoned one is fre-quently the youngest child of a family, a hero type known as "youngest-smartest," someone who, despite being despised or ignored or thrown away, proves to be the most gifted and intelligent of all, causing the adults who treated him badly to repent. Often the deserted child will be helped by a sibling or by animals, sometimes an animal or human "grandmother." Once the child has grown, there may be a reunion with family, but even so the child may decide to live with the animal benefactors, becoming one of them. This decision is a profoundly negative comment on the state of culture, since if a nation cannot nurture its children it has no future. In this way, the stories may have served as a warning to those who listened.

Pukeelāūwau (Thrown Away)

Tenskwatawa (One With Open Mouth, The Prophet, 1775-1836), Shawnee

T he idea of abandonment is particularly poignant here, for the teller is Tecumseh's brother, known to whites as The Prophet. After the British abandoned their Native allies in the War of 1812, sacrificing his brother in the process, Tenskwatawa told this story and others during long interviews with the Indian agent at Detroit and his secretary, who were charged with the task of collecting information to answer a US government questionnaire about indigenous nations. Tenskwatawa gave straightforward answers, but he also told stories in the Native fashion, since the white man's "facts" left much out, particularly nuances a good listener would have recognized and responded to. Did the white men recognize how powerfully the ancient stories the aging, one-eyed man told—he and his famous brother abandoned, their nation in ruins and soon to be removed west-ward—resonated with the present?

Haa! *Kautaupee!* (Pay Attention!)

In ancient days, when the Indians were much in the habit of wandering about from place to place, and when they had changed so often as to have arrived at an extreme easterly point on the earth, the great chief of a village, whose name was Peeāatāūkoothaumoa (Rising Sun), became much dissatisfied with his youngest son and was anxious to rid himself of him. One day he told his people that they must all prepare to remove from the village, that they would leave Pukeelāūwau, or Thrown Away, behind, and that each person must be careful to do his part in extinguishing the fire, that the son might be left without any. But one of the sisters of the boy, seeing him naked and destitute and being much affected with the prospect of him freezing to death, determined to deceive her relatives, and accordingly she stole a brand of fire which she secretly carried to a hole in the ground where her mother had been accustomed to dress skins, and having deposited it there, she covered it with some clay prepared for the purpose. Soon after, the bustle of preparation for departure was heard. The villagers made up their packs, and at a given signal from the chief they severally poured some water upon their fires and departed. When the sister of the boy was about to part with him, she informed him of the fire and directed him to be very careful in its preservation as his own existence depended upon it.

When they had all gone, the boy added fuel to the fire and, having secured it so that he thought it would not go out, he went about the village to find something to appease his hunger, which was extreme. He picked up a few ears of corn and carried them to his fire where he roasted them. In one of these excursions he heard the moaning of a dog and, pleased to think that he was not entirely destitute of company, he proceeded to the lodge where he heard the noise, and there he found one of the village dogs almost frozen and starved. He took him to his fire. When the dog had got warm, he addressed the boy. "My brother," said he, "hereafter I am going to talk with you and prevent you from being lonely. We will live here together, for such appears to be our lot, and we will select the tightest lodge in the village for our habitation, as we are entirely destitute of covering. Now brother, let us go and gather all the corn you can find in the village, and we will endeavor to procure from some of the lodges a bow and arrows. With these and the corn which you may find we will try to live through the winter."

The boy obeyed the directions given him and succeeded beyond his expectations in procuring a quantity of corn, a bow, some arrows, and some feathers to trim them with. With his bow he frequently killed small birds and squirrels which he shared with great exactness with his brother, the dog. In this way they lived through the winter, and in the spring they planted the remains of their corn, a very small quantity, in which labor the dog rendered his part of the service by scratching the holes for the seed. When autumn came and the corn was gathered, the dog said to the boy, "Now brother, I think we will try and find our friends who left us here, no doubt supposing that we would starve. You are large enough now to kill deer, and I am so meager, crooked, and ugly that, if we can procure some venison to eat, my appearance will be much improved, as well as your own. Our friends are not very distant from us, and the undertaking is not a great one."

Pukeelāūwau assented to the proposition of the dog, upon whose back he fastened a pack of corn and, taking another pack for himself, together with his bow and a stone knife, which he had found in the village, they sat out.[168] After traveling all day they encamped. About midnight the dog rose up and called out, "Brother are you asleep?"

"No," answered the boy.

"Well then," said the dog, "good fortune awaits us. I smell a bear, and we shall overtake him in the morning, about sunrise. He will be difficult to kill, but we will approach very near to him before the attack and, as soon as you discharge one of your arrows, I will seize him by the hinder legs, and by following the discharges of your arrows three or four times we will finally kill him."

In the morning the travelers sat out, and at the time mentioned by the dog they came in sight of a huge bear. They crept slyly towards him and, by pursuing the plan proposed, they killed him. Here they remained some time, feasting the bear's flesh. The boy dressed the skin and took care to put some of the oil upon the dog, who returned the compliment by licking him all over the body. Very soon the hair, which had fallen out in consequence of his poverty, began to appear, and both became quite fat and healthy. When the bear's meat was exhausted, the travelers recommenced their journey. On the first day they had the good fortune, by their united efforts, to kill a deer, and they remained two days to feast upon it when, the boy having dressed the skin and packed the remains of the venison upon the dog, they continued their route. They soon arrived at an encamping place where their friends had wintered after leaving them, and dog here proposed to Pukeelāūwau to leave him and go see the situation of matters at the village, which from appearances they judged to be near them.

In the morning dog cleaned himself by rolling in the leaves and, having a compliment from Pukeelāūwau on the improvement his appearance, he started for the village. In the afternoon he returned with the following account. "Brother, I have been to the village, I find close at hand. There I found all your relations and mine. I saw a great many handsome dogs. They appeared glad to meet me, and I treated them as they deserved, throwing down every one that came in my way. Tomorrow we'll set out for the village, and we will stop at the house of an old woman near the town, where you will live as her grandson.[169] In case your friends should suspect who we are, they may come to see you, but do not speak to or shake hands with them, for when they thought you a poor boy and expected no assistance from you, they left you to starve. But if your youngest sister should come to you, it will not be amiss to treat her better than the others because she pitied you. However you must not shake hands with her or anyone else.

In the morning the travelers set out, and they had not proceeded far before they arrived at a great hunting ground where they killed a great many bears, deer, and turkeys, after which they proceeded to the house of the old woman, the dog first having informed Pukeelāūwau that he would never speak to him in presence of anyone, so that he need not be betrayed.

The old woman inquired of the young man whence he came and manifested so much suspicion of his origin and true character that he revealed to her the whole story, excepting so far as related to his dog. He then told her that he had hunted near her house and had collected a large quantity of game, which [was] at her service, if she would cause it to be sent for. She informed him that his father still continued to be chief of the village and would be happy to recognize him and to send for the game, but he forbade her mentioning this subject and declared to her that he did not intend to recognize his relatives. But the old woman prevailed on him to consent to an application on her part to the Chief for assistance to bring in the game, and in the morning she went to the village, where she told the Chief whom she informed that her grandson had been out hunting and had collected more game than he could bring home alone and that a little assistance from him would be very acceptable. The Chief told his people, and they, thinking it an uncommon thing for hunters to solicit this kind of assistance, proposed to go in a body so that they might have a laugh at the young fellow. They accordingly assembled at the old woman's lodge and desired to be led to the wonderful sight of which she had told them. On the way they amused themselves in remarks about the ugly arrows of the young hunter, but some thought he possessed a remarkably fine dog, which made up for the want of arrows.

But all were astounded when Pukeelāūwau led them to the vast piles of venison and bear meat which he had collected. Their suspicions were excited, and they soon recollected that all the grandchildren of the old woman had been reported long since dead. When they had arrived at the village with one-half of the game, which the old woman had given them for their services, they asked the opinion of the Chief about the strange circumstances which they had witnessed and suggested the possibility that the young hunter was his discarded son. Whereupon, the Chief immediately dispatched a messenger to inquire his name. The old woman informed him of this, and the Chief, upon hearing it, assembled his relations and, having told them of the discovery, set out with them to see him. They soon reached the old woman's lodge, where they manifested much joy at the sight of their newly found relative. But Pukeelāūwau told his father that as he had thrown him away and abandoned him to starve or freeze to death, he was under no obligations to him and should not trouble himself with acknowledging such relatives, but his sister, who endangered herself to leave him a little fire, should be rewarded.

In the meantime the dog went again to village to make a visit, and Pukeelāūwau, who obeyed his directions in all things, was very industrious during his eight day's absence, collecting game for him, so that he might feast himself upon fine venison upon his return. When the dog returned, they went out to hunt, and during their absence the dog told Pukeelāūwau that something important was to be transacted and that he would go to the village and ascertain what it was. He went, and when he returned, he informed Pukeelāūwau that he had visited every lodge and at last went to the council house, where he saw a great number of warriors who listened to the plan of their Chief, and his proposal that they would take two prisoners and return home. Pukeelāūwau was much pleased with this news and manifested a desire to join the war party, which the dog advised him to do. So he went immediately to the village and offered his services, which were gladly accepted. The party set out, and the dog accompanied them four days when he parted with Pukeelāūwau, having first directed him to make a feast of bear's meat on the following day and [saying that] if his companions could not eat the whole of the meat, he should sit down and dispose of the remains.[170]

The next day Pukeelāūwau sent out two young men to hunt and, when they returned with a large bear, he caused it to be dressed and spread upon a parcel of brush, where it was cooked. In the meantime he painted himself with paint and ornamented his head with feathers and his neck with a crow skin. When he had done this, he sung the war song and then directed the warriors to begin to eat. After they had eaten as much as they could, there still remained a large quantity of the meat, and Pukeelāūwau, addressing himself to his brother (the dog) for assistance, commenced at the remains. His request for assistance was answered by a deputation of wolves, who were invisible to all but Pukeelāūwau, and the bear's meat disappeared, to the great astonishment of all present.

On the following morning the party resumed the march, and toward the close of the day they supposed themselves near the village which they were about to attack, upon which Pukeelāūwau proposed to go and reconnoiter. He reached the village in the night and, finding the inhabitants asleep, he went to their several lodges and took the strings from the bows and the flinty points from their arrows and stole their war clubs, after which he returned to the party, and having informed them of his success, they all set out the same night and reached the village about daylight where they attacked and easily overpowered the unsuspecting villagers. The head warrior was so charmed with Pukeelāūwau's prowess and good management that he surrendered to him his authority, and the whole party returned to the village, where they found the old Chief in much grief at the reception which he had met with from his son. Nothing could satisfy him, but a surrender of all his power in expiation of his offence, and Pukeelāūwau immediately became invested with the power and authority which his father had so long possessed. He lived in this way very happily for some time, but at length he grew weary of that kind of life and assembled all his people, to whom he recounted his history and then by advice of his faithful counselor, the dog, he chose to be transformed into a wolf and was accordingly changed. His people, despairing of ever having another chief like him, prayed to be also transformed, and some were bears, others deer, turkeys, beaver.

1824

I'm Making You Up

Chrystos, Menominee

Grandma we all need
partially deaf & busy with weaving
listens through a thick blanket of years & sore feet
nods   while I cry about everything they did to me
how horrible   & can't stand another
while brown wrinkled you smile at me like sun coming up
I stand next to you   pass wool absently
you lay aside the wrong colors without comment
I'm simply   Grandchild
babbling   your sympathy warm and comforting as dust
I sit in your lap   your loom pushed aside
you feed me fry bread with too much maple syrup
I pull your braids   you cradle me deeper in
your legs folded to make a basket for me
Grandmawho died long before I was born
   Come Back
     Come Back

1988

This poem is dedicated to Beth Brant.

An urban Native who was raised in the city, Chrystos (1946-   ) is a self-educated poet who makes politics a critical part of her life, working as an activist for land claims, treaty rights, and two-spirit (Gay) people. She is the author of six collections of poetry and the winner of the Audre Lorde International Poetry Competition and the Sappho Award of Distinction from the Astraea National Lesbian Action Foundation.

Mishosha, or the Magician and His Daughters

Bame-wa-wa-ge-zhik-a-quay (Woman of Stars Rushing Through Sky, Jane Johnston Schoolcraft, 1800-1842), Chippewa

"Mishosha"[171] is not a sacred story, which conveys important cultural information such as the origin of a clan totem, but was meant for entertainment during long winter evenings in the lodge. Set on Grand Island in Lake Superior, there are repeated trials of magic, and the story is discursive, as Ojibwa stories often are. But lodge stories were also meant for edification. "Mishosha" teaches proper behavior when one is angry; it suggests that bravery and aggressiveness against a foe will be rewarded; it reinforces the correct way to accomplish rituals and spells; and it describes how some personal guiding spirits, or manidog, are more powerful than others. Most importantly, it describes how an abandoned child of thoughtless parents can overcome adversity, here the infamous evil magician of Lake Superior.

In an early age of the world, when there were fewer inhabitants in the earth than there now are, there lived an Indian, who had a wife and two children, in a remote situation. Buried in the solitude of the forest, it was not often that he saw anyone out of the circle of his own family. Such a situation seemed favorable for his pursuits; and his life passed on in uninterrupted happiness, till he discovered a wanton disposition in his wife.

This woman secretly cherished a passion for a young man whom she accidentally met in the woods, and she lost no opportunity of courting his approaches. She even planned the death of her husband who, she justly concluded, would put her to death should he discover her infidelity. But this design was frustrated by the alertness of the husband, who having cause to suspect her, determined to watch narrowly to ascertain the truth before he should come to a determination how to act. He followed her silently one day at a distance and hid himself behind a tree. He soon beheld a tall, handsome man approach his wife and lead her away.

He was now convinced of her crime and thought of killing her the moment she returned. In the meantime he went home and pondered on his situation. At last he came to the determination of leaving her forever, thinking that her own conscience would in the end punish her sufficiently and relying on her maternal feelings to take care of the two boys, whom he determined to leave behind.

When the wife returned, she was disappointed in not finding her husband, having concerted a plan to dispatch him. When she saw that day after day passed and he did not return, she at last guessed the true cause of his absence. She then returned to her paramour, leaving the two helpless boys behind, telling them that she was going a short distance and would return but determined never to see them more.

The children thus abandoned soon made way with the food that was left in the lodge and were compelled to quit it in search of more. The eldest boy possessed much intrepidity, as well as great tenderness for his little brother, frequently carrying him when he became weary and gathering all the wild fruit he saw. Thus they went deeper into the forest, soon losing all traces of their former habitation, till they were completely lost in the labyrinths of the wilderness.

The elder boy fortunately had a knife with which he made a bow and arrows and was thus enabled to kill a few birds for himself and brother. In this way they lived some time, still pressing on they knew not whither. At last they saw an opening through the woods and were shortly after delighted to find themselves on the borders of a broad lake. Here the elder boy busied himself in picking the seed pods of the wild rose. In the meanwhile the younger amused himself by shooting some arrows into the sand, one of which happened to fall into the lake. The elder brother, not willing to lose his time in making another, waded into the water to reach it. Just as he was about to grasp the arrow, a canoe passed by him with the rapidity of lightning. An old man, sitting in the center, seized the affrighted youth and placed him in the canoe. In vain the boy addressed him. "My grandfather" (a term of respect for old people), "pray take my little brother also. Alone, I cannot go with you; he will starve if I leave him." The old magician (for such was his real character) laughed at him. Then giving his canoe a slap and commanding it to go, it glided through the water with inconceivable swiftness. In a few minutes they reached the habitation of Mishosha, standing on an island in the center of the lake. Here he lived with his two daughters, the terror of all the surrounding country.

Leading the young man up to the lodge, "Here my eldest daughter," said he, "I have brought a young man who shall become your husband." The youth saw surprise depicted in the countenance of the daughter, but she made no reply, seeming thereby to acquiesce in the commands of her father. In the evening he overheard the daughters in conversation. "There again!" said the elder daughter, "our father has brought another victim, under the pretence of giving me a husband. When will his enmity to the human race cease; or when shall we be spared witnessing such scenes of vice and wickedness, as we are daily compelled to behold?"

When the old magician was asleep, the youth told the elder daughter how he had been carried off and compelled to leave his helpless brother on the shore. She told him to get up and take her father's canoe and, [with use of] the charm he had observed, it would carry him quickly to his brother. That he could carry him food, prepare a lodge for him, and return by morning. He did everything as he had been directed and, after providing for the subsistence of his brother, told him that in a short time he should come for him. Then returning to the enchanted island, he resumed his place in the lodge before the magician awoke. Once during the night Mishosha awoke and, not seeing his son-in-law, asked his eldest daughter what had become of him. She replied that he had merely stepped out and would be back soon. This satisfied him. In the morning, finding the young man in the lodge, his suspicions were completely lulled. "I see, my daughter, you have told me the truth."

As soon as the sun rose, Mishosha thus addressed the young man. "Come, my son, I have a mind to gather gulls' eggs. I am acquainted with an island where there are great quantities, and I wish your aid in gathering them." The young man saw no reasonable excuse and, getting into the canoe, the magician gave it a slap and, bidding it go, in an instant they were at the island. They found the shore covered with gulls' eggs and the island surrounded with birds of this kind. "Go, my son," said the old man, "and gather them, while I remain in the canoe." But the young man was no sooner ashore than Mishosha pushed his canoe a little from land and exclaimed: "Listen, ye gulls! You have long expected something from me. I now give you an offering. Fly down and devour him." Then striking his canoe, he left the young man to his fate.

The birds immediately came in clouds around their victim, darkening all the air with their numbers. But the youth, seizing the first that came near him and drawing his knife, cut off its head and, immediately skinning the bird, hung the feathers as a trophy on his breast. "Thus," he exclaimed, "will I treat every one of you who approaches me. Forbear, therefore, and listen to my words. It is not for you to eat human food. You have been given by the Great Spirit as food for man. Neither is it in the power of that old magician to do you any good. Take me on your backs and carry me to his lodge, and you shall see that I am not ungrateful."

The gulls obeyed, collecting in a cloud for him to rest upon, and quickly flew to the lodge, where they arrived before the magician. The daughters were surprised at his return, but Mishosha conducted himself as if nothing extraordinary had taken place.

On the following day he again addressed the youth. "Come, my son," said he, "I will take you to an island covered with the most beautiful pebbles, looking like silver. I wish you to assist me in gathering some of them. They will make handsome ornaments and are possessed of great virtues." Entering the canoe, the magician made use of his charm, and they were carried in a few moments to a solitary bay in an island where there was a smooth sandy beach. The young man went ashore as usual. "A little farther, a little farther," cried the old man, "upon that rock you will get some finer ones." Then pushing his canoe from land, "Come thou great king of fishes," cried he, "you have long expected an offering from me. Come, and eat the stranger I have put ashore on your island." So saying, he commanded his canoe to return and was soon out of sight. Immediately a monstrous fish shoved his long snout from the water, moving partially on the beach, and opened wide his jaws to receive his victim.

"When," exclaimed the young man, drawing his knife and placing himself in a threatening attitude, "when did you ever taste human food? Have a care of yourself. You were given by the Great Spirit to man, and if you or any of your tribes taste human flesh, you will fall sick and die. Listen not to the words of that wicked old man but carry me back to his island, in return for which I shall present you a piece of red cloth." The fish complied, raising his back out of water to allow the young man to get on. Then taking his way through the lake, he landed his charge safely at the island before the return of the magician.

The daughters were still more surprised to see him thus escaped a second time from the arts of their father. But the old man maintained his taciturnity. He could not, however, help saying to himself, "What manner of boy is this who ever escapes from my power? His spirit shall not however save him. I will entrap him tomorrow. Ha! Ha! Ha!"

Next day the magician addressed the young man as follows: "Come, my son," said he, "you must go with me to procure some young eagles. I wish to tame them. I have discovered an island where they are in great abundance." When they had reached the island, Mishosha led him inland until they came to the foot of a tall pine upon which the nests were. "Now, my son," said he, "climb up this tree and bring down the birds." The young man obeyed. When he had with great difficulty got near the nest, "Now," exclaimed the magician, addressing the tree, "stretch yourself up and be very tall." The tree rose up at the command. "Listen, ye eagles," continued the old man, "you have long expected a gift from me. I now present you this boy, who has had the presumption to molest your young. Stretch forth your claws and seize him." So saying he left the young man to his fate and returned.

But the intrepid youth, drawing his knife and cutting off the head of the first eagle that menaced him, raised his voice and exclaimed, "Thus will I deal with all who come near me. What right have you, ye ravenous birds, who were made to feed on beasts, to eat human flesh? Is it because that cowardly old canoe-man has bid you do so? He is an old woman. He can neither do you good nor harm. See, I have already slain one of your number. Respect my bravery, and carry me back that I may show you how I shall treat you."

The eagles, pleased with his spirit, assented and, clustering thick around him, formed a seat with their backs and flew toward the enchanted island. As they crossed the water, they passed over the magician, lying half-asleep in his canoe.

The return of the young man was hailed with joy by the daughters, who now plainly saw that he was under the guidance of a strong spirit. But the ire of the old man was excited, although he kept his temper under subjection. He taxed his wits for some new mode of ridding himself of the youth who had so successfully baffled his skill. He next invited him to go a-hunting.

Taking his canoe, they proceeded to an island and built a lodge to shelter themselves during the night. In the meantime the magician caused a deep fall of snow with a storm of wind and severe cold. According to custom, the young man pulled off his moccasins and leggings and hung them before the fire to dry. After [the young man] had gone to sleep, the magician, watching his opportunity, got up, and taking one moccasin and one legging, threw them into the fire. He then went to sleep. In the morning, stretching himself as he arose and uttering an exclamation of surprise, "My son," said he, "what has become of your moccasin and legging? I believe this is the moon in which fire attracts, and I fear they have been drawn in." The young man suspected the true cause of his loss and rightly attributed it to a design of the magician to freeze him to death on the march. But he maintained the strictest silence and drawing his *conaus*[172] over his head thus communed with himself: "I have full faith in the Manito who has preserved me thus far. I do not fear that he will forsake me in this cruel emergency. Great is his power, and I invoke it now that he may enable me to prevail over this wicked enemy of mankind."

He then drew on the remaining moccasin and legging and, taking a dead coal from the fireplace, invoked his spirit to give it efficacy, and blackened his foot and leg as far as the lost garment usually reached. He then got up and announced himself ready for the march. In vain Mishosha led him through snows and over morasses, hoping to see the lad sink at every moment. But in this he was disappointed, and for the first time they returned home together.

Taking courage from this success, the young man now determined to try his own power, having previously consulted with the daughters. They all agreed that the life the old man led was detestable and that whoever would rid the world of him would entitle himself to the thanks of the human race.

On the following day the young man thus addressed his hoary captor. "My grandfather, I have often gone with you on perilous excursions and never murmured. I must now request that you will accompany me. I wish to visit my little brother and to bring him home with me." They accordingly went on a visit to the mainland and found the little lad in the spot where he had been left. After taking him into the canoe, the young man again addressed the magician: "My grandfather, will you go and cut me a few of those red willows on the bank. I wish to prepare some smoking mixture."

"Certainly, my son," replied the old man, "what you wish is not very hard. Ha, ha, ha! Do you think me too old to get up there?"

No sooner was Mishosha ashore than the young man, placing himself in the proper position struck the canoe with his hand, and pronouncing the charm, *n'chimaun poll,* the canoe immediately flew through the water on its return to the island. It was evening when the two brothers arrived and carried the canoe ashore. But the elder daughter informed the young man that unless he sat up and watched the canoe and kept his hand upon it, such was the power of their father, it would slip off and return to him. Panigwun watched faithfully till near the dawn of day, when he could no longer resist the drowsiness which oppressed him and fell into a short doze. In the meantime the canoe slipped off and sought its master, who soon returned in high glee. "Ha, ha, ha! My son," said he; "you thought to play me a trick. It was very clever. But you see I am too old for you."

A short time after, the young man again addressed the magician. "My grandfather, I wish to try my skill in hunting. It is said there is plenty of game on an island not far off, and I have to request that you will take me there in your canoe." They accordingly went to the island and spent the day in hunting. Night coming on, they put up a temporary lodge. When the magician had sunk into a profound sleep, the young man got up and, taking one of Mishosha's leggings and moccasins from the place where they hung, threw them into the fire, thus retaliating the artifice before played upon himself. He had discovered that the foot and leg were the only vulnerable parts on the magician's body. Having committed these articles to the fire, he besought his manito that he would raise a great storm of snow, wind, and hail and then laid himself down beside the old man. Consternation was depicted on the countenance of the latter when he awoke in the morning and found his moccasin and legging missing. "I believe, my grandfather," said the young man, "that this is the moon in which fire attracts, and I fear your foot and leg garments have been drawn in." Then rising and bidding the old man follow him, he began the morning's hunt, frequently turning to see how Mishosha kept up. He saw him faltering at every step and almost benumbed with cold, but he encouraged him to follow saying, "We shall soon get through and reach the shore," although he took pains at the same time to lead him in round-about ways, so as to let the frost take complete effect. At length the old man reached the brink of the island where the woods are succeeded by a border of smooth sand. But he could go no farther; his legs became stiff and refused motion, and he found himself fixed to the spot. But he still kept stretching out his arms and swinging his body to and fro. Every moment he found the numbness creeping higher. He felt his legs growing downward like roots, the feathers of his head turned to leaves, and in a few seconds he stood a tall and stiff sycamore, leaning toward the water.

Panigwun leaped into the canoe, pronounced the charm, and was soon transported to the island where he related his victory to the daughters. They applauded the deed, agreed to put on mortal shapes, become wives to the two young men, and forever quit the enchanted island. And passing immediately over to the mainland, they lived lives of happiness and peace.

1827

From *Night Flying Woman:* An Ojibwa Narrative
Ignatia Broker, Ojibwe

orn on the White Earth Reservation and educated at government boarding schools, Ignatia Broker spent most of her life in Minneapolis, working for the public schools and the Indian community as a writer, activist, and leader. *Night Flying Woman,* the story of her grandmother and Broker's only novel, is set primarily in the past. But Broker begins her grandmother's story with her own, one of the first about urban Native life and the changes it has meant, including the development of a pan-Indian, rather than band or nation, identity. Broker also hints at but does not describe in detail some of the problems faced by Natives who moved to the city, first during World War II and then in response to the US government's policies in the 1950s. As other writers will document in the selections that follow this, it is easy to become abandoned in the city as a child or an adult.

"When the forest weeps, the Anishinâbe who listen will look back at the years. In each generation of Ojibway there will be a person who will hear the *si-si-gwad,*[173] who will listen and remember and pass it on to the children."

I got off the city bus and walked the short one and a half blocks home as I have been doing for years around five o'clock each evening. Because this evening was warm, I walked slower than usual, enjoying the look and feel of the early spring. The earth that had been white was now brown, left uncovered by the melting snow. This brown was turning to green, and the air was fragrant with the opening of spring.

Daylight still lingered, and as I walked, I looked at my neighborhood and thought about it. When I first moved here in the mid-1950s this was a mixed neighborhood of Spanish-speaking people and Catholic whites, and there were many children. Now the Spanish-speaking people are all gone. They left when the parochial school closed its doors, although the church is still here. Now the neighborhood is only four blocks long and two blocks wide, whittled down by urban renewal and the freeways which reach their tentacles all around us.

I reached my doorstep and sat enjoying the good day and remembering the past. It was funny, really, when I think about it. That day thirty years ago when we moved here, me and my children, we were the aliens looking for a place to fit in, looking for a chance of a new life, moving in among these people, some of whose "forefathers" had displaced my ancestors for the same reason: looking for a new life. Their fathers were the aliens then, and now they, the children, are in possession of this land.

For a long time I was that Indian person with the two children. But it is good that children have a natural gift of accepting people, and so my children became a part of the neighborhood. Thirty years in this neighborhood. My children went to school from here, they went to church from here, they were married from here, and even though they are in faraway places, they seem to have their roots here, for they had lived no other place while growing up.

I talked to my children, even when they were very small, about the ways of the Ojibway people. They were good children, and they listened, but I had a feeling that they listened the same as when I read a story about the Bobbsey Twins or Marco Polo. I was speaking of another people, removed from them by rock and roll, juvenile singers, and the bobbing movement of the new American dance.

My two, born and raised in Minneapolis, are of that generation of Ojibway who do not know what

216

the reservation means, or the Bureau of Indian Affairs, or the tangled treaties and federal—so called—Indian laws which have spun their webs for a full century around the Native people, the First People of this land. Now my children are urging me to recall all the stories and bits of information that I ever heard my grandparents or any of the older Ojibway tell. It is important, they say, because now their children are asking them. Others are saying the same thing. It is well that they are asking, for the Ojibway young must learn their cycle.

I have been abroad in this society, the dominating society, for two-thirds of my life, and yet I am a link in a chain to the past. Because of this, I shall do as they ask. I can close my eyes, and I am back in the past.

I came to the Twin Cities from the reservation in 1941, the year Pearl Harbor was attacked. I went to work in a defense plant and took night classes in order to catch up on the schooling I had missed. I was twenty-two years old and aching for a permanent, settling-down kind of life, but the war years were unstable years for everyone and more so for the Indian people.

Although employment was good because of the labor demand of the huge defense plants, Indian people faced discrimination in restaurants, night clubs, retail and department stores, in service organizations, public offices and, worst of all, in housing. I can remember hearing, "This room has been rented already, but I got a basement that has a room I'll show you." I looked at the room. It had the usual rectangular window, and pipes ran overhead. The walls and floors were brown cement, but the man with a gift-giving tone in his voice said, "I'll put linoleum on the floor for you, and you'll have a toilet all to yourself. You could wash at the laundry tubs."

There was, of course, nothing listed with the War Price and Rationing Board, but the man said it would cost seven dollars a week. I know that he would have made the illegal offer only to an Indian because he knew of the desperate housing conditions we, the first Americans, faced. I remember living in a room with six others. It was a housekeeping room, nine by twelve feet in size, and meant for one person. It was listed with the price agency at five dollars a week, but the good landlady collected five dollars from each of us each week. However, she did put in a bunk bed and a rollaway, which I suppose was all right because we were on different shifts and slept different times anyway. It was cramped and crowded, but we had a mutual respect. We sometimes shared our one room with others who had no place, so that there might be nine or ten of us. We could not let friends be out on the street without bed or board. As long as our landlady did not mind, we helped and gave a place of rest to other Ojibway people.

Our paydays were on different days, and so whoever had money lent carfare and bought meat and vegetables. Stew was our daily fare because we had only a hot plate and one large kettle. I mention this practice because I know other Indian people did the same thing, and sometimes whole families evolved from it. This was how we got a toehold in the urban areas—by helping each other. Perhaps this is the way nonmaterialistic people do. We were a sharing people, and our tribal traits are still within us.

I think now that maybe it was a good thing, the migration of our people to the urban areas during the war years, because there, amongst the millions of people, we were brought to a brotherhood. We Indian people who worked in the war plants started a social group not only for the Ojibway but for the Dakota, the Arikara, the Menominee, the Gros Ventres, the Cree, the Oneida, and all those from other tribes and other states who had made the trek to something new. And because we, all, were isolated in this dominant society, we became an island from which a revival of spirit began.

It was not easy for any of us during the war years, and it became more difficult after the war had ceased. Many Native people returned to the reservations after our soldiers came home from the foreign lands, but others like me stayed and took the buffeting and the difficulties shown us by an alien society. The war plants closed, and people were without jobs. The labor market tightened up, and we, the Native people—even skilled workers—faced bias, prejudice, and active discrimination in employment.

I know because when I was released from my defense job I answered many advertisements and always I was met with the words, "I'm sorry, but we don't hire Indians because they only last the two weeks till payday. Then they quit." It was around this time that I met and married a veteran who was passing through to the reservation. He got a job with the railroad. To be close to that job and because of the bias in housing, we moved to the capital side of the river, to an area of St. Paul called the river flats. It was a poor area. Many of the houses had outdoor toilets; many were but tar-paper shacks. Surprising, but it was so in this very large city. It was here our two children were born, and I, like a lot of other Indian women, went out and did day work—cleaning and scrubbing the homes of the middle-income people.

Many Indian families lived on the river flats, which became vibrant with their sharing. People gave to each other because times were bad. No Indian family dared approach the relief and welfare agencies of the Twin Cities. They knew that they would only be given a bus ticket and be told to go back to the reservation where the government would take care of them as usual. This was the policy of the public service agencies, and we put up with it by not asking for the help to which we had a legal right. We also suffered in other ways of their making. My husband was recalled to service and died in Korea. After this I moved from the river flats. I took the clerical training and got my first job at a health clinic.

Because my husband died fighting for a nation designed for freedom for all, I felt that I must help extend that freedom to our people. I joined a group of Indians who had banded together to form an Indian help agency. We built a welfare case to challenge the policy of sending our people back to the reservation, and we were successful. After that, the tide of Indians moving to Minnesota's urban areas increased, and today there are ten thousand of us. As the number grew, new-fangled types of Indian people came into being: those demanding what is in our treaties, those demanding service to our people, those working to provide these services—and all reaching back for identity.

When I see my people every day and know how they are doing, I do not feel so lost in the modern times. The children of our people who come to our agency have a questioning look, a dubious but seeking-to-learn look, and I truly believe that they are reaching back to learn those things of which they can be proud. Many of these children were born and raised in the urban areas, and they do not make any distinctions as to their tribes. They do not say, "I am Ojibway," or "I am Dakota," or "I am Arapaho," but they say, "I am an Indian." Now they, too, are looking to their tribal identity.

These children are again honoring the Old People by asking them to speak, and I like other older people will search my memory and tell what I know. I, myself, shall tell you what I have heard my grandmother tell, and I shall try to speak in the way she did and use the words that were hers. . . .

1983

From *The Hiawatha*

David Treuer (1970-   ), Ojibwe

David Treuer

The family at the center of *The Hiawatha* came to the Twin Cities much like Ignatia Broker's did, but in this novel the ending offers little hope. When Treuer named his second novel after the great Haudenosaunee healer, he was being ironic, since the Hiawatha here is a defunct passenger train that sits on a siding. The author suggests the past and tradition are dead, unable to move, irrelevant. The plot begins when Simon's father is killed working in the woods and his mother, Betty, moves with her four children from the reservation to Minneapolis. The novel explores the fate of the family there, including Simon's drunken, unpremeditated murder of his younger brother, Lester and, later, the accidental shooting of Lester's child. Despite this grim scenario, an elegy for the American Dream, there are moments of hope. One-Two, the big Winnebago, who was named for how swiftly he could floor someone in a bar fight, takes care of Betty and her family to the end. There are also moments of triumph, and Simon's mastery of high-steel work—traditionally a Native profession—is a tribute to his skill and courage. The IDS Tower, where Simon walks beams in this excerpt from the novel, is eight hundred feet tall, an iconic Minneapolis landmark that rises over the city. David Treuer, a novelist who holds a Ph.D. in anthropology, is a professor at the University of Minnesota.

They sent the Indian crew skyward at noon. The other crews took the dawn and dusk shifts, when the wind was stilled in the absence of asphalt heat sent up from below like blasts from a large wing. They were allowed in the union because no one else wanted their jobs or the shifts they kept. The Indian men were from Black River Falls, Red Cliff, Eagle Butte, Wind River, Six Nations. They were from Lac Court d'Oreilles. The names rolling off their wind-dried tongues like scattered dimes. They'd worked in Chicago on the Sears, in Saint Louis and Kansas City. They had raised this new breed of buildings from the ball-tumbled rubble of ten cities.

They went up the lift in a silent huddle. The other crews were from across Europe—Polish, Czech, German, Swedish, Irish. The rest watched as the Indians gathered and did not break into their midst with jokes or conversation. They did not disrupt the silent communion between the Indians partly because they were, after all, Indian, and partly out of respect. The Indians worked the longest shifts during the summer swelter and the winter freeze. They were assigned the most extreme parts of the frame.

The lift shimmied and rose into the noon sky stretched thin under the weight of the June heat. Twenty men, and all that muscle slabbed tight over their hands and squared at their shoulders. They birthed the skeleton of the building, but if the elevator cable snapped, they would fall in a jumble of limbs. Even though they pulled the building together, they knew that what they did was more than their sum. No matter how good they were, how tightly they bolted the swinging I-beam, how carefully they set the crosses, they knew they could not argue with gravity. The earth would treat them with the same indifference as loose steel, a dropped hammer, a windblown lunch. This was the secret: the building wanted to stay standing, to grow; to sway but hold on, and so did they. The IDS Tower wanted to be noticed and admired, as did the Indian crew. Its bones of steel and skin of glass were treated roughly by the wind, heat, and ice as were their skin and bones. That was the secret they carried with them as they crammed into the steel cage that hoisted them upward. Under the watchful eyes of the ground crews and the earth itself they were silent until they were let off to climb the last three floors with their mallets and spud wrenches dangling like extra limbs from their belts and sack lunches tucked under their shirts. Once they were alone they began slight conversation, like tinkers banging out pots, trying not to wake a sleeping family. The newer members wore harnesses until they realized they were in more danger of getting trapped and crushed by beams than of falling. Soon they went without. After a while they, too, wore moccasins to give them a better feel for their footing.

Simon was no different. When he walked down to a Gateway site in 1963, he was green. One-Two had told him what to say, but he was still nervous. The foreman looked him up and down. Union? Simon shook his head. Permit? Simon shrugged. What tribe? Ojibwe. The foreman nodded and called over the Winnebago.

"You know him?" asked the pusher.

"Yeah. Know the family," said One-Two.

"He ever work steel before?"

One-Two looked at Simon. Simon didn't say anything.

"He did some burnin. He can cut, and works like a horse." All of it lies.

"Bullshit. If he knows what to do, then why the hell he come down here instead of the hall? You know better than that."

"Work's down here. They don't know him at the hall. He'd be sittin there twiddlin his fuckin thumbs all day. Besides, all the books are on the job already; you know we're short-handed. I'll take care of him."

The pusher shook his head.

"He's your responsibility. If he goes for a dive, it's your fault. If he gets someone else hurt, you're payin the widow. Go get a permit at noon."

That was that.

By the time they began work on the IDS, Simon had been working steel for seven years and had earned himself a place on one of the high steel crews. When Simon walked to the site at the corner of Eighth Street and Marquette, he grew silent and walked slower, letting the businessmen rush around him. When he got to the lot, he was brooding, looming over the other workers. He joined the Indians on the lift and walked out onto six inches of metal twenty stories above the sidewalk.

After they punched out, they walked into South Minneapolis together, ambling down the sidewalk, all of them marveling at the texture of the ground under their feet, shocked at the great expanse of it. It looked so smooth from above, so even and unbroken and simple.

During the summer they shuffled along until they found their way to Cressen's Bar or the CC Club.

They took up two tables and let their arms creep onto the chair backs of those next to them, expansive in their weariness and pride.

After the first nine months of construction at the IDS they started building up from the ground. Nine months just for excavating and sheeting, for pouring the pilings and the substructure concrete. Then Simon and the others urged the building into the sky. As they clipped and bolted the frame together, he always looked southward while his neighborhood came into perspective. It wasn't until they had been at work for eight months, when the IDS inched over the Foshay Tower, that Simon could make out the roof of their house peeking from behind the soiled brick of Stevens Community. He paused between loads of beam and searched the stunted buildings for some recognizable part of their house, and he saw it. Each day, as they circled the building adding floors, he looked to the house and knew Vera was there with Lester. Betty was at work, and the girls were at school. He was hanging high above the city. Lester and Vera were in the house alone. He was inside her, or she was biting his calf, his ear, his neck, marking him with a hidden map of their passion and time together. He thinks back, and as always, when waiting for his trial and then during ten years in prison, he rules out jealousy as a motive. He didn't want what Lester had, didn't really hunger for her young body. But maybe, maybe if he'd met her first, if he'd taken a different walk home, had reached out to her on the street, then everything would have been different.

They were putting in the spacing beams so the glaziers could begin to hang the skin, the mirrored glass panels that would clothe the building. It was 1971. It seemed that things were falling apart everywhere. The boys sent overseas were coming home broken. Different, at least. The news that came with them was hard to believe but impossible to refute in full color on the television. In Washington the president was denying everything.

Tucked away in the upper Midwest, Minneapolis was licking its wounds and thinking ruefully of Hubert Humphrey's lost bid, wondering how differently things might have turned out. The city looked outward from its perch on the edge of the nation and, given what it saw, everyone in the city was hurrying. One-Two, Simon, the rest of the crews, even the gnomelike architect who designed the building, were hurrying to finish it. They rushed because though the rest of the world seemed broken and unfinished they were determined to glass the sky with the IDS Tower, a home far better than the company that bore its name deserved.

They worked quickly, the masons running ahead of the iron-workers who scampered to clear their deck before the glaziers burned at their heels. After them came the mad scramble of electricians, plumbers, and the specialists who worked only on the ducting or interior walls.

They dared one another, urging speed, and every decision was weighed against the unspoken desire to make it whole in defiance of the dissolution affecting the rest of the country. They loaded the cranes with so much beam that the rear stabilizers almost left the ground. One load of beam took an hour to secure and hoist. If they piled on more, they could save days of work.

It wasn't that they were trying to stay under budget. It was too late for that. They simply felt it, felt it needed to be done. They rushed, pushed the equipment and men to capacity, overloaded the cranes, and turned on huge arc lights so the crews could work into the night. They pulled time and a half but drank up most of it as an antidote to the tensions of night work. The bar owners ignored the one o'clock closing law so when the crews checked out they could slip in the back and slump bone-weary and body-heavy in the booths. They were tired beyond anything they'd experienced except in war, but alert, strung as tight as crane cables.

On the building the usual method of communicating by hand signals was of no use at night. So they developed their own version of Morse which they beat out on the beams with their spud wrenches. The crew spoke in a metallic staccato that cut through diesel roar and hydraulic whine, above the rip of torches and grinders.

After work, in the bars, the men still didn't talk; ordinary speech was too difficult. Instead they carried the principle of code with them. They shouted out names, buildings and dates that carried within them their own stories. *Quebec Bridge, 1907!* someone would shout and the rest nodded and drank. *Chosa! Empire State, 1931!* The bar was solemn. Then some joker yelled *Lenny Whitebird, Sakura Massage Parlor, 1969!* They all laughed until it hurt. The list of fallen expanded to include those who got the clap.

They staggered home, or, often as not, slept in the booths until the bartender woke them with eggs and coffee. They walked out to the site again, ready to climb into the sky. One-Two, as one of the oldest, didn't allow himself much excess after his shifts. His responsibility to his crew lasted until well after they left the rig. He kept them company at the bar for a while, and even though high steel was solitary work, he left the bar alone and almost sober so he could walk home by himself. The darkened streets were what he imagined a decompression tank to be like—slowly giving him the ability to take full breaths and move unrestrictedly. He needed this time alone.

In the morning he retraced his steps and picked up the men who had slept at the bar and cajoled them into action. As for Simon, he kept a special eye on him. He never worried about the quality of Simon's work or if he'd show up—these were never issues for him. Rather, he tried to protect Simon for Betty's sake. Even though she hadn't opened the door for One-Two, hadn't given him much reason to hope, he hadn't talked himself out of loving her. Simon saw it plain as day.

"One-Two," he slurred though his whiskey, "she ain't gonna bend. She ain't the bendin type."

"Don't be so sure about your mom," cautioned One-Two. "She'll surprise you."

"She's always surprising. But her mind gets set and," he burped, "and that's that."

"Well, I ain't got nothin better to do. I might as well keep hopin."

"Go ahead." Simon clapped him on the back but kept his hand there, in quiet dialogue that said, I wouldn't mind it one bit.

And then there was the fall. The crane was loaded past capacity and the rear stabilizers weighted down with beam to keep it from tipping. One-Two was on the third floor signaling the load, and the cable snapped.

The beam crashed straight down, and the cable snaked and doubled and whipped through the corner of the third floor. It could have been worse. If the braided steel had hit One-Two directly, it would have cut him in half. He'd seen it happen. Strange that metal rope, when swung fast enough, acts like a knife. One-Two turned in, as if the shelter of his shoulders could stop it, but the instinct remained, the way he saw men cringe against an onslaught of rifle fire in Korea though it did no good. The cable passed over his head and made the same sound as a gull's wings when it locked and rocketed in, making the air rip.

It passed overhead, and on the way back it hit a generator and a stack of steel plate. The half-inch steel flew off the ground and slammed into One-Two's shoulder, thigh and arm. His shoulder socket was crushed, his hip shattered. The impact sent him flying off the third story. He landed in the torn sand of the construction lot, flat on his back, and he can't remember what his back hit. It could have been a lunch box or a piece of beam end, a boot, or even a small block of two-by-four left over from a foundation form. It could have been anything, and he landed with his spine directly on it.

He is proud he never lost consciousness. His body was numb from the middle of his back down. His shoulder felt shredded. Simon had been on the second floor, and he didn't wait for the lift or a ladder. He slid down the beam to the first floor, and he jumped the rest of the way.

One-Two could talk, and the foremen gathered, and the site manager was there. They knew, and One-Two knew, that they'd lost the rest of the day.

You feel okay? asked the site manager, a bald man with a permanently sunburned crown. We're gonna move you to the trailer until the ambulance gets here, he said.

One-Two nodded to say that he understood. Simon stepped in front of him.

"Like hell you're movin him."

"We'll lose a whole day here."

"You'll lose your fuckin head if you touch him," said Simon, lifting his spud wrench from his belt. One-Two was scared: he couldn't feel his legs. He couldn't sit up, and the pain in his shoulder and arm was spreading. He looked at the site manager, framed by Simon's spread-legged stance.

"Simon, you don't understand. If we lose a day, it means we lose about ten thousand dollars."

"You ain't touchin him unless you want to fight me now and the union later," stated Simon. "That'll slow you down right quick."

That's how it went. Simon stood guard over One-Two's body until the paramedics came and strapped him on the body board and took him to the hospital. One-Two thinks back; he counts it out and is surprised: Simon was only twenty-six years old at the time.

One-Two's body was ruined. They put a steel pin in his hip, gave him a new shoulder joint, and immobilized his back for six weeks to give it a chance to heal. He'd crushed two vertebrae.

After the accident the crew visited him in the hospital, and when he was released, Simon kept him up-to-date on construction. He talked crew politics and union position. He filled in One-Two on the gradual emergence of the building.

Neither he nor Simon was there when it was finished. Simon was in the middle of his trial, and One-Two was learning to walk again, and he read about the completion of the steelwork in the papers with a mixture of pride and anger. They had put the last beam in upside down: painted white and signed by the mayor and many of the steel workers, there was so much writing on it that the placement markings were impossible to read.

While he was still in the hospital, the crew took turns visiting his room, telling jokes, and smoking out the window. Betty came with Lester and the girls, and the men excused themselves under her fierce stare, promising not to smoke or drink in the hospital room. They gave him so much morphine he doesn't remember a lot about his time in the hospital except the melting in Betty's eyes. She wiped at them impatiently and complained about the smoke in the room, but One-Two thought maybe she was worried.

Once he healed enough to walk, he took the money the union gave him and looked for work. He couldn't get back on the crew; his body couldn't take it anymore. Instead, the manager at the Windsor, where he had lived since 1964, offered him the maintenance job. He was able to stay near Betty, his only consolation. As he settled into the mind-numbing work of shoring up the old building, he had only one comfort: that maybe Betty had been crying for him.

1999

I Know What You Mean, Erdupps MacChurbbs: Autobiographical Myths and Metaphors
Gerald Vizenor (1934-   ), Ojibwe

Gerald Vizenor's experience growing up in the city could have led him into darkness and failure; instead it made him into what he calls a "Trickster of Liberty": someone who looks at creeds, dogma, politics, fatuousness, and self-pity as nonsense that needs to be mocked. There are people, Vizenor declares, who are "Terminal believers, those believing only in one vision of the world, [and they] are never known to the little people. Terminal believers are too important to laugh at themselves." Despite the deaths and abandonments, Vizenor always retained that ability to laugh at the tricks fate played on him. Rather than becoming bitter, a Terminal believer, he developed the persona of a Trickster, Nanabush reincarnated. Now a distinguished professor and a prolific author, here Vizenor looks back at how a small, forsaken boy learned to survive and, with the help of an imaginary friend, to thrive. Like a true Trickster, he pokes fun not only at himself, but at the things his cultures—both white and Indian—wish to hold above reproach.

1936 Measuring My Blood
My Anishinâbe grandmother told me that my young father was a trickster, a compassionate trickster, who was not mindful of the sinister tribal stories about the great evil gambler when he left the White Earth Reservation.

"The land you intend to visit is infested with many evil spirits . . . ," the legendary tribal grandmother of the woodland people once told her brave grandchildren. "No one who has ever been within their power has ever been known to return."

Clement William Vizenor, one of six sons born to Henry Vizenor and Alice Beaulieu, did not return. Smiling and laughing most of his life, he came to Minneapolis a painter and paperhanger and bled to death in a downtown alley three years later.

A story dated June 30, 1930, on the front page of the Minneapolis Journal reported that "Police sought a giant Negro to compare his fingerprints with those on the rifled purse of Clement Vizenor, a twenty-six-year-old half-breed Indian . . . found slain yesterday with his head nearly cut off by an eight-inch throat slash . . . . He was the second member of his family to die under mysterious circumstances within a month. His brother, Truman Vizenor, was found in the Mississippi River, after he had fallen from a railroad bridge. . . ."

In a later story the Minneapolis Journal reported that "The arrest of a Minneapolis Negro in Chicago promised to give Minneapolis police a valuable clue to the murder of Clement Vizenor. . . . Three half-breed Indians were being held by police for questioning as a part of the investigation . . . . Seven Negroes were questioned and then given the option of getting out of town . . . . Captain Paradeau said he was convinced Clement had been murdered but that robbery was not the motive. The slain youth was reported to have been mild tempered and not in the habit of picking fights. Police learned that he had no debts and, as far as they could ascertain, no enemies.

Family Photograph

among trees
my father was a spruce

corded for tribal pulp
he left the white earth reservation
colonial genealogies
taking up the city at twenty-three

telling stories
sharing dreams from a mason jar
running
low through the stumps at night
was his line

at twenty-three
he waited with the old men
colorless
dressed in their last uniforms
reeling on the nicollet island bridge
arm bands adrift
wooden limbs
men too civilized by war
thrown back to evangelists and charity

no reservation superintendents there
no indian agents

pacing off allotments twenty acres short
only family photographs ashore

no catholics on the wire
tying treaty money to confirmations
in the city
my father was an immigrant
hanging paper flowers
painting ceilings white for a union boss
disguising saint louis park

his weekend women
listened to him measuring my blood at night

downtown rooms were cold
half truths
peeling like blisters of history
two sizes too small

he smiles
holding me in a photograph then
the new spruce
half white
half immigrant
taking up the city and losing at cards

Clement Vizenor was survived by his mother, his wife, three brothers, two sisters, and his son Gerald Robert Vizenor, one year and eight months old.

When my father was murdered, I was living with my Anishinâbe grandmother and aunts and uncles in a small cold-water apartment near downtown Minneapolis. The only personal memory I have from then is my grandmother hiding my nursing bottle, which, she said, I carried around all day clenched between my front teeth. When I was older, she told me between pinches of snuff that she stopped hiding my bottle when I learned the game and started hiding her bottles of whiskey. When she laughed, her round brown cheeks shook and her jumbo stomach jumped up and down under her dress of printed flowers.

Twenty-five years after the death of my father I met with police officials to examine the records of their investigation. Several people had been questioned, and the case was closed as an unsolved homicide. The chief of detectives, who was surprised to remember that he was the first officer called to investigate the crime, defended his superficial report: "We never spent much time on winos and derelicts in those days . . . who knows, one Indian vagrant kills another."

"Clement Vizenor is my father!"

"Maybe your father was a wino then," he said, looking at his watch. "Look kid, that was a long time ago, take it on the chin, you know what I mean?"

1938   Crossing the Wires

When I was four years old, my mother claimed me from my Anishinâbe grandmother for the beginning of a new life. We moved into a cold two-room apartment above a trunk manufacturing plant located on Washington Avenue in north Minneapolis. One warm spring morning I awakened early, climbed up on the cupboard, and searched the shelves for something to eat. I found only a box of soft prunes. Leaning from the kitchen window, I ate the whole box of prunes and one by one spit the pits like bombs at empty whiskey bottles in the oil and mud on the ground below.

My mother found a job as a waitress, but her salary was little more than the cost of our rent. Her eyes were always filled with tears, especially during birthdays and holidays. The electricity was terminated for nonpayment the day after she had trimmed a small Christmas tree with one threadbare string of lights. She was so distant and alone then. We sat in the dark; she cried and retold the tragedies of her twenty-two years of life. She confessed her deepest fears and guilt and stared at me through her tears before withdrawing into a depressive silence. Then it was time for me to melt the ice floating on the window or follow in silence a new crack in the flooring from one room to the next. I scraped the dirt from the cracks in even rows and then plowed it back again. During the night she summoned all her courage and broke the seal on the electricity meter, crossed the wires, and called me awake to see a lighted tree. She was so happy. The tree with one string of lights was her symbolic triumph over poverty and loneliness. She was crying again, but this time she touched me and hugged me and kissed me and told me her dreams and fantasies of a happy life for us sometime in the future. We were both so young.

During the next five years of my life I was placed with three different foster families, all of whom lived in poverty and had their electricity terminated for nonpayment, while my mother worked very hard for our future and suffered with her growing guilt. From my small places in the world then I learned how to recognize the sounds of poverty and the smell of brackish water in the city.

1941   Apples from the Evangelist

The old man had a deep white frown across his forehead and a shriveled unnerving arm and hand, which he would swing from the shoulder to beat his biological son. He was my first foster father. We lived near Pierce elementary school in northeast Minneapolis, next door to a soft-spoken and cold-fingered evangelist who was building his first church on the narrow lot in front of his small house. After school he would invite the neighborhood children in to sing and listen to his religious stories. None were worth remembering, but when his bare-breasted wife nursed her child in front of us, and when he offered us free apples once a day for helping him help the Lord build his church of concrete blocks, we sang high and mocked his strange stories. For months we hauled blocks to the wall, and when the blocks were set in concrete by the evangelist, who wagged his tongue and pinched his lips over his work, we would stuff newspapers in the holes for insulation. When my foster parents objected to their children seeing a bare breast, the woman and her child were hidden from us when we came to sing and work. We never saw her again.

When war was declared, we were all instilled with racial hate. The assumption was that the racism and hate of children at home would help defeat the evil enemy in Asia. The evangelist enlisted for the war. There were no more apples, the church was never finished, and the foster father became more obsessed with his disability—he beat his biological son all the more. When he caught me stealing food or wandering off for hours along the railroad tracks playing war without permission, he would never beat me but only stare at me with one hand on his hip—the other hand hanging limp—and turn away in silence. I never felt like his son because he never hit me with that shriveled arm. My fosterage was only for the money.

His wife, my first foster mother, was very gentle and kind. She would smile for us and plan things with her daughter, but when her husband was home she would seldom speak. He became more abusive and started drinking and staying away from home, which delighted and animated us, but soon his wife joined him, and they would both come home drunk.

He lost his job, and we looked after ourselves. One night when the electricity was terminated and the space heater ran out of fuel, we fell asleep waiting by the window in our winter coats for him and his wife to come home from drinking. Everyone contributed something to the war which lasted so long at night.

1943   Silence in the Third Grade

My mother married Elmer Petesch, a burly and balding man who left the security of a successful farm family to become an insecure, hard-drinking stationary engineer for a millworking company in the city. He carved his thick curling toenails with a broken pocketknife, ate large bowls of boiled cabbage, carried a pocketful of farmer matches to burn off the effluvial odor of his stomach gas, and was slow to show his love for people.

We lived in a small one-bedroom double bungalow in north Minneapolis across the street from an undeveloped cemetery where I spent most of my time alone with my dog. I built dugouts covered with woven grass and forts in the trees to watch for the evil gamblers of the city.

I entered the third grade at Hamilton elementary school and do not remember speaking an audible word for the whole school year. I had created a life of benign demons and little people from the woodland of love in my head. There was no reason then to leave my fantasies for academic prisons and cold rooms, which, until then, had been peopled with violence and promises and parental guilt. I sat at my little desk seven rows back, never gesturing for recognition or uttering a word. It was a peaceful time. By the end of the school year I had earned the affectionate reputation of being a very well behaved slow learner. At night, in a secret corner of the basement I would sit reading parables to my dog.

During the summer my cemetery territory was overrun and occupied by the enemy who became my friends: Myron Game, whom we called The Frog because he lost his breath on every other word when he was excited; Randolf Mullins, whom we called Black Foot Broth because he was so big and stupid and unclean; Wilbur Wannum, who owned his own real gun. These and others invaded my shelter, rebuilt my esthetic woven fortresses, competed for the loyal affection of my dog, and taught me the good times and places to peep in bathroom windows for a glimpse at naked female bodies.

The leaders of the cemetery legion were always the biggest and toughest but never the witless. Black Foot Broth never had a chance at leadership—we only used him as a servant. For my new place among new friends I practiced the roles of dutiful follower for favors, the daredevil trickster and clown, and as a last resort the intellectual, but I was never successful enough at any role to command the attention of my new friends for more than ten minutes at a time.

The following school year, my second in the third grade, I protested the arbitrary demands of authority—since I had been identified the year before as the well-behaved slow learner, my efforts to be the daredevil intellectual were not convincing—and wandered in my own fantasy of time, defining my own free space. I often skipped school with The Frog to explore the sewers and woods along the river. I was free and guiltless until a very savvy art teacher told me I was a brilliant painter. She displayed my watercolor paintings of setting suns over peaceful lakes, birch trees and moss, canoes, and jumping deer, while brainwashing me with the need for personal discipline. For a time, in the slow course of therapeutic art on the third-grade level, she was very successful. She told me, with an affectionate pat on the head, that I would be famous some day if I worked hard and obeyed the rules.

1946 Petunias in Juvenile Court

Come in, Zero Three, this is Zero Four. Suspects have just removed cartoon films from the department of children and are proceeding to the escalator near aisle seven, over.

This is Zero Three. Have visual contact with suspects, one in brown winter coat with matching fake fur collar and the other suspect in surplus blue parka . . . will pursue on escalator.

Check, Zero Three. Zero Two will intercept next floor. Believe suspects are destined for winter mittens and sports department, over.

Check, Zero Four.

Silence.

Zero Four, suspects are leaving winter sports department with ski poles and mittens, advise Zero One immediate interception on elevator and notify police, over.

Check, Zero Two.

Main floor, please.

"We made it, Wannum," I said.

"The mittens are mine," he demanded.

"But I thought you wanted the ski poles. Idiot, I wanted the mittens, you already have a pair, and I don't," I argued. Looking over my shoulder, I noticed a gray-haired man holding a portable shortwave radio.

"Let's get another pair then," said Wannum, washing his solid-gold-capped front tooth.

"Never mind, dummy."

Zero One grabbed us by the coat collars. "I see you boys have been shopping for ski poles and mittens," he said. "Have you stolen anything else today?"

"Oh shit . . . you asshole, Vizenor," yelled Wannum, backing away from me. "This wasn't my idea, I didn't take a thing," he pleaded as we were dragged from the elevator to a Big Zero office.

My first shudder of fear, having nothing to do with knowing right from wrong or my public image, was the thought of my stepfather Elmer stumbling at me with his big hairy arms and jerking my body and beating me until he was breathing so hard he could not swing again.

"Hey mister, I'll do anything, anything," I pleaded to the man in his Zero One office, "but please, do you have to tell my father, do you have to tell him?"

"Are you ashamed for what you have done?" Zero One asked, leaning back in his executive chair behind his desk.

"No, I mean yes, but do you have to tell my father?" I pleaded a second time. "You don't know what he will do to me when he finds out about this."

"Well, I don't think it is my place to tell your father what to do or not to do," Zero One said in dictation tones. "At any rate, we are pleased with your confessions, and when the police come along any minute now, the whole matter will be out of my hands."

Four two-hundred-pound police officers came puffing into the Zero One office. Zero One gave them the facts while they looked us up and down. We were dragged to a police car and driven in silence to the courthouse.

In a dark room juvenile officers questioned us about other crimes, while we confessed again and again to the shoplifting, and then they called our parents. About an hour later burly Elmer picked me up for the long ride home. He smelled of boiled cabbage and sulfur from burning matches.

Silence.

Turn right, turn left, next corner, but we were not going home. Elmer was taking me out to dinner and a man-to-man talk, he said. His kindness was a new form of torture because I could only measure the long seconds to the belting when we got home.

"Are you going to hit me?" I pleaded.

"No, not this time, and you know I don't like doing that any more than you like getting it," said my stepfather.

"You won't beat me?"

"No."

"Ever again?"

"Well, there might be a time when you'll need it again, but you're old enough now to talk about things man to man."

"When?" I asked, telling myself that I was always old enough to talk about things in place of a beating.

"You just eat now, and let's just talk about tonight before I lose my temper and change my mind," he said, beating the bottom of a ketchup bottle. "You and that kid you were with have to appear in juvenile court and that will be punishment enough for stealing. The judge will be tough, but you need the lesson."

We were well dressed for the event in juvenile court. Wannum was even wearing a new necktie his mother bought for the occasion. We waited for the judge to sentence us for our crimes. He looked down from his cruddy bench and said it was not the first time we had stolen something. We fell for the bait and confessed everything we had ever even thought about lifting.

"Do you want to grow up to be criminals and spend the rest of your natural lives in prison . . . do you?" he asked, but never waited for an answer. "Let me tell you this, young man," he said leaning over the bench and pointing at me, "and you too, young Wannum; if it was not true that our two juvenile training schools were filled I would send you both there in a minute for your crimes . . . you deserve no less . . . but because Glen Lake and Red Wing are filled, I am giving you a chance to do good by placing you both on probation for six months . . . and if during that time you ever steal, or do anything wrong again, I will let someone out just to make room to put you in. Do you understand what I have just said?"

We looked at each other, nodded, and listened again. We were scared and knew the judge was very serious, but we did not understand what he said about institutions and probation.

"You will report to your probation officer every Monday afternoon for six months . . . and you will tell the principal of your school that you are on probation for stealing and he will permit you to leave early to report to your probation officer. Do you understand what I have just told you?"

"Yes sir . . . sir."

"Have you learned your lesson?"

"Yes sir . . . sir."

Wannum's parents blamed me for influencing their son in the evil life of crime, and my mother blamed me first and then Wannum for leading me into a life of crime. But both parents agreed on one thing: we were never to see each other again. Close your eyes, they said, and turn the other way when you see each other in school or on the street. We listened, nodded, and went on looking at each other and playing together in the cemetery. We were always together on Monday afternoon when we went to see our probation officer at the courthouse.

There were no more than two or three probation officers for the whole city of juvenile criminals on probation. Every Monday every juvenile on probation would line up at the same time in the courthouse waiting to report. We were petunias on the low road in the juvenile world of crime. Shoplifting was no crime at all compared to the things the northeast bandits boasted about: rape, armed robbery, extortion, burglary, and car theft. The Frog and I had been kidnapped the summer before by the northeast toughs and hauled across the river where we were stripped and tortured. Being the smallest and petunia criminals, we waited in line the longest while the northeast bandits came late and took their places at the head of the line to see the probation officer.

His face was cracked like old yellow paste. "Did you go to church?" the probation officer asked. He waited for my answer with his head down and his pencil poised to enter my answer on a large yellow card.

"Yup."

"Attending school every day?"

"Yup."

I never saw his legs behind the desk.

"Staying away from other known criminals and juveniles on probation?" he asked, rubbing his forearm on the edge of the desk. Behind me was another probation officer asking the same questions.

"Yup."

He could be a cripple without legs.

"Very good, Gerald . . . you are making very good progress, and I think in a month or so if you behave yourself and stay out of mischief and follow the rules, we may release you from probation early."

"Really?"

"Yes, but don't forget to attend church every week," he said. He flashed a one-second smile and told me to send in the next boy. "Keep your nose clean, kid, you know what I mean. . . ."

I looked under the desk before I left to see if he had legs. He did, but he could still be a cripple.

1947 Trustworthy and Brave But Not Stupid

Many Point Scout Camp
Sunday

Dear Mother,

You never told me when I left for camp that they were sending me back to the reservation. You should have said something. My father grew up here you know, everybody knows that we are on the White Earth Reservation. There are animals and birds everywhere, but I don't like the people very much here. Everybody is always telling me what to do all the time. They think they own this place. I can't even swim when I feel like it, everything is on time, go here and go there, and I am hungry.

I am living in a tent with another scout and he eats sardines all the time and leaves the cans in the tent. He said he can do it because he is a Norwegian. He smells like a fish in the tent. He never gave me any either.

One of the scout leaders started a fire in the big fireplace in the main lodge with his mouth. I was fooled at first, but then I saw the gasoline he drank and spit at a match he was holding in front of the logs. But don't worry because he told us never to drink gasoline.

Yesterday they killed a whole pig and roasted it over a fire outside. I didn't eat any because it smelled awful.

Everybody tells us to work all the time. We wanted to explore around the lake but nobody would let us. One kid has all the merit badges they make. He's an eagle scout and everything, but he looks dumb with his thick glasses. He walks like Black Foot Broth—you know, my dumb friend across the alley.

We learned about canoeing and life saving and fire building. In the morning they give us cold toast and cold eggs. They gave us time after church today to write to you.

Your Loving Son,
Jerry

Wednesday

Dear Mother,

You won't believe this but they took us away from the camp yesterday to find our way back with a compass, but we went for a walk around the lake and they said we were lost. The kid with the thick glasses said he hoped we would get lost for the day on purpose. We had a great time. Nobody told us what to do all day. We circled the camp and walked around the lake until dark. We saw a nest of bald eagles. We knew where we were and didn't need a compass. Nobody could get lost walking around a lake anyway. It was really wild.

When we came back, they thought we were lost so now we have to stay here all the time. The kid with the thick glasses laughs at us all the time. Nobody believes we were not lost. Another dumb thing here is the order of the arrow when all the scouts pretend they are Indians. Tell The Frog I will be home next weekend.

Love,
Your Son, Jerry

Envoi: The Many Point Scout Camp Reservation is operated on twenty-four thousand acres of valuable wilderness tribal land on the White Earth Reservation by the Viking Council of the Boy Scouts of America. Few loyal and trustworthy scouts are aware of how the land was obtained from tribal people.

1948   Jaunty Pirates on Green Lake

Mean Nettles was born a squatter. He played high school football without practicing, drank hard booze from a jar, smoked two packs of cigarettes a day, had sex with older women before he was fifteen, and owned his own lake below a concrete block factory on the shores of the Mississippi River. He was very quiet and very mean, so mean that even the great river mosquitoes circled beyond his reach.

The Frog and I were enchanted by the river woods in the summer. We were small and quick and took pleasure in the excitement of tormenting giants like Mean Nettles. We waited in the brush pinching blood from mosquitoes and watched the mean giant build his sailboat. He hauled oil drums, deck joists, and boxcar siding to his dockyard on Green Lake. The lake, once a huge gravel pit near the river, was filled with limewater waste from the concrete block factory up the hill. The lake was chartreuse in color with a fuzzy gray bottom that turned yellowish at dusk. The water was thick and clear like cough medicine. We tried it as a mosquito repellent, but it only turned our skin into fine white wrinkles. Mean Nettles once threatened to baptize his enemies there.

The six cross-eyed Pitcher brothers squatted in the house next to Nettles about a mile below the bridge in north Minneapolis. Unlike Mean Nettles, the Pitchers talked all the time—talking twice as much about what they saw with double vision—and they were always together like a pack of hungry reservation tribal dogs. The Pitchers had equal rights as squatters, but they were not welcome at Green Lake. Mean Nettles ruled the lake.

In the evening before dark when Mean Nettles was away drinking and having sex with the river sirens, we entered the dockyard and sabotaged the construction of his sailboat. We punched holes in the drums and set them afloat on the thick chartreuse water. The giant had nailed a book, opened to a schematic drawing of a schooner, to a box elder tree near the dockyard. His oil drum sailing vessel was a rectangle about six feet long. We wrote obscene phrases about giants on the book.

Next day Mean Nettles rescued his drums and with the help of the Pitcher brothers set a trap for Vizenor and Game. They dug a six-foot hole on the running path along the river and covered it with a thin layer of earth and leaves. In the morning the little Pitcher was placed as a scout on the bridge to signal our arrival. Once we were on the river path, the three biggest Pitchers jumped from the brush and chased us along the path. Two more Pitchers joined in the chase. At a curve in the path we both dropped into the pit. When the dust settled, we looked up and saw Mean Nettles straddling the hole and heard him grinding his teeth. It was the only sound he made. Then six faces with crossed eyes looked into the hole.

"Let's just bury 'em," said the little Pitcher, out of breath. He kicked dirt at us in the hole.

Mean Nettles ground his teeth again.

"No," said another Pitcher, who covered his mouth when he spoke to hide his rotting front teeth. "Let's strip 'em, Nettles, and dump 'em in the lake."

"Badtize 'em, badtize 'em..." the others chanted.

"Hey, come on, you guys, you know us," I said with a graceful hand gesture. "We didn't do nothing… let us out of here."

Mean Nettles ground his teeth again.

"You sonnofabiches," said Game, losing his voice, "goddamit, you sonnofabiches, open this hole and let me out of here!"

"Throw it up," said Mean Nettles.

"Throw what up?" we asked.

"Throw it up," he repeated, grinding his teeth.

"Throw what?" The little Pitcher kicked dirt into my mouth and stumbled away in hysterical laughter.

We knew what to throw up, but we protested as long as possible, hoping that what we would throw up would spare us from a beating or a baptismal ceremony in Green Lake.

"Throw it up."

"My uncle is a cop, and he gave me this knife," said Game, holding his hunting knife out and losing his voice again on every other word.

"Throw it up, assholes, throw it up like we said," said the little Pitcher, kicking more dirt on our heads in the hole.

"My brother in the army overseas sent me this watch," I said in protest.

"What brother?" Game asked.

"What brother . . . what brother . . ." I snarled at Game, "the same one as your uncle cop, you idiot, give up your goddam hunting knife! Hey, Nettles, how about it, let me keep the watch, just the watch."

"Throw it up."

We threw up our hunting knives, the watch, billfolds, coins, rings, belts, sacred stones, and a pair of pigskin climbing gloves.

The Pitchers grabbed everything and ran off fighting over the booty while Mean Nettles, still straddling the hole and grinding his teeth, unbuttoned his pants, pulled out his giant penis and, while we protested and waved our hands, urinated on our heads.

When he left, we dug our way out of the hole and plunged into the river, scrubbing the urine of the giant from our hair and clothes. We had tormented the giant and got caught, but we knew with careful planning we could outwit him and his cross-eyed followers. We applied our abstract movie-matinee knowledge of piracy on the high seas and planned to plunder his dockyard and capture his sailboat.

Weeks later when the sailboat was built, we staged our assault on the dockyard. Our strategy was to capture the sailboat about noon, sail back and forth across the lake tiring the giant, who we knew would chase along the shore after us, and then, when the giant was near exhaustion, we knew he would run to the house of the Pitcher brothers for help.

He did everything according to plan. We knew he would not jump into the limewater lake after us, but twice he almost caught us near shore. We had never sailed before and forgot to reef at a turn at one end of the lake and almost capsized. The second time he almost caught us in a doldrum with only a small board to paddle the heavy four-drum vessel into deeper water. We yelled at him as he ran back and forth around the lake and gave him the finger and other obscene high signs. He went for help when we said things about his mother and his riverfront breeding.

We ran the sailboat ashore according to plan. Rather than running for the bridge and the security of home, which later proved to be our only mistake, we climbed to the top of two box elder trees which we had selected earlier along the river path, believing that the giant and his cross-eyed followers would think we were hiding deep in the woods. I waited like a crow at the top of the tree holding my breath and laughter, listening to the Pitcher brothers plunging through the thick brush below.

Pounding through the brush, they yelled at us and threatened to baptize us in the lake, whip the bottom of our feet until they bled, drive soft sumac stakes into our armpits, pound shit in our mouths and ears, and pull our eyelashes out.

We waited in the top of the trees, swaying peacefully in the afternoon sunlight. The katydids sounded, the leaves rattled on the breeze, and my foot fell asleep. I was dreaming of soaring as a crow or an eagle. I rubbed my wings against the limbs and sent my eyes above the trees.

Mean Nettles was a silent squatter, but we discovered he was not stupid. While the cross-eyed Pitcher brothers were searching deep in the woods, the giant walked down the river path looking for signs of our escape. He stopped beneath us and examined the scuff marks on the soft bark. He called for his followers, and with their hunting knives, which were once ours, they chopped us down. When we swung to the ground, the cross-eyed brothers grabbed us. I was beaten and kicked until I felt as numb as a bird with broken wings.

The little Pitcher kept spitting at us while our hands were tied behind our backs. With ropes around our necks we were led like animals to the dockyard where the giant, smoking cigarette after cigarette and drinking from a jar, told us he was holding a trial to find us guilty of messing with his sailboat. Point by point, Mean Nettles listed the evidence against us. We denied everything at first—it was a case of mistaken identity because we had been in the trees all day—but then we admitted to the theft of the sailboat only as a practical joke. "Have you lost your sense of humor?" we pleaded.

The cross-eyed jury found us guilty, and the giant sentenced us to be stripped, whipped with leather thongs, and banished to an island in the river for the rest of our lives.

The stripping was embarrassing, because between The Frog and me we had a total of no more than a dozen dark pubic hairs. The whipping was painful but less frightening than the hand of my stepfather, and the banishment was far better than being baptized in the limewater of Green Lake. We were transported to the island on a raft and left naked with our hands and feet tied to trees.

It was late in the afternoon. Hot and humid. Blackflies bit the top of my head. The giant river mosquitoes, too bloated with our blood to fly, just fell from our bodies into the moist grass and crawled away.

We loosened the ropes just before dark and swam down the river to the bridge. The cool dark water soothed the welts on our bodies. Naked, we ran home through the alleys. My dog was waiting for me in the basement. He listened to me curse the evil giants of the world and praise the courage of the little people.

1949 Every Threshold an Internal Fire

The benign demons and little woodland people of love who lived in my thoughts and fantasies during my year of silence in the third grade came to life as real people with real names. They are the stature of the people and images in my dreams, moving through my head at night, nudging me in daydreams along the river and leading my visions through boring and repetitive rhythms of controlled learning in school. They are the little people who raise the banners of imagination on assembly lines and at cold bus stops in winter. They marched with me in the service and kept me awake with humor on duty as a military guard. The little people sat with me in baronial ornamental classrooms and kept me alive and believable under the death blows of important languages.[174]

The little people told me stories when I cracked my elbow, cut my wrist to the bone, and stood in line waiting to report to my probation officer, and when I was shot in the lower lip during a real quick-draw gunfight on a dusty road with The Frog. The little people know how to distract me with humor when I am desperate enough to become a spiritual victim and to make promises to religious warlocks offering to change my life for the better again.

The little people came to life this year under velvet throws in the loft of a garage where I was hiding on a summer afternoon. The world around me was buzzing with the energy of little lives. Old trees from the woodland swayed and creaked as beams and joists and shiplap siding in the haunting memory of the wind. Insects etched their vibrations on wings and millions of little feet through cosmic space and violet visions of the sun. The little people told me they make themselves known when there is trust in knowing the world through different visions. Terminal believers, those believing only in one vision of the world, are never known to the little people. Terminal believers are too important to laugh at themselves.

Erdupps MacChurbbs walked across the red velvet throw and introduced himself to me.

"We have been traveling together in dreams for a long time, and now we are one and know our names as little people. You are me, and I am you. You have become a little person, and I have become you," MacChurbbs told me, knitting the fingers of his little hands and bowing in mockery of the terminal belief in proper manners and high social breeding.

"But I am not a little person," I said, moving my fingers and toes to validate the great space between them.

"You are when you free yourself from the customs of civilized measurement," he told me, extending his arms. "We are so big, and so little at the same time. You have learned only one way to measure the world. Little people disappear when civilization and terminal beliefs surround them. Imagination and humor expire, and people grow too big for their eyes when they seek cultural perfection through the exalted structures of the past. Civilization is a burnished skull for those who will never know the space between dreams . . . I will show you." Standing on my shoulder with his head cocked in front of my left eye, he continued to speak. He said we were flowers and birds and at times only members. "I am in your eye and you are in mine, and I see you back again as a little person. I will disappear when you think about what you will be in the future but are not now, by the measures of the past. What will you be when you grow up? What civilized attention will you demand from the world? Who will you be?"

"Just me."

"But whose skull will you be?"

"A famous writer...."

Erdupps MacChurbbs snapped into dust before my eyes. I searched the velvet throws calling his name. I felt large and mechanical. My hands were numbers, massive and improper, as I patted the red velvet folds for his little body. He was gone. I had been tricked by my own thoughts and felt stupid. I laughed at myself. I was nervous. Who cares what I will be? I said to myself. I will be nothing, no matter who I think I will be.

I leaned back and changed my mind again. The window in the loft was open. On the breeze of warm air great flowers of dust floated through the pillars of sunlight. I was dust when a dragonfly hovered at the opening of the window. Her shadow reached to the floor at my feet and examined every ridge and crater on the wood. When the dragonfly entered the loft closer to her shadow, I took up warm wings and watched my shadow move across time and space. I could only feel my eyes as the loft turned in shadowless circles of marbling greens and violets. In spiral space I saw MacChurbbs and other little people a hundred times my size. They were everywhere the same as if my vision had crossed and crossed without end. I bounced with my wings on the sunlight and listened to my eyes.

Bishop Bartholomew Baragga,[175] a little Old World missionary and linguist dressed in a scarlet gown and a black satin hat with a ragged tassel and carrying a sprig of white pine, moved across my eyes a hundred times with his head swung backward reciting a strange litany that no one answered. Then he stopped and stared at me in silence. Hundreds of bushy eyebrows moved with his wide lips. He explained that he carried white pine because bald eagles always have a fresh sprig in their nests.

"There are so many of you," I said, trying to blink away the many images of his stern face. "Which one of you is real?"

"The one you see."

"But I see you everywhere."

"Then you must be everyone to see me everywhere."

"Did you come through the window?"

"Yes, always through the windows of the world," the bishop chanted with his elbow resting in his hand. "You see, I am burdened with five glorious centuries of terminal belief in celibacy and the virgin birth, and I am not able to pass through time and cross thresholds. . . . My life is waiting at the edge of time in the past. I can move only as a spirit through windows."

"But you could fly across thresholds."

"Only windows."

"Why?"

"Every threshold is a fire."

"Would you burn up if you crossed?"

"No, but the internal fires would go out."

MacChurbbs appeared a hundred times in my eyes of the dragonfly with a beautiful dark-skinned woman dressed in leather and white linen. Her dark hair was drawn back with silver and turquoise jewelry. Her skin was soft and moist. On her left hand she wore a gold ring with tiny bells. Sophia Libertina, who first met MacChurbbs when he was wandering in the mountains seeking the mystery of translation, touched my face with her fingers, and I felt warm and clean. I saw her everywhere, and the sound of the tiny bells on her ring made us all smile and laugh a hundred times in my eyes.

"Famous writers spend too much time alone perfecting the style of their experiences from the past. No one has ever lived a life of humor and love in blank verse," MacChurbbs told me, poised on a rafter in the loft with one eye closed. "Love and passion are never left to the dull men who create history from all the words they have read. Some people put things together, some people take things apart, but little people float between words and dreams."

I found my shadow, and the little people in the loft came back to my eyes one by one. Leaning on my elbow in the velvet throws, I listened to the bishop move his eyebrows telling me that MacChurbbs was a wise clown, a cosmic jester who was never tricked even by believing in his own humor. He drew his humor from a moment of knowing the contradictions between passion and reason, between the terminal beliefs of men and women, between cats and dogs, between night and day, between up and down, between words and dreams. He tells fathers they are sons, criminals they are victims, women they are men, saints they are sinners—he turns the visions and cultural measures of the world around to share the humor of little people floating through their own shadows.

Bishop Baragga blessed himself, and we all joined hands and danced across the rafters and flew home before dark. The little people have been with me ever since, and I always remember to leave a window open for those who cannot cross thresholds for fear of extinguishing their internal fires.

1950 Masturbation Papers on the Double

I lied about my age to enlist as a private in the Minnesota National Guard. For two hours once a week I learned how to march, with hundreds of older men, back and forth in the Minneapolis Armory. After six months of marching and memorizing the mechanical parts of my rifle, I was ready for two weeks of summer training at Fort Ripley near Little Falls in northern Minnesota.

"Private Vizenor," the loudspeaker rang out one Sunday morning at summer camp. "Private Vizenor . . . get your ass to the orderly room on the double."

I was there on the double.

"Vizenor, I have been going through your service file," the sergeant said with disdain, "and I have not found your masturbation papers."

"My what, sir?"

"Your masturbation papers, soldier."

"Sorry sir, but . . . ."

"Well, get your sweet ass over to headquarters and get them right now, soldier," said the sergeant. "On the double, soldier."

"Yes sir," I said, not knowing about masturbation papers, worried that I had failed to do my duty to my country as a proud and brave soldier in the Minnesota National Guard.

"Private Vizenor, sir, reporting for my masturbation papers," I told the sergeant at headquarters.

"Where the hell have you been, soldier? Your masturbation papers are at the command post! Get your skinny ass up there and ask for the colonel."

"Yes sir," I said and double-timed from the headquarters tent to the command tent about two blocks away.

"Sir, Private Vizenor requests permission to see the colonel, sir," I said.

"At ease, soldier," he said, returning my salute. "What is so urgent that you must see the colonel, soldier?"

"My masturbation papers, sir."

"Your what?"

"Masturbation papers, sir."

"Who sent you here?"

"My company sergeant, sir."

"Just a minute, soldier, I think the colonel will want to talk with you about this," he said, cranking the field telephone to call the colonel. When the colonel entered the command tent, I snapped to attention and saluted. I knew I was in for real trouble when he frowned and returned my salute with a nubby swagger stick.

"Private Vizenor, sir, reporting for my masturbation papers, sir," I said in a loud and strong voice which I had learned by calling marching commands in the armory.

"Yes, where did you lose your papers?"

"I don't know, sir."

"Do you know what masturbation means?"

"No sir."

"Then how can you find your papers?"

"I don't know, sir."

"Do you know what jacking off means?"

"Yes, sir."

"Masturbation means the same thing, soldier. You can pick up your jacking off papers from your company sergeant," the colonel said. "You tell him I sent you."

"Yes sir."

"Hang in there, soldier."

"Yes sir."

"You know what I mean, soldier?"

"Yes sir."

"Carry on."

"Yes, sir!"

The company sergeant was not pleased when he learned that I had told the colonel who had sent me looking for my masturbation papers so he ordered me to clean the urinals for three days. Two weeks at summer camp as a soldier had taught me what masturbation meant, how to march in the sand, how to wire a field telephone, how to field-strip a machine gun, and how to keep the urinals clean.

1951 We Both Need a Good Home

Elmer Petesch returned from the mill right on schedule and found a short note from his wife of eight years. She told him she was moving on to a warmer climate and a better life, leaving him with the mortgage, a secondhand piano, and some old wedding gifts, and as a parting gesture of ironic affection she also left behind her only son. Elmer did not appreciate the reminder. A few months after the departure of my mother I also rejected his authority and violence and left his house.

We had just finished another boiled dinner with ring bologna when he struck me on the back while I was washing the dishes. He cursed me for my mother and hit me again. I left his house in silence determined never to return.

Elmer was alone for four days, and on the fifth day he began searching for me. He left thoughtful messages around the neighborhood that he wanted me to return. I ignored his rapprochement and peddled my own defensive stories about his violence to my friends and their parents. The Frog invited me to stay at his house, which pleased me because his father told great stories about his adventures in the wilderness and drank whiskey like a man—winking at us when his wife complained. We were willing listeners and eager conspirators of his boyhood memories. The old man was convincing because he had a bullet hole in his leg from a gunfight at a mining camp in the mountains. He even had the gun he said he took away from the man who shot him.

We were playing basketball in the backyard of the Game house when Elmer found me. I told him to leave because I would never listen to him again.

"Let's just talk it over," he said. Before he left, he told my friends to tell me that he would be back the next night to talk again. It gave me a feeling of personal power to have him on the defensive.

On the sixth night he met me in the alley with my friends. We first agreed that he would stand across the alley and that we would listen to each other without interruptions. He was the first to speak.

"Please believe me . . . . I am very sorry. I know you want to be with your friends now, but I want you to know how sorry I am for taking your mother out on you. I have been very lonely since you left, and I know it was wrong to hit you. It was not your fault, but sometimes we hurt the people we love the most. You know what I mean? I want you to come back home. We need each other now. I have never had a good home, and you have never had a good home either; now we need to make one together."

He was crying. Tears were running down his fat cheeks. He took his glasses off and pleaded to me with his hands. I felt like reaching out to him, but I had been hurt too many times in the past to yield only to tears and a stand-up promise. My thoughts were overburdened with his violence. My friends were embarrassed because we had all been taught to believe that tears were a sign of weakness in a man.

"I wish I could take back all the times I have hurt you," he said. "Leaving home was the best thing for you to do, and I have no right to expect you to trust me now and come back home . . . but I do want you to believe me this time." He blew his nose.

"I don't believe you," I said in a cold voice. "You have said all those things before. Go take it out on my mother, not me. Go away."

"Can we talk tomorrow again?"

"Maybe."

I would not yield. As a visitor I had fantasized my ideal place as a new son in the Game family, in which I was at least free of the fear of physical abuse. But visitors are visitors, and that night I was encouraged to return home.

The next night in the alley Elmer faced not only my friends but their parents and other neighbors who had learned from gossip about the negotiations in the alley. The women stood behind their children with their arms folded over their breasts. The men stood in the shadows of open garage doors chewing toothpicks and looking down. I was silent. The audience was tense.

"I will come every night to tell you I want you to come home, but not the way it used to be. I promise you, and you have your friends here listening, that I will never again mistreat you. We both need a good home. Please come home."

"Let me think about it," I said.

Elmer turned and walked down the alley toward his home. The neighbors and friends looked at each other; husbands and wives walked home with their children between them. Screen doors banged closed. Kitchen lights went on. I could smell the young trees and the moist leaves. Fireflies blinked and disappeared in the dark grass. The apples and plums were still green. My hands were swollen from clenching my fists. I was alone.

Watching the summer sky and listening to my uneven breath, I walked toward the river. That night I slept beneath the bridge with the little people and fell between dreams of flight over the woodland.

The house was cool and smelled of mold and dust. My ears buzzed with excitement. I walked through the house touching things like a stranger, putting thoughts from the past to rest, and was overwhelmed with a good feeling. I cleaned the house, washed the dishes, cut the grass, and baked a blueberry pie, his favorite, and waited in the kitchen for him to return from the mill. He walked in without speaking, took my hand, pulled me out of the chair, and embraced me. It was the first time he had touched me with affection. We both wept and never spoke of the past.

We lived together as equals, sharing our time and space without rules. We both became sons and fathers and brothers and friends at the same time. If I had not had the will to trust him again, I would not have known that Elmer was a very compassionate and loving man.

Five months after our negotiations in the alley, Elmer fell two stories down an elevator shaft while working at the mill. His pelvis was crushed, and he died three days later in the hospital. He was buried in the cemetery across the street from the house.

1952 Is the Little Man Ready?

We stopped a crowd of boys playing baseball in the street and asked them directions to 314 John Street. They looked at each other and then burst into laughter. The pitcher for the team, slapping a ball in his mitt and snapping his gum, asked us what we wanted there.

"Just a friend," I replied, squeezing the steering wheel of my 1934 Ford with a crank-out front window to flex my triceps in his face. He backed away from the car and extended his arm and mitt to the west and yelled the directions: "Two blocks that way! Down and at 'em, boys!" The team laughed. I raced the eight-cylinder engine, which burned a quart of oil every fifty miles, and peeled rubber on bald tires, heading for the first real live sex purchase of my life.

At 314 John Street, an address we had heard for two years in high school, was a house, or rather a duplex, of prostitution that looked like any other house on the block. It was painted white with black shutters and had a front porch and a swing. We had expected at least some sign or symbol advertising the business of sex.

We drove by the duplex three times and parked several blocks away. We hid our billfolds, rings, and watches in the car and took only folding money with us. Matthew Bridge, my friend from high school who was called The Candidate because he talked and laughed like a politician, took five dollars and I took three.

The Candidate knocked at the door of the duplex of prostitution. The shades were drawn. We waited. A boy and his dog ran down the street. Two cars stopped at the end of the block. The palms of my hands were sweating. He knocked again. The door opened, and we were greeted by a sweet grandmother in a print dress and apron. I knew we were at the wrong place.

"May I help you, boys?" she asked.

"Well. . . ." The Candidate said, hesitating and scratching arms, which I knew was a sign of great anxiety.

"Are you collecting for the paper?"

"No," said The Candidate, "we were wondering if you by chance had any propositions . . . you know what I mean?"

"Propositions?"

I was ready to run. The Candidate scratched his arms and jerked his head back and forth looking at the street and her face and her feet. She was wearing pink slippers.

"How old are you boys?"

"Twenty-five," said The Candidate.

"Twenty-three."

"I see," the sweet grandmother said. "Well, come in now, but be sure not to get your noses out of joint."

We followed her into a room where there was a wide ascending stairway. She told us to sit down and wait and to obey the rules of the house. The rules were to pay in advance, enter by one door leave by another, and stay out of the hallway when the red was on, which meant that someone was leaving who did not want to be seen. We sat in leather chairs facing the stairway and waited our turn. The Candidate scratched his arms. I picked at a black-head in my ear.

"How much will it cost?"

"Five dollars," said The Candidate.

"I only have three."

"You can hold hands for that."

"Propositions . . . who told you that word?"

"Do they come for us?"

"She said from the stairway."

"This is it," The Candidate said, jumping out of his chair, bounding up the steps to meet a big blond woman with large breasts. They walked up the stairs laughing. A door closed. I was alone. My wet hands squeaked on the arm of the leather chair.

"Are you waiting for me?" she asked, standing at the foot of the stairs dressed in a pink strapless high-school-prom formal evening gown. She was tall with long brown hair and small breasts, and she spoke with a southern accent.

"Well, yes, but . . ."

"But what?"

"Nothing . . . which way do we go?"

She led me into a small room with a window overlooking the backyard, three pink plastic flamingoes, and the alley. The room was very warm and smelled sweet from lilacs and roses. When I turned from the window to tell her about the three dollars, she was standing naked by the bed.

"Do you want to talk or play?" she asked, mounting the brass frame bed and rolling over on her back. I watched her naked body as I undressed. The leg of my trouser caught on my shoe and the lace on one shoe was knotted. When I was undressed, I sat next to her on the bed. She touched me, and I asked her how much.

"How much am I worth?"

"Three dollars?"

"We better hurry then," she said, running her fingers across my back and humming. Everything was so distracting. Every odor, every sound, every touch, everything was distracting me from the thought of sex. I wanted to look and talk for a while the way we did in the back seat of the car by the river. I could not stop talking and thinking. Everything was so easy.

"How did a nice girl like you end up in a place like this?" I asked with interest and affection.

"No words," she said, touching my lips with her fingers. They were sticky and smelled sweet. I said so. Then she ran her hand through my hair and told me to come down on the bed next to her. When she kissed my ear, the one with a blackhead in it, I jerked my head around to look into her big brown eyes.

"Is the little man ready?" she whispered.

1956 In a Low Voice without Words

A good game hunter is never competitive. Hunting with friends turns the hunt into a passionless and destructive contest. The instincts of a survival hunter are measured best when he is alone in the woods. In groups, people depend on each other for identity and security, but alone the hunter must depend on his own instincts of survival and must move with the energy of the woodland.

I walked into the woods alone and found a place in the sun against a tree. The animals and birds were waiting in silence for me to pass. They felt my coming from the lifeless energy of mechanical things. They knew my evil thoughts, the thoughts of a cunning killer. Falling asleep brought my mind and energy in touch with the life around me. When I opened my eyes, after a short rest, the birds were singing and the squirrels were eating without fear and jumping from tree to tree. I was jumping with them but against them as the hunter.

I raised my rifle, took aim, and fired at a large red squirrel running across an oak bough. He fell to the ground near the trunk of the tree, bounced once, and started to climb the tree again. The bullet passed through his shoulder, shattering the bone. His right front leg hung limp from torn skin. He fell to the ground and tried to climb the tree again. He instinctively reached up with his shattered paw, but it was not there to hold him. He fell again and watched me watching him. Blood was spreading across his body. He tried to climb the tree again and again to escape from me.

He was a survivor. He knew when and where to hide from the hunters who came in groups to kill—their harsh energies were burned in the memories of his animal tribe. I was alone. My presence and my intention to kill squirrels were disguised by sleep and camouflaged by my gentle movements in the woods.

I did not then know the secret language of squirrels. I did not know their suffering in the brutal world of hunters.

The overbearing hunter learns not to let an animal suffer. As if the hunter were living up to some moral code of tribal warfare, wounded animals must be put out of their miseries. When the squirrel started to climb the tree again, I fired one shot at his head. The bullet tore the flesh and fur away from the top of his skull. He fell to the ground still looking at me. In his eyes he wanted to live more than anything I have ever known. I fired a second time at his head. The bullet tore his lower jaw away, exposing his teeth. He looked at me and moved toward the tree again. Blood bubbled from his nostrils when he breathed. I fired again. The bullet shattered his forehead and burst through his left eye. He fell from the tree and watched me with one eye. His breath was slower. In his last eye he wanted to live again, to run free, to hide from me. I knelt beside him, my face next to his bloody head, my eye close to his eye, and begged him to forgive me before he died. I looked around the woods. I felt strange. I was alone. The blood bubbles from his nose grew smaller and disappeared. I moved closer to his eye. Please forgive me, I pleaded in tears. Please live again, I begged him again and again.

He blinked at me. His eye was still alive. Did his blinking eye mean that he had forgiven me? Please forgive me, I moaned again and again, until my self-pity fell silent in the woods. Not a bird was singing. The leaves were silent. He blinked again. I moved closer to him, stretching my body out on the ground next to him, and ran my hand across his back. The blood was still warm. I wept and watched the last of his good life pass through me in his one remaining eye. I sang a slow death song in a low voice without words until it was dark.

1972 We Came Here to Die

Thirteen armed leaders of the American Indian Movement, including Russell Means and Dennis Banks, filed into the tribal Head Start classroom on the Leech Lake Reservation and took their seats on little-people chairs.[176] They sat with their knees tucked under their chins, dressed in diverse combinations of Western cowboy clothes and traditional tribal vestments from the turn of the last century. Dennis Banks, who was a charismatic wanderer then, was wearing his fur-trimmed mountain man outfit. Most of the leaders of the militant organization were from urban centers.

Simon Howard, then president of the Minnesota Chippewa Tribe, entered the classroom, took his little seat, and twirled his thumbs beneath his heavy stomach while the leaders argued about their places in the chain of command—who would stand next to whom at the next television press conference. Howard wore a nylon bowling jacket and a floral print fishing hat in contrast to the renascence of traditional vestments worn by the militants. Howard was born on the reservation and had lived there all his life. He was at the meeting as an elected tribal official to keep peace between white people and the militants. The militants were there for an armed confrontation with white people on the opening day of fishing. I was there as a press officer for the tribal government to modulate threats and rumors at scheduled press conferences. The militants were not happy, and the press was not happy, but Howard avoided a confrontation.

"All right boys, quiet down now, and take your seats again," Howard said. The tribal leaders and militants had agreed to meet twice a day with each other and then with the press. "Now, I don't know everyone here, so let's go around the room and introduce ourselves," Howard said. "Let's start with you over there. Stand up and introduce yourself."

The man stood up, dragging his feet forward and swinging his rifle. "My name is Delano Western, and I am from Kansas," he said in a trembling voice. Western, leaning forward and looking down like a shy school child, was dressed in a wide-brimmed black hat with an imitation silver headband, dark green sunglasses with large round lenses, a sweatshirt with "Indian Power" printed on the front, two bandoliers of heavy ammunition, none of which matched the bore of his rifle, a black motorcycle jacket with military colonel's wings on the epaulets, "Red Power" and "Custer Had It Coming" patches, and a large military bayonet strapped to his body next to his revolver.

"We came here to die," Western said in a loud voice and sat down. He and about six hundred militant followers had come to Cass Lake on the Leech Lake Reservation to fight for treaty rights to hunt and fish on the reservation, which had already been won by reservation tribal officials in the federal court.

When white officials from Cass Lake had refused to pay the money demanded by the militants, who were camping on treaty land given over to a church group by the federal government for a summer camp, the leaders held a press conference on a rifle range to scare the public.

Means, smiling for television cameras, was plinking with his small-caliber "white people shooter," as he called his pistol, while Banks, my hero then, was preparing for fast-draw target practice. Dressed in a black velvet shirt with ribbon appliqué, he stood before a collection of empty food cans placed like the faces of white racist fishermen, dropped to one knee, and attempted to draw his small-gauge sawed-off shotgun. It stuck on the rope holder attached to his belt. Banks stood up and tried again, but it still stuck. Then he untied the rope, walked away embarrassed and angry, and never carried his shotgun-pistol again. Banks, a new hip-shooter from the city, was out of the running for a lead role in my imaginary hall of fame for fast-draw heroes.

"We came here to die defending our red brothers and sisters from those white racist fishermen," blared the loudspeaker voice across the church camp headquarters. "Dinner will be served in one hour, and there will be a dance contest tonight. We need volunteers to help out in the kitchen, and some brothers and sisters who know how to hunt deer . . . make that just the brothers for now."

The television newscast had reported the indiscriminate slaughter of deer on the reservation by militant hunters in violation of state laws. In fact, the brothers out hunting for two days missed every deer they shot at. One deer, pictured on television being dressed by militants at the church camp, had been killed in an accident with an automobile and was delivered to the encampment by the local game warden, who knew the militants needed food. While the militants were "shining" deer one night, they fired seven rounds at the big brown eyes of a cow. The owner of the cow fired back, and the militant hunters scrambled a fast retreat to the church camp, declaring that they were under attack by white racist fishermen.

My boyhood dream, after good food and a dentist to plug up the black holes in my front teeth, was to have in my employ a good listening chauffeur—someone to take the place of my dog and move me in peace through heavy traffic. The impossible dream was to be an unemployed radical and to have a chauffeur. My hero Dennis Banks had a chauffeur during his one-week administration of the militant encampment. The chauffeur was a good listener employed by the community relations service of the United States Department of Justice.

Two burly and bare-chested brown militant tribal guards stopped me at the entrance of the church camp because of my light skin color.

"No whites allowed, honky. This is a sovereign camp now," said one bandit with a shotgun leveled at my neck.

"Back this heap out of here, honky," said the other charming bandit. He had a self-styled tattoo recognizing his mother on his arm and wore reflecting sunglasses. Somewhere behind the mirror over his eyes I knew he was aiming his buffalo gun at my head.

"Drop the color shit," I said with an aggressive snarl. "Since when do all tribal people look like you two? Put the guns down before you lose your chance for a press conference."

"Who are you, honky?"

"I am the new little mixed-blood press chauffeur for Dennis Banks; now put your guns down and open the goddamn gate please. . . ." My bluff and blood pressure, measured by the little people at the cosmic laboratory of human relations and survival, rang the right bells, and the gate opened. Inside I parked my car like a good chauffeur for the little people.

"Vizenor!" Erdupps MacChurbbs called from the back seal. "You have given too much thought in your life to the violence of terminal believers! Show more humor and give yourself more time for the little people and compassionate trickery . . . remember you are over the hump and holding, you know what I mean?"

"I know what you mean, Erdupps MacChurbbs."

1976

SUMMER

Summer/Fall Moons

July, August, September[177]

Miami

paapahsaahka niipinwiki	midsummer moon	Midsummer.
kiišiinkwia kiilhswa	green corn moon	First corn is fit to eat.
mihšiiwia kiilhswa	elk (rutting) moon	Elk mating; kill by imitating calls.

Shawnee

miini-kiishthwa	blackberry moon	Blackberries are ripe.
po'kamaawi-kiishthwa	plum moon	Plums are ripe.
ha'shiimini-kiishthwa	papaw moon	Papaws are ripe.

Mohawk (old | modern)

sahdegagenhahenh	*ohyarihkó:wa'*	summer's dividing line	great June	Midsummer.
jaysgihgah	*sehskéha*	beginning of small mists	Morning mists begin now.
jaysgihneh	*sehske'kó:wa'*	green corn	great August	First corn is ripe.

Ho-Chunk in Wisconsin

waaxóčra wíi	corn-tasseling moon	Corn tassels evident
watajóxwíi	corn-popping moon	Corn is ripening.
hųųwážukwii	elk-whistling, elk rut moon	Elk mating season.

Meskwaki

Penāwikīceswa	summer moon	Summer
Nīpenwikīceswa	midsummer moon	Midsummer.
Āmanōwikīceswa	rutting moon	Deer and elk are breeding.

Ojibwe/Odawa

minigi-gisiss	blueberry moon	Blueberries are ripe.
manomini-gisiss	wild rice moon	Rice harvest begins now.
wake-baga-gisiss	weak leaves	Leaves are getting dry, turning.

Potawatomi

Nipiné kises	summer moon	Midsummer.
Mishèwě̂ kises	red deer, roebuck	Deer mating season.
Mimúkwosè kises	harvest moon	Harvest begins.

Menominee

men keso'	blueberry moon	Blueberries are ripe.
matchmen keso'	great ripening moon	Many crops are ripe.
onawipimek keso'	turning leaves moon	First leaves turn.

 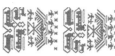 

# ❖ SUMMER ❖

Chant to the Firefly

Wau wau tay see! Flitting white-fire insect!
Wau wau tay see! Waving white-fire bug!
E mow e shin. Give me light before I go to bed.
Tshe bwau ne baun ewee! Give me light before I go to sleep.
Be eghaun—be eghaun—ewee!

Wa wau tay see! Come little dancing white-fire bug!
Wa wau tay see! Come little flitting white-fire beast
Was sa koon ain je gun. Light me with your bright white-flame instrument.
Was sa koon ain je gun. Light me with your little candle.

Henry Rowe Schoolcraft, 1845

Waawaatesi waawaatesé amawishin Firefly, flash light for me
ji-bwaa-nibaayaan E WEE before I sleep.
bi-izhaan! Bi-izhaan! E WEE Come here, come here!
Waawaatesi, waawaatesi Firefly, firefly,
waasakonenjigan, waasakonenjigan A lantern, a lantern.

John D. Nichols, 1991[178]

The art of story is learned over many years and cannot always be translated into a different culture without loss or change in meaning. There is no better example than many of the stories collected in this section, which describe spirit creatures of the water and sky. To understand them, it is helpful to know that one essential characteristic of the Native world is balance, where the forces of the universe are held in stasis so that neither the sky spirits nor the underwater beings are in control. That does not stop the underwater creatures from trying, however, and from those attempts come stories about the Thunderers' battles with the great horned snakes, such as the Seneca Doonongaes, and with the Ojibwe underwater lion, Micipijiu (Missipeshu: Big Lynx). The underwater beings are always dangerous, despite giving great gifts to humans. The Thunderers know this and so spend much of their time keeping the underwater beings in line, trying to prevent them from seducing humans with gifts, as malign creatures are wont to do.

The battles between these creatures inspired stories of all types: sacred stories about the formation of clans, youngest-smartest stories, Trickster stories, moral fables. This indicates that both the creatures who battle each other and their stories are ancient, perhaps even earlier than the first agricultural peoples in the

Great Lakes basin who built earthworks that functioned as calendars and observatories for celestial events, such as the Great Serpent Mound in Ohio.

Almost all North American Native nations believed in a water monster, usually a great horned snake that, from ancient times, has been associated with the fertility of soils and crops. The 1370-foot Great Serpent Mound in Ohio, the largest effigy mound in the world, is designed so that the serpent's head aligns with the sum-

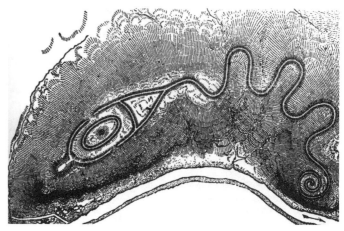

Great Serpent Mound, 1847

mer solstice sunset and the coils of its tail align with the winter solstice sunrise. This marks the limits of the agricultural sun, from the end of its longest day on June 21 to the beginning of its shortest on December 21 on contemporary calendars. In addition, the serpent fits precisely into a group of stars in the snake-like constellation Draco, with the position of an ancient North Star, Thuban (Arabic: serpent), or Alpha Draconis, coming at the seventh coil. Scientists carbon dating the mound have theorized that it may be linked to the explosion from a supernova that created the Crab Nebula in 1054, an extreme astronomical event that provoked an equally extreme effort at construction on earth, perhaps to appease the great serpent who rushed through the sky. Geologists have determined that the mound is placed on the site of an ancient meteor strike from the Permian period 248 to 285 million years ago, so the location may have been considered sacred before the Serpent Mound was constructed.

Scientists are still learning about the Great Serpent Mound and other Midwestern earthworks built between AD 700 and 1200, during the Hopewell and Mississippian culture periods. The Newark Earthworks in Ohio, the world's largest ancient mound site, once occupied four square miles and was designed to align with the northernmost point of the moon's rise, which occurred every 18.6 years. The earthworks are accurate enough to predict when lunar eclipses will occur at or near the summer or winter solstices, a darkening that earlier peoples believed endangered the sun's journeys through the year. Cultures that flourished during these centuries lived in villages and practiced intensive agriculture, so they were at the mercy of the weather and the seasons to survive. Since the available arable land was filled nearly to its carrying capacity and many later techniques for retaining the fertility of the soil were unknown, weather was critical. The reverence with which farmers held the sun and the moon is logical.

Agriculture had begun in the lakes' region by 6500 BC, when farmers were managing natural stands of several wild vegetable foods that were an important part of everyone's diet. Marsh elder (*Iva annua*) was the most common domesticated native plant, flourishing in river bottoms as early as 3000 BC. Goosefoot (*Chenopodium berlandieri*), knotweed (*Polygonum erectum*), maygrass (*Phalanx caroliniana*), and little barley (*Hordeum pusillum*), all now considered weeds, were important cereal grains; goosefoot was the earliest cultivated plant. Gourds and squashes (*Cucurbita pepo* and var.), first raised for their seeds, were cultivated by 2300 BC. Wild sunflowers (*Helianthus annuus*) were grown in the lakes' region as early as 2265 BC. One variant, the Jerusalem artichoke (*Helianthus tuberosus*), might have been farmed as well, though it is a prolific wild plant. Initially, these foods were supplemental to hunting and fishing, but as management of wild vegetables and seeds gradually became true cultivation, including land clearing and terracing, more semipermanent settlements could be created because crops helped buffer any scarcity of game. It was not until the introduction of maize in the first millennium, however, that agriculture became a primary source of food in the warmer regions of the Great Lakes, changing landscapes, politics, and arts. Natives today do not, for example, tell stories about early cereal grains, but there are many different stories about the origin of corn.

Indian corn

Corn is a miracle of plant breeding by generations of farmers over thousands of years who turned a tiny, wild, desert plant into the sweet corn so eagerly anticipated by both humans and raccoons today. Maize cultivation in North America began in the Southwest sometime before the first millennium BC, and the hard flint corn grown there was the first to spread across the continent. As experimentation improved genetics, the hardier *maíz de ocho* became the staple across the lower Midwest and East, with intensive cultivation beginning about AD 700-750. Archaeologists currently believe that maize agriculture came into the Great Lakes region sometime between AD 800 and 1200, whereas cultivated beans, as opposed to wild varieties that Mountain Wolf Woman describes "stealing from the mice" (p. 343), were introduced about 1000 and became common after 1200. By the nineteenth century, indigenous peoples grew over sixty varieties of beans across the region. Together with the far more ancient squashes, of which no lakes stories seem to have been collected, corn and beans formed the Three Sisters, which provided sustenance where large-scale hunting and gathering became impossible and also provided the foundation for an entirely new economy. The Seneca believe that *onenha* (corn) came in a dream to a dying man who had protected the seeds of the Three Sisters. She taught him corn dances, planting knowledge, and harvest rituals. For centuries, Great Lakes Native nations have celebrated the first ripe corn with the Green Corn Dance and again at final harvest or *Gondagonwisas*, where homage is paid to the Three Sisters as well.

The greatest grain in some northern parts of the Great Lakes is wild rice—*manoomin*—a shallow-water grass (*Zizania* species) revered by the ancients and harvested today. The problem, as Winona LaDuke points out, is that the increasing pollution of all waters and the commercialization of agriculture across the world, led by US chemical companies, have put even this sacred grain at risk. One solution would be a return to traditional ways, but reestablishing a balance between land, animals, and humans will not be easily done, if at all. Most North Americans now live insulated from the natural world, confident that abundant food, medicines, and human comforts will always be available, so asking for sacrifices—common to people who began adulthood with vision quests—will require either great foresight or great desperation.

Although summer could be a time of peace and plenty, it was also the season for the vision quest, a traditional way to reach out to the spirits and ask their blessings. For many centuries, no self-respecting male could avoid this arduous, dangerous, sometimes frustrating ritual of entry into manhood when he went without food and water to reach a trace-like state where the spirit-helpers would visit a helpless mortal in a dangerous world and give him *tatahkesewen* (Menominee: power). Extreme fasting brought extreme powers, no matter who attempted it or for what purpose, good or evil. This has not been lost on contemporary writers, and in the selection from her novel *The Bingo Palace,* Louise Erdrich mocks the vision quest of a so-called new tradition-alist who has only his own gratification in mind. Can anyone manage to balance on the slippery poles flung across the turbid river called Gaming? What happens to real tradition when money wields more power than true respect for the past? Historically, missionaries (both Native and white) and the governments of the USA and Canada attempted to eradicate indigenous spiritual traditions. But Natives were resilient, creating new ceremonies such as the Dream Dance to attempt to heal the ills created by armed aggression or incorporating Christian elements into older rituals to create communities of believers, such as the Native American Church, that could reach out to those who no longer fit in either the old, traditional world or the new Christianized one.

Summer is also the time for travel over the lakes, and their frequently violent waters inspired a unique class of stories about a creature far more dangerous than the stars or the snake. The Odawa and Ojibwe, who traveled the lakes extensively, found an explanation for the deadly storms in the water spirit Micipijiu, the underwater lynx or lion, perhaps inspired by panthers who were sometimes seen swimming. Known only as the lynx before the British came to North America, Natives began calling him a lion after noticing his resemblance to the lion on the British flag. As a creature of story, Micipijiu is one of the most powerful and malevolent spirits in the universe. Folklorists classify creatures like him as demon lovers, animal beings who try to become the mates of human women. Stories with this theme are told the world over, but the endings differ according to the culture. In societies where relations between the sexes are egalitarian, women are usually able to resist being pulled down into the underworld to be mated to the monster. In the Great Lakes region, only those who dreamed of the Thunderers as personal manidog, commonly young men who would become warriors or excep-tional women, would be empowered to survive Micipijiu's attacks. Those who dreamed of Micipijiu during their vision quests were instructed to refuse the dream lest they become sorcerers, capable of great power but con-demned to live alone forever. Ordinary folk who needed to cross water were frequently given a protective charm and a new name, such as Âjawac (Âjawash: Wafted Safely Across the Water) to help ensure safety.

Summer is not only journeys, fireflies, stars, visions, monsters, and ripening corn, it is also mosquitoes, a reminder that the Great Spirit has a sense of humor. Here is their story, related by David Cusick (*c.*1780-*c.*1831). Cusick was a Tuscarora physician, painter, and veteran of the War of 1812, who wrote the first narrative history of a Native nation in English, *Sketches of the Ancient History of the Six Nations,* from which this short tale is taken:

> About this time a great musqueto invaded the fort Onondaga; the musqueto was mis-chievous to the people, it flew about the fort with a long stinger and sucked the blood of a number of lives; the warriors made several oppositions to expel the monster but failed; the country was invaded until the Holder of the Heavens was pleased to visit the people; while he was visiting the king at the fort Onondaga, the musqueto made appearance as usual and flew about the fort; the Holder of the Heavens attacked the monster; it flew so rapidly that he could hardly keep in sight of it, but after a few days chase the monster began to fail; he chased on the borders of the great lakes towards the sun-setting and round the great country; at last he overtook the monster and killed it near the salt lake Onondaga, and the blood became small musquetoes.

1827

❖ SPIRITS OF THE WATERS AND THE SKY ❖

THE THUNDER SPIRITS

The Thunderers are grandfather spirits, giant bird-creatures who build their nests high on cliffs and represent supernatural powers over which most people have no control. Rumbling caused by the flapping of their wings is a sign of the return of warm weather, bringing rain so that the crops will flourish. These mammoth birds are the arch enemies of the underwater beings, such as the great horned snakes and Micipijiu, the underwater lynx or lion. The Thunderers cannot destroy the underwater beings—the powers of both kinds of creatures are too equal for that—but they can destroy the occasional underwater snake, as they do here in the first story here, an early tale transcribed by C. C. Trowbridge. Thunderers were the personal manidog of those chosen for the warpath. More darkly, they, along with Micipijiu, became the manidog of medicine women and men who would be given great power to heal but also to do harm. The ethics of the individual made the difference. Thunderers talk among themselves, and humans who are gifted can understand that speech.

Monaatoowaukēē—Young Tshingwüzāūkee—The Thunder Spirits

Le Gros, Miami

Le Gros undoubtedly came from a small Miami village on the Wabash River called Les gros (the big ones), a place that might have been named after one of his ancestors. C. C. Trowbridge, who spent the winter of 1825-1826 among the Miami in the service of the US Indian Department, hired Le Gros, for thirty dollars, to help him with his research. In addition to answering all the white man's questions, Le Gros, like Tenskwatawa, told stories as well, which Trowbridge copied and filed with the papers he sent to headquarters.

Very many ages ago one of the Tshingwütizāū or Young Thunder or Sons of the Thunder went to the falls of Niagara for the purpose of destroying the Mōnetoo (manido) that reigns in that tremendous work of nature, but after a long and very severe conflict he was overpowered, made prisoner, and remains there to this day. A long time after his capture his brothers, ten in number, set out to rescue him. A Miami was out in the woods and had just leveled his arrow at a fine deer, when a rumbling noise behind him caused the removal of his eye for a moment from the game, and upon looking up he saw coming towards him ten, very large, winged animals apparently half-birds, half-men. Each of them was armed with an immense *pukemāūgun* (*pakamaakani*), or war club, proportioned to the size of the bearer. Nine of these beings passed the Indian without regarding him, but the last one stopped and, having interrogated him about his pursuit and success, he drew from his right wing a feather and presented it to the hunter, who upon accepting it immediately became transformed into the shape of his companion. The Thunder then disclosed the plan of the party and the object of their excursion and, the hunter having acceded to a proposition to accompany them, the two set out and

253

Thunder Spirit pictograph, Minnesota

soon overtook those who had gone before. The hunter and his story were made known to the warriors by their brother, and the whole party proceeded on.

When they arrived at the falls, they were much perplexed for a plan by which they might call the attention of the Mōnetoo to such place as would afford them good battleground. At length he came out himself—a wonderful serpent, of immense size, of black colour, and having on his head two horns as large as those of the elk. The brothers were at first sight intimidated at the frightful appearance of the Mōnetoo, but at length one of them resolved to attack him. He did so, but his pukemāūgun had no effect. Another succeeded him, but though stronger than his brother, the Mōnetoo did not appear to know that any thing was near him but his native rocks and cascade, so little did he regard the oft-repeated blows of the warrior. Finally the brothers requested the Miami ally to try the effect of his pukemāūgun. He approached cautiously and, by a well-directed blow, he gave the Mōnetoo a death wound. The pain induced by this caused him to writhe and to sigh, and the air was so convulsed by this effort as to occasion an increased noise in the waters around. The Miami was carried by it a great distance off, and he fell to the ground with a force which caused a suspension of life. Here his adopted brothers found him. They exerted themselves a little, and he recovered sufficiently to accompany them to the battleground in front of the Mōnetoo's cave where they saw the fallen enemy lifeless. They drew him out of the cave and, having separated his head and horns from the body, they placed it upon a pole in the same manner that they now serve scalps and proceeded to return home, having first searched in vain for the prisoner, their brother.

When they reached the place where they had met the Miami, they thanked him for his assistance and told him that he was at liberty to return to his friends and enjoy the reputation of the greatest warrior in the nation, or to accompany them as he then was. He chose the former and, surrendering the feather to the person from whom he had received it, he found himself again a human being pursuing the pleasures of the chase. He returned to his village, the people of which had despaired of seeing him again and, having recounted to them the history of the excursion which he had taken, he sat down with the character of the most extraordinary man of his age and was ever after esteemed a great warrior, with whom it was folly to compete.

*c.*1820s

254

The Origin of the Sun-Shower

Yäh-rōhn-yäh-äh-wǐh (Deer is Sailing in the Sky, Catherine Coon Johnson, *c.*1850-†), Wendat

The Huron were premier agricultural people. When the Jesuit fathers came to Huronia in the sixteenth century, they expected to get lost in the woods. Instead, they got lost in corn fields, which produced grain the Huron used for barter with other nations, particularly those whose surplus was fur. Stories of how rain happened would be critically important information to these productive farmers, and so the ancient beginnings of sun showers

Yäh-rōhn-yäh-äh-wǐh at 60 with her granddaughters, 1912

are related here. Despite the young woman's repeated mistakes—being too picky about choosing a husband, not watching her child—people receive a benefit.

Yäh-rōhn-yäh-äh-wǐh, whose name is also translated as "The Deer Goes into the Sky and Everywhere," was born into the Deer clan on the Wyandot reservation in Oklahoma about 1850 and spoke Wendat almost exclusively when she told stories to Marius Barbeau in 1911.

A young woman, the most beautiful of all, was not pleased with her suitors, whom she scorned one after the other for a very long time. One day, however, a very handsome young man came around, whom she at once fell in love with. Now she was, indeed, willing to converse with him, so that they soon agreed to get married. The young man said, "Well then, tomorrow at night, I shall come and take you away." The young woman spoke to her mother and said, "I am very much in love with him, for he is far more handsome than the others. Tomorrow, at night, he is going to come and take me along with him." The mother gave her consent.

The next night, the young man came over as expected. The mother of the bride saw him, as he came into her house. They spoke to one another, and he said, "I have come for your daughter." The old woman replied. "Be it so!"

He, therefore, went away with the young woman. When they had traveled but a short distance, he said, "Here, let us take the shorter way across the forest yonder." And they went across the forest, so that, although they had traveled a long way, it did not seem long to her.

Upon reaching home, as he found his mother and three sisters all sitting there together, he brought the young woman in. And the young man and his bride then got married. Now her husband went out

255

hunting as if he were to bring back deer meat. And his bride kept on sitting there waiting for him. She was thinking that this was the abode of human beings. But after a while, she was very much scared when she found out that her husband was only a big snake. She had taken him for a young man, but there, in her lap he rested his head and said, "Louse me!" So she just looked on one side, and then she glanced at the other side. It was only a big snake whose head was in her lap. She cried out and started up quickly.

The husband's mother spoke to him and said, "Why did you ever want to marry this woman if really you could not transform yourself forever into a human being?" The young woman, by this time, knew that, truly, he was not a human being, and she was most frightened. The husband's mother scolded him still more bitterly. He remained only a snake, however, and the girl thought, "He was only man-like, the one whom I have married."

The mother took the young woman aside and said, "Next time, when he goes out hunting again, indeed you had better run back home. I have scolded him, but I shall not he able to prevent him from killing you, as he is one of us and we are not human beings, but snakes." And, she added, "This really happened because you did not want for so long to get married. That is why he said, 'As it is, I shall be transfigured into a human being and shall marry her.' This could not be so, however, and he could not forever retain the shape of a human being."

The young woman then took to flight and made for her home, because the old woman had said, "Be off! And go straight to the north, and run all the way as fast as you possibly can. It is a long way, but exert yourself to the utmost and run all the way home." Now she started out, running northwards with all her might.

When the young man came back from the hunt, nowhere could he see his bride. Soon, finding out that she had run away, he pursued her. The girl was quite far already, for she had been running as fast as she could all this time. It so happened, however, that the water rose all around her, and it became so deep that she could no longer run along. Now, her husband, swimming with his head out of the water, was on the point of overtaking her. Several men, however, could be seen standing at a distance. Their chief shouted to the young woman, "This way! Come and stand behind me. I shall defend you against him."

But the snake was getting still closer to her, while swimming with his head out of the water. The chief spoke to his men saying, "Shoot right there!" So it was done, and they killed the big snake, the one who had been the young woman's husband. The air at once became dark with smoke, as her protectors were the Thunder and his three sons, whose darts were lightning. The old man took the young woman along with him. She knew nothing of the place whither she was being taken. This time, she got married to one of the Thunder's sons and soon gave birth to a child.

She was constantly longing, however, to go down and visit her mother. As she had no idea of the way down to her mother's home, the Thunder, her husband, said, "I am willing to take you down to your mother's home. But you will have to take the young one along with you and pledge yourself to take the utmost care of him, as he must always he good-natured. He should never strike anybody, for if he does, he will surely kill outright, as he is of our family. And should this happen, I would at once take him away from you."

The chief (Thunder) had three young men with him, his own sons, and the young woman's mother had five sons.

Now the child grew in size. When he had reached his fourth year, he could go out and play with the other boys, and he was given a bow. As the other children one day came around, one of them got hold of his bow. The Thunder child, at once, took it back and with anger drew it at the other boy, and a thunder peal resounded.

The Thunder, his father, looked for the woman, and the air was filled with smoke. When the smoke had cleared off, nowhere was the Thunder-child to he seen. His father, indeed, had fulfilled his promise, for he had said to his wife, "I shall take him away from you if he breaks the custom and kills anybody."

Nobody had been killed, however, when the child drew his bow, for he had not hit anyone.

Then the Thunder spoke again to the young woman and said, "I have now taken him along with me and, whenever it rains while the sun is shining, the people shall think and say that Tsĭju´tŏo, the Wyandot, is making the rain."

1911

The Legend of the Thunderers

Chief Mandarong (We Are Unwilling, Joseph White) and Mrs. White, Wendat

Horatio Hale collected stories from a remnant Huron-Wendat band on what was once known in Canada as the Anderdon Reserve, near Lake Erie, in 1872 and 1874. His interpreter was Chehteh (War Club, Alexander Clarke), brother of Peter Dooyentate Clarke, who wrote the first history of the Huron-Wendat people. Hale writes in his introduction to this story that: "The Chief [Mandarong] remarked that the Indians held the opinion that each species of animal had for its spiritual representative one of its own kind, very much larger than the ordinary size, and endowed with preternatural powers, among which was the power of assuming the human form. Some of these powers could be communicated by them to any human beings who might form an alliance with them. Thus all the Wyandot men had their particular friends among the animals which surrounded them; that is, each man had selected one as his special ally, much as a Roman Catholic might select a patron saint. When the missionaries came among them and urged them to become Christians, one of their strongest objections was that they could not give up their forest friends. The chief added that since the white men came, these peculiar animals had disappeared. The Indians, he averred, and he seemed fully to share in the opinion, held that they are not extinct, but being alarmed by the throng of white people and the destruction of their ancient haunts, they have fled to a distance, perhaps, he added, under the sea. Even in the ancient times they kept mostly underground, being afraid of the thunder and, as the following narrative shows, with good reason." Here the Hīnōn, or Thunderers, help a human, who in turn helps them kill a grub that would destroy corn. Hīnōn usually live in a cave under Niagara Falls and taught people how to use tobacco.

From the earliest period the Wyandots and the Cherokees have been at war. The war was carried on sometimes by large expeditions, sometimes by parties of two or three adventurers, who would penetrate into the enemy's country and return proud of having slain a man. On one occasion in the ancient times,

257

three Wyandot warriors set out on such an expedition. When they were far distant from their own land, one of them had the misfortune to break his leg. By the Indian law it became the duty of the others to convey their injured comrade back to his home. They formed a rude litter and, laying him upon it, bore him for some distance. At length they came to a ridge of mountains. The way was hard and the exertion severe. To rest themselves they placed their burden on the ground and, withdrawing to a little distance, took evil counsel together. There was a deep hole or pit, opening in the side of the mountain, not far from the place where they were sitting. Returning to the litter, they took up their helpless comrade, carried him near the brink of the pit, and suddenly hurled him in. Then they set off rapidly for their own country. When they arrived, they reported that he had died of wounds received in fight. Great was the grief of his mother, a widow, whose only son and support he had been. To soothe her feelings they told her that her son had not fallen into the enemy's hands. They had rescued him, they said, from that fate, had carefully tended him in his last hours, and had given his remains a becoming burial.

They little imagined that he was still alive. When he was thrown down by his treacherous comrades, he lay for a time insensible at the bottom of the pit. When he recovered his senses, he observed an old gray-headed man seated near him, crouching in a cavity on one side of the pit. "Ah, my son," said the old man, "what have your friends done to you?"

"They have thrown me here to die, I suppose," he replied.

"You shall not die," said the old man, "if you will promise to do what I require of you in return for saving you."

"What is that?" asked the youth.

"Only that when you recover you will remain here and hunt for me and bring me the game you kill."

The young warrior readily promised, and the old man applied herbs to his wound and attended him skillfully until he recovered. This happened in the autumn. All through the winter the youth hunted for the old man, who told him that when any game was killed which was too large for one man to carry, he would come and help to convey it to the pit in which they continued to reside.

When the spring arrived, bringing melting snows and frequent showers, the youth continued his pursuit of the game, though with more difficulty. One day he encountered an enormous bear, which he was lucky enough to kill. As he stooped to feel its fatness and judge of its weight, he heard a murmur of voices behind him. He had not imagined that any human beings would find their way to that lonely region at that time of the year. Astonished, he turned and saw three men, or figures resembling men, clad in strange, cloudlike garments, standing near him. "Who are you?" he asked.

In reply, they informed him that they were the Thunderers (Hīnōn). They told him that their mission was to keep the earth and everything upon it in good order for the benefit of the human race. If there was a drought, it was their duty to bring rain. If there were serpents or other noxious creatures, they were commissioned to destroy them and, in short, they were to do away with everything that was injurious to mankind. They told him that their present object was to destroy the old man to whom he had bound himself, and who, as they would show him, was a very different being from what he pretended to be. For this they required his aid. If he would assist them, he would do a good act, and they would convey him back to his home, where he would see his mother and be able to take care of her.

This warning and these assurances overcame any reluctance the young man might have felt to sacrifice his seeming friend. He went to him and told him that he had killed a bear and needed his help to bring it home. The old man was anxious and uneasy. He bade the youth examine the sky carefully and see if there was the smallest speck of cloud in any quarter. The young man replied that the sky was perfectly clear. The old man then came out of the hollow and followed the young hunter, urging him constantly to make haste and looking upward with great anxiety. When they reached the bear, they cut it up hurriedly with their knives, and the old man directed the youth to place it all on his shoulders. The youth complied, though much astonished at his companion's strength. The old man set off hastily for the pit, but just then a cloud appeared, and the thunder rumbled in the distance. The old man threw down his load and started to run. The thunder sounded nearer, and the old man assumed his proper form of an enormous porcupine, which fled through the bushes, discharging its quills, like arrows, backward as it ran. But the Thunderers followed him with burst upon burst, and finally a bolt struck the huge animal, which fell lifeless into its den.

Then the Thunderers said to the young man, "Now we have done our work here and will take you to your home to your mother, who is grieving for you all the time." They gave him a dress like that which they wore, a cloudlike robe, having wings on the shoulders, and told him how these were to be moved. Then he rose in the air and soon found himself in his mother's cornfield. It was night. He went to her cabin and drew aside the mat which covered the opening. The widow started up and gazed at him in the moonlight with terror, thinking that she saw her son's apparition. He guessed her thoughts. "Do not be alarmed, mother," he said, "it is no ghost. It is your son, come back to take care of you." As may be supposed, the poor woman was overjoyed and welcomed her long-lost son with delight. He remained with her, fulfilling his duties as a son.

When the Thunderers bade farewell to the young man, they said to him, "We will leave the cloud-dress with you. Every spring, when we return, you can put it on and fly with us, to be witness to what we do for the good of men." They told him that the great deity, Hamendiju, had given them this authority and commission to watch over the people and see that no harm came to them. Accordingly the youth hid the dress in the woods that no one might see it and waited 'til the spring. Then the Thunderers returned, and he resumed the robe and floated with them in the clouds over the earth. As they passed above a mountain, he became thirsty and, seeing below him a pool, he descended to drink of it. When he rejoined his companions, they looked at him and saw that the water with which his lips were moist had caused them to shine, as though smeared with oil. "Where have you been drinking?" they asked eagerly.

"In yonder pool," he answered, pointing to where it lay still in sight.

They said, "There is something in that pool which we must destroy. We have sought it for years, and now you have happily found it for us." Then they cast a mighty thunderbolt into the pool, which presently became dry. At the bottom of it, blasted by the Thunderers, was an immense grub of the kind which destroys the corn and beans and other products of the field and garden; but this was a vast creature, the spiritual head, patron, and exemplar of all grubs.

After accompanying his spirit friends to some distance and seeing more of their good deeds of the like sort, the youth returned home and told his people that the Thunder was their divine protector and narrated the proofs which he had witnessed of this benignant character. Thence originated the honor in which the Thunder is held among the Indians.

The Wyandots were accustomed to call Hīnō their grandfather (*tsutaa*). Only three thunder-spirits were required on this occasion, but there were many of them. When thunder is heard to roll from many parts of the heavens, it is because there are many of the Thunderers at work. They are all called Hīnō, who may be regarded as one god or many, the Thunder or the Thunderers.

The young man learned from his divine friends the secret of rain-making, which he communicated to two persons in each tribe. They were bound to strict secrecy and possessed, Chief Mandarong affirmed, the art of making rain. He had often known them to accomplish this feat. He himself had become partly possessed of this secret and had been able in former days to bring rain. Of late years, in obedience to the injunctions of the church, he had forborne to exert this power.

1874

The Legend of the Thunderbird
Edward Bracklin, Chippewa

This short tale, retold by a student at the Carlisle Indian School, is remarkable in several ways. The medicine man walks west to the Great Lakes, not east, from the buffalo plains, the thunderbird in the story is small enough to be carried, it is colored like a tropical bird, and it ends a drought. There were several periods of drought during the Archaic Period (8000-1000 BC) when the climate of the Great Lakes sometimes became much warmer and drier than at present. There was also a severe drought during the Little Ice Age, AD 1400-1850. Again, because areas of the lakes region have been agricultural since late Archaic times, drought would be remembered and marked in stories. There were buffalo throughout the Great Lakes until the nineteenth century, when they were destroyed by overhunting and loss of habitat. Tropical birds are sometimes blown very far off course and into the Great Lakes, especially by storms originating in the south that also bring rain.

Long, long time ago, many, many moons before the white man came, when the buffalo were as blades of grass on the prairie, there came a great dry spell. No rain fell and the grass grew brown and the rivers dried up; the buffalo went away and my people could get nothing to eat but a few berries and they grew hungry and thin. Every day they prayed to the Great Spirit for rain and made much medicine, but the rain did not come. The Great Spirit was angry.

Among the greatest of the medicine men was Nashewa. He made much medicine. All day he prayed to the Great Spirit, and all night, and finally the Great Spirit came to him in a dream and said, "Nashewa, awake, and travel west until you receive a sign." And Nashewa heard and was glad.

The next morning he started and he went a long way to the west until he came to what is Gechigome (Great Lakes). He saw there a bird that was sitting near the edge of the water. He walked towards it. When he was looking at it, he knew that the bird did not belong to this country. Its feathers were all of different colors, it bill was green and its legs were colored the same. It would not open its eyes. Then he took it and

260

came back home. He entered his lodge, and all the chiefs were invited. The bird sat at the upper end of the lodge and Nashewa told these chiefs, "Now here is a bird that you may look at it to know what it is." It was not known—nobody could tell what kind of a bird it was, so they called it the Awneemekee (Animiki: Thunderbolt). After a while Nashewa pushed it, then it opened its eyes and they flashed lightning. The door was opened and the bird flew out. As he got outside, the sky darkened and the thunder roared and it rained. Many days it rained and the grass grew green again and the buffalo returned and my people got fat once more. This is the story of the Awneemekee (Thunderbird).

My grandfather told it to me, and his grandfather told it to him.

1914

Buffalo pictograph, Ontario

The Language of Weather

Ray A. Young Bear, Meskwaki

The summer rain isn't here yet,
but I hear and see the approaching
shadow of its initial messenger:
Thunder.
The earth's bright horizon
sends a final sunbeam directly
toward me, skimming across the tops
of clouds and hilly woodland.
All in one moment, in spite
of my austerity, everything
is aligned: part-land, part-cloud,
part-sky, part-sun and part-self.
I am the only one to witness
this renascence.
Before darkness replaces the light
in my eyes, I meditate briefly
on the absence of religious
importunity; no acknowledgment
whatsoever for the Factors
which make my existence possible.
My parents, who are hurrying
to overturn the reddish-brown dirt
around the potato plants, begin to talk
above the rumbling din.

"Their mouths are opening.
See that everyone in the household
releases parts of ourselves
to our Grandfathers."
While raindrops begin to cool
my face and arms, lightning
breaks a faraway cottonwood
in half; small clouds of red
garden dust are kicked into
the frantic air by grasshoppers
in retreat.
I think of the time I stood
on this same spot years ago,
but it was under moonlight,
and I was watching this beautiful
electrical force dance above
another valley.
In the daylight distance,
a stray spirit whose guise
is a Whirlwind, spins and attempts
to communicate from its ethereal
loneliness.

1991

Young Bear (1950-   ), whose first language is Meskwaki, is a poet and novelist who blends an ancient-sounding poetic voice with modern technique. In his novel, *Black Eagle Child,* he wrote, "To be ignorant, uninformed, and oblivious to one's origins was to openly defy 'the one who created you' and invite adversity." He strives to "maintain a delicate equilibrium with my tribal homeland's history and geographic surrounding and the world that changes its face along the borders."

THE UNDERWATER SPIRITS

Now Great-Lynx

Chief Kāgigē Pinase (Forever-Bird, John Penesi), Ojibwe

The following two stories show the underwater lion wreaking his threats on women and children. The first, "Now Great-Lynx," was collected north of Lake Superior during the years 1903-1905 by William Jones from the chief of the Fort William band. The second, "The Underwater Lion," was transcribed fifty years later south of Lake Superior by Robert Ritzenthaler at Lac Court Oreilles. In the latter, a young woman who has dreamed of Thunderers and followed their instructions always to carry a small cedar paddle is able to triumph over Micipijiu and to enrich her family because of her courage. The references to copper in this story are suggestive. Although there is no way of knowing when copper became imbued with magical and wealth-giving properties, it was associated with the sun and was mined for objects and trade in the Lake Superior region beginning with the Old Copper Culture in 3000 to 2500 BC. Between then and the coming of the Europeans, it was traded across the Eastern and Central United States, becoming rarer and more valuable the farther it traveled through the trade networks.

Long ago people often used to see something in places, especially where the current was swift. The people feared it; and that was the reason of the practice of sometimes throwing offerings to it into the water, even tobacco. Now, once yonder, at what is called Shallow-Water [Ross Port, Ontario], was where some women were once passing by in a canoe. Accordingly there happened to rise a mighty current of water, nearly were they capsized; exceedingly frightened were they. While they were paddling with all their might, they saw the tail of a Great Lynx come up out of the water; all flung themselves up into the forward end of the canoe in their fright. Now, one of the women that was there saw that the canoe was going to sink; accordingly, when she had gone to the stern, she raised the paddle in order to strike the tail of Great-Lynx.

And this she said: "While I was young, often did I fast. It was then that the Thunderers gave me their war-club." Thereupon, when she struck the tail of Great-Lynx, she then broke the tail of Great-Lynx in two. Thereupon up to the surface rose the canoe, after which they then started on their way paddling; and so they were saved.

Now, one of the women was seized by Great-Lynx. Therefore she it was who had told at home that Great-Lynx was continually harassing the people. And though the master of the Great-Lynxes would always speak to his son, saying, "Do not plague the people," yet he would never listen to his father.

Once, yonder at the Sault, together in a body were the people living. Once against a certain wigwam was leaned a child bound to a cradle-board; and then the child was missed from that place. They saw the sign of the cradle-board where it had been dragged along in the sand.

Thereupon they heard the voice of the child crying beneath a rugged hill. Even though the people made offerings in the hope that Great-Lynx might set the child free, even though for a long while they besought him with prayers, yet he would not let it go. So at length the people said that therefore they might as well slay Great-Lynx. Accordingly they began digging straight for the place from whence the sound of the child could be heard. And after a while they had a hole dug to the den of Great-Lynx. They saw water coming in and out (like the tide). It was true that even then they spoke kindly to Great-Lynx, yet he would not let the child go. Still yet they could hear the voice of the child crying. Accordingly they said: "Therefore let us dig to where he is, that we may kill him."

Truly they dug after him, following him up. By and by out came the cradle-board, floating on the water, together with the child that was bound to it. And when they caught hold of the cradle-board, they observed that the child had a hole crushed into its head; Great-Lynx must have slain it. Thereupon they followed him up, digging after him; and one man that was famed for his strength said that he would kill Great-Lynx. When drawing upon him, as they dug after him, round towards them turned Great-Lynx. Thereupon him struck he who said that he would kill Great-Lynx. Sure enough, he slew him.

And when they pulled him out, they saw that his tail was cut off. That was the one that had been struck at Shallow Water; by a woman with an oar he had been struck. That was what happened. Only not long ago was seen the place where the people had once dug the hole; it is over toward the Big-Knife country [United States], over by the Sault.

1903-1905

The Underwater Lion

Pete Martin, Chippewa

There was a big lake; Indians lived on both sides of it. There was a big island of mud in the center, and if anyone wanted to go to the other village across the lake, they would have to paddle around the edge of the lake. If they tried to go straight across, something would happen to them. A bad manido lived there in the island.

One day there was a medicine dance across the lake, and people started around the lake in their

Pictograph of Micipijiu, Great Snakes, and canoe,
Lake Superior Provincial Park

264

canoes. Two women started later, after the others had gone. They were sisters-in-law. One of them was rather foolish. She was steering in the stern and headed straight across. The other warned her not to do it, but in vain. The first girl had a little cedar paddle with her. She never left it out of her sight—always took it along, even when she went out gathering wood. She held it but did not use it for paddling. As they got to the middle, they crossed the mud, and in the center of the mud was a hole of clear water. The water was swirling around the hole and, as they started to cross it, a lion came out of the middle and switched his tail across the boat, trying to turn it over.

The girl picked up her little paddle and hit the lion's tail with it, saying, "Thunder is striking you." The paddle cut off the lion's tail, and the end dropped into the boat. When they picked it up, it was a solid piece of copper about two inches thick. They watched the lion running away through the mud, and the steerer laughed hard. She said, "I scared him. He won't bother us again."

When they got across, the girl gave the piece of copper to her father, and he got rich through having it. The copper had certain powers. People would give her father a blanket just for a tiny piece of that copper. They would take that bit for luck in hunting and fishing, and some just kept it to bring good luck.

1946

Mashenomak, the Great Fish

Chief Niopet Oshkosh (Four in a Den, 1829-†), Menominee

Nearly all cultures of the world tell tales of humans being swallowed by a giant fish. In this regard, Jonah was exceptional only for his dour grieving. In this Menominee version, Manabush, the culture hero, contrives to get himself swallowed so that he can fix a problem: a fish eating creatures it is not supposed to eat. The fish in this story is not like the snake or the lynx and does not usually raise storms or chase young women. A likely candidate for stories about giant fish is the sturgeon (*Acipenser fulvescens*), which has lived in the lakes since their beginning and can grow more than nine feet long, weigh over three hundred pounds, and live more than a century.

The people were much distressed about a water monster, or giant fish, which frequently caught fishermen, dragging them into the lake and there devouring them. So Manabush asked his grandmother to hand to him his singing sticks[179] and told her he was going to allow himself to be swallowed that he might be enabled to destroy the monster. Manabush then built a small raft and floated out on the lake, singing all the while, "Mashenomak, come and eat me; you will feel good." Then the monster, Mashenomak, saw that it was Manabush and told his children to swallow him. When one of the young Mashenomak darted forward to swallow Manabush, the latter said, "I want Mashenomak to swallow me." This made the monster so angry that he swallowed Manabush, who thereupon became unconscious. When he recovered, he found himself in company with his brothers; he saw the Bear, the Deer, the Porcupine, the Raven, the Pine-squirrel, and many others. He inquired of them how they came to meet with such misfortune and was very sad to find that other kinsmen also were lying dead.

Then Manabush prepared to sing the war song, during which it is customary to state the object of making the attack and the manner in which it is to be attempted. He told his brothers to dance with him, and all joined in singing. The Pine-squirrel alone had a curious voice and hopped around rapidly, singing, "Sĕk-sĕk-sĕk-sĕk," which amused the rest, even in their distress.[180] As the dancers passed around the interior of the monster, it made him reel, and when Manabush danced past his heart, he thrust his knife toward it, which caused the monster to have a convulsion. Then Manabush thrust his knife three times toward the monster's heart, after which he said, "Mashenomak, swim toward my wigwam," and immediately afterward he thrust his knife into the heart, which caused the monster's body to quake and roll so violently that everyone became unconscious.

How long they remained in this condition they knew not, but on returning to consciousness Manabush found everything motionless and silent. He knew then that the monster was dead and that his body was lying either on the shore or on the bottom of the lake. To make sure, he crawled over the bodies of his brothers to a point where he could cut an opening through the monster's body. When he had cut a small opening, he saw bright daylight and immediately closed the hole, took his singing sticks, and began to sing:

Kē-sik-in-nâ-min, kē-sik-in-nâ-min
(I see the sky! I see the sky!)

As Manabush continued to sing, his brothers recovered. The Squirrel alone was the one who hopped around singing the words, "Sĕk - sĕk, sĕk - sĕk, sĕk - sĕk, sĕk - sĕk."

When the dance was concluded, Manabush cut a large opening in the monster's belly through which they emerged. As the survivors were about to separate to go to their respective wigwams, they all complimented the Pine-squirrel on his fine voice, and Manabush said to him, "My younger brother, you also will be happy, as you have a good voice." Thus Manabush destroyed Mashenomak.

1890s

The Enchanted Bears
Unidentified Potawatomi

In addition to underwater snakes and panthers, the Potawatomi and Menominee believed in an underwater creature in the form of a great white bear with a long copper tail who lived in Lake Michigan. He is the traditional ancestor of the Menominee people and a force of great evil who was also the patron of all earthly bears. Here he is attacked by men who belong to the Thunder clan and so have the power to fight underwater beings.

A man named Wapiskinini, or the White-Man (loon), said that he had seen grizzly bears that lived both in land and water, so some people got in a canoe with him and went northward along the west shore of Lake

Michigan to the islands at the mouth of Green Bay (Potawatomi Islands) to see them.

The father of White-man, named Pitwánkwût, or Between the Clouds, saw something moving under the water. They all looked and, behold, it was a great bear. They could scarcely believe it, but not long afterwards another came out of the water and went on shore, and they saw still another. No one had ever heard of or seen such a sight before, so the Potawatomi desired to kill one of the animals. They therefore crossed over to one of the islands and, following one of the bears, saw it standing, swaying from side to side. At length it walked into the water and beneath it, where it went to sleep.

These men were all of the Thunder clan, so their leader got out his sacred bundle and took two arrows which he shot through the water right into the neck of the bear. It came out, and they shot it again. Five more emerged from the water and were likewise shot. The Indians blew upon the cane whistles from their bundles and then skinned the bears and, after their hides were removed, Wísakä (Trickster) changed them all into white beavers. Wísakä was just malicious about it.

1927

Getting Bounty from the English

Maskwawā´nahkwatōk (Red Cloud Woman, Louise Dutchman, *c.*1870-†), Menominee

Birchbark canoes are the most beautiful and most functional of Great Lakes vessels. Made of native materials and easily repairable on nearly any beach, they are also extremely light and allow portage without difficulty yet are capable of carrying cargoes in excess of four tons. Without them the lakes could not have been explored so easily, nor could the fur trade have developed as it did. But for all their beauty and their usefulness, they are also extremely tender and liable to swamp in even a moderate sea. They are best suited to rivers and inland lakes, yet they were the only mode of transport for Natives on the open lakes and, after Contact, their white passengers. There are numerous traveler's accounts, beginning with the Jesuits in the seventeenth century, that describe long, painful days spent sitting absolutely still so the canoe would not ship water and sink.

Besides the fragileness of the canoe and the ever-present threat of water monsters like Micipijiu, many Natives believed that to drown was to have one's soul wander cursed, forever to haunt the place where one died, and to pass that curse onto one's children. It is understandable then that any voyage was taken with much trepidation, even after careful preparations had been made to appease the spirits. Those who embarked without proper rites—a fast, a black dog sacrificed to the water, a new name and a protective charm, some tobacco left on a sacred rock or burned—were liable to die like those warriors who crossed too hastily from Washington Island to the Door Peninsula in pursuit of their enemies and were struck by a storm and lost, giving Death's Door the name it holds today. This story tells of a voyage to collect bounty payments which began from a Menominee village in Wisconsin ended at the British garrison on Mackinac Island sometime between 1763, when the French left the lakes, and 1814, when the British left. Even today, in a technologically sophisticated sailboat, this is a taxing trip; we can scarcely imagine what it must have been like in an open canoe steered by the stars.

Canoe of Indians, 1856. Eastman Johnston

When my grandmother was as big as this, being twelve winters old, then the people were summoned by the English, who wished to give them money and things to wear and things to eat.

Then the Menominee made birch bark canoes; four fathoms long were the canoes. And then, when they had completed them, they put into them their blanket-robes and their kettles. And then—there were many children—then all the children were put on board. Then four grown people got in, to take along their children. Then all the Menominee as many as were able went along, all the canoes being launched at the same time.

Then they started forth on their voyage. They did not see any land by which to direct their course; they observed the sun and moon; they went due east.

When they were about to start, they made a great burnt-offering, making prayer to the spirits of the water that they might safely reach their goal and return. They were heard. Not once did the wind blow while they voyaged. For ten days they voyaged, all day and all night; the grown people who did the paddling slept by turns.

Then, from some quarter a wind did spring up; the water to some slight degree came into motion; the women grew frightened and wept. Then one man was given tobacco, a man who had performed a great fast and had seen a vision of the waters. He accepted the tobacco and made a speech, dropping the tobacco into the water. Then, when he had finished his speech, then they all sang: thereupon the wind stopped.

So then they again started to paddle. As they paddled on and on, when they had eaten all of what little provision they had on the way, then they would eat only a little salt. Thereupon they would drink water; in this way their hunger was stilled.

As they voyaged along, a wind came up. Of course, they were as good as dead, if the wind grew strong. So then they made four tiny vessels of birchbark; and into each little vessel of birchbark they set an insect, namely a louse, and then they placed those little vessels into the water.

Then those little vessels tipped over; then were the children made to weep, so that they wept loudly;

268

and then all the grown people spoke. "Now they are all dead!" cried the women. At that the wind ceased, and the water lay quiet. Then they went on with all speed, all of them paddling, that they might quickly arrive.

At last they came in sight of land; they had reached their destination. When they had disembarked there in the Englishman's town, they were given plenty to eat, the Englishman giving them raised bread, pork, and all sorts of things. When they had eaten, they were at ease. Some of them did not eat any bread; they did not know what it was, or pork either.

On the next day the English gave them silver coins, such and such a number, giving a large sum of money to each and every one of these Indians and giving them also garments, blankets, broadcloth, and all things.

So much did I hear my grandmother tell when I was little. That is all. "Unbounded Space" was my grandmother's name.

1928

Lake of Dreams

Susan Power (1961-   ), Dakota

A member of the Standing Rock band, Susan Power's 1994 novel, *The Grass Dancer*, won the 1995 PEN-Hemingway Award for first fiction. In this autobiographical essay about growing up in Chicago, Power describes the relationship of mingled love and respect for the waters of the Great Lakes that many know. Portraying herself as a "small, anonymous fish," her memoir traces how she became baptized in and finally a part of the waters she loves.

My mother used to say that by the time I was an old woman, Lake Michigan would be the size of a silver dollar. She pinched her index finger with her thumb to show me the pitiful dimensions. "People will gather around the tiny lake, what's left of it, and cluck over a spoonful of water," she told me.

I learned to squint at the 1967 shoreline until I had carved away the structures and roads built on landfill and could imagine the lake and its city as my mother found them in 1942 when she arrived in Chicago. I say "the lake and its city" rather than "the city and its lake" because my mother taught me another secret: The city of Chicago belongs to Lake Michigan.

But which of my mother's pronouncements to believe? That Chicago would swallow the Midwestern sea, smother it in concrete? Or that the lake wielded enough strength to outpolitick even Mayor Richard J. Daley?

Mayor Daley, Sr., is gone now, but the lake remains, alternately tranquil and riled, changing colors like a mood ring. I guess we know who won.

When my mother watches the water from her lakeside apartment building, she still sucks in her breath. "You have to respect the power of that lake," she tells me. And I do now. I do.

I was fifteen years old when I learned that the lake did not love me or hate me but could claim me nevertheless. I was showing off for a boy, my best friend, Tommy, who lived in the same building. He usually accompanied me when I went for a swim, but on this particular day he decided the water was too choppy. I always preferred the lake when it was agitated because its temperature warmed, transforming it into a kind of Jacuzzi.

Tommy is right, I thought, once I saw the looming swells that had looked so unimpressive from the twelfth floor. Waves crashed against the breakwater wall and the metal ladder that led into the lake, like the entrance to the deep end of a swimming pool.

I shouldn't do this, I told myself, but I noticed Tommy watching me from his first-floor window. "I'm not afraid," I said to him under my breath. "I bet you think that I'll chicken out just because I'm a girl."

It had been a hot summer of dares, and sense was clearly wanting. I took a deep breath and leapt off the wall into the churning water. How could I possibly get out? I hadn't thought that far ahead. When I bobbed to the surface, I was instantly slapped in the face and smashed under again and again, until I began gasping for air. *I'm going to die now,* I realized, and my heart filled with sorrow for my mother, who had already lost a husband and would now lose a daughter. I fought the waves, the sound of breakers swelling in my ears, unnaturally loud, like the noise of Judgment Day. Here we go, I thought. Then I became unusually calm. I took a quick gulp of air, plunged to the bottom of the lake where the water was a little quieter, and swam to the beach next door until I reached shallow waters. I burst to the surface then, my lungs burning, and it took me nearly five minutes to walk fifteen feet to shore, continually knocked off balance by the waves that sucked at my legs. Tommy was no longer watching me, bored by my private games, unaware of the danger. I didn't tell my mother what had happened until hours later. I was angry at myself for being so careless with my life, but I was never for a moment angry at the lake. I didn't come to fear it, either, though it is a mighty force that drops 923 feet in its deepest heart. I understood that it struck indifferently; I was neither target nor friend. My life was my own affair, to lose or to save. Once I stopped struggling with the great lake, I flowed through it and was expelled from its hectic mouth.

My mother still calls Fort Yates, North Dakota, home, despite the fact that she has lived in Chicago for nearly fifty-five years. She has taken me to visit the Standing Rock Sioux Reservation, where she was raised, and although a good portion of it was flooded during the construction of the Oahe Dam,[181] she can point to significant hills and buttes and creeks. The landscape there endures, outlives its inhabitants. But I am a child of the city, where landmarks are human-made, impermanent. My attachments to place are attachments to people, my love for a particular area only as strong as my local relationships. I have lived in several cities and will live in several more. I visit the country with curiosity and trepidation, clearly a foreigner, and envy my mother's connection to a dusty town, the peace she finds on the prairie. It is a kind of religion, her devotion to Proposal Hill and the Missouri River, a sacred bond that I can only half-understand. If I try to see the world through my mother's eyes, find the point where my own flesh falls to earth, I realize my home is Lake Michigan, the source of so many lessons.

As a teenager I loved to swim in the dark, to dive beneath the surface where the water was as black as the sky. The lake seemed limitless, and so was I, an arm, a leg, a wrist, a face, indistinguishable from the wooden boards of a sunken dock, from the sand I squeezed between my toes. I always left reluctantly, loath to become a body again and feel more acutely the oppressive pull of gravity.

It was my father who taught me to swim, with his usual patience. First he helped me float, his hands beneath my back and legs, his torso shading me from the sun. Next he taught me to flutter-kick, and I tried to make as much noise as possible. I dog-paddled in circles, but my father swam in a straight line perpendicular to shore, as if he were trying to leave this land forever, just as he had left New York State after a lifetime spent within its borders, easily, without regret. His swim was always the longest, the farthest. Mom and I would watch him as we lounged on our beach towels, nervous that a boat might clip him. It was a relief to see him turn around and coast in our direction.

"Here he comes," Mom would breathe. "He's coming back now."

My father also showed me how to skip a stone across the water. He could make a flat rock jump like a tiny, leaping frog, sometimes five or six hops before it sank to the bottom. It was the only time I could imagine this distinguished, silver-haired gentleman as a boy, and I laughed at him affectionately because the difference in our years collapsed.

My mother collects stones in her backyard—a rough, rocky beach in South Shore. She looks for rocks drilled with holes, not pits or mere scratches, but tiny punctures worn clear through.

"I can't leave until I find at least one," she tells me.

"Why?" I ask.

"There are powerful spirits in these stones, trying to tunnel their way out."

What I do not ask is why she selects them, these obviously unquiet souls, why she places them in a candy dish or a basket worn soft as flannel. What good can it do them? What good can it do her to unleash such restless forces on the quiet of her rooms?

I finger my mother's collection when I'm home for a visit and sometimes even press a smooth specimen against my cheek. The stones are mute and passive in my hand. At first I think it must be a failing on my part: I cannot hear what my mother hears. Then I decide that the spirits caught in these stones have already escaped. I imagine them returning to the lake, to the waves that pushed them onto the beach and washed their pebble flesh, because it is such a comfort to return to water.

And then I remember my own weightless immersion, how my body becomes a fluid spirit when I pull myself underwater, where breath stops. And I remember gliding along the lake's sandy bottom as a child, awed by the orderly pattern of its dunes. Lake Michigan is cold, reliably cold, but occasionally I passed through pockets of tepid water that always came as a surprise. I am reminded of cold spots reputedly found in haunted houses, and I wonder: Are these warm areas evidence of my lost souls?

A young man drowned in these waters behind my mother's building some years ago. Mom was sitting in a lawn chair, visiting with another tenant on the terrace. They sat together facing the lake so they could watch it, though it was calm that day, uninteresting. A young man stroked into view, swimming parallel to the shore, and headed north. He was close enough for them to read his features; he was fifteen feet away from the shallows, where he could have stood with his head above water. He called out and asked in a calm voice how far south he was. The 7300 block, they told him. He moved on. A marathon swimmer, the women decided. But eventually my mother and her friend scanned the horizon and were unable to see his bobbing head and strong arms. They alerted the doorman, who called the police. The young man was found near the spot where he'd made his cordial inquiry.

"Why didn't he cry for help? Why didn't he signal his distress?" my mother asked the response unit.

"This happens all the time with men," she was told. "They aren't taught to cry for help."

So he is there too, the swimmer, a warm presence in cold water or a spirit in a stone.

I have gone swimming in other places—a chlorinated pool in Hollywood, the warm waters of the Caribbean, the Heart River in North Dakota—only to be disappointed and emerge unrefreshed. I am too used to Lake Michigan and its eccentricities. I must have cold, fresh water. I must have the stinking corpses of silver alewives floating on the surface as an occasional nasty surprise, always discovered dead, never alive. I must have sailboats on the horizon and steel mills on the southern shore, golf balls (shot from the local course) clustered around submerged pilings, and breakwater boulders heavy as tombs lining the beach. I must have sullen lifeguards who whistle at anyone bold enough to stand in three feet of water, and the periodic arguments between wind and water that produce tearing waves and lake-spattered windows.

When I was little, maybe seven or eight, my parents and I went swimming in a storm. The weather was mild when we set out, but the squall arrived quickly, without warning, as often happens in the Midwest. We swam anyway, keeping an eye on the lightning not yet arrived from the north. There was no one to stop us since we were dipping into deep water between beaches, in an unpatrolled area. The water was warmer than usual, the same temperature as the air, and when the rain wet the sky, I leapt up and down in the growing waves, unable to feel the difference between air and water, lake and rain. The three of us played together that time; even my father remained near shore rather than striking east to swim past the white buoys. We were joined in this favorite element, splashing and ducking. I waved my arms over my head. My father pretended to be a great whale, heavy in the surf, now and then spouting streams of water from his mouth. He chased me. My mother laughed.

Dad died in 1973 when I was eleven, before my mother and I moved to the apartment on the lake. We always thought it such a shame he didn't get to make that move with us. He would have enjoyed finding Lake Michigan in his backyard.

We buried him in Albany, New York, because that is where he was raised. My mother was born in North Dakota, and I was born between them, in Chicago. There is a good chance we shall not all rest together, our stories playing out in different lands. But I imagine that if a rendezvous is possible—and my mother insists it is—we will find one another in this great lake, this small sea that rocks like a cradle. We are strong swimmers in our separate ways, my mother like a turtle, my father like a seal. And me? I am a small anonymous fish, unspectacular but content.

1997

⁂ SUMMER STARS AND SKY BEINGS ⁂

Stories of the Sky

Chief Shunien Josette (Silver Money, 1827-†), Menominee

The Moon

Once on a time Kēso', the Sun, and his sister Tipäkēso' (Last Night Sun), the Moon, lived together in a wigwam in the East. The Sun dressed himself to go hunting, took his bow and arrows, and left. He was absent such a long time that when his sister came out into the sky to look for her brother she became alarmed. She traveled twenty days looking for the Sun, but finally he returned, bringing with him a bear which he had shot.

The Sun's sister still comes up into the sky and travels for twenty days; then she dies and for four days nothing is seen of her. At the end of that time, however, she returns to life and travels twenty days more.

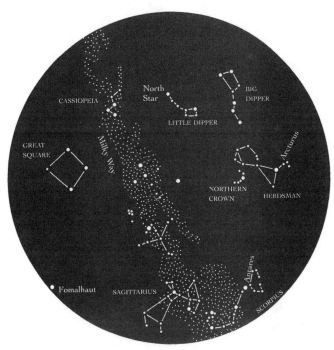

Summer star map

The Sun is a being like ourselves. Whenever an Indian dreams of him, he plucks out his hair and wears an otter skin about his head, over the forehead. This the Indian does because the sun wears an otter skin about his head.

The Aurora Borealis

In the direction of the north wind live the *manabaiwok* (giants), of whom we have heard our old people tell. The manabaiwok are our friends, but we do not see them any more. They are great hunters and fishermen, and whenever they are out with their torches to spear fish, we know it, because then the sky is bright over the place where they are.[182]

Meteors

When a star falls from the sky, it leaves a fiery trail; it does not die, but its shade goes back to the

273

place whence it dropped to shine again. The Indians sometimes find the small stars in the prairie where they have fallen. They are of stone and are round, with a spot in the center, and four or five small points projecting from the surface. I have myself found some of these fallen stars.

1890s

Fishing By Torchlight, 1848-56. Paul Kane

The Boy Who Caught the Sun
Unidentified Menominee

Tales about children who snare the sun occur in several cultures and might once have been used to explain eclipses. Sometimes the child repents and releases it; sometimes a mouse chews the strings or netting, and the sun flies free again, rewarding the mouse. Although several lakes nations believed the rainbow could be a snare, here the little boy uses basswood twine. He has begun to learn to hunt, shooting small birds, as young boys do when first given bows and arrows. But he must also learn responsibility and recognize that although revenge is a cherished right, it must be tempered by common sense.

A little boy was once living alone with his mother. The boy had a little bow and arrows and he went out and shot small birds. When he killed two, he brought them to his mother, who skinned them and stretched them on a frame. She cooked the two birds, split them in two, and when they were finished, she gave them to her son, who ate them. When the boy had killed twelve, they made a tiny feather coat. The boy kept it on, and one day he said, "This time I'll go fishing." He put on his bird skin coat and went out. He soon heard the Thunderers coming and ran home, but was overtaken by rain when nearly there and got wet. He took off his coat and dried it. The coat hung out to dry too long so that it crumbled to pieces when he put it on. He turned about and scolded the sun for being too strong. He told his mother, "That bad sun has dried my coat too much, or else he has chewed it up."

"It is your fault," said the mother, "you left it out there too long."

"Mother, you should have taken it in, for you know I am always busy," he said and scolded the sun again. "Sun you will get it," he said. "Mother, you had better gather some basswood twine as I intend to snare the sun."

His mother tried to prevent it. "If you do this, it will be dark," she said and refused to make the twine. The boy then started out himself and made it. He made it in three-strand braid and worked until he had a big ball of twine. Then he watched until he saw a winter hawk[183] and called it over. "Grandpa, would you please take me up and carry me to the sun, I want to talk to it." The hawk carried the boy up there with the rope hidden in his bosom. When there, the boy tied a loop around the sun's neck and returned to the earth with the rope, unwinding the ball as he went. When on earth, he had plenty of twine left. He pulled up the slack, ran, and choked the sun until it began to get dark.

His mother wondered and thought something was wrong. She ran out to find out and looked again to see that the sun was dark, the rest light. "What have you done?" she demanded of her boy.

"I am choking the sun in revenge," he answered.

The mother was alarmed and scolded him saying, "If you kill the sun, there will be no daylight, and you will be unable to see to hunt." She then inquired how he got up there where the sun dwelt. The boy told her that his grandfather hawk took him there and back. Soon when it was nearly dark, they saw the hawk and called him back. The mother told her boy to go and release the sun, and she gave him a knife to cut the string near the sun's throat. The boy released the sun and returned with the hawk again. So the sun came to life once more.

1915

The Worship of the Sun

Audaname, Odawa

This story of a man who marries the moon was related by a man from L'Arbre Croche, near Little Traverse Bay on Lake Michigan. The story is notable in several ways: it highlights the resistance of some children to fasting and the results that follow when parents force them. It mentions the Anishinâbe belief of a hole in the sky, which allowed communication between the sky and the earth. Some researchers believe the entrance to this hole is the constellation Corona Borealis or Northern Crown which is near Arcturus. O-no-wut-a-qut-o's marriage illustrates the idea that once committed to a sky being, humans could never return permanently to earth. In addition, the teller has explained what causes sickness and what happens to sacrificial goods offered to the gods for healing. In many tales Moon is the Sun's wife; here she is his sister.

A long time ago, there lived an aged Ojibwa and his wife on the shores of Lake Huron. They had an only son, a very beautiful boy, whose name was O-no-wut-a-qut-o, or He That Catches the Clouds. The family was of the totem of the beaver. The parents were very proud of him and thought to make him a celebrated man, but when he reached the proper age, he would not submit to the *we-koon-de-win,* or fast. When this time arrived, they gave him charcoal, instead of his breakfast, but he would not blacken his face. If they denied him food, he would seek for birds' eggs along the shores, or pick up the heads of fish that had been cast away and broil them. One day, they took away violently the food he had thus prepared, and cast him some coals in place of it. This act brought him to a decision. He took the coals and blackened his face and went out of the lodge. He did not return but slept without and, during the night, he had a dream.

He dreamed that he saw a very beautiful female come down from the clouds and stand by his side. "O-no-wut-a-qut-o" said she, "I am come for you—step in my tracks." The young man did so and presently felt himself ascending above the tops of the trees—he mounted up, step by step, into the air, and through the clouds. His guide, at length, passed through an orifice, and he, following her, found himself standing on a beautiful plain.

A path led to a splendid lodge. He followed her into it. It was large and divided into two parts. On one end he saw bows and arrows, clubs and spears, and various warlike implements tipped with silver. On the other end were things exclusively belonging to females. This was the home of his fair guide, and he saw that she had, on the frame, a broad, rich belt of many colors, which she was weaving. She said to him: "My brother is coming, and I must hide you." Putting him in one corner, she spread the belt over him.

Presently the brother came in, very richly dressed and shining as if he had points of silver all over him. He took down from the wall a splendid pipe, together with his sack of *apakozegun* (*apâkosigan*), or smoking mixture. When he had finished regaling himself in this way and laid his pipe aside, he said to his sister: *"Nemissa* (*nimissé*: elder sister), when will you quit these practices? Do you forget that the Greatest of the Spirits had commanded that you should not take away the child from below? Perhaps you suppose that you have concealed O-no-wut-a-qut-o, but do I not know of his coming? If you would not offend me, send him back immediately."

But this address did not alter her purpose. She would not send him back. Finding that she was purposed in her mind, he then spoke to the young lad and called him from his hiding place. "Come out of your concealment," said he, "and walk about and amuse yourself. You will grow hungry if you remain there." He then presented him a bow and arrows and a pipe of red stone,[184] richly ornamented. This was taken as the word of consent to his marriage; so the two were considered husband and wife from that time.

O-no-wut-a-qut-o found everything exceedingly fair and beautiful around him, but he found no inhabitants except her brother. There were flowers on the plains. There were bright and sparkling streams. There were green valleys and pleasant trees. There were gay birds and beautiful animals, but they were not such as he had been accustomed to see. There was also day and night, as on the earth; but he observed that every morning the brother regularly left the lodge and remained absent all day; and every evening the sister departed, though it was commonly but for a part of the night.[185]

His curiosity was aroused to solve this mystery. He obtained the brother's consent to accompany him in one of his daily journeys. They traveled over a smooth plain, without boundaries, until O-no-wut-a-qut-o felt the gnawings of appetite and asked his companion if there were no game. "Patience, my brother," said he, "we shall soon reach the spot where I eat my dinner, and you will then see how I am provided."

After walking on a long time, they came to a place which was spread over with fine mats where they sat down to refresh themselves. There was, at this place, a hole through the sky, and O-no-wut-a-qut-o looked down, at the bidding of his companion, upon the earth. He saw below the Great Lakes and the villages of the Indians. In one place, he saw a war party stealing on the camp of their enemies. In another, he saw feasting and dancing. On a green plain, young men were engaged at ball. Along a stream, women were employed in gathering the *a-puk-wa* (rush) for mats.[186]

"Do you see," said the brother, "that group of children playing beside a lodge? Observe that beautiful and active boy," said he, at the same time darting something at him from his hand. The child immediately fell and was carried into the lodge.

They looked again and saw the people gathering about the lodge. They heard the *she-she-gwun* (drum)[187] of the meet-a (Midé) and the song he sung, asking that the child's life be spared. To this request, the companion of O-no-wut-a-qut-o made answer: "Send me up the sacrifice of a white dog." Immediately a feast was ordered by the parents of the child, the white dog was killed, his carcass was roasted, and all the wise men and medicine men of the village assembled to witness the ceremony.

"There are many below," continued the voice of the brother, "whom you call great in medical skill, but it is because their ears are open and they listen to my voice that they are able to succeed. When I have struck one with sickness, they direct the people to look to me. And when they send me the offering I ask, I remove my hand from off them, and they are well." After he had said this, they saw the sacrifice parceled out in dishes for those who were at the feast. The master of the feast then said, "We send this to thee, great Manito," and immediately the roasted animal came up. Thus their dinner was supplied and, after they had eaten, they returned to the lodge by another way.

After this manner they lived for some time, but the place became wearisome at last. O-no-wut-a-qut-o thought of his friends and wished to go back to them. He had not forgotten his native village and his father's lodge, and he asked leave of his wife to return. At length she consented.

"Since you are better pleased," she replied, "with the cares and the ills and the poverty of the world than with the peaceful delights of the sky and its boundless prairies, go! I give you permission, and since I have brought you hither, I will conduct you back. But remember, you are still my husband. I hold a chain in my hand by which I can draw you back whenever I will. My power over you is not, in any manner, diminished. Beware, therefore, how you venture to take a wife among the people below. Should you ever do so, it is then that you shall feel the force of my displeasure."

As she said this, her eyes sparkled—she raised herself slightly on her toes and stretched herself up, with a majestic air, and at that moment O-no-wut-a-qut-o awoke from his dream. He found himself on the ground, near his father's lodge, at the very spot where he had laid himself down to fast. Instead of the bright beings of a higher world, he found himself surrounded by his parents and relatives. His mother told him he had been absent a year. The change was so great that he remained for sometime moody and abstracted, but by degrees he recovered his spirits. He began to doubt the reality of all he had heard and seen above. At last, he forgot the admonitions of his spouse and married a beautiful young woman of his own tribe. But within four days, she was a corpse. Even this fearful admonition was lost, and he repeated the offense by a second marriage.

Soon afterwards, he went out of the lodge one night but never returned. It was believed that his Sun wife had recalled him to the region of the clouds, where, the tradition asserts, he still dwells and walks on the daily rounds, which he once witnessed.

1830s

The Evening Star

David Lee Smith (1950-   ), Winnebago[188]

T he Evening Star" is a contemporary retelling of the origin of what may be Venus, the brightest of the planets, known also as the Evening Star. Depending on its orbit relative to the sun, Venus appears in either the morning or the evening sky. Like narratives about corn, the stories of the sky beings—the stars, planets, and other solar events—can show tantalizing traces of influences from Mesoamerica, such as the characteristics of Venus, but it is difficult to prove a connection. The Maya charted Venus because they believed it had great power—as well as brightness—during its heliacal rising, when it emerges before the sun as the Morning Star, or after it emerges from behind the sun once again to become the Evening Star. This was when the Maya made war. Mesoamerican stories characterized Venus as male and feared the beams of the star in the household because of their power. Mercury, which also appears as a morning or evening star, was nearly as powerful. It may be that some stories came to the lakes region along with their peoples during the Mississippian migrations about AD 1000 and became transformed through time.

The summer solstice (literally "sun stop"), where all the trouble starts in this story, has been marked by cultures since time immemorial. It occurs about June 21, the longest day of the year, when the sun seems to stop for a few days at its northernmost rising point before beginning to rise in a slightly more southern position every day until the winter solstice in December. In addition, the shaman here might be what the Ojibwe call a *wâbenowinini orwaiâbanowid* (man of the dawn sky), fire handlers who could interpret dreams and were known for their love potions. *Wâbenos*, who consider themselves brothers of Winabojo [Nanabozho], have a secret society similar to the Midéwewin that meets at night. They emerge just as dawn breaks in the sky; thus they are associated with the stars and celestial events. In the past they were most likely the guardians of an extensive star lore. If so, they would have been able to predict celestial events and share in the power of the Sky Beings, giving the wâbenos great power.

Thousands upon thousands of seasons ago, when the Winnebagos were still in the lake country, there lived a powerful shaman. This shaman was once known far and wide for his power, and all people, enemy and friend alike, respected him.

At first he used his power only for the good of the people. Then he fell in love with the chief's daughter, who was the prettiest young woman of the tribe. The trouble was that the chief's daughter did not like the shaman. He tried everything to please her. He brought her honey, furs, and flowers, but nothing he did could change her opinion of him. So the shaman resorted to the thing he never used before, and that was evil magic.

The shaman knew that if he used it, the evil magic would turn against him, but he was deeply in love. Nothing else mattered to him except the chief's daughter. So one dark night he called upon the evil spirits, who gave him a bag of love medicine to use on the chief's daughter. He then laid his plans very carefully, so no one would become suspicious of him. He planned to use the evil magic at the dance of the summer solstice.

The chief's daughter had plans of her own. She fell in love with a young warrior of the nearby Beaver tribe.[189] This tribe was reputed to be large and strong. The daughter's father, who was the chief, welcomed the idea of the mating, for in the process they would gain a strong ally. So, little known to the shaman, the marriage was to be consummated on the summer solstice.

As the day approached, the shaman was ordered to prepare a ritual drink for the marriage. When he found out who was getting married, he about fell over dead. He had worked hard and was not about to lose the chief's daughter to someone else.

That night, as the village lay sleeping, he turned himself into an owl and flew to the chief's lodge. Once there, he sprinkled dust over the sleeping form of the daughter and, before anyone awakened, he returned to his own lodge. The next day, the celebration would start at sunrise, so he went to sleep with an evil smile on his lips.

The next morning, after the sun appeared on the eastern horizon, the brave young warrior of the Beaver tribe appeared with his people. The chief ordered his daughter to get ready and sent word to the shaman to bring the ritual drink. The shaman arrived when the marriage ceremony was just about over. The ritual drink that he brought would be the final act to the marriage vows. When the daughter saw the shaman, her mind seemed to snap, and she fell in love with the shaman. The evil magic that the shaman used had done its purpose. When the chief asked his daughter to give the ritual drink to her new husband, she gave it to the shaman, and the marriage was done.

Both the chief and the Beaver warrior stood there aghast. Then both men flew into a rage. The warrior promised that war would be arranged, for no one would make a fool out of him. The chief answered that his people would be waiting. After the Beaver party left, the chief ordered his daughter and the shaman from the village. He loved his daughter dearly, but he could not break up the marriage. That would go against tribal tradition.

As the months passed, the chief's daughter became pregnant for the shaman. At the night of the birth, the daughter died after giving birth to a little deformed girl. The shaman now knew that his own evil magic had turned against him. The shaman was very heartbroken, but he buried his wife, took his daughter, and moved still further from his old village than before.

As the years went by, the old shaman used what good powers he had left to raise his daughter right. She became a mighty hunter and a powerful warrior. The only thing she lacked was her own people. The old shaman knew that her own people would never want her because she was deformed somewhat in the face. So his young daughter stayed with him until he died.

After the daughter laid her father to rest, she had a vision from her dead mother. Her mother appeared to her in a dream. "My daughter," she said, "forgive your father for what I am about to tell you. Long ago, your father used love medicine on me and won me away from my true husband-to-be. Now his tribe and our tribe are still fighting an endless war, and they need your help." The mother touched her daughter's hand and continued, "My father, the chief, is very old, but tell him I am sorry for what has happened. I hope in his heart he can forgive me." Tears seemed to flow from her mother's eyes. "Now go my daughter, and help your people, for the last battle is about to start, and remember I love you always."

As the vision faded, the mother said, "Follow the river to its mouth; there you will find your people." With that, the mother vanished and the daughter woke up.

In her hand she saw a small, red stone hanging on a string.[190] She had seen it once before, hanging from her mother's neck, so she knew her dream was more than a dream. The red stone was her mother's personal medicine, given to her by her father, the chief. Quickly she gathered her weapons and proceeded south, following the raging river.

Days later, she approached the mouth of the river. On the opposite bank she saw a large village, and she knew she had found her people. She then climbed the tallest pine and looked far to the west. There she saw smoke rising from four camps, with hundreds of men forming ranks. "So there's the enemy," she said aloud. "I better help my people, for they are outnumbered and will suffer greatly." Then she climbed down the tree and prepared herself a sweat lodge. If she was going to fight, she had to purify herself, as her father, the shaman, told her to.

During the night, as the stars came out, she prepared her own medicine, for she was not the shaman's daughter for nothing. She knew she had to cross to her people's village in order to approach the enemy. She did not want them to know that she was fighting for them, because her mother was the cause of the war and she did not know how her people would react. So when the clouds darkened the night, she changed herself into a small owl and flew over her people's village.

About the same time she was turning into an owl, her grandfather, the chief, came out of his lodge to pray to Ma-ona (*Mạ'úna*: Earthmaker) for victory the following day. He was tired and growing older each day. His thoughts kept going back to the scene eighteen years ago, when he exiled his daughter from his village. Now he was ready for death, and his only hope was that the Creator would forgive him for what he had done. Just then he looked up to the heavens and seemed to see an owl passing though the broken clouds. "An omen," he said to himself. "An omen of death, but whose death?" he said quietly.

At sunrise the next day, the chief gathered his warriors and marched out to meet the enemy. There was no enemy, for all the enemy were dead. In the middle of the dead Beaver warriors, he spotted a young girl in tribal dress, dying from many mortal wounds. Then he saw around her neck a small, pretty, red stone, hanging on a string. Tears formed in his eyes as he knelt down and cradled the girl's head in his arms. She slowly opened her eyes and said, "Grandfather, please forgive my mother and my father, and please take me home to our people." The grandfather grabbed his granddaughter in his arms and with his warriors marched back to the village.

Just as the sun was going down, the chief's granddaughter died. The whole village went into mourning. Then a strange thing happened. The dead girl was lifted into the heavens by the four spirit-winds. For Ma-ona himself felt very bad, and he wasn't about to let the little girl die after saving his own people. So as the sun disappeared, Ma-ona placed the chief's daughter in the evening sky. She became the evening star. Now she guards the people forever. If you ever look real hard, people say you can see the star shine brightly as if it is smiling. Smiling that she is now home with her people.

1997

The Bear Maiden

Pä-skin´ (Pä´skineu, *c.*1798-*c.*1900), Ojibwe

When Albert Jenks was gathering materials at Lac Courte Oreilles in Wisconsin in 1899 for *The Wild Rice Gatherers of the Upper Lakes,* he collected this tale from Pä-skin´, a woman he described as over a hundred years old. Jenks believed the little bear in this tale represents Venus as the Morning Star, the old woman and her daughters personify the earth, and the men carrying lights are stars. If so, that would suggest this is an eclipse story that might have roots in Mesoamerica where the Morning Star was considered to have great power and eclipses were dreaded because they released evil spirits that caused sickness. As Jenks noted, the pony is a later addition.

There was an old man and woman who had three daughters, two older ones and a younger one who was a little bear. The father and mother got very old and could not work any longer, so the two older daughters started away to find work in order to support themselves. They did not want their little sister to go with them, so they left her at home.

After a time they looked around and saw the little bear running to overtake them. They took her back home and tied her to the door posts of the wigwam and again started away to find work; and again they heard something behind them and saw the little bear running toward them with the posts on her back. The sisters untied her from them and tied her to a large pine tree. Then they continued on their journey. They heard a noise behind them once more and turned around to find their younger sister, the little bear, running to them with the pine-tree on her back. They did not want her to go with them, so they untied her from the pine-tree and fastened her to a huge rock and continued on in search of work.

Soon they came to a wide river which they could not get across. As they sat there on the shore wondering how they could cross the river, they heard a noise coming toward them. They looked up and saw their younger sister running to them with the huge rock on her back. They untied the rock, threw it into the middle of the river, laid a pine tree on it, and walked across. This time the little bear went with them.

After a short journey they came to a wigwam where an old woman lived with her two daughters. This old woman asked them where they were going. They told her that their parents were old and that they were seeking work in order to support themselves. She invited them in, gave them supper, and after supper the two older sisters and the two daughters of the old woman went to sleep in the same bed.

The old woman and the little bear sat up, and the little bear told many stories to the old woman. At last they both appeared to fall asleep. The little bear pinched the old woman and, finding her asleep, went to the bed and changed the places of the four sleeping girls. She put the daughters of the old woman on the outside and her own sisters in the middle. Then she lay down as though asleep. After a short time, the old woman awoke and pinched the little bear to see whether she slept. She sharpened her knife and went to the bed and cut off the heads of the two girls at the outer edges of the bed. The old woman lay down and soon was sleeping. The little bear awoke her sisters, and they all three crept away.

In the morning when the old woman got up and found that she had killed her two daughters, she was very angry. She jumped up into the sky and tore down the sun and hid it in her wigwam, so that the little bear and her sisters would get lost in the dark. They passed on and on and at last met a man carrying a light. He said he was searching for the sun. They passed on and soon came to a large village where all of the men were going around with lights. Their chief was sick because the sun had vanished.

He asked the little bear whether she could bring back the sun. She said: "Yes, give me two handsful of maple sugar and your oldest son." With the maple sugar she went to the wigwam of the old woman and, climbing up to the top, threw the sugar into a kettle of wild rice which the old woman was cooking. When the old woman tasted the rice, she found it too sweet, so she went away to get some water to put in the kettle, and the little bear jumped down, ran into the wigwam, grabbed up the hidden sun, and threw it into the sky. When the little bear returned to the village, she gave the oldest son of the chief to her oldest sister for a husband.

The old woman was angry, very angry, to find that the sun was again up in the sky, so she jumped up and tore down the moon. The good old chief again became sick because the nights were all dark. He asked the little bear whether she could bring back the moon. She said: "Yes, if you give me two handsful of salt and your next oldest son." She took the salt, climbed on top of the wigwam of the old woman, and threw it into her boiling kettle. Again the old woman had to go away for water. The little bear then ran into the wigwam and, catching up the moon, tossed it into the sky. The little bear returned to the village and gave the chief's second son to her other sister.

Again the old chief got sick, and he asked the little bear whether she could get him his lost horse which was all covered with bells. She answered: "Yes, give me two handsful of maple sugar and your youngest son." The little bear went to the old woman's wigwam and, doing as she had done before, she made the old woman go away for water. She then slipped into the wigwam and began taking the bells from the horse which was there. She led the horse outside, but she had neglected to take off one bell. The old woman heard the bell and ran and caught the little bear. She put the bells all back onto the horse and put the little bear into a bag and tied the bag to a limb of a tree. When this was done, she went far away to get a large club with which to break the little bear's neck.

While she was gone, the little bear bit a hole in the bag and got down. This time she took all of the bells from the horse, and then she caught all of the dogs and pet animals of the old woman and put them and her dishes into the bag and tied it to the limb. Pretty soon the old woman returned with her large club, and she began to beat the bag furiously. The little bear could see from her hiding-place and could hear the animals and hear the dishes breaking as the old woman struck the bag.

When the little bear took the horse to the chief, he gave her his youngest son. They lived close to the other two brothers and sisters. The little bear's husband would not sleep with her, so she became very angry and told him to throw her into the fire. Her sisters heard the noise and came in to see what the matter was. The young man told them what their sister had ordered him to do. When they went away, he turned toward the fire, and a beautiful, very beautiful maiden sprang out from the flames. Then this beautiful maiden would not sleep with her husband.

1902

The Pole Star

Unidentified Haudenosaunee

Here is a story about the Little People, small creatures who lived in rocks or enchanted places in the landscape and were known to all Great Lakes nations.[191] Although some could be mischievous, meeting them was often considered extremely good luck. In this tale they rescue a lost party of hunters and then teach them how to navigate by using what Haudenosaunee called Ti-yn-sōu-dǎ-go-êrr (Star That Never Moves), the North Star, which moves so slowly—over centuries, rather than months—that it seems to be fixed in the sky. Depending on the age of this story, the star may or may not be Polaris, the present-day North Star. Northern nations described the star as the Bow Paddler, because he always steers straight and true, and the three stars in the belt of Orion as the Stern Paddler. (See winter star map, p. 116.) Between them was the great canoe of the sky, holding the stars and all their stories.

A large party of Indians, while moving in search of new hunting grounds, wandered on for many moons, finding but little game. At last they arrived at the banks of a great river, entirely unknown to them, where they had to stop, not having the material to build boats. Lost and nearly famished with hunger, the head chief was taken very ill, and it was decided to hold a council to devise means for returning to their old homes. During the dance and while the tobacco was burning, a little being-like a child came up, saying she was sent to be their guide. Accordingly they broke up their camp and started with her that night. Preceding them, with a *gi-wǎh,* or small war club, she led them on until daylight and then commanded them to rest while she prepared their food. This they did, and when awakened by her, they found a great feast in readiness for them. Then she bade them farewell, with the assurance of returning to them again in the evening.

True to her word, at evening she reappeared, bringing with her a skin jug, from which she poured out some liquid into a horn cup, and bade them each to taste of it. At first they feared to do so, but at last yielding they began to feel very strong. She then informed them that they had a long journey to make that night. Again they followed her and in the early morn arrived at a great plain, where she bade them rest again for the day, with the exception of a few warriors who were to be shown where they could find plenty of game. Two of the warriors had accompanied her but a short distance when they encountered a herd of deer, of which she bade them kill all they wished in her absence, and then, again promising to return at night, she took leave of them.

At nightfall she returned, saying her own chief would soon follow her to explain to them how they could reach their own homes in safety. In a short time he arrived with a great number of his race, and immediately all held council together and informed the Indians that they were now in the territory of the Little People, who would teach them a sign, already in the sky, which would be to them a sure guide whenever they were lost. The Little People pointed out the pole star and told them that in the North—where the sun never goes—while other stars move about, this particular star would stand still as the Indians' guide in his wanderings. If they were then but to follow its light, they would soon return to their tribe, where they would find plenty of game.

Then they thanked the good Little People and traveled every night until they arrived safely in their homes where, when they had recounted all their adventures, the head chief called a meeting of all the tribes and said they ought to give the star a name. So they called it Ti-yn-sō-dă-go-êrr, (The Star Which Never Moves), by which name it is called unto this day.

1883

The Lone Lightning

Unidentified Ojibwe

Critics have often faulted Schoolcraft for editing and embroidering the indigenous stories he collected; he and his wife, Jane, added Victorian poetry, cut sections, and removed some episodes they believed were scatological. Unless he published a story several times, however, it apparently remained much as it was transcribed. "The Lone Lightning" appears to have been left largely untouched: a story about a boy who fails in a war against the manidog in the heavens and becomes the occasional single bolt of lightning seen in the summer sky. But who are these manidog in the north that change shape and must be killed?

Many Natives thought the *jeebyug neemeid dewaud* (*jiibayag niimihidiwaad*: spirits of the departed are dancing together, aurora borealis) predicted the future. The Haudenosaunee believed that if they were white, frosty weather would follow; if yellow, disease and pestilence. Red predicted war and bloodshed. Some Native nations believed the aurora consisted of evil spirits who needed to be shot at until they had all been killed. Nineteenth-century travelers reported that the voyageurs dreaded the northern lights as sure precursors of storms. Since they learned their Great Lakes weather lore from Natives, it is probable that the evil spirits manifested as the northern lights were connected with bad weather. The Menominee version that opened this section is more positive, perhaps because the Menominee were more agricultural than nations farther north and saw wet weather as good for gardens. The aurora may also be associated with meteors, as it is here, perhaps the Quadrantid shower that occurs in the northeast and appears to come from the constellation Draco, which is long and snake-like. Meteors sometimes fall to earth as rocks, the form the last manido takes to elude death in "The Lone Lightning."

The hero of the story is "lone" because of his orphaned state, and he is punished by becoming lightning, reflecting his "thin and light" shape from starvation. Lightning also mimics the powerful streaks of his twelve arrows, which might correspond to moons. Although this story appears to be a "how-so" tale describing how something came to be, it is also about how vulnerable humans, once again an orphaned child, could be used by powerful competing spirits, and how a balance of power—harmony—must be maintained.

A little orphan boy who had no one to care for him was once living with his uncle, who treated him very badly, making him do hard things and giving him very little to eat, so that the boy pined away. He never grew much and became, through hard usage, very thin and light. At last the uncle felt ashamed of this treatment and determined to make amends for it by fattening him up. But his real object was to kill him by over-feeding. He told his wife to give the boy plenty of bear's meat, and let him have the fat, which

284

is thought to be the best part. They were both very assiduous in cramming him, and one day came near choking him to death by forcing the fat down his throat.

The boy escaped and fled from the lodge. He knew not where to go but wandered about. When night came on, he was afraid the wild beasts would eat him, so he climbed up into the forks of a high pine tree, and there he fell asleep in the branches and had an *aupoway*[192] or ominous dream. A person appeared to him from the upper sky and said, "My poor little lad, I pity you, and the bad usage you have received from your uncle has led me to visit you. Follow me, and step in my tracks."

Immediately his sleep left him, and he rose up and followed his guide, mounting up higher and higher into the air, until he reached the upper sky. Here twelve arrows were put into his hands, and he was told that there were a great many manitoes in the northern sky, against whom he must go to war and try to waylay and shoot them.

Accordingly he went to that part of the sky and, at long intervals, shot arrow after arrow, until he had expended eleven, in a vain attempt to kill the manitoes. At the flight of each arrow, there was a long and solitary streak of lightning in the sky—then all was clear again, and not a cloud or spot could be seen.

The twelfth arrow he held a long time in his hands and looked around keenly on every side to spy the manitoes he was after. But these manitoes were very cunning and could change their form in a moment. All they feared was the boy's arrows, for these were magic arrows, which had been given to him by a good spirit, and had power to kill them if aimed aright.

At length the boy drew up his last arrow, settled in his aim, and let fly, as he thought, into the very heart of the chief of the manitoes. But before the arrow reached him, he changed himself into a rock. Into this rock, the head of the arrow sank deep and stuck fast.

"Now your gifts are all expended," cried the enraged manito, "and I will make an example of your audacity and pride of heart for lifting your bow against me." And so saying, he transformed the boy into the *Nazhik-a-wä wä sun*[193] or Lone Lightning, which may be observed in the northern sky to this day.

1830s

VISIONS

Personal Manitous and the Vision Quest
Basil Johnston (1929-   ), Anishinâbe

The concept of fasting for guidance and for a personal manido, or spirit helper, was central to Native life until it was replaced with Western religions. As soon as the weather warmed, young people were encouraged to begin fasting for a vision, and so, although summer meant freedom from harsh weather, it also meant the demanding duty of the fast and vision quest. Johnston embeds his descriptions with stories to illustrate the points he makes, and the stories contained in this section serve as examples.

. . . From the beginning, animals, birds, fish, and insects have served not only humankind but the manitous, spirits, and deities that abide in the supernatural, to enable them to fulfill their earthly purposes.

When Nanaboozoo, the prototype of all Anishinaubaek and of all human beings, was cast away on the sea in yet another flood, he, too, called for the delivery of a moiety of soil, and it was an animal who delivered the soil that enabled him to recreate and restore the world.

In human experience, as exemplified by Nanaboozoo in the flood, it was not this prototype human being with all the advantages and attributes of humanity who retrieved the soil, but a little muskrat without a single outstanding quality to compare with those of his kind and kin.

Nothing is more graphic than the image of Nanaboozoo, half-manitou, half-human who symbolizes all humankind, clinging to a makeshift raft and begging the animals to fetch a pawful of soil as a last, desperate measure to stave off death. Without the animals, he would die; with them, he lived. He ate; survived; created an island, his world; and, in the end, restored the Earth. The story exemplifies humankind's relationship to the animals, a dependence that is absolute.

Although the animals are neighbors and co-tenants with men and women on the Earth, they are much more than mere nearby dwellers. They are indispensable to humans, not only as sacrificial victims, whose flesh, blood, bones, fur, and tissue sustain men and women in their struggle for life, but as exemplars whose habits, character, and works provide insights and knowledge that humans would not otherwise have.

Long ago, when our ancestors had only the bow and arrow, club, spear, snare and deadfall as weapons with which to slay an animal, they had a higher regard for their co-tenants and neighbors than many do today. They knew that they owed their lives, much more than they could ever imagine, to the creatures that dwelt in the sky, forest, meadows, seas, and underground.

From infancy, children were taught that the sudden calls or unexpected shadows of animals or birds meant no harm, that these calls were talk in the animals' and birds' own languages, and that all creatures had their own purposes and affairs to conduct. Men and women had less reason to fear bears and such than they did their fellow humans. Children were advised to give animals and birds their distance and not to provoke them.

If children would attend to and understand the languages of humankind's neighbors, they would profit. The chatter of animals and the cries of birds were the key to understanding what was taking place in the woods beyond one's vision, as well as to gaining foreknowledge of the weather in the near future and the climate in the coming seasons. What the animals did and said were nothing less than public proclamations of the presence of enemies, danger, or death. Once children understood the languages and the habits of birds, animals, and small creatures, they would know things that they would not normally get to know as human beings.

How did the eagle, the bear, the wolf, the turtle, and the butterfly know what they know? Did they learn by listening to the words of others, as humans learn? Men and women have other humans, animals, and an inner sense to tell them what they want and need to know, but who tells the loon, the skunk, or the gnat when to take cover and when to emerge; when winter is coming and they must go, and when it is safe for them to return; where to go and what direction to take; what to eat and what not? Instinct? Sense? The manitous?

Only a higher being, a manitou, could tell them what they need to know and give them foreknowledge of events and changes and the wisdom to take measures for their well-being and safety.

Experience and observation lent strength to the conviction that there was something, someone, presiding over the affairs of the animals and safeguarding them. How else could one explain and understand success and failure? Every person has the same skills in marksmanship; similar training; and equal knowledge of the weather, the seasons, and the dwelling places and habits of the quarry, yet some hunters return home from almost every expedition with cargoes of meat, whereas others return home empty-handed, failures more often than not.

In the belief that manitous directed the fate and safeguarded the well-being of birds, animals, small creatures, and fish, men and women began the practice of entreating the manitous, asking for leave to take the lives of animals and soliciting the sanction of the higher, supernatural beings. In their supplications, the hunters adverted to need . . . .

Afterward, a hunter offered tobacco in thanksgiving to the manitou of the victim and, more remotely, to Kitchi-Manitou, the Master of Life, for sanctioning the taking of life and for fulfilling the hunter's family's needs. For the victim to come within range of an arrow or to stumble into a deadfall or a trap was seen as nothing less than the tacit approval of the manitou for the hunter to take the life of the quarry. It was only fitting that the hunter express his apologies to his victim and his thanksgiving to the manitou for allowing the killing.

In many respects, the manitou and Kitchi-Manitou were more generous with birds and animals than with men and women, bestowing on them faculties, aptitudes, and qualities that they did not bestow on humans: speed, flight, sight, smell, strength, patience, and length of life.

Men and women coveted these attributes and the advantages they conferred. If they themselves were not meant to be so gifted, then might they not at least hope to derive advantages and benefits from those so endowed with the goodwill of the manitou?

Human beings had special regard for certain qualities and virtues of the animal world. To possess and exercise comparable qualities and virtues would exalt and dignify the human spirit and soul, and men and women aspired to deeds that would make them proud. Few men or women, for example, will dare what every sparrow will do: to stand up to an assailant many times stronger and bigger . . . and drive him off for the sake of her young, exercising two virtues in the one act. Few men or women have the self-control and patience of the heron, the persistence of the wolf, the foresight of the eagle, or the resourcefulness or industry of the beaver.

Men and women especially valued attributes that would enable them to achieve their dreams and visions more readily, to carry out their duties and responsibilities more easily, and to safeguard their lives and health in times of great need. They wished that they had been as endowed and favored by Kitchi-Manitou as were the eagles, sparrows, bears, deer, turtles, butterflies, and sturgeon.

To obtain the benefits of the attributes that they did not possess, the Anishinaubae peoples dedicated their families to birds, animals, small creatures, and fish in the hope that these beings, by the exercise of their attributes and faculties, would obtain for men and women the favors that were needed.

The animals that were chosen as patrons also served as emblems that identified and distinguished families who were dedicated to the same ideals and were entrusted with certain duties. The Anishinaubae peoples called their patrons "totems," a term derived from *dodaem*, meaning action and duty serving as inspiration. Men and women who belonged to the same totem regarded themselves as brothers and sisters of the same family.

But a family's dedication and commitment to a particular totem did not bar the family members from seeking the patronage of the manitous of other creatures of the animal world as their personal manitous.

Men and women sought patrons to conduct them through crises, to protect them from sorcery, and to overcome difficulties that they would not be able to surmount alone. The image of the creature, its spirit, became their personal manitou.

Men and women did not always have to dream to conjure a manitou. Sometimes a manitou came unasked, knowing better than men and women what was needed. Whereas only a limited number of birds, animals, small creatures, and water beings served as totems, any nonhuman being could become a personal patron, manitou, of any man or women.

1995

The Vision

"No man begins to be until he has received his vision" perhaps best expresses the Anishinaubegs' fundamental understanding of man's purpose in life and, by distinguishing between living and being, posits the existence of a moral order. In turn, this basic understanding is predicated upon the concept of the essence and nature of a human being.

According to the Anishnaubeg, man was a spontaneous being made out of nothing; that is, created from new substances unlike those out of which the physical world was made. Out of corporeal and incorporeal substances was man created according to and in fulfillment of a vision of Kitche Manitou. Man was, in the abstract metaphysical sense, a composite being.

But as the Anishnaubeg conceived man as a being endowed with a capacity for vision much like his creator, man became more than an abstract being, a creature of the mind. Man was bound to seek and fulfill visions and as such was a moral being. His life, therefore, was to be regarded in a moral sense.

Men were required to seek vision; moreover, they had to live out and give expression to their visions—it was through vision that a man found purpose and meaning to life and to his being.

There was another aspect to the nature of man. In scope and depth and breadth, every man was very different; some were gifted; others possessed lesser powers. Still each was obligated to seek in his own capacity, his purpose not outside himself, but within his innermost being. And because each man was differently endowed, every man attained a different vision; each fulfilled his vision as he and not someone else understood it.

For the Anishnaube the vision became the theme and quest in his life that attained the character of force; as a force, it could alter the course of individuals, bend the nature of living, enhance the tone of life, and change character. For the fulfillment of vision, aspirations were reluctantly forsaken, and a new mode of life taken up if necessary.

The vision as a force could alter conduct, mode of life, and even character; it wrought yet another change. For with the coming of vision, existence became living; that is, man entered a moral order where his individual acts and conduct assumed character and quality that they did not previously possess. Prior to this event, a man was, in a moral sense, incomplete, a half-being; by vision he gained purpose that conferred meaning upon his actions and unity to his life.

Purpose without quest is empty; a vision without fulfillment is vain. Just as Kitche Manitou received a vision and created matter, being, and life, so man in receiving a vision had to live it out.

Besides fulfillment, vision required preparation. The capacity for vision, like other faculties, was only a capacity whose growth required nourishment. And because man was a composite being, man's two substances needed preparation in order to attain a state of harmony necessary for reception of the vision. Not until these corporeal and incorporeal substances were ready and worthy did the vision come. Not until a man was ready to live out the vision did he receive it.

Preparation rendered the body worthy through physical testings and the inner being worthy through dreaming and vigils ready for vision; both substances had to be worthy of each other. For the body there was to be strength, endurance, agility; for the inner being, patience, discipline, silence, and peace. Only when there was a state of readiness did man receive his vision.

There were two dimensions to a man's life: one existence, the other a moral sense. By far, the most significant was the latter. The physical because of the difficulty of survival was considered to comprise four hills, infancy, youth, adulthood, and old age; the moral also consisted of the preparation, the quest, the vision, and the fulfillment which corresponded to the four physical phases.

Life was difficult in physical terms. Few survived infancy. Many more died in the stage of youth. Men and women, on attaining adulthood, endured privations in discharging their duties; and in old age, they faced frailty, disappointment, deafness, and blindness. Through all stages, there was illness, frequently hunger.

Though existence was hard, the vision had to be sought. There was no better way to achieve understanding of self and life. Moreover, it impressed merit upon a man and enabled him to endure the difficult life and to fulfill his purpose in life.

While it was almost mandatory for a man to seek a vision, the quest did not always lead to vision. It was a gift that came to those who were prepared and came only when a man was ready.

For women there was no such comparable obligation to seek a vision. Any obligation that might have pre-existed was removed by the first of mothers, who gave birth to men and completed the cycle of life and time, creation, destruction, and recreation. By this act, a woman was complete in herself. A woman, by giving life, fulfilled the first portion and requisite of being; man had to give meaning to that gift of life. But a woman was free to quest for a vision . . . .

The Quest

In their twelfth year boys were deemed ready to begin their quest for vision. After purification ceremonies, a boy was conducted by his father to a place of visions, a remote, solitary place, unique by virtue of its mood and spirit for the reception. There, the boy was left alone in a specially constructed lodge, to contemplate life, his being, and existence. In solitude he endeavored to bring his inner being and body together in accord as he attempted at the same time to be conjoined with the earth and the animal creatures and plant beings who resided in the place of vision. To be at one with the world, or to discover one's meaning through peace and silence, was not easy.

For some, the vision came early, ending the quest and inaugurating a new phase of life, being. For others, the vision came late.

Whether the boy had received his vision or not, at age sixteen he received from his mother a three-cornered blanket which served as his coat, blanket covering, and cushion. The blanket was a gift, a symbol of love, and an emblem of an attachment. With the gift of blanket was signified partial dependence, partial independence. The young man was now on his own, independent. After this he could set up his own shelter as it pleased him. As the blanket was incomplete, it symbolized a bond, a sign of continuing motherhood.

Until a young man had performed an act of courage, he was considered physically a boy. It was an act of courage that admitted him into the company of warriors and gave him the status of manhood. And there was no better way of demonstrating physical quality and worth than by exposure to injury and even death. Overcoming the danger entitled a man to wear a feather or a bear claw in his necklace as a symbol of his deed.

But courage was more than a single act of bravery. It was an attribute of manhood that was almost synonymous with the term "man." In some instances, courage or some proof of courage was required of a young man before marriage. With the performance of the first brave deed, a man embarked upon a course in which courage would become a part of his being.

Through this stage of preparation, those who had not attained the vision continued the quest annually in summer.

Before going out to the place of visions to keep vigil, the vision seeker first had to cleanse his body in the purification lodge. There, his body would be cleansed by vapours created from the four primal elements: fire, rock, water, and the breath of life; the soul-spirit was cleansed by contemplation and denial and privation. Then for four days or until the vision, the questor remained in vigil abstaining from food.

Man's soul-spirit hunger had to be filled; his bodily hunger, more easily fed, could wait. There was to be no distraction; no weakening of resolve. Food had to be forsaken. The vision seeker had to surrender completely to self and to the place around him.

In silence and peace would vision come to him who was prepared.

The Vision

The Anishnabeg recognized at least three kinds of vision, the distinction based upon the mode of coming of the vision. In form and nature, the different visions were similar.

By *Waussayauh-bindumiwin* was meant vision that was received during vigil and whose meaning was complete. No further or additional visions were required. The message was unified.

The word *Waussayauh-bindumiwin* (*wâsséiâbandamowin*) issues from two terms; the first, *waussayauh* (*wâsséia*), meaning light and clarity; the second, *inaubindum* (*inâbandam*: dream something in a certain manner), meaning perception by sight or insight. Within the context of the purpose, nature, and essence of vision, waussayauh-bindumiwin means many things: self-understanding, enlightenment of self, while at the same time, suggesting destiny and even career.

But not all visions came complete and entire. Perhaps the majority were of the kind known as *mauzzaubindumiwin* (*manzhâbandamowin* or *mânâsabandamowin*); that is, unclear and incomplete. A vision could come in stages under different circumstances and over a long period. Only after a number of partial visions had been received would the entire vision become clear.

The term, mauzzaubindumiwin itself means hazy or fuzzy and even vague, owing probably to the incomplete nature of the various portions of the vision received.

In form, nature, and mode, the *apowawin* is similar to the waussayauh-bindumiwin. Like the waussayauh-bindumiwin, it is complete. It differs only in that it comes during sleep. Because it occurs during sleep, often rousing the dreamer to consciousness, and because it makes the dreamer aware of himself, the term means "awakening" or self-revelation.

Self-revelation or awakening could come to either man or woman; it was not necessarily the privy of man. But when it did come, it was regarded as personal, not to be disclosed to others; nor were others to interfere with the vision or the quest of another person. It was said, "Do not give away your soul-spirit. Do not attempt to enter the soul-spirit of another." To reveal one's spirit was tantamount to surrender of self and a loss of freedom. An attempt to enter the inner being of another person was construed as an act of possession.

The individual and his individuality were inviolable; his vision was equally inviolable. No person was to surrender to another; no person was to seek dominion over another man or woman. The principle was binding. . . .

Living Out the Vision

Living out the vision was not less difficult than the quest. Men made errors in judgment; they forgot. That the path of life was tortuous was portrayed on birchbark scrolls—seven and sometimes nine branches digressed from the main road. Men and women straying from the main road were considered to have betrayed their vision; such a state was tantamount to non-living in which acts and conduct had no quality. To avoid such a state, men and women went on annual retreats to review their lives and to find where they had strayed and to resume the true path.

Man in the last phase of life, old age, was considered to have acquired some wisdom by virtue of his living on and by fidelity to his vision. Wisdom was knowing and living out the principles of life as understood.

1976

Getting Nowhere Fast

Louise Erdrich (1954-   ), Chippewa

This is a chapter from *The Bingo Palace*, Erdrich's novel about the clash of traditional cultural values and contemporary reservation gambling, which is part of her series of novels about a reservation in Minnesota. The narrator here is Lipsha Morrissey, great-grandson of a traditional shaman, Fleur Pillager, whose spirit-helper is Micipijiu (Missipeshu) and who lives on the shore of Matchimanito (Bad-Spirit) Lake. Lipsha is the inheritor of Fleur's powers, and he will eventually be blessed by Micipijiu in a dream-vision or apawewin, but because he lacks both parents and the traditional culture to support his gifts, he flounders in school and with drugs. His mother, June, had cast him into a slough to drown when he was a baby, but like Moses cast into the Nile, he was miraculously saved, perhaps by Micipijiu. June died of alcoholism, though she occasionally appears to Lipsha. His father, Jerry, is in prison. Lipsha has fallen in love with Shawnee Ray, Miss Little Shell, a powwow dancer. Her name is Erdrich's reference to the Little Shell Band of Pembina (cranberry) Ojibwe, who are still fighting for federal recognition, and to the small shells used in Midé healing ceremonies. Shawnee is also being pursued by the older, wealthier tribal leader Lyman, who may be the father of her son and who is determined to build a casino on land that belongs to Fleur near the shores of Matchimanito Lake.

In this excerpt, Lyman and Lipsha embark on a traditional vision quest to impress Shawnee. The result reflects the Native principle that those who have the most power are the least likely to show it. Erdrich questions the use and misuse of the traditional vision quest. She satirizes hypocritical traditionalists like Lyman (lie-man) who use culture and religion for personal gain and, by having Lipsha's attempts for transformational experience disrupted, she points out that tradition divorced from culture or used for personal aggrandizement is doomed to failure. The scene is funny like a Trickster story, but the point is telling: Erdrich is confronting her characters, and metaphorically her nation and her readers, with the implications of insincere use of ceremonies and a rush to development through gambling and casino building.

I believe in the wandering son, the missing father, and the naked spirit of the Holy Ghost. I believe in the crush of night, the ragged holes in the feet of the plaster Jesus, through which you see the wires cross. I believe in the single malt whiskey if you're rich, the bottle of white port if you're broke. I believe in the peace of worms. I believe in the extension ladder and the angel with the torn mouth at the bottom,

292

waiting to wrestle. I believe in the one on one, in the hands and voice of Jimi Hendrix, and that I will always love Shawnee Ray, even though I come to know a side to her that's fearful.

Before I go on out with Lyman to my vision fast, I feel it is important for me to have just a word, a normal conversation, with Shawnee Ray Toose. After all, she is the one I hope will be there with the feasting food when we return. She is the reason I am going off on what seems, the more I think about it, a desperate and foolish mission. And I am worried, too, about the way Zelda Kashpaw and Lyman have managed to get Shawnee under their control although she did what she said, earned some money, made a college hunt.

Zelda took Redford from the Toose house, using the system, and now that Shawnee Ray is back from her nearly big time second-place jingle-dress finish, there is no sign of her. She lives again with Zelda. But no one sees her, no one hears what she's up to, no one reports on her the way they used to. She has dropped out of my line of vision, or maybe she is a prisoner fed scraps in Zelda's house. In Lyman's company, however, we will be admitted for a visit.

We swirl into Zelda's driveway, get out of the car, and immediately, looking so anxious and tense my heart cranks over, Shawnee Ray walks slowly down the steps with a cookie-smeared Redford in her arms. She hesitates. There is a sadness about the way she looks at us, and her movements seem quiet and shocked. In a dazed way, she hands Redford over to his father, who holds him with a sort of neat authority and starts fussing with and dusting up the little boy right off. I think they look natural together, Lyman and his son, and in my heart I feel a plucked string.

"Hey," I greet Shawnee Ray.

She nods. I look very serious and searching into the unknowns of her face.

Suddenly Redford lets out a belly shriek at nothing in particular. To prove the efficiency of his fatherhood status, then Lyman is forced to resist tossing him back to his mother and begins to try all sorts of methods to divert the boy's attention. He jiggles, he prances, he hops and changes his voice to high, odd coos, but nothing works. At last he turns away from me and Shawnee Ray and walks around the back of the house, where there is a little sandbox set up and a couple plastic trucks.

I take my chance, turn to Shawnee Ray again, with urgent haste. There is an eager look in her face for me, I am sure of it. I think she is about to bloom toward me like the flowers in my dreams. In spite of knowing Lyman is just around the corner, my lips part and my whole face yearns for her face, and I have to jerk my arms around my back to keep them from winding around her waist, from gliding down the fountains of her soft, thick hair, from holding the delicate seashell structure of her chin, her cheeks, from smoothing the lids of her eyes and the sweet, short eyebrows. I stand there with my mouth open, waiting for inspiration.

"Would you marry me?"

At first Shawnee Ray draws back like she is insulted at my request, as though she maybe thinks it is a joke. The edges of her mouth go down and she starts to turn away, and then, giving me one slight glance, she sees the something in my face. The ravaged something. The diet of Polish sausage and old cookies, the dreams, the anguish and the tea, the sacrifice of half my sanity, the religion. She stares hard at me, and I cleave tenderly toward what I anticipate as the equal longing in her look. I hold out my arms, but she bats at the air, leaning backwards, her face changing, moving.

"Get real." Her voice is high-pitched, strained, and her eyes are shining too bright.

"I am real."

I say these words so desperate that my knees buckle. I go down before her on my knees, and then I put out my arms and tenderly clasp the worn blue spots on the knees of her jeans. It is like I never saw a thing so beautiful as those two lovely pieces of fabric, rubbed smooth. She tries to move away, but my arms tighten in spite of myself and she's hobbled. She almost loses her balance. She stands still a moment, and then she bends over and she pushes at me in a panic. I loosen my grip of her knees in surprise, and then her foot plants itself under my chin with such force I go tumbling backwards.

"Get out of my way. . . ." Her voice is too even, too low, trembling underneath the tone with a kind of threat I've never heard. I scuttle backwards like a crab, out of reach of her hard leather toes, away from that scorching voice.

"What'd I do?"

"What'd he do?"

It is Lyman, returning with a now sand-over-cookie-caked Redford round the side of the yard. The two make their way evenly toward us, but Shawnee abruptly strides over to Lyman and grabs Redford from his arms. Too shocked to wail, Redford looks at us with big eyes, back and forth.

"What'd he do?" Shawnee's voice is a ripped screen. She is not my sweet Shawnee, not my tender air-brush picture. Suddenly she shows the undertone, the strokes of which she is created. Her hair flows like snakes, shaking down, and in her cornered anger she is jiggling Redford so fast that his cheeks bounce.

"He asked me to marry him!" She says these lovely words in an intense and awful voice of scorn.

"And I mean it," I say humbly, falling back onto my knees, dazed and addled as a sheep.

"Oh, shut up," says Shawnee Ray. "And you," she addresses Lyman as he starts for me, "stay away from him. I won't marry you either. Get that idea out of your bingo brain."

Lyman stands in paralyzed surprise like he was frozen with a laser gun.

"Shawnee Ray," he says gently. "You don't know what you're saying."

There is a silence, and then, taking one deep breath, she screams loudly—an incoherent, strange cry, like a baboon in the desert. The air vibrates. I put my hands over my ears. She does that same robbed and naked scream again, a sound that makes my neck crawl. Her face is working, witchy, so frightful that Redford buries his face in her shirt, hanging on like a frightened little monkey as she whirls. She seems to grow larger, her shirt billows, her hair is dark leaves in a storm.

"Get out of here! I won't marry either of you. Period. You . . ." she looks down at me, her mouth twisting, "you talk so big about your feelings and you can't even make it back to school."

Lyman steps toward her.

"Don't you come near me, don't you even try. If you ever go to court again, if you ever get in my way . . . ."

"I'm Redford's father," says Lyman gently.

Shawnee turns. She walks back to the house with Redford, talking to him in a soothing and familiar voice. She opens the door, goes inside, and we hear a cupboard slam. A short wail, more calm talk. Lyman shuffles around, and I back toward the car, both of us uncertain, hoping that the scene is over. But no, just as we are tentatively confident in our leave-taking Shawnee Ray comes back down the steps and stands in front of Lyman. She puts her hands on her waist. She is like that tough lady in *The Big Valley*, hips thrust out in tight pants, heeled shoes, mouth held in a bold sneer.

"You're Redford's father? Says who? You weren't there when it counted. You're too late. I'm Redford's mother."

Her voice becomes musical and horrible, for it is falsely charming with a loathing current underneath. "Think back, Lyman," she warbles. "You weren't my only boyfriend, remember? I had three other guys, and I only made a birth control mistake with one of them."

She leans close to Lyman, chin jutting, and pushes her face into his face.

"Want to take a blood test?"

Lyman is smiling foolishly now, with a look of glazed wonder. I put my hands on his shoulders, guide him backwards, open the car door, and put him in, still with that amused and quizzical indulgent expression on his face. It's like an expression made of china, one that can easily shatter to its opposite, and I know it's time to get moving, get out of there.

The funny thing is that as we drive along no silence grows between us, and we have no reaction to what just happened. Not two miles onward, we begin to talk about inconsequential things. We wonder about the sky, if it looks rainy or the day will hold. We anticipate the road and what comes next. We have a lot to think about, but we can't talk. We can't make the past half-hour real. It is as if neither one of us can take in the Shawnee Ray we both saw. We can't understand, can't absorb, can't admit, and will not let that woman be her.

* * *

We drive the small roads, the back roads, leading surely and slowly farther on toward the house that belongs to Xavier Toose. He lives at the edge of an allotment that blends into the land around Matchimanito, the land that belongs to Fleur Pillager. I can't figure Lyman here. We are nearing the very same rolling, sweet, wooded hills that he wants to use for the big casino that he plans, the luck place, the money-maker scheme that will build day cares, endow scholarships, cure the ills of addiction of which it is a cause. I know that Lyman has thought out the consequences and the big-time benefits, but I believe, now, that he hasn't really examined the personal. Maybe that's what his quest is about, the bigger picture of an operating genius. Or maybe Lyman Lamartine is deep down religious. And then again, maybe given what we've just been through, we have a lot of things to think about regarding Shawnee Ray.

We take a turnoff, and the brush closes. I am still stunned by Shawnee's knees so close, her ankles so perfect to grip. Luckily, by this time, Lyman is concentrating on the world beyond this one and has let go of that final scene. As we bounce down the last, long drive, just wheel ruts, to Xavier's, he is trying to instruct me about a sweat lodge, the proper way you enter it and crawl around in it, but I am dizzy. There was a moment back there when I felt that Shawnee Ray wasn't really angry, that she was screaming hard to cover up the true feeling that she has for me. I try to recast the whole scene in my thoughts. I wonder if she wasn't putting on her tantrum for the benefit of Lyman and planning to wink at me as we left. I never turned around! I never looked in the rearview! If I had, what would I have seen? If I had only stayed, I think now, ditched Lyman, let her rage herself into my arms, maybe she might have bent to my life. I fear I may have blown it, may have lost my narrow chance. I still can't admit that she really might be furious. For one thing, there is no reason, is there? How could she? I have done nothing but over adore her.

We come to a halt in the yard of Xavier Toose's place, and we get out of the car. Xavier walks lightly toward us, easily, like his joints were new oiled. He's wearing a light green shirt and blue jeans. He is a kind of medium-looking man all around. You wouldn't pick him out in any crowd as holy; that's for sure. He has no blessed airs about him; he is not like a priest and not spooky like Fleur. He has no manner of the Touch Me and I'll Strike You Dead. He is sort of round, just tall enough, not fat in the face or thin, and cheerful. He is not like Russell Kashpaw, who works with him, a Mount Rushmore-looking Indian. No, Xavier has a kind of big, arched nose, extremely black and shining eyes, thin and surprised-looking eyebrows, and a humorous mouth. The one different thing besides his hand with the fingers gone is that he wears an earring, one little shell. We touch his arms, and right away, from the warm current in his presence, I am reassured. Here is not a man who will allow me to waste away and die or be eaten by wild animals in either the spirit or the natural realm. I am encouraged by the kind gaze upon my face, the joking forbearance.

"I almost chickened out," I tell him.

His only answer is, "Some do."

He motions for us to walk out in back of his small, brown house and down a trail. I take deep breaths, for at any moment I expect a flash to hit, some kind of electric power to jolt on, a message to seep into my feet through this holy land that stretches from Xavier's backyard all the way to the shore I don't want to think about, the waters of Matchimanito Lake. I expect some unearthly voice to blare on with each footstep, worry that I might be smote from the days of old. What happens, however, is that Xavier Toose puts us to work.

"Heavy labor's good for body sculpting," says Lyman, an hour into what we're accomplishing.

"I thought we were coming here to get enlightened," I complain. It has turned into a muggy, hot, scratchy day, and we are in deep and windless bush searching out nice-size and bendable willow poles, slogging through the steaming, spongy grass near a slough. I have a small hatchet, not near sharp enough, with which I am chipping at the base of a tough sapling. Lyman, lucking out as always, has a keen bow-shaped Swedish saw with which he dispatches three times as many trees.

When we have enough leaf-stripped poles, we drag them back, and then there is the careful twine-tying with tight lodge knots, the post hole digging, the gathering of the stones that pass muster. And for the last, standing at the shores of the lake I don't want to think about, there is a lot of argument over which kind of rock heats up best. Not that I know enough to argue—it is just that by then I am in all respects pissed off at Lyman.

"Who cares?" I pick up one that I hope Fleur has cursed. "I mean, take this smooth black one here. Hot's hot."

"Hot's not just hot," he answers. "There's qualities of heat. Take this speckled one."

"That looks like an egg, like it would explode."

"Rocks don't blow up."

"If they get hot enough and if there's any water in their seams, they do." I make this up.

Lyman bites his lip, tries to control himself.

"I'm worried about this idea of superheating stones," I continue, annoyed he doesn't believe my scientific theories. "The physics of it sounds dangerous."

"I'm sick of babying you."

"Who asked you?"

Lyman sighs and hefts another big rock in his weight lifter's arms. For him, the heavier the better-heating.

"Wouldn't a banana split taste good about now?"

Lyman kind of laughs.

"How hot could it really get?" I wonder after a few minutes.

"Real hot," Lyman answers in a relishing voice.

Later on, I find out. The lodge looks too little for us all to enter, and I wish we'd made it three times as big. There is this person attending to the fire, a big Terminator-muscled convict type with a lot of tattoos—probably free, courtesy of Russell Kashpaw. The whites of his eyes show, and he grins too much. A red bandanna is tied onto his head, and he is getting the instructions, too, even as he prepares the fire for us and then keeps heating up the rocks fiery red. They're placed in a little half-circle next to an altar made of earth, sprinkled in a line with cedar. A bowl of tobacco, just a small wood bowl, is set to one side. When Xavier says he is ready, the guy, Joe, puts the rocks in the fire pit with a shovel. Xavier goes inside the sweat lodge. Lyman and I take our clothes off and get in too. The big guy closes the flap. Xavier throws a dipperful of water down on the stones, and then it starts getting hot.

Xavier prays and talks to us and instructs us. Out of the blue, Lyman comes up with a very insightful, long, and meaningful prayer that sounds like it could be used to open up a conference. I am worrying about what I'll say, since I don't believe exactly in who—or whatever I am talking to, but when the turn is mine I find that heat adds to my praying ability. My words flow, as if my syllables are thinned honey. Amazingly hot, surprisingly hot. So hot I can't take it. But then I do take it, and I get hotter yet. I try to cool off by talking faster, praying louder, as if my tongue is a little fan, but then I give up and fall quiet. Xavier has given us this teaching that the sweat lodge is female, like a womb, like our mother we have to crawl on the earth to re-enter. He has encouraged us to let ourselves feel that connection we must have forgot, and I think I do without trying, for as I am getting hot, as I am praying, I find myself slipping away from the present, into a dark dream that hasn't a forwards or a backwards. I stop talking, or thinking, or even feeling the blasting heat that sizzles out of the rocks every time Xavier splashes them with water. I just exist, float, my ears stopped, my mind doused. After a while the heat feels bearable, then it feels like the most perfect embrace there ever was. Then Lyman says he wants it hotter and splashes more water on the stones.

I could kill Lyman. I'm a cooked steak. My breath feels cold on my hands, and I know that I'll never leave the place alive. Panic grabs me. I begin to pray in a maniac's voice, desperate and pure, until I slip from the present in which Xaiver Toose's voice is wide and soothing as the sky. I don't get gist of his instructions, but I feel the comfort. Again, I want to stay there, and stay, but it's all over. We emerge into the normal sunlight, the day which before had been low and humid now seems fragile, fresh and cool. I should be a newborn baby, but instead I feel strange, unrocked. A roar of disappointment builds inside my head.

I look around for June, through the trees, toward the road as if I'd see the flash of the blue car speeding into the mint-conditioned day. But there's no sign of her, no return.

I mope around half-listening to Xavier tell us what we must do, but I'm only there in the flesh. We walk down to the lake, dive in to wash ourselves entirely clean. The water doesn't thrill me, doesn't want me. I close my eyes against the darkness and get out as quickly as I can without looking either the annoying perfection of Lyman's muscle-toned wrestling star's build, or at the beefy collisions of scars and tattoo snakes and women in eventful positions that round the thighs of the helpful convict. Xavier douses himself, too, and teases Joe about his snakes and women. But I can't get into tone of the day, for sadness inhabits me.

"What's wrong?" Lyman whispers to me once, impatient, probably thinking I am hurt by Shawnee Ray.

I considered. What is wrong? What is my problem?

"I miss my mother," I say.

Lyman snorts, puts his hand before his face, and I know at that moment he is sorry that he ever asked me to go with him on this spiritual journey. I try to whip myself back into mental shape. I am hardly managing to do the least thing that is required, just go along with what is happening, truck off into the woods behind Xavier's house. In the long shadows of that afternoon I find myself wandering alone looking for a place where I can spend as long as it takes for a vision to come my way. The choices are numerous, but I am supposed to pick a personal spot to gather power.

I try, but I just stumble around for the longest time until I lose track of where I am, but nothing matters. By that time, being lost is a trivial detail.

I lower myself onto a hard, cold rock and get depressed still worse when I look up and see that I am in eyeshot of the damn old lake where bad things happen, where I visited the old woman, where in deep fear I listened to her bear talk. In Matchimanito Fleur Pillager drowned and came back to life, and her cousin Moses haunts the island with the howls of cats. I don't care though. If the horned thing, the grappling black thing that lives down there, bellies after me, I won't run. What's the point? There is no good book to help me, and once again I have no motive, no reason for staying alive.

"This is great," I say out loud, building myself a little nest out of pine needles and wood moss and leaves. "If I was feeling like myself, I'd be so fucking scared I'd never sleep."

I have only three pieces of equipment—my sleeping bag with the blue elks in rut pictured on the inside flannel, a plastic bottle of water, and a garbage bag. That last, my supposed tarp for rain, I fill with more leaves to make a mattress. That is probably cheating. Oh yes, I have some tobacco too, and a little cedar that Xavier pressed into my hand. Beyond that, nothing. Although it is still daytime, and the light is falling dappled through the twins and leaves, I crawl into my sleeping bag.

I don't know what time it is when I wake. In sleep, my dragging-down feeling vanished and is now replaced with the normal instinct for self-preservation, only crazed beyond sense. I can't believe I've gotten myself into this situation. The wind picks up, the dark is pure and intense, and I hear the terrible rustles of surrounding animals, and even the monster hoot of Ko ko ko, the owl, sounding in my ears.

From all sides, fears grab and shake me. I put my head in my hands, rock back and forth, wish at least I'd built a little place for myself up in the trees. Deer could step on me down here on the ground. I think of their pointed hooves. Then I think of teeth. Fangs, tusks, rabbit incisors. Jaws for tearing. Sharks. Forget sharks. Bears. Raccoons. In this overbearing dark, I won't see it coming. Slashing death. Of course, I know there have been no bear attacks, no packs of wolves descending on lone campers, no owl or squirrel flocks reported tearing up a human, not in all the time I have ever been around here, and yet, and yet there is always a first for a freak occurrence. That's what makes the news.

I groan out loud and curl into myself, and for the rest of the night whenever some noise startles me I jump up, shout, then settle back again to wait for the next advance of nature. In this way, with frequent yells, I fend off the invisible intruders. I keep peering and staring into the faceless dark that is not even lit by the glow of wild eyes.

Morning. Morning. Night. Night. Morning. I go through two cycles and then I lose track. The first day I am hungry, and all my visions consist of Big Macs. The next day nothing matters again. I drink water from the lake and wait to die of an old paralyzing curse, but nothing happens. Upon waking, sometime after, I begin to take an interest in my surroundings. I watch an ant kill a bug of some kind and saw it into pieces and carry it away. A small brown bird hops from one branch to another. Then it hops back to the first branch again. A weasel flashes through once, looks straight at me, curious, and vanishes. A blue jay lands, squawks, and disappears. I try to interpret these things as signs of something bigger, but I can't jack up their meanings.

I sleep, becoming weaker, and when I wake my head feels light and fat as a balloon. I fall into a dreamy and unpleasant mood, and all of a sudden I am annoyed that I turned out as an Indian. If I were something else, maybe all French, maybe nothing, or say, a Norwegian, I'd be sitting in comfort, eating pancakes. Or Chinese. Longingly, I shut my eyes and imagine the snap of fried wontons between my teeth at HoWun's. I taste sweet-and-sour fried batter. Hot crispy noodles. No fair. I resent the lengths that I am driven by the blood. I take mental revenge, then, by imagining what would happen if all the Indians in the country suddenly disappeared, went back where they came from.

In my mind's eye I see us Chippewas jumping back into the big shell that spawned us, the Mandan sliding down their gourd vine, Navajos climbing underground and covering themselves up, the Earthmaker accepting Winnebagos back into primal clay, the Senecas hoisting themselves into the sky, the Hopis following their reed to the Underworld.

And then what? I study on that only for a moment before I know the answer. Lyman Lamartine would somehow wangle his way out of the great Native apocalypse. Lyman would finally, and entirely, be in charge. Policies and programs would flow from his desk, examining this problem. He'd issue directives with a calm born of disaster, marshal all his forces. Even if no Indian returned to this world, Lyman Lamartine's paperwork would live on, even flourish, for the types like him are snarled so deeply into the system that they can't be pulled with unraveling the bones and guts. Cabinets of files would shift priorities, regenerate in twice-as-thick reports.

Yet, in that same daydream, I get even with Lyman too. He sheds his turquoise and inlay rings, his Hush Puppies shoes, his go-to-Washington two-hundred-dollar suit and bolo tie, and he stands along with everybody else. I make Lyman run for the shell along with all the other Chippewas, but too late. The shell claps shut around me and Shawnee Ray and Redford, and it sails off, leaving Lyman on the shore. He's left to watch until it's just a pearl in the distance, until it winks over the edge of the world.

Of course, this is just a dream. It won't be so easy to get rid of him.

By throwing my lot in with Lyman I've gotten to be part of something very big, very muddy, and very slow. A megalith of mediocrity, somebody said, but he was a dropout from the Bureau, fired, and Lyman and I have our fates intertwined, mixed up like the roots of two plants. I kept on seizing in my mind on that comfortable feeling we once had together, when Lyman said he remembered the day he and his brother Henry lay and dozed under the powwow trees, the pine arbor, listening to dancers pound dirt.

Nowadays, they put a rug of Astroturf down on the arena, and there is no dust, no grit to chew on. Still, I fall asleep imagining those good food-filled days and more like them before us, with the bingo money I've accumulated. I wake wishing that I had a book to read, my Walkman. I play back all the Hendrix in my memory, then heavy metal, and around the time the sun goes down I make a surprising discovery that I don't really need a stereo cassette. I am hooked up to my own brain. This is not a major vision, but it helps pass the time. Movies come back. Books. I rewatch all the Godfather series, then reread the Dune trilogy and my Kashpaw dad's favorite, Moby-Dick. I go on and on back below the surface of my mind. Of course, Shawnee Ray is there at each bend. The thought of her is so troubling, every time I look out toward the lake, especially, that I have to try and stow it. I imagine a little cardboard box, and then I wrap her up tenderly, even though she fights me, and I put her inside. I mail her to myself. Open on arrival. I feel better once she is temporarily contained.

I have gotten used to the rustlings and squeaks and calls by then. I have given up on getting scared. I am just bored, and now I realize I've never been that way before. Something was always happening in my real life, at every minute, compared to out here in the woods. What is so great, what is so wonderful, what is so outrageously fantastic about the woods? I ask this of myself as I sit there. There's not a goddamn thing to do but think. From time to time, I get disgusted. I start talking to myself, mutter a curse on all I see.

"Let Lyman build his old casino here, what's the difference? What does it matter where he puts the thing? At least there would be other human voices. I wouldn't mind a little slot machine right here, by this rock, with a big dollar lunch and free Pepsi. That would be fine with me."

For the purposes of his plan, this is a spot like none other: lake view, perfect for a large-scale resort. And now, as I sit here, my mind a blank for long hours, I have to agree.

Morning. Night. Night. Morning. I have no idea what is passing, time or space. I am still falling in and out of deep despairs, plus I am still not getting what I define as a vision. Where is it? I think that after I have dealt with the hunger, which gets so bad sometimes I put leaves in my mouth and chew them and spit them back out, some bright picture will approach me. I now settle into the frame of mind where nothing frightens me, or surprises me, where I would welcome a bear walking into my little camp and saying something conversational.

That's another thing: I am getting lonelier and lonelier. After a while, it is a toss-up between the loneliness and the hunger. Shawnee arrives during one of my periods of wakefulness, and I can't help untie the package and take out her memory. From then on, her face before she flew into the rage is on a line with the image of the hot dog I so regret not having eaten back at the Dairy Queen. I taste mustard, sweet relish, and most agonizingly, the light salt sweat on Shawnee's neck. How I regret the waste of all the ice cream that smashed on people and the floor. Towering concoctions rise in my mind. Walnut toppings. Shawnee Ray spoons large quantities of frozen slush into my open mouth, or drops in loaded nachos, one by one. I try to heighten this, to make it into something like a vision to light my path, but I know that it isn't the real thing. I get stubborn. I am positive that Lyman is having by-the-book visions right and left and that I will be completely smoked if I don't have something deep and amazing to balance him off. But nothing happens, nothing happens, and still nothing more happens, until I began to call this my getting nowhere fast.

Then early in the morning something does occur. Not the thing that should have, of course. The light is gray in the trees when I wake, like old silver, and the sleeping bag feels snug, warmer than usual. I drift in and out of sleep twice more before I surface to the consciousness that there is something else warming me up. I feel the weight suddenly, the other presence, and as I uncover my head and peer out of the bag, the smell hits me before the sight of the shaggy round ball of fur nestled at my hips. Black fur, white stripes. The mother of all skunks. I don't know why but I think it's a she. Maybe it's the self-assurance, the way she continues to sleep heavily on the most comfortable part of my body. I begin to ease myself back from her, carefully intending not to drop her or damage or even wake her with my movements, but of course, there is no hope of that. All of a sudden, her black eyes open gleaming bright, her mouth yawns, full of pointy teeth.

This ain't real estate.

I hear a crabby, drowsy voice in my head. Now is it the skunk who says this, or is it that my mind has finally sprung a leak? I panic at the thought that I've finally flipped, and scramble backwards, dumping her, rude and sudden. She rises on her tiptoes, this skunk. She stiffens. And then I swear, frozen as I am in place, that she pats down with her front paws, drumming a little tune. Then, just before she lifts her plumed tail, she glances over her shoulder at me and gives me a smile of satisfaction.

This ain't real estate, I think, and then I am surrounded and inhabited by a thing so powerful I don't even recognize it as a smell.

There is no before, no after, no breathing or getting around the drastic moment that practically lifts me off my feet. I stand, drenched, but not alone, for the skunk odor is a kind of presence all of itself. It is a live cloud in which I move. It is a thing I can feel and touch—and then Xavier Toose appears. He is there so suddenly and looks so real that I just gape. I think at first he's been shot, had a heart attack, that he's finally bought it, for he collapses on the ground and begins to roll this way, that, over and over so quick it looks like he's in agony. But now, as I run to him, as I try to help, his arms flap helplessly, his face is screwed up but not with suffering. He's laughing, and laughing so hard there is no use talking to him, no use at all.

I walk back in silence, without my spiritual guide. I enter the area set up for us underneath a tarp near Xavier's house. Well ahead of me, Joe the convict dives for cover. I see that there is food underneath clean white and blue dish cloths, all centered on the picnic table. But the skunk has shut off all of my senses. I have to imagine from a long distance. Wild rice cooked with mushrooms, Juneberry jelly on fresh bannock and bangs. I have to imagine the taste of Kool-Aid and iced tea and picture steam rising in the sealed thermoses of coffee. Sliced melon and the cake. Angel cake. I dig in and no one stops me. The skunk smell rings in my head so loud I can't hear, can't face them. I just know they're somewhere else, around me, howling at the outcome. I swallow down a hot dish thick with hamburger and tomatoes. I chew jerky—beef and buffalo.

No one dares to approach me. They make a circle, call to me from the edges of Xavier's yard. But that's too far away, and I don't answer, just keep eating, though I'm full sooner than I can believe. I see the smoke that rises from the little fire, but I don't go there to sit. They're all weeping with laughter now, heady with my story.

I am completely shamed out by Lyman.

Eventually, I creep close to the circle around the low flames.

"I was begging for a vision," Lyman begins quietly, his voice low but very pleased with what is coming. "I was begging for a vision." He sets his preface out again.

The drama of it! I look unhappily from side to side, and everyone's eyes are fixed with solemn satisfaction upon Lyman, even as they discreetly hold their noses because of me. Lyman it is, and will always be. Never Lipsha. I settle into the bones of my defeat, sit there quiet with my hands in my lap. In my heart, I hate Lyman, but on my face a look of expecting love is pressed.

1994

▲▲
▼▼▼

The Origin of Gambling

Ě′niwûb′e (Sits Farther Along), Chippewa

Ě′niwûb′e

Long before casinos, gambling was part of indigenous cultures, a gift from the gods. Frances Densmore, who collected this story at Lac du Flambeau in Wisconsin in the process of transcribing songs related to gambling, wrote that, "It is the belief of the Chippewa that gambling was taught the Indians by a manido in order to relieve their distress from hunger and ill fortune. Three games were taught them for this purpose—the hand game (onínjiwatâgéwin), the moccasin game (makizínatâdiwín), and the plate game (bûgeséwin, bagesewin).[194] Songs were sung during the first two games, but there was no music with the plate game, as the play was very brief and the computing of the score required considerable time . . . .

"The [screw-shaped] spiral pieces of metal [used in the hand game], ending in a sharp point, called "gun worms," were secured from traders at an early day. The hand game is probably the oldest and most widely distributed of Indian games. Since it was played entirely by gesture, the game could be carried on between individuals who had only the sign language in common.

According to Ě′niwûb′e, the hand game soon came into general use among the Chippewa. The numerous players were seated in two long rows facing each other, while the pile of wagered articles, placed between them, was often so high that the opposing players could scarcely look over it. The spectators danced around the players, singing the hand game songs."

302

Long ago there was a Chippewa who had two wives, each of whom had two children. The man was a great hunter and could kill any animal that he desired. He once took his family and went on a hunting expedition. They went far away from all other Indians. Suddenly one of his children died, and the next day another died. He and his wives buried them. The third day another child died, and on the following day the last of his children died. The fourth day one of his wives died, and on the following day his other wife died. He buried them both. Then he wondered what would become of him. Should he kill himself with his knife or with his arrow? He decided not to do so. A death as certain awaited him if he wandered about worn out with exhaustion, and he decided on this course. Day after day he walked continuously. If he saw water he did not drink, for he was determined to die. He staggered on his way until at last he fell and could not rise. His clothing of skins had been entirely torn from him. He had lost everything—his family, his strength, his tattered raiment; at length life itself departed.

At last he heard someone coming toward him, stamping heavily on the earth. With returning consciousness he saw a man standing before him. The stranger was dressed all in black, even to his mittens. The stranger (who was a manido) spoke, saying, "Brother, why do you lie here?" He who had been dead then rose to a sitting posture.

The stranger said "Brother, let us gamble." The man answered, "Very well," though he did not know what game was to be played. The stranger, seating himself opposite the man, took a skunk-skin bag from his hip pocket. In this were a piece of flint and a small screw-shaped piece of metal used in removing the wad from a gun. The stranger tossed the flint to the man, saying, "You may use this"; he himself used the piece of metal.

The stranger showed the man how to play the hand game. Laying his coat across his knees, he concealed his hands beneath it; in one hand was the metal object. He then passed his closed hands rapidly before his opponent. Skill in the game consisted in transferring this from one hand to the other while both were closely watched by the opponent, who attempted to guess in which hand the object was concealed. The man who had been dead won the game from the stranger, although it had just been taught him.

The stranger, though defeated by the man who had been dead, asked him to try another kind of game. The stranger then took off his moccasins and, laying them on the ground, taught the man to play the moccasin game exactly as it is played by the Chippewa at the present time. At this, as well as at the first game, the man who had been dead was victorious.

Song of the Hand Game

Sung by Ĕ′NIWÛB′E

Then the stranger took from his belt a small shallow wooden plate, which hung there by a cord, and from his tobacco bag some tiny figures made of bone. Placing these figures in the plate, he showed the man how to toss them in the air and note their positions as they fell. The former dead man was winner in this game also.

Plate game plate and pieces

After being defeated at the plate game the mysterious stranger rose and said to his opponent: "Brother, we will part now. Look, yonder is an Indian village. Go there and gamble as I have taught you. I will now tell you who I am. Watch me as I depart."

The man looked up and saw a large black bear walking away from him. The bear turned and said, "Brother, do you know me?" and the man answered, "Yes, I know now who you are."

The man then went the Indian village and began to gamble. According to E´niwub´e, the man won back his dead—that is, two women and four children were staked on the game, and he won; so he felt as though he had the same ones back again.

*c.*1910

▲▲▲
▼▼▼

From The Life, History, and Travels of Kah-Ge-Ga-Gah-Bowh

Kah-ge-ga-gah-bowh (George Copway, 1818-1869), Ojibwe[195]

Kah-ge-ga-gah-bowh

Born near Trenton, Ontario, Copway here describes his conversion experience to Methodism, which is reminiscent of the vision quest of traditional spirituality that he rejected. Copway later served as a missionary, but after being accused of embezzlement and defrocked by the church, he and his wife left for New York City, where Copway had begun his career as a writer and editor. *The Life, History, and Travels* was the first book published by a Canadian First Nations author, and it was followed by six more. Copway began his own Native newspaper, which folded after a few months, and he died in relative obscurity in Quebec. What is intriguing about this excerpt from his autobiography are his descriptions of the missionaries' vigorous proselytizing among the Lake Superior Natives and those Natives' attempts at resistance as their cultures were becoming overwhelmed by whites. Natives sometimes converted to Christianity because they saw religion as a contest between figures of power and white religion seemed more powerful as settlers took their lands. Missionaries held camp meetings that took the place of Midéwiwin ceremonies and, in many ways, attempted to supplant Native spiritual leaders by conducting many of the same ceremonies with different religious figures. What is most troublesome here is that Copway appears to have absorbed the nineteenth-century Christian ideal that Native people were intrinsically less worthy than whites.

In the summer following my mother's death (1830), *I was converted.* The following are the circumstances connected with my conversion. My father and I attended a camp meeting near the town of Colbourne.[196] On our way from Rice Lake, to the meeting, my father held me by the hand, as I accompanied him through the woods. Several times he prayed with me and encouraged me to seek religion at this camp meeting. We had to walk thirty miles under a hot sun in order to reach the place of destination. Multitudes of Indians, and a large concourse of whites from various places, were on the ground when we arrived. In the evening, one of the white preachers (Wright, I believe was his name) spoke; his text was "For the great day of His wrath is come, and who shall be able to stand." He spoke in English, and as he closed each sentence, an Indian preacher gave its interpretation. He spoke of the plain and good road to heaven; of the characters that were walking in it; he then spoke of the bad place, the judgment, and the coming of a Saviour. I now began to feel as if I should die, *I felt very sick in my heart.* Never had I felt so before; I was deeply distressed and knew not the cause. I resolved to go and prostrate myself at the mourners' bench, as soon as an opportunity offered. We were now invited to approach. I went to the bench and knelt down by the roots of a large tree. But how could I pray: I did not understand how to pray; and besides, I thought that the Great Spirit was too great to listen to the words of a poor Indian boy. What added to my misery was that it had rained in torrents about three quarters of an hour, and I was soaking wet. The thunder was appalling, and the lightning terrific. I then tried again to pray, but I was not able. I did not know what words to use. My father then prayed with and for me. Many were praising God, all around me. The storm now ceased, and nearly all the lights had been extinguished by the rain. I still groaned and agonized over my sins. I was so agonized and alarmed that I knew not which way to turn in order to get relief. I was like a wounded bird, fluttering for its life.

Presently and suddenly, I saw in my mind something approaching; it was like a small but brilliant torch; it appeared to pass through the leaves of the trees. My poor body became so enfeebled that I fell; my heart trembled. The small brilliant light came near to me, and fell upon my head, and then ran all over and through me, just as if water had been copiously poured out upon me. I knew not how long I had lain after my fall; but when I recovered, my head was in a puddle of water, in a small ditch. I arose; and O! how happy I was! I felt as light as a feather. I clapped my hands, and exclaimed in English, *"Glory to Jesus."* I looked around for my father, and saw him. I told him that I had found "Jesus." He embraced me and kissed me; I threw myself into his arms. I felt as strong as a lion, yet as humble as a poor Indian boy saved by grace, by grace alone. During that night I did not sleep. The next morning, my cousin, George Shawney, and myself went out into the woods to sing and pray. As I looked at the trees, the hills, and the vallies, O how beautiful they all appeared! I looked upon them, as it were with new eyes and new thoughts. Amidst the smiles of creation, the birds sang sweetly as they flew from tree to tree. We sang, "Jesus the name that charms our fears."

O how sweet the recollections of that day! "Jesus all the day long was my joy and my song."[197] Several hundred were converted during this meeting. Many of the Indians were reluctant to leave the camp ground when the meeting was broken up. When we reached our homes at Rice Lake, everything seemed to me as if it wore a different aspect; everything was clothed with beauty. Before this, I had only begun to spell and read. I now resumed my studies with a new and different relish. Often, when alone, I prayed that God would help me to qualify myself to teach others how to read the word of God; Sabbath mornings I read a chapter in the New Testament, which had been translated for my father before we went to meeting.

During this summer, one of our chiefs, John Sunday, with several others, departed from Rice Lake for the West, with a design to preach to the Ojebwas. When they returned, they told us that the Indians were very eager to hear the word of God and that many had been converted. John Sunday informed us of a certain Indian who was so much opposed to the meetings that he confined his wife and children to one of the islands, to prevent her attending them. But this poor woman was so anxious to obey God in attendance on worship that she was in the habit of fording the river every night and carrying her children on her back. Her husband was afterwards converted. He mentioned also an instance of an Indian who brought his medicine sack[198] with him to the meeting, but on being converted he scattered its contents to the four winds of heaven. These sacks were held very sacred among the Indians. He spoke likewise of the conversion of many chiefs and of the flocks of children anxious to hear the word of God. He left such an impression on my mind that often, while alone, I prayed that God might send me to instruct the children in the truths of religion . . . .

* * *

I now began to feel the responsibilities resting upon me. The thought of assuming the station of a teacher of the Indians, with so few capabilities, was enough to discourage more gifted men than myself. Frequently did I enter the woods and pour out my soul to God in agony and tears. I trembled at what was before me and said, "Who is able for these things?" But a still small voice would answer, "My grace is sufficient for you." Soothing words indeed, especially to an unlearned and feeble Red man—a mere worm of the dust.

Having provided everything necessary for our journey and a residence of eight months at the Kewawenon[199] Mission, we started in company with Rev. Mr. Chandler, Uncle John Taunchey, and the traders who intended to winter on the shores of Lake Superior and do business with the Ojebwas. We were more than three weeks on our journey—three hundred and fifty miles.

At one place we were weather-bound for one week. Our French companions were the most wicked of men. They would gnash their teeth at each other, curse, swear, and fight among themselves. The boat, oars, the winds, water, the teachers, etc., did not escape their execrations. I thought now that I understood what *hell* was in a very clear manner. My very hair seemed to "stand erect like quills upon a fretful porcupine," when they gave vent to their malevolence and passions. They would fight like beasts over their cooking utensils, and even while their food was in their mouths. I will just say here that I have often seen them eat boiled corn with tallow for butter.

On our road, we saw the celebrated Pictured Rocks, Sand Banks, and Grand Island. On a point of the latter place we encamped. Every Sabbath I devoted about one hour in sighing and crying *after home.* What good can *I do,* when I reach the place of labor? was a question that often occurred to my mind. Still we were going farther and farther from home. We were obliged too, to do our own cooking, washing, and mending.

At last, in September, we arrived at the Aunce Bay.[200] Here, our house was no better than a wigwam; and yet we had to occupy it as a dwelling, a school house, a meeting house, and a council room.

We commenced laboring among our poor people, and those that had been Christianized were exceedingly glad to see us. Brothers Sunday and Frazer had already been among them more than a year. We began to build quite late in the fall, and although we removed a house from the other side of the bay, yet we experienced much inconvenience. We visited the Indians daily, for the purpose of conversing and praying with them. There were about thirty, who had, for more than a year, professed to experience a change of heart. As my uncle was experienced in conversing with the unconverted, I endeavored to pursue his course in this respect. Each day we took a different direction in visiting the unconverted. We would sing, read the scriptures, and then pray with them. Sometimes they would be impudent and even abusive, but this did not discourage us or deter us from our duty. By persevering, we soon discovered that the Lord was about to bless our efforts. While my uncle was visiting some four or five wigwams, I was visiting as many others, their wigwams being near us. Our influence, with God's blessing, was now felt among them. Singing and praying were their constant employment; and some of them seemed to know nothing else but the enjoyment of the truth of the gospel and that God can and does "forgive sin." They became the happiest of beings; their very souls were like an escaped bird whose glad wings had saved it from danger and death. Brother Chandler preached twice every Sabbath and taught school every other week. One Sabbath, in January, 1835, Brother Chandler preached from these words, *"And they were all filled with the Holy Ghost."*[201] He spoke with unusual liberty; I caught some of the *same fire* with which the sermon was delivered and interpreted it with much ardor. O what a melting season it was! The anxious and expressive looks of the Indians, the tears streaming down their cheeks, all tended to add to the occasion. My readers, here was comfort; here was one bright spot, at least, in my checkered life, that I never can forget. My poor brethren appeared to swallow every word of the sermon as I interpreted it. One John Southwind, who had been notoriously cruel and revengeful, was among the humblest and the happiest. He had been a great *Conjurer.*[202]

On Sabbath evenings, every converted Indian would try to induce his relatives to embrace religion and pray in the wigwams of their unconverted relatives. These happy scenes often made me forget home.

Many of the unconverted were very revengeful; but we let them expend their vengeance on the air. One of them, Kah-be-wah-be-ko-kay (Gâ-bîwâbiko-ke), i.e. Spear Maker, threatened to tomahawk us if we should come to his wigwam "with the white man's religion, for," said he, "already some of my family are very sick and crazy." Notwithstanding this threat, we commenced our visits, and with no other weapon than a little calico bag containing our Testament and Hymn Book. Whenever he saw us near his wigwam (we were obliged to pass near his in visiting other wigwams), he would run out and grumble and growl like a bear escaping from its den for life. In this way we continued our visits and had opportunities to converse with the family, which resulted in the conversion of all his children. In the month of February, he himself came to us and pled earnestly for our forgiveness. He had gone out to hunt the martin, with his youngest daughter who was about ten years old. While her father was preparing a martin trap, or dead-fall as it is sometimes called, the daughter slipped behind a tree, knelt in the snow, and prayed for her father. The Lord heard her prayer. The old man "felt sick in his heart," and everything he looked at appeared to frown upon him and to bid him, "Go to the missionaries, and they will tell you how you can be cured." He returned home three days earlier than he had intended. Just after day-dawn we heard a number of Indians praying. John Southwind came in and said to us, *"Ke-ge-ke-wa-ye-wah, Ka[h]-be-wah-be-koo-[k]ay, ke-che-ah-koo-sey,"* (*Gîjikiwenyiwâ, Gâbîwâbikoke, gichi-âkozi*), i.e. "Your friend Spear Maker is very sick; he wishes you to call at his wigwam and pray with him." This was good news indeed! We went at once and prayed with him. He could not speak but sat sobbing and sighing over the fire. We conversed with him and then left him; but before breakfast he entered our house with his large medicine sack containing little gods of almost every description. He stood before us and said, *"Ah bay, was ah yak mook,"* (?*Ambe, awas ayaamok*: Hey, away you have it!)—here, take this. He cast the bag, or sack, down upon the floor and wept and sobbed bitterly, saying, "I have done all I could against you, but you have been my friends. I want you to pray for me and to burn these gods, or throw them where I can never see them." Shortly after this interview, he obtained religion and became truly happy in the Lord.

1847

Speech of Mononcue

Chief Mononcue (1778-1838), Wendat

Mononcue

Once Natives converted to Christianity, they discovered that they had not escaped prejudice or bad behavior. The hypocrisy of whites was often their biggest complaint, as it is here, in an address by Mononcue, a converted Christian and an "exhorter" in the Methodist Episcopal Church, who is speaking to a white congregation near Sandusky, Ohio, in the 1820s. His command of rhetoric is sophisticated as he begins with compliments, but his logic spares no one. Monocue belonged to the Ohio Wendat, a Christianized nation who hoped to retain their land rather than be removed to the West. They could not persevere against the whites, however, and were removed to Kansas in 1843.

"Fathers and brothers, I am happy this night before the Great Spirit that made all men, red, white, and black, that he has favored us with good weather for our meeting and brought us together that we may help each other to do good and get good. The Great Spirit has taught you and us both in one thing—that we should love one another and fear him. He has taught

308

us by his Spirit, and you white men by the Good Book, which is all one. But your Book teaches us more plainly than we were taught before what is for our good. To be sure, we worship the Great Spirit sincerely with feasts, rattles, sacrifices and dances, which we now see was not all right. Now some of our nations are trying to do better, but we have many hindrances, some of which I mean to tell.

"The white men tell us that they love us, and we believe some of them do and wish us well, but a great many do not, for they bring us whisky, which has been the ruin of us and our people. I can compare whisky to nothing but the devil, for it brings with it all kinds of evil. It destroys our happiness; it makes Indians poor; it deprives our squaws and children of their food and clothing; makes us lie, steal and kill one another. All these, and many other evils, it brings among us. Therefore you ought not to bring it to us. You white people make it; you know its strength; we do not. But it is a great curse to your own people. Why not cease making it? This is one argument used by wicked Indians against the Good Book. If it is so good, say they, why do not all white men follow it, and do good? Another hindrance is that white men cheat Indians—take their money, skins and furs for a trifle. Now, your Good Book forbids all this. Why not, then, do what it tells you? Then Indians would do right, too. You say the Great Spirit loves all—white, red, and black men—that do right. Why do you, then, look at Indians as below you and treat them as if they were not brothers? Does your Good Book tell you so? I am sure it does not.

"Now, brothers, let us all do right; then our Great Father will be pleased and make us happy in this world, and after death we shall all live together in his house above and always be happy."

1820s

The Origin of the Dream Dance

Maskwawā´nahkwatōk (Red Cloud Woman, Louise Dutchman, *c.*1870-†), Menominee

The Dream Dance, or Drum Dance, probably arose among the Santee (knife) Sioux branch of the Dakota sometime after the 1870s when a girl fled from US soldiers taking over her band's camp. Tailfeather Woman hid in a lake under the pond lilies, forced to remain there for four days without food until she saw a cloud settle over the water. In it was the Great Spirit, who had come to rescue her. He taught her the ceremony of the dance and instructed her to take it back to her people. The purpose of the dance was to recreate Tailfeather Woman's vision to bring peace rather than war, friendship instead of hatred, and to ask for the blessings of the Great Spirit. As with other songs and dances, it was considered a sacred ceremony and a form of prayer.

The dance took place in a circular enclosure, outside or in a building, four times a year. The center of the ceremony was the sacred drum, which was supported by four legs that kept it from touching the ground. This was a larger drum than most Natives had used before, and the drumhead was painted half red (symbolizing south) and half blue (symbolizing north), with a yellow stripe, signifying the path of the sun, dividing the colors. Dancers believed the Great Spirit imbued the drum with sacred power and that it symbolized the world; thus it was addressed as *gimishoomisinaan* (our grandfather), treated with the greatest respect, and aligned so that the yellow stripe would exactly mimic the path of the sun. The beating of the drum, combined with smoke from ceremonial pipes, carried the prayers to the Great Spirit.

309

Drum (or Dream) Dance drum

During the dance, the drummers knelt in a circle around the drum, and each beat the drumhead with a slender stick. As they drummed, they sang, assisted by women who sat behind them and hummed in a nasalized fashion, while the dancers moved clockwise around the circle in time to the rhythm of the songs. Dancing was interspersed with speeches, prayers, stories, and the recitation of the creed of the drum; there was also a feast that was frequently centered around wild rice. The ceremony took place during the day and usually lasted four days, though some meetings could be longer.

At the edge of a lake dwelt these people. When they were dwelling there, some soldiers came to them to fight them. Then a certain woman took her child on her back and ran down to the lake to go lie in the water. Where many reeds stood, there she went and hid in the water. When she had lain four days in the water, she began to starve. In great number had those Indians been killed. Some of them had broken through and got away; they alone remained alive.

There by the shore, then, those soldiers were encamped. At night that woman would nurse her child, to keep it from crying; by day she would lie with only her mouth above the water. When she had lain four days in the water, a Spirit came to her: "Now then, go out of the water; go and eat where those soldiers are camping! They will not see you, when you eat there with them," she was told by someone who addressed her.

Then accordingly, she went out from the water.

"Go, go and enter the place! They are eating their meal. Go there, you too, and seat yourself at the table!" she was told by that Spirit. But she did not see that Being which was speaking to her.

When she had reached that house: "Now, enter!" it said to her. "They will not see you," it told her.

Then she entered and went and ate at the table. With no attention to her the soldiers went on eating. They did not see the woman.

When she was done eating, she went out of the place. A wash-tub was lying outside.

"Take it up. Take it along to where your people dwell," she was told by him who spoke to her. "You will tell your men-folk to go slay the creature [a deer] that you are to use on this drum, so that you may make a drum. Let them hurry about it. Then when they have completed the drum, they will dance to-gether. But you women will merely sit by and join your men-folk in singing the songs. And you will always cook, whenever there is going to be a dance, and in the evening, when it is over, you will give food to your men. Let no one run out from the ceremony. When these soldiers hear the drum, they will go there to slay you. Take heed what you do. Pay no attention to them but pray earnestly to the Spirit our Father. Do not notice the soldiers. Let no one run out; let no one fight back; let them, unheeding, sing loudly and let them dance hard. The soldiers will not be able to go and slay you. All those soldiers will reel and fall. They will not be able to fight you there.

The reason the dream drum exists is that this brown-skinned Indian was given it by the Great Spirit. The reason they all frequent this dream-dance ceremony is that they may deal kindly with each other, that they may never fight each other, that they may never kill each other, that they may there treat each other as brothers and sisters, that there at the ceremony of the dream dance they may feel pity and sympathy for each other, exchanging things by way of reciprocal gifts. That is why the brown-skinned man dances the dream dance—that Indians may deal kindly with one another, and feel pity for one another, and love one another.

1920s

From The Autobiography of A Winnebago Indian

Hágaga (Third-Born Son, Big Winnebago, Sam Blowsnake/Carley, 1875-†), Ho-Chunk

Hágaga

Blowsnake wrote his autobiography in Hocąk, one of the first to do so in an indigenous language rather than English. He spoke English with difficulty and would never have written about his life except that the ethnologist Paul Radin was willing to pay him and Blowsnake needed the money. He had no models, but he had worked for several years with his brother Jasper, helping Radin collect infor-mation on the Ho-Chunk, and that may have influenced him to write as he did. He was also influenced by the Peyote religion where public confession relieved communicants of their guilt, particularly about past events the Peyotists frowned upon. Blowsnake's writing gives a snapshot of his culture at a time of great turmoil: the old ways no

311

longer sufficed, but the new were still being invented. The Peyote religion, which was ancient and had spread to the Great Plains from Mexico in the mid-nineteenth century, offered the people a new spirituality that combined Christianity with traditional elements. Peyote (entheogen peyote, *Lophophora williamsii*), a spineless cactus with hallucinogenic effects, is still used today as part of the sacraments of the Native American Church.

The Indians were celebrating their midsummer ceremony [Midé]. I went there and took part, and I drank all the time. I considered myself a brave man and a medicine man, and I also thought myself a holy man, a strong man, and a favorite with women. I regarded myself as being in possession of many courting medicines. I am a great man, I thought, and also a fleet runner. I was a good singer of Brave Dance songs. I was a sport, and I wanted whiskey every day.

My mother and father had gone to Missouri River[203] and left me in charge of the two horses they possessed, as well as a vehicle which I was using at the time. Later on, in the fall, when the cranberry season started, I lived with three women. I never did any work but simply went from one of these women to the other. After a while an annuity payment was made. I went around "chasing the payments," and I sold the horses at that time and spent the money.[204]

My First Acquaintance with Peyote

Then my father and mother asked me to come to the Missouri River, but I had been told that my father and mother had eaten peyote, and I did not like it. I had been told that these peyote eaters were doing wrong, and therefore I disliked them; I had heard that they were doing everything that was wicked. For these reasons we did not like them. About this time they sent me money for my ticket, and since my brothers and sisters told me to go, I went. Just as I was about to start, my youngest sister,[205] the one to whom we always listened most attentively, said to me, "Older brother, do not you indulge in this medicine eating [peyote] of which so much is said." I promised. Then I started out.

As soon as I arrived in Nebraska, I met some people who had not joined the peyote eaters and who said to me, "Your relatives are eating the peyote, and they sent for you that you also might eat it. Your mother, your father, and your younger sister, they are all eating it." Thus they spoke to me. Then they told me of some of the bad things it was reported that these people had done. I felt ashamed, and I wished I had not come in the first place. Then I said that I was going to eat the medicine.

After that I saw my father, mother, and sister. They were glad. Then we all went to where they were staying. My father and I walked alone. Then he told me about the peyote eating. "It does not amount to anything, all this that they are doing, although they do stop drinking. It is also said that sick people get well. We were told about this, and so we joined and, sure enough, we are practically well, your mother as well as I. It is said that they offer prayers to Earthmaker [God]," he said. He kept on talking. "They are rather foolish. They cry when they feel very happy about anything. They throw away all of the medicines that they possess and know. They give up all the blessings they received while fasting, and they give up all the spirits that blessed them in their fasts. They also stop smoking and chewing tobacco. They stop giving feasts, and they stop making offerings of tobacco. Indeed they burn up their holy things. They burn up their war-bundles. They are bad people. They give up the Medicine Dance. They burn up their medicine bags and even cut up their otter-skin bags. They say they are praying to Earthmaker, and they do so standing and crying. They claim that they hold nothing holy except Earthmaker. They claim that all the things that they are stopping are those of the bad spirit [the devil], and that the bad spirit has deceived them; that there are no spirits who can bless; that there is no other spirit except Earthmaker.

Then I said, "Say, they certainly speak foolishly." I felt very angry towards them.

"You will hear them for they are going to have a meeting tonight. Their songs are very strange. They use a very small drum," said he.

Then I felt a very strong desire to see them.

After a while we arrived. At night they had their ceremony. At first I sat outside and listened to them. I was rather fond of them. I stayed in that country, and the young peyote eaters were exceedingly friendly to me. They would give me a little money now and then, and they treated me with tender regard. They did everything that they thought would make me feel good, and in consequence I used to speak as though I liked their ceremony. However I was only deceiving them. I only said it because they were so good to me. I thought they acted in this way because the peyote was deceiving them. . . .

After a while we moved to a certain place where they were to have a large peyote meeting. I knew they were doing this in order to get me to join. Then I said to my younger sister, "I would be quite willing to eat this peyote ordinarily, but I don't like the woman with whom I am living just now and I think I will leave her. That is why I do not want to join now, for I understand that when married people eat medicine they will always have to stay together. Therefore I will join when I am married to some woman permanently."

Then my brother-in-law came, and she told him what I had said, and he said to me, "You are right in what you say. The woman with whom you are staying is a married woman, and you cannot continue living with her. It is null and void, this marriage, and we know it. You had better join now. It will be the same as if you were single. We will pray for you as though you were single after you have joined this ceremony, then you can marry any woman whom you have a right to marry legally. So, do join tonight. It is best. For some time we have been desirous of your joining, but we have not said anything to you. It is Earthmaker's blessing to you that you have been thinking of this," said he.

I Eat Peyote

Therefore I sat inside the meeting-place with them. One man acted as leader. We were to do whatever he ordered. The regalia were placed before him. I wanted to sit in some place on the side, because I thought I might get to crying like the others. I felt ashamed of myself.

Then the leader arose and talked. He said that this was an affair of Earthmaker's and that he could do nothing on his own initiative; that Earthmaker was going to conduct the ceremony. Then he said that the medicine was holy and that he would turn us all over to it; that he had turned himself over to it and wished now to turn all of us over to it. He said further, "I am a very pitiable figure in this ceremony, so when you pray to Earthmaker, pray also for me. Now let us all rise and pray to Earthmaker." We all rose. Then he prayed. He prayed for the sick, and he prayed for those who did not yet know Earthmaker. He said that they were to be pitied. When he had finished we sat down. Then the peyote was passed around.

313

They gave me five. My brother-in-law said to me, "If you speak to this medicine, it will give you whatever you ask of it. Then you must pray to Earthmaker, and then you must eat the medicine." However I ate them immediately for I did not know what to ask for and I did not know what to say in a prayer to Earthmaker. So I ate the peyote just as they were. They were very bitter and had a taste difficult to describe. I wondered what would happen to me. After a while I was given five more, and I also ate them. They tasted rather bitter. Now I was very quiet. The peyote rather weakened me. Then I listened very attentively to the singing. I liked it very much. I felt as though I were partly asleep. I felt different from my normal self, but when I looked around and examined myself, I saw nothing wrong about myself. However I felt different from my normal self. Before this I used to dislike the songs. Now I liked the leader's singing very much. I liked to listen to him.

They were all sitting very quietly. They were doing nothing except singing. Each man sang four songs and then passed the regalia to the next one. Each one held a stick and an eagle's tail feather in one hand and a small gourd rattle, which they used to shake while singing, in the other. One of those present used to do the drumming. Thus objects would pass around until they came back to the leader, who would then sing four songs. When these were finished, he would place the various things on the ground, rise, and pray to Earthmaker. Then he called upon one or two to speak. They said that Earthmaker was good and that the peyote was good and that whosoever ate this medicine would be able to free himself from the bad spirit; for they said that Earthmaker forbids us to commit sins. When this was over, they sang again.

After midnight, every once in a while, I heard someone cry. In some cases they would go up to the leader and talk with him. He would stand up and pray with them. They told me what they were say-ing. They said that they were asking people to pray for them, as they were sorry for their sins and that they might be prevented from committing them again. That is what they were saying. They cried very loudly. I was rather frightened. I noticed also that when I closed my eyes and sat still, I began to see strange things. I did not get sleepy in the least. Thus the light of morning came upon me. In the morning, as the sun rose, they stopped. They all got up and prayed to Earthmaker, and then they stopped.

During the daytime, I did not get sleepy in the least. My actions were a little different from my usual ones. Then they said, "Tonight they are going to have another meeting. Let us go over. They say that is the best thing to do and thus you can learn it right away. It is said that their spirits wander over all the earth and the heavens also. All this you will learn and see," they said. "At

Peyote. *Curtis Botanical Magazine*, 1847

times they die and remain dead all night and all day. When in this condition they sometimes see Earth-maker, it is said." One would also be able to see where the bad spirit lived, it was said.

So we went there again. I doubted all this. I thought that what they were saying was untrue. However I went along anyhow. When we got there, I had already eaten some peyote, for I had taken three during the day. Now near the peyote meeting an Indian feast was being given, and I went there instead. When I reached the place, I saw a long lodge. The noise was terrific. They were beating an enormous drum. The sound almost raised me in the air, so pleasurably loud did it sound to me. Not so pleasurable had things appeared at those peyote meetings that I had lately been attending. There I danced all night, and I flirted with the women. About day I left, and when I got back, the peyote meeting was still going on. When I got back, they told me to sit down at a certain place. They treated me very kindly. There I again ate peyote. I heard that they were going to have another meeting nearby on the evening of the same day. We continued eating peyote the whole day at the place where we were staying. We were staying at the house of one of my relatives. Some of the boys there taught me a few songs. "Say, when you learn how to sing, you will be the best singer, for you are a good singer as it is. You have a good voice," they said to me. I thought so myself.

The Effects of the Peyote

That night we went to the place where the peyote meeting was to take place. They gave me a place to sit and treated me very kindly. "Well, he has come," they even said when I got there, "make a place for him." I thought they regarded me as a great man. John Rave, the leader, was to conduct the ceremony. I ate five peyote. Then my brother-in-law and my sister came and gave themselves up. They asked me to stand there with them. I did not like it, but I did it nevertheless. "Why should I give myself up? I am not in earnest, and I intend to stop this as soon as I get back to Wisconsin. I am only doing this because they have given me presents," I thought. "I might just as well get up, since it doesn't mean anything to me." So I stood up. The leader began to talk, and I suddenly began to feel sick. It got worse and worse, and finally I lost consciousness entirely. When I recovered, I was lying flat on my back. Those with whom I had been standing were still standing there. I had as a matter of fact regained consciousness as soon as I fell down. I felt like leaving the place that night, but I did not do it. I was quite tired out. "Why have I done this?" I said to myself. "I promised my sister that I would not do it." So I thought and then I tried to leave, but I could not. I suffered intensely. At last daylight came upon me. Now I thought that they regarded me as one who had had a trance and found out something.

Then we went home, and they showed me a passage in the Bible where it said that it was a shame for any man to wear long hair. That is what it said, they told me. I looked at the passage. I was not a man learned in books, but I wanted to give the impression that I knew how to read, so I told them to cut my hair, for I wore it long at that time. After my hair was cut, I took out a lot of medicine that I happened to have in my pockets. These were courting medicines.

There were many small bundles of them. All these, together with my hair, I gave to my brother-in-law. Then I cried, and my brother-in-law also cried. Then he thanked me. He told me that I understood and that I had done well. He told me that Earthmaker alone was holy; that all the blessings and medicines that I possessed were false; that I had been fooled by the bad spirit. He told me that I had now freed myself from much of this bad influence. My relatives expressed their thanks fervently.

On the fourth night they had another meeting, and I went to it again. There I again ate peyote. I enjoyed it, and I sang along with them. I wanted to be able to sing immediately. Some young men were singing, and I enjoyed it, so I prayed to Earthmaker, asking him to let me learn to sing right away. That was all I asked for. My brother-in-law was with me all the time. At that meeting all the things I had given my brother-in-law were burned up . . . .

I Am Converted

On one occasion we were to have a meeting of men, and I went to the meeting with a woman with whom I thought of going around the next day. That was the only reason I went with her. When we arrived, the one who was to lead asked me to sit near him. There he placed me. He urged me to eat a lot of peyote, so I did. The leaders of the ceremony always place the regalia in front of themselves; they also had a peyote placed there. The one this leader placed in front of himself this time was a very small one. "Why does he have a very small one there?" I thought to myself. I did not think much about it.

It was now late at night, and I had eaten a lot of peyote and felt rather tired. I suffered considerably. After a while I looked at the peyote, and there stood an eagle with outspread wings. It was as beautiful a sight as one could behold. Each of the feathers seemed to have a mark. The eagle stood looking at me. I looked around thinking that perhaps there was something the matter with my sight. Then I looked again, and it was really there. I then looked in a different direction, and it disappeared. Only the small peyote remained. I looked around at the other people, but they all had their heads bowed and were singing. I was very much surprised.

Some time after this I saw a lion lying in the same place where I had seen the eagle. I watched it very closely. It was alive and looking at me. I looked at it very closely, and when I turned my eyes away just the least little bit, it disappeared. "I suppose they all know this, and I am just beginning to know of it," I thought. Then I saw a small person at the same place. He wore blue clothes and a shining brimmed cap. He had on a soldier's uniform. He was sitting on the arm of the person who was drumming, and he looked at every one. He was a little man, perfect in all proportions. Finally I lost sight of him. I was very much surprised indeed. I sat very quietly. "This is what it is," I thought, "this is what they all probably see, and I am just beginning to find out."

Then I prayed to Earthmaker: *"This, your ceremony, let me hereafter perform."*

As I looked again, I saw a flag. I looked more carefully, and I saw the house full of flags. They had the most beautiful marks on them. In the middle of the room there was a very large flag, and it was a live one; it was moving. In the doorway there was another one not entirely visible. I had never seen anything so beautiful in all my life before.

Then again I prayed to Earthmaker. I bowed my head and closed my eyes and began to speak. I said many things that I would ordinarily never have spoken about. As I prayed, I was aware of something above me, and there he was; Earthmaker to whom I was praying, he it was. That which is called the soul, that is it, that is what one calls Earthmaker. Now this is what I felt and saw. The one called Earthmaker is a spirit, and that is what I felt and saw. All of us sitting there, we had all together one spirit or soul; at least that is what I learned. I instantly became the spirit, and I was their spirit or soul. Whatever they thought of, I immediately knew it. I did not have to speak to them and get an answer to know what their thoughts had been. Then I thought of a certain place, far away, and immediately I was there; I was my thought. . . .

I have written of some of these matters, and I have spoken out clearly. I talked about this to the older people, but they refused to do it. I thought I would write it down so that those who came after me would not be deceived. Then my brother had us do this work, aided by my older brother and my younger brother.

Before my conversion I went about in a pitiable condition, but now I am living happily, and my wife has a fine baby.

This is the work that was assigned to me.

This is the end of it.

1920

❖ SUMMER/FALL HARVESTS ❖

CORN AND ITS SISTERS

The Magician of Lake Huron
Nabunwa, Odawa

This version of the origin of corn, collected by George Johnston, places the beginnings of corn and pumpkins on Manitoulin Island,[206] the largest freshwater island in the world, located in northern Lake Huron and home to the Odawa for centuries. The time of the story is shortly after the Haudenosaunee have driven the Huron from nearby Huronia in the seventeenth century. Nabunwa not only relates the magical origin of corn, which always comes as a gift from the body of a spirit, but also describes the Little People, beloved by all Great Lakes nations. Many nations tell of dwarves who give corn to the people, but here they also grant the Odawa great success in trade.

At the time that the Ottowas inhabited the Manatoline Islands in Lake Huron, there was a famous

Guarding the Corn-Fields, 1853. Seth Eastman

magician living amongst them whose name was Masswäwëinini, or the Living Statue.[207] It happened, by the fortune of war, that the Ottowa tribe were driven off that chain of islands by the Iroquois and obliged to flee away to the country lying between Lake Superior and the Upper Mississippi, to the banks of a lake which is still called by the French, and in memory of this migration, Lac Courtoreille[s], or the Lake of the Cut-Ears,[208] a term which is their *nom de guerre* for this tribe.[209] But the magician Masswäwëinini remained behind on the wide stretching and picturesque Manatoulins, a group of islands which had been deemed from the earliest times a favorite residence of the manitous or spirits. His object was to act as a sentinel to his countrymen and keep a close watch on their enemies, the Iroquois, that he might give timely information of their movements. He had with him two boys; with their aid he paddled stealthily around the shores, kept himself secreted in nooks and bays, and hauled up his canoe every night into thick woods and carefully obliterated his tracks upon the sand.

One day he rose very early and started on a hunting excursion, leaving the boys asleep and limiting himself to the thick woods, lest he should be discovered. At length he came unexpectedly to the borders of an extensive open plain. After gazing around him and seeing no one, he directed his steps across it, intending to strike the opposite side of it; while traveling, he discovered a man of small stature, who appeared suddenly on the plain before him and advanced to meet him. He wore a red feather on his head and, coming up with a familiar air, accosted Masswäwëinini by name and said gaily, "Where are you going?" He then took out his smoking apparatus and invited him to smoke. "Pray," said he, while thus engaged, "wherein does your strength lie?"

"My strength," answered Masswäwëinini, "is similar to the human race and common to the strength given to them, and no stronger."

"We must wrestle," said the man of the red feather. "If you should make me fall, you will say to me, 'I have thrown you, Wa ge me na.'"

As soon as they had finished smoking and put up their pipe, the wrestling began. For a long time the strife was doubtful. The strength of Masswäwëinini was every moment growing fainter. The man of the red feather, though small of stature, proved himself very active, but at length he was foiled and thrown to the ground. Immediately his adversary cried out, "I have thrown you: Wa ge me na," and in an instant his antagonist had vanished. On looking to the spot where he had fallen, he discovered a crooked ear of *mondamin* or Indian corn,[210] lying on the ground, with the usual red hairy tassel at the top. While he was gazing at this strange sight and wondering what it could mean, a voice addressed him from the ground.

"Now," said the speaking ear, for the voice came from it, "divest me of my covering—leave nothing to hide my body from your eyes. You must then separate me into parts, pulling off my body from the spine upon which I grow. Throw me into different parts of the plain. Then break my spine and scatter it in small pieces near the edge of the woods and return to visit the place after one moon."

Masswäwëinini obeyed these directions and immediately set out on his return to the lodge. On the way he killed a deer and, on reaching his canoe, he found the boys still asleep. He awoke them and told them to cook his venison, but he carefully concealed from them his adventure.

At the expiration of the moon he again, alone, visited his wrestling ground, and to his surprise found the plain filled with the spikes and blades of new-grown corn. In the place where he had thrown the pieces of cob, he found pumpkin vines growing in great luxuriance. He concealed this discovery also, carefully from the young lads, and after his return busied himself as usual in watching the movements of his enemies along the coasts of the island. This he continued till summer drew near its close. He then directed his canoe to the coast of that part of the island where he had wrestled with the Red Plume, drew up his canoe, bid the lads stay by it, and again visited his wrestling ground. He found the corn in full ear and pumpkins of an immense size. He plucked ears of corn and gathered some of the pumpkins, when a voice again addressed him from the cornfield.

"Masswäwëinini, you have conquered me. Had you not done so, your existence would have been forfeited. Victory has crowned your strength, and from henceforth you shall never be in want of my body. It will be nourishment for the human race." Thus his ancestors received the gift of corn. . . .

Masswäwëinini now returned to his canoe, informed the young men of his discovery, and showed them specimens. They were astonished and delighted with the novelty.

There were, in those days, many wonderful things done on these islands. One night, while Masswäwëinini was lying down, he heard voices speaking, but he still kept his head covered, as if he had not heard them. One voice said, "This is Masswäwëinini, and we must get his heart." "In what way can we get it?" said another voice. "You must put your hand in his mouth," replied the first voice, "and draw it out that way."

Masswäwëinini still kept quiet and did not stir. He soon felt the hand of a person thrust in his mouth. When sufficiently far in, he bit off the fingers and thus escaped the danger. The voices then retired, and he was no further molested. On examining the fingers in the morning, what was his surprise to find them long wampum beads, which are held in such high estimation by all the Indian tribes. He had slept, as was his custom, in the thick woods. On going out to the open shore, at a very early hour, he saw a canoe at a small distance, temporarily drawn up on the beach; on coming closer, he found a man in the bow and another in the stern, with their arms and hands extended in a fixed position. One of them had lost its fingers; it was evidently the man who had attempted to thrust his arm down his throat. They were two *pukwudjininees* or fairies.[211] But on looking closer, they were found to be transformed into statues of stone. He took these stone images on shore and set them up in the woods.

Their canoe was one of the most beautiful structures which it is possible to imagine, four fathoms in length and filled with bags of treasures of every description and of the most exquisite workmanship. These bags were of different weight, according to their contents. He busied himself in quickly carrying them into the woods, together with the canoe, which he concealed in a cave. One of the fairy images then spoke to him and said: "In this manner, the Ottowa canoes will hereafter be loaded, when they pass along this coast, although your nation are driven away by their cruel enemies the Iroquois."

The day now began to dawn fully, when he returned to his two young companions, who were still asleep. He awoke them and exultingly bid them cook, for he had brought abundance of meat and fish and other viands, the gifts of the fairies.

After this display of good fortune, he bethought him of his aged father and mother, who were in exile at the Ottowa lake. To wish and to accomplish his wish were but the work of an instant with Masswäwëinini. One night as he lay awake, reflecting on their condition, far away from their native fields and in exile, he resolved to visit them and bring them back to behold and to participate in his abundance. To a common traveler, it would be a journey of twenty or thirty days, but Masswäwëinini was at their lodge before daylight. He found them asleep and took them up softly in his arms and flew away with them through the air and brought them to his camp on the Manatoulins, or Spirits' Islands. When they awoke, their astonishment was at its highest pitch and was only equaled by their delight in finding themselves in their son's lodge in their native country and surrounded with abundance.

Masswäwëinini went and built them a lodge, near the corn and wrestling plain. He then plucked some ears of the corn and, taking some of the pumpkins, brought them to his father and mother. He then told them how he had obtained the precious gift, by wrestling with a spirit in red plumes, and that there was a great abundance of it in his fields. He also told them of the precious canoe of the fairies, loaded with sacks of the most costly and valuable articles. But one thing seemed necessary to complete the happiness of his father, which he observed by seeing him repeatedly at night looking into his smoking pouch. He comprehended his meaning in a moment. "It is tobacco, my father, that you want. You shall also have this comfort in two days."

"But where," replied the old man, "can you get it—away from all supplies and surrounded by your enemies?"

"My enemies," he answered, "shall supply it—I will go over to the Nadowas of the Bear totem, living at Penetanguishine."[212]

The old man endeavored to dissuade him from the journey, knowing their bloodthirsty character, but in vain. Masswäwëinini determined immediately to go. It was now winter weather, the lake was frozen over, but he set out on the ice, and although it is forty leagues, he reached Penetanguishine the same evening. The Nadowas discerned him coming—they were amazed at the swiftness of his motions and, thinking him somewhat supernatural, feared him and invited him to rest in their lodges, but he thanked them, saying that he preferred making a fire near the shore. In the evening they visited him and were anxious to know the object of his journey at so inclement a season. He said it was merely to get some tobacco for his father. They immediately made a contribution of the article and gave it to him.

During the night they however laid a plot to kill him. Some of the old men rushed into his lodge, their leader crying out to him, "You are a dead man."

"No, I am not," said Masswäwëinini, "but you are," accompanying his words with a blow of his tomahawk, which laid the Nadowa dead at his feet. Another and another came to supply the place of their fallen comrade, but he dispatched them in like manner as quickly as they came, until he had killed six. He then took all the tobacco from their smoking pouches. By this time the day began to dawn when he set out for his father's lodge, which he reached with incredible speed, and before twilight spread out his trophies before the old man.

When spring returned, his cornfield grew up, without planting or any care on his part, and thus the maize was introduced among his people and their descendants, who have ever been noted, and are at this day, for their fine crops of this grain and their industry in its cultivation. It is from their custom of trading in this article that this tribe is called Ottowas.[213]

1830s

The Origin of White Corn, or Kaněňhagěňät

Truman Halftown, John Armstrong, Henry Stevens, Senecas

Before 1900 and the introduction of a yellow variety known as Country Gentleman, corn was usually white or multicolored. Here is the story of how the sweet, succulent white corn everyone loves to buy in August was given to an elder, rich with experience and wisdom, of the peaceful, industrious Tuscaroras when they still lived in present-day North Carolina. J. N. B. Hewitt (1857-1937), a bilingual Tuscarora linguist and ethnologist, collected this story at the Cattaraugus Reservation in New York during the last part of the nineteenth century.

In ancient times there lived a community of people at the foot of a very high, steep, and rugged cliff. There came a day when they heard the plaintive singing of a woman, who seemed to be on the top of this almost inaccessible mountain. The mysterious woman directed the words of her songs to a very old but highly respected man of this small community. The burden of the songs was expressed by the words: "Oh! Kinsman of my father's brother, come up here. I, indeed, desire greatly to become your wife." These words gave much anxiety to the people who heard them, but the old man paid no attention to them.

The woman, seemingly on the mountaintop, continued to sing daily, however, and finally some of the people urged the old man to go up to the summit to learn the designs of the persistent singer. But he excused himself, saying: "The mountain is so steep and rugged, and I am now become so aged that I do not feel able to make the attempt to climb its side."

But the woman on the height, continuing her singing from day to day, and the anxiety of the people becoming very marked, the chiefs of the community in council finally requested the old man, whom they highly respected, to go to the mountaintop to unravel, if possible, the meaning of the mysterious singing. They represented to him the importance of this mission, since the persistent singing might have some relation to the welfare of the community at large.

After long meditation he replied to the request of the council, "Oh, my chiefs! At your request I will go to the mountaintop to learn, if it be possible, the meaning of this woman's singing."

Having made the necessary preparations, the old man started and, after overcoming many difficulties, he finally reached the summit of the mountain. There he saw a young, fine-looking woman, who stood not far from the brink of the cliff. She had been standing in that position while he was painfully wending his way up the mountainside and urged him to have patience and courage to persist in his attempt to climb the mountain. Seeing that he had reached the top of the mountain, the young woman beckoned him to her side, at the same time saying: "Do thou come to me, oh, my friend! I desire to share my mat with thee."

Drawing near to the young woman, the aged man said kindly to her: "I am unfortunately past the age when it might have been in my power to comply with your request."

But the young woman replied: "Fear not, but draw near me. I will endow thee with the power which will enable thee to comply with my desire. So come close to me. Now, mark my words and carefully cherish them. Out of the ground at the spot whereon I have lain a plant shall sprout and grow. Care tenderly for this, for it shall be a boon to your people, a chief source of food to them; and it shall be called Kanĕñhagĕñät; that is to say, White Corn. In five days from now you must return to care for what you will find growing out of the ground, as I have already told you. As for me, I shall die."

The aged man drew near the woman and embraced her. Time passed and he swooned. When he finally recovered his senses he discovered that the young woman had disappeared—vanished into thin air—and he believed that he had embraced a vision. Arising from the ground, he returned to his people at the foot of the mountain.

Remembering the words of the young woman to the effect that he must return to the mountaintop to obtain a mysterious plant, at the end of five days the old man returned to the summit. There he found on the spot whereon the young woman had lain a growing corn plant.

He carefully pruned away from it all weeds and placed rich, fine earth around its rootlets and also watered it from a neighboring spring. Taking great delight in caring for this corn plant, the aged man came frequently to the mountaintop to attend to it. In course of time it had grown to maturity, bearing three ripened ears of white corn. These he carefully husked and carried back to his lodge.

In the spring he assembled all the people of the community and divided the corn among them equally, a few grains to each family, and he instructed them in the method of planting and caring for the corn, telling them that in time it would become one of their staple food plants. Such is, it is said, the manner in which the white corn originated among the Tuscarora, who have generously shared the seed with neighboring tribes and kindred.

The Bean Woman (A Fragment)
Truman Halftown, John Armstrong, Henry Stevens, Senecas

J.N.B. Hewitt did not say why he, Halftown, Armstrong, or Stevens considered it a fragment. Perhaps it is extremely old and only a portion survived into the nineteenth century. Certainly it is rare. The suitors "The Bean Woman" rejects are all creatures of the older hunting and gathering world: the panther, the deer, and the wolf. Only when the fourth suitor—corn—offers marriage does the woman accept, completing not only a family, but also reflecting the complementary protein that beans and corn form for the human body and the way they grow entwined together.

In ancient times a people dwelling near a river bank were startled by the sound of singing, which came apparently from downstream. The voice was that of a woman, and tradition says that it was indeed the Bean-Woman who was singing. The Bean-Woman sang, it is said, "Who shall marry me again? Let him ask me in marriage!"

The Panther-Man, answering this challenge, said: "I will marry you if you will accept me for your husband."

Pausing in her singing, the Bean-Woman asked, "If I marry you what shall be the food which I shall regularly receive from you to eat?"

The Panther-Man replied: "You shall always have meat in great plenty to eat."

The Bean-Woman answered: "In that case it is very probable I should die, for I do not eat that kind of food under any circumstances." Thereupon the Bean-Woman resumed her singing: "Who will marry me again? Is there one who is willing to marry me again? If so, let him ask me."

Then the Deer-Man approached the Bean-Woman and said: "I will marry you if you will accept me for your husband."

The Bean-Woman asked him: "What food will you regularly provide for me to eat?"

The Deer-Man replied: "Browse and buds and the tender bark of trees, for these are the things which I regularly eat."

The Bean-Woman answered: "Such a marriage would not bring good fortune to me, because I have never eaten that kind of food." So the Deer-Man departed. Then the Bean-Woman resumed her song: "Is there not someone who is willing to marry me? If there be, let him ask me." As she sang, she heard the Bear-Man say to her: "I will marry you if you will accept me." Whereupon she asked him: "What kind of food will you regularly provide for me to eat?"

He replied, "I will provide you with nuts of various kinds, for even now I have many bark receptacles filled with nuts for food."

The Bean-Woman replied: "In this event I should most certainly die, for I have never been in the habit of eating that kind of food; so I cannot accept you." Without feeling disappointed she resumed her singing: "Is there not someone who will marry me again? If so, let him ask me."

Then the Wolf-Man approached her, saying: "I am willing to marry you if you will accept me."

Once again the Bean-Woman asked: "If I should marry you what kind of food would you regularly provide for me to eat?"

The Wolf-Man answered: "I will provide you with meat and venison."

At this the Bean-Woman said with scorn: "It is, indeed, quite proper for you to offer me meat and venison for food, but I have never had the desire to eat meat which has been stolen."

Thereupon the Wolf-Man departed. The Bean-Woman resumed singing, as before: "Is there anyone who is willing to marry me again? If there is, then let him ask me."

Then the Corn-Man, drawing near, said: "I am willing to marry you if you will accept me."

In reply she asked: "If I should marry you what will you give me for my regular food?" The Corn-Man's answer was: "You shall have sweet corn to eat at all times."

In reply the Bean-Woman said: "I pray that it may so come to pass. I am, indeed, thankful for this offer, for it is a well-known fact that I am in need of it."

When the Corn-Man had heard her answer, he said to her: "Come to me." Rushing forward, she threw her arms around his neck and embraced him, saying: "This is, indeed, a condition established by Him who sent us, by Him who created our bodies, beginning with the time when the earth was new."

They dwelt together contented and happy. This is the reason that the bean vine is at all times found entwined around the cornstalk.

1896

WILD RICE

Wild rice (*Zizania aquatica*), called manoomin by the Ojibwe, is one of the most important crops that Great Lakes Natives harvest, and they have been doing so for millennia. The grain is so important that the word became the name of the Menominee nation: Wild Rice People. This cereal grain, a type of grass, is used ceremonially as well as for food; its origin is the subject of legends. Wild rice early became a diet staple for those people lucky enough to live near lakes and rivers that had mineral-rich waters where the plant would thrive, and with good reason: rice was the single most nutritious item available. More than any other vegetable or meat Natives could raise or hunt, rice is rich in carbohydrates, low in fat, and contains protein and vitamins.

Traditional harvesting is done from a canoe with two long sticks, called knockers, one to bend the rice plant over the canoe, the other to knock the grains off the plant. Nineteenth-century artists George Catlin and Seth Eastman recorded large canoes with three or more people—one to paddle and two to harvest. Now smaller canoes hold only two people, one to pole, the other to knock. Because rice is an annual, it is necessary to let some of the rice fall into the water during harvesting to seed the next year's crop. Once the canoes return to shore, the rice is dried in the sun and parched by smoking or in kettles; then the husks are thrashed by treading or "dancing" the rice to separate the grains from the husks. Finally the rice is winnowed: tossed into the air from large trays to separate the grains from the chaff.

Ojibwa Gathering Wild Rice Near the St. Peter's River, 1836. George Catlin

Nänabushu and the Mallard

Midāsuganj (Ten Claw), Ojibwe

This story, collected at Bois Fort near northern Lake Superior, recounts the traditional origin of rice as coming from the dung of the Mallard duck. This is also a classic folktale of the "bungling host" type, where the animal host's magical creation of food cannot be duplicated by another, in this case Trickster. Indeed, when Mallard's children find Nänabushu's hidden mittens, the clever duck knows exactly what's going to happen: his ability to produce rice will be taken advantage of once again.

Well, already was Nänabushu again becoming hungry. And one other time he came to some people, and they also had two children. And now, as he looked about, "What in the world must they have to eat?" he thought.

Presently said the man: "Please do you go and hang up the kettle," he said to the woman.

Thereupon truly the woman went and hung up the kettle. Presently the man painted himself with a green color; all around over his head did he put it. In time he was done with painting himself. And while yet seated, and of a sudden, he started forth from the place, uttering: *"Kwīsh, kwīsh, kwīsh, kwīsh!"* Such was the sound of his voice.

Nänabushu observed him muting [defecating], while at the same time he heard him saying: "Ho, ho, ho, old woman! Keep it stirring," he said to her. And all the while the Mallard muted, he was saying: "Ho, ho, ho, old woman! Keep it stirring."

Thereupon Nänabushu truly heard the sound of his rice boiling. When it was boiled, then down from aloft came the Mallard. "Now, therefore shall you eat, Nänabushu," he was told. "What you do not eat, then to your children may you take."

Thereupon truly, while about to return, he again put his mittens in among the balsam boughs. And later on he was again heard calling with a loud voice: "Oh!" he was heard calling out.

"Nänabushu may want to say something to you," the Mallard said to his children. "Truly, he has forgotten something! Now look yonder where he sat!" And there truly were his mittens.

"'My nephews may fetch them,' he will say. And from a distance shall you fling them to him. He will not avoid saying something to you."

Thereupon truly, when from afar they intended throwing them to him, he then said to them: "Oh, come give them to me!" he said to them. And so truly the boys went and gave them to him.

"I say," he said to them, "would that when tomorrow is here, your father might come over! You people must be in want of food."

So thereupon, truly, on the morrow thither went the man. Naturally in waiting was Nänabushu. Presently he heard them say: "Halloo! A visitor!" Thus he heard them say. Then presently in he came.

Then Nänabushu said to his wife: "Oh, for goodness' sake, do hang up the kettle! For it is our duty to feed the visitor."

Thereupon he was told by his wife: "For mercy's sake, what have we to feed him!" he was told by his wife.

"What possesses you to talk that way whenever I tell you to do something! Simply go on and hang up this kettle!" he said to her.

The woman truly hung up the kettle. He had his green paint spread out; in painting himself he colored his head green. Presently he was done painting himself; and while seated, and of a sudden, up he sprang. *"Kwīsh, kwīsh, kwīsh, kwīsh!"* was the sound he uttered. It was a long while before he was able to get to yonder cross-pole; he was a long while getting there. Finally he was perched over the place where hung their kettle, he could be heard uttering: *"Kwīsh, kwīsh, kwīsh, kwīsh!"* Now they watched him perched aloft, with his anus opening and closing. He was not able, with all his efforts, to ease himself; but after a long while there fell a miserable droplet of dung.

"Oh, oh!" he was told by his wife.

Now, down at once their visitor lowered his head, for round about in the boiling water whirled Nänabushu's sorry droplet of dung. So then accordingly down climbed Nänabushu.

"Pray, give me your paint," he was told by their guest. "Now, go wash your kettle," he said to the old woman.

So it was true that soon she had finished with washing her kettle. Then she hung up the kettle with a different kind of water.

And when their visitor was done painting himself, then began the sound of the Mallard, who then was alighting upon their cross-pole. So thereupon he began muting, and forthwith some rice came pouring out. When their kettle began to fill, then down he alighted. Thereupon he said: "Nänabushu, therefore, now shall your children have enough to eat," such was said to Nänabushu.

Well, so then upon his way he went, and accordingly did Nänabushu's poor children eat.

1905

Under the Wild Rice Moon
Winona LaDuke (1959-   ), Anishinâbe

Winona LaDuke, writer, environmental activist, and vice-presidential candidate in 1996 and 2000 on the Green Party ticket, addressed the United Nations on environmental issues when she was eighteen. This Harvard-educated activist founded the White Earth Land Recovery Project and continues to press for indigenous rights and environmental reform. Here she describes the problems currently facing the wild rice harvest. Native rice will not tolerate chemical pollution, and it needs a precise alkalinity of water to thrive—both conditions that are less available than in the past. In addition, the growth of machine-planted, insecticide-sprayed, machine-harvested "wild" rice has depressed the prices the people can receive for their harvest and threatened the genetic purity of wild rice. The sacred grain is now endangered as never before.

Ponsford, Minn.—It is the wild rice moon in the North Country, and the lakes teem with harvest and a way of life.

"Ever since I was bitty, I've been ricing," says Spud Fineday of Ice Cracking Lake. Spud, with his wife,

Tater, this year started ricing at Cabin Point and then moved to Big Flat Lake, lakes within the borders of the Tamarac National Wildlife Refuge.

"Sometimes we can knock four to five hundred pounds a day," he says, explaining that he alternates the jobs of "poling and knocking" with Tater, a.k.a. Vanessa Fineday.

The Finedays, like many other Anishinaabeg from White Earth and other reservations in the region, continue to rice to feed their families, to "buy school clothes and fix cars," and to get ready for the ever-returning winter. The wild rice harvest of the Anishinaabeg not only feeds the body; it feeds the soul, continuing a tradition that is generations old for these people of the lakes and rivers of the North. The ricing tradition that Spud Fineday has practiced since childhood is a community event, a cultural event that ties the community in all its generations to all that is essentially Anishinaabeg, Ojibwe.

As the story is told, Nanaboozhoo, the cultural hero of the Anishinaabeg, was introduced to rice by fortune and a duck.

"One evening Nanaboozhoo returned from hunting, but he had no game. . . . As he came toward his fire, he saw a duck sitting on the edge of his kettle of boiling water. After the duck flew away, Nanaboozhoo looked into the kettle and found wild rice floating upon the water, but he did not know what it was. He ate his supper from the kettle, and it was the best soup he had ever tasted. Later, he followed in the direction the duck had taken and came to a lake full of manoomin. He saw all kinds of ducks and geese and mudhens, and all the other water birds eating the grain. After that, when Nanaboozhoo did not kill a deer, he knew where to find food to eat. . . ."

Manoomin, or wild rice, is a gift given to the Anishinaabeg from the creator and is a centerpiece of the nutrition and sustenance for our community. The word manoomin contains a reference to the creator, who is known as Gichi Manidoo. In the earliest of teachings of Anishinaabeg history, there is a reference to wild rice known as the food that grows upon the water, the food the ancestors were told to find so we would know when to end our migration to the west.

It is this profound and historic relationship that is remembered in the wild rice harvest on the White Earth and other reservations—a food that is uniquely ours and a food that is used in our daily lives, our ceremonies, and our thanksgiving feasts. It is that same wild rice that, ironically, exemplifies the worldwide debate on issues of biodiversity, culture, and globalization.

The crispness of early fall touches my face as we paddle through the rice on Blackbird Lake. Four eagles fly overhead, and a flock of geese moves gracefully across the sky. Through the rice, I can see officers of the law, ensconced in their work. They are ricing. Eugene Clark, a.k.a. Beebzo (Ogema mayor and Becker County Deputy Sheriff), and John MacArthur, a Mahnomen County Sheriff, are Anishinaabeg, and they are police officers. Today they are continuing the harvesting tradition. As they move swiftly through the rice bed, MacArthur is knocking and Clark is poling.

Both men began ricing as teenagers. "We're out here to eat, not to make money," they tell me. They are ricing for their families. On this day, they bring in a couple of hundred pounds of green rice.

Ronnie Chilton is working at the Native Harvest (White Earth Land Recovery Project) rice mill. He too has a long connection to ricing. "I've riced my whole life, most of the time with my dad." He considers ricing a part of his family's tradition as well and wishes he were on a lake, even as I am interviewing him.

It's said that there are fewer rice buyers this year on the reservation, although Beebzo maintains that "there were more people at the rice permit drawing [for Tamarac Lakes] than vote in most elections." There are also lots of ricers. By two weeks into ricing season, Native Harvest bought from thirty or forty ricers.

There is always a debate about the rice crop—this year is deemed by many to be better than the last few. However, Big Rice Lake, in the northwest corner of the reservation, is seen as a sort of the Shangri-La of rice—the paradise for ricers. A perceived reduction in the crop on that lake causes opinions to fly. The reasons are speculative: high water levels, agricultural herbicide runoff, the usual suspects.

"It used to be you would get lost in the rice on that lake," Russell Warren, a twenty-year rice processor, tells me. "They used to have to put flags up at the landings, so you could find your way back. It's the fertilizer, and the runoff, that ruins the crop."

As with farmers anywhere, there's much discussion as to the status of the crop, the international markets and their subsequent impact on local production and the preservation (or lack of preservation) by state officials of the water quality around the rice crop. There may well be a diminished interest in the Native-harvested rice, as the big food companies—Stouffer's, Uncle Ben's, Gourmet House and the others—drive a paddy wild rice market, the vast majority of it out of state.

Mirror of Change

This fall, the state's Agriculture Department discusses a probable ten percent decline of the farmers in this northwest region, attributed to the economy, the weather, and yet-another bad year. I am struck by how the transformation of agriculture from family farms to large corporate farms is mirrored in the wild rice industry. Consumer and biodiversity scholars maintain that the recent enactment of multilateral trade agreements (i.e., GATT) means that, for the first time, multinational corporations are within reach of controlling the planet's genetic wealth. Indeed, this is reflected in food production, processing, and marketing, where today corporate agribusiness manufactures and markets over ninety-five percent of the food in the United States. We increasingly rely upon a smaller group of sources for food.

The concentrated control over not only food production but the seeds themselves has become a significant controversy, as local varieties disappear and farmers lose control over their seeds. Patents are bought and sold, and the actual life itself becomes a market commodity. Many of the seed companies have been acquired by multinational chemical corporations. According to the most recent issue of *Consumer Reports* magazine, Monsanto, for example, has spent nearly eight billion since 1996, purchasing seed companies. Dupont is buying Pioneer Hi-Bred. According to the Worldwatch Institute, these combined purchases make Dupont and Monsanto, respectively, the world's largest and second-largest seed companies.

A similar concentration is underway in the wild rice industry. Minnesota's paddy wild rice production began aggressively in 1968, representing roughly twenty percent of the state's crop by the harvest of that year. Paddy rice production increased the available quantities of wild rice and by 1973 had increased the yield to some four million pounds. The increase in production and interest by the larger corporations (i.e., Uncle Ben's, Green Giant and General Foods), in many ways skewed perceptions of wild rice and altered the market for traditional wild rice. In 1977 the Minnesota Legislature designated wild rice as the official state grain. That was perhaps the kiss of death for the lake wild rice crop.

With an outpouring from state coffers, the University of Minnesota began aggressively to develop a domesticated version of wild rice. By the early 1980s, cultivated wild rice had outstripped the indigenous varieties in production. Ironically, Minnesota lost control over wild rice production to California, which by 1983 produced more than eight million pounds, compared with Minnesota's five million pounds. By 1986, more than ninety-five percent of the wild rice harvested was paddy grown, the vast majority produced in northern California. When the glut of wild rice hit the market in 1986, the price plummeted, not only affecting the newly emerging domesticated market but devastating the Native wild rice economy.

Now, ricer Joe LaGarde, the White Earth Tribal Council, and other Indians are concerned not only with economics but also with biology. "Man thinks he can improve on something that's been developing over thousands of years. Eventually, he might end up with nothing," LaGarde says. He's concerned about the genetic strains of paddy rice and their possible impact on the lake rice crop. Every ricer knows that the rice is distinct between lakes.

"There's sand-bottom rice (usually shorter grains), muddy-bottom rice, all of that," Joe explains. "We're concerned about the possible [crossbreeding] of these 'hybrid cultivated varieties' with our lake rice." The White Earth Tribal Council even wrote a letter to the University of Minnesota asking it to "quit messing with the rice," Joe says.

He is worried and remembers a childhood spent ricing at Mitchell Dam on the Refuge, camping for a week or so. He'd like to keep that memory a part of a living culture, not a relic of the pre-industrialized agriculture age.

Meanwhile, the wild rice market now serves consumers who demand a big black grain, rice that boils up exactly at the same pace as white rice. That market is huge. Jerry Schochenmaier is the general manager of Indian Harvest Wild Rice Co., in Bemidji, Minnesota. An affable fellow, Schochenmaier is a major promoter of wild rice and is interested in the preservation of the wild harvesting of the rice and the Native community.

Interestingly enough, Indian Harvest, which is the nation's largest wild rice processor, is pretty much an operation with few "Indians," although some lake rice is in its program. The plants and operations, for the most part, are in California, where this year Schochenmaier expects to process around seventy-five percent of the national crop. Indian Harvest reflects the national trends and market in wild rice, which remains focused on the cultivated varieties.

Schochenmaier has been in the wild rice business since the fall of 1997. In 1989, Indian Harvest processed some one million pounds. By 1994, production was up to six million pounds, increasing to a projected thirteen million pounds this year. "The rice mill was originally designed to be in Bemidji"—the footings for the building are still at Bemidji's industrial par—"but California was identified as the place to produce rice if you were going into the business," he says.

The rice found in the major markets is quite different from the rice most of us see in northern Minnesota. Commercially processed wild rice, for Uncle Ben's, Gourmet House, Pillsbury, Stouffer's, General Mills, ConAgra, and the other big companies, is processed black and scarified, so as "to get its cook time to match that of white rice," explains Schochenmaier. That way, those who seek to create "gourmet" meals can ensure that their meals are brought to the table in a timely manner.

While international taste buds and global corporations have one idea of what wild rice is, their market-driven impacts have been felt on the lakes of Becker County and throughout the North Country.

Return in the Rain

A pickup pulls up at the rice mill. Eugene Davis and Tony Warren bring in around three hundred pounds of rice from South Chippewa Lake. They are tired, wet from the recurring morning rain, but they are happy.

"This is the only job we can make a hundred fifty an hour at up here," nineteen-year-old Eugene Davis tells me. "I like it when it rains out there. It's nice; you can't hear anything but the rain."

It is that peace which brings the ricers back. It is also the memories. I ask Eugene Davis what he thinks about the fact that probably five or ten generations of his family have been on that same lake. "I like knowing that they were on the same lake. It makes me feel good," he responds and smiles.

Receiving the rice are Ronnie Chilton, Pat Wichern, Pete Jackson, and a few other men who gather under some tarps at the offices of the White Earth Land Recovery Program on Round Lake. The sweet smell of parching rice wafts through the dusty air, ancient machines shift and creak as the husks blow off, and the rice slowly moves through a long chain of events. The air is filled with dust from the rice. Ronnie, Pat, and Pete look a bit like Anishinaabeg chimney sweeps, covered in rice hulls, but smiling beneath all of it.

The equipment is ancient, and much of it handmade—a 1940s Red Clipper fanning mill, a handmade thrasher, a 1980s set of George Stinson (a Deer River celebrity) parching drums, a '50s-vintage gravity table.

The men fiddle with the machines, fine-tune the gravity table, and then the rice comes out—colors of dark green, tan and brown. They are local producers, and this is the perfection of the small batch, and the simple joy of this life. Ronnie, Pete and Pat grin through the dust. They are doing their job. This rice, like that of their ancestors, is going to feed families and feed spirits.

To Pat, Ronnie, Spud, Tater and the rest of the ricers of White Earth, this season, the Ojibwe Ricing Moon—*Manoominigiizis*—is the season of a harvest, a ceremony and a way of life.

"I grew up doing that," reflects Spud Fineday. "You get to visit people you haven't seen for a whole year, because just about everyone goes ricing."

Far away a combine is harvesting wild rice in California, and consumers are eating a very different rice. The Anishinaabeg would not trade for the rice, or the combine. In the end, this rice tastes like a lake, and that taste cannot be replicated.

1999

Dancing the Rice

Denise Sweet, Anishinâbe

For Mr. Bill Sutton
The fall season enters the rhythms of our pace
leaves gather like whorls on a spindle of wind
twisting and coiling around our feet;

the old man sits in front of the fire stirring
and singing low in whispers to himself, tossing
the rice slowly in the bottom of the black pot;

the good grain, *manomin,* turns slowly from green
to darkened fibers in the heat, we watch it turn
small swirls of steam wisp away from the parching;

when we dance, he says, we caress the earth
we carry power in the way we present ourselves
as dancers, as singers, bringing the rice home;

this power enters each stem of *manomin*
but it must be a gentle step, the padding of feet
against the good grain; they hold our dreams

and we must be slow and gentle when we dance the rice
or they can quickly turn to broken stems and then to dust
then we have nothing and the *manomin* will not return.

He lowers himself into the barrel of parched rice
placing his feet gently against the heated grain
slowly lifting one foot, and twisting the other

he shifts his hips side to side; hoisting his weight
on the sides of the barrel, he gently kneads the grain
pressing each step in a circle against the barrel's bottom

"Everything tries to go in a circle. Everything in nature.
You and me. Yuh." The old man watches while the rice is tossed
from the basket into the air—tiny whirlwinds of chaff spring

forth like dervishes released from a magic lamp. The wind
sails them away from the winnowed rice—the grain chinks against
the birchbark basket in cadence with the dropping wrists and
the young man's swaying black hair—it is a dance of sweet and
gentle love—warming hearts and pleasing the old man who watches
and sees in circles, our survival embodied in the winds of October.

1990s

Denise Sweet, author of several books of poetry and recipient of numerous awards, was named Wisconsin Poet Laureate for 2004-2008. "Poetry is the way I tell my story," she says. "The role of remembering in tribal community is held in high regard, as it is a powerful act of survival—verifying our tribal histories through stories of our own making, through words of our own choosing. The storyteller and poet come from the same territory of the imagination." Sweet believes that the storyteller and the poet are carriers of culture, "demonstrating how the world comes together and invariably transforms before our eyes in profound and magical ways. . . . In some indigenous languages, the words used to express the act of breathing are one and the same with the description of singing or expressing poetry. For many tribes, artful expression is as essential as breathing."

FALL

Fall/Winter Moons
October, November, December[214]

Miami

šaašakaayolia kiilhswa	grass burning in streaks	Agricultural burning. Leaves are green; fire does not spread
kiiyolia kiilhswa	smoky-burning moon	Agricultural burning.
ayaapeenhsa kiilhswa	young buck moon	Two-year-old bucks rut now.

Shawnee

kini-kiishthwa	long moon	Long month?
wa'shilaatha	eccentric moon	Changeable weather.
ha'kwi-kiishthwa	severe moon	Cold weather brings hard ground.

Mohawk (old | modern)

*gasahginehah	kenténha'*	greater frosts begin	?	Weather is colder now.
*gasahgineh	kentenhkó:wa'*	ripened fall	great October	Leaves fall; late crops are ripe.
*johtoh	tsyothórha'*	cold moon	Coldest moon.

Ho-Chunk in Wisconsin

čaamą́ąhinągǒwii	deer pawing earth moon	Buck deer fight before breeding.
čáikirúxewii	deer-mating moon	Deer breed now.
čaahéwakšų́wii	deer antler-shedding moon	Buck deer shed fighting horns.

Meskwaki

Tagwatä'a	frosty time	Frost bites everything.
Pagamä'ikīceswa	strikes it moon	Muskrat dens speared to kill muskrats inside.
Ke'tcima'kwa	big bear moon	Bears mating and hunted before hibernation.

Ojibwe/Odawa

binakwi-gisiss	combing-shedding leaves moon	Leaves are stripped from trees.
gashkadini-gisiss	it freezes over moon	Ground freezes.
manito-gisissons	Spirit little moon	

Potawatomi

Yamino kises	rutting moon	White-tailed deer take the male.
Pinőne kises	antler loss moon	White-tailed deer lose their antlers.
Kitché mukő kises	big bear moon	Bear hunting before hibernation.

Menominee

pinipimek	falling leaves moon	Leaves fall.
pokiwakomi/wemonoso	frozen ground/deer rutting	Ground freezes hard; deer breed.
häwätûk	God	

❖ FALL ❖

The Corn Husker

Hard by the Indian lodges, where the bush
   Breaks in a clearing, through ill-fashioned fields,
She comes to labor, when the first still hush
   Of autumn follows large and recent yields.

Age in her fingers, hunger in her face,
   Her shoulders stooped with weight of work and years,
But rich in tawny coloring of her race,
   She comes a-field to strip the purple ears.

And all her thoughts are with the days gone by,
   Ere might's injustice banished from their lands
Her people, that today unheeded lie,
   Like the dead husks that rustle through her hands.

Tekahionwake

Tekahionwake, 1903[215]

This season begins with a lesson about traditional fall activities, taught by Mountain Wolf Woman, who grew up when everyone gained their livelihoods from the natural world. People knew a place, its plants, its stars, and its creatures intimately, not because they worshiped nature, as later North Americans would do, but because their lives depended on their knowledge. This place is where the wild potatoes grow. If you look carefully, you can see where the mice have hidden their harvests of wild beans. Here is where the fish will come in this moon or that one. This is what is required for killing deer. While the writers in the Spring section celebrated joy of maple syrup and those in Summer gave thanks for rice and the Three Sisters, the narratives here describe a world apart from agriculture, one where hunters dance to the first snow and a young moose learns humility. *"Hok'íkun*: Teachings," by three Ho-Chunk, details how children and young adults were trained to take their places in the world before knowledge became institutionalized and put in books.

  The section on "Warfare" begins with an account of traditional warfare as practiced by the Ho-Chunk, with the rituals of supplication, power, and politics that accompany war in all cultures. In the fall, after food was gathered, harvested, and stored, and before snow made winter hunting possible, many bands and nations preferred to go to "war," which consisted of raiding parties that minimized loss to both enemies and combatants by the practice of counting coup. Before Europeans introduced the concept of total war to North America, killing everyone including women and children and destroying all crops and structures was the exception. When Natives first encountered white Europeans' methods, they were appalled. "Who will be left to fight another time?" one of them asked a Puritan leader and minister during the Pequot War in 1637.

Much has been written about Native brutality in war, and there are examples of that here, but it is necessary to put that brutality in context. In the 1830s, after talking with George Johnston, Jane Johnston Schoolcraft's brother, about Indian warfare, Anna Jameson, wife of the Canadian governor general and the first white woman to run the Sault rapids in a canoe, wrote in her journal:

> There is a sensible proverb about taking care of our own glass windows: and I wonder if any of the recorded atrocities of Indian warfare or Indian vengeance, or all of them together, ever exceeded Massena's retreat from Portugal—and the French call themselves civilised. A war-party of Indians, perhaps two or three hundred (and that is a very large number), dance their war-dance, go out and burn a village, and bring back twenty or thirty scalps. They are savages and heathens. We Europeans fight a battle, leave fifty thousand dead or dying by inches on the field, and a hundred thousand to mourn them, desolate; but we are civilised and Christians. . . . Really I do not see that an Indian warrior, flourishing his tomahawk, and smeared with his enemy's blood, is so very much a greater savage than the pipe-clayed, padded, embroidered personage, who, without cause or motive, has sold himself to slay or be slain: one scalps his enemy, the other rips him open with a sabre; one smashes his brains with a tomahawk, and the other blows him to atoms with a cannon-ball: to me, femininely speaking, there is not a needle's point difference between one and the other. If war be unchristian and barbarous, then war as a science is more absurd, unnatural, unchristian than war as a passion.

Jameson's point, which still applies, is that no matter who wages it, war of any type is always brutal, always involves the death of noncombatants, and always causes irreparable losses. As for Natives making war as a sport or passion, readers will discover that there were strict conventions to be met before war parties set out and before they engaged the enemy. The war party could be stopped at any time by someone who objected, thus short-circuiting the possibility of war for personal glory causing too many casualties. If European armies had operated on a like principle, Napoleon's disaster in Russia would never have occurred. Defensive war against whites was a different matter, and Natives quickly learned that to survive, they must fight as whites fought.

As white settlement began pushing Natives west across the Great Lakes region, the people already occupying those lands were pushed west in turn. Thus, the Dakota and Lakota, who once resided in the present-day Upper Peninsula of Michigan, were pushed onto the inhospitable climate of the Great Plains, where initially they nearly starved. The result was the Chippewa-Dakota War, which raged for more than a century over territory in Wisconsin and Minnesota, despite the attempts of white traders to stop it because it interfered with business. William Warren devotes much of his *History of the Ojibwa People* to that war, which neither side ever won and stopped only when the combatants were forced onto reservations. That the Dakota later adapted to their Plains environment to become one of the most romantically portrayed cultures in North America would have been small comfort against what they had lost and, after the coming of the whites into their Plains territory, would lose again. Warren's history also demonstrates that while Natives may have fought in the white men's wars, such as the American Revolution, when they came to tell their own histories, white wars were not all that important. Natives often acted as little more than mercenaries in white conflicts, playing the European and North American powers against each other to attempt to retain as much of their lands as they could.

The chronology at the end of this book lists in mind-numbing succession the major wars that inflamed the Great Lakes region from 1641, when the Haudenosaunee attacked the Huron, to 1862, when a force of Dakota led by Little Crow to fight the ravages of white settlers was defeated and thirty-eight warriors were publicly hung in Mankato, Minnesota, the largest mass execution in United States history. The two centuries of warfare leading up to that humiliation saw Native nations forced to give way, mile by mile and treaty by treaty, some of the most beautiful and productive land in the world. Black Hawk's narrative, the first autobiography written by a Native American, describes in painful detail what it was like to come home, only to discover strangers who insulted him, beat him, stole his possessions and, when he tried to protest and enforce his treaty rights, called in the militia to massacre his band's women and children. Although the wars produced some brilliant Native military leaders, they also led to the complete disappearance of many nations and inspired a literature of loss and trauma. As Tecumseh once said, "Where are the Narraganset, the Mohican, the Pakanoket and many other once powerful tribes of our people? They have vanished before the avarice and oppression of the white man, as snow before a summer sun."

Paradoxically, the decentralized practices of Native warfare were what left them vulnerable to the organized ruthlessness of European and American opponents. Even charismatic war chiefs such as Pontiac and Tecumseh—who could foresee what was going to happen if whites were allowed to continue encroaching upon Native lands—were unable to convince enough bands and nations to align and remain together long enough to repel settlers permanently. Tecumseh, who was born into a land already threatened and nurtured in a cradle of war, observed that white people did not care how many soldiers they lost since there were always more to replace the ones killed, whereas for Natives to lose a warrior in an ill-advised battle was a disgrace. In addition, whites seldom played fairly. Their wars were not about ritual; they were about territorial expansion, based on faraway European politics or uncontrollable backcountry settlers like Daniel Boone. Native allies were pawns in a white political game. When it was no longer convenient to support their allies, the Europeans or Americans abandoned them to their fates.

By the nineteenth century, that fate was the reservation, and a new type of war began. Christian missionaries and "Friends of the Indian" pushed through the General Allotment Act of 1887 (Dawes Act), which, as many historians have noted, was a subversive way to allow timber and mining companies, and then white settlers, to buy Native land that otherwise would have remained part of a reservation. The Dawes Act was rendered obsolete by the Indian Reorganization Act of 1934, which supposedly gave a "New Deal" to the Natives and did offer much help. But less than twenty years later, the Termination Resolution attempted to end all federal payments to Natives and led to nearly the same result as the Dawes Act. If Termination had not been reversed by

Menominee Ada Deer and her group of activists, few reservations or reserves would remain today in the USA or Canada.

As many accounts in this book attest, whites have never stopped coveting Native land or artifacts, no matter how much they have already taken. The new "Indian wars" are now fought in air-conditioned courtrooms by Harvard-educated attorneys, but the rituals are no less complex and the stakes are just as high. Ted Williams describes his nation's battle to keep territory from being sliced away, a piece at a time, by state and federal governments using eminent domain. Ironically for whites, the unintentional result of late nineteenth- and early twentieth-century racist policies to deprive Native children of their lifeways and languages by forcing them into boarding schools was to create, several generations later, a cadre of skillful Native attorneys backed by the deep pockets of gaming revenue who routinely win cases against US and Canadian governments. But as Oren Lyons suggests in "Sovereignty and the Natural World Economy," in the process of winning this war, Natives have come too close to losing the values of their cultures and adopting the destructive beliefs that have motivated whites. As he notes, if the planet is to survive, this must stop. The respect for the natural world that informs Basil Johnston's descriptions of our elder brothers, the animals, has frequently been lost to industrialization, greed, and revenge.

In the preindustrial world, the sky was alive with songs and stories that were later made to seem quaint or obsolete by industry, technology, and the dispersal of cultures intimately tied to hunting and farming. But the star lore of Native peoples is rich and deep, even near the Great Lakes, parts of which suffer as many cloudy days as the Pacific Northwest. When the clouds part, the stars are still there, as they have been ever since the Paleoindians first came to the lakes. The stars those hunters watched have moved a bit since then—their Pole star isn't ours—but they may have used constellations to predict the winter solstice, even as we can today. One dramatic group of stars that never falls below the horizon in the northern parts of the world, Ursa Major, was to them as they are to us. Some Great Lakes nations know these stars as the Fisher Stars and told a tale about their creation at the spring equinox (see p. 167). But stories about Ursa Major can also some mark the fall activities of hunting and gathering, as they do in stories that follow. Northern peoples used these constellations as a clock by following their nightly movements from east to west, as some nations also did with another distinctive group that rises in fall, the Pleiades, here described as the Seven Sisters, which are frequently associated with agriculture or harvesting wild or domesticated crops. When the Pleiades become visible in fall, it is time to make the last harvests before killing frosts; when they disappear in spring, the weather is safe for planting.

The fall equinox marks the halfway point between the longest and shortest days of the year, June 21 and December 21. Now the hours of daylight seem to shrink more quickly. At the winter solstice (literally "sun stop") on the shortest day, the sun reaches its most southerly point on the horizon. It seems to stop for a few days and then begins rising a little farther north each day, bringing longer days and warmer weather. The solstice is a sign that spring will return, and it has been celebrated by cultures around the world since people first tracked the movements of the sun. Lakes Natives had more reason than most to mark the solstice, since it meant relief was coming from the punishment of winter, even though it be months away. The Great Bear/Fisher Stars can be used as a tracking device to predict when the winter solstice will occur, since they are at their lowest point in the sky in December, only fifteen degrees above the horizon. At that time the leaders responsible for predicting the changes of the seasons would know the solstice was imminent and could tell stories about it to give people hope.

Would that ethnoastronomy were always so easy as deciphering stories about the Great Bear and the Pleiades. Stories such as "The Women of the Eastern Sky" may refer to a Mesoamerican past long transformed by immigration and time. When this story was collected, white cultures seldom navigated by the stars or paid much attention to them except as a romantic backdrop, so although the story exists in several versions, no one, apparently, thought to ask the most obvious question: Which stars does the story describe? How do the stars in this story serve as a marker for the winter solstice, since that seems to be part of the plot? How did a story that appears to be about heart sacrifice, a practice of the Maya and Aztec cultures, come to be told in Wisconsin in the early twentieth century? Some scholars have attempted to make a case for Mesoamerican stories carried north with emigrants during the past ten millennia, but their guesses outnumber facts. This does not mean it didn't happen or dim the radiance of this and all the other star stories that remain imperfectly understood. They are a reminder of what everyone in North America lost—not just Natives—when land and the stars that were part of a way of life were gone. Land was lost. Lifeways were lost. Many stories, fortunately, were not because they can survive when little else does, persevering like archaeological remains when the people who created them are dust. Stories survive to testify that people, no matter how long the war or how fierce the struggle, can endure to tell new stories with the old.

❖ FALL HARVESTS ❖

Livelihood: Fall and Winter (from *Mountain Wolf Woman*)

Kéhachiwinga (Mountain Wolf Woman, 1884-1960), Ho-Chunk

Kéhachiwinga

When various foods were ripe, the people dried them. They also steamed things underground. They harvested a lot of corn and carried it home on their backs. When I was a little girl, our family was large. I was the youngest, and I had three older brothers and two older sisters. Another older sister and I were the younger ones. When they harvested the gardens, they harvested a great amount. They steamed the corn. In the evening they dug a pit and heated stones there in a big fire. They put the stones in the pit, and when the stones became red hot, they took out all the wood and embers and put in the corn husks. Then they put in the fully ripe corn and covered it with more husks. Finally they covered it with the earth that had been dug out. They covered the pit, but they left four holes in which they poured water. We used to hear the red hot stones make a rumbling sound.

Then, very early in the morning they opened the pit with great care. They removed the earth very carefully, and finally when they reached the husks, they took them out. Eventually they reached the corn, and it was thoroughly cooked. It was really hot! They took the corn out and put it on the husks. Sometimes other people heard about it and worked with my family. The helpers came and spread out a big piece of canvas on which they put the corn. Then they used metal teaspoons or clamshells to scrape the corn off the cobs. They used to dry it, and after it was dried, you could see sackfuls of corn standing here and there. They dried the corn in the sun and put it in white flour sacks. Some corn was allowed to remain on the stalks after it was ripe. This they saved for seed. In addition to saving seed, they made hominy of this dried corn. They mixed it with ashes and popped it to make hominy.

Squash was also dried. The women pared the squash, cut it in two and sliced it to form rings. They cut down forked trees, peeled them, and strung the squash on poles they laid across the forks. A lot of squash hung on this framework. The Indians generally dried squash in this way and saved it for winter.

They used to dry blueberries too, berries they did not sell. They dried the blueberries and cooked them in the wintertime. The blueberries were boiled with dried corn, and I used to think this was delicious. That is what we used to eat.

They used to dig a hole to save whatever they were not going to use during the winter. They kept out whatever they thought they would need for that winter, and they saved in the hole what they would eat in the spring. Seed was also buried in the ground. They made a hole and buried things in it and took them out as they were required. "Dig up that which is buried," they used to say.

They also dried Indian potatoes. My grandmother and my mother's younger sister and I used to gather them. Indian potatoes grow wild, where it is wooded with dense hazel bushes, near creeks. The vines of the Indian potatoes are like strings stretched out, a lot of strings extending in all directions. That is the way the vines grow, tangled up around the bushes. The women would try poking here and there with a hoe, and then they would hit upon them. The potatoes would be linked to each other as if they were strung together. Then they would dig a lot of them. After they dug them up, they cut up the links and dried them. When they cooked these things, they added sugar and boiled them until the water was gone, and then we peeled off the skins. Oh, they were really delicious things!

Stealing from mice is something I never did but aunt and grandmother told me about it. They would go off in the brush, in the woods, and steal wild beans from the mice. These mice know how to store things. Running back and forth, the mice carried things to a particular place. Their little trails showed the way they went into their little holes in the ground. There they gathered very many of those wild beans. Grandmother said that when a family had a lot of little boys it used to be said of the last born, the youngest one, that he is married to one of these mice. It was that boy who used to find the storehouses. That is why they used to say the little boys married little mice. Mother's brothers were all big, and they did not have any little boy. Even my youngest uncle was grown up, but they used to say, "Squeaking Wing's wives have stored some things; let us go look for some of them." They always found some. Grandmother used to say that some women knew very well how to look for wild beans. They would stand some place and look around. "There is one over there!" they used to say, and "There is one right here too!" When they scraped away the leaves and the earth [w]here the holes used to be, [it was] just all full of wild beans. They would take them and save them. Sometimes they said they found a bucketful, I do not know how big a bucket they meant. Those beans were very good; I ate some of them. When I went to Nebraska, they gave me some there. I cooked them in the same way I cook any beans. The beans that we eat today are good, but wild beans are much more delicious.

When I was small, the Winnebago generally went to pick cranberries after they were through taking care of their gardens. We used to do that too. When we arrived at the marsh, there were many Indians who camped together there and picked cranberries. The men used rakes, and the women picked by hand. As the women were picking and they reached the edge of the ditch, they all sat on the edge of the ditch in a long row, side by side. They picked ahead of themselves in a straight line, a bushel-sized box at each woman's side. They would put aside as many boxes as they thought they would fill so that they would not run out of boxes. They left their boxes as they filled them, and if you looked down a line, you could see the row of filled boxes. As they filled each box, they took along another empty box. At noon they went back to the camp to eat. Some people even brought their lunches along and ate there at the marsh. I used to think it was great fun when we took food and ate outside.

That is what people did in the fall. They were making money to save. When they finished there, they went deer hunting. They were trying to earn money for themselves, and they probably earned quite a bit, but I did not know what they were earning. The women used to pick into a big dishpan, and when it was full, it was emptied into the box. We children used to pick too. We used small pails. Wherever mother sat, I used to sit next to her, and I would pick cranberries. When I filled the pail, I emptied it into mother's bushel box. My sister did the same thing on the other side of mother. That is what I used to do.

When we were there, a peddler of general merchandise often came around. When he said the word for a white man's shirt, he would say, *"sorot."* He was a white man with black hair and black mustache, and he did not know how to speak English. When this peddler came, they would all call out, "Oh, sorot is here!" They used to call him sorot.

The Indians were making money, and that is why they used to come around and sell things. Somebody came around selling pies. I used to think that was very nice. Mother often bought things from these peddlers, and then we used to eat pie. After all, the Indians were using campfires outside and could not bake pies and cakes, and so they had a bakery shop there at the marsh.

That cranberry picking place is gone now. Iron Mountain Marsh they used to call it, and I do not even know the English name for it. That cranberry marsh no longer exists because at one time a big forest fire came through there. When the people fled, they said that they had to put the old people in the ditches. They could not flee with them in time, and so they put the old people in the water in the ditches. I believe the marsh ceased to exist at that time. The entire stand of cranberry bushes was burned up.

After cranberry time they went on the fall migration to hunt deer. That is what we always did; we went traveling to hunt deer. At that time my father did not have to buy any deer license. They never used to pay for such things. When they went deer hunting, the white people did not spy on them. That is how it used to be at that time. They killed as many deer as they deemed necessary. We used to travel a certain distance east of Neillsville [Wisconsin] where there used to be a woods. There were not many white people around at that time. That is where we used to go in the fall. That is where we used to live and almost immediately the hunters used to bring in deer. They wrapped the deer in autumn leaves and carried the deer on their backs. As they were approaching, you could see the red leaves moving along here and there, as they came home with the freshly killed deer. Just as soon as we arrived, the first day, they always brought home game. It was always this way. Sometimes they even used to bring in a bear.

Four or five households of Indians migrated to this area where they built long wigwams; my father and my brothers, also my brother-in-law Cloud and another brother-in-law Little Náqiga (Fourth-Born Son) as well as their relatives and sometimes our uncles, came there too. Our family was large enough to require a two-fireplace wigwam. We lived in a rush wigwam. My grandmother and my mother made our house of cattail matting. The wigwam was covered with mats of cattail stalks. The inside of the house was never smoky. I suppose that was because it was properly made. It was very pleasant to live in a rush wigwam. My older sister White Thunder and my brother-in-law Cloud lived next door, but they lived in a large round wigwam. Another person who lived in a big round wigwam was Cloud's brother who was called Big Thunder. Big Thunder's wife's name was Axjinwinga[216]—and I do not know what that would mean in English. Her mother's name was Four Women, and her husband's name was Daylight.

One time when we had been living there only a short time, as I recall, this old man, Daylight, died. When he was about to die, he was very sick. He was really very sick, but he said that he wanted to see the daylight, he wanted to go outside. He said this as he lay there. Upon hearing this, my mother came home. She had evidently gone to visit him. She said, "My sons, he is to be pitied that he is saying this. Go and carry him. Take him outside. Let him see the daylight." So, my older brothers did as they were told to do.

Then the old man said as he lay there, "Daylight, at one time I knew this daylight well. That accounts for my name; they called me Daylight. But nothing can be done to help me, so I am going away. At one time there was a certain food of which I was fond, skunk meat. If you should kill a skunk, cook it and think of me as you do so. Think of me and scatter some tobacco for me. Whatever you want when you do this, it will be granted to you." That is what the old man said. That is the way the old people were; the old people were supposed to be respected. "Respect those old people," mother and father used to say to us. That is what we used to do. We respected the old people, but today they do not respect the old people.

1958

The Chestnut Tree Guarded by the Seven Sisters

Unidentified Seneca[217]

The linguist Jeremiah Curtain (1839-1906), who collected this story at the Cattaraugus Reservation in New York in the late nineteenth century, wrote that: "There are several versions of [this] story. In one version the tree is guarded by geese. The lad entered one of the geese, and as the seven sisters were bathing, he slipped from the goose into the person of the youngest sister, and she thereby became pregnant. Being born of her, he became the master of the chestnuts." Curtain's observation suggests that this story is old and important, perhaps sacred, especially because it is linked with the Seven Sisters, the Pleiades, one of the most revered cold-weather constellations. As they rise in the east, they signal fall and the harvest, here of venison and chestnuts. When they disappear in spring, they are the signal for planting to begin.

Chestnuts and other nuts, called mast, are critical food sources for many animals. Mast was one of the great gifts of the deciduous forest that began covering the Great Lakes region as the climate recovered and warmed from the last glacier. Long before Natives became farmers, they collected, processed, and stored nuts, even though some, such as oak acorns, required much labor to overcome their natural bitterness from tannic

American chestnuts

acid. That a nut so easily collected and made into so nutritious a food as the chestnut should become sacred is logical, but such a rich bounty would be guarded by powerful beings as well. "The Chestnut Tree Guarded by the Seven Sisters" is built around several ancient folktale formulas—a magic bowl that grows larger and larger, celestial guardians, a small underground animal as a helper to humans, and a magic kind of food—but the chestnut is pure North American.

Unfortunately, Chestnut blight killed the North American Chestnut trees in the 1930s. Like the Native peoples, these majestic native trees had no resistance against European diseases, so a food source for millennia vanished in only a few years. There are now attempts to regenerate a moderately disease-resistant variety, but the great forests of chestnuts that once covered the eastern half of North America, giving shelter and food to the beings who resided there, will never return.

In a small lodge, deep in a dense forest, a man lived alone with his nephew. It was the custom of the uncle to cook every day the food required by his nephew, but he never ate with him. There came a time, however, when the little nephew asked his uncle to eat with him. The only reply was, "No; I have already eaten my food." Then, urging his nephew to be quiet, he would remark, "I have cooked this food for you alone."

As the little nephew grew older, he began to wonder at this strange conduct of his uncle. Finally he asked him: "Oh, my uncle, I never see you eat! How is this?" But the uncle made him no reply. So the little nephew decided to try to catch his uncle eating by spying on him. One night after this, when the little nephew had eaten his supper, he said: "Oh, uncle, I am very tired and sleepy. I am now going to bed to get a good rest." With this remark he lay down on his bed and, drawing over him the deerskin cover, soon began to snore as if he were sound asleep.

The wily old uncle waited a while, and then assuming that his nephew was fast asleep, he decided to begin getting his own evening meal. Going to his bed and carefully searching among the skins with which it was covered, he drew forth a small kettle and a very small bundle. Then placing the kettle on the bench near the fire and opening the bundle, he took out of it some substance, a small quantity of which he scraped into the kettle. After putting water into the kettle, he hung it over the fire. When the water began to boil, the old man, taking a wand from its wrappings of skin, began to strike gently on the kettle while he sang the words, "Now, my kettle, I want you to grow in size." Obedient to the words of the song, the kettle began to increase in size, and its contents grew in bulk. Repeating the words and continuing to tap gently on the kettle, the old man watched it becoming larger and larger. He kept up the singing until he decided that the kettle would hold enough of the mush which he was making to satisfy his hunger; then he stopped singing and tapping on the kettle. Carefully replacing the rod, or wand, in its skin wrapping, he removed the kettle from the fire and sat down to eat. After finishing his supper, he carefully washed his kettle; then he shook it until it decreased to the size it was when he took it from the hiding place under the bed, to which place he now returned the rod, the bundle, and the kettle.

The nephew, who was still feigning sleep, was watching his uncle through a hole in the bed covering. He decided to take breakfast with his uncle in the morning, and in order to do this he resolved to arise much earlier than usual. When he arose, however, the youth found that his uncle had finished breakfast and was preparing something for him to eat.

After the uncle had gone out to hunt, the youth brought into the lodge a large quantity of bark to make a good fire. About midday be said to himself: "I am going to be very kind and good. My uncle will be tired when he returns, so I shall have his supper all ready for him. I think that I can prepare it just as he does." For a long time he searched in his uncle's bed for the bundle; at last he found it. On opening it he discovered that it contained a small fragment of a chestnut. Beside the bundle he found the kettle, which was very small. These were the only articles he found under his uncle's bed. He wondered and wondered at what he had discovered, for he could not understand how it was that with this bit of chestnut and the tiny kettle his uncle could make enough mush to feed him. Finally he decided on his course of action, saying to himself: "Well, I must do this exactly as my uncle did. This chestnut must be enough for one more meal."

Kindling a good fire, the youth carefully scraped all the chestnut into the kettle; and then he poured water into the kettle and set it over the fire. Then taking the wand from its skin wrapping, when the water began to boil, he gently tapped on the kettle, saying, "I want you to grow, my kettle." He was so much amused by the increase in size of the kettle that he kept on tapping it and repeating the magical words, until there was hardly room enough in the lodge for him, because the kettle and the mush which it contained had grown so large; so, climbing to the roof, he continued to tap the kettle until it touched the sides of the lodge. He was so busy that he did not see his uncle approaching. The latter from a distance saw him on the roof and watched his actions. As he approached the lodge, he heard the nephew say, "Oh, grow! my kettle. Oh, grow! my little kettle," and then he knew that the youth had discovered everything. This made the uncle very sad and depressed. He called to his nephew: "What have you done now, my nephew?" The youth replied in delight: "Oh, I have so much pudding that we shall have a grand feast." Then he told his uncle everything.

The uncle asked, "Did you use all the chestnut?" The youth replied, "Yes. There was only a small bit here." Thereupon the poor uncle exclaimed: "By doing this you kill me. That is the only kind of food I can eat. I shall die of hunger now. That kind of chestnut does not grow everywhere, and only a person who has great orenda (magic power) can get it."

"Oh, pshaw!" replied the nephew; "I know where there are whole trees full of chestnuts of this kind. I can get a large bagful for you, my uncle. So do not worry."

The uncle, unconsoled, replied: "No, it is not possible for you to do so. This is a bad thing that you have done. This chestnut would have lasted me for years. Now I never can get another; I shall starve to death. I may as well tell you about it, for I must soon die."

Then, shaking the kettle slightly to decrease its size so that he could get into the lodge, the uncle said: "There is but one tree in the world that bears such chestnuts. Seven sisters who are great sorcerers own that tree. Many men have lost their lives in trying to get these chestnuts."

The youth confidently replied, "I am sure that I can get you one."

The uncle answered: "No, you can not. You are yet only a small boy. You would lose your life. These seven women have a great eagle perched upon a very tall tree to watch it. Night and day he guards it. Not a living thing can come near the tree, for if even a man try his utmost, the eagle would discover him and scream out a cry of distress. Thereupon the sisters would come forth and beat the intruder to death no matter who he might be. Men have often taken the forms of various birds and animals to try to deceive them, but so far they have all failed in their attempts. These seven sisters have beaten to death everything that has come near that chestnut tree."

But this kindly advice did not change the youth's resolve to make the attempt to get some of these well-guarded chestnuts. The next morning he said to his uncle, "You must tell me where the tree stands, for I am going to try to find it."

When the fond uncle saw that he could not repress his nephew's desire to go, he replied: "Go toward the rising sun, and after you have passed through the forests intervening, you will come to a large open space. In the middle of this great clearing you will see a very tall tree near which stands a lodge. On the top of this tree sits the eagle with his sharp eyes looking in all directions; and it is in this lodge that the seven sisters dwell."

Taking a bag, the young nephew said: "Now, cheer up, uncle. I will bring you a whole bagful of chestnuts before you have finished eating the pudding in that kettle." With this remark the youth started toward the sunrise. After traveling for some time he killed a deer, which he cut up, filling his bag with the venison.

Finally the nephew came to a place where he began to see through the forests to an opening, whereupon he resolved that he must put forth all his caution and craft. So, having the mole as his fetish,[218] he called out, "Now, my friend, I want you to come to me; come to me, you mole!"

In a short time the leaves began to rustle at his feet, and a mother mole appeared and asked him, "What do you want of me?"

The youth replied: "I have done a great mischief to my uncle by scraping away all his chestnut. Now I want you to help me get more for him. I shall enter your body, and you will carry me underground to that tall tree yonder on which the eagle is sitting. When you are under the tree, thrust out your nose a little so that I can see. I shall have to carry my bag with me. Do you think that you can bear me and it, too?"

The mole answered, "Oh, yes! I can carry all."

After reducing his size magically, the youth entered the body of the mole, and then it made its way to the tree indicated. As the mole arrived directly under the tree, thrusting its nose out of the ground, it said, "The eagle is looking." In a flash the youth, stepping out of the mole, scattered venison all over the ground under the tree. The eagle flew down and began to eat voraciously of the meat. In the meantime the youth stuffed his bag with the chestnuts, which he gathered in handfuls, and just as the eagle was finishing the last morsel, the mole was engaged in carrying the youth with his bag back to the forest. When the meat was all eaten, the eagle uttered a loud scream, and out ran the seven sisters with their clubs. When they saw that the chestnuts were already stolen and that no one was in sight, they fell upon the eagle and beat it until they had nearly killed him.

Arriving in the forest, the youth said to the mole: "Now, I will hide my chestnuts here, and you must then take me back to the lodge of the seven sisters, so I can hear what they say, in order to learn whether they intend to follow us in an attempt to recover the chestnuts."

Having again entered the body of the mole, the youth told it to go under the ground until it came to the lodge. The mole obeyed him literally. When the mole reached the lodge, it thrust out its nose and mouth. The youth then stuck his ear out of its mouth and listened to what was being said in the lodge. He finally overheard one of the sisters say: "It must be a young man just grown. No one has succeeded since his uncle in stealing the chestnuts. Perhaps he has a nephew now who is as crafty as he used to be, and it may be that he, too, is going to live on chestnuts."

Another answered her, saying: "Well, they are stolen. We may as well let them go."

After hearing this last speech, the youth asked the mole to bear him back to the forest at once. After reaching the forest, the youth dismissed the mole with thanks for its aid and then hurried home. When the youth reached home, he found his uncle sitting by the fire, singing his death song, "I must now die of hunger, for my nephew will never return to me."

Then the nephew rushed into the lodge, saying, "Oh, my uncle! I have brought you here a bag full of chestnuts." The old man welcomed his nephew home and gave thanks to their guardian spirits for the latter's success, and he was very, very happy. He is still making chestnut puddings. His nephew became a great hunter. He obtained whatever he desired, because he had the mole for his guardian spirit and aid.

1883-1887

Manabus Frightened by the Birds

Unidentified Menominee

Here Trickster and his grandmother, First Woman, are harvesting fish and nuts for the winter. What sets this story apart is the ending, where Trickster creates the constellation Ursa Major from the pieces of his grandmother's lover, the bear, calling it the Bear's Buttocks. This Ursa Major story celebrates the fall equinox, a time of equal day and night, halfway between the longest day of the year in June and the shortest in December. After the equinox the "handle" of the constellation points up toward the north, leaving the four stars of the "dipper," here the ghost's coffin, pointing down. Thus it resembles a bear walking away on its hind legs. The constellation—and perhaps the story—marked the season to complete harvesting before winter began.

One time Manabus told his grandmother he was going to build a dam to catch fish, so he cut poles and made a dam across the river. When he had made it, he fished nearby and caught great quantities of fish. The old lady was kept busy cleaning and drying them, so she built a shack in which to dry his catches.

At last the news leaked out that Manabus was catching and drying fish, and all the great birds heard and saw it. So they counseled together to go and scare him. They appointed Horned Owl, Long-Eared Owl, Screech Owl, and Bittern, who looks always at the sun.[219] These four were the ones selected to scare Manabus for Manabus was young. They were to take turns in whooping at him, while he was hunting and fishing.

While he was at work, he heard them and never knew or saw who they were. When he heard the first one calling, he threw down his spear and ran home to tell his grandmother. "Grandmother, I have heard a God."

349

Bear's Buttocks

"What way did he call?"

Manabus imitated him.

"Oh, that's only a Horned Owl, Wiwicmianiw, that's what your uncles call him."

So back he went, and soon he heard another noise that scared him and he ran back to tell his grandmother.

"What kind of sound did he make?" and Manabus imitated him. "Oh, that's only Totopa, the Screech Owl, that's what your uncles call him."

When the three owls had tried unsuccessfully to drive off Manabus, the bittern took his turn, and Manabus heard him and ran back for the fourth and last time. "What sound did you hear?"

"*Wi-kum-uk!*" imitated Manabus. "I've heard a powerful God!"

The old woman said, "Yes, sure enough you did hear a great power," and she was frightened too.

Manabus left all his food and started off with his grandmother on his back. When they had traveled a long way off, they stopped and camped. Then the old lady began to pick acorns and prepare them. But she prepared them for her sweetheart, a bear. Manabus did not want to go, but his grandmother coaxed, until finally he went. When he arrived, he noticed his bear grandfather was growling. "Oh my, what's the matter with you? Grandmother sent me here to give this to you," he said, so the bear became quiet.

Manabus stayed there that night with bow and arrows. When they were nearly ready to sleep, they told each other stories. Then Manabus pretended to go to sleep and made no answer to his grandfather. After a while he pretended to have a nightmare.

"Oh grandson, what's the matter with you?"

"Oh grandfather! I've had a vision."

"What did you dream?"

"I just dreamt that they are going to kill both of us with stone-headed lances and when I was ready to fight you'd get in my way or hold me back."

"Oh that's nothing! Go to sleep. It would only have been true if you had dreamt that they used a copper-tipped weapon, then we would have to do something."[220]

Now Manabus was only doing this in order to find out what medicine the bear was afraid of. Manabus watched his grandfather until he fell asleep, then he went out and defecated all around the lodge in different spots. He said to each: "You watch here like a brave warrior and, just before dawn, blow on your war whistle and whoop and begin the attack." When he had surrounded the lodge with these, he took his copper spear and went back to sleep. Just before dawn the clamor of whistles and whooping aroused his grandfather.

"Didn't I tell you so. Here they are!" Manabus grabbed his weapons, feigned to shoot at the door, and pretended to run out, with his grandfather running behind on his hind legs. Then Manabus turned around and shot his copper-tipped arrow right into the old bear, who died. At dawn Manabus skinned and dressed his grandfather. He then started for home with the bear's stomach fat and ate the acorns himself that his grandmother had sent to the bear.

When he got home, his grandmother cried: "My! My! My! Manabus, maybe you ate that yourself," for she saw remnants of the feast between his teeth.

"Oh no, they fed me." Then Manabus said: "My aunts used to boil bones to get the marrow. You ought to do that too."

So his grandmother said, "Yes," and began to crack and split deer bones to boil them for the marrow.

"Another thing my aunts generally do is to dance when it commences to boil, and that makes more marrow come out."

"Yes, all right, if your aunts used to do so, I'll do it." She tied up her dress to dance so Manabus began to sing and rap with a stick. "Grandmother! Grandmother is cooking to get more marrow."

He told his grandmother to keep her eyes closed while dancing. While she was doing that, he dropped his grandfather's fat into the kettle. When the dance was over, she knew what Manabus had done, and they started out to butcher his bear grandfather. "What part of the bear do you prefer?" said Manabus, and he offered her the forequarter.

"Oh no! I don't want that part, for he will scratch me!" She refused the hind quarters, because they would claw her. Then Manabus offered the back, but she was afraid of that. "Well now," said Manabus over and over, "what part will grandmother really accept? Well, won't you? take the head?"

"No, then he will bite me."

"Then take this," and he offered her the spine.

"All right. Your uncles will say in the future that Manabus was liberal in giving his grandmother the backbone of the bear."

Then they started home with their heavy load of the bear's meat. Manabus started first and got home earlier; then he started back and met her and took her load away. "I'll take this away from you and give it back to my uncles," and he threw it upwards, and it became a constellation called "Bears Buttocks" by the Indians today. It is sometimes called the "Ghost's Coffin."

1915

❖ ANIMALS: OUR ELDER BROTHERS ❖

In *Ojibway Heritage,* Basil Johnston teaches that Kitche Manitou, the Great Spirit, created the world in a specific order. First were Father Sun, Grandmother Moon, Mother Earth, stars and northern lights and thunder. Second was the world of plants: trees, flowers, grasses, and fruits. Plants, Johnston teaches, "could exist alone; they were not dependent upon other beings for their existence or well-being." Indeed, plants would give to others—animals and people—and allow life for those creatures to flourish, so they deserved great respect. Gahadondeh (Woodland Border), a Seneca, described the reverence that accompanied the gathering of medicinal herbs:

> He goes into the woods where they grow and builds a small fire. When there is a quantity of glowing embers he stands before it, and as he speaks, at intervals he casts a pinch of tobacco on the coals. He speaks to the spirits of the medicines telling them that he desires their healing virtues to cure his people of their afflictions. "You have said that you are ready to heal the earth," chants the gatherer of herbs, "so now I claim you for my medicine. Give me of your healing virtues to purge and cleanse and cure. I will not destroy you, but plant your seed that you may come again and yield fourfold more. Spirits of the herbs, I do not take your lives without purpose, but to make you the agent of healing, for we are very sick. You have said that all the world might come to you, so I have come. I give you thanks for your benefits and thank the Creator for your gift." When the last puff of tobacco smoke has arisen, the gatherer of herbs begins his work. He digs the plant from the roots and, breaking off the seed stalks, drops the pods into the hole and gently covers them over with fertile leaf mold. "The plant will come again," he says, "and I have not destroyed life but helped increase it. So the plant is willing to lend me of its virtue."

After Kitche Manitou had created the world and the plants, he then turned his attention to animals, the elder brothers of humans. This organization of the world is different from a traditional Judeo-Christian view, where the Bible teaches that animals are servants of people. Perhaps no other single idea illustrates the difference between indigenous and western viewpoints as well as this. Natives believe humans owe respect and reverence to the plants and animals that support human life. Humans are not "masters of the universe," but so weak and helpless they cannot survive without the more important creations that came first. Thus the proper way to approach plants and animals is with humility, not arrogance and selfishness, since failing to treat them with respect means destruction for all.

The Nature of Animals

Basil Johnston (1939-   ), Anishinâbe

Third in the order of creation were the animal beings. There were those who flew, those who swam, those who crawled, and those who walked.

From the very first, all animals possessed a special affinity with Mother Earth and with plants. They lived by the Great Laws, and they somehow had a precognition or preknowledge of events.

Besides this great gift, which all possessed, each species and each individual creature was endowed with unique and singular powers proper to himself and his kind. Each had his sphere on earth, each his own time for the performance and fulfillment of his purpose and powers. Such was the general nature of animal beings.

In the beginning, animals were created without powers. They were required to approach Kitche Manitou on a high mountain to receive his gifts.

The eagle received strong wings, keen sight, and aloofness. His sphere was the mountain and the heights. He was content.

To the hummingbird was given the power of hovering. He was entrusted with tending the flowers and blossoms. As his nourishment the hummingbird was to feed upon the sweet nectars and to share them with the bees. He was content.

Kitche Manitou gave to the vulture flight, and patience, and watchfulness. His task was to keep the meadows clean and the wind pure. He, too, was content.

The bear received strength; the otter, playfulness; the butterfly, beauty; the tadpole, transformation; the dog, a loving nature; the beaver, peace; the wolf, fidelity; the fox, resourcefulness; the owl, care; the deer, grace; the trout, fertility. All animal beings received a portion of the power of Kitche Manitou, and most were content.

Only the wolverine was discontented. When he saw the extent of the gifts of the other animals, he grew envious. Soon he wanted the strength and the size of a bear, the elegance of deer, and the swiftness of the fox. In his increasing disappointment, the wolverine began to despise himself and his gifts and feel bitter at Kitche Manitou. At length, he resolved to return to the mountain top and ask the Master of Life for greater and better gifts.

When the wolverine attained the crest, he boldly called out, "Kitche Manitou! Hear me! You have not been just to me. You have not been just to all the animals. To some you have given greater scope and a greater measure of gifts. By this uneven distribution you have made some great and some less."

More audacious, the wolverine continued, "I demand that you redress this great wrong. For myself, I wish more strength, more comeliness, more speed."

But Kitche Manitou's thunderous voice broke through the selfish list of wolverine. "To each animal being I have given sufficient power for the fulfillment of his being and form. The power I have conferred on each is a form of my power and is a reflection of my gifts.

"No injustice has been done. If you have not developed and fostered the gifts I have presented to you, it is you who have perpetrated an injustice upon yourself. You have betrayed yourself. For your presumption, you shall wander alone and despised. And for your refusal to develop your attributes you will, henceforth, feed upon what has been left over by your fellow creatures who have nurtured their talents. Go!"

Wolverine left the mountain top more bitter and envious than before. He had not been daunted by Kitche Manitou himself!

As Kitche Manitou ordained, so the wolverine became solitary, vicious, and avoided. Hungry ever, he must feed upon the portions left by other animals.

Very different was the manner of the snake upon receiving his form and powers. Legless, armless, and wingless, he nevertheless kept the little plants in the fields and meadows safe. Not once did he complain of his condition or covet the better fortune of others. Cheerful and satisfied he made the most of his least of powers.

Unfortunately for the poor snake and his brothers, there were rabbits, the most mischievous of creatures. While the snakes could repel the smaller rodents from the gardens, they were unable to discourage the fleet and numerous rabbits. The ordeal for the snakes began not out of evil or malice on the part of the rabbits, but arose out of the playful dispositions of the long-eareds and their voracious appetites.

The rabbits ate and ate. Try as they might the snakes were unable to prevent the rabbits from destroying plants and gardens. Instead of selecting a few succulent leaves from each plant, so that more leaves could grow and the plants benefit, the greedy rabbits ate all the leaves, the stalks, the flowers, and often the roots as well. They stripped the bark from seedling trees. No plant was safe from them. The snakes warned and fought as best they could; the rabbits merely snickered and ate some more.

Discovering that snakes were feeble, the rabbits made sport of them. In play the rabbits pulled their tails, sat on them, dragged them around, and even tossed them in the air. The snakes were helpless; they suffered injuries and indignities. In their grief and to bring their torments to an end, the snakes pleaded with the rabbits to stop. It was useless.

At last, wearying of the abuse heaped upon them, the snakes called upon Kitche Manitou for help.

They went to the Mountain of Gifts where they called out to Kitche Manitou, "Hear us, Kitche Manitou! We are oppressed. The rabbits have inflicted harms and insults upon us. We are defenceless against them; we cannot fulfill our duties to the plant beings. Kitche Manitou, help us!"

Kitche Manitou took pity on the poor snakes. He gave some of them venom and to others the ability to wrap themselves tightly around creatures and crush them. He warned them: "Do not abuse the power I have given to you. Use it as a last resort; use it properly. Before resorting to poison, warn your enemies, and perhaps, by a threat, you can avoid destroying other creatures."

The snakes thanked Kitche Manitou for the additional gifts and then returned to their homes.

Before long the other animal beings learned of the potency of the snake.

A rabbit was in a merry mood. Watched by his brothers, he began to tease the snake who was busy guarding corn.

It began harmlessly enough. Rabbit blocked the snake's way, pulled at his tail, and nipped him behind the head. Such treatment did not hurt the snake but prevented him from carrying out his duties and gave insult to his dignity as a guardian. Still, he said nothing. Soon the merriment grew abusive.

Rabbit cuffed and then picked up the snake and tossed him into the air. The snake fell to the ground dazed and bleeding.

"That's enough. No more," the snake hissed, rattling his tail in anger.

Rabbit laughed; the other rabbits chortled. "An empty threat. Threats ought not to be made by one incapable of carrying them out," smirked the rabbit as he darted toward the coiled snake.

The snake lashed out and sank his fangs deep into the rabbit's nose. Rabbit jumped back, reeled, and fell to the ground. He moved no more. The other watching rabbits fled in terror.

Such stories reflect the composite nature of all animal beings. Each member is made up of two substances: one corporeal; the other, incorporeal. The scope and nature of the soul-spirit of an animal is expressed in his mood and temperament. Perhaps deeper than this is the certain belief that the power of a creature was an extension of Kitche Manito's powers conferred in an animal creature.

The animal beings lived in concord with the laws of the world. Initially, they lived in harmony with one another and with all beings, subject to the same laws of nature. It is said they understood one another.

Man's Dependence on Animals

When the world was flooded, all the land animals perished; only the fishes and birds and animals who lived in the water survived.

With their prescience and preknowledge, the animals sensed the supernatural conception of man in the spirit of woman. It was their feeling of compassion for the spirit woman that prompted the animals to invite her down to rest upon the turtle's back. Even the smallest and the least of the animals, the muskrat, served. When all the others failed, the muskrat brought back from the bottom of the sea the small portion of soil requested by the spirit woman. Without the animal, the world would not have been; without the animals the world would not be intelligible.

At birth man was helpless. Again it was the animals who assisted the spirit woman in nourishing the newborn infants by bringing fruits, vegetables, berries, and drink, while the birds and butterflies brought joy.

That winter, when food was scarce and the winds cold, the animals sheltered man. The bear, who loved the newborn beings, offered his flesh so that the Anishnabeg would survive. Following the example of the bear, the deer, moose, porcupine, beaver, ground hog, grouse, and goose, and almost every animal being offered himself to sacrifice.

Even when the first man and woman were fully grown and had many descendants, the animals continued to serve. Man relied on the creatures for all his needs. He did not work because there was no need for labour. Life was easy. More and more the Anishinabeg relied upon the animals. And as life was easy for mankind, it was difficult for the animal beings. The animals' burdens became more onerous.

Men and women understood the utterances of the animals; the animals understood man. It was this mutual understanding that enabled man to impose greater burdens upon his brothers. What was worse, man set animal against animal.

Instead of doing his own fishing, man dispatched a loon or a kingfisher to catch fish for him. If he wanted a rabbit, man would send an eagle or a hawk; if he wanted a partridge, he would send a fox; if he wanted the sap of trees, he ordered the woodpecker to drill holes in the trees for him; if he wanted a new lodge, he commanded the beaver and the porcupine to fell the trees. The animals did all the work; man did none.

For a long time the animals served without complaint. But what was worse than burdens was the apparent indifference of the Anishnabeg to the needs of the animals themselves. Little could be collected and stored to keep them during the long winter, and what was set aside was often taken by man. Service brought poverty.

At last, weary of service, the animals convened a great meeting to gain their freedom. All came at the invitation of the courier.

The bear was chosen to be the first speaker and to act as chairman of the session. He explained the purpose of the meeting. "We are met to decide our destiny. We have been oppressed far too long by man. He has taken our generosity and repaid us with ingratitude; he has taken our labours and repaid us with servitude; he has taken our friendship and fostered enmity among us.

"Either we continue to serve him or we withhold our labours. Are we to continue to serve? We shall come to an end. If we deny our labours, we shall live. Should you choose the former, you must resign yourselves to your fate. Should you prefer the latter, then you must consider the manner by which it is to be accomplished. Consider carefully."

The bear had scarcely finished when the groundhog shouted out, "I am for man's death. We have suffered enough. The Anishnabeg have killed us; they have been unkind; and they have subjected us. Only with the death of man will these injustices cease. Man must die."

"Hey! Hey! Let him die," concurred the animals.

"I am for life. I am for mercy," said the dog on rising. "While it is true that man has been unkind, he has not been unkind to all. There are many in this company who have not suffered. The cat, the vulture, the whippoorwill, the frog, the butterfly, the mouse, the hummingbird have, all of them, lived and worked and rested without harm. To them man has been kind. Perhaps he has been somewhat thoughtless. Is this a good reason to wish him dead? Man does not deserve death; he deserves to live, even as we live."

"Hey! Hey! Let him live," chorused the dog's supporters.

The wolverine rose to his feet, visage dark and threatening. "Let the Anishinabeg neither live or die, but let him suffer. If you have suffered at man's hand, you are partly to blame, for he who allows himself to be servile deserves servitude. He bears as much guilt as he who subjects. Man is not entirely to blame and ought not pay the entire penalty for your folly." As he sat down, the wolverine taunted, "And if man is to die who will kill him?"

The meeting buzzed with the consternation of the animals. Questions were asked, "If man is to die, who will kill him?"

All the animals looked at one another, but not one spoke to answer this final question. "Bear, will you kill him?" asked the wolverine sardonically

"Yes! The bear! He is strong and brave," shouted the animals.

The bear cringed, turning somewhat grey. "I am too slow. I am unwilling. There are too few of us," he replied to excuse himself.

"Then the wolves must do it. They are fast and strong," offered the wolverine.

Not expecting to be named, the startled wolves managed to sputter, "We cannot, and we dare not. Man is too clever."

"Cowards!" jeered the wolverine. "The rattlesnake shall do it."

But the rattlesnakes refused, saying, "We are too slow. Man is too swift. We are not big enough."

While the debate raged, a dog stole away from the meeting. A vigilant wolf spied him and trailed him.

The debate continued and became a clamour. The bear, realizing that nothing could be resolved with opinion divided and feelings heated, called the meeting to order. "We cannot kill man. He is too strong, too many, and too cunning. Nor should we want to kill him or injure him. He, too, is entitled to life and well being. We can resolve our state without man's death."

It was at this time that the wolf dragged the errant dog into the meeting and near the central fire.

Without waiting to be asked to speak, the wolf angrily shouted above the din. The whimpering of the dog and the ululating snarl of the wolf instilled silence.

"This dog has betrayed us. He must be punished. A little while ago he made off almost unnoticed. But I saw him and followed. He went directly to the village of the Anishnabeg and divulged what we were discussing. This one and all the dogs must be punished."

The assembled animals were outraged. They seized the dogs and began to pummel them. But though the bear was as outraged as his brothers, he maintained his composure. He thundered out, "Brothers, it is too late. To kill the dogs would be without purpose and substance. Rather let him endure his servitude. Let him serve man. Let him hunger. Let him hunt for man. Let him guard man. Let him know man's fickleness."

Turning to the dog, the bear speaking on behalf of his brothers said, "For your betrayal, you shall no longer be regarded as a brother among us. Instead of man, we shall attack you. Worse than this, from now on you shall eat only what man has left, sleep in the cold and rain, and receive kicks as a reward for your fidelity."

The bear turned again to the crowd. "To make it difficult for man to enslave us again, no longer will we speak the same language. Instead we shall speak in different languages. From now on we shall live to ourselves, for ourselves. Let men learn to fend for themselves without our help."

With that the meeting broke up, and the animals went their separate ways.

Man was dependent upon the animals for his food, clothing, and tools; man was also dependent upon animals for knowledge of the world, life, and himself.

There is in animals a unique capacity to sense the changes of the world, the alteration of seasons, and the coming state of things. Man does not have the preknowledge possessed by bluebird, or trout, or squirrel. For man to prepare, he looked to his elder brothers.

Eagles, geese, and robins knew of the advent of autumn and would leave for the south. The squirrels sensed the quality of the coming winter and in preparation played less, stored large quantities of provisions, and made deep dells. What bees sensed dictated how high or how low they built their nests, and how much honey they would produce. Bluebirds and robins knew when to return to their summering grounds. Men did not possess this facility. Not having it, they had to find preknowledge through the animal beings.

* * *

Animals were more than flesh for food, more than the reflections of coming changes, and more than images of character. They were living beings entitled to life and existence. But for men to live, the animal beings had to die.

To acknowledge their dependence upon the animal beings for almost all aspects of life, the Anishnabeg included them in almost all their stories.

Such was the totality of that dependence that the Anishnabeg related stories of the disappearance of animals and tried to conceive the consequences that would follow. Perhaps the annual departure of animals prompted such stories. Even if this were the case, the fact remains that with the departure of the animal beings, the quality and the tone of life changed.

For some inexplicable reason the deer, the moose, and the caribou once vanished from the land of the Anishnabeg. With their going, the life of the Anishnabeg was not what it had been. To restore the quality of life the Anishnabeg went in search of them.

Assisted by the other animal beings whose state of being, too, had been altered, the Anishnabeg roamed the world in quest of the vanished animals. An owl, who had gone north more in search of rest than labour, came upon the herd confined in an immense enclosure as if imprisoned. Yet they seemed quite content, grazing upon the spruces, pines, cedars, and balsams.

Curious, the owl flew down to a low-hanging branch to question the deer. But as he alighted upon the branch, a flock of crows attacked him and drove him from the country. The owl barely got away. That it was night, no doubt, enabled the owl to escape. The owl left the land as fast as he could.

Back in the land of the Anishnabeg, the owl reported his discovery immediately. The Anishnabeg speedily organized a large war party to rescue the imprisoned deer. Owl guided the expedition.

When the war party arrived at the very gates of the enclosure, it was attacked by a vast flock of fierce crows. Days of battle followed with neither side victorious. The Anishnabeg fought ferociously; the crows stormed relentlessly. But at no time during the conflict did the deer attempt to escape; they simply looked on in curiosity. Their seeming indifference dismayed the invaders.

Discouraged, the Anishnabeg asked for a truce. The crows granted the request and looked on smugly as the chief of the Anishnabeg addressed the deer. "Why are you unconcerned with our efforts to rescue you from your enforced confinement? We have endured hardship and risked death on your behalf. Still you appear indifferent."

The chief of the deer replied, "You have assumed wrongly that we are here against our wishes. On the contrary, we choose to remain here and are quite content. The crows have treated us better than you have ever treated us when we shared the same country with you."

"How did we offend you?" asked the chief, astonished.

The deer chief spoke quickly and sadly. "You have wasted our flesh; you have despoiled our haunts; you have desecrated our bone; you have dishonoured us and yourselves. Without you we can live. But without us, you cannot live."

"How shall we make amends? Know that our seeming indifference was not ill will. How shall we atone for your grief? Tell us," said the Anishinabe chief.

Again the deer chief spoke. "Honour and respect our lives, our beings, in life and in death. Do what you have not done before. Cease doing what offends our spirits."

The chief promised, and the crows released the deer, the moose, and the caribou from their bondage. The animals who had been in captivity willingly followed the Anishnabeg back to their homeland.

This and similar stories reflect a recurring theme in the life of the Anishnabeg and their outlook.

> All life must be honoured.
> The quality of life for one order depends upon another.
> Take life but not in anger.
> Life for one means death for another.
> By honouring death, life itself is honoured.
> Animal beings deserve life. They deserve honour.

Many animal beings quit the land for the winter; life changed for the Anishnabeg. From this annual circumstance and from the periodic disappearance of animals began many customs and practices connected with the taking of game. There were prayers said or thought at the death of an animal being, prayers that expressed sorrow and need and apology.

Prayer to a Deer Slain by a Hunter

I had need.
I have dispossessed you of beauty, grace, and life.
I have sundered your spirit from its worldly frame.
No more will you run in freedom because of my need.

I had need.
You have in life served your kind in goodness.
By your life, I will serve my brothers.
Without you I hunger and grow weak.
Without you I am helpless, nothing.

I had need.
Give me your flesh for strength.
Give me your casement for protection.
Give me your bones for my labours
And I shall not want.

Not only was the primacy of animal beings acknowledged in prayer, it was memorialized in the instruments of ceremony. Attached to the sacred Pipe of Peace were the plumes of the eagle and the tegument (skin) of animal. Each of the four orders of life and being were represented in ritual. Only when the four orders were present was the instrument complete and the ceremony fulfilled. Without the four dimensions there was no unity.

In the Midéwewin, animal beings and the world of animal beings were represented. Often animal beings were represented as contraries, or contradictions. One time the bear represented good; another, he imaged evil. This portrayed a fact of being and life, that there are two aspects to everything, appearing as opposites. Birth and death, youth and old age, day and night, man and woman, water and fire, wind and rock, sadness and joy, triumph and defeat, body and soul-spirit, good and evil. That life and being are paradoxical is stated in prayer and tangibly represented in the Midéwewin.

The *tegument* of ermine constitutes an essential portion of the medicine bag. By it the medicine man or woman is reminded that the knowledge of the curative properties of plants comes through animals.

For the third order members of the Midéwewin who practised the *jeesekeewin* (*jiisakiwin*: communion with the incorporeal world), the turtle symbolized the celerity of thought and the means by which the different dimensions and orders of beings communicated.

Other animal beings were similarly honoured in prayer and ritual. At the practical level, animals were respected in the following ways:

Female animals with young were spared. Only males were to be taken.
Young were to be allowed to grow.
A pair of animal beings were to be allowed to live to insure continuation of life.
The bones of game were to be used, not wasted. The bones of fish were not to be cast into the water.

Such was the way the Anishnabeg endeavoured to honour the life, death, and knowledge of the animal beings. Men and women called them "Our Elder Brothers."

1976

One, Two, Three
Dawendine (The Dawn, Bernice Loft Winslow, 1902-†), Mohawk

This is the story of three field-mice who became my true friends. I named them Anskyah, Dekani, Ahssenh, the Mohawk words for one, two, three (*enhskat, tekeni, ashen*). This is how it began:

Outside our log home on the Six Nations Reserve was a shed. Here, in a cupboard off the dirt floor, were stored milk, cream, butter, and other foods, because it kept them quite cold. From rafters would hang a dressed fowl or two and, at times, small strings of braided corn. Sometimes there were bunches of herbs, used for medicines or seasoning foods.

Two or three steps led from the door of the house into this storage shed. Nearby was another door in this outer room, which led to the out-of-doors. Here, there was just a low sill.

On this lovely September morning I was getting breakfast for my father, the Chief. Going to the outside cupboard for cream for his porridge, I was surprised by what I saw. The squat pitcher of cream had been churned almost into butter and peering from it were two little blinking coal-black eyes. On the whiskers and eye-lashes were bits of cream, but the body was covered. I thought, "No cream for father's porridge today." Then I thought, "How you must have wanted to live, my little friend!" There must be a reason or purpose for this. I knew the little mouse must have struggled all night to have reduced the cream to this state and must have been too weary to try and get out. Why was she looking for food so desperately?

Now I heard my father's voice calling to me, wondering what had kept me so long. I asked him to come and, as he stood in the door-way looking down at me, I showed him the pitcher. His amused, gentle smile showed me he knew what I was thinking. His only remark was, "Do you think we shall be over-run with mice?"

But, as we took the pitcher inside and breakfast was forgotten, he helped me wash the little creature with lukewarm water and cotton, cleansing the little eyes, too. Then the oven door of the wood stove was let down, and I placed the mouse there in warm cotton, in a small woven basket, to dry off. While the mouse was drying off in the basket, and father had had his breakfast, I kept thinking and wondering: "Why had this mouse made such a heroic struggle to live?" I felt there must be a reason. For the time being, all my chores were forgotten.

When the little creature was dry, I was moved to take the basket and put the mouse on the ground at my feet, as I sat on the lower step in the shed. Then I watched the mouse make its way slowly, painfully to the door-sill and over it. Going to the door, I saw her creep around the corner of another small, brick-lined storage building. It was here that my mother used to keep the churn for making butter out of cream. Now it was used to keep cool the big earthen crocks of food. Around this building the mouse made its way very slowly, and I went quietly back to sit on the step and wait.

I sat there for some time, thinking, thinking about the mouse. Then, to my amazement, the mouse returned, holding in her mouth one of the tiniest mouse babies I had ever seen—a tiny, hairless pink body, less than an inch long, with unopened eyes. Only then did I realize the reason for her great struggle. On she came, over the sill, so very slowly still, and there, between my feet, she released the little baby. I sat, unmoving. Then she turned and resumed the same slow journey outside, while I watched and waited. After a long while she returned again, this time with two babies clinging to her breasts. This was an epic journey I was witnessing, for once when she paused, I saw her tiny heaving chest, and at times, her body almost fell over, but she would right herself and keep on. Some instinct, however, must have made her babies not loose their hold. Very, very slowly, she kept coming toward me until finally she reached my feet, and there she fell over and died. I carefully detached the two small babies and placed them in the basket with the first one. But as I looked down at the mother, something inside me broke in worship of such heroism. I knew, also, that I was committed to raise her children. I wondered and marveled at the love this little mother had for her babies and the trust she had placed in me in return for the kindness she had received.

So, after suitably burying the little mother's body, I took her children in the basket inside the house, keeping them warm with cotton heated in the oven, I dipped my finger in warm milk and held it beside the tiny mouths. To my great surprise, they were able to take the nourishment. I kept on with this for a few days. Later on, with a very small eye-dropper, I was able to get them to take more. In a few weeks they could eat oatmeal gruel with the milk.

I watched them as they grew, day by day, until they were eating some cereals and crushed grain. Finally, after some weeks, they were able to play about the house but always returned to their basket for rest. I had gathered milkweed silk and thistle downs to line their wee bed. By now I had learned to love these dainty creatures with their erect deer-like ears tipped with black. I loved their grey white-chested bodies, contrasted with the black shoulders, ending with long, graceful tails.

My father, in kindly amusement, watching my devotion to the wild babies, asked me one morning if I had named them. It was then we decided to name them in Mohawk, One, Two, Three.

Behind our wood-burning stove was a box in which we stored firewood. Now extra care had to be taken in replenishing the supply for this box, since any skittering noise here told us the babies were exploring. We knew a careless move could crush them.

What mischief my family got into was both amusing and unpredictable. After a quiet interval one day I missed them. Then I noticed movement inside the cloth top of our flour bag. So I knew where they were. What a sight met my eyes! Three small figures, almost resembling sculptures, were covered with the white flour we use for baking bread. To wash them meant I would have dough-like images. I had to find a brush with soft-enough bristles to clean them off without hurting them.

A few days later, the sound of falling baking pans told me they were exploring the cupboard. I looked to see one small body in an over-turned pan and two pairs of eyes looking at me from the side of the other pans. This escapade resulted in an over-turned box of rolled oats, which was easily swept up.

What fanatic care was taken not to leave the oven door of the hot stove open, lest they would be burned. They loved, also, to explore the tufts of the corn-husk mats just inside the doors, so extra care had to be used in opening or closing these entrances. However, their great curiosity for everything only endeared them to us the more.

To my great surprise, our faithful, gentle, old watch-dog of uncertain lineage took this family addition very casually. One small mouse, perched atop his shoulder, bothered him not at all, nor the two resting between his paws. He just stared at them until he fell asleep.

When night came, I placed their little basket at the foot of my bed. While there was still light, they scampered over my pillows and coverlet. When I blew out my lamp, they ran back to the basket until morning.

Some time later, I realized that these little mice must be returned to their natural home. They had made a joy of my life for a short period and made a great impression upon me. It will always amaze me that such a tiny creature of the wild had recognized kindness and had placed so much trust in me to take over the care of her babies. It seemed as if the Great Spirit had spoken to me, that this was my task. We, the mouse and I, were a part of all life. The mouse mother had known kindness and love and, in return, had placed joy and love in my hands.

Finally one day, with both happiness and regret, I put the babies in a basket and started across some meadows towards the woods. I looked back at the places where they had romped, and this was the happiness. My regret was to lose them, but I knew they belonged to the wild. So there beside the woods, in some deep meadow grasses, I left them, with a little prayer to the Great Spirit for their welfare and happiness.

c.1940s

White-footed mouse

Waikun: A Fable

Chashchunka (*Tcactcâka*: Wave, Peter Sampson), Ho-Chunk

Once there were some mice under a crooked log, and they believed they were the only people in the whole world. One of them, standing up and stretching his little arms, could just touch the underside of the log. He thought that he was very tall and that he touched the sky. So he danced and sang this song:

Mo-zhun-na-le,	Throughout the world
Pe-zhe ya-ki-ske shun-non-nink na-gi-kche!	Who is there like little me! Who is like me?
Mo-zhun-na-le,	Throughout the world
Pe-zhe ya-ki-ske shun-non-nink na-gi-kche!	Who is there like little me! Who is like me?
Ne-sha-na ma-chi-nik-gla ya-ki-o-o!	I can touch the sky, I touch the sky
	I can touch the sky, I touch the sky indeed!

c.1910

How Graywolf Became Guardian of the World
David Lee Smith (1950-   ), Winnebago

Nebraska Winnebago tribal historian David Lee Smith describes this tale as a legend, that is, a story that has been passed down through the generations but is not a sacred story. Himself an oral traditionalist—a storyteller who retells stories that may be hundreds of years old—Smith here relates the story of the four wolves, their powers, and the gifts they give to humanity. But it is only Graywolf, because he is willing to go to war, who receives the greatest powers and becomes the protector of mankind. Humans and wolves are the two most widely distributed species on earth and once competed for the same food, but Natives respected wolves because of their intelligence, loyalty to each other, and hunting abilities. They were, indeed, elder brothers who were better than humans in nearly every respect.

At the time of Creation, Ma-ona (Mą'úna: Earthmaker) made four brothers, Green Wolf, Black Wolf, White Wolf, and Gray Wolf. These four brothers at first roamed the surface of the world, but three brothers went beneath the earth and are still there, appearing to Wolf clan people occasionally. Gray Wolf is the only one that is seen above the ground.

Ma-ona named the green wolf Kera-co-ra (Kératcóra: Blue Sky). This wolf was in charge of the day. The second wolf that Ma-ona created was the black wolf, who was in charge of the night. His name was Shunk-cank-sep-ka (Cúnk-tsánk Sep-ga: wolf-black-one who). The third wolf carried the name of Shunk-cank-ska (Cúnk-tsánk Ská: wolf-white), or White Wolf. This wolf was in charge of all things sacred. The last wolf that Ma-ona created was Hin-rhoc-ka (Hina-xótc-ga: fur-gray-one), the gray-haired wolf. His duty was the protection of mankind. This is the legend of the four wolves.

There was once an old man who lived all alone except for the company of four dogs. These dogs kept him company and supplied him with friendship in his elder years.

One day, while out picking berries, the old man fell and broke his ankle. As the days went by, he became so hungry that he started to eat his bear rugs because he could not hunt for his food. This brought some concern to the dogs. One night, while the old man slept, the dogs held council. The first dog said, "We should go hunt for our master, for he is very hungry." The second dog cut in and said, "No! No! He was always unkind to us and treated us like dogs." This brought a laugh from the third dog, "Ha ha, we are dogs, you fool, that is why Ma-ona created us with four legs and a tail." After the laughter died down, the fourth dog said, "Our brother is right, it is our duty to hunt for our master, for he has kept us with him through all our young years." So it was agreed on that they would go hunting the next morning.

At daybreak, all four dogs left, but first dog was the only one who came back with food. The old man blessed him and called him Kera-co-ra and gave him powers to hunt during the day. Not to be outdone, the second dog left during the night and brought back to the old man some food by morning time. So the second dog was blessed by its master and named Shunk-cank-sep-ka. He was given powers to hunt during the night.

The third dog saw what his master had done to his brothers, and he decided to outdo both of them. With sacred herb and the wood of the cedar tree, the third dog eased the old man's pain and fixed his leg.

The master was very pleased and made him in charge of everything that is sacred. He named the third dog, Shunk-cank-ska.

The only dog that wasn't given any power was the fourth dog, and all his brothers looked down on him because of this. One day, while out hunting for himself, the fourth dog spotted a large war party coming. He knew his brothers could not help him because first dog was out hunting, second dog was sleeping, and third dog was praying. Therefore, fourth dog attacked the war party himself.

All day the battle raged, and at sundown the enemy retreated. The fourth dog went back to his master's lodge to lick his wounds. Seeing that he was hurt, the master said, "Anything wrong?" The fourth dog said, "No, master, for I am going to sleep." The next day, the fourth dog again left and battled the war party. And for the next two days after, he did the same thing. At the end of the fourth day, the enemy was all killed. All this fighting brought a change over Fourth Dog. He became wild and mean.

The master, finally seeing what he did, said, "Fourth Dog, from this day forward, I will give you special powers to hunt both day and night and powers to be unafraid of anything." After blessing him, the master said, "Your job now is to run the wilds, for I am going home to Ma-ona, and you will be the protector of mankind from this day forward." As a parting gesture, the old master placed Fourth Dog's brothers beneath the earth. They would become protectors of the underworld.

From time to time, humans call on White Wolf, who always brings them good luck. Hunters call on Green Wolf, who brings them good luck hunting during the day. The night people call on Black Wolf, who guards their camp during the night. But Gray Wolf is free, and his call is always heard the world over, for he is the mightiest wolf of them all. He is the protector of the human race.

1997

The Dogs of the Chief's Son
John Bear, Ho-Chunk

This story has been retold many times; it is linked to "How Graywolf Became Guardian of the World," since Black-Dog is revealed as a *cunktcenk wilukana* (*cúnk-tsánk wirúkana*: wolf-ruler), or wolf spirit, perhaps originally the same wolf Ma-ona put in charge of the night. The lesson is that man must trust the four-leggeds and must put their needs first if his own are to be met. There is humor here as well; notice that Spotted-dog won't move without being fed and resents being treated like a dog. Some nations went further in their beliefs about dogs. This small Onondaga story is an example:

> Men should be good to their dogs, for kindness is due to those that aid us, and if they are unkind, there may be a penalty. There is an abyss between us and the land of souls, and over this two dogs hold a log by their teeth. Over this log, if fortunate, the soul passes to the happy hunting grounds. If voices are heard saying, "He fed us, he sheltered us, he loved us," then the dog at each end grips hard with his teeth, holding the log with all his might, and the soul passes safely over. But if the voices say, "He starved us, he beat us, he drove us away," then, when he is halfway over, the dogs let go, and he falls into the depths of woe.

365

Once a Ho-Chunk chief had one son who had two dogs. One was a black dog, and the other was spotted black and white. One day the chief's son went hunting. His father advised him not to take his wife. "If anything happens to you, don't come home without her," the chief said, "for then the people would despise you." But the chief's son took his wife and the two dogs with him.

They came to the hunting place and set up a lodge there. It was the fall of the year. Although the man hunted constantly, he had no success. There came a light snowfall. "Now the hunting ought to be good," the man thought. But there was no sign of any game. Every day he hunted all day long but got nothing. The supply of food was getting very low.

The chief's son loved his two dogs very much. He awoke in the middle of the night. There was a noise: it was someone talking. He had never heard those voices before. Then he realized that the two dogs were talking together. He could understand every word they said. Black Dog was older and larger than Spotted-Dog. Black Dog said, "Younger brother, I have failed to help find any game. You are younger than I am. Why don't you try to find something? Our brother the chief's son needs help."

Spotted Dog said, "Oh, I could find something if I wanted to for his sake, but our sister-in-law—his wife—treats me badly. I am sorry, but I don't feel like helping. She treats me like a dog!"

Then Black Dog said, "You are always thinking of yourself. How about our older brother? He's always treated us very well. We should scare up some game so they won't go hungry."

"Well," said Spotted Dog, "I could do that easily if he would give me the rest of the food they have, but I'm hungry myself. I can't hunt without food."

The man awoke at daylight. He roused his wife and told her to prepare what remained of their food supply. She did as she was told. When it was cooked, the man told her to put it in a bowl. She did this and brought it to him. Then he cooled the food, stirring it with a spoon, after which he gave it to the two dogs. Then the man spoke to the dogs. He said, "Brothers, since you have lived with me I have always treated you right. I have taken good care of you and brought you up to be my companions. The food we had is all gone, and I am giving the last of it to you now. I won't eat a bite of it. I wish that you would go and find some more food, so that we can eat again. I am hungry now." Then he gave the food to the dogs, and they ate it all.

After eating, the dogs left the lodge. Immediately Spotted Dog ran away. Soon they heard him barking a short distance from the camp. The man had hunted at that spot many times and caught nothing. This time, however, he saw that Spotted Dog had found a very large bear. They killed the bear right in his nest, but the bear was so large that they could not pull him out. The man called his wife to help, and they got the bear out. It was still early in the morning, so she cooked some bear meat for their breakfast. The dogs also were fed again. After that they hunted again. Spotted Dog located another bear, and the chief's son killed a deer. From that time on they found plenty of game and dried it on a rack for safe keeping.

Once again the chief's son awoke in the middle of the night. Again he heard the dogs talking together. Black Dog spoke to his younger brother. "There is a fire coming this way," he said, but he was really talking about an enemy. "You can run faster than I can, younger brother. You should go spy on them."

"All right, I can do that," said Spotted Dog, "but I would like to have something to eat before I go."

So the man got up and built a fire. Then he told his wife to prepare some food. When it was ready, he gave the food to the dogs.

After eating, Spotted Dog started out. He traveled for four nights and then came upon the enemy. He heard the leader say that they were going after a man, his wife, and two dogs. The dog hurried back to the chief's son. Using his spirit power, he was able to make the journey more quickly and arrived home just before daylight. He told the man that the enemy was four days distant. "They are coming after us," he said.

The chief's son then said to Spotted Dog, "Take the news back to the village."

Spotted Dog said, "All right, but first give me something to eat." So the man fed him again.

The village was also four days' journey away. Spotted Dog arrived there in one morning. The people knew that the chief's son had two dogs. They were alarmed to see only one dog return. They thought that all had been killed but this dog. Spotted Dog entered the chief's lodge. He licked the chief's hands and whined. The chief could not understand what the dog was trying to say. The chief sent for an old woman who was blessed by the spirit of a dog and who was able to converse with dogs. She talked with Spotted Dog and said to him, "Your people are anxious to know why you returned home all alone. Have your brothers and sisters been killed by an enemy?"

Spotted Dog said, "I have been trying to tell them, but they do not understand me. Stranger enemies are coming. I was sent here to get you to come and help my brothers. They are waiting there for the enemy to come. Give me something to eat, and I shall return to help them. Follow my tracks, and you will be guided to the place where they are."

The chief sent two town criers to tell all the people. They made preparations and started right away. Each man took extra moccasins with him. Spotted Dog finished eating and started on his return journey. He arrived there that same day. Since they lacked his spirit power, the war party arrived two days later. Spotted Dog spied on the enemy to find out just where they were. Black Dog said, "Our enemy's dream will not come true. I have more power than they have."

When the reinforcements arrived, they were given plenty of food from the hunter's supplies. Then they prepared to fight. There was snow on the ground. Spotted Dog said that the enemy would come the next morning. A great number of the enemy were approaching, so the people set a trap for them and hid on either side of the approach to the camp. The dogs were to give the signal to start fighting because the enemy would pay no attention to the dogs.

As soon as the enemy came within the wings of the trap, the dogs cried four times as instructed.[221] Then those lying in wait started to shoot. The enemy knew then that they were trapped. They were tired from their long journey. Those attacking them had had plenty of food and rest and were fresh for the battle. That is why they killed the enemy easily. Then the victors started for home. They carried with them all the meat supplies and the scalps of the enemy.

From that time on the two dogs were very useful. Black Dog used to know when an enemy was coming, and Spotted Dog acted as a spy. He was also clever at hunting.

When Black Dog grew very old, he said to Spotted Dog, "Brother, I am going to leave you. I urge you to remain with our brother, the chief's son, and to help him as long as you live. When you, too, are ready to go, you must come to the place where I will dwell." Black Dog was actually the wolf spirit.

*c.*1932

HUNTING

They That Chase After the Bear

Unidentified Meskwaki

This story, an ancient one that has been told around the northern reaches of the world for millennia, describes how the constellation Ursa Major serves as a calendar and a clock. In northern latitudes, where it never drops below the horizon, it serves as a clock, making a circle around the North Star every twenty-four hours. The changing position of these stars relative to the horizon and to the Corona Borealis throughout the year forms the calendar. In the story, the Great Bear stars move from the northeast in late fall to overhead in the spring and to the northwest in late summer. As one looks north in May, the bear seems to be climbing out of her den, the Corona Borealis, a higher part-circle of stars. As the season progresses and the bear gets fatter, ready for hibernation, the star bear seems to be falling on her back. In midwinter, she's lying on her back when the den appears in the east. The story begins in early winter at the fall equinox and moves through the seasons as the hunters and their puppy, sometimes identified as Alcor, the faintest star in the constellation, chase a bear who eventually takes them all into the sky. The Seneca call these stars Niágwai' Hades'he' (Nyakwai' Hatis'he'), or Bear They Pursuing Are.

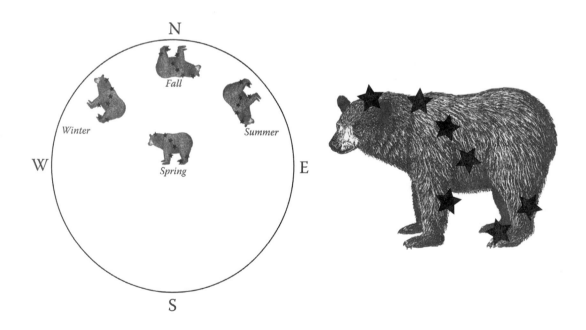

Ursa Major as a bear through the seasons

It is said that once on a time long ago in the winter, at the beginning of the season of snow after the first fall of snow, three men went on a hunt for game early on a morning. Upon a hillside into a place where the bush was thick, a bear they trailed. One of the men went in following the trail of the bear. And then he started it up running. "Towards the place whence comes the cold is he speeding away!" he said to his companions.

He that headed off on the side which lay towards the source of the cold, "In the direction of the place of the noonday sky is he running!" he said.

And then again he that stood guard on the side of the way towards the noonday sky, "Towards the place of the going-down of the sun is he running!" he said.

Back and forth amongst themselves they kept the bear fleeing.[222] They say that after a while he that was coming up behind chanced to look down at the ground. Behold, green was the surface of the earth lying face up! Now of a truth up into the sky were they conveyed by the bear! When round about the bush they were chasing it, then truly was the time that up into the sky they went. And then he that came up behind cried out to him that was next ahead: "O River That Joins Another, let us go back! We are being carried up into the sky!" Thus said he to River That Joins Another. But by him was he not heeded.

Now River That Joins Another was he who ran in between the two, and little puppy Hold Tight he had for a pet.

In the autumn they overtook the bear; then they slew it. After they had slain it, then boughs of the oak they cut, likewise boughs of the sumach;[223] then laying the bear on top of the leaves, they flayed and cut up the bear; after they had flayed and cut it up, then they began flinging and scattering the meat in every direction. Towards the place of the coming of the morning they flung the head; in the winter-time when the morning is about to appear some stars usually rise; it is said they came from the head of the bear. And also his backbone, towards the place of the morning they flung it too. They, too, are commonly seen in the winter-time; they are stars that lie huddled close together; it is said that they came from the backbone.

And they say that these four stars in the lead were the bear, and the three stars at the rear were they who were chasing after the bear. In between two of them is a tiny little star, it hangs near by another; they say that it was the puppy, the pet Hold Tight of River That Joins Another.[224]

Every autumn the oaks and sumachs redden in the leaf because it is then that the hunters lay the bear on top of the leaves and flay and cut it up. Then red with blood become the leaves. Such is the reason why every autumn red become the leaves of the oaks and sumachs.

That is the end.

1907

An Old Hunter's Memories

Hudaju (His Arrow Kills, John Kayrahoo, *c.*1840-*c.*1913), Wendat

The Seneca described deer as *hustoyowanen* (long-snouted one), *dodjenendogeni* (cloven hoofed), and *ono-gengow* (great horned one), and they have always been an important food for Great Lakes peoples. The great hunter Hudaju was interviewed in Wyandotte, Oklahoma, in June 1912, a year before he died at 73 years of age. Here he describes a hunting charm he found when he was about 45 and to which he attributed much of his success. The following text is a combination of two separate accounts: "The Deer Charm" and "An Old Hunter's Reminiscences."

When I was a child, the only one to take care of me was an uncle; and it seems to me that I was quite unlucky. When I was a young fellow, my regular occupation was hunting game. At first I used to kill wild turkeys, and it was real fun to hunt them after a snowfall and to follow their tracks in the snow.

As I grew up, I became a good hunter. There were no deer to be found in the country where I was then living (Kansas), but after we came to this place (Oklahoma), it took me about a year to become quite familiar with the habits of the deer. Then I began to slay quite a number of them. At the first snows I would often shoot down as many as five deer in a single day. That is really because I knew the country quite well.

I was not so successful at the very first. Twice I went out hunting without catching anything, as I was still young and inexperienced. But the third time the folks looked at me when I returned home, for I was bringing back loads of meat. In the distant woods, far away, the game usually repaired. So there I used to hunt.

Once I killed a deer. Having bled it in the throat with my knife, a long stream of blood flowed out. When the deer was dead, I cut its body open and removed the skin. When it was done, I hung up the venison on a tree. As I was puzzled about the great quantity of blood which lay coagulated on the ground, I ran my hand through the heap to see what was the cause for so much blood. And I discovered the body of a small deer, a *huñot*.[225] I had often heard the people say that the one who finds such a thing is always lucky thereafter. So it happened.

I washed the little deer, and I went back home. There I dried it. I wrapped it when it was dry, and I put it into a bag which I used to carry in my hunting pouch when in the woods. I became a very lucky hunter. So it really happened, for it seems to me that I made a wish to this effect. That is the reason why this experience occurred to me and made it easy for me to kill as much game as I wanted. Such was the cause of my good fortune.

And from that time on my assistance was often requested by people who were in need of venison, whenever people wanted to make a feast. And if they so requested me to hunt, it was, indeed, because they knew how easily I could always do what they wished.

In those days the meat was never paid for. It was distributed free to the people. That was always the way with us Indians. We were generous to one another; and our livelihood depended upon the game.[226] Times, however, have now changed. Now everyone has to pay. That is why we, Indians, prefer the old customs. I, for one, understand the old ways much better. Here is what I think: There are two kinds of things, the old customs and the modern ways. Everybody in this land has to follow one or the other. I have picked up just a little of these new things, that is, only insofar as it seemed useful to me. So it has happened; and, in that manner, we have become mixed in the country where we are now living. While some still retain the old customs of long ago, others have adopted modern habits. It was not possible, in fact, to keep up all the old Indian ways; for we had to improve our condition with what is of some benefit. In the old time our costumes were made of tanned hide. But today there is no game here. So, as I have already said, our old fashion had to disappear. Long ago we used to fare well on all kinds of game. It is all a thing of the past now. That is what happened to me, an Indian. Now I have to work to get something to eat. No game is left on which to subsist.

Could one still live according to the customs of long ago? No, that is not possible. That time is gone. But one kind of custom is now bound to exist for all in this country. The same thing happens to all the Indians. We were all advised to take up work. The old customs of the time past are merely what we talk about. That is all. Moreover, we have now forgotten most of these things. The many kinds of animals of long ago are only the familiar subjects of our talks.

Now, if I really wished to speak of all the modern things that are not good, it would take a great deal of time. There would be a number of stories to tell here. Quite a number of changes, I suppose, should really be welcome; and much might be said on this matter.

But I do not wish to add anything more. It would not be worthwhile, for I am a man of the past. My ways are the old ones, and the only things I know well are those of long ago.

1912

Hunting Song
Bécǐgwíwizäns (Beshwi-gwiiwizens: Nearby Boy), Ojibwe

Anun´guň	Like a star
Nǐndinábamǐg	I shine
Awesin´	The animal, gazing, is fascinated by my light

*c.*1909

371

Snowshoe Dance

Kapahpwah (Looking Over the Top, Chief Clarence Godfroy, 1880-1962), Miami

Kapahpwah

apahpwah was a descendant of the last Miami war chief and wealthy Métis trader, François Godfroy, and a great-grandson of Frances Slo-cum, a Quaker child taken by Delaware in 1778 who later married a Miami chief and spent her life as Maconaquah in the Great Lakes country. The Miamis, or Twightwees (said to be from the alarm call of a crane), were an agricultural Algonquian nation that lived near the Great Lakes at Contact and then moved into the Wabash country and western Ohio. Although they lost most of their lands after the War of 1812, the prominence of Godfroy's family allowed them to retain small grants where Chief Clarence was living when he recorded his stories and memories. He was one of the last fluent speakers of the Miami language.

According to tradition the early Indians prepared themselves for the Snow Dance when the first snow arrived or it was about time for it to arrive. The Snow Dance was given in honor of the Great Spirit who had sent the snow to help them track wild game for their food during the long winter months. Since their food was principally the flesh of wild animals, the snow was of great service to the red man for it helped him find animals which could be killed.

When all the Indians were ready to dance, their spears, hunting knives, and bows and arrows were all placed in a pile on the ground. Each Indian who wanted to dance this particular dance had to put on his snowshoes. The leader started out dancing in a circle about the weapons lying on the ground. All of the other Indians followed their leader.

Snowshoe Dance at the first snowfall, 1835-1837. George Catlin

While dancing, each Indian, one at a time, danced up to the pile of weapons, chose the one he wanted to hunt with and then danced back to the edge of the circle. All the time he was singing his hunting song. At the same time he had to go through the motions of catching the game he hoped to bring back to the camp as his spoil. If he was pretending he was hunting deer, he danced by leaps and bounds, throwing his head up in the air and looking from side to side. If he was imitating hunting a bear he ran at a pacing run around the circle. He tried to imitate the animal he hoped to catch. Each Indian had to be dressed in his hunting garments if he wished to take part in the Snow Shoe Dance. This particular dance was quite interesting and exciting to watch.

1950s

A Moose and His Offspring

Kūgigēpinäsíkwä (Forever Bird Woman, Marie Syrette), Ojibwe

Kūgigēpinäsíkwä grew up at Lake Nipigon, on the north shore of Lake Superior, and she would have heard stories not only from her band but also from those who came from the highlands and rivers that flow farther north into Hudson's Bay. These are hunting cultures, and no other story expresses quite so beautifully the conflicted feelings Natives have about killing animals they call older brother, yet on whom their sustenance once depended. There is wistfulness here, as well as humor: Kūgigēpinäsíkwä clearly knows teenagers well. But in her description of the tearful reunion of a mother and her son there is not only great fondness, but the reflection of a culture's wish that those they hunt may live forever.

"A Moose and His Offspring" was collected by William Jones, who translated it into a formal, late-nineteenth-century English that reflected as closely as possible the original Ojibwe. This makes for some convoluted sentences, which have been left as Jones rendered them. To appreciate Kūgigēpinäsíkwä's artistry, imagine beyond language to hear the humor, fear, and pathos of this wonderful story with its small touches of inventiveness: the mother threatening to attack humans with her old moccasin, the recalcitrant young moose ignoring everyone's advice and only learning by hard experience, the mother sympathetically trying to fix his nose. It is beautifully structured, with two sets of fathers and sons, beginning and ending with the father moose, who keeps repeating lessons about human power and who is just as repeatedly ignored. Even the dogs' barking is rendered conversationally.

Since stories are told not only to entertain, but also to teach, "A Moose and His Offspring" may also be referring to history. Reading this story from the perspective of the twenty-first century, the young moose's fate can be seen as the failure of individualism, with wounds that can be healed only by maternal love. The story undermines the idea that an individual can control fate, and it reinforces the Native world view that survival comes from being part of a group.

373

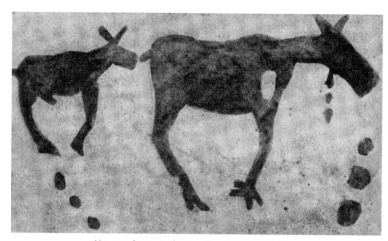

Moose pictograph, Quetico Provincial Park

The Moose was about to go into camp for the winter, and also his wife. Two in number were their children, and there was a youth among them; therefore they were five. It was so that they were in fear, of people they were in fear. On very long journeys frequently went the youth, whereupon continually was the old man trying to dissuade him not to go so far. "Upon your trail might come the people." But the youth paid no heed. Once he saw the tracks of another Moose; he knew it was a cow. Accordingly he followed after her, whereat, on seeing her, he took her to wife. During this time that he had her for wife, by another Moose were they visited; and by her, as by the other, was he desired for a husband; to be sure, he married her. Therefore two were the wives he had. In truth, very frequently did they fight.

And once he went away, to his father he went. After he was come, he spoke to his son, saying: "My son, do not bring it about that there be two women for you to have. Perhaps they might do harm to each other."

"Ay," he said to his father. And then on the morrow he went back home; in a while he arrived at where they dwelt. Whereupon, sure enough, (he found) that one of his wives had been killed.

And once there arrived two other Moose. Presently they spoke to him, saying: "Why did you have two wives? You should not have done so."

Now in secret the youth had plucked out his testes, afterwards he flung them straight toward the west.

And then said the women: "Therefore we will follow after your testes."

Thereupon he became exceedingly ill, hardly was he able to go back to his father. In time he arrived within the wigwam, whereupon then he began to undergo treatment from his father.

"Such was the reason why I tried to dissuade you from your purpose. Because of this disobedience you became sick. Therefore now you should remain quietly by."

By this time the winter was halfway gone. In certain places roundabout where they lived wandered the calves. When it snowed, then sang the young Moose. Truly happy they were when it snowed: "May more snow fall, may some more snow fall! May more snow fall, may some more snow fall! May more snow fall, may some more snow fall! May more snow fall, may some more snow fall!" Thus sang the young Moose. They were heard by their mother, by whom they were then addressed: "Do not sing such a song, lest perhaps you be laid low with a club on the hardened crust, if much snow falls." Thereupon they ceased.

And in course of time to very much better health was the youth restored. Therefore then he started off, trying to see how he could travel; and very comfortably did he walk along. And once he saw where the cloud had cast a shadow; in truth, he believed that he could outstrip it. Accordingly, when he ran it a race, a very great distance behind he left it. Truly pleased was he to have outrun the cloud. Then on his homeward way he went. When he entered into where they lived, he spoke to his father, saying: "My father, of a truth, you deceived me when you said that speedy is a human being. On this day now past I raced with the cloud, far behind I outran it. Not so swift as that would a human being be."

Thereupon he was addressed by his father saying: "My dear son, of a truth, you are greatly to be pitied for regarding with contempt a human being. Of the nature of a manitou is a human being. Today you shall learn, if very far you intend to go, how it is that a human being is of the nature of a manitou. He makes use of bird-hawks and swans, and on that account speedy is a human being."

It was then growing dark when the youth departed, far away went the Moose. And once, while traveling along, he saw the tracks of someone; it seemed as if someone had been dragging two poles, such was the mark of someone's trail.[227] "It must be a human being that has made the trail," he thought. Then he followed in the path behind him. Of a truth, he made great fun of the human being; he held him in contempt because of the tracks he made. "It is impossible for him ever to overtake anyone, too ungainly are his tracks."

And then back home he went; when he arrived, a heap of fun he made of his father: "My father, now perhaps"—while at the same time he was laughing at his father—"upon the tracks of a person did I come. No doubt, you must have been beside yourself, my father, when you said that a human being was speedy. When I was on his trail, two poles was he dragging behind. Verily, never anything could that good-for-nothing human being overtake." Thereupon then again he was addressed by his father saying: "In a little while we shall be visited by a human being."

It was now growing dark. And suddenly in came a pipe.[228] First to the girl's mouth came the stem, whereupon then the girl smoked; next to the old woman, and she also smoked; next to the boy, likewise to the old man, who smoked; then next to the youth. The moment that the stem was entering into his mouth, he dealt it a hard blow. Thereupon then he said: "Never can I be slain by a human being." Thereupon then he was addressed by his father saying: "Oh, my dear son! Therefore now have you played the mischief with yourself."

And then in a while they lay down to sleep. After they had lain down to sleep, they heard the sound of a kettle-drum beating; and it was on their account that it was beating; they were being overcome with manitou power. The old man then rose from his bed. "It is in the morning that we shall be sought for. My dear son, come, harken to what I tell you! Don't think of trying to flee away, for I am really telling you the truth in what I am saying to you. Of bird-hawks and swans the people make use, such are the things the people use."

Early in the morning, while it was yet dark, there came a sudden crunching of the crust of the snow.

Not even did he see any one. Very close he heard the sound of some one. "Halloo!" exclaimed the other. It so happened that the dogs were scattered about everywhere barking. The calves rose to their feet; they saw some one walking hitherward. Not at all did they fail to make out every part of him, and exposed to view were his entrails. They saw him pointing the gun at them, whereupon they were then shot at. Now, there were two human beings. When they all had been shot at, then in that place were they all killed. Then for tracks did the man seek. In truth, one he found trailing off the other way. Before following it up, he turned about, he went to where his father was. "Therefore you had better look after the dressing of these moose."

Then away he started, following after the lone moose. On his way went the man, keeping ever on the trail of the moose. Now, two in number were his dogs, and so upon them he depended. Now, with an easy gait at first did the moose move along; and later, while on his way he went traveling, he suddenly heard the dogs as they came barking. And then with great speed went the moose. And as he was on the point of slowing up, already again was he being overtaken. In lively manner was he barked at, whereupon truly as fast as he could go he went. For a little while he got out of sound of the dogs' barking. Now, by this time he was very much out of wind, but yet of a truth he tried running. It was impossible for him to outstrip the dogs, for by this time he was very much out of strength.

And by and by, *"Kan 'kan, kan 'kan, kan 'kan!"* he heard. Then it was that he became mindful of what he had been told by his father, who had tried in vain to dissuade him from going. Thereupon truly he tried with all his might to go, but he was not at all able to outrun the dogs. At the same time he cried as he went walking along. And once, when unable to go, he saw back on his trail a human being walking hitherward, he came saying: "Well, Moose, does it seem that you have walked far enough?"

"Not at all have I yet walked enough."

Then at yonder place the man leaned his gun; an axe he drew from his belt, a stick he cut. After cutting the stick he came over to where the Moose was; a hard blow on the back was dealt the Moose.[229] He was addressed by the man saying: "Go on! Not yet have you walked enough."

Poor fellow! In spite of his efforts, he tried to go, but he was not even able to take a step. Next the man drew a knife from his scabbard. Then he went up to the Moose; taking him by the nose, he cut it off. After hanging the nose to his belt, he turned the head of the Moose about and said to him: "Yonder is where you shall be eaten by your fellow-dogs."[230] Forthwith then away went the man.

Accordingly then, in truth, he was much disturbed in mind, fearing lest he might bleed to death. Then he became mindful of what in vain he had been told by his father; and of his mother he also thought.

And now, after those were disposed of that had been killed at yonder place, then back again to life they came. Forthwith they fixed up the place where they lived. It was now growing dark. And after a while there came someone to invite them, whereupon all that were there were asked to come. They departed on their way to where the people dwelt. After they had gone inside, then they smoked. They also were fed, and they were given raiment. Truly happy were they. The old woman was given ear-rings and leggings. And all the various things that people have they were given. And the boy was given a cedar-bark pouch to keep powder in. Ever so pleased was the boy after putting over his shoulder the powder pouch.[231]

And in a while back home they went; after they were come at home, gone was their youth. In a while it began to grow dark, but they would not go to sleep. And by and by in the night the old woman heard the sound of somebody out-of-doors coming softly up (and) stopping by the door. "That may be my dear son," she thought. "Some evil fate, perhaps, may have befallen my dear son." Rising to her feet, she then went outside.

Poor thing! There he was with his hand over his nose. "Ah, me! My dear son, what has been done to you?"

"Nothing is left of my nose."

When the old woman saw him, very bitterly she wept. After she had finished weeping, she took up some earth that was very black; when she rubbed it over his nose, then back as it used to look became his nose. When within entered the old woman, she spoke to her son, saying: "Come inside!" Of a truth, the man accordingly entered.

Then spoke the old woman, saying: "Verily, with my old moccasin will I strike at a human being if he purposes to shoot at me."

Thereupon spoke the old man, saying: "Hush! Speak not thus of the people, for they are truly endowed with manitou power."

And so the buttocks of the ruffed grouse now hang aloft.[232]

*c.*1900

Chai Vang and Relationships in the Wisconsin Northwoods

Oshcabewis (Little Attendant in Ojibwe, Paul DeMain, 1955-   ), Oneida

On November 21, 2004, a Hmong immigrant, Chai Vang, shot several white deer hunters while hunting on state land in northern Wisconsin. Six died; two were wounded. Vang was tried, convicted, and sentenced to prison. In this essay from *News From Indian Country,* one of the largest circulating Native publications in North America, editor Paul DeMain asks the difficult question of how much prejudice affects behavior in the woods. DeMain is no stranger to tough questions. A past president of the Native American Journalists Association and a Wisconsin Governor's Policy Advisor during the term of Governor Anthony S. Earl, his investigation and coverage of the murder of Anna Mae Aquash earned him the Payne Award for Ethics in Journalism and the Wassaja Award for courage in reporting from the Native American Journalists Association.

The trial of Chai Vang brought an unprecedented deluge of media and attention to our quiet little north woods city of Hayward, Wisconsin, recently. Despite the record number of stories written about the event that led up to the shooting death of six Wisconsin hunters, what seemed to be missing was another perspective only miles from the center of attention: the Chippewa reservation eleven miles southeast of Hayward. Not that anybody from this reservation didn't find the death of six hunters appalling, or in need of condolences for the six victims and their families, including the Vang family who have lost one of their own in the incident.

Vang, who was convicted of six charges of murder in the first degree and attempted murder, will spend the rest of his life in prison, depriving their family of the major bread winner and father, grandfather, brother, and son. If justice is done, there will never be a feeling of justice in its complete form for either party, but that is the way our judicial system works, and the jury has spoken. What wasn't said in all the media frenzy, and in part it was not just because of the fear of retribution to the Indian community, is how many tribal hunters and family members felt about this incident—which in the opinion of many, was an event waiting to happen. I can tell you that from the day the event occurred, many of my friends and neighbors on the reservation always felt there was more to the story than was being heard.

Denials to the media by local law enforcement officials, the Attorney General, and non-Natives in the region that racism played any part in the incident flies in the face of the facts of the case. The Native community remembers the thousands of protesters that lined up at the lakes of southern Sawyer County to denounce not only reserved treaty rights to hunting and fishing in the ceded territory, but to rain upon the Native fishers epithets, death threats, gunshots, and vandalism to vehicles.

The mere fact that Sawyer County school officials had a contingency plan to protect the children at a nearby elementary school in Hayward in case violence broke out, following an acquittal, speaks volumes to what even some non-Native authorities thought white hunters and spectators at the trial were capable of doing if their opinion of justice was not rendered.

Just about every group in northern Wisconsin has some kind of village idiot in its crowd that under the right circumstances can be both embarrassing and cause an incident.

The fact that Vang had apologized and was leaving the area when five members of the hunting party decided they needed to teach Vang a lesson and roared up on ATVs to confront him with foul language [and] derogatory racial remarks while preventing him [from] leaving for a period of time, according to court testimony, helped fuel the end result. (By the way, this part of the incident was one part that nobody read about in any major incident reports released by the police or printed by the media last fall.) Whether death was justified or not, and to what extent, at this point only the Creator knows the real truth. Conflicting testimony about a pot shot being taken in the direction of Vang and how he reacted to it, is still a question in my mind.

From conflicting reports from one of the surviving victims (Hessebeck) who last fall claimed that another hunter (Willers) took a shot at Vang after Vang had shot at him, then retracted it, to the missing shell casing that nobody could find from their gun, like somebody had cleaned up the scene, to court testimony from another hunter who heard one shot, then a number of rapid shots (Vang had a semi-automatic), there were questions in my mind that were never answered to my satisfaction.

Needless to say, the jury did not believe Vang's version of the story that he was shot at first, over that of the non-Native hunters. And even then, it was hard for me to understand how the incident ended up with six dead people, other than the glaring fact that maybe this group, after confronting other hunters in the area in the same way in past years, finally messed with the wrong man.

Despite taking the stand and doing fairly well in explaining some of the events of the day, Vang, a trained military sniper—whose training focuses on taking out all the danger of the enemy, and who came from Laos some twenty or more years ago to become a vibrant citizen of this country—I could still see the cultural differences and language barriers in the questions and answers.

In asking who deserved to die that day, Vang responded to the Attorney General by naming three of the six victims. Had the Attorney General asked who was responsible for the events that occurred that day, the answer might have been less dramatic in the media and less appalling to the jury, but nevertheless exactly the same.

Hopefully the end of the trial will bring some closure to these events. But with that, not much has changed in the north country where tribal hunters in recent years have been confronted and left the woods out of an inner uneasiness of what could happen. Vandalized cars with smashed windows and flattening of tires have occurred as well. Of course, local officials and many of the non-Native community where these events have happened know for sure that it has nothing to do with racism, or ethnic intolerance.

They seem to ignore what is directly in front of them at times. I learned long ago that honkys and niggers came in all colors of the rainbow, including copper-toned brown. Racism is something that our own Native community must battle on a regular basis as much as anybody else. Most of the communities of northern Wisconsin claim they are not racist, but they are untested. The don't live next to a Black, Hispanic, or Hmong community—they think they are tolerant but bar talk and casual chatter tell me they have not come the full circle.

I have had my sons in hockey for several years now, and one of my son's coaches is a well respected member of the Sawyer County law enforcement community. I still have the greatest respect for him, and I have no doubt if some fan or parent called my son out in some racist fashion, he would be the first to get back in their face. But sitting around a table one day he neither blushed nor hesitated to describe the latest trend of our young (Indian and non-Indian) listening to what he called "nigger" music.

Those are the little things that tell me what might be under the hidden layer that people cannot see in themselves, the cease fire and uneasy peace that the Indian community here didn't want to offend by saying what was on their minds about the events of November 21, 2004, nor other incidents we still put up with.

If you ask around, there are very few people who really understand the Chippewa community that lies only a few miles from this town. Our community, and I mean our community both off and on the reservation, knows even less about the Hmong, and their courageous fight as allies of the U.S. government in Southeast Asia against the Communists.

Most of our Native hunters will be out this season, but in the back of their minds there is the unsettling question of how they might have reacted had it been them that had been confronted. At what point is it right to defend yourself in the face of humiliating factors, or if you're surrounded, or in face of fear, or in responding to an alleged pot shot by one of our northern Wisconsin idiots. What if? And what if the all white jury doesn't believe you?

2005

In 2007, another Hmong hunter, who did not speak English, was shot and killed in the Peshtigo Harbor Wildlife Area of northern Wisconsin.

Wolf

Mike McDougall, Anishinâbe

The blue wolf shivers in the shadows.
In Grand Marais, men who stick
signs on their trucks like "Sierra Club Kiss My Axe"
load their guns,
feel like champions,
and the wolf and the moon wait.

1977

Mike McDougall wrote this poem during class one day when he was in junior high. The class was part of COMPAS (Community Programs in Arts and Sciences) in St. Paul, Minnesota, which had begun as a Minnesota Poets in the Schools Program. McDougall is a plumber in Detroit Lakes, Minnesota, and a member of the White Earth Anishinâbeg.

⋅◈⋅ EDUCATION ⋅◈⋅

What would education be like without classrooms filled with rows of desks, without bells, rules, and books? What if education took place every day, teaching skills that are immediately useful and necessary, the lessons taught by family and neighbors? The young always need to be taught the values of their culture and how to apply those values to life, but North American culture gives over a large part of this instruction to institutions and groups such as churches, schools, and youth organizations. Before whites interfered with Native lives, education was the privilege and duty of elders. Grandfathers, fathers, and uncles taught young boys; grandmothers, mothers, and aunts taught young girls, and their primary lessons were respect and the interconnectedness of all things. These lessons underscored everyone's duty to be humble and self-effacing, since people were the puniest creatures in the universe, creatures who could never get through life without the help of more powerful spirits.

As the first selection reprinted here shows, education in traditional Native cultures was demanding because it involved the duty of fasting. Once children were compelled to leave their communities for academic training in English, however, the challenges changed to learning new languages while enduring separation and, frequently, racism. The deliberate destruction of fluency in traditional languages was one of the greatest evils wreaked by westernized schoolmasters; as several writers here suggest, that loss echoes down the decades to the present.

Hok'íkun: Teachings

Warudjáxega (Terrible Thunder-Crash, Jasper Blowsnake), **Hágaga** (Third-Born Son, Big Winnebago, Sam Blowsnake/Carley), **John Rave**, Ho-Chunks

Paul Radin, who collected these instructions from Ho-Chunk who were also Peyotists, writes that they conveyed "a series of precepts on aspects of life, such as the duty of fasting, of being a warrior, of behavior to one's parents and relatives, how to treat one's wife and women in general, how to bring up children, how to behave to strangers, etc. These precepts were called *hok'íkun*: precepts or teachings. Foremost among them was the duty to fast. By regularly fasting, and so suffering, the spirits would take pity and grant requests. Fasting and the discipline it required were central to leading the well-lived life. Radin notes that "one of the objects of the old men was to draw the most alluring pictures of the rewards that would fall to the lot of those who followed in the footsteps of their ancestors and, on the other hand, to draw the most lurid pictures of the wretchedness that befell those who deviated, no matter in what details, from the customs sanctioned by age."

Instructions to the son

"My son, when you grow up, you should see to it that you are of some benefit to your fellow men.

There is only one way in which you can begin to be of any aid to them, and that is to fast. So, see to it that you fast. Our grandfather, the fire (*pétc*),[233] who stands at all times in the center of our dwelling, sends forth all kinds of blessings. Be sure that you make an attempt to obtain his blessings.

"My son, do you remember to have our grandfathers, the war chiefs, bless you. See to it that they pity you. Someday when you go on the warpath, their blessings will enable you to have specific foreknowledge of all that will happen to you on that occasion. This will likewise enable you to accomplish what you desire without the danger of anything interfering with your plans. Without the slightest trouble you will then be able to obtain the prizes of war. Without any trouble you will be able to obtain these and in addition glory and the war honors.[234] If, in truth, you thirst yourself to death, our grandfathers who are in control of wars—to whom all the war powers that exist in this world belong—they will assuredly bless you.

"My son, if you do not wear out your feet through ceaseless activity in fasting, if you do not blacken your face for fasting, it will be all in vain that you inflict sufferings upon yourself. Blessings are not obtained through mere desire alone; they are not obtained without making the proper sacrifices or without putting yourself time and again in proper mental condition. Indeed, my son, they are not to be obtained without effort on your part. So see to it that, of all those spirits whom Earthmaker created, one at least has pity upon you and blesses you. Whatever such a spirit says to you that will unquestionably happen.

"Now, my son, if you do not obtain a spirit to strengthen you, you will not amount to anything in the estimation of your fellow men. They will show you little respect. Perhaps they will make fun of you. . . .

"My son, it will indeed be good if you obtain war powers, but our ancestors say it is difficult. Especially difficult is it to be leader on the warpath. So they say. If you do not become an individual warranted to lead a war party, yet mistaking yourself for one although really an ordinary warrior and you "throw away a man," your act will be considered most disgraceful.[235] A mourner might harm you in revenge for the fact that you have caused him to mourn and burn you with embers. Your people will all be sad, both on account of your disgrace and on account of the pain inflicted upon you.

"My son, not with the blessing of one of the spirits merely, nor with the blessing of twenty, for that matter, can you go on the warpath. You must have the blessing of all the spirits above the earth, and of all those on the earth, and of all those who are pierced through the earth; of all those under the earth; of all those who are under the water; of all those that are on the sides of the earth, i.e., all the four winds; of the Disease-giver; of the Sun; of the Daylight; of the Moon; of the Earth; and of all those who are in control of war powers—with the blessings of all these deities must you be provided before you can lead a successful war party.

"My son, if you cast off dress [belongings], men will be benefited by your deeds. You will be an aid to all your people. If your people honor you, it will be good. And they will like you even the more if you obtain a limb [war honor]. They will indeed like you very much if you obtain a limb, even better, two or three. If you do thus, wherever people boil an animal with a head [give a Winter Feast], you will always be able to eat.

"If on account of your bravery you are permitted to tell of your exploits during the Four Nights' Wake for the benefit of the soul of the deceased, do not try to add to your glory by exaggerating any exploit, for by so doing you will cause the soul to stumble on its journey to the spirit land.[236] If you do this and add an untruth to the account of your war exploit, you will die soon after. The war spirits always hear you. Tell a little less. The old men say it is wise.

"My son, it is good to die in war. If you die in war, your soul will not be unconscious. You will have complete disposal of your soul, and it will always be happy. If you should ever desire to return to this earth and live here again, you will be able to do so. A second life as a human being you may live, or, if you prefer, as an inhabitant of the air [a bird] you may live, or you may roam the earth as an animal. Thus it is to him who dies in battle.

"My son, fast for an honorable place among your fellow men. Fast, so that when you are married you may have plenty of food; that you may be happy and that you may not have to worry about your children. If in your fastings you have a vision of your future home, the members of your family will be lacking in nothing during their life. Fast for the food that you may need. If you fast a sufficiently large number of times, when in after life you have children and they cry for food, you will be able to offer a piece of deer or moose meat without any difficulty. Your children will never be hungry.

"My son, never abuse your wife. The women are sacred. If you abuse your wife and make her life miserable, you will die. Our grandmother, the earth, is a woman, and in mistreating your wife you will be mistreating her. Most assuredly will you be abusing our grandmother if you act thus. And as it is she that is taking care of us, you will really be killing yourself by such behavior.

"My son, when you keep house, should anyone enter your house, no matter who it is, be sure to offer him whatever you have in house. Any food that you withhold at such a time will most assuredly become a source of death to you. If you are stingy about giving food, the people will kill you on this account. They will poison you. If you hear of a traveler who is visiting your people and you wish to see him, prepare your table for him and have him sent for. In this manner you will be acting correctly. It is always good to act correctly and do good, the old people used to say.

"If you see an old, helpless person, help him with whatever you possess. Should you happen to possess a home and you take him there, he might suddenly say abusive things about you during the middle of the meal. You will be strengthened by such words. This same traveler may, on the contrary, give you something he carries under his arms and which he treasures very highly. If it is an object without a stem [a plant root], keep it to protect your house. If you thus keep it within your house, your home will never be molested by any bad spirits. Nothing will be able to enter your house unexpectedly. Thus you will live. Witches, instead of entering the house, will pass around it. If, in addition to possessing this medicine, you also fast, your people will be benefited by it greatly. Earthmaker made spirits up above and some he made to live on this earth, and again some he made to live under the water, some to live in the water, and all these he put in charge of something. Even the small animals that move about this earth, the creator put in charge of some power. Thus he created them. Afterwards he created us human beings, and as he had exhausted all the powers to be disposed of, we were not in control of anything. Then he made a weed and placed it in our charge. And he said that no matter how powerful are the spirits that exist, they would not be able to take this weed from us without giving something in return. He himself, Earthmaker, would not be able to demand it for nothing. So he spoke. This weed was the tobacco plant. Earthmaker said that if we would offer a pipeful of tobacco to him, whatever we should ask of him he would immediately grant.

Not only he, but all spirits created, longed to have some of this tobacco. It is for this reason that when we fast and cry piteously for some spirit to take pity on us, if we give them tobacco they will bless us with those powers that the creator gave them. So it will be. Earthmaker made it thus.

"My son, you must fast. If you breathe upon sick people, I mean if you are blessed with that kind of power, you will be able to restore people to health. You will be of help to your people. If you can, in addition, draw out the pain from within the body of an individual, you will indeed be a help to your people. They will respect you. You will not even have to work for all your necessities, for those whom you treat will cheerfully support you as long as you live. If you should die, your name will be held in great respect, and people will frequently talk about you. Ah, that man he had indeed great power!

"My son, if you are not able to fast, try at least to obtain some plants that are powerful.[237] There are people who know the qualities of the different plants, who have been blessed by the spirits with knowledge. It is pitiable enough that you could obtain nothing through fasting, so ask those that are in possession of these plants at least to have pity upon you. If they have pity upon you, they will bless you with one of the plants they possess, and you will thus have something to help you in life and to encourage you. One plant will be enough. Of all the plants that cover the earth and lie like a fringe of hair upon the body of our grandmother, try and obtain knowledge of these, that you may be strengthened in life. Then you will have reason to feel encouraged. A real medicine man has more justification for feeling encouraged than an ordinary one, because such a one has been blessed with life by the Water-spirits—then some day, when your children are in need of medicine, you will not need to go and look for a medicine man, but you will only have to look in your medicine bundle. Whatever trouble your children have, you will be able to cure it. Should anything be the matter with the people of your tribe, they will call upon you. You can then open your medicine bundle, and the individual who is wanting in life will be benefited from the stock of medicines that are in your possession. You will indeed never be embarrassed. You will know just wherein his ailment lies. As you have obtained your power with great effort, therefore what you say will be so. If you say, "He will live," he will live. If the relatives of the patient make you good payments, you may perform what you are accustomed to in your treatment of people. Then you can ask your medicine to put forth its strength for you, and it will do so. If you make good offerings of tobacco to the plants and if you make feasts in their honor, if, indeed, you make much of your medicine, if you talk to it as though it were a human being, then when you ask it to put forth its strength, it will do so. The payments that you receive you can take with a good conscience, and your children will wear them and will be strengthened thereby. So be very diligent in the care you bestow upon them.

The medicines were placed here by Earthmaker for a good purpose. We are to use them to heal ourselves. For that purpose Earthmaker gave them to us. If anyone tries to obtain the life-sustainers—that is, the medicines—and inflicts suffering upon himself in order to obtain them, our grandmother will know about it. So whatever you spend upon it, be it in labor or in goods, she will know about it. All that you gave in obtaining your medicines she will know. They will be returned to you. The people will thus be providing themselves with something for the future. The people always look forward to the future, and for all possible happenings they will have some medicine provided. You must try to obtain some of the medicines that most people possess. If you want paint-medicine, make yourself pitiable. If your paint-medicine overcomes your enemy and you keep it in your home, you will never be wanting in wealth. The most valued possessions of the people will be given to you. The people will love you, and the paint-medicine will be the cause of it. Whatever you receive will be in consequence of the possession of the paint-medicine. The paint-medicine is made of the blood of the Water-spirits, and therefore it is holy. People used to fast and thirst themselves to death, and a Water-spirit would appear to them and bestow his blessings upon them. Whatever he told them would come true. The Earthmaker put the Water-spirit in charge of these things so that he would bless the people with them. That was his purpose.

"Some people who wished to find good medicines obtained the race medicine. Try and learn of it. Others had gambling medicine, and still others again had hunting medicine. There are medicines for every purpose. There is a courting medicine and a medicine to prevent married people from wishing to separate, and there is a medicine for making one rich. If one wishes to make a person crazy, there is a medicine for that purpose. If someone had made another one sad at heart and he wished to revenge himself, he would use a medicine that would make that person crazy. Thus he would poison him. If a person wished to marry a certain girl and she did not want him, he would poison her with a medicine that would make her become a harlot. All the men would fall in love with her by reason of the medicine he gave her. If they wished a man to be continually running after a woman, they had a medicine for that purpose. All these medicines they possessed. You can obtain any of them you like if you ask for them in the proper way.

"Some people have knowledge of plants that will cause a person to sleep all the time. Others again have medicines that will cause them to stay awake all the time. Some know how to overcome the viciousness of dogs that watch over women by means of medicines; some again have medicines that will make people single them out even in crowds. If this person uses his medicine in a crowd of people, the one on whom it is used will consider him a great man no matter how many there should be in the crowd. Some have a medicine to be used for preventing an individual from getting tired. Others have a medicine to be used when they have dog contests.

"Whatever they did, for that they would have medicines.

"Whenever they plant a field, they protect it with medicine tied on to a stick. No one will then go through that field without suffering for it. If you did not have that protection, people could go through your field whenever they wished. In short, try to obtain as many medicines as you possibly can, for you will need them all. People should always look out for themselves so that they may learn what is necessary to make life comfortable and happy. If you try to obtain the knowledge of these things, you will get along in life well. You will need nothing, and whenever you need a certain medicine, instead of being compelled to buy it, you will have it in your own possession. If you act in this manner and keep on fasting, you will never be caught off guard during your life. If you have a home, it will always look nice, and you will be lacking in nothing. So do what I tell you, and you will never regret it in after life. Try and learn the way in which your ancestors lived and follow in their footsteps.

"If you thus travel in the road of the good people, it will be good, and other people will not consider your life a source of amusement [they will not ostracize you].

"If you cannot obtain a blessing from the spirits, try also to have some good plant take pity on you. This I am telling you, and if you do not do it, you will suffer for it. All that I am saying will be of great benefit to you if you pay heed to me, for you will need medicines for whatever you do in life, if you are not fortunate enough to obtain blessings from the spirits. If you are ever on the warpath, you will need medicine in order to escape being hit or in order to prevent yourself from getting exhausted or from feeling famished. If you manage to be fortunate in all these things, you may be certain that the medicines have caused it.

"My son, help yourself as you go along life's path, for this earth has many narrow passages, and you can never tell when you will come to one. If, however, you have something with which to strengthen yourself, you will come safely through the passages you meet.

"Let every one think you a desirable person to know. Associate with people. If you act in this manner, every one will like you. You will live a contented life. Never do anything wrong to your children. Whatever your children ask you to do, do not hesitate to do it for them. If you act thus, people will say you are good-natured. If you ever lose a friend by death and if you have riches, cover the expenses of the funeral of the deceased. Help the mourners to feed the people at the wake. If you act thus, you will be acting well. Then you will be truly a helper of the people, and they will know you as such. Indeed, all of them will know you. For the good you do, all will love you.

"My son, do not become a gambler. You might, it is true, become rich, but in spite of your wealth all your children will die. No gambler ever had children. It is an affair of the bad spirits entirely. Now if you do all that I have told you, you will unquestionably lead a happy and contented life. . . .'"

Instructions to the daughter

This is the way the old men used to speak to the little girls:

"My daughter, as you go along the path of life, always listen to your parents. Do not permit your mother to work. Attend to your father's wants. All the work in the house belongs to you. Never be idle. Chop the wood, carry it home, look after the vegetables and gather them, and cook the food. When in the spring of the year you move back to your permanent settlements, plant your fields immediately. Never get lazy. Earthmaker created you for these tasks.

"When you have your menses, do not ask those in your lodge to give you any food, but leave the lodge and fast and do not begin eating again until you return to your own lodge. Thus will you help yourself. If you always fast, when you marry, even if your husband had amounted to nothing before, he will become an excellent hunter. It will be on account of your fasting that he will have changed so much. You will never fail in anything, and you will always be well and happy. If, on the contrary, you do not do as I tell you—that is, if you do not fast—when you marry, he will become very weak, and this will be due to you. Finally he will get very sick.

"My daughter, do not use medicine. If you marry a man and place medicine on his head, he will become very weak and will not amount to anything. It may be that you do not want to have your husband leave you, and this may induce you to use medicine to keep him. Do not do that, however, for it is not good. You will be ruining a man. It is the same as killing him. Do not do it, for it is forbidden. If you marry a man and you want to be certain of always retaining him, work for him. With work you will always be able to retain your hold on men. If you do your work to satisfaction of your husband, he will never leave you. I say again it is not proper to use medicine. Above all, do not use medicine until you have passed your youth. You will otherwise merely make yourself weak. You will lead a weak life. It may even happen that you will cause yourself to become foolish.

"Do not use a medicine in order to marry. If you marry, remain faithful to your husband. Do not act as though you are married to a number of men at the same time. Lead a chaste life. If you do not listen to what I am telling you and you are unfaithful to your husband, all the men will jeer at you. They will say whatever they wish to, and no one will interfere. Every man will treat you as though he were on the "joking relationship" with you.[238] If you do not listen to me, therefore, you will injure yourself.

"Thus the old people used to talk to one another. Thus they would warn one another against certain actions. They used to instruct the young girls as they grew up just as I am doing to you now. That is why I am telling of these things now.

"My daughter, as you grow older and grow up to be a young woman, the young men will begin to court you. Never strike a man, my daughter. It is forbidden. If you dislike a man very much, tell him gently to go away. If you do not do this and instead strike him, remember that it frequently happens that men know of medicines, or if they themselves have none they may know from whom to get them. If you make a man feel bad by striking him, he may use this medicine and cause you to run away with him and become a bad woman. It is for this reason that the old men used to warn the young girls not to strike the men who are courting them but whom they dislike. Pray with all your heart that you do not become such a woman.

"Do not act haughtily to your husband. Whatever he tells you to do, do it. Kindness will be returned to you if you obey your husband, for he will treat you in the same manner.

"If you ever have a child, do not strike it. In the olden times when a child misbehaved, the parents did not strike it, but they made it fast. When a child gets hungry, he will soon see the error of his ways. If you hit a child, you will be merely knocking the wickedness into him. Women should likewise never scold the children because children are merely made wicked by scoldings. If your husband scolds the children, do not take their part, for that will merely make them bad. In the same way, if a stranger makes your children cry, do not say anything to the stranger in the presence of the children, nor take their part in his presence. If you wish to prevent a stranger from scolding your children, keep them home and teach them how to behave by setting them a good example. Do not imagine that you do the best for your children by taking their part, or that you love them if you talk merely about loving them. Show them that you love them by your actions. Let them see that you are generous with donations. In such actions they will see your good work, and then they will be able to judge for themselves whether your actions equal your words.

"My daughter, do not show your love for other children so that strangers notice it. You may, of course, love other children, but love them with a different love from that which you bestow on your own children. The children of other people are different from your own children, and if you were to take them to some other place after you had been lavishing so much love upon them, they would not act as your children would under the same circumstances. You can always depend upon your own children. They are of your own body. Love them, therefore. This is what our ancestors taught us to do.

"If a wife has no real interest in her husband's welfare and possessions, she will be to him no more than any other woman, and the world will ridicule her. If, on the other hand, you pay more attention to your husband than to your parents, your parents will leave you. Let your husband likewise take care of your parents, for they depend on him. Your parents were instrumental in getting you your husband, so remember that they expect some recompense for it, as likewise for the fact that they raised you.

"My daughter, the old people used to teach us never to hurt the feelings of our relatives. If you hurt their feelings, you will cause your brothers-in-law to feel ashamed of themselves. Do not ever wish for any other man but your husband. It is enough to have one husband. Do not let anyone have the right to call you a prostitute.

"Do not hit your relatives at any time. For if you did that or if you were on bad terms with one of them, it may chance that he will die, and then the people will say that you are glad that he is dead. Then, indeed, you will feel sad at heart and you will think to yourself, 'What can I best do' to make up for my conduct. Even if you were to give a Medicine Dance in his honor or donate gifts for the Four Nights' Wake, many people will still say, 'She used to be partial and jealous when he was alive. Now that he is dead she loves him. Why does she act this way? She is wasting her wealth. She really does not love him and therefore she ought not to spend so much money upon him now.' Then, indeed, my daughter, will your heart ache; then, indeed, will you get angry. That is why the old people would tell their children to love one another. If you love a person and that person dies, then you will have a right to mourn for him, and everyone will think that your mourning is sincere. Not only will your own relatives love you, but everyone else will love you likewise. If, then, in the course of your life you come to a crisis of some kind, all these people will turn their hearts toward you.

"My daughter, all that I am trying to tell you relates to your behavior when you grow up. In your own home the women all understand the work belonging to the household and that relating to camping and hunting. If you understand these and afterwards visit your husband's relatives, you will know what to do and not find yourself in a dilemma from which you cannot extricate yourself. When you visit your husband's people, do not go around with a haughty air or act as if you considered yourself far above them. Try to get them to like you. If they like you, they will place you in charge of the camp you happen to be visiting. If you are good-natured, you will be placed in charge of the home at which you happen to be visiting. Then your parents-in-law will tell your husband that their daughter-in-law is acting nicely to them."

Instruction to Children

I still keep up the old system of teaching my children at the campfire. In the morning I wake them up early and start to teach them as follows:

"My children, as you travel along life's road, never harm anyone, nor cause anyone to feel sad. On the contrary, if at any time you can make a person happy, do so. If at any time you meet a woman in the wilderness, away from your village, and if you are alone and no one can see you, do not scare her or harm her but turn off to the right and let her pass. Then you will be less tempted to molest her.

"My children, if you meet anyone on the road, even though it is only a child, speak a cheering word before you pass on. Fast as much as you can, so that when you grow up you can benefit your fellow men. If you ever get married, you must not sit around your lodge near your wife but try and get game for your wife's people. So fast that you may be prepared for your life.

"My daughters, if at any time you get married, never let you husband ask for a thing twice. Do it as soon as he asks you. If your husband's folks ever ask their children for something when you are present, assume that they had asked it of you. If there is anything to be done, do not wait till you are asked to do it, but do it immediately. If you act in this way, then they will say that your parents taught you well.

"My son, if you find nothing else to do, take an ax and chop down a tree. It will become useful some day. Then take a gun and go out hunting and try to get game for your family."

As soon as I see that the children are showing signs of restlessness, then I stop immediately.

1908-1913

Who Was Really the Savage?

Majigikwewis (First-Born Girl, Rose Mary Shingobe Barstow, 1915-†), Ojibwe

Beginning in the early nineteenth century in the United States and Canada, governments and churches began a policy of forced assimilation of Native children by sending them to a network of hundreds of boarding or residential schools far from their families for many years. Children were compelled to attend; once there they were stripped of their lifeways and languages. If they resisted or tried to run away, they were severely punished. When they were allowed to leave at sixteen or eighteen, many could no longer communicate with their parents because they spoke only English. The schools concentrated on manual skills training, as did the more advanced "colleges," such as Haskell Institute in the US, so that students would learn a trade such as tailoring or blacksmithing. Intellectual university training was not available. Several generations of Native children were pushed through this system, one reason many indigenous languages lost the necessary number of speakers required to survive. The following reminiscence of boarding school is by a language teacher and bilingual education consultant for the Minneapolis Public Schools.

I was born at four o'clock in the morning at ricing time in Onamia, Minnesota. The year was 1915. My mother was a converted Catholic. She didn't abide by all the traditional rites that were a part of the life pattern of Ojibwe families, so I didn't go through a naming ceremony. When I was two or three, an old lady felt sorry for me and gave me her name, Majigikwewis, and a feast. . . .

I was seven when my mother died. She had been in the hospital for a long time. My grandmother and grandfather raised me. When I turned eight, I went away to a Catholic mission boarding school. My mother had requested that I be sent there. Such a request was always honored by the old people. It was the first time in my life that I was left alone with absolute strangers.

The sisters at the school wore black, and I was afraid of them. One of the first things they did was cut my braids off. They made me wear a gingham dress with a big bow. I looked like everybody else. I felt really lost.

They put me in a kindergarten class because I could speak only Ojibwe. I was willing to learn English. One of the girls was asked to read out loud in English. She made a mistake, and the whole class began to laugh. I had been brought up not to laugh at a person who made a mistake—if he made it over and over, you felt sorry for him. I thought those children were crude. Even the teacher had a glint in her eye. So I zipped up my mouth and made up my mind that nobody was going to laugh at me for trying.

I was dumb all that year; never spoke a word. But I was learning internally. I worked so hard at learning English, I almost forgot my Ojibwe. When I returned home in the summer, I could hardly talk to Grandma and Grandfather. I was embarrassed. My aunt didn't understand what was wrong with me. She accused me of having foolish pride in myself—*bishigwadis* (immoral, unchaste)—that's a terrible insult to our people, because we're taught that you're never an entity by yourself. You're always a part of something. So I made up my mind to show her, to relearn Ojibwe so I could converse properly with my grandparents. By the end of the summer I was fluent in the language.

Our summers were happy. On Sundays, Grandfather would catch the horse, we'd jump in the buggy, and go to church in the town where our relatives lived. One Sunday it was Episcopal, the next Methodist. We sat in the back row and learned to respect other religions. We learned that what's important is not what religion you practice but believing in what you've been taught. Others will respect you for it.

I went back to school in the fall. Now I could speak English; I never kept my mouth shut. We read a history book about "the savages." The pictures were in color. There was one of a group of warriors attacking white people—a woman held a baby in her arms. I saw hatchets, blood dripping, feathers flying. I showed the picture to the Sister. She said, "Rose Mary, don't you know you're an Indian?" I said, "No, I'm

Mt. Pleasant, Michigan, Indian School, 1890s

390

not." She said, "Yes, you are." I said "No!" and I ran behind a clump of juniper trees and cried and cried. I spent a week in the infirmary. I didn't eat. I was really sick.

When I went home, I told Grandfather. He said, "I've heard about those books. They call us savages. Some of our old people wonder who was really the savage. Whites came here with a man nailed to a cross and used it to subdue us. They took everything from us. They said that we scalped our enemies. But you know, they bought Indian scalps for a dollar a head. That's not in those history books. You must return to school, Rose Mary. The Great Spirit gave you a mind of your own. Someday, my girl, you will write the truth in our language. You will write of the goodness of our people, and the tranquility."

1979

Sehià:rak
Gail Tremblay, Onondaga

Always the memories come rising like smoke
from burning fields, from smoldering towns—
the soldiers whose grandfathers came from Europe
destroying hundred weights of corn, torching
storehouses of dry beans, orchards of nut trees,
fruit trees, and every longhouse they could find.
The sacred objects and household tools turn
to ash as the newcomers try to obliterate our words,
to write the history of a continent where no one
lived, a place they claim—they wish
even our ancestor's bones that make this ground
to become their heritage. They create myths
in which we disappear and make us study them
in school. Their teachers tell our children to be ashamed
of our old ones, our old ones who say:
"Thó nonkwá ionsasewe' tsi nisewaweiennó:ten."
"Sehià:rak nitesewehtahkwen."
They say our words sound funny, ridicule us
for thinking in ways they cannot understand.
They report we are too much like our savage parents.
In boarding schools, they tell us, "Don't let
your people hold you back." And, "Earth

is no one's mother; we have dominion over it."
They tear and dig and destroy, build bigger
and more awesome instruments with which to kill.
Always the memories come rising like smoke
from death camps and bombed cities; it no longer
surprises us the world is mad; images
tear up the pages and speech grows raw.
The grief wells up in us and overwhelms
our tears. To forget is to become part of a lie;
to forget is impossible. Even the maggots
are part of the sacred circle, devouring the rot,
cleaning the earth; even the maggots can
teach us to survive. We struggle to grow,
to grow corn, to feed the people,
to keep the dream of peace alive.

                                                            1980s

Sehià:rak: Remember it.

Thó nonkwá ionsasewe' tsi nisewaweiennó:ten: That way   go back there   to your culture.

Sehià:rak nitesewehtahkwen: Remember it   your belief.

Born in Buffalo, New York in 1945, the poet and artist Gail Tremblay graduated from the University of New Hampshire and the University of Oregon. She began teaching at Evergreen State College, Olympia, Washington, in 1981. She has published several books of poetry and her artwork has been exhibited in the USA and internationally.

Iah Enionkwatewennahiton'se': We Will Not Lose Our Words

James Aronhiotas Thomas Stevens (1966-   ), Mohawk

The author of this meditation on language and culture is a professor and an award-winning poet. Here he examines in detail what is lost when a language is lost.

"The Mush Hole," also known as the Mohawk Institute, founded in 1831 in Brantford, Ontario, Canada, by the New England Company, a Protestant mission based in Britain. Renovated as Woodland Cultural Centre.

Thomas Asylum for Orphaned and Destitute Indian Children, later known as "Thomas Indian School" was founded in 1854 in Irving, New York, Cattaraugus Seneca Reservation, by Philip E. Thomas, a wealthy Quaker merchant of Baltimore, Maryland. Main building standing but windowless.

Language in the Burnham and Bero families; dismantling begun in the late nineteenth century. Structure unsound and listing badly, but possibility of future renovation.

The loss of the Mohawk language in my mother's family began with her paternal grandfather, my great-grandfather, or double-*totah*, as Mohawk kids might say today. Totah is the word for any respected elder but is most often used for a grandparent. My great-grandfather James Burnham was born on the Six Nations Reserve, bordering the city of Brantford, Ontario. Orphaned as a child, he was schooled at "The Mush Hole" and grew up not speaking his own language, Kanienkehaka (Firesteel-at-People), or Mohawk. Later he would marry Ida Anderson. Ida was from a farming family in Ohswekenand still spoke Mohawk fluently, but as English was the language of their interpersonal communication, the children, including my grandfather Earl, did not learn it.

My grandmother, Esther Hero, was born at the Saint Regis, or Akwesasne (Where the Partridge Drums) Mohawk Reservation, in upstate New York. Her mother, Harriet, died when my grandmother was fifteen, with six children even younger. The three eldest, Esther, Mary, and Irene, were old enough to stay with their father. The next three, Thomas, Ray, and Leona were sent away to the Thomas Indian School on the Cattaraugus Reservation, where their language was dissolved. My aunt Lena at Akwesasne adopted the baby, Eva, born while my great-grandmother was bedridden. Her language remained intact, along with that of the three eldest children.

At the age of seven, while my iron-working great-grandfather had taken his family to Syracuse, a white man abducted my grandmother, the totah in my family. At seven she spoke no English other than her name and address, not her true name, Kanarathakwas, but Esther Hero. As the man dragged my grandmother through the side streets of Syracuse, they passed a young couple, and my grandmother was able to tear away from her abductor and cling to the legs of the passing woman, repeating her name and address over and over. The man, of course, took the opportunity to escape. This event most likely signaled to Esther's parents the importance of learning English.

My grandparents, Esther and Earl, met at an Indian Defense League function in Niagara Falls, New

York. My grandfather's family from Six Nations, though no longer Mohawk speaking, was very active in Indian rights, especially concerning border issues, since his whole family had by then moved stateside. Meanwhile, my Totah's father had brought her and her siblings to live in Niagara Falls. Totah and Grandpa met for one date; then Totah had to leave to go back to Akwesasne; however, they remained in touch and were married after her return. My mother, Judith, is the first of six children born to them. Though involved in Indian functions, the children were never taught Mohawk. Again, English was the shared language between their parents. Certain phrases have survived, such as *Kanaron'kwa* (*kenaronhkwa'*: I love you); *Shékon, skennonkówa?* (Hello, are you well?) and others, but there is no fluency.

The transliteration of Mohawk to English letters, while making the language more accessible to non-Native scholars, actually aided in its deterioration. Most people I know who are fluent in the language do not read it in its written form, as the chosen letters don't function in a way that makes sense to them. My Totah, who can readily say *Kanaron'kwa* in her mother tongue, writes *Gonalunkwa* on birthday cards. Why is it that a word as simple as the word for "yes," *hen* (*hen'en*), can confuse a reader? Because the word is pronounced as two trochaic syllables with a nasal, sounding more like *huh'uh* (*hunh 'unh*); Hello, or *shékon*, is pronounced say'go. These are the small words. Imagine how daunted one feels on encountering a word like *enionkwatewennahton'se*, meaning "We will lose our words."

Early dictionaries, before it was settled upon that *t* and *th* equal *d*, *k* is *g*, *r* is *l*, and so on, are often easier to read, as they are simply written phonetically; although, one must take into account the rules of the translator's language, for example the Dutch *j* as *y* in the following texts, beginning with a short Mohawk vocabulary list written in 1624 by Nicolaes Janszoon van Wassenaer. This would be followed by van den Bogaert's 1635 text and Johannes Megapolensis's list of 1644. These brief lexicons are of very little use to modern-day Mohawks for two reasons. First, many of us have become familiar now with the accepted transliteration system, and secondly, lexicons such as Megapolensis's are full of phrases indicative of missionary zeal.

For example: *Tkoschs ko aguweechon Kajingahaga kouaane Jountuckcha Othkon* means "Really, all the Mohawks are cunning devils."

This phrase has never come into use in my own life, nor have I found much more in Megapolensis's text useful. This example is from one of the two dictionaries I had available to me as a teenager. The other is actually a small pamphlet, which was compiled at Akwesasne in 1975. The words are only roughly in alphabetical order, with corrections made in pen before photocopying.

At least twenty years during my childhood and young adult life were spent visiting my grandparents' home on the Tuscarora Reservation, six miles from my own family's home. Though I was surrounded by great leaders and activists like their neighbors Chief Clinton Rickard and Mad Bear Anderson, my ancestral language—obviously a key element in language acquisition—did not surround me.

Due to the availability of work at factories in Niagara Falls, and my grandfather's job at the Carborundum Company, my grandparents sought a place to live at the nearby Tuscarora Reservation. This push toward the cities in order to find work is responsible for some of Native American language loss. In particular, so many Iroquois and Anishnaabe men left for the cities to find ironwork. My grandparents were lucky, as they could at least live surrounded by Iroquois culture, if not language. The Tuscaroras, one of the six nations of the Haudenosaunee Confederacy, readily accepted them, and they stayed for a period of some twenty years. In the time I spent on that reservation while growing up, I don't remember hearing anything other than English, unless it was at an official gathering such as the Tuscarora picnic, a much-anticipated event with its nighttime fireball game. Now the Tuscarora School has implemented a language program, and signs on the reservation, including traffic signs, are written in Tuscarora.

Ironically, I first became seriously interested in the Mohawk language upon moving to New York City after high school. I lived in the Williamsburg section of Brooklyn before its gentrification, and although I had originally moved to the city in order to attend the School of Visual Arts, monetary problems forced me to withdraw, and I took a job at a cafe. I later began to work at the Museum of the American Indian— Heye Foundation, now relocated from its Spanish Harlem site to the old New York Custom House and soon to move to the Washington Mall as the Smithsonian's National Museum of the American Indian.

Being surrounded by other Natives who were employed there, Potawatomis, Cherokees, Aymara, Salish, and Hunkpapa Lakota, I was quickly reabsorbed into the Indian world. I began attending pow-wows at the YMCA and became involved in the American Indian Community House on Broadway and their gallery in SoHo. I was exposed to Spider Woman Theater and the Shinnecock Drum. It was obviously a very different Indian world, dancing on a basketball court at the McBirney Y, but nevertheless it was Indian.

I began reading as much translation as I could, fascinated by the more comfortable structure of Native languages. I began writing at this point, and Blue Mesa Review published the first three poems I wrote, "3 Songs of the Medicine Bundle." This style of writing became more developed when I attended the Institute of American Indian Arts in Santa Fe. By the time I reached graduate school at Brown University's Creative Writing Program, I was working on poetic forms that involved direct translation from Mohawk, meaning instead of translating a word like akohsátens as horse, I translated it as its linguistic parts: "the that aside." This alludes to the way Mohawk people first saw this animal, as reined together, pulling wagons and plows. Ironically, everyone thought I was deeply influenced by "language poetry."

My first book, titled *Tókinish* (*Wake Him*), a single poem, began formulating in my mind during graduate school. I worked briefly at the Narragansett Tribal House on Friendship Street in Providence as a data collector for a program called Wahteauonk (Knowledge). It was designed to keep children off the city streets after school by providing classes in Native tradition. Many of the children spoke Spanish, but none of them spoke a tribal language. I remember being surprised at two children who were, at least hereditarily, from the Acoma Pueblo. They had never been there, and I recall their delight when I showed them photographs I had from a feast day I had attended at the pueblo.

I was interested in the fact that the Narragansett words I saw written on the after-school projects were taken from Roger Williams's 1643 grammar of Narragansett. People were left to choose Indian names from Williams's *A Key into the Language of America,* as there were no fluent speakers. This forced loss of language has affected the self-identity of countless tribes. I began to relate it to the loss of individual identity in personal relationships also. What happens when we first call another person mine and begin our own colonization process? This question, using the Narragansett language as a guide, became *Tókinish.*

Most recently I have used the Mohawk language in a series of poems from my book *Combing the Snakes from His Hair.* These poems stem from a project I deemed *sui*-translation, translations for the self. These translations are executed in a way that allows for the words to change, in order to create relevancy in one's own life. The following is an example, beginning with Mohawk words, followed by the literal translation, and the *sui*-translation:

Canoe Song
Teiohonwa:ka ne'ni akhonwe:ia. Kon'tatieshon iohnekotatie.
Wakkawehatie, wakkawehatie.

> The canoe is very fast. It is mine. All day I hit the water.
> I paddle along. I paddle along.

> I am the hull—rapid against your stream.
> Birch beneath the ribs
> Circumnavigating your body.
> Endless propeller of my arm
> As it circles to find the flow.
> I move this way against you.
> I move this way.

This traditional song is originally intended to be sung while paddling, much like work songs that developed in African-American slave communities, rhythmic tunes to help one get through a task. Seeing as I don't often have to travel any distance by canoe, this song could be written off as being useless to me. However, it can and should change in order to become relevant to my life. This goes against what ethnographers and anthropologists have imposed on us since they first began to study us.

As early as the 1930s anthropologists like Elsie Clews Parsons in her two-volume work *Pueblo Indian Religions* were declaring tribes such as the Laguna Pueblo lost causes, due to the fact that their stories had changed since the earliest recordings. That it is one of the tenets of the oral tradition that stories must evolve to create relevancy was never even considered by anthropologists.

How is a canoe song relevant to my life? Every day I move against a stream of other lives, currents of emotion, eddies of fear or pain. Each day my arms reach for another, birch ribs under skin, trying to find a flow of unity. This is how a canoe song helps me. This is what I am trying to show in my work, specifically in the work that relies on the Mohawk language for imagery and meaning.

In a recent interview with Mark Anthony Rolo in *The Progressive,* Ojibwe author Louise Erdrich states: "The real life, blood, and guts of a language is in the everyday interactions between people," and "If it's not taught in the home from the very beginning, is that a real language, or is that an academic exercise?"

I wholeheartedly agree with Erdrich, and sadly I recognize my own knowledge of my language as academic exercise. I love the sound of Mohawk, and its construction is so beautiful to me, but I am a professor, and college teaching positions are not available on the Mohawk Reservation, or even close enough that I could immerse myself in the language. Presently I teach between the Cattaraugus and Allegheny Seneca reservations, to whom I'm indebted for the opportunity to attend occasional lacrosse games and socials; however, I find myself in a place not unlike that of my grandfather and great-grandfather, moving for job opportunity and forced to sacrifice language, if not culture.

In 1997 I moved to Lawrence, Kansas, where I taught at Haskell Indian Nations University for five years until moving back to New York in 2001. I saw many students go through courses in the Choctaw and Cherokee languages, and it was clear the pride with which they would greet me or say good-bye in these languages, but I never knew any of these students to actually have a group in which to converse or move beyond useful phrases. The fact that these courses are offered at all is a great step toward preservation, but the main element lacking in language preservation is a base of Native speakers large enough to support daily conversation. I envy the Diné for their Diné language radio station. And although many of my Diné friends have also ended up in urban areas to find work, there is a large community to return to for interaction with their language.

Recently I did a reading at the University of Maine in Orono and was glad to see an exhibit at the Hudson Museum concerning the Penobscot Primer Project, where a Native speaker was shown pictures and asked to describe them in Penobscot. The spoken language is recorded and also transliterated on a computer screen. While this provides a record of the language, I feel that until there are committed people willing to create "language nests," as Erdrich calls them, communities of people speaking a single language and passing it on, we are all in danger of losing the thing most important to our tribal identities.

Dorothy Ann Lazore writes in "Iehatien: tere'skwe'" ("Prophecy") in the anthology *Kanien'keha' Okara'shon:'a: Mohawk Stories*:

> *On:wa'ki' wenhniserá:te kerihwaién:tere's oh nahó:ten' rati:ton! Ne kí:ken kén' nón:we nikaná:taien' tenwatté:ni! Iáh ó:ni' onkwehonwehnéha' thenhshako'nikonhrotákwen iáh ó:ni' ónhka' thaonsaiontatíhseke' nonkwawén:na' enionkwattewennáhton'se' ok ó:ni nonkwaianerénhshera' tenwatté:ni! O:nen ki' tiotáhsawen tsi teiottenionhátie!*

> (Now, today, I understand what they meant by these stories. This very place will change. We Indians will no longer speak our language and, along with our words, we will lose our law. Even now it has begun. It is changing.)

In looking through this book of Mohawk stories today, I come across one of the most beautiful phrases, and it haunts me as I write this—*Ó:nen iehióhe naienenhstaienthó:ko'* (Now is the time when one should unplant the corn). This idea of harvesting as unplanting what one has planted is one of those typical linguistic structures I admire. It is the time for us to unplant our languages, to gather together what has been sown in the generations before. May the prophecy go unfulfilled as we all work toward its unfulfilling.

2003

My Hair Was Shorter Then

Eric Gansworth, Onondaga

In the months between graduate school
and my first class as instructor,
having never learned
to braid my hair, looking more
like Jerry Garcia than Geronimo
knowing the economics of a pathetic
job market, I cut my losses and hair
for the interview, and passing entered
my 8:00 a.m. American Literature class
where I knew I would be
forced, at Canon point to verbally
grant William Bradford and Jonathan Edwards
their roles as seminal voices in this country's
identity and worrying about how I was
going to do them justice, as it were, tried
breaking the pale ice of an early morning
class with a story of my own, how I had barely made it
to school that morning as an aggressive
driver transforming a left turn lane into a passing
one nearly hit me head on, only to witness
in response a blond haired young man in the front
row look around the room quickly and seeing no
evidence, informed me it had to be one
of those crazy ass drunk Indians from down the road.

                                                          2000

Eric Gansworth was born about 1965 and grew up at the Tuscarora Indian Nation in western New York. He began his career as a visual artist and expanded to storytelling. He has published five books of poetry and fiction and has been honored with numerous gallery exhibitions, and his short fiction is part of many anthologies. He is a professor of English and Lowery Writer in Residence at Canisius College in Buffalo, New York.

✦ WAR ✦

aul Radin, who transcribed the narrative that begins this section, wrote: "War was one of the most important elements in the life of a Winnebago. The life of the warrior was the ideal toward which all men strove. It not only satisfied certain emotional needs, but it was so inextricably interwoven with social standing in the community and with individual prestige that Winnebago life is unthinkable without it.

"When a man went on a warpath for the sake of glory, he generally led a large party and all sorts of special arrangements were made, because then a war leader was necessary and volunteers were always needed. It is believed that the same holds true for larger war parties . . . a special blessing was necessary for this purpose. . . .

"Before entering the village that warrior who has counted first coup is offered a pipe, from which he always takes a few puffs. The same pipe is then handed to the one who counted coup second, and so on, until the fourth man is reached. Then the prizes are given to the victors, who afterwards give them to their sisters. The scalps are not taken into the village but are left outside, and warriors who have remained at home rush out to count coup upon them. Then the scalps are carried around the village four times.

"The widely known Plains custom of counting coup is also practiced among the Winnebago. The individual who strikes the dead body of the enemy first obtains the first honor, the one striking it second the second honor, the one striking it third the third honor, and the one who actually killed the enemy obtaining the fourth and least important honor."

✦ ✦ ✦

Warfare
Member of the Thunderbird Clan, Ho-Chunk

If a man wishes to go on the warpath, he must fast and be blessed by the spirits in a specific manner. If a man is thus blessed, he gives a feast and announces his intention of leading a war party. The chief always has a representative at such a feast [a member of the Buffalo clan], and as soon as it is over this man goes to the former and reports to him. If the chief thinks that the blessing is insufficient and might cause the death of many men, he takes the war leader's pipe and lays it across his path, and the war leader is then compelled to abandon his undertaking. This action on the part of the chief is sacred and must be accepted as final. The war leader dare not step across the pipe. Should the chief, however, not do this, then the war leader knew that there was no objection. Usually some members of every clan go along, but especially members of the Thunderbird, Warrior, and Bear clans

The action of the war leader is controlled by many rules. He must be the one who has fasted and been blessed with all that is essential for conducting a war party. He must have his food provided for him by the spirits, know the exact location of the enemy, their numbers, and their sex.

After the war party has traveled for about four days, the men offer tobacco to the leader, and he tells them where he is going, the number of the enemy, etc. If, after that, any of the members of the war party do not approve of the undertaking, then they place a pipe across his path and the war leader is compelled to return. If nothing is said, then all is well. The war leader always goes ahead of his party and his attendants behind him, followed by the other members of the party. Whenever the chief stops, his attendants run to his side, take his war bundle, and place it in front of him.[239] Then the leader sits down, neither turning to the right nor to the left but looking straight ahead. The attendants get two poles and place them on each side of him and bend the ends over to form an arch, on each side of which are placed small oak sticks, arranged in a row. Under this structure the war leader stands. Here he sleeps and is fed by his attendants. No one is permitted to go ahead of this improvised structure. On each side of him two fireplaces are placed, two for the Upper clans.[240] If a man is going on a warpath for the first time, he stays in the rear of the party and has a little fire of his own. He remains in the rear in this way until the battle begins. Then he joins the others.

A member of the warrior clan is selected by the war leader to act as guard and goes back and forth behind him encouraging the men and telling them not to steal away alone or go too far ahead of the party, since that always results in the loss of life. It is for this reason that it is not considered correct for a man to try and steal away and perhaps obtain a war honor in this selfish manner. Whenever the war leader stops, he tells his companions what they must do in order to obtain food, all this information having been provided for in his blessing. If he tells someone to go to a certain place and kill a deer, he is certain to find a deer at the place specified. Whenever the leader gets up and steps over his war bundle, the attendants come and place his bundle on his back, and he then proceeds on his march, followed by the other members of the party. Whenever he comes to a river, he takes some of the tobacco which is always kept on hand and offers it to the spirit who controls this particular war party. The others do the same. Then he would cross the river. Whenever he drank any water, the others would also do so and, if he refrained, so would the others. If at any time during the night when they are camping the war leader should wake

Pipe, pipestem, club, 1845. Paul Kane

up and sing some songs, be they grizzly bear, black root paint, or night songs, all those others who knew similar songs would likewise begin to sing.

War honors—"It is the ideal of every Winnebago youth," says an informant, "to kill an enemy in full sight of his friends and thus to gain for himself a headdress and an eagle feather." Most deeds considered valorous, according to Winnebago ideas, have associated with them certain insignia which are always worn in public, giving evidence to all that the person has performed a particular valorous deed. These insignia consist of the following:

Headdress and feather—Denote that an individual has scalped and killed a man and torn off his scalp still bleeding. He is entitled to a red headdress and eagle feather. This also includes the man who counted first coup (*sarinîgwahína*).

Red headdress—If he has killed the enemy and not scalped him (*tcasî´ntc wak'érê*).

Eagle feather—Worn by one who has counted second coup.

Hanging eagle feather—Worn by one who has counted third coup.

Eagle feather stuck crosswise in hair—Worn by one who has counted fourth coup.

Wangirusgitc—Consists of a rope worn around the neck by the leader of that warpath who has captured an enemy.

Uâ´nkerê—Arm band worn by the person who did the actual capturing. If two enemies are captured, he can wear an arm band on each arm.

Red-dyed eagle feather—A red-dyed eagle feather worn by a war leader who has brought a captured enemy to camp and tortured him with embers.

Ankle-band of skunk or polecat—An ankle-band of the skin of a skunk or polecat worn by one who has seen an enemy dead on the battle field and kicked him. If he does it for the second time, he may wear skunk skins on both legs below the knee. If the leader does it, he is allowed to use an otter skin.

Rope tied to belt—A rope of any desirable length tied to a belt may be worn by an individual who has succeeded in either capturing or killing an enemy's horse. At a dance no one would dare step on it. If an individual does not want to wear this, he may in its place wear a rope around his body.

Legs painted white—An individual who has been on the warpath in winter may paint his legs white, from the knee down.

Gun painted red—An individual who has killed an enemy with a gun may carry this gun at a dance and paint it red.

Spear—If a person kills an enemy with a spear, he may carry this and tie to it any symbol eagle feather etc. that he has gained.

Kokê´reûn—An individual who was a well-known warrior and had fought in front of his comrades, and one whom the enemy respected, was entitled to a long stick with eagle feathers. At a dance he had the privilege of dancing with the stick in front of his comrades.

Hand on face—Any warrior making all four coups, who did not care to wear a dress, might paint a man's hand in black upon his face.

Raven's skin around neck—If an individual captured more than one woman in war, he was entitled to wear a raven skin around his neck.

Body painted yellow and wounded spot red—If a man had been wounded on the warpath, he had the right at a dance to paint his body yellow and the wounded spots red, with red streaks running from the wounds.

Otter skin around knee and *nangiso*—A great warrior, one who has gained all the war honors, can, if he does not wish to wear his separate insignia, wear instead an otter skin attached below the knee, whose ends are not quite united. He may also wear a nangiseo consisting of a stick, whittled and painted red, in his hair.

Valorous deeds are also perpetuated on the grave posts when the warriors who have accompanied the corpse to the grave count coup and draw a picture symbolizing their particular deed on the post. It should therefore be remembered that the markings on these posts do not refer at all to the valorous deeds of the deceased but to those of warriors who happened to count coup at the grave.

1908-1913

A War Adventure
Yäh-rohn-yäh-äh-wih (Deer is Sailing in the Sky, Catherine Coon Johnson, *c.*1850-†), Wendat

The attacking party described here may have been Haudenosaunee, since they were responsible for the nearly total extermination of the Huron/Wendat in the mid-1600s. Notable here is the Wendat chief's use of the animals in his warbundle—the wolf to find the track, the crow to follow the trail, and the small, quiet quail to reveal the enemy camp. The torture here is fairly typical of early warfare. What mattered to the tellers was that the Wendat triumphed and treated their enemies as they had been treated.

Yäh-rōhn-yäh-äh-wĭh, whose name is also translated as "The Deer Goes into the Sky and Everywhere," was born into the Deer clan on the Wyandot reservation in Oklahoma about 1850 and spoke Wendat almost exclusively when she told stories to Marius Barbeau in 1911.

The story I am now about to tell you is one that I have often heard from the old folks, when I was a child. It goes back to the very old times, and nobody now could say, for certain, where all these things happened.

The Wyandots used to hunt in the winter and attend to their gardens in the summer. During the hunting season, three or four large bands of our people would camp at different places, where game was plentiful, in the woods far away. When the hunting season was over, they would break up their winter camp and return to their cultivated lands, there to scatter in small bands and sow corn, beans, and squashes in their gardens.

Once, a large crowd of our people moved out to their winter quarters for the hunting season. All the able-bodied men went out hunting, leaving behind the old folks, women, and children, as was the custom. When they came back to their camp, after a very long hunt, they found that their people had been killed or had taken to flight. The scalps of all those that were strewing the ground had been torn and taken away. It became clear, after the dead had been counted, that some were likely to have escaped. Several hunters, therefore, started out and went in various directions, yelling in a peculiar manner, so that their voices might be heard a long way off. This was a friendly warning to all those that had run away and were still hiding in the bushes. Several times over the hunters went around, repeating the same familiar call, until, having heard the yells, all those that were hidden soon joined their folks. As a child was still missing, however, it was thought that the enemies had possibly taken it along with them.

The head chief at once summoned the warriors for a big war dance. And all the young fellows and nimble-footed men painted their bodies, picked up their spears, bows, and tomahawks, and fixed themselves up for the dance. The head-man made a very small fire, a mere handful of red embers, in the center of the dancing-ground, just as the Senecas still do at the present day. Then he pulled out a small pouch of sacred Indian tobacco, the leaves of which are tiny and round. During the dance, at intervals, he threw a few pinches of tobacco into the small fire and, while glancing at the smoke that curled upwards, he was speaking right along to himself, but in such a way that those who stood by could hear what he said. He was speaking out his wishes for a terrible revenge upon the slayers of his people. This was, truly, a kind of worship.

When all the tobacco had passed into smoke, the warriors began the war-dance. They were now on the war-path. The chief came forward holding a complete dried wolf-skin, with a short opening from the neck to the breast, a part of which had been sewn. He shook the skin and then threw it to the ground, and there a real, live wolf was now standing at the very place where the dried skin had hit the ground. The wolf at once began to howl and wiggle his tail. "Now, Cousin Wolf," said the chief, "you have to follow their trail!"

The wolf jumped around for a little while, until the chief ordered him to rush ahead. The wolf started off, followed at a distance by the hustling warriors. This was the only possible way for our warriors ever to find out where the enemies were now camping. The oft-repeated howls of the wolf guided the scouting party ahead, all through the night. At the dawn of the next day, they stopped and had a short war-dance, different from that of the first night. After having had something to eat, again they ran ahead. The wolf was, as ever, guiding them in the daytime, although without howling, as they could see him.

At night, they stopped. The Chief caught the wolf, shook it, and once again it became a mere dried skin. Then he made another small fire and, while throwing pinches of sacred tobacco on the red embers, he repeated his wishes for a great revenge. He now pulled out the dried skin of a kind of large, mythic raven, called Korekome, shook it, and threw it to the ground. The raven became alive and flew around several times. The chief said, "Uncle Korekome, it is now your turn to follow the trail!" And the raven flew ahead all the night long, croaking from time to time, so that the warriors might follow the right trail. The next morning they stopped and ate a little. All through the day, they followed the raven as they could see it flying slightly above the ground. They soon became aware that they were getting near the enemy, as the raven was not often seen flying back and forth.

At night they stopped, and the head chief seized the raven and shook it. It had now become a mere dried skin, to be put away. In the small fire that he had just made, he threw some tobacco and again spoke out, saying that his wish was soon to overtake the enemies. When all the tobacco had been burnt into smoke, the chief pulled out a dried quail skin with an opening from the neck to the breast. He shook the bird skin and threw it to the ground, and there it was now a live quail. The chief then spoke to the quail as if it had been a relative, called it brother, and said, "Now it is your turn; follow up the trail!" The quail ran around for a little while. "Go ahead!" ordered the chief, and off it went. The warriors did not see the quail any longer, as it was lost sight of in the grass, but could from time to time hear it cackle. It was now clear that they were getting quite close to the enemy, for the quail was often going back and forth and almost incessantly repeating its warnings. The warriors were no longer running but marching slowly. The quail then came back, flew up, and fell down to the ground. This was a sure sign that the end of the chase had now almost come. The pursuers kept crawling ahead for a while and then stopped. Two men were sent ahead. While crawling forward, they detected their foes as they were just erecting their camp. The spies came back to their own people and gave them warning. The Wyandot warriors then quickly scattered and crawled all around the camp, while the others, not suspecting the presence of their foes, were building up a fire for a big war dance. With the first whoops of the war dance, the warriors came forth with the Wyandot scalps tied on to sticks. Every one of the dancers had a stick, some with many scalps, others with but a few. And, high above their heads, they were brandishing their sticks, while dancing the war dance. This was, truly, a big war dance; and they had a big time, for they were unconscious of the keen, eagle eyes of the watchful Wyandots.

The child that had, in fact, been stolen from our people was soon brought out and handed over to the head chief of the dancing warriors. Some other warriors also offered him a long stick, sharpened on both ends. While the dance was still going on around him, the chief first brandished the stick and then pushed it right through the child's body, from the thighs up to the neck. He now came up to the big log fire and began roasting the child while it was still alive. And the others had a good time as the child was roasting. "Here is the Wyandot child roasting! Pretty good roast it is, for the Wyandot is my meat!" From the fat body of the child, the grease was dripping slowly into the fire.

And all this while, the Wyandots were all around, seeing and hearing everything. They were, indeed, getting quite impatient and furious, while standing nearby under the brush, and they wanted badly to spring forward and at once kill all the dancers to the very last one. But their chief said, "Wait! Keep on waiting! At daybreak, our turn!"

Once the child's body was roasted, it was put away; and the dance was broken up. It was now time to sleep. The Wyandots were more watchful. They had noticed the place where the child's body had been hid; and they named two of their own men to keep track of the spot where the enemy's head chief was going to sleep, so that they might capture him alive.

About daybreak, while every one of the doomed warriors was sound asleep, the impatient Wyandots were still waiting for the war yell, for, according to the custom, the one gifted with the best voice among the warriors had to yell in a certain manner, thus calling the others at once to rush upon their victims. The warwhoop then resounded, clear and loud, and all the Wyandots sprang forward for revenge upon those who had slain their people. They killed them outright, all but the head chief, whom they captured alive, and they took away their scalps. All but one, in fact, were dead.

The Wyandots then started off homewards taking their captive, the head chief, along with the roasted body of the Wyandot child. They traveled all day and camped at night. A fire was built for a big war dance. And all the warriors fixed themselves up for the dance. The prisoner was fastened to a post just near by, so that he could see the Wyandots dancing their war dance and brandishing their enemies' scalps, fastened, as usual, on to sticks. Some of the dancers, passing by the chief, their prisoner, would, in turn, cut his left and right ears, his nose, his lips, and his fingers; and they would torture him while dancing around. They still were in a great fury against him for all the atrocities that they had endured at his hands. They cut his body at different places, tore his phallus off, and burnt him all over. The Wyandot chief then started to roast the child's body, and again the grease began to drip off into the fire. When it was quite hot, he placed it against one side of the prisoner's face, saying, "Here is your Wyandot meat!" Then he applied it to the other side of his face and repeated: "Here is your Wyandot meat!"

Now they knew that their captive would not live much longer. They untied him. The Wyandot head chief pushed him off, saying, *"Hedi cateduto same tame tahe sarenewadat."* That is, "Go ahead! And tell your people how the Wyandots have treated you!" And he added, "If it hurts their feelings, let them come back and get even with us, if they dare to!" Then he pushed him off again, seeing that he was about to die.

When it was all over, the Wyandots started on their way home, carrying the dead child along with them, for they were to bury it in their camp, according to their custom.

This is the end.

*c.*1911

Traditional Wyandot History
Peter Dooyentate Clarke, Wendat

After the Huron were attacked by the Haudenosaunee, most fled Huronia [Ontario] and began migrating onto more western Great Lakes country, where they became known as the Wendat or Wyandot. There they came into contact and eventually war with the Cherokee and the Meskwaki, whose home it was at that time. An episode from that war is recounted here by the son of a European-Canadian Indian officer and the daughter of a Huron-Wendat chief. Clarke, who became chief himself in 1871, had for many years collected information about his nation. This became *The Origin and Traditional History of the Wyandotts,* and Sketches of Other Indian Tribes of North America, the first history of the Huron-Wendat, published in Toronto in 1870 and from which the following account is taken. The story he includes describing how animals resuscitate a warrior is common to many Native nations.

Between the years 1710 and 1721, the Wyandotts had commenced venturing southward through the vast wilderness to the Ohio River and beyond, occasionally coming into contact with strange Indians. They discovered some Cherokees inhabiting the banks of the Miami who came from the southwest.

A roving band of savages sojourned in the forests of Michigan, whom the Wyandotts named Foxes,[241] from their predatory raids into the neighbourhood of the French and Indians about Detroit, and who would occasionally return after being chastised and driven away by the French and their Indian allies.

At one time, whilst a party of Wyandotts were gone to their hunting grounds, leaving some of their old and young people to take care of their village some distance from Detroit, a party of the Fox Indians suddenly made their appearance and encamped near the Wyandott village and who, on finding that the warriors were absent, commenced annoying the old and young people by taking provisions from them. They would

405

come into their habitations and take a kettle of partly cooked meats or corn off the fire and carry it away, or otherwise ill-treat them. In the meantime some of the older Wyandott boys were sent to tell their friends at the hunting grounds. The old Fox chief of this marauding band had some of his young men on the lookout, and no sooner had he learnt that the Wyandotts were all returning home than he started with his party westward, but the retreating Foxes were soon within rifle and arrow shot of their pursuers. On, on through the wide forest and across plains went the Foxes, who were decimated by the rifle and tomahawk in the hands of their pursuers before reaching the shores of Lake Michigan. Here the Wyandotts turned back and left the remnant of the savages fleeing towards the Mississippi.

Overcome by fatigue they were soon fast asleep. Next morning the party found themselves completely covered up by a deep snowdrift; hearing the cold winds whistling through the branches of the scrubby oaks over their heads, each one dreaded getting up out of his hidden couch, and now and then one would scratch a hole through the encrusted surface of the snow, peep out, and exclaim, *"Whoo, nootendewaugh"* (It is terrible). The Chief of the party, losing all patience in waiting for some of his men to get up and start a fire, got up himself, and with a poking stick in his hand jumped on them, tramping and scattering the snow about their heads, exclaiming, "Get up out of this you sleepy-headed set!" and thus instantly roused up his men. Such was the Indian warrior's regard for his brave leader that no thought of insubordination ever prompted him to show any resentment, be he ever so roughly handled for being slow to obey his Chief.

During this decade (between the years 1720 and 1731), the Wyandotts and Cherokees became hostile to each other, and their long protracted warfare has been supposed to have originated from kidnapping one another's women and children for adoption. If this was the main source of strife between them, there was evidence enough from there being persons of Cherokee blood among the Wyandotts before and ever since the two nations made peace with one another; but whatever was the cause, a savage warfare was kept up between them for years through the forest to the Ohio River and beyond. . . .

At one time . . . a party of Wyandotts were overtaken north of the Ohio River and attacked in their camp by about double their number of Cherokees, and nearly all slain. But four of the former made their escape after the encounter and returned to the camp in two or three days; and as they were nearing the desolated camp, a swarm of different kinds of carrion birds flew up and scattered off. Some with bloody beaks looked down on them from their lofty perch, within gun shot. A strange and frightful sight caused them to shudder whilst gazing about the camp among the fleshless remains of their friends. One lay untouched by the carrion birds and, apparently in the calm sleep of death, tomahawked and scalped! They concluded that their friend lay in a trance; they would see what could be done for him with medicine to bring him back to life.[242]

In his vision he saw carrion birds around him instead of his friends. A bald eagle seemed to be guarding his body and allowed none of the birds to touch him. He concluded that the rapacious birds would soon commence devouring his carcass in spite of the eagle, but the bald eagle now began to speak and reasoned with them in this wise: "I think that instead of devouring this noble son of the forest, it would be doing him a kind and grateful act if we were to bring him back to life. We all know that he was a great hunter; many a deer we have known him to kill—stripped it of its skin and left the carcass for us to eat. Never, since I first came here, could I divest myself of the thought that there is life yet in his body, though apparently dead. Let us then all go to work and try to resuscitate him.

"Here, Blackhawk, you go get the medicine root, and you," said the eagle to a large northern hawk, "take a southern course and go to the Cherokee's camp, and you will find his scalp, among others, strung up on a tall pole over their camp, and bring it here."

Both birds started on their errand as they were ordered, and both were successful.

"Here, Raven, help the hawk put the scalp on this Indian."

"But the scalp has contracted," said the hawk, "and does not fit well."

"Soak the scalp in water," replied the eagle, "and stretch it to its full size, and you, Blackhawk, steep the medicine in that little kettle over the fire."

"Hey, all of you on the ground there, stop pecking at them bones and come rub this Indian's body, his feet, hands, legs, and arms. Steady there, all of you, and don't you relax one moment."

"I think," said the Blackhawk, "this medicine is steeped enough."

"Well, bring it here," said the eagle.

"But we have no spoon," said the other.

"Take that duck's bill on the ground there, and use it for a spoon," was the sharp reply. "Here, some of you help me about his head, rub his eyelids, nose, and lips with the medicine, put some on his tomahawk wound. Steady, friends, we can bring him back to life yet, and he will live to kill many a deer and leave the carcass for us as he has done between here and his home in the North."

The Indian in a trance thought he heard his winged friends around him singing the Indian medicine feast song while they were rubbing his body.[243]

"Now Buzzard," continued the eagle, "try and open his mouth a little, so that I can pour some of this medicine down him. Easy, easy, don't open his jaws as you would that of a dead deer's head." Little by little the eagle poured the medicine into the Indian's mouth. Fortunately for the Indian it was a glancing blow he received on the head and did not injure the brain. Presently they heard a gurgling sound, the liquid medicine was forcing its way down his throat, a shout of joy went up from the motley group, "Ye, hey!"

"Steady, friends," exclaimed the eagle, "we will soon have this noble son of the forest on his feet again. Don't stop rubbing him yet. Hey, you sluggish Buzzards sitting up there, cease craving for some of this Indian's carcass now, and be gone."

The evening shades were closing around him again as the Indian thought, and his winged friends still striving to restore him to life, until late in the night when they all suddenly disappeared. He thought he felt the next morning's sun touching his feet, hands, and face. His Wyandott friends now began to perceive unmistakable signs of returning life; his eyelids began to quiver, and his fingers and toes were moving. He suddenly opened his eyes and looked up, then turned and stared at them in mute astonishment. They stood watching their friend in silence, until he was asked by one of them if he was aware of his being yet on earth. This question made him stare the more wildly at them.

Presently they observed his lips moving as if trying to speak. At last he uttered in a scarcely audible voice, from weakness, saying, "If you are on earth, my friends, I am still with you." Raising up his head and looking around him with surprise, said he: "Where is the bald eagle and the other birds that brought me back to life."

"Ha! Ha! Ha! Ha!"

"What are you laughing about?" asked the resuscitated Indian, who was now sitting up.

"Your spirit," said one of his friends, "has been playing pranks on you. Ha! Ha! Ha! Ha! The eagle," he continued, "and his companions you speak of, betook themselves to flight on our approach, and had we not come as soon as we did, they might have pecked a hole through your body and extinguished the last spark of life in you."

"It may seem very strange to you," said the resuscitated Indian, "my friends, when I tell you that from the moment I first saw the bald eagle here, in advance of the other birds, he seemed to have singled me out from the rest of our slain friends, and from what I heard him say to the other birds, he had often seen me in the forest and seemed to know that I left deer carcasses purposely for his own and other kinds of flesh eaters of the flying species. It is wonderful to me," he continued, "when I think of the wanderings of my spirit during the last few days. I thought I followed and saw the hawk snatch off my scalp from a tall pole over our enemy's camp; it commenced, from a great height, sailing round and round, down gradually over the open camps of the Cherokees, who were watching the strange maneuvering of the hawk. Suddenly it swept by the pole over their camp, with the keen sound of whistling wind, and snatched off one of the scalps. In a moment the hawk was high up in the air again, with my scalp dangling from its talons, then flew northward, leaving the group of Indians, at the camp, with upturned faces and utterly confounded." Putting his hand on his head, "Whoo!" he exclaimed, "What is this? This is not my scalp!"

A roar of laughter preceded the response from his friends, when he was told that they had stuck a piece of raw otter skin on his head in the place of his original and missing scalp and that they went to work as soon as they concluded he was in a trance, instead of burying him, and brought him back to life with medicines.

"I thought one time," he continued, "that the bald eagle and his companions had brought me back to life and that I returned home, but my mother would not notice me. I told her repeatedly I was her son and that I had come home, but she would not listen to me. I then thought I pushed her elbow, which caused her to thrust her hand into a kettle of boiling corn and venison, over which she was leaning, giving her great pain from the scald. I thought too that I left home in sorrow for not being noticed by my mother. All seems like a dream to me now."

The now five surviving Wyandott warriors commenced their journey homeward.

1870

The Legend of Ho-poe-kaw
David Lee Smith (1950-   ), Winnebago

One of the greatest of Winnebago chiefs was not a man but a woman. Her name is still spoken whenever contemporary Winnebagos talk about political leadership. It has been more than two hundred years since the passing of Ho-poe-kaw,[244] but the legend lives on.

They said it was during the month of the Digging Moon (May) when Ho-poe-kaw was born. She was

408

the only child of the last true chief of the Winnebago people. On a clear, bright, sunny morning, she was presented to her people. To the Winnebago people it was an omen—an omen of good after suffering all spring with thunderstorms. It was also a time of great war, when the Winnebago joined their ally the Mesquaki Indians against the hated French. Ho-poe-kaw's father was of the Thunder Clan, and her mother was of the Eagle Clan.

As the years went by, young Ho-poe-kaw was taught the Winnebago way by her mother's sisters and her mother's brothers. Then one stormy night, she was called to her father's lodge. The old chief had passed away in his sleep. The entire tribe went into mourning, and the Grand National Council of the twelve clans debated on the issue of succession. Ho-poe-kaw found peace in the forest among her friends the animals. As a young girl of eighteen, she was unprepared for what lay in store for her. But the spirits of the dead chiefs were with her, and they made a pact with the thunder-beings that she would be the greatest chief of all of them.

During the closing of the Corn Popping Moon (August), the council elected her first chieftainess of the Winnebago people. Half of the tribe left for the Mississippi, because a woman chief was unheard of in that day and age.

At the age of nineteen, she became an ally of the French people, who named her Glory of the Morning, a translation of Ho-poe-kaw. In the first week of the Elk-Calling Moon (September), she was wed to a French military officer and, out of that union, would arise the famous DeCorah family.[245]

In the cool days of the Deer-Digging Moon (October), young Ho-poe-kaw and her war chiefs were invited to a council with the Upper Great Lakes tribes. After the council, they fell upon a Mesquaki hunting party and sent every one of the enemy to the spirit world. Ho-poe-kaw was finally caught at Little Butte des Morts Lake, and she almost went to the Spiritland herself. It was said the Thunder-beings intervened and turned the tables on the Mesquaki. The Mesquakis were caught at Starved Rock, Illinois, and almost terminated to the last man.

Ho-poe-kaw felt sorry for her people's former allies, and she pleaded with other tribes on their behalf to the French. Much to the displeasure of the French, they granted Ho-poe-kaw's request. Peace finally came to the Winnebagos, and the smile was once more on the face of Glory of the Morning, who had just turned twenty-six years of age.

The smile on Ho-poe-kaw's face seemed to vanish overnight. Her husband for the last seven years left her and returned to Quebec with his daughter Oakleaf. But deep in her heart, Ho-poe-kaw knew the Thunder-beings were putting her to a test—a test she would pass with flying colors. With a man out of her life, she devoted herself fully to the warpath. In 1752, under her orders, Winnebago warriors attacked their age-old enemies the Michigamia and the Cahokians. In 1755, Ho-poe-kaw sided with the French in the great war for the empire.

Under her eldest son's leadership, the Winnebago joined other Great Lakes tribes and attacked the British at Pickawellany and destroyed Edward Braddock on his way to Fort Duquesne. Then during the month of the Deer-Mating Moon (November), Ho-poe-kaw's warriors raided into Pennsylvania, Maryland, Virginia, Kentucky, and Tennessee. In all her victories, Ho-poe-kaw never fully forgot her one true love. Then came the tragedy at Quebec, when the only man in her life was killed while fighting alongside their son Choukeka (Tcugiga: spoon). The year was 1759, and Ho-poe-kaw had just turned forty-eight years of age.

In 1763, something seemed to come over Ho-poe-kaw. She seemed to be withdrawn and tired. When Pontiac went to war with the Long-Knives, she declined. Day after day, Ho-poe-kaw went into the forest and prayed for her people, and the Thunder-beings were kind, for they brought peace to the Winnebagos again. The legends say that one day, while walking through the pine trees, Ho-poe-kaw heard an owl calling her name. She knew it was an omen of death. Ho-poe-kaw was both sad and proud for what she had done for her people. Sad, because so many of them died in fighting for their land, and proud, that her sons would carry on the fight for her. One night in the Deer Antler Shedding Moon (December), Ho-poe-kaw had a vision from her father. He was calling her name.

The snow was falling heavily when daylight broke, and the stillness of the morning was shattered by the rumblings of thunder. This was odd, since the fall storms had passed two months before. Ho-poe-kaw's sons ran quickly to her lodge, and when they got there, they found Ho-poe-kaw dead. The chief lay wrapped in her furs with a smile playing on her lips. Ma-ona, (Earthmaker) the Creator, had called her home.

The legend of Ho-poe-kaw will never die as long as there are Winnebagos left in the world. And when the last Winnebago passes on, Ho-poe-kaw will walk with that person as they both enter the Spirit-land of the Creator forever.

1997

THE SEVEN YEARS' WAR IN AMERICA
(FRENCH AND INDIAN WAR)

Speeches of Pontiac at Detroit
Pontiac, Odawa

Pontiac[246] was one of the first leaders in the Great Lakes region to understand the danger whites posed to the Native way of life. Born in an Odawa village near Detroit about 1720, he had grown up in a Native/French world where power was shared and the relations between races were deep and long-lasting. When the French were forced to surrender New France to the English after Montcalm's defeat in 1759, suddenly the English were no longer just a bothersome foe and ally of the Haudenosaunee to the east, but they became an unpredictable presence on the lakes from Green Bay to Montreal. Moreover, it soon became apparent that they had little love for the Natives, drove churlishly hard bargains for sometimes shoddy merchandise, and were unable and unwilling to prevent settlers from invading Native lands. They were not the benevolent "fathers" the French had always been.

When he recognized what the English were and the eventual threat their control could pose, Pontiac formed a confederacy of allied tribes and Frenchmen to attack the western Great Lakes forts and return power to the French. He nearly succeeded, capturing all the western lakes forts except Detroit [Fort Pontchartrain], Fort Pitt, and Niagara. If French military commanders, exhausted and exiled beyond the Mississippi, had joined him, the English might have found themselves once again fighting for ground they had just won.

Pontiac was inspired not only by his own observations and experiences, but also by Neolin, a Nativist reformer living near the Ohio River called the Delaware Prophet.[247] Like Handsome Lake who would follow him, Neolin merged Christian doctrine with traditional customs, injected a large component of strict self-denial, and preached return to a pre-white past where Natives would live independently. He believed that without rifles, trade goods, or liquor, the dream of the past could be recaptured, provided that the whites were first driven out of the lakes. Pontiac made Neolin's message specifically anti-British, rather than generically anti-white, and used the Prophet's ideas as a divine justification for his campaign.

On April 27, 1763, Pontiac met with nearly 500 allies from several tribes near Detroit. After a reconnoitering visit to the fort, he then held another meeting on May 5 at the Potawatomi village downriver. No women were permitted; sentinels were stationed around the town. Robert Navarre, a French resident of Detroit who acted as Pontiac's scribe, recorded the war chief's speech in his journal.

May 5, 1763

It is important for us, my brothers, that we exterminate from our lands this nation which seeks only to destroy us. You see as well as I that we can no longer supply our needs, as we have done from our brothers, the French. The English sell us goods twice as dear as the French do, and their goods do not last. Scarcely have we bought a blanket or something else to cover ourselves with before we must think of getting another;

and when we wish to set out for our winter camps, they do not want to give us any credit as our brothers the French do.

When I go to see the English commander and say to him that some of our comrades are dead, instead of bewailing their death, as our French brothers do, he laughs at me and at you. If I ask anything for our sick, he refuses with the reply that he has no use for us. From all this you can well see that they are seeking our ruin. Therefore, my brothers, we must all swear their destruction and wait no longer. Nothing prevents us; they are few in numbers, and we can accomplish it.

All the nations who are our brothers attack them; why should not we strike too? Are we not men like them? Have I not shown you the wampum belts which I received from our Great Father, the Frenchman? He tells us to strike them. Why do we not listen to his words? What do we fear? It is time. Do we fear that our brothers, the French, who are here among us will prevent us? They do not know our plans, and they could not hinder anyway, if they would. You all know as well as I that when the English came upon our lands to drive out our father, Bellestre,[248] they took away all the Frenchmen's guns and that they now have no arms to protect themselves with. Therefore, it is time for us to strike. If there are any French who side with them, let us strike them as well as the English. Remember what the Master of Life told our brother, the Delaware, to do. That concerns us all as well as others.

I have sent wampum belts and messengers to our brothers, the Chippewas of Saginaw, and to our brothers, the Ottawas of Michilimackinac, and to those of the Thames River to join us. They will not be slow in coming, but while we wait, let us strike anyway. There is no more time to lose. When the English are defeated, we shall then see what there is left to do, and we shall stop up the ways hither so that they may never come again upon our lands.

> Pontiac failed to take the fort because the commander was warned in advance. One version places the blame on Angélique Cuillerier, who overheard her father and Pontiac plotting at her home. She informed her lover, a fur trader who lived at the fort, who notified the commandant, and Pontiac was kept out of the fort. Later historians blame an Odawa named Mahiganne (wolf?). By July 1 the fort had not fallen and the siege was at an impasse. Fearing that the French residents of Detroit, who had declared themselves neutral but had been compelled to help support the besieging Natives, would begin to side with the British inside the fort, Pontiac called a meeting. The French were too clever to take part openly in the rebellion and thus risk British reprisals if it didn't succeed, but Pontiac forced their hands and succeeded in getting some of the young men to join him temporarily. His address, once again copied by Robert Navarre, is a masterpiece of coercion.

July 1, 1763

My brothers, I am beginning to grow tired of seeing our lands encumbered by this carrion flesh [the English], and I hope you feel the same. I believe you are about ready to conspire with us to destroy them; still, it has seemed to me that you have been abetting them to our hurt. I have already told you, and I say it again, that when I began this war it was for your interest as well as ours. I knew what I was about.

I know Fort Presqu'Isle has fallen. I say I know it, and this year all the English in Canada, no matter how large their force, must perish. It is the Master of Life who commands it; He has made known His will unto us; we have responded and must carry out what He has said, and you French, you who know Him better than we, will you all go against His will? I have not wished to speak, hoping that you would let us take our course; I have not wished to urge you to take up arms against them, for I did not think you would side against us. I know very well you are going to say that you do not side with them, but you are siding with them when you report to them all that we do and say. For this reason there is only one way open today: either remain French as we are, or altogether English as they are.

If you are French, accept this war belt for yourselves, or your young men, and join us; if you are English, we declare war upon you, which will show our valor all the more because we know you to be children of our Great Father as well as we; to make war upon our brothers for the sake of such dogs pains us, and it will cost us an effort to attack you inasmuch as we are all French together; and if we should attack, we should no longer be French. But since we are French, it is wholly the interests of our Father, yours and ours, that we defend. Therefore answer, my brothers, that we may come to an understanding; and behold this belt which makes its appeal to you and your young men.

> Nothing came of this, however, and in September Pontiac was told by the French that they would not help him and he should make peace. His dream dead, he left Detroit for a village on the Maumee River where he hoped to establish a new base of power, but he was unsuccessful. In 1769 he was clubbed and stabbed by a Peoria in the French village of Cahokia.

Ending of the French Supremacy
William Warren (1825-1853), Ojibwe

William Warren, the son of an Ojibwe-French mother and a white fur trader descended from Mayflower pilgrims, wrote *The History of the Ojibway People*, the first history of the Ojibwe, from which this episode of the fall of Michilimackinac (Mishiwi-makinâk: Big Turtle) is taken. Educated at mission schools and in New York, Warren, who became an interpreter for the US government and an elected member of the Minnesota territorial legislature, received the blessing for his history in 1847 from Buffalo, an elder at La Pointe. Warren's method was to use many informants, checking accounts against each other, to collect "all the events of importance that had happened to their tribe in former times, especially the battles that their ancestors had fought with their many and different enemies." Like many Métis on the Great Lakes frontier, he moved easily between cultures, and he does that here, narrating from his Native informants while using quotations from Alexander Henry, an eyewitness to the fall of the fort, who had been a trading partner of Warren's French grandfather, John Baptiste Cadotte. Ill with tuberculosis, Warren worked desperately hard to finish one volume of the several he had envisioned, but he died at 28.

The excerpt reprinted here describes one of the most famous battles of the Great Lakes: the capture of Fort Michilimackinac during what was known as "Pontiac's War," as part of the Seven Years' War in America (French and Indian War) from 1754-1763. The fort controlled commerce on three lakes and was central to the fur trade; thus the neighboring Odawa had received a war belt from their fellow Odawa, Pontiac, signifying his desire for their help. When they hesitated, the nearby Chippewa seized the initiative and made plans to storm the fort, using a game of lacrosse as a ruse. Warren's version of events states that the Chippewa were under the control of Pontiac and that the leader of the attack was Minavavana who was known as Le Grand Saulteur by the French. White historians believe the war chief who actually led the attack was Matchekewis,[249] whose cleverness and success stunned the British and left the grumbling Odawa to insist on sharing the spoils—the prisoners who could be taken to Montreal for ransom. Warren, ever the politician caught between two cultures, may have been throwing a bone to the Odawa by suggesting the Chippewa took orders.

We have now brought forward the history of the different sections of the Ojibway tribe to the time when the French nation were forced to strike their colors and cede their possessions in America (comprising the great chain of lakes), into the hands of the British Empire.

The time during which these two powerful nations battled for the supremacy on the American continent is an important era in the history of the Algic tribes who occupied a great portion of Canada and the areas of the great western lakes.

Induced by their predilection to the French people, the causes of which we have given in a previous chapter [not supplied here], the eastern section of the Ojibway tribe residing at Sault Ste. Marie, Mackinaw, and the shores of Lake Huron joined their warriors with the army of the French and freely rallied to their support at Detroit, Fort Du Quesne,[250] Niagara, Montreal, and Quebec. The Ojibways figured in almost every battle which was fought during these bloody wars, on the side of the French against the English. A party of the tribe from their central village of La Pointe on Lake Superior even proceeded nigh two thousand miles to Quebec, under their celebrated war chief Mamongeseda (Big Foot/Big Feet), and fought in the ranks of Montcalm on the Plains of Abraham, when this ill-fated general and the heroic Wolfe received their death wounds.[251] According to the late noted British interpreter John Baptiste Cadotte, the name by which the Ojibways now know the British, Shaugunaush,[252] was derived from the circumstance of their sudden and almost unaccountable appearance on that memorable morning on the heights of Abraham. It is a little changed from the original word *saugaushe* which signifies "to appear from the clouds."

With the deepest regret and sorrow, the Ojibways, in common with other Algic tribes, at last viewed the final delivery of the northwestern French forts into the hands of the conquering British. With aching hearts they bade a last farewell to the kind-hearted French local commanders, whom they had learned to term "Father," and the jovial-hearted *"coureur du bois"* and open-handed *"marchand voyageur,"*[253] many of whom took their final departure from the Indian country on its cession to Great Britain. The bonds, however, which had been so long riveting between the French and Ojibways were not so easily to be broken.

The main body of the French traders and common voyageurs who had so long remained amongst them had, many of them, become united to the Indian race by the ties of marriage; they possessed large families of half-blood children whom the Indians cherished as their own and in many instances actually opposed their being taken from their midst. These Frenchmen, as a body, possessed an unbounded influence over the tribes amongst whom they resided, and though they did not openly aid and advise them in the strenuous efforts which they continued to make even after the French as a nation had retired from the field, to prevent the occupation of their country by the British, yet their silence and apparent acquiescence conduced greatly to their noble and protracted efforts headed by the great Algic leader Pontiac.

The fact of their love and adherence to the French people cannot be gainsaid, and to more fully illustrate this feeling, as it actuated their conduct even after the great French nation had delivered them over to the dominion of the British, I will refer to the respected authority of Alexander Henry, the first British trader whom the Ojibways tell of having resided with them after the termination of the disastrous war which we are about to notice.

In 1760, the French forts on the northern lakes were given up to the British, and for the time being the northern tribes of Indians apparently acquiesced in the peace which their Great Father, the French King, had made with Great Britain. In the spring of the following year, Mr. Henry, the well-known author of *Travels and Adventures in Canada and the Indian Territories Between the Years 1760 and 1766*, tells of making a trading voyage from Montreal to Michilimackinac. He came across a large village of Ojibway Indians on the small island of La Cloche in Lake Huron[254] who treated him in the kindest and most friendly manner, till, "discovering that he was an Englishman," they told his men that the Michilimackinac Indians would certainly kill him and that they might as well anticipate their share of the pillage. They accordingly demanded a part of his goods, which he prudently gave them. He observed afterwards that from the repeated warnings which he daily received, his mind became "oppressed and much troubled," and learning that the "hostility of the Indians was exclusively against the English," this circumstance suggested to him a prospect of security in securing a Canadian disguise, which eventually enabled him to complete his journey.

He arrived at Michilimackinac, where he found his difficulties to increase and where he fully learned the nature of the feelings which actuated the minds of the Ojibways against the occupation of their country by the English; nor were his apprehensions allayed, till he received a formal visit from the war chief of the eastern section of the tribe, who resided at Michilimackinac. Mr. Henry describes this man as a person of remarkable appearance, of commanding stature, and with a singularly fine countenance.

He entered the room where the traveler was anxiously awaiting the result of his visit, followed by sixty warriors dressed and decorated in the most formal and imposing fashion of war. Not a word was spoken as they came in one by one, seated themselves on the floor at a signal from the chief, and began composedly to fill and smoke their pipes. The Ojibway chieftain meanwhile, looking steadfastly at the trader, made various inquiries of his head boatman, a Canadian. He then coolly observed that "the English were brave men and not afraid of death, since they dared to come thus fearlessly among their *enemies.*"

When the Indians had finished smoking their pipes, the chief took a few wampum strings in his hand and commenced the following harangue—

"Englishman! It is to you that I speak, and I demand your attention!

"Englishman! You know that the French king is our father. He promised to be such; and we, in return, promised to be his children. This promise we have kept.

"Englishman! It is you that have made war with this our father. You are his enemy; and how then could you have the boldness to venture among us, his children? You know that his enemies are ours.

"Englishman! We are informed that our father, the king of France, is old and infirm and that being fatigued with making war upon your nation, he is fallen asleep.

"During his sleep, you have taken advantage of him and possessed yourselves of Canada. But his nap is almost at an end. I think I hear him already stirring and inquiring for his children, the Indians—and when he does awake, what must become of you? He will destroy you utterly.

"Englishman! Although you have conquered the French, you have not yet conquered us! We are not your slaves. These lakes and these woods and mountains were left to us by our ancestors. They are our inheritance, and we will part with them to none. Your nation supposes that we, like the white people, cannot live without bread and pork and beef. But you ought to know that He—the Great Spirit and Master of Life—has provided food for us in these broad lakes and upon these mountains.

"Englishman! Our father, the king of France, employed our young men to make war on your nation.

"In this warfare, many of them have been killed, and it is our custom to retaliate, until such time as the spirits of the slain are satisfied. Now the spirits of the slain are to be satisfied in either of two ways. The first is by spilling the blood of the nation by whom they fell; the other, by *covering the bodies of the dead,* and thus allaying the resentment of their relatives.[255] This is done by making presents.

"Englishman! Your king has never sent us any presents, nor entered into any treaty with us, wherefore he and we are still at war; and until he does these things, we must consider that we have no other father or friend among the white men than the king of France. But for you, we have taken into consideration that you have ventured your life among us, in expectation that we should not molest you; you do not come armed with an intention to make war. You come in peace, to trade with us and supply us with necessaries of which we are much in want. We shall regard you therefore as a brother, and you may sleep tranquilly without fear of the Chippeways. As a token of our friendship, we present you with this pipe to smoke."

Mih-neh-weh-na, the name of the chieftain who delivered this noble speech, now gave his hand to the Englishman. His sixty warriors followed his example. The pipe, emblem of peace, went round in due order and, after being politely entertained by the anxious trader, from whose heart they had taken a heavy load, they all quietly took their leave.

So many more able writers than myself have given accurate accounts of the memorable events which occurred during this important era in American history, that I desist from entering into details of any occurrence, except in which the Ojibways were actually concerned.

For upwards of four years after the French had ceded the country to the British, the allied Algic tribes, after a short lull of quiet and comparative peace, under the masterly guidance of Pontiac, maintained the war against what they considered as the usurpation, by the British, of the hunting grounds which the Great Spirit had given their ancestors.

Such was the force and accuracy of the organization which this celebrated leader had effected among the northern tribes of his fellow red men that, on the same day, which was the 4th of June, 1763, and the anniversary of the king's birth (which the Indians knew was a day set apart by the English as one of amusement and celebration), they attacked and besieged twelve of the wide-spread western, stockaded forts and succeeded in taking possession of nine. In this alliance, the Ojibways of Lake Huron and Michigan were most active parties, and into their hands was entrusted by their common leader, the capture of the British fort at Mackinaw. "That fort," according to the description of an eminent writer, "standing on the south side of the strait between lakes Huron and Michigan, was one of the most important positions on the frontiers. It was the place of deposit and point of departure between the upper and lower countries; the traders always assembled there, on their voyages to and from Montreal. Connected with it was an area of two acres, enclosed with cedar wood pickets, and extending on one side so near to the water's edge that a western wind always drew the waves against the foot of the stockade. There were about thirty houses within the limits, inhabited by about the same number of families. The only ordinance on the bastions were two small brass pieces. The garrison numbered between ninety and one hundred."

The important enterprise of the capture of this important and indispensable post was entrusted into the hands of Mih-neh-weh-na, the great war chieftain of the Ojibways of Mackinaw, whom we have already mentioned, and by the manner in which he superintended and managed the affair to a complete and successful issue, he approved himself a worthy lieutenant of the great head and leader of the war, the Ottawa chieftain, Pontiac.

The Ottawas of Lake Michigan, being more friendly disposed to the British, were not called on by the politic Ojibway chieftain for help in this enterprise, and a knowledge of the secret plan of attack was carefully kept from them, for fear that they would inform their English friends and place them on their guard.[256] In fact, every person of his own tribe whom he suspected of secret good-will towards any of the new British traders, Min-neh-weh-na sent away from the scene of the intended attack, with the admonition that death would be their sure fate should the Sauguna[u]sh be informed of the plan which had been formed to take possession of the fort.

In this manner did he guard with equal foresight and greater success than Pontiac himself against a premature development of their plans. Had not the loving Indian girl informed the young officer at Fort Detroit of Pontiac's secret plan, that important post, and its inmates, would have shared the same fate as befell the fort at Mackinaw.

Of all the northern tribes who occupied the great lakes, the Ojibways allowed only the Osaugees [Sauk] to participate with them in their secret councils, in which was developed the plan of taking the fort, and these two tribes only were actively engaged in this enterprise. The fighting men of the Ojibways and Osaugees gradually collected in the vicinity of the fort as the day appointed for the attack approached. They numbered between four and six hundred. An active trade was in the meantime carried on with the British traders, and every means resorted to for the purpose of totally blinding the suspicions which the more humane class of the French population found means to impart to the officers of the fort, respecting the secret animosity of the Indians. These hints were entirely disregarded by Major Etherington, the commandant of the fort, and he even threatened to confine any person who would have the future audacity to whisper these tales of danger into his ears. Everything, therefore, favored the scheme which the Ojibway chieftain had laid to ensnare his confident enemies. On the eve of the great English king's birthday, he informed the British commandant that as the morrow was to be a day of rejoicing, his young men would play the game of ball, or Baug-ah-ud-o-way (*baaga'adowe*: he plays lacrosse), for the amusement of the whites, in front of the gate of the fort. In this game the young men of the Osaugee tribe would play against the Ojibways for a large stake. The commandant expressed his pleasure and willingness to the crafty chieftain's proposal, little dreaming that this was to lead to a game of blood, in which those under his charge were to be the victims.

During the whole night the Ojibways were silently busy in making preparations for the morrow's work. They sharpened their knives and tomahawks and filed short their guns. In the morning these weapons were entrusted to the care of their women who, hiding them under the folds of their blankets, were ordered to stand as near as possible to the gate of the fort, as if to witness the game which the men were about to play. Over a hundred on each side of the Ojibways and Osaugees, all chosen men, now sallied forth from their wigwams, painted and ornamented for the occasion and, proceeding to the open green which lay in front of the fort, they made up the stakes for which they were apparently about to play and planted the posts towards which each party was to strive to take the ball.

This game of Baug-ah-ud-o-way is played with a bat and wooden ball. The bat is about four feet long, terminating at one end into a circular curve, which is netted with leather strings and forms a cavity where the ball is caught, carried, and if necessary thrown with great force, to treble the distance that it can be thrown by hand. Two posts are planted at the distance of about half a mile. Each party has its particular post, and the game consists of carrying or throwing the ball in the bat to the post of the adversary. At the commencement of the game, the two parties collect midway between the two posts; the ball is thrown up into the air, and the competition for its possession commences in earnest. It is the wildest game extant among the Indians and is generally played in full feathers and ornament with the greatest excitement and vehemence.

The great object is to obtain possession of the ball, and during the heat of the excitement no obstacle is allowed to stand in the way of getting at it. Let it fall far out into the deep water, numbers rush madly in and swim for it, each party impeding the efforts of the other in every manner possible. Let it fall into a high enclosure, it is surmounted, or torn down in a moment, and the ball recovered; and were it to fall into the chimney of a house, a jump through the window, or a smash of the door, would be considered of no moment, and the most violent hurts and bruises are incident to the headlong, mad manner in which it is played. It will be seen by this hurried description, that the game was very well adapted to carry out the scheme of the Indians.

On the morning of the 4th of June, after the cannon of the fort had been discharged in commemoration of the king's natal day, the ominous ball was thrown up a short distance in front of the gate of Fort Mackinaw, and the exciting game commenced. The two hundred players, their painted persons streaming with feathers, ribbons, fox and wolf tails, swayed to and fro as the ball was carried backwards and forwards by either party, who for the moment had possession of it. Occasionally a swift and agile runner would catch it in his bat and, making tremendous leaps hither and thither to avoid the attempts of his opponents to knock it out of his bat or force him to throw it, he would make a sudden dodge past them and, choosing a clear track, run swiftly, urged on by the deafening shouts of his party and the bystanders, towards the stake of his adversaries, till his onward course was stopped by a swifter runner, or an advanced guard of the opposite party.

The game, played as it was by the young men of two different tribes, became exciting, and the commandant of the fort even took his stand outside of his open gates to view its progress. His soldiers stood carelessly unarmed, here and there, intermingling with the Indian women who gradually huddled near the gateway, carrying under their blankets the weapons which were to be used in the approaching work of death.

In the struggle for its possession, the ball at last was gradually carried towards the open gates, and all at once, after having reached a proper distance, an athletic arm caught it up in his bat and, as if by accident, threw it within the precincts of the fort. With one deafening yell and impulse, the players rushed forward in a body, as if to regain it, but as they reached their women and entered the gateway, they threw down their wooden bats and, grasping the shortened guns, tomahawks, and knives, the massacre commenced, and the bodies of the unsuspecting British soldiers soon lay strewn about, lifeless, horribly mangled, and scalpless. The careless commander was taken captive without a struggle, as he stood outside the fort viewing the game which the Ojibway chieftain had got up for his amusement.

The above is the account, much briefened, which I have learned verbally from the old French traders and half-breeds, who learned it from the lips of those who were present and witnessed the bloody transaction. Not a hair on the head of the many Frenchmen who witnessed this scene was hurt by the infuriated savages, and there stands not on record a stronger proof of the love borne them by the tribe engaged in this business than this very fact, for the passions of an Indian warrior, once aroused by a scene of this nature, are not easily appeased, and generally everything kindred in any manner to his foe falls a victim to satiate his blood-thirsty propensities.

Alexander Henry, one of the few British traders who survived this massacre, gives the most authentic record of this event that has been published, and to his truthful narrative I am indebted for much corroborating testimony to the more disconnected accounts of the Indians and old traders. A few quotations from his journal will illustrate the affair more fully, and I have no doubt will be acceptable to the reader as being better told than I can tell it.

After disregarding the friendly, cautionary hints of Wa-wat-am, an Ojibway Indian who had adopted him as a brother, but who dared not altogether disclose the plan of attack formed by his people, Mr. Henry resumes his narrative as follows:

"The morning was sultry. A Chippeway came to tell me that his nation was going to play at Baggati-way with the Sacs or Saukies, another Indian nation, for a high wager. He invited me to witness the sport, adding that the commandant was to be there, and would bet on the side of the Chippeways. In consequence of this information, I went to the commandant and expostulated with him a little, representing that the Indians might possibly have some sinister end in view, but the commandant only smiled at my suspicions.

"I did not go myself to see the match, which was now to be played without the fort, because, there being a canoe prepared to depart on the following day to Montreal, I employed myself in writing letters to my friends; and even when a fellow trader, Mr. Tracy, happened to call on me, saying that another canoe had just arrived from Detroit and proposing that I should go with him to the beach to inquire the news, it so happened that I still remained to finish my letters, promising to follow Mr. Tracy in the course of a few minutes. Mr. Tracy had not gone more than twenty paces from the door, when I heard an Indian war-cry and a noise of general confusion. Going instantly to my window, I saw a crowd of Indians within the fort, furiously cutting down and scalping every Englishman they found. In particular, I witnessed the fate of Lieut. Jenette. I had, in the room in which I was, a fowling piece, loaded with swan shot.[257] This I immediately seized and held it for a few minutes, waiting to hear the drum beat to arms. In this dreadful interval, I saw several of my countrymen fall, and more than one struggling between the knees of an Indian who, holding him in this manner, scalped him while yet living! At length, disappointed in the hope of seeing resistance made to the enemy and sensible of course that no effort of my own unassisted arm could avail against four hundred Indians, I thought only of seeking shelter. Amid the slaughter which was raging, I observed many of the Canadian inhabitants of the fort calmly looking on, neither opposing the Indians nor suffering injury. From this circumstance I conceived a hope of finding security in their houses."

After describing the many hair-breadth escapes which befell him at the hands of the savages, Mr. Henry was eventually saved by Wa-wat-am, or Wow-yat-ton (Whirling Eddy), his adopted Ojibway brother, in the following characteristic manner, which we will introduce in his own words, as an apt illustration of Indian custom:

"Toward noon (7th June), when the great war chief, in command with Wen-ni-way, was seated at the opposite end of the lodge, my friend and brother Wa-wa-tam, suddenly came in. During the four days preceding, I had often wondered what had become of him. In passing by, he gave me his hand but went immediately toward the great chief, by the side of whom and Wen-ni-way, he sat himself down. The most uninterrupted silence prevailed. Each smoked his pipe, and this done, Wa-wa-tam arose and left the lodge, saying to me, as he passed, 'Take courage.'

"An hour elapsed, during which several chiefs entered and preparations appeared to be making for a council. At length Wa-wa-tam re-entered the lodge, followed by his wife, and both loaded with merchandise, which they carried up to the chiefs and laid in a heap before them. Some moments of silence followed, at the end of which Wa-wa-tam pronounced a speech, every word of which, to me, was of extraordinary interest—

"'Friends and relations,' he began, 'what is it that I shall say? You know what I feel. You all have friends and brothers and children whom as yourselves you love, and what would you experience did you, like me, behold your best friend, your brother, in the condition of a slave—a slave exposed every moment to insult and to the menaces of death! This case, as you all know, is mine. See there,' pointing to myself, 'my friend and brother among slaves, himself a slave!

"'You all well know, long before the war began, I adopted him as my brother. From this moment he became one of my family, so that no change of circumstances could break the cord which fastened us together. He is my brother—and because I am your relation, he is therefore your relation too; and how, being your relation, can he be your slave?

"'On the day on which the war began, you were fearful lest, on this very account, I should reveal your secret. You requested, therefore, that I should leave the fort and even cross the lake. I did so but did it with reluctance. I did it with reluctance, notwithstanding that you, Mih-neh-weh-na, who had the command in this enterprise, gave me your promise that you would protect my friend, delivering him from all danger, and giving him safely to me.

"'The performance of this promise I now claim. I come not with empty hands to ask. You, Mih-neh-weh-na, best know whether or not, as it respects yourself, you have kept your word. But I bring these goods, to buy off every claim, which any man among you all may have on my brother, as his prisoner.'

"Wa-wa-tam having ceased, the pipes were again filled, and after they were finished, a further period of silence followed. At the end of this, Mih-neh-weh-na arose and gave his reply:

"'My relation and brother,' said he, 'what you have spoken is the truth. We were acquainted with the friendship which subsisted between yourself and the Englishman, in whose behalf you have now addressed us. We knew the danger of having our secret discovered and the consequences which must follow. You say truly that we requested you to leave the fort. This we did in regard for you and your family; for if a discovery of our design had been made, you would have been blamed, whether guilty or not, and you would thus have been involved in difficulties, from which you could not have extricated yourself. It is also true that I promised you to take care of your friend; and this promise I performed by desiring my son, at the moment of assault, to seek him out and bring him to my lodge. He went accordingly but could not find him. The day after I sent him to Langlade's [a French trader], when he was informed that your friend was safe; and had it not been that the Indians were then drinking the rum which had been found in the fort, he would have brought him home with him, according to my orders. I am very glad to find that your friend has escaped. We accept your present: and you may take him home with you.'

"Wa-wa-tam thanked the assembled chiefs and, taking me by the hand, led me to his lodge, which was at the distance of a few yards only from the prison lodge. My entrance appeared to give joy to the whole family. Food was immediately prepared for me, and I now ate the first hearty meal which I had made since my capture. I found myself one of the family and, but that I had still my fears as to the other Indians, I felt as happy as the situation could allow."

Mr. Henry says further: "Of the English traders that fell into the hands of the Indians at the capture of the fort, Mr. Tracy was the only one who lost his life. Mr. Ezekiel Solomons and Mr. Henry Bostwick were taken by the Ottawas and, after the peace, carried down to Montreal, there ransomed. Of ninety troops, about seventy were killed; the rest, together with those of the posts in the Bay des Puants[258] and at the river St. Joseph, were also kept in safety by the Ottawas till the peace and then either freely restored or ransomed at Montreal. The Ottawas never overcame their disgust at the neglect with which they had been treated in the beginning of the war by those who afterwards desired their assistance as allies."

That portion of the Ojibways forming by far the main body of the tribe, who occupied the area of Lake Superior, and those bands who had already formed villages on the Upper Mississippi and on the sources of its principal northeastern tributaries, were not engaged in the bloody transactions which we have described, or at most but a very few of their old warriors who have now all paid the last debt of nature were noted as having been present on the occasion of this most important event in Ojibway history.

1885

THE WAR OF 1812

Speech of Tecumseh at Vincennes
Chief Tecumseh (*c.*1768-1813), Shawnee

Tecumseh ? B. J. Lossing

"Brothers—My people wish for peace. The red men all wish for peace. But where the white people are, there is no peace for them, except it be on the bosom of our mother."

Born under the sign of a great comet, Tecumseh was the last hope for the Great Lakes nations to unite and drive white settlers from their lands, many of which had been seized by fraudulent treaties or by force. Like Pontiac before him, Tecumseh understood what was at stake, and he spent years traveling in the eastern part of the continent, attempting to convince the nations to present a unified front to the Americans and reclaim their lands. He almost succeeded, but his dream was betrayed by his brother, Tenskwatawa (One With Open Mouth, The Prophet), who allowed himself to be decoyed into a premature fight with William Henry Harrison while Tecumseh was absent. The alliance tribes scattered after their defeat, and the larger war was lost by Tecumseh's outgunned and outmanned British allies who retreated into Canada and left him facing overwhelming odds in the Battle of the Thames in 1813.

When Tecumseh gave this speech at Vincennes, Illinois, on August 15, 1810, in a meeting with Governor William Henry Harrison at his mansion, Grouseland, the war chief still believed it was possible to call the Americans to account for their dishonest dealings. Harrison had called the meeting to discuss Tecumseh's fury over a treaty the USA had made with the Miamis for land the Shawnees considered theirs. The governor had arranged for the meeting to be held on the columned portico, saying that it was the order of the "great father" in Washington that Tecumseh be treated well. Tecumseh refused, saying, "The sun is my father; the earth is my mother, who nourishes me, and on her bosom I will recline." By this time Tecumseh had already created Tippecanoe[259] the settlement where he had gathered many of the allies who supported the confederation of tribes, and he was powerful enough to pose a real threat to the settlement of the land on the Wabash River between Ohio and Illinois. This was a meeting of equals, and Harrison knew it. A little over a year later, however, Tenskwatawa would provoke Harrison's troops into attacking and essentially destroying Tippecanoe, shattering Tecumseh's carefully constructed confederation. The translator for this speech was Tecumseh's nephew, who had decided to become loyal to the whites and was an aide to Harrison.

"Brother, I wish you to listen to me well. As I think you do not clearly understand what I before said to you, I will explain it again. Brother, since peace was made, you have killed some of the Shawnees, Winnebagoes, Delawares, and Miamis and you have taken our lands from us and I do not see how we can remain at peace if you continue to do so. You try to force the red people to do some injury. It is you that are pushing them on to do some mischief. You endeavor to make distinctions: you wish to prevent the Indians doing as we wish them—to unite and let them consider their lands as the common property of the whole; you take tribes aside and advise them not to come into this measure; and until our design is accomplished, we do not wish to accept your invitation to go and see the president. The reason I tell you this: you want, by your distinction of Indian tribes in allotting to each a particular tract of land, to make them war with each other. You never see the Indian come, do you, and endeavor to make the white people do so? You are continually driving the red people; when, at last, you will drive them into the Great Lake, where they can't either stand or walk.

"Brother, you ought to know what you are doing with the Indians. Perhaps it is by direction of the president to make those distinctions. It is a very bad thing, and we do not like it. It is true that I, with the help of my brother, Tenskwatawa, who is The Prophet, and many others, have organized a Combination of all the Indian tribes in this quarter to put a stop to the encroachments of the white people and to establish a principle that the lands should be considered common property and none sold without the consent of all. Since my residence at Tippecanoe, we have endeavored to level all distinctions—to destroy village chiefs, by whom all mischief is done. It is they who sell our lands to the Americans. Our object is to let our affairs be transacted by warriors.

"Brother, this land that was sold and the goods that were given for it were done only by a few. The treaty was afterwards brought here, and the Weas were induced to give their consent, because of their small numbers. The treaty at Fort Wayne was made through the threats of Winnemac, but in the future we are prepared to punish those chiefs who may come forward to propose to sell the land. If you continue to purchase them, it will produce war among the different tribes and, at last, I do not know what the consequences will be to the white people.

"Brother, I was glad to hear your speech. You said if we could show you that the land was sold by people who had no right to sell, you would restore it. Those that did sell did not own it. These tribes set up a claim, but the tribes with me will not agree with their claim. If the land is not restored to us, you will see, when we return to our homes, how it will be settled.

"Hear me! We shall have a great council at which all the tribes will be present, when we shall show to those who sold that they had no right to the claim that they set up. And you will see what will be done to those chiefs that did sell land to you. I am not alone in this determination; it is the determination of all the warriors and red people that listen to me. I now wish you to listen to me. If you do not, it will appear as if you wished to kill all the chiefs that sold you the land. I tell you so because I am authorized by all the tribes to do so. I am the head of them all! I am a warrior, and all the warriors will meet together in two or three moons from this. Then I will call for those chiefs that sold you the land and shall know what to do with them. If you do not restore the land, you will have a hand in killing them!

"Brother, do not believe that I came here to get presents from you. If you offer us any, we will not take them. By our taking goods from you, you will hereafter say that with them you purchased another piece of land from us.

"It has been the object of both myself and my brother to prevent the lands being sold. Should you not return the land, it will occasion us to call a great council that will meet at the Huron village, where the council fire has already been lighted, at which those who sold the lands shall be called and shall suffer for their conduct.

"Brother, I wish you would take pity on the red people and do what I have requested. If you will not give up the land and do cross the boundary of your present settlement, it will be very hard and produce great troubles among us. How can we have confidence in the white people? When Jesus Christ came on the earth, you killed and nailed him on a cross. You thought he was dead, but you were mistaken. You have Shakers among you, and you laugh and make light of their worship. Everything I have said to you is the truth. The Great Spirit has inspired me, and I speak nothing but the truth to you.

"Brother, I hope you will confess that you ought not to have listened to those bad birds who bring you bad news. I have declared myself freely to you, and if any explanations should be required from our town, send a man who can speak to us. If you think it proper to give us any presents—and we can be convinced they are given through friendship alone—we will accept them. As we intend to hold our council in the Huron village that is near the British, we may probably make them a visit; but should they offer us powder and tomahawk, we will take the powder and refuse the tomahawk. I wish you, Brother, to consider everything I have said as true and that it is the sentiment of all the red people that listen to me."

At this point Harrison said that the Wabash lands had belonged to the Miamis and they alone were able to determine what happened to them.

You are a liar! Everything you have said is false! The Indians have been cheated and imposed upon by you and by the Seventeen Fires.[260] Nothing you have said—before, or now at this council—can be trusted. You lie and you cheat!"

After this dramatic confrontation, Tecumseh and his party stalked off, leaving Harrison and the Americans alone.

1810

THE BLACK HAWK WAR

Black Hawk, 1832.
George Catlin

Black Hawk lost his battle with the Americans in 1832 in what came to be known as the Black Hawk War, but the beginning of his fight reached back to the Treaty of 1804, negotiated by William Henry Harrison and made without the consent of all members of his nation. It sold a large tract of land along the eastern shore of the Mississippi in Illinois to the Americans for a pittance—a thousand dollars—while granting Natives the right to remain on the lands until they were surveyed and developed. Had the government kept to the terms of the treaty, the surveying would have taken years and Black Hawk could have lived and died without moving. The problem, as usual, was that after the War of 1812, the USA looked the other way as thousands of white squatters poured into the area in violation of the treaty. When Sauk leaders complained, the US authorities promoted Keokuk as the tribal leader and suggested all Natives follow him to a new settlement across the Mississippi. Black Hawk, who had spent most of his life at Saukenuk, the Sauk settlement along the Rocky River in Illinois, refused. The settlers, who were carving homesteads out of some of the richest farmland in the world, refused to move as well.

Black Hawk began a war to protect his homeland, counting on support from the Winnebago and Potawatomi, which never came. The war lasted fifteen weeks, until the massacre of the women and children of his tribe at the Bad Axe River by Illinois militia convinced him resistance was futile. He surrendered and gave up his medicine bag to save his people. He was taken to Washington to meet with President Andrew Jackson and then paraded around the East Coast of the United States before being sent to the Sauk settlement in Iowa. There he approached the government interpreter to write down his autobiography, the first ever written by an indigenous person in the United States. He lived a relatively peaceful retirement, dying in 1838, but his body was stolen from the grave. Stripped to the bones, the skeleton hung for many years in the office of a doctor in Burlington, Iowa, until it was destroyed when the building burned in 1855. The following is from *The Life of Black Hawk*.

Ma-ka-tai-me-she-kia-kiak (Large Black Hawk, Chief Black Hawk, 1768-1838), Sauk[261]

On my arrival at the village, I was met by the chiefs and braves and conducted to a lodge that had been prepared to receive me. After eating, I gave an account of what I had seen and done. I explained to them the manner the British and Americans fought. Instead of stealing upon each other and taking every advantage to *kill the enemy and save their own people*, as we do (which, with us, is considered good policy in a war chief), they marched out, in open daylight, and *fight* regardless of the number of warriors they may lose! After the battle is over, they retire to feast and drink wine, as if nothing had happened; after which they make a *statement in writing,* of what they have done—*each party claiming the victory!* and neither giving an account of half the number that have been killed on their own side. They all fought like braves but would not do to lead a war party with us. Our maxim is, *"to kill the enemy and save our own men."* Those chiefs would do to *paddle* a canoe but not to *steer* it. The Americans shoot better than the British, but their soldiers are not so well clothed, or provided for. . . .

We can only judge of what is proper and right by our standard of right and wrong, which differs widely from the whites, if I have been correctly informed. The whites *may do bad* all their lives, and then, if they are *sorry for it* when about to die, *all is well!* But with us it is different: we must continue throughout our lives to do what we conceive to be good. If we have corn and meat and know of a family that have none, we divide with them. If we have more blankets than sufficient and others have not enough, we must give to them that want.

We were friendly treated by the white chiefs and started back to our village on Rock River. Here we found that troops had arrived to build a fort at Rock Island. This, in our opinion, was a contradiction to what we had done—"to prepare for war in time of peace." We did not, however, object to their building the fort on the island, but we were very sorry, as this was the best island on the Mississippi and had long been the resort of our young people during the summer. It was our garden (like the white people have near to their big villages) which supplied us with strawberries, blackberries, gooseberries, plums, apples, and nuts of different kinds; and its waters supplied us with fine fish, being situated in the rapids of the river. In my early life, I spent many happy days on this island. A good spirit had care of it, who lived in a cave in the rocks immediately under the place where the fort now stands, and has often been seen by our people. He was white, with large wings like a swan's, but ten times larger. We were particular not to make much noise in that part of the island which he inhabited, for fear of disturbing him. But the noise of the fort has since driven him away, and no doubt a bad spirit has taken his place!

Our village was situated on the north side of Rock River at the foot of its rapids and on the point of land between Rock River and the Mississippi. In its front, a prairie extended to the bank of the Mississippi; and in our rear, a continued bluff, gently ascending from the prairie. On the side of this bluff we had our corn-fields, extending about two miles up, running parallel with the Mississippi, where we joined those of the Foxes, whose village was on the bank of the Mississippi, opposite the lower end of Rock Island and three miles distant from ours. We had about eight hundred acres in cultivation, including what we had on the islands of Rock River. The land around our village, uncultivated, was covered with blue-grass, which made excellent pasture for our horses. Several fine springs broke out of the bluff, near by, from which we were supplied with good water. The rapids of Rock River furnished us with an abundance of excellent fish, and the land, being good, never failed to produce good crops of corn, beans, pumpkins, and squashes.

We always had plenty—our children never cried with hunger, nor our people were ever in want. Here our village had stood for more than a hundred years, during all which time we were the undisputed possessors of the valley of the Mississippi, from the Ouisconsin [Wisconsin] to the portage des Sioux, near the mouth of the Missouri, being about seven hundred miles in length. At this time we had very little intercourse with the whites, except our traders. Our village was healthy, and there was no place in the country possessing such advantages, [or any] hunting grounds better than those we had in possession. If another prophet had come to our village in those days and told us what has since taken place, none of our people would have believed him! What! To be driven from our village and hunting grounds and not even be permitted to visit the graves of our forefathers, our relations and friends?

This hardship is not known to the whites. With us it is a custom to visit the graves of our friends and keep them in repair for many years. The mother will go alone to weep over the grave of her child! The brave, with pleasure, visits the grave of his father, after he has been successful in war, and repaints the post that shows where he lies! There is no place like that where the bones of our forefathers lie, to go to when in grief. Here the Great Spirit will take pity on us!

But how different is our situation now, from what it was in those days! Then we were as happy as the buffalo on the plains—but now, we are as miserable as the hungry, howling wolf in the prairie! But I am digressing from my story. Bitter reflection crowds upon my mind and must find utterance. . . .

That fall I visited Malden[262] with several of my band, and [we] were well treated by the agent of our British Father, who gave us a variety of presents. He also gave me a medal and told me there never would be war between England and America again but, for my fidelity to the British during the war that had terminated some time before, requested me to come with my band and get presents every year, as Colonel Dixon had promised me.

I returned and hunted that winter on the Two-Rivers. The whites were now settling the country fast. I was out one day hunting in a bottom and met three white men. They accused me of killing their hogs. I denied it, but they would not listen to me. One of them took my gun out of my hand and fired it off—then took out the flint, gave back my gun, and commenced beating me with sticks, and ordered me off. I was so much bruised that I could not sleep for several nights.

Some time after this occurrence, one of my camp cut a bee-tree and carried the honey to his lodge. A party of white men soon followed and told him the bee-tree was theirs and that he had no right to cut it. He pointed to the honey and told them to take it; they were not satisfied with this but took all the packs of skins that he had collected during the winter, to pay his trader and clothe his family with in the spring, and carried them off!

How could we like such people, who treated us so unjustly? We determined to break up our camp, for fear that they would do worse—and when we joined our people in the spring, a great many of them complained of similar treatment.

This summer our agent came to live at Rock Island. He treated us well and gave us good advice. I visited him and the trader very often during the summer and, for the first time, heard talk of our having to leave my village. The trader explained to me the terms of the treaty that had been made and said we would be obliged to leave the Illinois side of the Mississippi and advised us to select a good place for our village and remove to it in the spring. He pointed out the difficulties we would have to encounter if we remained at our village on Rock River. He had great influence with the principal Fox chief, his adopted brother, and persuaded him to leave his village, go to the west side of the Mississippi River and build another—which he did the spring following. Nothing was talked of but leaving our village. Ke-o-kuck had been persuaded to consent to go and was using all his influence, backed by the war chief at Fort Armstrong and our agent and trader at Rock

Island, to induce others to go with him. He sent the crier through the village to inform our people that it was the wish of our Great Father that we should remove to the west side of the Mississippi—and recommended the Ioway river as a good place for the new village—and wished his party to make such arrangements, before they started on their winter's hunt, as to preclude the necessity of their returning to the village in the spring.

The party opposed to removing called upon me for my opinion. I gave it freely—and after questioning Quàsh-quà-me (Jumping Fish) about the sale of our lands, he assured me that he "never had consented to the sale of our village." I now promised this party to be their leader and raised the standard of opposition to Ke-o-kuck, with a full determination not to leave my village. I had an interview with Ke-o-kuck, to see if this difficulty could not be settled with our Great Father—and told him to propose to give other land (any that our Great Father might choose, even our lead mines), to be peaceably permitted to keep the small point of land on which our village and lands were situate. I was of opinion that the white people had plenty of land and would never take our village from us. Ke-o-kuck promised to make an exchange if possible and applied to our agent and the great chief at St. Louis (who has charge of all the agents) for permission to go to Washington to see our Great Father for that purpose. This satisfied us for some time. We started to our hunting grounds, in good hopes that something would be done for us.

During the winter I received information that three families of whites had arrived at our village and destroyed some of our lodges and were making fences and dividing our corn-fields for their own use—and were quarreling among themselves about their lines in the division! I immediately started for Rock River, a distance of ten days' travel, and on my arrival found the report to be true. I went to my lodge and saw a family occupying it. I wished to talk with them, but they could not understand me. I then went to Rock Island and, the agent being absent, told the interpreter what I wanted to say to these people, viz: "Not to settle on our lands—nor trouble our lodges or fences—that there was plenty of land in the country for them to settle upon—and they must leave our village, as we were coming back to it in the spring." The interpreter wrote me a paper, and I went back to the village and showed it to the intruders but could not understand their reply. I expected, however, that they would remove, as I requested them. I returned to Rock Island, passed the night there, and had a long conversation with the trader. He again advised me to give up and make my village with Ke-o-kuck, on the Ioway River. I told him that I would not. The next morning I crossed the Mississippi, on very bad ice—but the Great Spirit made it strong, that I might pass over safe. I traveled three days farther to see the Winnebago sub-agent and converse with him on the subject of our difficulties. He gave no better news than the trader had done. I started then, by way of Rock River, to see the prophet, believing that he was a man of great knowledge. When we met, I explained to him everything as it was. He at once agreed that I was right and advised me never to give up our village, for the whites to plough up the bones of our people. He said that if we remained at our village, the whites would not trouble us—and advised me to get Ke-o-kuck, and the party that had consented to go with him to the Ioway in the spring, to return and remain at our village.

I returned to my hunting ground, after an absence of one moon, and related what I had done. In a short time we came up to our village and found that the whites had not left it—but that others had come and that the greater part of our corn-fields had been enclosed. When we landed, the whites appeared displeased because we came back. We repaired the lodges that had been left standing and built others. Ke-o-kuck came to the village; but his object was to persuade others to follow him to the Ioway. He had accomplished nothing towards making arrangements for us to remain, or to exchange other lands for our village. There was no more friendship existing between us. I looked upon him as a coward, and no brave, to abandon his village to be occupied by strangers. What right had these people to our village and our fields, which the Great Spirit had given us to live upon?

My reason teaches me that *land cannot be sold.* The Great Spirit gave it to his children to live upon and cultivate as far as is necessary for their subsistence; and so long as they occupy and cultivate it, they have the right to the soil—but if they voluntarily leave it; then any other people have a right to settle upon it. Nothing can be sold but such things as can be carried away. . . .

> Black Hawk spent some time across the Mississippi in 1831, but in 1832, counting on help from the British and from Native allies, he led his band back to his home on the Illinois shore. He fought bravely, retreating and trying to outflank the militia by going to the Wisconsin River, but allies deserted him and the whites had overwhelming numbers.

Here some of my people left me and descended the Ouisconsin, hoping to escape to the west side of the Mississippi, that they might return home. I had no objection to their leaving me, as my people were all in a desperate condition—being worn out with traveling and starving from hunger. Our only hope to save ourselves was to get across the Mississippi. But few of this party escaped. Unfortunately for them, a party of soldiers from Prairie du Chien was stationed on the Ouisconsin, a short distance from its mouth, who fired upon our distressed people. Some were killed, others drowned, and several taken prisoners, and the balance escaped to the woods and perished with hunger. Among this party were a great many women and children.

I was astonished to find that Ne-a-pope (Na-pope: broth) and his party of spies had not yet come in—they having been left in my rear to bring the news, if the enemy were discovered. It appeared, however, that the whites had come in a different direction and intercepted our trail but a short distance from the place where we first saw them—leaving our spies considerably in the rear.

Ne-a-pope and one other retired to the Winnebago village and there remained during the war! The balance of his party, being brave men, and considering our interest as their own, returned and joined our ranks.

Myself and band having no means to descend the Ouisconsin, I started, over a rugged country, to go to the Mississippi, intending to cross it, and return to my nation. Many of our people were compelled to go on foot for want of horses, which, in consequence of their having had nothing to eat for a long time, caused our march to be very slow. At length we arrived at the Mississippi, having lost some of our old men and little children, who perished on the way with hunger.

We had been here but a little while before we saw a steamboat, the *Warrior,* coming. I told my braves not to shoot, as I intended going on board, so that we might save our women and children. I knew the captain, Throckmorton, and was determined to give myself up to him. I then sent for my *white flag.* While the messenger was gone, I took a small piece of white cotton and put it on a pole and called to the captain of the boat and told him to send his little canoe ashore and let me come on board. The people on board asked whether we were Sacs or Winnebagoes. I told a Winnebago to tell them that we were Sacs and wanted to give ourselves up! A Winnebago on the boat called to us *"to run and hide, that the whites were going to shoot!"* About this time one of my braves had jumped into the river, bearing a white flag to the Boat—when another sprang in after him and brought him to shore. The firing then commenced from the boat, which was returned by my braves and continued for some time. Very few of my people were hurt after the first fire, having succeeded in getting behind old logs and trees, which shielded them from the enemy's fire.

The Winnebago on the steamboat must either have misunderstood what was told, or did not tell it to the captain correctly, because I am confident that he would not have fired upon us if he had known my wishes. I have always considered him a good man and too great a brave to fire upon an enemy when sue- ing for quarters.

After the boat left us, I told my people to cross if they could and wished, [because] I intended going into the Chippewa country. Some commenced crossing, and such as had determined to follow them re- mained—only three lodges going with me. Next morning, at day-break, a young man overtook me and said that all my party had determined to cross the Mississippi—that a number had already got over safe, and that he had heard the white army last night within a few miles of them. I now began to fear that the whites would come up with my people and kill them, before they could get across. I had determined to go and join the Chippewas, but reflecting that by this I could save only myself, I concluded to return and die with my people if the Great Spirit would not give us another victory! During our stay in the thicket, a party of whites came close by us but passed on without discovering us.

Early in the morning a party of whites, being in advance of the army, came upon our people, who were attempting to cross the Mississippi. They tried to give themselves up—the whites paid no atten- tion to their entreaties—but commenced *slaughtering* them! In a little while the whole army arrived. Our braves, but few in number, finding that the enemy paid no regard to age or sex and seeing that they were murdering helpless women and little children, determined to *fight until they were killed!* As many women as could commenced swimming the Mississippi, with their children on their backs. A number of them were drowned, and some shot, before they could reach the opposite shore.

One of my braves, who gave me this information, piled up some saddles before him, when the fight commenced, to shield himself from the enemy's fire and killed three white men! But seeing that the whites were coming too close to him, he crawled to the bank of the river, without being perceived, and hid him- self under it, until the enemy retired. He then came to me and told me what had been done. After hearing this sorrowful news, I started, with my little party, to the Winnebago village at Prairie La Cross. On my arrival there, I entered the lodge of one of the chiefs and told him that I wished him to go with me to his father—that I intended to give myself up to the American war chief and die, if the Great Spirit saw proper! He said he would go with me. I then took my medicine bag and addressed the chief. I told him that it was "the soul of the Sac nation—that it never had been dishonored in any battle—take it, it is my life—dearer than life—and give it to the American chief!" He said he would keep it and take care of it, and if I was suf- fered to live, he would send it to me.

During my stay at the village, the squaws made me a white dress of deer skin. I then started with sev- eral Winnebagoes and went to their agent at Prairie du Chien and gave myself up.

On my arrival there, I found to my sorrow, that a large body of Sioux had pursued and killed a number of our women and children, who had got safely across the Mississippi. The whites ought not to have permitted such conduct—and none but cowards would ever have been guilty of such cruelty—which has always been practiced on our nation by the Sioux.

The massacre, which terminated the war, lasted about two hours. Our loss in killed was about sixty, besides a number that were drowned. The loss of the enemy could not be ascertained by my braves, exactly, but they think they killed about sixteen during the action. . . .

1834

THE LONG BATTLE

Once Native nations were consigned to reservations, most non-Native Americans and Canadians tended to think of them as tourist attractions or inspirations for woodcrafts and camping expeditions. Unfortunately, the last brutal chapter of Black Hawk's War and all the barbarous wars on the Plains and in the West that followed were only a prelude to the fight to retain rights granted by treaties in exchange for the lands relinquished. The reservation period created new sets of problems. Then, in 1953, the United States enacted a Termination Resolution to end tribal sovereignty and federal obligations specified in past treaties or acts of Congress, including education and health care. The objective was to make Native nations completely independent and self-sufficient, but the results were a disastrous repetition of the land losses and suffering that followed the Dawes Act in the nineteenth century. When Natives abruptly became responsible for all services and support, including taxes on land, they were living on circumscribed reservations that had few industries or other ways of earning money.

Although Termination was eventually stopped, it was still difficult for many nations to protect their lands from white encroachment and to provide for people, until the beginning of legalized gaming in the 1970s, which generated enough cash flow so that bands and nations could meet basic needs and begin land-repurchase programs. Gaming, however, has as many opponents as it has supporters, since many believe that it destroys traditional values and causes social problems more intransigent than the ones it solves. And, as many have discovered, even land repurchase programs could not stop all land losses, since USA and Canadian federal governments have attempted several times to exercise their rights of eminent domain to build on and across tribal lands. The long battle, begun so many centuries ago, has not ended yet.

The Power Came from the People

Ada Deer (1935-   ), Menominee

When Termination began, the Menominee were one of the first nations to feel its effects. Ada Deer had already earned her master's degree in social work from Columbia University and was enrolled in law school, but she dropped out when she saw what Termination was doing to her people. She led a grassroots movement called DRUMS—Determination of Rights and Unity for Menominee Shareholders—that stopped land sales to pay taxes and began the drive to reverse federal policy. Deer, more than any other single person, was responsible for ending Termination, which was finally fully repealed for all nations in 1988, more than ten years after Deer pushed through her bill restoring federal recognition for her nation.

I was born on the Menominee reservation in Wisconsin and lived there for eighteen years. As a teenager I saw the poverty of the people—poor housing, poor education, poor health. I thought, "This isn't the way it should be. People should have a better life."

I wanted to help the tribe in some way, but I wanted to have something to offer. I decided that going to college and developing my skills was the best way to break out of the bonds of poverty. After college, I entered law school.

In 1961 the tribe was terminated; that is, federal support was withdrawn. Some of us opposed termination from the start, but we were overruled. Only five percent of the people voted; they were lured by the cash payments offered in return for giving up government services. Most of the people were uninformed; they did not protest termination because they did not foresee its drastic implications. The government pushed it through without preparing the people. It was "an experiment."

The years 1961-1973 were a political, economic, and cultural disaster for the Menominee. Formerly, under the tribal system everyone had been equal, with one vote per tribal member. Under the new corporate structure just a few people had the power to make decisions.

We were the state's poorest county, with just one small industry, a lumber mill. We were suddenly faced with massive tax burdens. Our hospital and school were forced to close. The people suffered a great deal. To survive, the tribe had to sell some of its land.

Land is very dear to the Menominee. We have a beautiful reservation—over 234,000 acres of mountains, streams, and lakes. Our reservation is our homeland, guaranteed by a treaty. Our cultural identity is bound to the land.

With termination, many of the people moved to the cities in search of jobs. They lost their connection with their traditional culture and way of life. Then too, termination canceled tribal membership for children born after 1954.

The government had tried for two hundred years to eliminate the Indians. They tried wars, disease, putting us on reservations. They tried acculturation—shipping us off to cities. Termination was the ultimate expression of that....

I wanted to get involved. People said I was too young, too naïve—you can't fight the system. I dropped out of law school. That was the price I had to pay to get involved. It was worth it.

In 1970 we started our movement called DRUMS. We sought an end to land sales, the restoration of federal support, and full participation of the people in tribal government. To present our goals to our congressman, we staged a march covering one hundred and fifty miles from our reservation to Madison. Our congressman said he didn't think our legislation had much of a chance, but he'd introduce it.

Menominee Tribal Restoration. Ada Deer at far right

I spent six months in Washington influencing

congressmen and mobilizing the support of our people throughout the country. We were able to get our legislation through the House of Representatives 404 to 3; an exciting day. It went through the Senate on a voice vote with no protest and was signed into law on December 1, 1973. The land was restored to trust status; roles in government were opened to young people and to women.

Where did the manpower and womanpower come from to accomplish this? It came from the people. Men and women working together as a total community. Now we Indian people believe we can do anything!

1975

From The Reservation

Ted C. Williams (1930-2005), Tuscarora

Ted C. Williams

The Tuscaroras, who were driven out of their extensive traditional lands in the Carolinas by white colonization and sold as slaves in Pennsylvania, eventually settled with the Haudenosaunee in New York and Ontario, becoming the sixth nation of the Iroquois Confederation. They didn't have much land, only a small portion near Buffalo and Niagara, and so any threat to their holdings was met with fierce protectiveness. This chapter, from Williams's sometimes humorous and sometimes bittersweet memoir of growing up on the Tuscarora Reservation in the 1940s and 1950s, describes what happened when the New York State Power Authority decided to build a dam on the Niagara River that would flood part of the Tuscaroras' land. A modern Indian war ensued, with the small tribe pitted against the politicians and attorneys of the State of New York.

The Reservoir

It's a son-of-a-gun to monkey with the kids in big families. Some are fighting while others are playing, but any minute the ones who seem mad enough to kill each other are both on the same side, beating up on the ones who just got done helping them fight or have fun. But, of course, the worst thing is to not belong to that family and jump in and try to rescue a victim getting beat up. The whole family jumps on the rescuer with the victim jumping on the rescuer the hardest. The reservation is like that; like one big family.

In fact, if the United States is at war, the Indians from different reservations enlist like it was an attack against their family. But then, they are just as ready to fight city hall or the state or the United States. At this time, the Indians unite as a separate nation, which nobody seems to know if they are or are not. Also, a lot of Indians don't worry about that, as long as there is a bit of excitement in the family once in a while. Also, just as Indians are not sure how much of a separate nation they may be, there are Indians on the reservation who are not Tuscarora and who defend, sometimes better than some Tuscaroras, the reservation. At other times, they might kick up a ruckus at feeling not accepted, and often for good reason.

If the State of New York is like a big brother in one big family, one day big brother wanted a bite of little brother's candy. More like sister's candy because the women on the Tuscarora Indian Reservation outdid the men in many ways. What happened was that big brother got the bright idea that the Niagara River should do more than just create something to look at at Niagara Falls. It could be making boo-coo more power. What the idea was was that as long as the Niagara River made a bend just before it fell over the Falls, why not dig a channel and take a shortcut to Lewiston. Then as the water wants to pour down the gorge into the Lower Niagara River, why not let it pour through electricity-making machinery? Better yet, why not let the water rest up first at the top of the gorge in a lake or reservoir? All that water could REALLY make electric then, couldn't it? Well, this is what happened. But as big ideas often pop up in beautiful weather, they sometimes don't look so good in bad weather.

Weather, in fact, did have something to do with one of the things that big brother forgot about. Six or seven years later, when all of the hassles that big brother's idea caused were all worked out and the idea was starting to work, ice came from Lake Erie and jammed the channels to the reservoir. Dynamite was tried. Nothing happened. Probably a good-sized sturgeon would of done more. So now icebreakers or tugboats are needed, or the Big Idea of big brother isn't so big.

How the Tuscarora Indian Reservation happened to find itself part of the Big Idea was that part of the reservation was where the reservoir would need to be. Another, bigger, part of the reservation was where a beautiful state park would be which, in the Big Idea, would surround the reservoir. It seemed like, one day nobody knew this, the next day EVERYBODY knew it.

The news was like an explosion on the reservation, and it traveled about like the fuse on a firecracker. It was like looking out your window and seeing a stranger pulling boards off your house and saying, "I bought your house last night, didn't you know that?"

Big brother's name was the State Power Authority and many eyes were on his scalp. The war was on. The name State Power Authority was shortened to SPA, and some Indians got the letters mixed up sometimes and said "ASP or SPCA."

The first SPA "troops" were the poor surveyors. I say poor because they got the worst of it. Though it was not a real war, it was very much like a real war with privates and sergeants and generals. Sometimes rank came in handy, and other times, I suspect, a "four-star general" wished he had taken up some other sport.

In the old laws of the Iroquois, the chiefs were called lords, and since the clan mothers chose the lords, the Tuscarora Indian Reservation had some fairly high-rank, monkey-farting among the privates. Much higher than the SPA realized at first.

Believe you me, it ain't easy to see what's going on all over the place at the same time at a shindig like this.

Nor could it be known what was going on at different headquarters where, likely, headquarters didn't know and would like very much to stay out of the fields. The action was where the best and bravest of the Indians were. They were women. Of course, during the day most men were working, but when they did come off the jobs, they still weren't often the most active.

One man didn't stand still, though. G-By came charging through the bushes because he didn't like to see these surveyors sighting along his land. He had a stout cane, and in about a minute he gave some free lessons in how to cross-check with a lacrosse stick. The surveyors picked themselves up and took on off out of there. The reason G-By wasn't on a job was because he was over seventy years old.

As fast as the surveyors put stakes into the ground, the women gathered them up for fire to cook donated food on. One small girl held a large American flag and stood in front of a surveyor's transit.

Just the same, it was a simple thing for a surveyor to stand on the spot where the first hole for test borings into the rock would be made. And here came the huge bulldozer towing the drill rig. It came rumbling up Garlow Road, and to the worried surveyors, it probably felt like help in the form of a General Sherman tank. It never got off Garlow Road. Jeet-niiht (Čî'nę̀: Bird) went and met it and threw herself right in the way, and the big diesel Cat ground to a halt.

The drill rig had been rented from Kroening, who had drilled wells for Indians for drinking water.

By this time some men had drifted in from jobs, and Oxen was one of them. He was small but powerful. He stepped up to Kroening. Kroening stepped back.

"Don't be afraid of me," Oxen said, "I'm not afraid of you."

"What's the matter?" Kroening asked. "What's going on here?" There was two, maybe three hundred Indians as far as you could see.

"If you find your drill rig upside down tomorrow morning, it might pay you to find out," Oxen said.

Different other things like this were happening, but it was what can be called the first few skirmishes. Now it was time for the SPA to put a stop to this nonsense, and in the morning air a chorus of sheriff car sirens wailed from the substation to the reservation. Sheriff Murdock had just been elected.

Now here were real bullets. Some of the oldest Indians who could hardly walk began to cry. In a little while the deputies were out in the fields keeping order while the surveyors' sledgehammers began pounding on stakes. I looked out across the field, and there was only one Indian moving. But, man, he was moving. The dust balls behind him were ten feet apart. It was Fox, and he was running like foxes run across a big field, in a straight line. Fox was the grandson of Babymind who was the fastest runner at Carlisle,[264] and Fox was no slouch either. I figured he had discovered a nest of yellow jackets.

The next thing that happened was, there was a cloud of dust at the far end of Garlow Road. Pretty soon you could see that a car was leading it. Out of the car jumped Fox. Turquois was chairman of the chiefs' council. He came out of the other door wearing a Bear Claw necklace. Fox had driven the car up the left-hand side of the road and had stopped just short of Sheriff Murdock's front bumper. Murdock was standing by his car door with his hands on his hips, near his gun. The dust caught up now and went all over both cars. This drew all the Indians and some of the deputies like a magnet.

The wind blew the dust off to the east. "Get your men out of here, and you go with them!" Turquois boomed at the sheriff.

The chief had a country preacher's voice. His thumb was up, pointed towards the substation.

"I'll do nothing of the kind," Murdock said, leaning comfortably against his car.

The chief didn't look much different from any other wrinkled old Indian with long hair, and the sheriff didn't look much different from any other sheriff in uniform with big rosy cheeks. Together, even though they were both medium size, their looks was saying, "I'm on the opposite side of you!" Only one thing was in common. They were both wearing cuffs. Murdock's was black leather and part of his gloves. Turquois wore beaded cuffs. They were light blue with white flowers.

"You're trespassing," Turquois said.

"I'm the law," Murdock said.

"This is the Tuscarora Indian Reservation," Turquois said. "This land is under federal jurisdiction. You better go get a federal marshal before I have you arrested." Turquois put his hand on his car door. "You better hurry," he said, "I'm drafting an injunction against the State Power Authority." Then he got in the driver's seat and drove away.

By then all the deputies had gathered nearby. "Let's go," the sheriff said, jumping into his car and gunning it around in a half-circle. "The chief's up to something," he called out the window as he stepped on the gas. In a few seconds it looked like chickens do when one gets a worm. There were no sirens though, and out near Gill Creek I saw an Indian girl running with her hands above her head. She had both hands on a stick, and a spool of yellow ribbon was unreeling off it in the breeze. It was the ribbon that the surveyors used to mark the trees. It wouldn't be hard to track her until the ribbon ran out and she jumped Gill Creek.

Like the tides in the ocean and the tides in war, so did the events of the battle for Indian land go. The newspapers had a picnic. It didn't matter to them if they reported the tide in when it was out as long as there was matter to be printed. And there was plenty to print; enough to last through any lulls in battle when the battlefields waited to be taken into court. Also, the never-ending family squabbles that the reservation seemed to enjoy never let up either.

The Power Project was the name of the Big Idea, and it was the SPA's pet baby. The SPA wasn't going to let this baby die although it was going through the mumps and the measles and the whooping cough like any other baby.

If the Baby was having these short-lasting diseases such as hundreds of contractors fighting over bids and then trying to back out when they found out how much limestone lived in Niagara County, then the illness of the fight for Indian land might better be called the seven-year itch. In order to stop the seven-year itch the SPA began using many "doctors" with many ways of cure. One of the best medicines expected to do the trick was called the Bribe. Nobody knows how many doses were given or if some was swallowed or spit out. The Tuscarora Indian Reservation, as a family, had enough squabbles within itself to show that some of the medicine probably got into the bloodstream.

When the federal marshal arrived, surveying and test boring began, and Indians felt powerless to stop the work, and here's where the squabbles began. Some Indians, needing work and seeing the work being done anyways, went to work. Trees were being cut, and Indians were good at it. Others, who had factory jobs already, called them traitors. Those Indians, including chiefs, whose land fell within the part where the reservoir and the park would be, began to give up hope. Some of them began to see dollar signs if they owned large parcels of land. Then along with the medicine called Bribe, another medicine might be called Shock Treatment. At least, it had to be pretty scary for those men, women, and children whose home, favorite trees, and playground fell in line with these little stakes with the yellow ribbon on them. They might find it easy to start looking for the next best spot on the reservation before all the best spots are already taken. But those that moved out had to face the "boos" of those that didn't have to move and

437

more so from those that wouldn't move. A lot of Indians were involved because the outside edge of the park was a deep bite into the reservation.

Some never gave up, and many were women. The army to harass never seemed to get smaller even though now they were facing jail sentences and fines. The chiefs, meanwhile, had not really allowed any moss to grow under their feet either, although the wheels of justice of the courts seemed to be lacking in grease. The chiefs held meeting after meeting to decide who could be trusted and who could not, especially of lawyers; when to use stalling tactics and when to hurry; if it was best to listen to one lawyer's advice to hold out for a big, big price or to never give in; what, if anything, to tell the newspapers; and decisions on endless questions and pressures from the Tuscarora Reservation family. Many other meetings were also taking place in homes and fields and woods. Into all this, the doctors were trying to feed Bribe medicine and Shock Treatment.

Very Bear, of the Bear Clan, whose mother was clan mother, was one of the fiercest of fighters of Indian rights on the Tuscarora Indian Reservation or maybe of any reservation. During all this struggle, he seemed not to be doing much. Some wondered why, while others knew what was going on. Very Bear's reputation was well known, and the U. S. Marshal was well informed that here was a dangerous Indian to be watched carefully and thrown into jail for the first false move he made. Very Bear, though, figured on this, and during the day he sat in a car in plain sight with his lawyer. A .35 Remington pump was also in plain sight in the car. Now this automatically caused the marshal to post some men near-by, and while they were guarding Very Bear, the Indians whose meetings Very Bear had sat in and made plans with were that much more free to go about their harassments.

Some Indians just naturally thrived on the excitement and practically lived on Garlow Road. Others went home and tried to think of ways of stopping the taking of Indian land and hunting grounds. There were photographers around, and sometimes these Indians would return to Garlow Road with signs and banners hoping to have the papers carry pictures of their messages for public sympathy. Sometimes it worked. Sometimes non-Indians joined the harassers, or owners of stores donated food to the Indians who continued to resist. Usually, though, the photographers would not take pictures of the signs or banners, or if they did, the papers would not print them; sometimes because the words were unprintable.

Just the same, many pictures were printed, and if you just read the papers, the Indians seldom won. Also, in those pictures, the pictures of whoever might be familiar to local judges or sheriff's deputies or state police would be pointed out to the marshal as being a ringleader and watched more closely. On one particular morning, Hoodoo and Crane were listening to the eight o'clock news on the radio, and they heard that they had been arrested on Garlow Road that very morning. So they went out to Garlow Road to show the other Indians that the radio report was a lie, and at nine-thirty they DID get arrested.

Moonflower was big and strong and beautiful and had long black hair and big white teeth. She was mad enough that the reservoir would replace the new house that her husband and she had built. Then she heard that a state trooper had knocked her husband flying through the air with his car as he flagged traffic near the Stauffer Plant in Niagara Falls. The news was that the trooper claimed Warwhoop was struck by another car; that he, in fact, chased the hit-and-run because he thought Warwhoop was dead. But Warwhoop never died at all, even though his legs were mangled, and he told Moonflower the truth. Now she got madder.

The thing that looked the worst to her was the drill rig drilling holes in a line with her house. The men on the drill rig had huffed and puffed to remove a huge stone out of the drill bit's way. With what looked like no effort, Moonflower picked up the huge stone and heaved it into the hole as the drill bit came down. WHAM! The drill bit bent like a flybeard on a big carp's back. The men ran to the marshal to tell on her.

The marshal's name was Cranden, and he itched to catch the harassers and have them jailed because every contractor was crying the blues and scared to death of bankruptcy, and so far the harassers were hard to catch. He said, "Even the old women can run like the devil."

"This one's a mean one, I think," said one of the drillermen, "I mean she's strong, and she's right over by your car waiting for you."

Cranden says, "I'll handle her," and he started off with long steps. He was well over six foot.

At Cranden's car, Moonflower was not alone. Pheebee Willy was with her. Pheebee was so old she was almost dead. She was one of the ones that cried quite a bit. Moonflower had a long stick and was standing lazy-like near the back of the car. The end of the stick was letting air out of Cranden's tire s-s-s-s-s-s-s-s. She had asked Pheebee Willy to stand in the way so Cranden couldn't see what she was doing. So now here came Cranden.

Pheebee Willy says, "Stay right where you are, you boogey-man, or I'll witch you."

Cranden never paid any attention to her and started to walk right around her. WHAM! Pheebee Willy came across with a terrific haymaker, and it flattened Cranden's nose. Pheebee said later, as though she had been the one getting punched, "I don't know where that punch came from."

Cranden went around Pheebee and blinked back the tears. "All right," he said, pulling out a pair of handcuffs. "You're gonna have to come along with me."

Moonflower reached in her pocket and pulled out a long, scaly sand lizard. She put it on her palm, holding it by the tail with the other hand. She looked at it. "You got deadly poison, haven't you?" she asked the lizard.

She squeezed its tail, and it answered by sticking out its long tongue and hissing. And then she threw it on the marshal's chest.

"Yeow!" he said, running backwards with his eyes popping.

Next, buttons were flying all directions as he ripped his jacket off, not knowing where the lizard was and probably imagining it to be running all over his back or something.

Actually the lizard had streaked off in another direction, Moonflower in another, and Cranden was dancing around for nothing. Pheebee Willy just stood there. She was crying again. But this time it was because she was laughing so hard. Pretty soon Cranden took off in his car to get another jacket. "BEH-BEH-BEH-BEH-BEH-beh-beh-beh-beh-beh-," went the flat tire as he drove out of sight.

Moonflower went home to change clothes and do her long hair up under a straw hat so she wouldn't be noticed so quick when Cranden came back. She got there just in time to see a brush-cutter cut off the little walnut tree she had planted when the house was finished.

Now she was running, but she was running kind of zig-zaggy. Why she was zig-zaggy was because she was so mad she was wanting to find something to pick up to hit the man that cut the tree down with. Of all the things she could get her hands on, what do you think she grabbed? A PITCHFORK! And before you could say "Pretty blue skies," that man turned into SOME kind of runner.

Now both of these runners had terrific reasons for speed. In Moonflower's mind, she was going to run this man so far away that he'd starve to death trying to get back. And him, well he just wanted to live to a riper older age; that's all he was running for.

The man had a pretty good start on Moonflower, and he was headed towards the bushes, hoping to lose her. She cut off to the opening to the right of the bushes because the bushes were made of prickly ash. "YEOW!" The man had hit the bushes and was fighting his way back out of them. "YEOW!" he said again. There was a slight downward hill starting at the opening, and the man saw it and began shifting gears.

Moonflower's house was right out in the open on Garlow Road, and most of us had seen her take after the brush cutter. We were also running at high speed too, thinking he might have stolen something or something.

The man hit the opening at full throttle, and so did Moonflower. Just as he broke over the hill, he glanced back. Here was the pitchfork starting downward and aimed perfectly for his butt.

Now I'm sure you can understand where he got some extra speed from. The same place that Pheebee Willy got her haymaker from. The man was a little heavy, but it didn't hold his legs back any, and what with Moonflower's hair blowing in the wind I thought it looked a little like Moby Dick and Captain Ahab.

ZING! The pitchfork, from where I was, looked as though it struck a rock and bounded upwards. The man, though, went downwards and out of sight.

When we got there, Moonflower was just standing there looking at the man. There was blood all over the place, and the man, white as a ghost, sitting there, was staring at the blood squirting out of his ankle. The pitchfork had gone all the way through his ankle and through his shoe, which was still stuck to the bent fork of the pitchfork.

I could tell that Moonflower was worried, but she put her hands on her hips as though to give the man a stern lecture. But all she said was, "Don't cut any more trees." Then she went back to her house to change her clothes and left us to take care of the man who had received some of the Shock Treatment that was going around. He was, in fact, in a perfect state of shock.

In the harassment meetings it was many times agreed on never to hurt anyone. Strictly harassment. And probably the pitchfork thing was about as hurty as it got, except for some fist-fights that were pretty evenly matched and nobody was hospitalized. As I say, it was about impossible to know what was going on all over, but in general, the women were capable of Moonflower's courage, except maybe they couldn't pick up that huge rock. And maybe now, she couldn't do it either.

If it wasn't for the harassments, much more of the reservation would have been destroyed. The work was going slow, sometimes even stopped. Sometimes workers would quit, either from sympathy or from fright. That was one thing. If the Indians were frightened, so were a lot of the workers. A lot of them tried to get on other parts of the power project. Many had even gone to school with some of the Indians, and for that reason would not work there, or else they would offer money for food for the harassers. Some though, were strangers to the area and sort of thought of Indians as most history books tell about them. I mean, maybe these workers liked to read paperbacks about Indian fighters. Like this one surveyor helper. He was thickset and never wore a shirt, maybe to show off his muscles. None of the Indians paid any more attention to him, other than to let the air out of his tires or whatever the children were doing to any other worker. How he was different, was, he began making remarks like, "I'd like to smash one of them redskin's teeth in," or "I'm gonna take me a couple of them good-looking squaws home to bed with me sometime." Or, "I ain't ascared of these dumb injins, what the hell's the matter with you guys."

So the surveyor boss sent him in on G-By's property. Not much had been done on G-By's land because a lot of Indians liked G-By and had harassed the surveyors pretty badly in that area. Maybe it was more like because G-By himself sat on his porch with a full-choke double leaning against the railing and nobody knew if BB's or double 00 buckshot or slugs were in the chamber.

Anyways, a few of us Indians went along to see what we might do to slow down the surveying on G-By's land. Pretty soon we see the surveyors put on shirts, and so did the tough surveyor helper. Pretty soon we can see why. There were lots of mosquitoes, and pretty soon there was just me and Fox left because the others said, "They won't last there long, and even if they do, they're getting harassed anyways."

I was sort of thinking the same thing except I wanted to get a line on where they were going to set the stakes so we could come back to the right place and pull them back up again. The surveyor's helper had a stake in his hand, and a surveyor had another. They were working furiously, and it looked as though they'd be getting in a lot of stakes. Just as the helper put a stake down on point to drive it in, a .270 exploded from about two hundred yards or more. The stake blew up in the helper's hand, and the echo vibrated through the swamp. In the moment that the surveyors and the helper froze before they ran, another .270 bullet roared, and the other stake that the surveyor held blew up. The bullets were hollow points, and there wasn't anything left in either stake carrier's hand. And by the time the second echo died out there wasn't any surveyors or helper left in sight either.

There were a few Indians that shot like that, but only one or two used a .270. And maybe just one could shoot that fast. Oxen's brother, White-Corn. If meat got low on the reservation in the late fall, White-Corn would spotlight some deer at night and pass the venison to the needy. If there were three or four deer standing up to three hundred yards off, the biggest one would get it between the eyes. The rest got it in the lungs.

Offhand now, I'd figure that most or all of the SPA workers that sort of had that Indian fighter feeling like the helper I was using for an example, might quit or go to another contractor on another part of the Power Project. In this case, the example did not. He did not come back the next day, but probably he was getting a permit because on the day after that, he came back wearing a Colt .45. And bullets.

This raised a few eyebrows, including Marshal Cranden's. He knew of the disappearing stakes, and he didn't tell the helper not to wear the Colt, but he did get everybody together. "No more shooting," he said. "Harassment is one thing, but shooting is something else. We don't want anybody getting killed here." Five workers had already died on the Power Project but from work accidents. One had fallen into a huge cement pour. He was from the state of Oregon and was now buried under thousands of yards of Portland cement.

"O.K. I won't shoot," Hroo-saa-noo (Ruhsè·nu': crab) said. She had never shot a gun in her life, and she was about fifty-five years old. Her feet were bare, and she was curling her toes in the sandy dirt.

"Young lady," the marshal said, looking at Hroo-saa-noo, "I'm going to ask you if you won't personally do me one big favor." He had learned that she was Very Bear's aunt and had singled her out as a ringleader, which, by the way, he was right. She had pulled off a few pretty good tricks after a bulldozer had gouged a big ditch right across her long driveway for no real reason. "I want you to promise me that you and your friends won't take the yellow ribbon markers off the trees," Cranden said. "Do you think that you could promise me that much?"

"Yes, I can," she said.

"I mean, would you, please?" the marshal pushed.

"Yes, I'll promise you that," Hroo-saa-noo said.

The next day all the trees that had the yellow ribbons on them still had them on. But so did every other tree in the area.

The surveyors' helpers and the surveyors were there too, and they finished up another small job before going in among all the yellow ribbons and mosquitoes. So it was quite warm then, by the time they got to G-By's property. This time they brought hand pumps of two-gallon size to spray the area of mosquitoes. Right away they pushed themselves through the *nu-heehk* bushes, spraying them as they went. Then one of them said, "Hey John, did you shit?"

"No, but somebody did," came the reply.

Come to find out, Hroo-saa-noo and some others had dipped into some backhouses and, walking backwards, had mopped all the bushes with a watered-down paste of *ood-gwe(t)-hreh* (*utkwéhreh*: excrement). All of that surveying crew quit, including Colt .45.

Gradually, now, even though the harassments continued, the work went on, and it began to seem as though there really wasn't much use fighting the SPA. Patience was running low towards the chiefs, and rumors flew left and right. Homes were being moved, and new home sites were being bought. Some of the Indian women had infiltrated engineering and project offices as secretaries, and much information came from that direction. There had been an effort by the marshal to starve out the harassers because some contractors were falling farther and farther behind schedule. All stores were asked to refuse food to Indians, and police or sheriff cars were placed near store entrances with a lawman there to pressure the storekeeper. So food had to be gotten from farther and farther distances. Some stores and restaurants brought food out at night, but probably some of it never got to anybody because the person bringing the food would not know where to bring it to and any cars cruising on Garlow Road at night might be stopped. So despair began to creep into the ranks of the resisters.

And no wonder. The injunction to stop work, which the chiefs had obtained, had been overridden by a higher court. The surveyors had been granted permission to survey, but that was all. Twenty-five or thirty state police had also come around at the time of the injunction, but they respected the injunction and stood back. The sheriff had not.

Hiring a lawyer is usually fairly easy. But when the legal matter involves a versus-the-United-States, many lawyers shy off. Of those that don't, it then becomes a case of who to trust. The chiefs settled on a man named Laws. However good Laws was, or regardless of how many times he gave advice to accept the most money that the Tuscarora Indian Reservation could get, he stuck it out through all the courts and all the appeals, winning a few and losing more. Now I can't tell you how many decisions and appeals or reverses there were because I'm not a lawyer. And all I knew was, SOMEBODY was taking over Gill Creek, and I wanted to stand by the water, every springtime, next to G-By, and watch for pike and listen to the *hhu-deg-khroth* (*ruté·krar*: green frog). So that's where I was, in the fields, not the courts. That's how I can get goofed up on exactly what was going on in them. Or when.

Very Bear knew, though, and about this time he said, "Them rich Jews in New York City that floated out them bonds for this project ought to be getting a little itchy and worried. They like to get a project like this moving on schedule. The courts are holding them up, and so are we."

Almost as a prediction, we got word that a group from New York City and Albany wanted to meet with the chiefs. The meeting was for Tuesday night.

On Tuesday night the chiefs went into the Council House and locked the door. I was standing outside with the crowd when these big black limousines pulled up. A picture of the state seal was on each car door.

First, the driver of the first car rolled down the window and asked if this was the Council House. Someone told him it was, and all the men in suits got out. They went up to the door, and one of them knocked. Nobody opened it. The man knocked again, as loud as he dared without hurting himself too much.

After a while you could hear some shuffling, and the latch rattled. Chief Tom Isaac stuck his head out. "What you want?" he says.

"We're the delegation from Albany," the knockerman said. "We're the people you want to see."

"That's just it," Old Tom says. "We don't know yet. We're having a meeting to see if we want to talk with you." He pulled in his head and locked the door again.

"See here!" the man shouted, "We've driven all this way. . . ." But the door didn't open. The men in suits went back to the cars.

No sooner had they got settled down when my father came to the door and let them in. He was a sachem chief now, and his name had become Saa-gwa-hree(t)-thre(t) (Sekwarí'θre·: Spear-Carrier, Turtle Clan chief). He let the men in and everybody else that could fit into the building with the door open.

The meeting itself was not much except maybe the end of it. Laws, the lawyer, was there and sat with the chiefs. Some of the chiefs, like Chew, didn't speak English the best, but they understood.

At one point, the main speaker of the suited ones was telling about the benefits of the project to the Indians. He was saying, ". . .and on the whole east side of this dike will be a huge sign, TUSCARORA INDIAN RESERVOIR. . . ."

June Bug jumped up and interrupted him. "Maybe you should have brought some beads," he said.

The man, I think he was introduced as a past-Lieutenant Governor, got red in the face and raised his voice, "See here. I didn't come here with that frame of mind!" he said.

All the talk that went on during the meeting didn't mean anything. When it got late and nothing was agreed to, the main speaker got up again. He was through bargaining. I don't remember what the first offer in dollars was for the Reservation property. Maybe one or one and a half million, which I don't know the meaning of anyways. "Well," he says, "we're not getting anywheres, and we've all got some important business to conduct tomorrow. I have to hand it to you Indian people. You drive a hard bargain. And a good one." Here he paused to let that sink in. "I have," pause, "in my power," pause, "one final offer." Pause. "You'll have a short time to decide this, and then we're leaving. And I know—and I know your attorney knows—that you don't have much chance in court." He paused again and looked around. Then he pulled what he expected to be his ace up his sleeve. "Ladies and gentlemen, I offer you eight million dollars for said property on this reservation!" He sat down.

He had said that we had a short time to decide, and Turquois used it right away.

"You don't understand," Chief Turquois said, standing up. "The land is not for sale. It is not for me that I speak; it is for my children's children and their children's children." The meeting was over.

After the meeting I sat up all night and talked with my father. We had talked before, but I had to tell him I was getting the first of a giving-up feeling, and it took most of the night to dare to tell him that. His clan was Turtle, mine was Wolf, after my mother. One of my chiefs was in the position of having to move, it looked like, and he then became one of the ones who was caught in that die-if-you-do and die-if-you-don't feeling. His name was Thqwah-hree-nih-huh (θkwarì·nę-eh: Wolf Little), and often he was furious at any Indian who would work for the SPA and cut trees on the reservation, and yet he himself was forced to give in to the SPA and to prepare to move and accept a new home. I asked my father what he thought was going to happen.

He said, "You're big enough to understand what can happen. Some day there might not even be a reservation here."

He talked slowly. "Whoever is president of the United States can have a lot to do with it. Now take this Power Project. At the first smell of it, Chief Turquois went to President Eisenhower's inaugural. It seemed like a good play. Turquois usually attracts the newspapers, and here was a chance to see what kind of a president Ike was. Turquois asked him to uphold the Treaty with the Tuscaroras if the State of New York tried to take some land. Ike passed the buck and turned the matter over to the Department of the Interior. The Interior turned it over to New York State, and the chiefs' council fought that. Before we could bring our case up, Harriman went ahead and condemned the land that the SPA wanted. Maybe some money changed hands, maybe not, but the condemnation was processed on a Saturday. The chiefs didn't get a letter about it until Tuesday. On Sunday, the day after the condemnation, some SPA men were already spotted on Garlow Road. The letter of condemnation with a permit to survey came around one o'clock in the afternoon on Tuesday, but the surveyors had already started in that morning."

This was all going over my head, so I ran out towards Garlow Road in the wee hours of morning. It was up to me to give up or not, and I so much did not want to give up that I was running like the wind. Only I wasn't sure where or what I was running to.

Big noises of big engines could now be heard for miles. Some came from as far as the gorge where drilling and rock removal was going on. Those big machines made me feel so small. It would soon be *hraw-thek-gyeh-huh* (*rahθé'kye-eh*: little autumn, September), and I'd have to get back in school. Funny how I could stand and watch a huge shovel scoop out the very earth and stone I wanted left alone and yet still just like to see the action.

I sort of woke up doing this just in time to see Nehts-eh(t) (Nér'ę: Skunk) being chased away from a bulldozer. He had dark skin and light hair. I joined up with him, and he said, "I used to play in that swamp. They're filling it all in." The 'dozer was pushing boulders into the swamp, which seemed to swallow them up. "It's like quicksand in some places," Skunk says. "Stay here. I'm going to see if I can make it out to that little island."

He sure knew his way around the swamp, and quick like a frog, he was on the island. He waved but didn't look at me, so I turned and saw Jewel coming from the East. Just as I looked back at Skunk, BAM!-BAM!-BAM! A gun went off. Black mud was spattered all over Skunk. "I told you, get the hell out of here, kid!" It was the surveyor helper with the Colt .45; only this time he was doing pick and shovel work. He laughed and shot again. BAM! Skunk went back the way he came.

Jewel said nothing but started off towards the contractor's office. She was now clan mother of the Snipe Clan. I could feel how mad Skunk was, and no matter how much I asked him to leave and go back to Garlow Road, he wouldn't. After a while Jewel came back and joined us. I wasn't even sure if we were on the reservation or not because the looks of the place was changing so fast. Jewel was mad too. She said, "I told the boss there about the shooting, and he just said, 'Well get the hell out if you don't like it.'" She tried to get Skunk to leave too, but Skunk seemed all the more stubborn.

I was wondering what to do when up staggered Sky High, and that's what he was too. Drunk. We told him what had happened, and he said, "Well I'd jes go over and drive that big 'dozer into the swamp."

What he said made me look at the 'dozer. It made Skunk look too. Nobody was on it, and it sat puffing away by itself. Way down the haul road I could see men hurrying towards the red coffee truck. Skunk was already running towards the 'dozer. He looked like a flea on an elephant when he finally got into the seat. First the 'dozer backed up; then it went forward. It went so slow I don't think anyone but Jewel and me and Skunk knew it was moving. Skunk rode it quite a ways because I think he was trying to get the blade up. But it didn't matter. Jewel took off towards Garlow Road. I got into some low elders and hid. Sky High just wandered off towards the coffee wagon. Skunk jumped off the 'dozer and started after Jewel. I gave him a sound like cock pheasants do when they fly up. He came into the elders with me. We watched the 'dozer, together, as it idled out to the edge of the stones. Before it went down into the swamp, it balanced a little bit. I felt like it was time for me to leave, and I left. Again, I couldn't get Skunk to go with me. It was his swamp, and he was wanting to see the most of it that he could.

I followed Gill Creek back to Garlow Road and found out that Jewel had told more about being chased out of the contractor's office. She told around that she had warned the contractor that he'd be sorry if he didn't get that man with the gun off the job. I knew that when Skunk's father, Hroo-Snek'kree (Ruhsné·kri': Big Horned Owl), heard about this, he'd be rough. And he was maybe stubborner than Skunk. I was getting hungry, but there was a big line to the sandwich and soup kettle. After a while I got in line. Skunk came from the swamp, and I let him cut in line. He was a stubborn hero to me. He was still mad. "It never went out of sight," he said. "The exhaust pipe is still sticking out. About a foot of it. If that engine would of just kept going a little longer, I think it would of gone out of sight. And talk about swearing, you should of heard them men swear when they seen what happened. Then they all went down to the office arguing whose fault it was."

That night at a meeting at Double Ugly's the news was that Sky High had been arrested for destroying a bulldozer. The meeting broke up when Heavy Dough came to the door and, through puffs from running, said that there had been some heavy shooting out towards Garlow Road direction. We questioned him as to who all did he think was shooting. "Well," he said, thinking, "maybe it was just one person. About ten or fifteen shots. Damn loud though."

Several meeting members wanted to jump into cars and go see. "Hold it," Very Bear said. "Take your cars home and go on foot cross lots if you gotta go over there. The law might be riding heavy right now."

Heeengs, the oldest woman there, said, "Maybe nobody better go." She was talking Tuscarora. "Your eyes will shine at night if they light you." Nobody went.

The next day we found out what had happened. Much machinery was damaged. Diesel engines had holes through them, and all the crane booms near the swamp were laying on the ground bent because the sheaves holding the hog rods were all smashed. It took a heavy rifle and a scope to do this. Skunk's father owned one. He sometimes hunted far north in Canada. Monkey Boy said he was in Johnson Sporting Goods store when Hroo-Snek'kree(t) picked up some special order bullets. They were .600 Nitros. "They ain't for Moose," was all he said, according to Monkey Boy.

Now I'm going to ask you to do something. I'm going to ask you to picture a big machine coming at you, maybe a D9 Caterpillar Bulldozer. You are in a fenced-in place, you and that machine. You can't see the operator of that machine, but it keeps coming at you. You can move faster than it can, but it never seems to tire. You keep wondering if it's going to run out of fuel before you get too tired and have to stop to rest, to get some sleep. After a while you won't know how many hours have gone by. Or days. Or years.

That's the way it seemed to me with this struggle with the Niagara Power Project. I mean, as far as time and events went. Maybe I haven't told of everything happening in the right order. I KNOW that many other things were happening where I wasn't. If so, that's the reason. Time likes to scramble. I don't know how many years went by.

I can remember one more thing happening. It seemed to say that the privates in the war were tired of the generals who hid and called the shots because it was the last harassing thing that I saw the harassers do, and the state trooper involved seemed to not care. Several Tuscaroras had New York State licenses as demolition experts. On this day I happen to see this state trooper sitting next to this brand-new giant yellow bulldozer, guarding it. He was tired, but not tired enough to take off his Smokey-the-Bear-type hat that New York State troopers wear. But he was too tired of it all to get excited when a woodchuck rifle bullet somersaulted that hat off of his head. He just sat there, hatless, for a minute or two, before he picked up his hat and walked slowly toward a field telephone to report the incident. When he was no more than fifty yards from the still-clean machine, an unknown number of dynamite sticks blew the machine apart. The trooper looked back at the wreckage, but he didn't hurry any extra as he went on towards the telephone. He would just report TWO incidents instead of one. And the harassments sort of died out with that machine.

Goo-ses-hehh-huhh (*kuhsérhę-eh*: little winter, November) came and snowflakes with it. The resistance pulled in its horns to think, worry, and wonder by the fire. It was a time of not much heart, but little did the Indians know the amount of their land they were saving.

In New York City lived a man who was no more than Mr. SPA himself. His name was Robert Moses. He had been in charge of building whatever huge projects the State of New York and the City of New York had thought of. He was getting up there in age, but he came on like a firebrand when the Niagara Power Project first began. Nobody knows how far the pressure of millions of dollars can go to take the heart out of a man like Robert Moses. Maybe he didn't know either because maybe he didn't feel like feeling any more of it, or maybe he felt so much he couldn't stand it any longer. I'm just pretty sure the Big Idea at Niagara Falls cost quite a bit. If impatience can be added up like money, then maybe there was about a squillion dollars worth of it riding on one man. The Big Idea belongs to New York State and not the federal government. But the decisions in court about a small piece of land on the Tuscarora Indian Reservation belonged to the federal judges in federal courts. However old Robert Moses was when the Indians pulled out the first surveyor's stake near Garlow Road, he added enough years before the reservoir was finished that it had nothing to do with his birth certificate anymore. He gave up.

Indians hated his guts and still do. In the long and bitter winter that never really went away when the summertime came, the reservoir slowly took shape while another chunk of Indian land waited to know if it would be a state park or Indian hunting grounds. Robert Moses waited too, and so did the blue teal, and the muskrats, and the Indians, including those that went to Europe and Asia to fight for the place they were born.

The case was in the last court of appeals. So was the patience of Robert Moses. When the judge gave the decision, it was in favor of the muskrats.

Robert Moses said, "I'm finished. I'll not appeal that."

The news was received on the Tuscarora Indian Reservation without too much jumping and dancing around because Laws, the lawyer, had chalked up a few wins before but they never had lasted. It just seemed like another temporary delay. And it was.

The federal commission, all by itself, appealed, and the case went to the Supreme Court. To no Indian's surprise, the Tuscarora Indian Reservation lost the decision. Maybe the commission felt obligated to Robert Moses. Maybe they respected him. Maybe they just liked him. Or even maybe the Bribe Medicine never stopped. For whatever reason, the Supreme Court handed Robert Moses the deed for the big bite of land into the Tuscarora Indian Reservation.

As I say, Moses was no longer connected correctly to his birth certificate, and the only thing that didn't stink to him anymore were the things he had seen with his eyes. He had seen the best lawyers in the land cross examine some chiefs who spoke so slow that the very slowness was making the lawyers go batty. "You don't understand. The land is not for sale. It is not for me. It's for my children's children and their children's children." And he had seen how hard it was to talk to them. Not because they wouldn't talk to him; they didn't talk with money. They talked with words. And he had seen the reports of contractors going bankrupt because some Indians, mostly women, were doing mischief. But mostly, this part of the earth was almost solid granite and limestone.

So what he did, he made the reservoir a little higher, just short of Garlow Road, which, by the way, is now paved. And he took the deed for the rest of the land and gave it back to the Tuscarora Indian Nation.

Maybe the cross examiners and some of the judges were big-eyed when he did that, but the Indians weren't. Some had added a few extra years to their age, too, and some were dead of old age. Probably the ones that care the least are the muskrats, and they ain't building no better or no worse houses than they were long before the Big Idea was born.

I was pissed off because the pike couldn't swim up Gill Creek anymore, and I still am. But just on the east side of Garlow Road a powerful medicine grows in that same creek. Nobody knows, but maybe all the struggling we did, did not have the power that that medicine has. All during the struggle it grew there in peaceful confidence, just as it does today. Maybe we lost our heads and forgot the power of Mother Earth. Maybe all we had to do was plant some of that *oo-nihh'gwo(t)'oit* (*yunęhkwa't*: medicine) on the opposite side of the road.

1976

Sovereignty and the Natural World Economy
Chief Oren Lyons (1930-   ), Onondaga

Oren Lyons is a Faith-Keeper of the Turtle clan, Onondaga Council of Chiefs. As Faith-Keeper, he is entrusted to maintain the customs, traditions, values, and history of the Turtle Clan and uphold Gai Eneshah Go Nah (Kaya·Nę·hsæ·'Kó·nah), the Great Law of Peace, while representing the people's message to the world community. He helped establish the United Nations Working Group on Indigenous Populations, and in 1992 he was invited to address the General Assembly of the United Nations to open the International Year of the World's Indigenous People at the United Nations Plaza in New York. Lyons was an All-American lacrosse player at Syracuse University and helped found a team called the Iroquois Nationals in 1983. In 1990, they traveled to Australia for the Lacrosse World Championship games, the first time in over a century that the Haudenosaunee carried their own flag and performed their own anthem in international competition.

Sovereignty is a term that we hear being used all the time and particularly in relation to Indians. It is a term that should be applied to Indians. However, I have noticed in the past ten years or so a certain change in terminology. Nationally and internationally, the term sovereignty is often being replaced by the term autonomy. I have noticed this in relation to the Nicaraguan conflict and the Mesquitoe Indians.

What is the difference between the two terms? What is sovereignty? We have always taken a rather simplistic view. We said that sovereignty is the act thereof. You are as sovereign as you are able to be. Generally, sovereignty is applied to nations and today to nation-states. Indians have always perceived themselves to be nations, sovereign and independent. Further, we apply sovereignty even further than nations. We apply it to individuals in the form of respect. Indian people, of all people, understand the concept of freedom and being born free with rights. Columbus landed here five hundred years ago. Across America and the world there was a tremendous preparation for 1992. I know that the President of the United States set aside some eighty-two million dollars for this celebration as they call it, and Spain has spent even more than that. All the world has become involved: the Catholic Church, for obvious reasons, Italy, the United States, as well as Latin America. Everybody is pointing to the year 1992.

Why? Since 1992 is a year of assessment, where we stand back and look at five hundred years of activity in the Western Hemisphere and assess what condition we are in. It can be a year of atonement for what happened to the indigenous peoples who caught the brunt of this invasion, or it can be a year of commitment to see that the next five hundred years are going to be better than the last five hundred.

This process of reflection will have to involve Indian nations. We have to make our own assessment of our condition. We have to present a position to challenge this idea of a celebration, to challenge this idea of a discovery. Discovery is a very arrogant perception; we were discovered, sort of like the flora and fauna of North America. In truth, there were free nations here with a real understanding of government and community, of the process and great principles of life. In fact, on the landfall of Christopher Columbus, freedom was rampant in North, Central and South America. Everybody was free and living in a natural world economy where they had economic security in perpetuity. They had adjusted themselves to working with the land and understood that every year that the land renewed itself.

Now, coming across the water were people with a different perception about economy. As a matter of fact, up to the present day, the governments of Canada and the United States have spent their time trying to get our people involved in this economy. They have spent a lot of time trying to tell us about the importance of private property as opposed to community property. We hear terms like development, progressive development, sustainable development, but our perception is that if you do not operate around the real laws of the universe, you are challenging fundamental cycles that you depend on for life.

So, there was obviously a conflict between Christopher Columbus's perception, and the people that he met. All of the writing says the first peoples were healthy, happy and well-fed, and not overly inclined to warfare. Yet, the process of domination began immediately. He said: these would make good slaves. That was his first message back to the Queen: We can make slaves of these people since they are easily subjugated, and they do not know much about warfare. Any ten of my men can take over this island with the technology and weapons we have brought over.

The basic conflict relates to the economy because Indian nations operated on the basis of a natural world economy. They had thanksgiving ceremonies that went around the clock and around the calendar year. Something was always coming up, so there was always thanksgiving in a land-based economy. It was part of the structure of a community. It was an instruction to respect what was growing. This was true across the Americas. Yet, our white brother kept telling us there was a better way: get rich. Our people had a hard time with that. They said, "No, our land is held in common; everyone owns the land. Water is free, air is free, everything you need for life sustenance is free." And he said, "I would like to buy your land." They said, "What do you mean by buying?" Now we have people buying his argument. We have people, our own people, who are now willing to sell long-term sovereignty for short-term personal gain. As we sit back and assess these last five hundred years, let us look at what has happened to our people. How have the Indian nations fared? How have our children? How are our institutions? Are they holding up? How are our principles? Are they holding up? We have to look at ourselves because as tough as these last five hundred years have been, the next five hundred or even fifty years are going to be tougher.

There is a fundamental issue here that we have to look at because human beings are displacing life around the world. Huge populations are displacing life, whether it is trees, the elephants in Africa, the tigers in India, or the buffalo in this country. They are not here anymore. Yet there are more and more people. There is a displacement going on here of things a fundamental economy needs. The Indians understood one thing: they understood that the law of flesh, blood, and bones is common to all living beings. We are under one common law here. We are animals, but we are animals with intellect. Intellect is what makes us dangerous because we have the foreknowledge of death. Animals know when death is coming, and they prepare for it. Yet, we know from a very young age that we are going to die. This is a tremendous knowledge, but how do you use that knowledge? How do you work with it?

When one speaks of generations the way the Indians speak of them, we must see that the next generations, those faces coming from the earth, have the same good that we have and can enjoy the same law that we do. Well, in assessing five hundred years in this country, we see that the next seven generations are not going to enjoy that. Every day, at least six species of life become extinct. So when you talk about the philosophy of sovereignty, you must talk of longevity and the future. This is the common sense that comes from the long experience of Indian nations being in one place: if you do not work with the laws that surround you, you will not survive. It is quite simple. We know that there is no mercy in the natural law whatsoever. It will exact retribution in direct ratio to violation. You cannot discuss this—there are no lawyers, only the retribution. The problem here is that we visit this retribution on our children and on our grandchildren. We leave them the problem of our excesses. What do we say to greedy individuals who say sovereignty is money?

I never believed the white man when he said his way was better. I never believed it. I always believed that our way was better, maybe just because I knew more about it. The truth is, if we sit back and really look at it, there is some hard news here for all of us no matter who we are.

When we speak of sovereignty, we have to have a large conceptualization of what it is we are talking about. With Indian nations, it is not just a political term, it is also a spiritual term. It may be even be more spiritual than political. One of our people once said that spirituality is the highest form of politics. So, let us keep the parameters of what we are talking about clear.

The parameters are beyond the oceans that surround us, and they are beyond our time here on earth. The parameters we are discussing reverberate into the future. If your economy does not function within those parameters, then you are shortchanging those future generations we talked about. Maybe it is only the Indians that talk about the seventh generation. I do not know. Since we have talked about it a lot, I have heard it again and again. I hear it from strangers; I hear it from strange places. Why not? It seems to us common law and common sense. So, let us say that sovereign is common sense in its most basic fundamental form: common sense and respect for all life.

Land is the issue; land has always been the issue. We cannot trade our jurisdiction over lands and territories for money. Our lands and our right to govern ourselves are all we have. If we gamble our lands for money, jurisdiction, and taxation, we will lose, because that is the white man's game.

1990

·❖· FALL STARS AND CELEBRATIONS ·❖·

THE WINTER SOLSTICE

For many peoples the winter solstice was the most important day of the year, and great festivals were held. The birth of Christ, which actually took place in spring, was celebrated at the solstice by early Christians to avoid persecution. Native North American cultures built earthworks or used natural landforms to predict when the solstice would occur. They could also track it by the movements of the stars, including Ursa Major.

The Women of the Eastern Sky

Maskwawā´nahkwatōk (Red Cloud Woman, Louise Dutchman, *c.*1870-†), Menominee

This is a story about some of the Wābanunäqsiwŏk, the Eastern People, who are associated with the sun, the Morning Star, and a group of stars known as the Sacred Sisters of the Eastern Sky. These star spirits may come to people in dreams, or they may choose to be reborn on earth, which is what happened to Maskwawā´nahkwatōk, who believed she was the reincarnation of one of the Sacred Sisters. Men blessed by male Wābanunäqsiwŏk may become Wābano sorcerers, or Men of Dawn, associated with the power of the sun and thunderbirds. If a woman who is under the guardianship of the Sacred Sisters neglects to give them attention, they can punish her by making her ill. If she dreams of them or is sick, she must pay for an offering as a ball game called double-ball, or shinny [women's lacrosse], played with a straight stick and two red-painted balls linked by a thong. She may play the dice game, which has ten pieces colored white on one side and dark on the other. The players dress in red or have some red decoration, since red signified happiness.

Fall star map

451

Plate game with dice and bowl, shinny stick, 1920s. Frances Densmore

Frances Densmore and Walter Hoffman, who studied the Menominee, were told by informants that there are eight spirit women in the East (*manitúkiwûg*). These women all had specific names and usually appeared to women, though they could be summoned by jessakids (jaasakiijig). The spirit women were Mādjíkikwáwis (Matsikihkwäwis, Oldest in a Group), Osáwapûnóke (Osáwāpanóhkiw, Yellow[-tinted] Dawn Woman), Kísigkóqkiu (Kēsekóhkiw, Sky Woman), and Wāpanómitáwe (East, or Sun Medicine Woman), Kískapanuq'kiu (Kískāpanúhkiw, Early Dawn Woman), Kashkíqkapan (Kaskīhkapan, Dark Haze at the Horizon), Páshapanoq'kiu (Pásapanóhkiw, Yellow Streak of Cloudy Vapor of Dawn Woman), Mä´tshiwiqkwáwis (Mǽciwihkwáwis, She Who Governs). The last two were evil. Osáwapûnóke is the youngest and marries the hero of this story, Pä´skineu. Densmore's informants related that

> Early in the morning, when the sky is red, the spirit women are playing their dice game, and the color in the sky is the color on their faces. According to Thundercloud, a Winnebago, there are four spirit women playing the bowl-and-dice game in the northern sky, and the eight stars in a circle known as the Northern Crown are their dice. Once, these stars dropped down to the earth and became the dice with which the Indian women play the game. The game played by the spirit women is that in which the dice are tossed upward in a bowl, and when they appear to a woman, they usually tell her to play this game. They tell her to play it once a year and whenever she is sick or beset by trouble and anxiety. They say that every morning, in the eastern sky, they are playing this game to give help and pleasure to their sisters on the earth. 'Look in the sky,' they say, 'play our game and give us a feast. So you will make us happy, all your troubles will vanish, and your health will be restored. At the feast you must make a speech and say that you are playing the game for us.' The spirit women did not always say the same thing, but they never told anyone to take material remedies, such as decoctions of herbs or roots.

"The Women of the Eastern Sky" might have been associated with the solstice because the heroine of the story, Osáwapûnóke, begins in winter as an old woman but then becomes young. In addition, the reed mat on which the women descend may be Ursa Major, which seems to touch the horizon during winter. The young men of the story may correspond to the constellation known as Orion, which is visible from winter through early spring. Maskwawā´nahkwatōk's story also may have nearly buried links to an ancient past related to Mesoamerican heart sacrifices, which often accompanied ball games played to the gods. These sisters and their mother are powerful, and powerful spirits, even if evil, provide great blessings if carefully propitiated. But what may have begun as an ancient legend has been transformed by a "youngest-smartest" heroine, here the youngest of the ten sisters, who is willing to reveal herself to a young warrior to stop her older sisters and mother from practicing cannibalism. This warrior is powerful by virtue of his puberty fast and the visions that have given him the protection of the sky beings [birds], land creatures [fox], and underwater creatures [fish]; thus he commands the entire universe. He and the old mother of the story are both sorcerers. The young man wins the contests with the sisters' mother because he is connected to the Thunderers, and it is they who eventually remove the women from earth to the sky.

Which constellation they become remains a mystery, especially since Maskwawā´nahkwatōk's version has ten women, rather than eight. The "rocky place" at the beginning of the story might be the Milky Way. The women appear at twilight; then, later in the legend, they move at dawn and go "halfway" to camp, a reference to how far the constellation moves in the night sky. They may be the Pleiades or the Hyades, and the young men may be the constellation Orion, which appears to chase the two constellations. Some nations did identify the Pleiades as having ten stars, rather than six or seven as was usual. In addition, the Skidi (Wolf) Pawnee, western neighbors of the Menominee, associated the Pleiades with the basket dice game.[265] Maskwawā´nahkwatōk prayed to the Thunderers for herself and for anthropologist Leonard Bloomfield, asking that he be given more money, which might have been the first time the Thunderers were propitiated for academic grant money.

Up above yonder, there must be a rocky place. That is where dwelt these ten women, with their mother they dwelt. Now, they used to throw down a reed mat to the earth here; it served as a ladder. On it they would descend. Then they started forth. They did not miss any men; wherever men were staying, they would always see them. There would be nine of these men who followed these women. When they camped somewhere on the way, they would take these men's hearts away from them. Here, into the braids of their headdresses was where they placed those hearts. Then, while these men were asleep, these women would start away. So then, when the men arose from sleep, the women would be gone. Then they would follow them. Then, when these women arrived at the place whence they had come, these men would be slain, and they would eat these men. That was what they always did. Many men had those women slain, for no one could keep from following them. Those women had taken their hearts. That was the way they always did.

Now, a certain woman went far away; into the deep wilderness she went, to give her young brother the puberty fast; too dangerous at this time were these women. When that youth had completed his fasting, a stick of wood he set up. He had a pet eagle, and up there that eagle used to perch. Also a fox that boy had as a pet, which he had been given in his fasting.[266] Then he kept hunting, killing very much game, that his sister might have ample food when he had left her. At one time he brought home two young bears.

"Now, sister," he told her, "set these two young bears to boil; some people are coming. And make me some moccasins," he told his sister. She did exactly as he told her.

And really, as twilight fell, some women came, one behind the other, out of the depths of the forest. Way in the very rear a little old woman came hobbling along on a cane. When they had come, then close to the wigwam they scraped the snow away. When they had scraped the snow away, the women cut down trees and dragged them near; some of them, you see, were cutting trees for building the lodge. When they had completed it, they broke off cedar boughs to make their flooring. Then they gathered firewood. Then, when they had built the fire, they rested. And then came these men, nine of them.

"Hee-hee-hee-hee!" they said, shivering in the cold, for their blanket robes had been taken away from them.

That youth then said to them, "Come in here!"

When the men came in, he took from the kettle the two young bears and gave these men a hearty meal. Truly then did these men eat with zest, drinking all the broth, besides. When they had finished eating, they filed out of the house and entered the lodge of these women and sat by them, each by his own. Then these women placed meat upon wooden spits and roasted it. When it was cooked done, then the oldest of the sisters, as she ate, left nothing for her husband. The first five women did not give their men anything to eat. The sixth one left a little food for her man. The last four kept back half of that meat for them.

Then that youth went and entered their lodge. By the cooking place sat the little old woman; by her side the lad took his seat. Indeed, then those women laughed loudly. "Fie, nasty!" they said, "What is this fellow doing, coming here and sitting by our grandmother?"

The lad did not heed it at all. The little old woman had eaten very little of her roast; she gave the food to her man. At last, in due time, they lay down to sleep. When the time had come for them to lie down to sleep, then, after all her older sisters were asleep, the little old woman said to the youth, "Now go about and undo my older sisters' braids. That is where these men's hearts have been placed. Go out of doors. Shape snow in your hands. Go and make nine snowballs. These you will put into my older sisters' braids here."

So when the youth came back, he undid the oldest sister's braid; there lay the heart of that man. The youth took it and placed the lump of snow into her braid. Thereupon he placed back this man's heart for him. Thus he did with all those women, restoring their hearts to all these men. When he had replaced them all, he came back and lay down.

Then the little old woman rose from the couch and went outside. After a short time she came back into the lodge. Truly, she was beautiful now, a young girl, having gone and put away her disguise of old age.[267]

"Now then, just before dawn we shall start," the youth's wife said to him. "Halfway we shall camp," she told him. When he was still asleep, the woman, who was now his wife, nudged him. "Now we are going!" she told him. "Truly, our eldest sister is fleet of foot."

Then the women arose, all of them taking away their men's blanket robes. The lad went off and waited for them ahead, in the direction they were taking. Behind a tree the youth took his stand. Matsikihk-wäwis came running in the lead. He struck her on the leg, breaking the bone. "Is this the way you imitate your grandmother when she takes a husband?" he said to his sister-in-law. Then truly in a great rage was Matsikihkwäwis.

"Truly, I hate him! Where in the world did she go and pick up this fellow dog of hers?" she said to her youngest sister. Then slowly enough did Matsikihkwäwis walk.

The youth then ran all the way back home. His sister had by this time finished her cooking. When those men awoke, at once they were going to start in pursuit.

"Let us eat before we start. They can't get very far, can they?" the youth said to them. So then they went and ate.

When they had eaten, "Now, sister, if anything anywhere happens to me, this eagle of mine will keep giving its call. He will keep guard over you," he said to his sister, as he departed.

So then they went in pursuit. In time they reached the place where the women had again made camp. They finished cooking and put the meat on spits. Matsikihkwäwis gave her man no food. Then the youth said to her, "Is that what you learn by watching your grandmother when she takes a husband?"—because she gave him nothing to eat.

When the next dawn was near, "Now we shall start," his wife told him. "At noon we shall arrive, slowly enough is Matsikihkwäwis traveling with her broken leg." Then they took away the blanket robes from their husbands.

"Leave those robes! Let them wear their robes. They too feel the cold," said the youth to them. Thereupon again those five women became very angry.

When they had departed, he roused all those men from their sleep. "Get up! We are pursuing our wives!" he said to them. The men jumped up and started in pursuit. At noon they came to the place where the women dwelt. Up on top of a cliff there stood a long lodge. When they reached the foot of the cliff, there was a vast number of bones, human bones, of as many people as they must have slain. Truly steep, like this in shape, was that solitary cliff. High, high, far up above, was where they dwelt. How were they to climb up? Then that youngest one threw down a reed mat; it was in form like a ladder.

"Now, exactly where I step, you too will have to take each step, as many as you are. Only in this way will you arrive," he said to his companions.

Then the youth started, and behind him came those men, clinging to him, At last they reached the top of the cliff. Then they went, one after the other, into that long lodge, each taking his seat by his wife.

"So now at any rate you have managed to come into the house," the youth was told by his wife.

Soon the old woman of the house called out, bidding Matsikihkwäwis come have her hair combed. "I truly love this daughter of mine, who always makes me glad, bringing me that whose taste I truly like." She lifted some red coals from the fire. On them she threw the lump of snow, for she thought it was a human heart. Soon she unbound another daughter's braid, to do her roasting in the flame, to cook on the coals. Thus she did with all ten of her daughters. Then, when she had undone all their braids, she wanted to lift out her roasts. But there! the glowing coals had been entirely put out by water. What was there for her to eat? For it was only snow.

"Look at that!" said the old woman. "What shall I feed these sons-in-law?" She took up her bag. When she had hung up the kettle, "Suppose I give them berries to eat!"

They were human eyes.

"Not at all do we eat that kind of food," said the youth to her.

"Yah, truly, I do hate him! What kind of a creature is this she has brought?" she said to her daughter. So then she put away her bag of human eyes. "I suppose I shall have to give them dried squash," said the old woman.

When she untied her bag, leeches were those things.

"Not at all is that our way of eating, to eat leeches."

So then the old woman gave up. Thereupon she became very ill; she was almost dying. "What is the matter with you?" Matsikihkwäwis asked her.

"If I ate the White Lynx, I should get well," said the old woman.[268]

"What does she say?" said the youth to her.

"If she ate the White Lynx, she says she would get well."

"Very well, I shall fetch it," said the youth. Off he went, only a short time he was gone, then he came with the White Lynx. When the old woman saw it, in truth she wept bitterly.

"What sort of creature has she brought here, to the undoing of my little brother?" she said to her daughter. For that lynx was the old woman's younger brother. To it the old woman, while it lived, had fed those youths.

On the next day she again became very ill; she was at the point of death.

"What is the matter with you?" Matsikihkwäwis asked her.

"If I ate the White Porcupine, I should get well."[269]

"Alas, you speak of hard things! Whence are we to get the White Porcupine?"

"Is that porcupine so hard to get? I shall go get it," said the lad. Off he went; in a short while he brought the White Porcupine. In truth the old woman again wept bitterly.

"So now all my younger brothers have been destroyed for me! Where did she get her hands on this creature she has brought, to the undoing of my brothers?" That was all.

Now the youth in turn became very ill. Soon Matsikihkwäwis again arose and went over to question him. "What is matter with you?"

"If some fetched me my eagle, I should get well."

"Is that eagle so hard to get? Why, I shall fetch it," said the old woman. Off she went to fetch the eagle. When the old woman came running close to that place, the eagle sounded the alarm. Then the fox came running out and fiercely attacked the old woman, and she did not succeed in getting hold of that eagle. So back home went the old woman.

The youth had a fish; on his settee in the wigwam that fish used to lie. Now again very ill grew the youth. "If someone fetched me my fish, I should get well."

"Very well, I shall go get that fish," said the old woman.

Off she started, on the run, and ran inside the wigwam to go seize that fish. Then again in truth did the fox and the eagle sorely maltreat her. They chased her to the edge of the earth, and out there they killed the old woman.

So then, when the old woman did not return to her dwelling, the youth called to the Thunderers, saying, "Now, let these women go stay in some fixed place. If they remain dwelling even here, no men will be left." Thus spoke the youth.

Thereupon the Thunderers started forth, and there was a great wind. The women shook themselves where they sat, like this, until they sank into the rock up to here. But as the great wind kept blowing, they were carried away into the air; truly they flew along with great speed. Over into the east the Thunderers went and set those women.

Now, that is all.

Those string-like objects—of about this length—which hang in the tamarack-swamps, they are the hair of those women.

My name is Red Cloud Woman; hither from that place I came to dwell in human form. They are my sisters.

Lo, I make unto you a burnt offering of tobacco, Women Who Dwell in the Eastern Sky. Graciously take pity on us, now that I have told of how you fared when here on earth you dwelt. Take pity on this man here; help him that he may remember this tale.

And you, O Thunderers, to you too I make a burnt-offering of a pipeful of tobacco. And this piece of money you are to accept. He gives it to you. Help him that he may secure more money. Amen.

1920s

The Red Swan

Unidentified Anishinâbe

This story, which may once have been sacred, has had nearly as many interpretations as scholars who have studied it. It may be an allegory of a celestial, seasonal occurrence, perhaps the winter solstice in conjunction with the movements of the planet Venus. The three brothers who begin and end this story symbolize the Three Fires nations—Ojibwe, Odawa, and Potawatomi—with the origin of the tale and its probable teller being Ojibwe, the name of the main character. Their parents, who have died as the story opens, would have been the two down-fended children[270] described in the creation stories. In some versions, when First Woman is thrown from the sky world, she comes to rest on the backs of swans, thus the significance of the swan as magical. Red comes from vermilion [mercuric sulfide pigment], a sacred mineral that was buried with the dead for centuries. The teller incorporates many classic folkloric elements: the quest journey of the youngest-smartest, help from magicians, a magic pot of food, humans becoming animals, a journey to the underworld. Equally important is the wounded magician who, once his scalp is restored, instantly becomes a young man, symbolizing renewal and the return of spring. The Red Swan may also symbolize Venus, whose orbit as the evening star shows the planet in the west soon after the sinking of the sun. In ancient times, there would have been a festival celebrating Venus as an evening or a morning star, for example, the planet's orbit relative to the solstice. In addition, Venus spends part of its orbit behind the sun, where it cannot be seen, a symbol of a journey to the underworld; when it emerges, it celebrates the return of life. That may be a foundation for this story, which shows the hero providing wives, and so children, to his brothers. The ending may have been added at a later time, after the buffalo had begun to disappear from the Great Lakes region and after the coming of the missionaries and their proscriptions about polygamy.

Three brothers were left destitute by the death of their parents, at an early age. The eldest was not yet able to provide fully for their support but did all he could in hunting, and with his aid and the stock of provisions left by their father, they were preserved and kept alive, rather, it seems, by miraculous interposition, than the adequacy of their own exertions. For the father had been a hermit (*pai-gwud-aw-diz-zid*)[271] having removed far away from the body of the tribe, so that when he and his wife died they left their children without neighbors and friends, and the lads had no idea that there was a human being near them. They did not even know who their parents had been, for the eldest was too young, at the time of their death, to remember it. Forlorn as they were, they did not, however, give up to despondency but made use of every exertion they could and, in the process of time, learned the art of hunting and killing animals. The eldest soon became an expert hunter and was very successful in procuring food. He was noted for his skill in killing buffalo, elk, and moose, and he instructed his brothers in the arts of the forest as soon as they became old enough to follow him. After they had become able to hunt and take care of themselves, the elder proposed to leave them and go in search of habitations, promising to return as soon as he could procure them wives. In this project he was over-ruled by his brothers, who said they could not part with him. Maujeekewis,[272] the second eldest, was loud in his disapproval, saying, "What will you do with those you propose to get—we have lived so long without them, and we can still do without them." His words prevailed, and the three brothers continued together for a time.

One day they agreed to kill, each, a male of those kind of animals each was most expert in hunting, for the purpose of making quivers from their skins. They did so and immediately commenced making arrows to fill their quivers, that they might be prepared for any emergency. Soon after, they hunted on a wager to see who should come in first with game and prepare it so as to regale the others. They were to shoot no other animal but such as each was in the habit of killing. They set out different ways; Odjibwa, the youngest, had not gone far before he saw a bear, an animal he was not to kill by the agreement. He followed him close and drove an arrow through him, which brought him to the ground. Although contrary to the bet, he immediately commenced skinning him, when suddenly something red tinged all the air around him. He rubbed his eyes, thinking he was perhaps deceived, but without effect, for the red hue continued.

At length he heard a strange noise at a distance. It first appeared like a human voice, but after following the sound for some distance, he reached the shores of a lake and soon saw the object he was looking for.

At a distance out in the lake, sat a most beautiful Red Swan, whose plumage glittered in the sun and who would, now and then, make the same noise he had heard.[273] He was within a long bow shot and, pulling the arrow from the bow-string up to his ear, took deliberate aim and shot. The arrow took no effect; and he shot and shot again till his quiver was empty. Still the swan remained, moving round and round, stretching its long neck and dipping its bill into the water, as if heedless of the arrows shot at it. Odjibwa ran home and got all his own and his brothers' arrows and shot them all away. He then stood and gazed at the beautiful bird. While standing, he remembered his brothers saying that in their deceased father's medicine sack were three magic arrows. Off he started, his anxiety to kill the swan overcoming all scruples. At any other time, he would have deemed it sacrilege to open his father's medicine sack, but now he hastily seized the three arrows and ran back, leaving the other contents of the sack scattered over the lodge. The swan was still there.

He shot the first arrow with great precision and came very near to it. The second came still closer. As he took the last arrow, he felt his arm firmer and, drawing it up with vigor, saw it pass through the neck of the swan a little above the breast. Still it did not prevent the bird from flying off, which it did, however, at first slowly, flapping its wings and rising gradually into the air and then flying off toward the sinking of the sun.[274] Odjibwa was disappointed; he knew that his brothers would be displeased with him. He rushed into the water and rescued the two magic arrows. The third was carried off by the swan, but he thought that it could not fly very far with it, and let the consequences be what they might, he was bent on following it.

Off he started on the run. He was noted for speed, for he would shoot an arrow and then run so fast that the arrow always fell behind him. "I can run fast," he thought, "and I can get up with the swan sometime or other." He thus ran over hills and prairies toward the west till near night and was only going to take one more run and then seek a place to sleep for the night, when suddenly he heard noises at a distance which he knew were from people, for some were cutting trees and the strokes of their axes echoed through the woods. When he emerged from the forest, the sun was just falling below the horizon, and he felt pleased to find a place to sleep in and get something to eat, as he had left home without a mouthful. All these circumstances could not damp his ardor for the accomplishment of his object, and he felt that if he only persevered, he could succeed.

At a distance, on a rising piece of ground, he could see an extensive town. He went toward it, but soon heard the watchman, Mudjee-Kokokoho[275]—who was placed on some height to overlook the place and give notice of the approach of friends or foes—cried out, "We are visited!" and a loud holla indicated that they all heard it. The young man advanced and was pointed by the watchman to the lodge of the chief. "It is there you must go in," he said and left him.

"Come in, come in," said the chief, "take a seat there," pointing to the side where his daughter sat. "It is there you must sit." Soon they gave him something to eat, and very few questions were asked him, being a stranger. It was only when he spoke, that the others answered him.

"Daughter," said the chief, after dark, "take our son-in-law's moccasins and see if they be torn; if so, mend them for him, and bring in his bundle."[276]

The young man thought it strange that he should be so warmly received and married instantly without his wishing it, although the young girl was pretty. It was sometime before she would take his moccasins, which he had taken off. It displeased him to see her so reluctant to do so, and when she did reach them, he snatched them out of her hand and hung them up himself. He laid down and thought of the swan and made up his mind to be off by dawn. He awoke early and spoke to the young woman, but she gave no answer. He slightly touched her.

"What do you want?" she said, and turned her back toward him.

"Tell me," he said, "what time the swan passed. I am following it. And come out and point the direction."

"Do you think you can catch up to it?" she said.

"Yes," he answered.

"Naubesah,"[277] she said. She, however, went out and pointed in the direction he should go.

The young man went slowly till the sun arose, when he commenced traveling at his accustomed speed. He passed the day in running, and when night came, he was unexpectedly pleased to find himself near another town. When at a distance he heard the watchman crying out, "We are visited," soon the men of the village stood out to see the stranger. He was again told to enter the lodge of the chief, and his reception was, in every respect, the same as he met the previous night, only that the young woman was more beautiful and received him very kindly. Although urged to stay, his mind was fixed on the object of his journey. Before daylight he asked the young woman what time the Red Swan passed and to point out the way. She did so and said it passed yesterday when the sun was between midday and *pungishemoo* (*pangishimo*: it sets) its falling place.[278]

He again set out rather slowly, but when the sun had arisen, he tried his speed by shooting an arrow ahead and running after it, but it fell behind him. Nothing remarkable happened in the course of the day, and he went on leisurely. Toward night, he came to the lodge of an old man. Sometime after dark he saw a light emitted from a small low lodge. He went up to it very slyly, and peeping through the door, saw an old man alone, warming his back before the fire, with his head down on his breast. He thought the old man did not know that he was standing near the door, but in this he was disappointed, for so soon as he looked in, "Walk in, *Nosis*,"[279] he said, "take a seat opposite to me, and take off your things and dry them, for you must be fatigued; and I will prepare you something to eat."

Odjibwa did as he was requested. The old man, whom he perceived to be a magician, then said, "My kettle with water stands near the fire," and immediately a small earthen or a kind of metallic pot with legs appeared by the fire. He then took one grain of corn, also one whortleberry,[280] and put them in the pot. As the young man was very hungry, he thought that his chance for a supper was but small. Not a word or a look, however, revealed his feelings.

The pot soon boiled, when the old man spoke, commanding it to stand some distance from the fire. "Nosis," said he, "feed yourself," and he handed him a dish and ladle made out of the same metal as the pot. The young man helped himself to all that was in the pot. He felt ashamed to think of his having done so, but before he could speak, the old man said, "Nosis, eat, eat." And soon after he again said, "Help yourself from the pot." Odjibwa was surprised on looking into it to see it full. He kept on taking all out, and as soon as it was done, it was again filled, till he had amply satisfied his hunger. The magician then spoke, and the pot occupied its accustomed place in one part of the lodge.

The young man then leisurely reclined back and listened to the predictions of his entertainer, who told him to keep on, and he would obtain his object. "To tell you more," said he, "I am not permitted; but go on as you have commenced, and you will not be disappointed. Tomorrow you will again reach one of my fellow old men, but the one you will see after him will tell you all and the manner in which you will proceed to accomplish your journey. Often has this Red Swan passed, and those who have followed it have never returned. But you must be firm in your resolution, and be prepared for all events."

"So will it be," answered Odjibwa, and they both laid down to sleep.

Early in the morning, the old man had his magic kettle prepared so that his guest should eat before leaving. When [Odjibwa was] leaving, the old man gave him his parting advice. Odjibwa set out in better spirits than he had done since leaving home. Night again found him in company with an old man, who received him kindly and directed him on his way in the morning. He traveled with a light heart, expecting to meet the one who was to give him directions how to proceed to get the Red Swan. Toward nightfall, he reached the third old man's lodge. Before coming to the door, he heard him saying, "*Nosis*, come in," and going in immediately, he felt quite at home. The old man prepared him something to eat, acting as the other magicians had done, and his kettle was of the same dimensions and material. The old man waited till he had done eating, when he commenced addressing him.

"Young man, the errand you are on is very difficult. Numbers of young men have passed with the same purpose but never returned. Be careful, and if your guardian spirits are powerful, you may succeed. This Red Swan you are following is the daughter of a magician who has plenty of everything, but he values his daughter but little less than wampum. He wore a cap of wampum, which was attached to his scalp, but powerful Indians—warriors of a distant chief—came and told him that their chief's daughter was on the brink of the grave, and she herself requested his scalp of wampum to effect a cure. 'If I can only see it, I will recover,' she said, and it was for this reason they came. After long urging, the magician at last consented to part with it, only from the idea of restoring the young woman to health, although when he took it off, it left his head bare and bloody. Several years have passed since, and it has not healed. The warriors coming for it w[ere] only a cheat, and they are now constantly making sport of it, dancing it about from village to village, and on every insult it receives the old man groans from pain. Those Indians are too powerful for the magician, and numbers have sacrificed themselves to recover it for him, but without success. The Red Swan has enticed many a young man, as she has done you, in order to get them to procure it, and whoever is the fortunate one that succeeds will receive the Red Swan as his reward. In the morning you will proceed on your way, and toward evening you will come to the magician's lodge, but before you enter, you will hear his groans. He will immediately ask you in, and you will see no one but himself. He will make inquiries of you, as regards your dreams and the powers of your guardian spirits; he will then ask you to attempt the recovery of his scalp. He will show you the direction, and if you feel inclined, as I dare say you do, go forward, my son, with a strong heart, persevere, and I have a presentiment you will succeed."

The young man answered, "I will try."

Early next morning after having eaten from the magic kettle, he started off on his journey.

Toward evening he came to the lodge as he was told and soon heard the groans of the magician. "Come in," he said, even before the young man reached the door. On entering he saw his head all bloody, and he was groaning most terribly. "Sit down, sit down," he said, "while I prepare you something to eat," at the same time doing as the other magicians had done, in preparing food. "You see," he said, "how poor I am; I have to attend to all my wants." He said this to conceal the fact that the Red Swan was there, but Odjibwa perceived that the lodge was partitioned, and he heard a rustling noise now and then in that quarter, which satisfied him that it was occupied.

461

After having taken his leggings and moccasins off and eaten, the old magician commenced telling him how he had lost his scalp—the insults it was receiving, the pain he was suffering in consequence, his wishes to regain it, the unsuccessful attempts that had already been made, and the numbers and power of those who detained it. He stated the best and most probable way of getting it, touching the young man on his pride and ambition by the proposed adventure, and last he spoke of such things as would make an Indian rich. He would interrupt his discourse by now and then groaning and saying, "Oh, how shamefully they are treating it!"

Odjibwa listened with solemn attention. The old man then asked him about his dreams, his dreams at the particular time he had fasted and blackened his face to procure guardian spirits.[281] The young man then told him one dream; the magician groaned, "No, that is not it," he said. The young man told him another. He groaned again. "That is not it," he said. The young man told him of two or three others. The magician groaned at each recital and said, rather peevishly, "No, those are not they."

The young man then thought to himself, "Who are you? You may groan as much as you please. I am inclined not to tell you any more dreams."

The magician then spoke in rather a supplicating tone. "Have you no more dreams of another kind?"

"Yes," said the young man and told him one.

"That is it, that is it!" he cried. "You will cause me to live. That was what I was wishing you to say," and he rejoiced greatly. "Will you then go and see if you cannot procure my scalp?"

"Yes," said the young man. "I will go, and the day after tomorrow, when you hear the cries of the *kakak* (*gegek*: hawk), you will know by this sign that I am successful.[282] You must prepare your head and lean it out through the door, so that the moment I arrive, I may place your scalp on."

"Yes, yes," said the magician. "As you say, it will be done."

Early next morning, he set out on his perilous adventure, and about the time that the sun hangs toward home (afternoon), he heard the shouts of a great many people. He was in a wood at the time and saw, as he thought, only a few men, but the farther he went, the more numerous they appeared. On emerging into a plain, their heads appeared like the hanging leaves for number. In the center he perceived a post, and something waving on it, which was the scalp. Now and then the air was rent with the *sau-sau-quan* (*sasâkwewin*: joyful shouts), for they were dancing the war dance around it. Before he could be perceived, he turned himself into a *no-noskau-see* (*nonôkâsi*: humming bird) and flew toward the scalp.[283]

As he passed some of those who were standing by, he flew close to their ears, making the humming noise which this bird does when it flies. They jumped on one side and asked each other what it could be. By this time he had nearly reached the scalp, but fearing he should be perceived while untying it, he changed himself into a *me-sau-be-wau-aun*[284] and then floated slowly and lightly onto the scalp. He untied it and moved off slowly, as the weight was almost too great. It was as much as he could do to keep it up and prevent the Indians from snatching it away.

The moment they saw it was moving, they filled the air with their cries of: "It is taken from us! It is taken from us!"

He continued moving a few feet above them; the rush and hum of the people was like the dead beating surges after a storm. He soon gained on them, and they gave up the pursuit. After going a little farther, he changed himself into a *kakak* and flew off with his prize, making that peculiar noise which this bird makes.

In the meantime, the magician had followed his instructions, placing his head outside of the lodge as soon as he heard the cry of the kakak, and soon after he heard the rustling of its wings. In a moment Odjibwa stood before him. He immediately gave the magician a severe blow on the head with the wampum scalp; his limbs extended and quivered in agony from the effects of the blow. The scalp adhered, and the young man walked in and sat down, feeling perfectly at home. The magician was so long in recovering from the stunning blow that the young man feared he had killed him. He was, however, pleased to see him show signs of life; he first commenced moving and soon sat up. But how surprised was Odjibwa to see, not an aged man far in years and decrepitude, but one of the handsomest young men he ever saw stand up before him.

"Thank you, my friend," he said. "You see that your kindness and bravery has restored me to my former shape. It was so ordained, and you have now accomplished the victory." The young magician urged the stay of his deliverer for a few days, and they soon formed a warm attachment for each other. The magician never alluded to the Red Swan in their conversations.

At last, the day arrived when Odjibwa made preparations to return. The young magician amply repaid him for his kindness and bravery by various kinds of wampum, robes, and all such things as he had need of to make him an influential man. But though the young man's curiosity was at its height about the Red Swan, he controlled his feelings and never so much as even hinted of her, feeling that he would surrender a point of propriety in so doing. While the one he had rendered such service to, whose hospitality he was now enjoying, and who had richly rewarded him, had never so much as even mentioned anything about her but studiously concealed her.

Odjibwa's pack for traveling was ready, and he was taking his farewell smoke, when the young magician thus addressed him. "Friend, you know for what cause you came thus far. You have accomplished your object and conferred a lasting obligation on me. Your perseverance shall not go unrewarded. If you undertake other things with the same spirit you have this, you will never fail to accomplish them. My duty renders it necessary for me to remain where I am, although I should feel happy to go with you. I have given you all you will need as long as you live, but I see you feel backward to speak about the Red Swan. I vowed that whoever procured me my scalp should be rewarded by possessing the Red Swan." He then spoke and knocked on the partition. The door immediately opened, and the Red Swan met his eager gaze. She was a most beautiful female, and as she stood majestically before him, it would be impossible to describe her charms, for she looked as if she did not belong to earth. "Take her," the young magician said. "She is my sister, treat her well. She is worthy of you, and what you have done for me merits more. She is ready to go with you to your kindred and friends and has been so ever since your arrival. My good wishes go with you both."

She then looked very kindly on her husband, who now bid farewell to his friend indeed, and accompanied by the object of his wishes, he commenced retracing his footsteps. They traveled slowly, and after two or three days reached the lodge of the third old man who had fed him from his small magic pot. He was very kind and said, "You see what your perseverance has procured you. Do so always and you will succeed in all things you undertake." On the following morning when they were going to start, he pulled from the side of the lodge a bag, which he presented to the young man, saying, "Nosis, I give you this. It contains a present for you, and I hope you will live happily till old age." They then bid farewell to him and proceeded on.

They soon reached the second old man's lodge. Their reception there was the same as at the first; he also gave them a present, with the old man's wishes that they would be happy. They went on and reached the first town, which the young man had passed in his pursuit. The watchman gave notice, and he was shown into the chief's lodge.

"Sit down there, son-in-law," said the chief, pointing to a place near his daughter. "And you also," he said to the Red Swan. The young woman of the lodge was busy in making something, but she tried to show her indifference about what was taking place, for she did not even raise her head to see who was come. Soon the chief said, "Let someone bring in the bundle of our son-in-law." When it was brought in, the young man opened one of the bags, which he had received from one of the old men; it contained wampum, robes, and various other articles. He presented them to his father-in-law, and all expressed their surprise at the value and richness of the gift. The chief's daughter then only stole a glance at the present, then at Odjibwa and his beautiful wife. She stopped working and remained silent and thoughtful all the evening.

They conversed about his adventures; after this the chief told him that he should take his daughter along with him in the morning. The young man said, "Yes." The chief then spoke out, saying, "Daughter, be ready to go with him in the morning."

There was a Maujeekewis[285] in the lodge, who thought to have got the young woman to wife. He jumped up, saying, "Who is he (meaning the young man), that he should take her for a few presents? I will kill him!" and he raised a knife which he had in his hand. But he only waited till someone held him back and then sat down, for he was too great a coward to do as he had threatened.

Early they took their departure, amid the greetings of their new friends, and toward evening reached the other town. The watchman gave the signal, and numbers of men, women, and children stood out to see them. They were again shown into the chief's lodge, who welcomed them by saying, "Son-in-law, you are welcome," and requested him to take a seat by his daughter, and the two women did the same.

After the usual formalities of smoking and eating, the chief requested the young man to relate his travels in the hearing of all the inmates of the lodge and those who came to see. They looked with admiration and astonishment at the Red Swan, for she was so beautiful. Odjibwa gave them his whole history. The chief then told him that his brothers had been to their town in search of him but had returned and given up all hopes of ever seeing him again. He concluded by saying that since he had been so fortunate and so manly, he should take his daughter with him, "For although your brothers," said he, "were here, they were too timid to enter any of our lodges and merely inquired for you and returned. You will take my daughter, treat her well, and that will bind us more closely together."

It is always the case in towns that someone in it is foolish or clownish. It happened to be so here, for a Maujeekewis was in the lodge, and after the young man had given his father-in-law presents, as he did to the first, this Maujeekewis jumped up in a passion, saying, "Who is this stranger that he should have her? I want her myself." The chief told him to be quiet and not to disturb or quarrel with one who was enjoying their hospitality. "No, no!" he boisterously cried and made an attempt to strike the stranger. Odjibwa was above fearing his threats and paid no attention to him. He cried the louder, "I will have her! I will have her!" In an instant he was laid flat on the ground from a blow of a war-club given by the chief. After he came to himself, the chief upbraided him for his foolishness and told him to go out and tell stories to the old women.

Their arrangements were then made, and the stranger invited a number of families to go and visit their hunting grounds, as there was plenty of game. They consented, and in the morning a large party was assembled to accompany the young man, and the chief with a large party of warriors escorted them a long distance. When ready to return, the chief made a speech and invoked the blessing of the great good Spirit on his son-in-law and party.

After a number of days' travel, Odjibwa and his party came in sight of his home. The party rested while he went alone in advance to see his brothers. When he entered the lodge, he found it all dirty and covered with ashes; on one side was his eldest brother, with his face blackened, sitting amid ashes, crying aloud. On the other side was Maujeekewis, his other brother; his face was also blackened, but his head was covered with feathers and swan's down. He looked so odd that the young man could not keep from laughing, for he appeared and pretended to be so absorbed with grief that he did not notice his brother's arrival. The eldest jumped up and shook hands with him and kissed him and felt very happy to see him again.

Odjibwa, after seeing all things put to rights, told them that he had brought each of them a wife. When Maujeekewis heard about the wife, he jumped up and said, "Why is it just now that you have come?" and made for the door and peeped out to see the women. He then commenced jumping and laughing, saying, "Women! Women!" That was the only reception he gave his brother. Odjibwa then told them to wash themselves and prepare, for he would go and fetch them in. Maujeekewis jumped and washed himself but would every now and then go and peep out to see the women. When they came near, he said, "I will have this one, and that one," he did not exactly know which—he would go and sit down for an instant and then go and peep and laugh. He acted like a madman.

As soon as order was restored, and all [were] seated, Odjibwa presented one of the women to his eldest brother, saying, "These women are given to me. I now give one to each. I intended so from the first."

Maujeekewis spoke and said, "I think three wives would have been enough for you."

The young man led one to Maujeekewis, saying, "My brother, here is one for you and live happily."

Maujeekewis hung down his head as if he was ashamed but would every now and then steal a glance at his wife and also at the other women. By and by he turned toward his wife and acted as if he had been married for years. "Wife," he said, "I will go and hunt," and off he started.

All lived peaceably for some time, and their town prospered, the inhabitants increased, and everything was abundant among them. One day dissatisfaction was manifested in the conduct of the two elder brothers on account of Odjibwa's having taken their deceased father's magic arrows. They upbraided and urged him to procure others if he could. Their object was to get him away, so that one of them might afterward get his wife. One day, after listening to them, he told them he would go. Maujeekewis and himself went together into a sweating lodge to purify themselves. Even there, although it was held sacred, Maujeekewis upbraided him for the arrows. He told him again he would go, and next day, true to his word, he

465

left them. After traveling a long way he came to an opening in the earth, and it led him to the abode of departed spirits.

The country appeared beautiful, the extent of it was lost in the distance; he saw animals of various kinds in abundance. The first he came near to were buffaloes; his surprise was great when these animals addressed him as human beings. They asked him what he came for, how he descended, why he was so bold as to visit the abode of the dead. He told them he was in search of magic arrows to appease his brothers.

"Very well," said the leader of the buffaloes, whose whole form was nothing but bone. "Yes, we know it," and he and his followers moved off a little space as if they were afraid of him. "You have come," resumed the Buffalo Spirit, "to a place where a living man has never before been. You will return immediately to your tribe, for your brothers are trying to dishonor your wife, and you will live to a very old age and live and die happily. You can go no farther in these abodes of ours."

Odjibwa looked, as he thought, to the west and saw a bright light, as if the sun was shining in its splendor, but he saw no sun. "What light is that I see yonder?" he asked.

The all-boned buffalo answered, "It is the place where those who were good dwell."

"And that dark cloud?" Odjibwa again asked.

"Mudjee-izzhi-wabezewin" (wickedness),[286] answered the buffalo.

He asked no more questions, and with the aid of his guardian spirits, again stood on this earth and saw the sun giving light as usual, and breathed the pure air. All else he saw in the abodes of the dead and his travels and actions previous to his return are unknown. After wandering a long time in quest of information to make his people happy, he one evening drew near to his village or town. Passing all the other lodges and coming to his own, he heard his brothers at high words with each other; they were quarreling for the possession of his wife. She had, however, remained constant and mourned the absence and probable loss of her husband, but she had mourned him with the dignity of virtue. The noble youth listened till he was satisfied of the base principles of his brothers.

He then entered the lodge, with the stern air and conscious dignity of a brave and honest man. He spoke not a word but, placing the magic arrows to his bow, drew them to their length and laid the brothers dead at his feet. Thus ended the contest between the hermit's sons, and a firm and happy union was consummated between Odjibwa, or him of the primitive or gathered voice, and the Red Swan.

*c.*1839

DEAD FEASTS AND GHOST SUPPERS

Many nations around the lakes practiced anciently founded rituals honoring the dead, often inviting them back to earth for a feast. Although the dead who have led good lives go to a wonderful place where everything is as people want it to be—ample food of the best kind, dancing, no work, and no death—still, humans and the dead miss each other and wish to communicate once again.

In the nineteenth century, Skanáwà·ti, Onondaga wampum keeper from Canada, wrote a letter, accompanied by a string of wampum to give it official sanction, explaining what he called the "Dead Feast." The "messenger" of the first line is the letter.

Dead Feasts
Skanáwà·ti (Across the Swamp, John Buck), Onondaga

Skanáwà·ti

I am John Buck's messenger. Therefore listen.

John Buck says in olden times of my forefathers was able to recall their departed relatives to see them again, the living ones will make one accord whatever the number they may be will get a feast at a certain house for the dead ones, and when the living ones assemble at the appointed place each of them will take a sliver off their bark door where it turns, this at their different one's houses, and enter noiselessly in the house where the feast is spread out for the dead, and they will now all set down next to the wall of the house on the ground all round the house, and the feast is spread out in the centre of the house, and one is appointed to address the Great Creator; at intervals he would throw an Indian Tobacco on the fire, he will ask the Creator to send their dead relatives, for they are desirous to see them again, and when he ends it, his speaking, he will sit down again, and they will let the fire go down till the light ceases, so that in the house becomes dark, and no one is allowed to speak or to make any noise, and in a little while they will hear people coming, outside, and they will enter the house and will set themselves around the spread feast, and the assembled living ones will wait till the dead ones are about done eating, then the living ones will kindle the slivers of bark which they have brought with them, and the dead are now seen through this light.

Here is the string of wampum.

So, dear friend, according what I have learned by of your letter which you sent and I have received, therefore I have wrote to you now of the above. I am your friend.

Chief John Buck
Firekeeper of Six Nations of Indians, Canada

1890s

Ghost Suppers

Chief Fred Ettawageshik (Both Day, 1896-1969), **Frank Ettawageshik** (Both Day, 1949-   ), Odawas

After surviving government boarding schools in Mt. Pleasant, Michigan, and Carlyle, Pennsylvania, Fred Ettawageshik returned home to the traditional residence of the Odawa on the northwest shore of Michigan at Little Traverse Bay. He became a businessman, a tribal leader, and in time, a great storyteller. The anthropologist who came to Michigan to record his stories fell in love with her informant and stayed. Their son, Frank, who trained as an artist at the University of Michigan, recreated the tools and methods of prehistoric Great Lakes ceramics. Like his father, he also became a storyteller and a band leader and was instrumental in achieving federal recognition for the Little Traverse Bay Band. Here they write of a continuing tradition of remembrance.

Fred Ettawageshik

Frank Ettawageshik

No longer do the council fires of the Ottawas burn in Michigan—no longer do the hills and forests resound with the echoes of the piercing yells of painted warriors on the war path. The echoes of the rhythmic beat of the *tom-toms*, and the chants of the Indians as they danced around their council fires are stilled forever. They have put away their feathers and buckskins and buried their tomahawks so many years ago that relics of these things of their yesterdays can now be seen only in museums.

It is, therefore, of special significance, to note the survival of any of the fine old customs in Michigan. One of the few to survive this period of transition is the giving of the "Ghost Suppers." It must be remembered also that those customs deeply imbued with a religious significance are hardest to eradicate.

Ghost Suppers are held each year during the first week of November by the Ottawas in the northern regions of the Lower Peninsula of Michigan. To mention a few of the places, there is Cross Village, Middle Village (the oldest Indian settlement in this region), Five Mile Creek, Harbor Springs, Petoskey, and Burt Lake. At this time one or more families in a community will cook a large supper, to which it is generally understood all the Indians are invited. The word just gets around that some family is getting up a supper commemorating the spirits of their departed, hence, the name Ghost Suppers. To especially honor the memory of those who have gone to the "Happy Hunting Ground," the family will invite a few people approximately of the same age as the deceased. Tobacco will be given to them if the person they are supposed to represent was a tobacco user; if not, some gift will be presented. Children are given candies or some little gift. Custom requires that these few especially invited guests come early enough, if possible, so that they will be among the first served.

The Indians go from one supper to the other, until they have made the rounds. Etiquette requires that they eat at least a little of each kind of food offered. After the last guest has been served, the remaining food is left on the table until midnight, or in some cases until morning so that the spirits may come and feast.

Years ago, it was not uncommon for as many as six or eight households in a community to have these suppers during an evening. Today with the smaller Indian population, fewer suppers are held, and an effort is made to spread them more evenly throughout the week. From fifty to seventy-five and as many as a hundred guests are served in some homes. Because of the limited space in the average home, the guests are served in relays. The first table is set and ready around six o'clock, seating from twelve to sixteen people; when these have finished, a second table is set, and so on until the last have been served.

A large variety of food is usually served at these suppers, because each family tries to outdo the other. Invariably, the main dish served at all the suppers is one of three kinds of corn soup: *binag gisig anak* (*binagiziganag, bnagziganag*: peel by heat; Indian hominy), made from corn that has been boiled with wood ashes to remove the hull; *wish ko bimi nak* (*wîshkobiminag*: sweet corns) made from dried corn, red kidney beans, and potatoes and seasoned generously with finely chopped meat (before the era of stoves, this corn was dried out in the open air, spread out on mats or rugs made of bulrushes; now it is dried on a hot stove and usually parched a little); *minda min abo* (*mindâmin-âbô*: corn soup) made from finely cracked corn.

A large bowl of one of these soups is placed in the center of the table and served with a *ma tik go em kwan* (*mitigo-êmikwân*: wooden spoon), an old-fashioned wooden ladle. The corn for the *minda min* is cracked in a *pota gan* (*botâgan*), a wooden mortar and pestle. The mortar is made from a short log about thirty inches long, ten to twelve inches in diameter, and hollowed at one end to a depth of about twelve inches. The pestle, *po tchi kwa nak* (*bochikwanag*), is made out of a hardwood pole four to five feet long, three to four inches in diameter, and shaved down in the middle to form the handle. In the "good old days" there was an abundance of venison, bear meat, wild fowl, muskrat, and other small game; today, however, the meat is usually "Chicago prime beef."

Some of the older Indians who are imbued with a profound belief in the significance of this custom have claimed to have heard the dishes rattling after everyone had retired for the night, saying that the spirits had come and feasted. Others have seen apparitions of people preceding them on their way to these suppers. There is the story, and a true one, of a man, while passing an old burial ground, having seen a group of people going ahead of him on his way to a Ghost Supper. Thinking that here was a chance for some company, he tried to overtake them, but no matter how fast he walked, they remained always the same distance ahead of him. Then his attention was attracted from the rear, and when he looked again, the people in front had disappeared from view. He said that they were near enough so that, had they been real people, they could not have gotten out of sight so soon.

Many of the early white settlers used to participate in these feasts. Recently a white man was a guest at one of these suppers, at which binag gisig anak (Indian hominy) was served. He was very profuse in praising it, saying, "This is the first time I have ever eaten popcorn soup." He undoubtedly got his idea from the fact that when this corn has been boiled for a long time, which is necessary to soften it, it will expand and burst, actually resembling popcorn. Another white man ate so much minda min abo soup that every time he met his Indian friends the Indian would call out "Minda min abo!" until all the Indians began calling him that. This pleased him very much because he thought he had an Indian name. This name stuck to him until he left the country.

This feast for the dead is observed each year. During bad times a few families will band together; in good times, more of them go on their own.

These feasts were not always held during the first week in November. Before the coming of the "pale-faces," they were held during the late spring and early summer and were accompanied with much dancing and singing and peace offerings. Groups of grown people and children would go from place to place saluting each other, saying, "We are going around as spirits." At each place they would feast, dance and sing, and throw food into the fire, believing that the spirits would come and eat the food as it was consumed by the fire. They would go for miles to reach some outlying home, trailing through the forests with birchbark torches and making merry as they went along. Today, a family piles into the old "jalopy" and goes long distances to one of these suppers, using this occasion also as an opportunity to visit.

The change in the time for these feasts from the early part of the year to the first week in November was brought through the influence of the missionaries, who saw the feasibility of aligning this custom with the feast days of their church, All Souls Day and All Saints Day. However, as of old, this custom remains non-sectarian, because all of the Indians, regardless of creed, still take cognizance of these Ghost Suppers.

So once each year, during good times and bad, the Ottawas in Michigan, even the humblest of them, hark back to the days of their ancestors and prepare feasts in memory of their departed.

1943

* * *

In the time since my father wrote about the ghost suppers much has changed in the world: we fly faster than sound, men walk on the moon, and we look deep into space with orbiting telescopes seeking to look back into the very beginnings of our universe. Our Odawa world has changed as well: the council fires once again are burning and the beat of the drums again echoes from the powwows where people are dancing for themselves, for their communities, and for Mother Earth. Those who have been keeping and guarding our ways have been reawakening the honor and respect for creation that is the central gift of our people.

Ghost suppers are still held all over northern Lower Michigan. In parish halls and in private homes, from Cross Village to East Jordan, from Peshawbestown to Petoskey, in Charlevoix, Harbor Springs, and Burt Lake, families are honoring their ancestors and keeping sacred fires burning. Minda min abo is still the central food served. The people now come by the hundreds to visit each other, tell stories, and honor the ancestors, teaching our children the old ways while preparing to walk with pride into the future.

1992

THANKSGIVING

We Are Still Here

Mark Anthony Rolo (1962-   ), Ojibwe

A member of the Bad River Band of Ojibwe in northern Wisconsin, Rolo is the former executive director of the Native American Journalists Association. He is also the former Washington bureau chief for the national weekly newspaper *Indian Country Today* and former editor of *The Circle,* a newspaper based in Minneapolis. He hosted and co-wrote *A Seat at the Drum,* a PBS documentary about contemporary Natives of Los Angeles. He published a novel, *The Wonder Bull,* in 2006, and UCLA American Indian Studies published a collection of his plays, *What's an Indian Woman to Do? And Other Plays By Mark Anthony Rolo,* in 2010. In this brief essay, Rolo quietly celebrates what most Americans take for granted but what Native people never do: simple existence.

You might think that Indians won't be in a party mood come Turkey Day. After all, given the historical record of how the founders of this country treated the first people of this land, it does not take much cultural sensitivity to understand why some Indians don't celebrate Thanksgiving. But there are those (myself included) who choose to find something to be thankful about during this season.

We are still here.

After wiping out whole tribes or rounding up the rest of us like cattle onto reservation land, the federal government believed it would only be a matter of time before Indians—as a race, as nations of people—would soon disappear from the geographical and political landscape.

The government enacted policies designed to terminate tribal systems and to assimilate Indians into the racial melting pot, such as sending young Indian people to boarding schools so they could learn to be like white man. Throughout the boarding school era, original tongues were banned, buckskin dresses had to be traded in for cotton skirts and starched white shirts, and braided hair was trimmed down into buzz cuts. But the goal of taking the Indian out of the Indian proved to be futile.

Today, despite the worst poverty rates among all population groups, despite staggering statistics that reveal how Indian country continues to be devastated by poor health care and a lack of education and employment opportunities, Indians still cling to their ancient ways, rituals, languages, and tribal values. Yes, many Indian people enjoy getting ensnared in the trappings of a consumer and pop-culture society. But many Indians manage to return to their place, their identity that is rooted in tribal, traditional ways of being.

This Thanksgiving there will be plenty of turkey, cranberries, and pie passed around the tables in many Indian homes. But above the roar of the football crowds, away from the sights and sounds of parades, you can bet that within the hearts of many Indians there will be a grand sense of gratitude. Indians will be thankful that we have not just survived—we have held onto a lifeline of tribal identity.

That's something to be cherished and passed on to the next generation.

2000

CHRISTMAS

Iesous Ahatonnia: A Huron Christmas Carol
Fr. Jean de Brébeuf

This carol, one of the most popular in Canada and becoming more well-known each Christmas season in the United States, has a long history. The version English-speaking persons know was created in 1927 by Jesse Edgar Middleton, a Canadian journalist. He did not speak Huron and perhaps not much French, but he was obviously an avid admirer of Tennyson and romantic Victorian poetry, which held sentimentally racist ideas about Natives. The carol he "translated" has little resemblance to the original. The reality, though less poetic to English-trained ears, is a good deal more interesting. George Laidler wrote that:

> In the first half of the seventeenth century, Jesuit priests from Quebec and Old France established missions in some of the villages of the Huron Indians, just south of the Georgian Bay, Ontario. Among these were Fathers Jean de Brébeuf and Gabriel Lalemant [Lallemant]. When the Iroquois attacked in March, 1649, these two were put to death at the village of St. Ignace, about six miles east of the mission's headquarters at Fort St. Marie. . . .

> Under persistent menace by the Iroquois, the Hurons and the Jesuits abandoned the district that summer and retired to Christian Island, off the Penetanguishene peninsula, where they spent a terrible winter of hardship and famine. Finding conditions intolerable, the community decided to disperse in the following spring. Some of the Hurons managed to reach distant tribes, others died at the hands of the Iroquois, and the rest accompanied the Fathers on their sad journey back to Quebec by the circuitous northerly route of the French River, Lake Nipissing, and the Mattawa and Ottawa Rivers.

> In the Jesuit Relations of 1642, written by the missionaries to their Superior at Quebec, Father Brébeuf reported that the converted Hurons were particularly devoted to the celebration of the Nativity. They built a small chapel of fir and cedar branches in honor of the manger of the Infant Jesus, observed a fast on the day preceding the anniversary, and met to sing hymns in praise of the newborn Child.

> One of these hymns in the Huron language was written by Father Brébeuf, under the title "Jesous ahatonhia" (Jesus is born). . . . It was preserved through tradition among the remnant of the Hurons who came down from Christian Island in 1650 and settled at Lorette, near Quebec, where their descendants are living today. A pastor of theirs, Father Etienne de Villeneuve, wrote down the stanzas, and on his death in 1794, the manuscript with a statement of its authorship was found among his papers.

John Steckley, a contemporary scholar of Huron who has also made a detailed study of the song, writes that:

> One major reason . . . why Jesuits such as Father Jean de Brébeuf decided on using music as a strategy in teaching Christianity to the Huron is because the Huron had a rich tradition of

472

song. This richness can be seen in the extensive vocabulary in the Huron language that pertains to song; [in addition] there was traditionally a strong connection between songs and the sacred in Huron culture. . . .

The oral tradition of the Huron long told that the Huron Carol was composed by Father Jean de Brébeuf. This makes sense, as Brébeuf was the first of the Jesuits (*hatitsihenstaatsi'*: they are called charcoal) to become fluent in their language. They called him Hechon, a combination of an attempt to pronounce his first name "chon," (with the -ch- pronounced like the English -sh-), with the masculine pronominal prefix "he." Although the name didn't originally have a translation or meaning, as such, it developed the meaning of an outsider who masters the language and uses that knowledge to try to help the people. . . . [287]

Rarely told is the sad story of the first published reference to the Huron Carol. This is because this reference is recorded as a translation of the title of the carol: "Iesus Ahatonnia" ("Jesus, he is newly made, just born"). The story was recorded in 1669 by Father Le Mercier. It refers to "the holy death of a Huron girl named Thérèse" (*JR* 52:239), who died on Christmas day, 1688. According to Le Mercier:

> During her illness, she often asked her mother, "When is it that JESUS will be born?
> At length being told, on Christmas eve, that he would be born that night, she began
> to sing, "Jesus is going to be born"—which is an air sung by the Hurons on Christ-
> mas Festivals. (*JR* 52:237).

The tune for the carol is that of a sixteenth-century folk song entitled "Une Jeune Pucelle" ("A Young Maid"), and the melody is built upon the aeolian scale, an old church mode that has half steps and whole steps in a relationship different from that of a modern major scale because instruments of the Middle Ages had problems properly playing tunes with many sharps and flats. The aeolian scale is a minor one, and so it gives the song a darker, more mournful sound. It may have seemed to European ears to be more like the traditional songs of the Huron than western music.

The carol is given here in four versions: the original Huron, a linear (word-by-word) translation underneath, a free translation in bold type, and Middleton's romantic verses last. All versions and the pronunciation guide were generously shared by John Steckley, a modern Hechon.

Iesous Ahatonnia (ee-sus a-ha-ton-nyah)
Jesus, He is born
Jesus is born
'Twas in the Moon of Wintertime

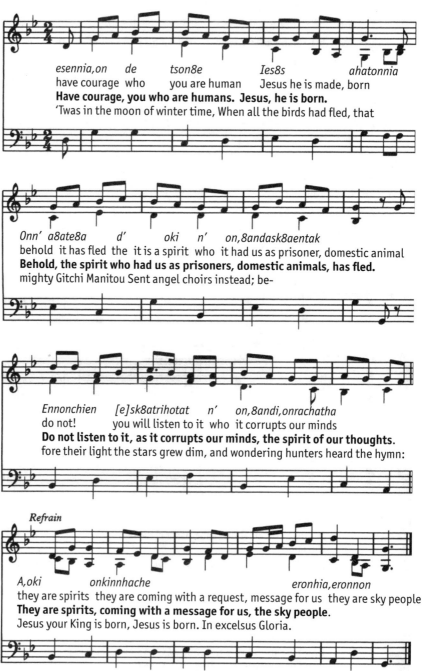

Original Huron:
Linear Translastion:
Free Translation:
Anglicized Hymn:

esennia,on de tson8e Ies8s ahatonnia
have courage who you are human Jesus he is made, born
Have courage, you who are humans. Jesus, he is born.
'Twas in the moon of winter time, When all the birds had fled, that

Onn' a8ate8a d' oki n' on,8andask8aentak
behold it has fled the it is a spirit who it had us as prisoner, domestic animal
Behold, the spirit who had us as prisoners, domestic animals, has fled.
mighty Gitchi Manitou Sent angel choirs instead; be-

Ennonchien [e]sk8atrihotat n' on,8andi,onrachatha
do not! you will listen to it who it corrupts our minds
Do not listen to it, as it corrupts our minds, the spirit of our thoughts.
fore their light the stars grew dim, and wondering hunters heard the hymn:

Refrain

A,oki onkinnhache eronhia,eronnon
they are spirits they are coming with a request, message for us they are sky people
They are spirits, coming with a message for us, the sky people.
Jesus your King is born, Jesus is born. In excelsus Gloria.

474

·❖· ·❖· ·❖·

CHRONOLOGY

▼▼▼▼▼▼▼▼▼▼▼

Significant legal decisions and titles are in *italic*. Major wars are in **bold**.

BC

12,000 BC	Wisconsin Glacier begins its retreat; large mammals follow the retreat north, pursued by hunters using knapped points and spears.
9200 BC	Knapped point types evolve; smaller animals hunted; new techniques used.
4000 BC	Archaic period peoples begin building permanent base camps near rivers.
2000 BC	Four native plants are domesticated in region: squash, sunflowers, marsh elder, and lamb's quarters (pigweed).

AD 100-1000

400-500	Bow and arrow are in use.
750	Mississippian period cultures develop, organized with chiefdoms and based on maize agriculture. Long-distance trade is important.
900	Hopewell mound builders active in Great Lakes region.
1000	Adena/Hopewell peoples build Serpent Mound in Ohio.

AD 1000-1500

1000-1300	Cultivation of maize begins in St. Lawrence River valley; longhouses built; villages fortified.
1050-1250	Cahokia flourishes.
1300	Deganawida, Huron spiritual leader residing in Ontario, establishes the Iroquois Confederacy. Cultivation of beans begins.
1500	Beginning of indigenous population decline from disease (not reversed until 1900).

CONTACT TO 1600

1506-1518	First French explorations of St. Lawrence.
1534-1541	Cartier makes three voyages up the St. Lawrence.
1542-1600	Iroquoian-speaking nations along the St. Lawrence are invaded and displaced by Algonkian-speaking nations from the north and west. Iroquoians retreat to lower Great Lakes.
1588	Fur trade monopolies granted by French king.

1600-1700

1603-1616	Champlain begins explorations. Sides with Hurons against Onondagas and so turns Iroquois Confederacy against the French.
1615-1640s	Huron trading empire reaches from James Bay to the Gulf of Mexico, from present-day Minnesota to Quebec.
1633-1650	Jesuits proselytize the Hurons.
1634	Nicolet explores the northwest Great Lakes region.
1635-1640s	Beavers are nearly extinct in both Iroquois and Huron country; furs for trade must be imported from peoples north and west.
1640	Dakota in northern Great Lakes move toward Lake of the Woods region and out onto the Plains; some eventually become Assiniboines of the Rocky Mountains. Floral designs in Northeast Native art begin in Quebec after being taught by Urseline nuns.
1640s-1700	**Beaver wars.** This period begins more than a century of warfare between the British and the French and their Native allies in the Great Lakes region to attempt to control the fur

	trade, retain territory, and receive trade goods. Alliances shift throughout the period as the Haudenosaunee attempt to assert hegemony over Great Lakes region. Huron trading networks destroyed by 1650; French fur trade largely stopped in Great Lakes region by 1660.
1640-1641	Potawatomi flee Attiwendaronk (Hurons and Neutrals) in Michigan to Ho-Chunk territory in Wisconsin. War results; 500 warriors lost in storm on Green Bay. Potawatomi are driven to Mackinac.
1641	Huron and Algonkian traders receive firearms. The Haudenosaunee seek peace and furs from Hurons and French but are rebuffed because French don't want furs supplied to English.
1642	Montreal founded. Haudenosaunee attack Hurons.
1642-1649	**Illinois-Winnebago war.** Illinois and Miamis capture southern Wisconsin, forcing Ho-Chunk to Green Bay.
1643	Iroquois Confederacy signs treaty with Dutch.
1643-1654	Sauk, Kickapoo, Meskwaki nations forced from Michigan-Ontario region.
1648-1669	Shawnee migrate to Ohio to escape trade wars.
1649	**Iroquois War against Huronia** begins, destroying or scattering entire population; some survivors move to Quebec, others flee west becoming known as Wendat (Wyandot; probably 'language', shortened from a longer term, F. Lounsbury 1975).
1650s	Haudenosaunee destroy Petun (Tobacco) and Neutral nations; raid west to Green Bay, north to Lake Superior; Erie nation attacked, and those not made slaves are dispersed to Ohio where they become the Mingo. By 1654 the entire peninsula of Michigan is uninhabited, and Wisconsin becomes a refugee camp for Algonkian-speaking tribes; Odawa move west to Green Bay, to Sault Ste Marie, finally to western Lake Superior to escape.
1660s	Chippewa, pushed west by Haudenosaunee, push Minnesota Dakota onto Plains.
1660s-1670s	Odawa and Wendat establish trading center at Chequamegon Bay (*Zhaagawaamikong*: at the sand bar), and other nations flock there.
1662-1680	Coalitions of Algonkian-speaking warriors and French push Haudenosaunee out of western Great Lakes; Haudenosaunee are attacked by Susquehannock in East.
1667	Haudenosaunee make peace with French, and Great Lakes are reopened to fur trade.
1669-1673	Joliet and Marquette explore the Great Lakes and Mississippi River.
1670	Hudson's Bay Company chartered.
1671-1679	French establish forts from Thunder Bay eastward.
1673	Dakota delegation sent to Sault Ste Marie to trade is killed by Chippewa; this begins a **Dakota-Chippewa war** that will last into the nineteenth century.
1673-1679	Miamis begin moving back into western Michigan; begin hostilities with Illinois over trade.
1670s	European trade goods—guns, beads, cloth—begin to replace indigenous manufactures.
1677	Haudenosaunee attack and negotiate with Ohio valley tribes, including Miamis, to control fur trade.
1677-1731	Shawnees, Delawares, other landless tribes are granted land in Pennsylvania as a buffer zone between English colonies.
1680s	Odawas control two thirds of the fur trade; Chippewas the rest. Caravans going to Montreal end because of Haudenosaunee attacks. Haudenosaunee attack Mackinac. Haudenosaunee attack French and Algonkian-speaking allies on the Illinois River and are defeated, ending Iroquoian monopoly attempts.
1689-1697	**King William's War**; the first of the French and Indian Wars between England and France.

1700-1800

1701	*Great Peace of 1701.* Delegates from 40 First Nations meet in Montreal to end war between French and Natives.
1713-1722	Tuscaroras migrate from North Carolina into Haudenosaunee (Oneida) territory.
1715	Iroquois Confederacy of Five Nations becomes Six Nations with addition of Tuscaroras.
1712-1734	**Fox Wars.** Resentful of Meskwaki demands for tribute, the French and Chippewas repeatedly attack the Wisconsin Mesquakis and their allies, the Sauk, Mascouten, Kickapoo, and Ho-Chunk, attempting complete extermination. Meskwakis are attacked near Detroit and in Wisconsin and eventually driven across the Mississippi.
1744-1748	**King George's War.** English and French hire Natives as mercenaries to fight. Haudenosaunee make Treaty of Lancaster with British, ceding territory near Ohio River.
1754-1763	**Seven Years' War in America (French and Indian War)** is the climax of the series of wars between England and France as they compete for supremacy in America. Wendat, Shawnee, Chippewa, Potawatomi, Odawa, Miami, Abenaki, Micmac, and Lenape align with French. Haudenosaunee align with English. French lose and begin to surrender Great Lakes territory.
1760-1763	Delaware Prophet preaches that Europeans must be driven from continent and the indigenous peoples return to traditional ways.
1763	British issue *Royal Proclamation* forbidding settlers to cross Appalachian Mountains; this is ignored. This proclamation also sets boundaries of Quebec; first document to require large land cessions in Canada.
1763-1764	**Pontiac's War.** Influenced in part by the Delaware Prophet, Odawa war-chief Pontiac's pan-Indian alliance against British takes all forts west of Niagara Falls except Detroit and Pittsburgh. In 1764-1765 Pontiac and other chiefs make peace with British.
1768	In the *Treaty of Fort Stanwix* the Six Nations cede land from south of the Ohio River to Kentucky, land belonging to the Shawnees, who do not sign the treaty. Tecumseh, born this year, will create a confederacy to drive the whites out and defend their territory.
1773-1774	**Lord Dunmore's War.** British and Shawnees fight in Ohio; Shawnees lose and must cede territory conveyed by Haudenosaunee in previous treaties.
1774	Approximately 50,000 whites have moved west of the Appalachians.
1777-1778	Iroquois Confederacy is split by divided loyalties to Britain or United States.
1776-1795	**Revolutionary War** period causes border wars in Great Lakes region as alliances of Native nations fight Americans to retain territories. Includes Little Turtle's War (1786-1795; Battle of Fallen Timbers, 1794) to retain Ohio and Kentucky.
1779	**Iroquois War.** General George Washington orders invasion of homelands in Pennsylvania and New York. Forty indigenous towns destroyed.
1783-1790	*Treaty of Paris* ends the US Revolutionary War. No Natives included in deliberations. US government claims all territory to Mississippi River and, to make money, begins land sales to developers.
1787	*Northwest Ordinance* calls for division of lands into territories to be mapped and sold once Native titles have been terminated by treaty. This establishes the precedent by which the USA will expand westward across North American by the creation of new states.
1791	**Little Turtle's War.** Confederated nations in Ohio annihilate the army of General Arthur St. Clair near Fort Wayne.
1794	General Anthony Wayne defeats Ohio Natives at the Battle of the Fallen Timbers. Jay Treaty allows Natives to pass freely between the USA and Canada.
1799	Handsome Lake begins teaching the Gaíwiio` code.

1800-1900

1809	*Treaty of Fort Wayne.* Delaware, Potawatomi, Miami, Kickapoo, and Eel River tribes cede three million acres.
1811-1813	**Tecumseh's War.** Shawnee, Potawatomi, Ho-Chunk, Chippewa, and Wendat fight for Ohio and Indiana. In the Battle of Tippecanoe in 1811 William Henry Harrison engages Tecumseh's brother in battle; warriors desert Tecumseh's carefully built confederation of nations, leading to his defeat and death in the War of 1812.
1812-1815	**War of 1812** finally ends British occupation of Great Lakes forts and opens region to American domination and unrestrained white settlement.
1813	**Peoria War** fought in Illinois between Potawatomis and Kickapoos and the US Army.
1815	Kickapoos migrate to Texas. They will flee to Kansas in 1861; between 1862 and 1865 many move to Mexico.
1820s-1840s	Hudson's Bay and North West fur companies merge.
1817	**Le Fèvre Indian War** with Ho-Chunk in Wisconsin.
1830	*Indian Removal Act* formalizes US policy begun by Thomas Jefferson.
1832	**Black Hawk's War.** At the Bad Axe River, US troops massacre unarmed women and children being led across the Mississippi by Black Hawk, who hopes to restore their villages and crops; Wisconsin Assembly apologizes in 1989.
1834	*Life of Ma-Ka-Tai-Me-She-Kia-Kiak or Black Hawk* published; first autobiography by a Native American.
1830s-1840s	Fur trade is in a state of near collapse. USA begins implementing Indian Removal policies to force tribes to Oklahoma.
1850-1862	*Province of Canada Treaties* require indigenous peoples to cede mineral-rich lands north of Lake Superior in return for reserves.
1850-1886	Reservation Era; removals are phased out for lack of land.
1858-1859	First Mohawk steelworkers begin construction of Victoria Bridge across St. Lawrence River at Montreal.
1862	**Minnesota Dakota War.** Dakotas under the leadership of Little Crow resist white aggression; 300 are captured; 38 are publicly hung in Mankato, the largest mass execution in US history.
1867	*British North American Act* gives Canada authority over indigenous peoples and their lands.
1870s	Peyote religion spreads into US from Mexico; the Native American Church, incorporating peyote rituals, is formally established in 1918.
1870s-1920s	Collectors strip bands and nations of art and artifacts for museums.
1871	*US Congress ends treaty-making with Native nations*; agreements will be made by congressional acts and executive orders because Natives are no longer seen as independent nations.
1876	*Canadian Indian Act* makes all Natives legal wards of the state and establishes residential schools; Métis are stripped of Native status, a position reversed in 2003.
1879	Carlisle Indian School opens in Pennsylvania, the first federally funded institution designed to "civilize" indigenous children by separating them from their cultures; its motto was "Kill the Indian and save the man."
1880	*Canadian Indian Act of 1876 revised* to allow federal government to impose elected band councils on reserves east of Lake Superior.
1884	*Religious Crimes Codes* forbid traditional indigenous "religious" practices. *Indian Advancement Act* authorizes Canadian minister of Indian Affairs to replace indigenous chiefs he deems unfit.

1886	*Indian Languages Policy*. US federal rules state that "no books in any Indian language must be used or instruction given in that language . . . the rule will be strictly enforced."
1887	*General Allotment (Dawes) Act* passed by US Congress; in 1907 Congress will authorize the sale of unclaimed lots or lots belonging to "incompetent" individuals.
1890-1934	Assimilationist policies determine US government treatment of Native Americans.
1891	*Indian Schools Act* formalizes building of industrial schools in the Great Lakes region.
1899	*Queen of the Woods* by Simon Pokagon published; it is the first novel by a Native American.

1900-PRESENT

1902	*Lone Wolf v. Hitchcock* determines the extent of the power US has over indigenous peoples, including selling their lands without their consent. US Commissioner of Indian Affairs prohibits "the wearing of long hair by the male Indian population"; refusal to cut hair meant loss of annuities.
1911	Society of the American Indian established at a meeting in Columbus, Ohio. Canadian government amends the Indian Act to expropriate land on Indian reserves regardless of treaties.
1913	Elmer Jamieson, Haudenosaunee, helps Canadian army develop a code based on the Mohawk language, the first Indian-language-based code used in wartime.
1923	*Canadian Williams Treaties* cost indigenous peoples their right to hunt and trap in ceded Great Lakes territories.
1924	US citizenship granted to Native Americans, partly in gratitude for their contributions to WW I.
1925	*Canadian Indian Act* bans cultural ceremonies, including powwows. Indian Defense League established; succeeds in reestablishing the Jay Treaty of 1794.
1934	*Indian Reorganization Act* renders the Dawes Act obsolete.
1941-1945	25,000 Native Americans join US military to fight WW II, including many from Great Lakes nations. In 1942 the Six Nations make a separate declaration of war on the Axis powers.
1944	National Congress of American Indians (NCAI) established to guard indigenous rights and preserve indigenous cultures and territories.
1946	*US Indian Claims Commission* created to allow Native bands and nations to press claims for dishonesty, fraud, and incompetence relating to treaties; Natives had pressed claims since 1881, but each nation had needed a special act of Congress before this act.
1950s-1970s	US federal government begins urging Native American families to move to urban areas as part of assimilationist policy by providing funds for training and moving; approximately 250,000 leave reservations.
1951	*Indian Act* reduces powers of Canadian Indian Affairs Department but retains provisions forcing assimilation.
1953	*Termination Resolution* enacted to end tribal sovereignty and federal obligations specified in past treaties or acts of US Congress, including education and health care. *US Public Law 280* empowers state legislatures to take over civil and criminal jurisdictions on reservations without consent.
1957	Mohawk leaders claim land under the Treaty of 1784 and deny validity of later acquisitions by New York State. Tuscarora Reservation land is condemned by the state for development.
1959	Ontario Indian Organization founded. The Haudenosaunee reestablish heredity chiefs and form an Iroquois police force.
1961	Kinzua Dam floods 10,000 acres of Seneca land in New York, including the Cornplanter Grant, a holy shrine; one third of the population must relocate; 1794 treaty violated. Canadian Indian Organization founded.

1968	American Indian Movement (AIM) founded in Minneapolis, ushering in a decade of Native civil disobedience in the USA and Canada.
1969	*Statement of the Government of Canada on Indian Policy*; this Canadian "White Paper" is nearly the same as Termination in the USA; it will be formally retracted in 1971.
1971	Native American Rights' Fund (NARF) founded to offer expert legal advice to tribes.
1970	US President Richard Nixon ends termination. AIM members seize a replica of the *Mayflower* and proclaim Thanksgiving Day a day of national mourning.
1973	*Menomini Restoration Act*, reestablishes relations with the US federal government. Canadian Office of Native Claims established to negotiate claims for lands taken without consent.
1975	*Indian Self-Determination and Education Assistance Act* allows Native Americans to administer their own federal programs, including tribal involvement in the management of federal lands.
1978	*American Indian Religious Freedom Act* guarantees freedom to practice tribal religions. *Federal Acknowledgment Program* established to provide a sanctioned way for tribes to receive federal recognition.
1979	*United States v Michigan* by Judge Noel Fox determines that the 1836 Treaty of Washington reserves the indigenous right to fish without regulation by the state.
1980	Kateri Tekakwitha, Mohawk-Algonquin, beatified by the Vatican. The Fox Decision on Chippewa and Ottawa fishing rights in the Great Lakes is upheld by the US Court of Appeals.
1982	*Canadian Constitution Act* restores Native status to all aboriginals.
1983	*Lac Courte Oreilles Band of Lake Superior Chippewa Indians v. Lester P. Voight*; the US 7th Circuit Court of Appeals finds that the Lac Courte Oreilles Band retains treaty-granted hunting, fishing, and gathering rights.
1985	*County of Oneida v. Oneida Nation* establishes a precedent for the Oneida Nation to sue for lands taken illegally in 1795.
1986	Smithsonian Institution agrees to begin returning indigenous skeletal remains for reburial.
1988	*Termination Act* repealed by US Congress. *US Indian Gaming Regulatory Act* determines how bands and states will cooperate to regulate gaming. Canadian Native Arts Foundation established by John Kim Bell, Mohawk conductor and composer; his *In the Land of the Spirits* is the first Native ballet.
1989	The State of New York agrees to return twelve wampum belts to the Onondaga Nation of New York. Wisconsin apologizes to Sac and Fox Nation (Meskwaki) for massacre at Bad Axe and Black Hawk War.
1990	Canadian plans to extend a golf course onto a sacred Mohawk burial site provoke a blockade; the crisis provoked at Oka lasted for 78 days. *Native American Languages Act* passed by US Congress to preserve, protect, and promote native languages, the exact reverse of nineteenth-century government schools' policies. *Native American Graves Protection and Repatriation Act* passed by US Congress. *Indian Arts and Crafts Act* passed by US Congress to safeguard Native Americans from competition with machine-manufactured, non-Native "crafts."
1991	The Oblate Conference of Canada apologizes for abuses Indians suffered at residential schools.
1992	Dickinson Mounds Museum in Illinois, the last American museum to display remains of ancient Natives, is closed by the governor.
1993	*Religious Freedom Restoration Act*; subsequent amendments in 1994 protected the rights of members of the Native American Church to use peyote.
1996	National Indian Heritage Month declared in USA.
2004	National Museum of the American Indian established on the Mall in Washington, DC.

PRONUNCIATION GUIDE
▼▼▼▼▼▼▼▼▼▼▼▼▼▼▼▼▼▼▼▼

Carl Masthay

Over the centuries there have been many spelling systems (orthographies) using Roman or Latin letters, and so it is difficult to establish the actual correct sounds. In addition, different speakers' habits change as time passes. As a result, these letter symbols are approximations for the uninitiated but sometimes a perplexity to the meticulous linguist. After much experimentation and discussion there arose the exact system called the IPA (International Phonetic Alphabet) to describe sounds definitively. A very loose version is used with some of the languages used in this book.

Ho-Chunk (Winnebago): Ho-Chunk ('voice-big' unless 'fish-big') is a Siouan language heavily nasalized marked by a tailed vowel as in *hųųč* 'bear' in this orthography, but a syllable-initial *n-* is like that in English; *š* = /sh/, *č* = /ch/; *x* is a voiceless velar fricative as in German *Bach* ('brook') and *ǧ* is its voiced counterpart; *é* somewhat as in *they* /e·/; *r* is a one-tap sound like the single *r* in Spanish; ' is a glottal stop, but ´ (acute accent) marks stress.

Huron: e = like 'eh' ; 8 = 'w' before vowel, 'u' before consonant; i = like 'ee' in 'freeze' = 'y'; a = like 'ah'; th = t followed by an aspiration; on = as in the French word 'bon'; en = as in the French word 'chien'; an = as in the French word 'viande'; Accents tend to fall on the second to last syllable.

Menominee: The vowels in Menominee have varieties under differing phonetic environments, especially *e*, a single pure sound best pronounced here somewhat as in *they* /e·/; the short *e* (as in *nepēw* 'water') is like short *i*: /nipeyw/; for *i*, pronounce it usually as in *machine*; *û* is like that in *put*; < ' > (elsewhere *q*) is the glottal stop.

Meskwaki (Fox): Meskwaki means 'red-earth.' Visually the former Bureau of Ethnology orthography looks overwhelmingly hard to pronounce! The normalized orthography that Michelson's Meskwaki uses is essentially phonemic and easily transliterated. (Rough breathing < ' > is /h/ except before <c> = /sh/ or <s>, where /h/ is redundant and has been omitted in 'moon.') *a* short as in *father*, *ā* (for *aa*) long as in *far* (without the *r*); *e* as in *led*; *ä* as in *they* (long *e·*); A (small capital A) is like *u* in *sun* or *a* in *sofa*; the single open-quotation mark < ' > is always /h/; *ī* is long *i* (as in *machine*); *c* = /sh/, *tc* = /tch/.

Miami: *a* short as in *father*, *aa* long as in *far* (without the *r*); *č* = /ch/; *ee* long as in *they* /e·/; *h* is pronounced; *i* short /ee/, *ii* long /i·/ as in *machine*; *o* short /o/, *oo* long /o·/.

Mohawk: Mohawk is a heavily nasalized Iroquoian language. The old spelling does not allow one to distinguish the sounds well: *n* before a consonant is usually nasalized (as in *nh*), *r* used to be a one-tapped front *r* but is now usually an *l* (el) depending on which of three Mohawk dialects (western, central, eastern); an *h* that closes a syllable is ambiguously *h* or ' (glottal stop), but the glottal stop is the better choice; the *g* and *d* are actually voiceless unaspirated *k* and *t* (not like those as initials in English words); modern *ts-* can be /ts/ or /j/ or better voiceless thus /ch/, but *th* is always *t* + *h* (not English *th*; so now try pronouncing "Hiawatha" formerly spelled /Haionʰhwaʹʹthaʹ/ but now /Hayęhwathaʹ/ with stress on the *yę*, nasalized /yunh/); the colon < : > means a long sound (as in -*kó:wa*ʹ 'big'). The grave accent < ` > usually indicates downward stress in Iroquoian languages, but alone it could also be the poor typographic merging of a raised dot for length and a glottal stop (as in -yo·').

Mohawk spelling may appear confusingly divergent for the exact same Mohawk word, yet the reason for the difference is quite clear. For example, "'Hello', or she'kon, is pronounced /say'go/." Actually that is still not accurate. It is an aspirated s (with lots of air) and not sh or just s; the e is IPA for traditional English /ay/, that is, long /e·/; the k is voiceless and unaspirated, sounding almost like a g but not an English g! And finally the on is nasalized /oon/ and not just o.

Ojibwe/Odawa: "Ojibwa, Ojibway, Ojibwe" have only one pronunciation: /o-JIB-way/; it is not the frequently heard */o-JIB-wuh/, which is a contamination from the now less-used and receding term "Chippewa" /CHIP-uh-wah/. "Odawa" is /o-DAH-wah/, but its variant "Ottawa" is /AW-tuh-wuh/; the Ojibwe spelling adaawe- ('trades it') indicates /uh-DAW-way/, as some pronounce "Odawa." Usually a as in sun; â and aa as in law, brought (with rounding and deeper than the other articulation by many Americans who don't distinguish words like cost standard /kawst/ versus /kahst/); e always long /e·/ as in they; i as in hit or higher as in Mary, but the first i in gisiss /ghee-siss/ is long (î, ii) as in machine; g is always hard g (not /j/).

Potawatomi: /pah-tuh-WAH-tuh-mee/. To spell it successfully remember that two middle a's are flanked by two outer t's and two external o's and then one i. Although the month set came from a French source, all letters were kept except for <ch>, which I have made into <sh> for clarity; a as in father, but ā is longer; the same with e, i, o; u is like that in sun; ê = nasal and a little guttural; ´ = stress; ˉ = long.

Shawnee: (as in **Miami**); ' = glottal stop (as in "written" /rɪ'n/); sh = sh, th = Engl. th as in thin.

Tuscarora: There are two dialects: Eastern and Western. Eastern Tuscarora is what is given by the standardized International Phonetic Alphabet forms as supplied by Rudes 1999. The spelling by Ted C. Williams diverges considerably from the standard. His use of "(t)" is obscure but sometimes for the glottal stop ('). Some speakers vary r and s, y and sh, y' and 'y, long and short vowels, hstr and hst, θ and s. The theta symbol θ is like English th in thin. The tailed ę is a nasalized vowel varying from hint to hunt or even to its absence as in hit. The Eastern-dialect short vowels remain the same whether stressed or not, but in the Western dialect short vowels are pronounced differently.

The consonants vary depending on their position in a word: As word final or when before a consonant (except y and w) t k r n y w are voiceless (t k s hn sh f), but before y, w, or a vowel they are voiced d g r n y w; the other consonants do not vary. In the Western dialect t and k are strengthened to 't and 'k; θ and s have merged to just s; finally voiceless y and w (that is, sh and f) disappear. ´ = high pitch; ` = low pitch.

NOTES

GREAT LAKES NATIVE LITERATURES

1.   Linguist Carl Masthay suggests that the final word of the poem should be *pesazmuk* (stars), not the usually printed *pemtenikek* (mountains). Because Leland and Prince were whites who did not speak Passamaquoddy fluently, Masthay checked everything with the Francis and Leavitt *Passamaquod-dy-Maliseet Dictionary* (2008) and with other scholars in June 2010. According to Conor McDonough Quinn, the Passamaquoddy words are garbled. According to Nicholas Smith, Peter Paul (who was fluent in Passamaquoddy) had examined the poem in the 1930s without changing the Passamaquoddy words but changed the translation to slightly more modern words: "We fly over the sky," "We make a road for the spirits, / For the spirits to pass over," but this latter line is clearly "A road for the Great Spirit." There are some slight punctuation differences. The withdrawn last line "This is the Song of the Mountain" appears to be an error from an inappropriate "echo" typing of Passamaquoddy pemtenikek (mountain) from the end of the previous line. For these reasons, Masthay suggests that although the poem was first published in 1882, only the 1902 original should be followed, except for pemtenikek (mountain).

2.   Robert L. Hall, *An Archaeology of the Soul: North American Indian Belief and Ritual* (Urbana, IL: University of Illinois Press, 1997): 169.

3.   Susan Martin, *Wonderful Power* (Detroit, MI: Wayne State University Press, 1999); John R. Halsey, Personal Communication, 2009.

4.   Brian Fagan, *Ancient North America* (London, England: Thames & Hudson, 2000).

5.   Richard White, *The Middle Ground* (New York, NY: Cambridge University Press, 1991).

6.   Patrick J. Jung, "Forge, Destroy, and Preserve the Bonds of Empire: Euro-Americans, Native Americans, and Métis on the Wisconsin Frontier, 1634-1856" (MA thesis, Marquette University, 1997); Walker D. Wyman, *The Chippewa: A History of the Great Lakes Woodland Tribe Over Three Centuries* (River Falls, WI: University of Wisconsin-River Falls Press, 1993); Robert H. Keller, "An Economic History of Indian Treaties in the Great Lakes Region," *American Indian Journal* 4 (February 1978): 2-20.

7.   Andrew J. Blackbird, *The Indian Problem from the Indian's Standpoint* (Harbor Springs, MI: Privately printed, 1900).

8.   Windigog is an Ojibwe word cognate to the Meskwaki word *wi·teko·waki* (owls), which were sometimes terrifying creatures that foretold death or suffering. Children who didn't behave could be scared with owl masks on sticks waved into the lodge at night. The Ojibwe had other words for the various kinds of owls but used windigog solely for the giant cannibals.

9.   David Rockwell, *Giving Voice to Bear* (Lanham, MD: Roberts Rinehart, 1991).

10. George Lankford, *Reachable Stars: Patterns in the Ethnoastronomy of Eastern North America* (Tuscaloosa, AL: University of Alabama Press, 2007).

11. Bruce Trigger, *The Children of Aataentsic* (Montreal, QE: McGill-Queen's University Press, 1976).

12. Jarold Ramsey, *Coyote Was Going There: Indian Literature of the Oregon Country* (Seattle, WA: University of Washington Press, 1977).

13. Lankford, 2007.

WINTER

14. Many Native nations used thirteen moons, not twelve, so their moons do not exactly match contemporary calendar months. Shawnee months, for example, were said to begin on the fifteenth day. Sources for the month names: **Miami:** Jacob Piatt Dunn, n.d. (*c.* 1920); David Costa's transcription, 1991 and 2010, pers. comm.; **Shawnee:** Ronald L. Christley. *An Introduction to the Shawnee Language*, ed. 2. Newark, OH: self-published (deceased), 1995; **Mohawk:** modern: David Kanatawakhon Maracle. *One Thousand Useful Mohawk Words.* Guilford, CT: Audio-Forum, 1992; **Ho-Chunk (Winnebago):** supplied by Johannes Helmbrecht, Allgemeine und Vergleichende Sprachwissenschaft, Universität Regensburg, Regensburg, Germany; **Meskwaki:** Truman Michelson. "Fox miscellany." Smithsonian Institution. *Bureau of American Ethnology Bulletin* 114. Washington, DC: Government Printing Office, 1937; reworked by Carl Masthay 2010; **Ojibwe/Odawa:** Sister M. Inez Hilger. "Chippewa Child Life and its Cultural Background." Smithsonian Institution. *Bureau of American Ethnology Bulletin* 146. Washington, DC: Government Printing Office, 1951; **Potawatomi:** Maurice Gailland. *Grammaire de la langue potêvatémie.* ms. NA 20 (Box X) Box 2 in Jesuit Missouri Province Archives, St. Louis, MO: 1868; **Menominee:** Alanson Skinner. "Social Life and Ceremonial Bundles of the Menomini Indians." *Anthropological Papers of the American Museum of Natural History*, vol. 13, pt 1. New York, NY: Museum of Natural History, 1913.

15. Isaac performed this song for an ethnologist near Pinconning, Michigan. *Chouqua* (/shoo-KWAH/ or /shoo-KWAY/) is not an indigenous word but appears to be from the French, meaning a jackdaw or a tough sailor who sets the blocks that hold masts tight. Its origin cannot be recovered.

16. Lankford, 2007: 240, 256.

17. Robert A. Brightman. *Ācaðōhkīwina and Ācimōwina: Traditional Narratives of the Rock Cree Indians*, Canadian Ethnology Service, Mercury Series Paper 113, Canadian Museum of Civilization, Hull, Quebec, 1989:65. Linguist Carl Masthy suggests that the name may be based on the Cree Wīsak, with the sense of "bitter" or "suffer."

18. The name is from the Huron Eiǎ'tǎgěn'tci': She Whose Body is Ancient, Ancient One.

19. Down-fended children were hidden from the sight of everyone except a trustee until puberty and were considered to have great *orenda*, or spiritual power. The term comes from the custom of scattering feather-light cattail flag down around the children so that no one could pass without disturbing it. The power of orenda is associated with song, a common way of communicating with the spirits. *Otgon*, the opposite of orenda, is poison or evil power.

20. This is Aataentsic (Eiǎ'tǎgěn'tci': She Whose Body is Ancient, Ancient One, Sky Woman), and she will be the mother of the earth and humankind.

21. Yellow dog-toothed violet (*Erythronium americanum*). This is not a violet but the yellow trout lily. Natives used the plant's leaves as greens and the corms as a vegetable. They brewed a root decoction for fevers and bacterial infections, made poultices for sores and splinters, and ate raw leaves for contraception. Different versions of this story use different trees, but all are light-giving replacements for the sun.

22. Young women who were to be married baked cornbread into a dumbbell shape and carried it to their prospective husbands.

23. Otherwise known as Gaasyendiet'ha (Traveling Torch of Light), or White Fire Dragon, a meteor and a powerful sorcerer. These dragons are forced to live in the deepest portions of lakes and rivers because the sparks and flashes from their bodies would set the world afire if they remained out of the water for any length of time.

24. These are not the European mute swans seen in parks but the large whistling swans native to North America (*Olor columbianus*).

25. Turtles are an ancient species, 200 million years old, having existed well before the dinosaurs. The largest, the Bolson tortoise (*Gopherus flavomarginatus*), weighed over one hundred pounds and was common throughout North America.

26. The American toad (*Bufo americanus*) is a logical choice for an agricultural people like the Wendat to use to create the world because toads are one of the most useful animals for people and their crops. Oehda grew to become the entire world.

27. Natives gathered several types of wild potatoes—arum-leaved arrowhead (*Sagittaria arifolia*), water nut or swamp potato (*Sagittaria latifolia*), groundnut (*Apios tuberosa*)—and cultivated one type of fingerling that was probably originally derived from wild tubers: Indian potato (*Solanum tuberosum*).

28. Niágwai' [h]adishé' (Ursa Major); Tgêñdêñ´withä' (Morning Star, Venus; less likely Sirius or Mars); Gatgwä´´dä' (Northern Crown?); De'hoñnoñt´gwěn' (Pleiades); Ieniú'ciot (Orion); Nanganiä´´gon Ga'sä´don' (Little Dipper).

29. Perhaps Snapping turtle (*Chelydra serpentina*).

30. The Twins are also known as Iouskeha (Tijuskeha: Good-Minded or Sapling); and Tawiskaron (Othegwenhda: Bad-Minded or Flint or Crystal). Tsesta, from the Oklahoma Wendats, has no supplied meaning, unless possibly "embers."

31. The turtle is the representative of the great underground bear and as such is particularly desirable as food at all feasts in honor of the thunderbirds, who prey on the underneath gods [note in original].

32. Probably the bald eagle (*Haliaetus leucocephalus*), an ancient species from the Pleistocene that winters south of the Great Lakes.

33. Flint, or Bad Mind.

34. Galls are irregular growths built around an insect, usually a wasp. The gall provides protection to the insect during a one- or two-year life cycle. Some galls may be one or two inches in diameter.

35. For many Native nations Trickster is a rabbit or a hare, which is the usual accepted translation for names like Nänabush, Menapos.

36. Probably a species of catfish, considered hairy because of its chin barbels or whiskers. The brown bullhead (*Ictalurus nebulosus*), a common type, has two barbels that stick up from its snout, like horns.

37. In the Ojibwe version Nanabozo travels to the far land by causing the water to freeze. He obtains fire by willing a spark to fall on his back and set himself afire. He then runs back over the ice to his grandmother, burning with a blue flame.

"And this he said to his grandmother when he came flying in, 'Rub the fire off from me, I am burning up, my grandmother!'

Whereupon truly off from him did the old woman rub the fire.

Therefore such was how they there came into possession of fire. And this said Nanabushu, 'Therefore such shall be the look of the hare in the summertime.'" (William Jones, *Ojibwa Texts*, 1917-1919.)

38. Grandmother or Mother of All the Earth or Toadwoman.

39. Chibiabósa (Tchīpaiyāpōswa, Ruler of the Dead) is also the manido of music and dance and laughter, which conquer death. As Kabeyun, or Kīyāpä‘tä, he is known as the West Wind.

40. The Wolves want to avoid Trickster because they know he will take advantage of their good manners and manipulate them into feeding and taking care of him.

41. Cedar knots were used as torches because of their shape and the quantity of flammable resin they contained.

42. Red (Norway) pine, a tall, northern tree that indigenous peoples use for construction materials and toys. With white pine it formed part of the old-growth coniferous forest of the upper lakes region.

43. Balsam fir (*Abies balsamea*) grows densely in swamps—not a good place to camp.

44. Flint was used to make a spark; punk is tinder, usually dry, decayed wood that will catch fire easily.

45. Tales of fruit confusingly reflected in water are common the world over. Highbush cranberry (*Oxycoccus macrocarpus*) is native to the lakes.

46. A white bear is sacred and powerful, such as the white bear that was the origin of the Menominee.

47. The great underwater horned serpent.

48. Painted turtle (*Chrysemys picta*).

49. Toadwoman. She is carrying basswood (American linden, *Tilia americana*) because the inner bark was used for twine. She would use rattles as part of a healing ceremony.

50. A small frog [note in original]; all frogs eat the flesh of other small animals.

51. This number refers to the Seven Generations. See The Seventh Fire (p. 114).

52. There are several types of ducks that are good divers: American pintail (*Anas acuta*), bufflehead (*Bucephala albeola*), and canvasback (*Aythya valisineria*). The last dives the deepest and can feed off-shore.

53. Probably the white-crowned pigeon (*Columba leucocephala*).

54. This is a satire of the belief that songs come to people in dreams from the divine, and because their expression in dance may be sacred as well, participants must follow the dictates of the dreamer, a duty that could become onerous [note in original].

55. A round, grass-covered, ceremonial lodge, not used for habitation, with a smoke hole in the top.

56. Wood duck (*Aix sponsa*).

57. What a warrior says after victory, especially in earlier times when enemies were sometimes made into soup. "Scabby-mouth" ducks may be a species of scoter, which are not good food because they feed on fish.

58. In some versions, Trickster punishes his anus by sliding down banks of bushes to water. His blood makes them red, accounting for the color of red osier dogwood (*Cornus stolonifera*).

59. At this point in his existence, Trickster's penis is so long he must carry it in a box on his back, a satire on men's wishes. Only a distinguished warrior would be allowed to have sex with the chief's daughter.

60. Several plants can be used as emetics; this may be wild leek (*Allium tricoccum*), which has bulb-shaped roots.

61. This is the opposite of what people did when attacked by a war party.

62. Probably white oak (*Quercus alba*), which grows on well-drained bottomlands, red oak (*Quercus rubra*), slippery (red) elm (*Ulmus rubra*), and basswood (American linden, *Tilia americana*). This episode teaches where certain trees grow so that by glancing around someone can guess how far water might be or what grows nearby.

63. Blowsnake, who was fond of dancing, is satirical here [note in original].

64. According to Ho-Chunk belief, elk came from the water, but Trickster is also satirizing dreams and visions.

65. Lily-of-the-lake: American lotus? (*Nelumbo lutea*); potatoes: swamp potato (*Sagittaria latifolia*); turnips: prairie turnip (*Psoralea esculenta*); artichokes: Jerusalem artichoke (*Helianthus tuberosus*); ground beans: wild beans *(Falcata comosa)*; dog teeth: yellow dog-toothed violet (*Erythronium americanum*); rice: wild rice (*Zizania palustris*); pond-lily: sweet white water lily? (*Nymphaea odorata*). Artichokes, which look like wild sunflowers, were harvested and perhaps cultivated for centuries in North America before being shipped to Europe in 1616 where they were additionally named "Jerusalem."

66. A medicine bag was made from the skin of an animal, and contained objects of power and guidance the owner had obtained during ceremonies or dreams. Otter-skin bags, given during initiation into the first level of the Midéwewin, were the most common. Medicine bags were used in healing ceremonies or vision quests and so were sacred.

67. "Marry" usually means the couple will sleep together and then announce that they are married. Feasts and ceremonies will be held and presents exchanged to formalize the union. Turtle's object, on the other hand, is simply sex.

68. Cāwano (c = /sh/) is the manido who is chief of the Thunderers.

69. This is Kīyāpā'tä, whose name changed when he became guardian of the dead.

70. Turtle is going to the ends of the four directions and to the powerful manidog who live there. Cāwano is the south wind; the Thunderers live in his lodge. Tcīpaiyāpōswa rules over the land of the dead. The underworld manidog are guardians of fire. The White River is the Milky Way, and manidog live along its banks. Gīshä Mŭ´nětōa, the chief manido, lives in a lodge on the White River.

71. When a person is ill, Nokanowa (no·ke·nawa: soul) crosses the river to the land of Tcīpaiyāpōswa. If it remains there, the person dies. Hence the power of this medicine, which Turtle knows is capable of keeping back Nokanowa on this side of the river. Since Nokanowa can live only in the breast of humans or in the land beyond the river, it will come back into the breast of humans if prevented from crossing the river. Turtle, by knowing the medicine that has this power, is able to give people long life [note in original].

72. This is backwards, an illustration of how little the youngest brother apparently knows.

73. The Night Spirits, Those Who Walk in Darkness, controlled war powers and caused the darkness of night.

74. Probably the painted turtle (*Chrysemys picta*), which has red marks on its shell. Turtle has planted turtles all along the race course.

75. This is a war bundle feast. War bundles contained the bodies of animals whose characteristics—fleetness, strength, vision, hearing—were given to the owner, and flutes with which to call the spirits for aid. Each clan had its own sacred war bundle, given to it by the spirits.

76. During his fast, the leader of a war party would be told the exact number of people he was going to capture or kill. The speed with which the food was consumed at the fast-eating contest determined whether any enemy predestined to be killed or captured would escape. Turtle is, once again, justifying being slow [note in original].

77. Go to the bathroom.

78. He is indicating that he has scalped an enemy, obtaining the first war honor. All other members of the war party may strike the fallen enemy, known as counting coup [note in original].

79. This tradition was the preferred way a war party returned home.

80. A man should accept moccasins only from his wife.

81. Turtle is never associated with a successful war party because he often insists on going his own way [note in original].

82. They are playing lacrosse, which mimics war and is called the "little brother of war."

83. These words indicate defeat.

84. He is beginning to fast, which children often did at five years of age but never on their own. To do so is a sign of superiority [note in original].

85. Wailing songs are sung by people about to die.

86. This is a typical departure for a spirit who has been reincarnated to help human beings [note in original].

87. The etymology of Hayęhwàtha' is uncertain, despite attempted translations of: He Makes Rivers, or Seeker After Wampum, or He Who Combs (snakes from the hair of Thatotaho').

88. Seneca *hotinohsyoni'*: they who are of the extended lodge.

89. The name may also be translated "setting his teeth together," but the meaning is uncertain.

90. The Bay of Quinte, among the Huron people.

91. This man is Thaęhyawá'ki (Mohawk Tharǫhyawâ·kǫ: He Who Holds Up the Sky), the Good Mind and the good son of Sky Woman's daughter.

92. He of the Great Voice, Great Being, the Thunder, Earthgrasper, the husband of Sky Woman.

93. Thaęhyawá'ki (Mohawk Tharǫhyawâ·kǫ: He Who Holds Up the Sky).

94. Some commentators believe that this passage shows Christian influences because Gibson and the translators adapted the original story to meet the needs of the largely Christian Haudenosaunee at the time Gibson narrated. It also describes the rituals and the duties of members of the Iroquois Confederacy when they meet.

95. A pine tree will become important in League of the Iroquois rituals, and a white pine becomes a symbol of the league.

96. In other words, completing the work he has set out to do will be as impossible to a mortal person as floating a stone canoe.

97. Tekánawíta' crosses over Lake Ontario. Kanyę'ke is a Mohawk settlement.

98. In some versions this is the man Tekánawíta' christens Hayęhwatha'.

99. The uprooted tree is a reference to the uprooted tree in the creation story, and it foreshadows the great tree at the center of the confederacy where the weapons of war will be buried at the founding of the league.

100. Tekánawíta' must prove himself to the Great Warrior who has the power to initiate wars.

101. Part of Tekánawíta''s task is to establish the names by which the confederacy chiefs will be known. Tekaihokę is the first Mohawk title in the roster. When a chief dies, the name passes to the next male who is a member of the title-holding matrilineage. The process of "raising up" someone to assume the name title of someone who has died is known as the Condolence Council and is a part of the rituals Tekánawíta' came to earth to establish.

102. That is, they would attempt to cure her.

103. No one comforts Hayęhwatha' because the people have become so used to fighting they are desensitized to grief and death.

104. Hayęhwatha' has created wampum, which will be used to send messages and to keep the records of the league. Later in the recital he comes to a lake, and ducks swimming there fly up, taking the water with them. He then uses shells from the lake bed to replace the sticks. Sections of this text are divided by drawings of wampum strings.

105. This episode explains the "invitation wampum" that will figure in the confederacy and condolence rituals.

106. The league's wampum keeper.

107. Here Tekánawíta' has established the symbolism of the central hearth, the confederacy fire. The rising smoke of a fire, which has occurred several times during the narrative, now becomes a symbol for the meetings of the confederacy and a symbol in much other Haudenosaunee literature.

108. Deer antlers symbolize his status as a confederacy chief. The circle comprises the other chiefs who symbolize a protective circle around their people, and it is symbolized by the Circlet of the League Wampum.

109. The white pine (*Pinus strobus*), the symbol of renewal.

110. Ganowogęs: rapids-smelly.

111. Seneca *káiwi·yo·h* (good message, good word, religion).

112. Drunks were put in the middle of canoes lashed together so they didn't fall out.

113. Handsome Lake, Skanyátaí·yo', one of the fifty hereditary sachems of the Longhouse as established by Tekánawíta'.

114. Awlbreaker, another of the fifty sachems.

115. Cornplanter, the half-brother of Handsome Lake.

116. The earliest of the wild strawberries are believed to be of great medicinal value and are eagerly eaten as soon as ripe. The strawberry is so sacred that it is believed to grow along the "heaven road." A person recovering from a severe illness says, "I almost ate strawberries."

117. The primary religious dance.

118. Many nations knew of herb abortificants. The Seneca and Onondaga belief was that every woman has a certain number of children predestined to her and that they are fastened on a stringlike runner like tubers, or like eggs within a bird.

119. Moje Manido (*maji-manido*: bad spirit); Panther (Micipijiu: Missipeshu or Great Lynx).

120. The concept of *pimâdiziwin* (*bimaadiziwin*: life) means wholeness: a good life, with a strong community and a commitment to ethical behavior.

121. Lankford, 2007: 181.

122. Faith-keepers are deacons of the Longhouse, charged with transmitting history and ritual.

123. The Milky Way.

124. In some versions the mothers' selfishness in refusing to provide food or help their sons is the reason the dancers are called into the sky.

125. Snowsnake is a game played by sliding long, smoothed sticks across the snow to see which one will go the farthest.

126. One of the stars of the constellation is less bright than the others. Parker may be imagining Djinaĕñ''dă' as a shooting star or meteor.

127. Windigog is an Ojibwe word cognate to the Meskwaki word *wi·teko·waki* (owls), which were sometimes terrifying creatures that foretold death or suffering. Children who didn't behave could be scared with owl masks on sticks waved into the lodge at night. The Ojibwe had other words for the various kinds of owls but used windigog solely for the giant cannibals.

SPRING

128. Many Native nations used thirteen moons, not twelve, so their moons do not exactly match contemporary calendar months. Shawnee months, for example, were said to begin on the fifteenth day. Sources for the month names: **Miami:** Jacob Piatt Dunn, n.d. (*c.* 1920); David Costa's transcription, 1991 and 2010, pers. comm.; **Shawnee:** Ronald L. Christley. *An Introduction to the Shawnee Language*, ed. 2. Newark, OH: self-published (deceased), 1995; **Mohawk:** modern: David Kanatawakhon Maracle. *One Thousand Useful Mohawk Words*. Guilford, CT: Audio-Forum, 1992; **Ho-Chunk (Winnebago):** supplied by Johannes Helmbrecht, Allgemeine und Vergleichende Sprachwissenschaft, Universität Regensburg, Regensburg, Germany; **Meskwaki:** Truman Michelson. "Fox miscellany." Smithsonian Institution. *Bureau of American Ethnology Bulletin* 114. Washington, DC: Government Printing Office, 1937; reworked by Carl Masthay 2010; **Ojibwe/Odawa:** Sister M. Inez Hilger. "Chippewa Child Life and its Cultural Background." Smithsonian Institution. *Bureau of American Ethnology Bulletin* 146. Washington, DC: Government Printing Office, 1951; **Potawatomi:** Maurice Gailland. *Grammaire de la langue potêvaté-mie*. ms. NA 20 (Box X) Box 2 in Jesuit Missouri Province Archives, St. Louis, MO: 1868; **Menominee:**

Alanson Skinner. "Social Life and Ceremonial Bundles of the Menomini Indians." *Anthropological Papers of the American Museum of Natural History*, vol. 13, pt 1. New York, NY: Museum of Natural History, 1913.

129. Rev. W. M. Beauchamp. *Iroquois Folk-lore Gathered from the Six Nations of New York* (Syracuse, NY: Dahler, 1922): 231. Parker, who was known as "The Reader" to his band, was the grandson of Red Jacket, who opposed white colonization. Trained as an attorney, Parker was not allowed to practice because he was Indian and so lacked USA citizenship. He subsequently became a civil engineer before becoming General Grant's secretary during the US Civil War. He later became commissioner of Indian Affairs.

130. There are several species of yellow water lily (genus *Nuphar*), a plant known as *cerap* (*c* = /ch/) to the Ho-Chunk [note in original].

131. "Mashkawshakwong," a longer and nearly identical story by Chief Nabinoi and George Johnston, names the hunter as Mashkawshakwong, or the Red Head. This may be the same Red Head described in "Meskwaunkwāātar" (p. 188); it may refer to Mercury or another star that shines red, such as Antares.

132. Also spelled *bâwitig* (pronounced /bao-tig/) or *bâwiting*: the rapids. In French *saut*: /so/; old spelling *sault*, pronounced in America /soo/. The present-day St. Mary's River rapids near Sault Ste. Marie.

133. Probably the Sandhill crane (*Grus canadensis*), flocks of which have nested near the lakes for millennia.

134. The crane is the dodem of the chiefs of the bands near the St. Mary's River. In "Mashkawshakwong," Schoolcraft noted that, "The small white shells that the whitefish live upon and the white substance found in its gizzard are to this day considered by the Indians to be the brain and skull of the woman. . . ."

135. *Shinnob* is slang for Anishinâbe. "Knockers" is a pun that also refers to the sticks used to knock wild rice from the plant into the canoe. Fond du Lac (the head of the lake) is the old name for the Duluth-Superior area.

136. "Deer shiners" use powerful spotlights on their vehicles to illegally locate and shoot deer at night, also known as "jacklighting."

137. A white skin suggests that they are underwater manidog who are sacred and powerful snakes or bears.

138. Dorcas S. Miller. *Stars of the First People* (Boulder, CO: Pruett, 1997): 44.

139. Paulette Jiles. *North Spirit: Travels Among the Cree and Ojibway Nations and Their Star Maps* (Toronto, ON: Doubleday Canada, 1995): 249.

140. Lankford, 2007: 2-19.

141. These animals are married to the daughters or granddaughters of Earthgrasper, Earthmaker, or Gitchi Manito (Great Spirit), who created the world.

142. A term for vulva [note in original].

143. Uttered by drawing in the breath [note in original].

144. A name referring to the giant Mesâbä (big-man).

145. Toward the north [note in original].

146. Which accounts for the position of the stars in the handle of the Dipper [note in original].

147. Referring to the time when the snow is deep and the crust hardened, when game is easily approached and killed [note in original].

148. The stories collected from Bois Fort often end with this sentence. It is a joke but also suggests the teller has "caught" the story, something requiring skill. Ruffed grouse (*Bonasa umbellus*) are among the finest of the upland game birds; they are more shy and wary than their close relatives, spruce or "fool" grouse (*Dendragapus canadensis*), which were the first game many children attempted to snare.

149. Flutes were used for courting. A magic one would have irresistible spirit power.

150. *c* = /sh/.

151. Lankford, 2007: 201-225.

152. Female spirit or prophetess [note in original].

153. Mudjikewis (Mâdjîkiwiss: First Born Son) is the first son of Ae-pungishimook (Epangishimog: the West) and Winonah (to nourish) a mortal. Schoolcraft's translation of Winona is faulty, however, because Winona is from the Santee Sioux and means First Born Girl child, a surprising match to that of Mâdjîkiwiss. Mâdjîkiwiss was a warrior and hunter of great power who led his brothers and his nation with courage, dignity, and care. He inherited his father's power.

154. Excrement

155. A better transliteration would be: *Muwis, nin-gi-waniwinig, niwaniwinig.* Schoolcraft translates the words as "Moowis, Moowis, you have led me astray—you are leading me astray." He described the name Moowis, derived from the Ojibwe noun *mo* (filth or excrement) as being one of the most derogative and offensive possible. Since the suffix *-is* denotes smallness, the name Moowis translates as Little Shit.

156. This would be symbolically toward death, but also literally across the Mississippi toward Kansas and Oklahoma where some nations were sent.

157. Carl Masthay has determined that Pokagan (/puh-KAY-gun/) once represented the Ojibwe word *pakâkwaan*: shield. Modern Potawatomis now say that the word is *pigegan* (/pih-GAY-gun/): rib. This is the inalienable noun with the required obviative suffix: *opigeganama* (/o-pih-GAY-guh-nuh-muh/: his rib).

158. Pokagon is assumed to have known some Potawatomi up to twelve years of age, but he may not always have remembered his first language well by the time he wrote *Queen of the Woods,* and he did not live to see the book through the press. He also appears to have used Baraga's Ojibwe dictionary (1880) and other sources, making grammatical and lexical errors. In 2010, Carl Masthay tried to supply the correct forms according to Pokagon's English, but "had to surrender to a few difficult ones." Masthay's supplied Potawatomi words follow Pokagon's in parentheses with Pokagon's translations, but Masthay notes that there are few Potawatomi sources, such as Gailland (1868).

159. Joseph Bertrand, Jr.

160. The Black River. There is a Black River in traditional Potawatomi country in southwestern Michigan in present-day Van Buren County. There is also a Black River in west-central Wisconsin where, after the sale of their lands, many Potawatomi trying to escape removal migrated, since that country was still wild. Pokagon may have thought that by setting his romance on the Black River, he could also highlight the plight of that band's removal from Indiana.

161. "Missionary Hymn" (1819); words by Reginald Heber (Acts 16:9), music by Lowell Mason (not supplied).

162. *Wâwâshkeshi nissâ animooshan*: The deer will kill the dog.

163. James Clifton. *The Potawatomi.* New York, NY: Chelsea House, 1987.

164. Perhaps more precisely, *wegimind okow súkisi*: you my-mother deer.

165. This is the wrong word. Perhaps it is *gi-git gigi-kijâdisiwinang indigo.*

166. *Pik-wan* is a person's back; perhaps it should be *Ajeshkâ, ajeshkâ.*

167. Ojibwe is *nin-dé*; Potawatomi is *nití.*

168. The detail of the stone knife allows Tenskwatawa to highlight the age of the story and call attention to the hero's return to a positive primitive simplicity. "Sat" here is an old form of "set."

169. This echoes traditional Shawnee stories of the grandson of Kokumthena (Snaggle-Toothed Woman, or Cloud), the world creator, who lives with her grandson and his dog near the land of the dead. She can be seen bending over her cooking pot in the full moon.

170. An eat-all feast before or on the warpath where all food must be consumed or bad luck will follow.

171. The name 'Mishosha' perhaps comes from *wemishoozhi* (he has a large boat), for the character Wemishoosh in Ojibwe oral tradition.

172. *Conaus* means 'hood' and comes from the Algonquin word *konàs*: dress or robe.

173. The sounds trees make.

174. Many nations of the Great Lakes believe in a separate race of tiny humans who often live in caves hidden in the cliffs above lakes and give great gifts to humans. Some call them *pagwâdj-inini-wag*: wild men.

175. Vizenor means the Slovenian Bishop Frederic Baraga (Friderik Baràga), who served Natives in the Great Lakes region from 1831 to his death in 1868. In addition to constant travel between bands, he wrote the first Chippewa (Otchipwe, Ojibwe) grammar (1850) and dictionary (1853) and several devotional books in Chippewa.

176. AIM (American Indian Movement) was founded in Minneapolis in 1968 by Dennis Banks, Clyde Bellecourt, Eddie Benton-Benai, and Russell Means to address discrimination and inequality by public protest. AIM seized a *Mayflower* replica on Thanksgiving in 1970, occupied the Bureau of Indian Affairs, Alcatraz Island, and later Wounded Knee on the Pine Ridge Reservation in 1973, the latter resulting in a standoff with FBI agents that left some dead and others permanently incarcerated. AIM is active in the USA and Canada and on behalf of indigenous peoples in the Americas.

SUMMER

177. Many Native nations used thirteen moons, not twelve, so their moons do not exactly match contemporary calendar months. Shawnee months, for example, were said to begin on the fifteenth day. Sources for the month names: **Miami:** Jacob Piatt Dunn, n.d. (*c.* 1920); David Costa's transcription, 1991 and 2010, pers. comm.; **Shawnee:** Ronald L. Christley. *An Introduction to the Shawnee Language*, ed. 2. Newark, OH: self-published (deceased), 1995; **Mohawk:** modern: David Kanatawakhon Maracle. *One Thousand Useful Mohawk Words*. Guilford, CT: Audio-Forum, 1992; **Ho-Chunk (Winnebago):** supplied by Johannes Helmbrecht, Allgemeine und Vergleichende Sprachwissenschaft, Universität Regensburg, Regensburg, Germany; **Meskwaki:** Truman Michelson. "Fox miscellany." Smithsonian Institution. *Bureau of American Ethnology Bulletin* 114. Washington, DC: Government Printing Office, 1937; reworked by Carl Masthay 2010; **Ojibwe/Odawa:** Sister M. Inez Hilger. "Chippewa Child Life and its Cultural Background." Smithsonian Institution. *Bureau of American Ethnology Bulletin* 146. Washington, DC: Government Printing Office, 1951; **Potawatomi:** Maurice Gailland. *Grammaire de la langue potêvatémie*. ms. NA 20 (Box X) Box 2 in Jesuit Missouri Province Archives, St. Louis, MO: 1868; **Menominee:** Alanson Skinner. "Social Life and Ceremonial Bundles of the Menomini Indians." *Anthropological Papers of the American Museum of Natural History*, vol. 13, pt 1. New York, NY: Museum of Natural History, 1913.

178. Of this little poem Schoolcraft wrote: "In the hot summer evenings, the children of the Chippewa Algonquins, along the shores of the upper lakes, and in the northern latitudes, frequently assemble before their parents' lodges, and amuse themselves by little chants of various kinds, with shouts and wild dancing. Attracted by such shouts of merriment and gambols, I walked out one evening, to a green lawn skirting the edge of the St. Mary's River, with the falls in full view, to get hold of the meaning of some of these chants. The air and the plain were literally sparkling with the phosphorescent light of the firefly. By dint of attention, repeated on one or two occasions, the following succession of words was caught. Metre there was none, at least of a regular character: they were the wild improvisation of children in a merry mood." John D. Nichols, a scholar of Ojibwe, retranslated the poem from Schoolcraft's version.

179. Singing sticks—*misásakiwîs*—were shaped like drumsticks and were tapped together to accompany songs.

180. Probably the red squirrel (*Tamiasciurus hudsonicus*), which prefers to live in evergreen forests.

181. *owáhe*: foundation to stand on.

182. Other nations referred to the northern lights as the dancing spirits of the dead, but some saw them as an evil portent. See "The Lone Lightning," p. 284-285.

183. A hawk that winters near the Great Lakes; perhaps the rough-legged hawk (*Buteo lagopus*).

184. Catlinite, or pipestone, quarried in present-day Minnesota.

185. The young wife is the Moon, but "Last Night Sun" was how several languages named the Moon.

186. *apakwei*: lodge mat; *apakweshkwai*: rush for mats.

187. Properly jishigwan: gourd bottle with shot inside, used as a rattle.

188. Many Winnebago, or Ho-Chunk, still live near the Great Lakes in Wisconsin, but the narrator of this story lives in Nebraska. The original Ho-Chunk were removed from Wisconsin to Iowa in 1840, to Minnesota in 1846, to South Dakota in 1863, and fled to Nebraska to escape starvation in 1864-1865, where they purchased land. When they lost fifty percent of their Nebraska land during the Allotment Era (1887-1934), half of the members returned to Wisconsin and formed a separate community.

189. This reference is unclear. Beaver tribe may mean the Ojibwe, since the actual Beaver Tribe is a Déné people who reside in northern Alberta, not "nearby" the Great Lakes.

190. This red stone may be from the quarry near Pipestone, Minnesota, where the people mined catlinite for pipes. Three large granite boulders, known as the Three Maidens, rest on a bed of red quartzite, which was once covered with pictographs. People from all over the Great Lakes region journeyed there. Contemporary researchers believe that most of these pictographs were related to spirit power.

191. Many nations of the Great Lakes believe in a separate race of tiny humans who often live in caves hidden in the cliffs above lakes and give great gifts to humans. Some call them *pagwâdj-inini-wag*: wild men.

192. The verb *aupoway* (he had a bad dream) is used here, but it should be the noun *âpawewin* (bad dream). Âpawewin is only an inadequate approximation for these terms that are not in conceptual use in Ojibwe.

193. *neshikewewe*: solitary sounding + *-sin?*

194. The moccasin game consists in hiding four playing pieces, one marked, under four moccasins. One person or team places the pieces; the other must guess where the marked one is. The plate game is a form of dice game, like the plum-stone game of the Plains nations. The object is to toss up the carved figures to have them land on the plate in certain positions, some of which count more than others.

195. Kâgige-gâbau: Perpetually He Stands

196. Colbourne, Ontario, on Lake Ontario.

197. "O For a Thousand Tongues to Sing" (1739), words and music by Charles Wesley.
    "Jesus all the day long. . ." is from a hymn by Charles Wesley (1743?).

198. For example, an otter-skin Midé bag earned with completion of the first-degree rites.

199. *giwewinon*: portage; carry back again something

200. American-French *anse*: bay

201. Acts 2:4

202. Jessakid (*tchessakid*). Ojibwe *jaasakiid*: conjuror making oracular pronouncements from a closed tent.

203. To the Ho-Chunk reservation in Nebraska.

204. Chasing women who have just collected their government payments to get money from them.

205. This is Mountain Wolf Woman (pp. 145-146, and 341-345), who later joined the Native American Church.

206. According to Ives Goddard, *manito:wa:link* means "spirit's-cave-at" in Odawa, superseding the formerly regarded "spirit-abode-island."

207. It's not clear what Masswäwëinini means. *Mazinichigan*: doll, image, statue; *miziwe*: everywhere; *mishewe*: stag; but there is nothing with an *a* in the first syllable or with an *sw* cluster. One could imagine a name like *Mezhewewi-inini* (with initial change in the first syllable) meaning Stag Man, but it doesn't match up. (Richard Rhodes 2010.)

208. Literally, short-ears.

209. Translated from the French, this means "name that each soldier formerly used to take on entering military service, now, pseudonym" (assumed name).

210. *mandâmin*; Odawa *mindâmin*.

211. Many nations of the Great Lakes believe in a separate race of tiny humans who often live in caves hidden in the cliffs above lakes and give great gifts to humans. Some call them pagwâdj-inini-wag: wild men.

212. The various forms of the term "Nadowe" (*na·towe·*) were used by many nations to mean enemy or stranger, but specifically "Wendat, Six-Nations Iroquois" and sometimes the "Senecas." The term actually describes the eastern Massasauga rattlesnake and comes from the Proto-Algonquian **na:tawe:wa*: **na:t* seek out + **-awe* condition of heat + **-wa* he/she/it: "seeker of heat," meaning a snake wanting to be near warm places or using its thermal sensory facial pits.(Summed up from Siebert 1996). Penetanguishene is on the Ontario mainland at the opposite or southern end of Georgian Bay from Manitoulin Island, a long and dangerous journey. "Penetanguishene" may be Odawa or Abenaki for "the place of the white falling or rolling sands."

213. *Odawa* means "trader."

FALL

214. Many Native nations used thirteen moons, not twelve, so their moons do not exactly match contemporary calendar months. Shawnee months, for example, were said to begin on the fifteenth day. Sources for the month names: **Miami:** Jacob Piatt Dunn, n.d. (*c.* 1920); David Costa's transcription, 1991 and 2010, pers. comm.; **Shawnee:** Ronald L. Christley. *An Introduction to the Shawnee Language*, ed. 2. Newark, OH: self-published (deceased), 1995; **Mohawk:** modern: David Kanatawakhon Maracle. *One Thousand Useful Mohawk Words*. Guilford, CT: Audio-Forum, 1992; **Ho-Chunk (Winnebago):** supplied by Johannes Helmbrecht, Allgemeine und Vergleichende Sprachwissenschaft, Universität Regensburg, Regensburg, Germany; **Meskwaki:** Truman Michelson. "Fox miscellany." Smithsonian Institution. *Bureau of American Ethnology Bulletin* 114. Washington, DC: Government Printing Office, 1937; reworked by Carl Masthay 2010; **Ojibwe/Odawa:** Sister M. Inez Hilger. "Chippewa Child Life and its Cultural Background." Smithsonian Institution. *Bureau of American Ethnology Bulletin* 146. Washington, DC: Government Printing Office, 1951; **Potawatomi:** Maurice Gailland. *Grammaire de la langue potêvatémie*. ms. NA 20 (Box X) Box 2 in Jesuit Missouri Province Archives, St. Louis, MO: 1868; **Menominee:** Alanson Skinner. "Social Life and Ceremonial Bundles of the Menomini Indians." *Anthropological Papers of the American Museum of Natural History*, vol. 13, pt 1. New York, NY: Museum of Natural History, 1913.

215. Stage performer, poet, and writer, Emily Pauline Johnson was born on the Six Nations Reserve near Brantford, Ontario, in 1861. Her father and grandfather were Mohawk chiefs; her mother was English. After her father was beaten to death trying to protect Mohawk land from white timber merchants, Johnson adopted her grandfather's name, Tekahionwake (Two Lives, Double Life), and began publishing

poems. When she needed money to support herself and her mother, she began a stage career began in 1892 and toured for fifteen years, becoming one of the most popular performers in Canada as she presented dramatic recitations of her poetry and skits about Native life. When entertaining paled, she turned to writing short stories for boys' and women's magazines, continuing her work even after being diagnosed with the inoperable breast cancer that would kill her in 1913. She had earned her retirement; historians estimate she probably traveled over more of Canada than any other woman of her generation.

216. John Koontz suggests that the Ho-Chunk name Axjinwinga may have been deliberately left untranslated because of the possibility of an offensive, possibly sexual connotation. The root *aas-* or *ąąs-* means 'be delicious', as in the stem *aasji-* 'be delicious, good-tasting' (considered offensive by some). The *x* replaces *s* in an augmented sense ('greatly'). The rest is *wi-* 'woman' + *-ga* 'that one (used in a title)'. It could mean one of the following: 'Babe, Delectable, Sweet Woman; Hot-looking Woman'. There is also a homophonous root *aas-* with the sense 'be open, spread, gaping' which exacerbates matters. The Ho-Chunk are as prone to puns as anyone.

217. Jeremiah Curtain obtained stories from the following persons: Abraham Johnny-John, Solomon O'Bail, George Titus, John Armstrong, Zachariah Jimeson, Andrew Fox, Henry Jacob, Henry Silverheels, Peter White, Black Chief, and Phoebe Logan. Any one or several of these could have told this story. Many versions of this Seneca story focus on two brothers, Hadjigwas (Mush Eater), the eldest, and Hadadenon (He, the Last), the youngest.

218. Spirit helper

219. Horned owl (*Bubo virginianus*), long-eared owl (*Asio otus*), screech owl (*Otus asio*), American bittern (*Botaurus lentiginosus*).

220. Copper, which has been mined in the Great Lakes region for thousands of years, was believed to have great magic power. See *Wonderful Power: The Story of Ancient Copper Working in the Lake Superior Basin* by Susan R. Martin. Detroit: Wayne State University Press, 1999.

221. David Lee Smith, in his version of this tale, describes this sort of ambush (*wirápe*), where the dogs cry from four different places, as a *waikecen* (*ʔwaikičą*).

222. The bear runs to the north and northwest (place of the cold) in late fall and early winter, to the to the south and northeast in spring and summer, and back to the north (late summer and fall).

223. *Makomic* (Meskwaki *mahkomiši*: sumac), bear plant, is another name for staghorn sumac (*Rhus typhina*) because bears are fond of the berries.

224. River That Joins Another is the star known to us as Mizar. Hold Tight, the puppy, is the small, faint star right next to Mizar known as Alcor. The "four stars in the lead" are the bowl of the Dipper.

225. A small deer charm is a tiny deer, about an inch and a half long, an exact replica of a living deer. Hunters believed it could be found only in the throat of an old buck, the leader of a deer herd, and brought good luck in hunting.

226. Translator Allen Johnson explained the custom to which Kayrahoo refers: "Whenever a hunter, who was hunting together with a party, happened to kill a deer, he used to let the other hunters skin the animal and divide it into parts. Each hunter of the party was given his share."

227. The tracks are made by a travois (/chruh-VOY/ or /CHRAV-voy/, a transport device made of two poles joined by a frame and pulled by an animal, here a dog. This is suggestive of a family or band moving to their winter hunting camp.

228. The pipe is magical, and whoever smokes it is agreeing to be killed by human hunters. This, along with the drum, refers to the hunters' spiritual ceremonies before beginning the hunt.

229. The hunter is counting coup, as if to signify that the moose is already as good as dead.

230. To be eaten by dogs is to be completely disgraced.

231. This refers to the custom of decorating the carcass of game, as a gesture of respect, once it is brought back to camp.

232. The stories collected from Bois Fort often end with this sentence. It is a joke, but also suggests the teller has "caught" the story, something requiring skill. Ruffed grouse (*Bonasa umbellus*) are among the finest of the upland game birds; they are more shy and wary than their close relatives, spruce or "fool" grouse (*Dendragapus canadensis*), which were the first game many children attempted to snare.

233. The fire is regarded as a spirit . . . and he possesses many gifts that are of use to human beings. . . . In order to obtain them, mortals must make offerings of tobacco. . . . In addition to his other powers, it is believed that he is the messenger of Earthmaker and the other spirits and that he transmits both the messages, as well as the offerings that mortals make to them, by means of the smoke that rises upward [note in original].

234. There are four war honors, the highest going to [he] who first touches a dead enemy, the second . . . to the one who kills him, and the last two to those who touch him second and third [note in original]. These are collectively known as the "four limbs," or counting coup.

235. That is, cause someone to be killed by giving poor leadership.

236. The souls of all the enemies one has killed become the slaves of the victor, and he may command them to do his bidding at any time. If the victor tells his exploit and then commands the enslaved soul to take care of the recently departed person in whose honor the wake is being given, the soul of the conquered enemy will be of considerable aid in overcoming the obstacles that are supposed to infest the path between this earth and the land of the spirits. . . . If, however, a warrior becomes vainglorious, the soul of the recently departed individual will fall into the abyss of fire. . . . [note in original]

237. Not everyone who fasts is blessed with power. For those who are unable to obtain blessings directly from the spirits, there is only one method of protection against evils—the purchase of plants with magical properties from those who have been blessed with them [note in original].

238. That is, men will not be respectful. The joking relationship exists in many indigenous North American cultures and allows certain relatives to play practical jokes and poke fun at other relatives without fear of reprisal or anger.

239. *Waruxawe* (*warughawe, warighabe, warighábera, wárughápara*: war bundles) were composed of objects that had spiritual significance for the owner to aid him in battle: plant medicines, symbols of his spirit helpers, sacred paint, and so forth. Medicine or healing bundles were called by the same name.

240. At the time Radin worked with the Ho-Chunk, they were divided into two major divisions: clans named after birds (upper) and clans named after land and water animals (lower). These were most important in marriage customs, where partners must be from different divisions, as well as from different clans.

241. The Meskwaki. The French, perhaps tutored by a Native ally, saddled them with this nickname because they could seldom outwit them or catch them.

242. The warrior's name is usually Bloody Hand, and the medicine the animals make is *nigahnegaha* (Small Dose), a potent medicine that only trained medicine people, or *hochinagen*, could administer.

243. Midéwiwin song.

244. *Hopók*: owl, as at end of story; less likely *hâmpgú*: dawn.

245. The DeCorahs are leaders.

246. A name based on *bâwatig*: rapids.

247. Neolin is traditionally translated as the "enlightened one," but this has no basis in any Algonquian language; the second translation by F. E. Hoxie 1996 is far better: "four" as in Delaware *newo*, plus an obscure suffix, perhaps for "man."

248. M. De Bellestre, Commander of operations at Detroit until deposed by the British in 1760.

249. Menehwehna, Chief Minweweh, Grand Chief Mivanon, (The One with the Silver Tongue, 1710-1770). *Mino*: good + *-oweh*: he speaks; *minowe*: he has a fine, clear voice; or *minwewi*: he is zealous). Le Grand Saulteur: The Great Saulteur. Saulteurs were a band/nation that lived near Sault Ste. Marie. Mâdjikiwiss: First-born Boy, possibly implying hereditary chief.

250. Fort Duquesne was near present-day Pittsburgh.

251. In 1759 the French under General Montcalm and the English under General Wolfe met on the Plains of Abraham, near Quebec. The English victory determined the outcome of the Seven Years' War in America and restricted French influence near the lakes to Quebec.

252. Warren's etymology is false. *Jâganâsh, zhaaganaash* is simply a deformation of "/En/gl/ish" and means "Englishman, Irishman."

253. A *coureur de bois* (woods runner) was someone who engaged in the fur trade without a proper license. A *marchand voyageur* (traveling merchant or trader) was an expedition leader who negotiated with the Natives.

254. La Cloche (bell-shaped hat) is between Manitoulin Island and the mainland. Some folktales report that the island cliffs rung like a bell when struck.

255. "Covering the bodies of the dead" was a custom of paying tribute to the family of the deceased to avoid protracted blood feuds.

256. According to white historians, the L'Arbe Croche (The Crooked Tree) Odawa felt little love for Pontiac; this does not mean he kept his intentions from them. He had sent them a war belt.

257. A large diameter of shot used for shooting large birds.

258. *La Baie des Puants*: the bay of the Winnebagos, Green Bay, Wisconsin.

259. Miami-Illinois */*kiteepihkwanonki/*: pike-at, buffalo fish-at, (Costa's translation).

260. States of the United States.

261. *Mahkate:wi-meši-ke:hke:hkwa*: black-large-*Accipiter* sp./duck hawk/pigeon hawk, (Goddard's and Thomason's translation).

262. Amherstburg, Ontario.

263. *ki:yohkaka*: to step on (it) about, (Goddard's translation).

264. Carlisle Indian School in Pennsylvania.

265. Miller (1997): 156, 222.

266. As a result of a dream vision during the fast [note in original]. In Mesoamerican stories, eagles are associated with men, the sun, and human sacrifice, which was the primary means of nourishing the sun. Foxes are associated with cleverness; in addition, witches frequently transformed themselves into foxes.

267. The tenth is transformed into the youngest of the sisters, which may be a reference to the transformation of Venus into the Morning Star, or to the coming of spring.

268. The lynx was the earthly representative of the underground panther, an extremely powerful spirit, made more so here by being white.

269. Porcupine (Kitä´mi, *ketaēmīw*) was a clan of great importance in Menominee life.

270. Down-fended children were hidden from the sight of everyone except a trustee until puberty and were considered to have great orenda, or spiritual power. The term comes from the custom of scattering cattail flag down around the children so that no one could pass without disturbing it (the fluffy down).

271. *Begwad-âdizid*: one whose lifeway is in the wilds.

272. Grandson of Sky Woman, brother of Nänabush, bringer of stories to the people, and the person who wrested sacred wampum from the grizzly bear. He is also often the butt of jokes and is portrayed comically as chasing after women and being impulsive.

273. This would be a magical, red version of the common whistling swan, not the ornamental mute swan of parks.

274. Pungish-e-moo, falling or sinking into a position of repose [note in original]. *Pangishimo*: it sets; *epangishimog, bangishimog*: (in the) west. This would signify the Red Swan as Venus, from its position as the first star to be visible after sunset.

275. A combination of Mudjeekawis (*mâdjîkiwiss*: first-born boy) and *kokoko* (*gôkôko'ô*), the word for owl, is suggestive that the watchman is overreacting.

276. Only a mother, sister, or wife should make or mend moccasins.

277. *Nâbese*: foolishness, or male bird.

278. If the Red Swan is Venus, this would refer to the point in its orbit when it is halfway between its occurrence as an evening or a morning star. Depending on what the story celebrates, this might have been a calendrical marker.

279. My grandchild [in the vocative case] [note in original].

280. Technically a bilberry; probably a blueberry in this context.

281. *Enaw-bandum* (*inâbandam*: as he saw when asleep), [note in original].

282. Awuss-Waubung (*awaswâbang*: the day beyond tomorrow), [note in original]. The hawk is a symbol for the sun.

283. Hummingbirds seem to be associated with ancient Mesoamerican symbols for war.

284. *Mishâbiwinân*: eyelash; the down of anything that floats lightly on the air.

285. Since Baraga clearly states in two places that *mâdjîkiwiss* is the first-born boy of a family, this suggests that Odjibwa is more powerful and to be more honored than any usual mortal.

286. *Matchi-ijiwebisiwin*: bad-so-conduct-oneself (noun).

287. Wikipedia supplies another etymology: The Natives called him Echon (Echon pronounced like Ekon), meaning Healing Tree, as a representation of how much Brébeuf had helped the Hurons and of the medicines he brought them from Europe.

BIBLIOGRAPHY
▼▼▼▼▼▼▼▼▼▼▼

Armstrong, John. "The Origin of the World" (Seneca Version). In *Iroquoian Cosmology*, by J. N. B. Hewitt. Twenty-First Annual Report of the Bureau of American Ethnology of the Smithsonian Institution. Washington, DC: Government Printing Office, 1903.

_____. "The Origin of White Corn"; "The Bean Woman (A Fragment)." In *Seneca Fiction, Legends, and Myths; Part 1 and 2*, by Jeremiah Curtain and J. N. B. Hewitt. Thirty-Second Annual Report of the Bureau of American Ethnology of the Smithsonian Institution. Washington, DC: Government Printing Office, 1918.

Audaname. "The Worship of the Sun." In *The Red Race*, by Henry Rowe Schoolcraft. New York, NY: [n.p.], 1847.

Bame-wa-wa-ge-zhik-a-quay (Jane Johnston Schoolcraft). "Moowis, the Indian Coquette." In *The Literary Voyageur or Muzzeniegun*, by Jane Johnston Schoolcraft and Henry Rowe Schoolcraft. Sault Ste. Marie, MI: 1826-1827.

_____. "Mishosha"; "The Forsaken Brother." In *Algic Researches, Comprising Inquiries Respecting the Mental Characteristics of the North American Indians*, by Henry Rowe Schoolcraft. 2 vols. 1839. Reprint. New York, NY: Garland, 1979.

Bear, John. "The Dogs of the Chief's Son." In *Year Book of the Public Museum of Milwaukee* 10 (February 19, 1932): 317-321.

Beauchamp, Rev. W. M. *Iroquois Folk-lore Gathered From the Six Nations of New York*. Syracuse, NY: Dahler, 1922.

Bécĭgwíwizäns. "Hunting Song." In *Chippewa Music*, by Frances Densmore. Smithsonian Institution. Bureau of American Ethnology Bulletin 45. Washington, DC: Government Printing Office, 1910.

Blackbird, Andrew J. *The Indian Problem from the Indian's Standpoint*. Harbor Springs, MI: Privately printed, 1900.

Blaeser, Kimberly. "Trailing You." In *Trailing You*. Greenfield Center, NY: Greenfield Press, 1994.

Bracklin, Edward. "The Legend of the Thunderbird." *The Red Man* 6:6 (February 1914): [n.p.].

Brightman, Robert A. *Ācaðōhkīwina and Ācimōwina: Traditional Narratives of the Rock Cree Indians*, Canadian Ethnology Service, Mercury Series Paper 113, Canadian Museum of Civilization, Hull, Quebec, 1989.

Broker, Ignatia. "Prologue: The Forest Cries." In *Night Flying Woman: An Ojibway Narrative*. St. Paul, MN: Minnesota Historical Society Press, 1983.

Chashchunka (Peter Sampson). "Waikun: A Fable." In *The Indians' Book*, by Natalie Curtis. New York, NY: Harper and Brothers, 1907.

Christley, Ronald L. *An Introduction to the Shawnee Language*, ed. 2. Newark, OH: self-published (deceased), 1995.

Chrystos. "I'm Making You Up." In *Not Vanishing*. Vancouver, BC: Press Gang Publishers, 1988.

Chusko. "Wassamo, or the Fire Plume." In *Algic Researches, Comprising Inquiries Respecting the Mental Characteristics of the North American Indians*, by Henry Rowe Schoolcraft. 2 vols. 1839. Reprint. New York, NY: Garland, 1979.

Clarke, Peter Dooyentate. "Traditional Wyandot History." In *Origin and Traditional History of the Wyandotts*. Toronto: Hunter, Rose, 1870.

Clifton, James. The Potawatomi. New York, NY: Chelsea House, 1987.

Cusick, David. "The Great Mosquito." In *Sketches of the Ancient History of the Six Nations*. Lewiston, NY: Privately published, 1827.

Dawendine (Bernice Loft Winslow). "The Dancing Stars, or the Pleiades"; "One, Two, Three." In *Iroquois Fires*. Ottawa, ON: Penumbra Press, 1995.

Deer, Ada. "The Power Came From the People." In *I Am the Fire of Time: The Voices of Native American Women*. New York, NY: Dutton, 1977.

Densmore, Frances. "Maple Sugar." In "Uses of Plants by the Chippewa Indians"; in Forty-Fourth Annual Report of the Bureau of American Ethnology of the Smithsonian Institution. 1926-1927. Reprint. New York, NY: Dover Publications, 1974.

_____. *Menomini Music*. Smithsonian Institution Bureau of American Ethnology Bulletin 102. Washington, DC: Government Printing Office, 1913.

Dunn, Anne M. "When Beaver Was Very Great." In *When Beaver Was Very Great: Stories To Live By*. Mount Horeb, WI: Midwest Traditions, 1995.

Ĕ´niwûb´e. "The Origin of Gambling." In *Chippewa Music II*, by Frances Densmore. Smithsonian Institution. Bureau of American Ethnology Bulletin 53. Washington, DC: Government Printing Office, 1913.

Erdrich, Louise. "Getting Nowhere Fast." In *The Bingo Palace*. New York, NY: HarperCollins, 1994.

Eshkwaykeezhik (James Red Sky, Jr.). "The Creation of the World." In *The Sacred Scrolls of the Southern Ojibway*, by Selwyn Dewdney. Toronto, ON: Toronto University Press, 1975.

Ettawageshik, Frank. "Ghost Suppers." Program, Festival of Michigan Folklife. Lansing, MI: Michigan State University Museum, 1992.

Ettawageshik, Fred. "Ghost Suppers." *American Anthropologist* n.s. 45 (1943): 491-493.

_____. "The Legend of Manitou Island and Sleeping Bear Point." Recorded by Jane Willets, Harbor Springs, Michigan, 1947. Ottawa Indian Manuscript. Library, American Philosophical Society, Philadelphia, Pennsylvania.

Fagan, Brian. *Ancient North America*. London, England: Thames & Hudson, 2000.

Gahadondeh. "The Ceremony of Gathering Herbs." Note 55:2 in *The Code of Handsome Lake, the Seneca Prophet*, edited and transcribed by Arthur C. Parker. Albany, NY: New York State Museum, 1913.

Gailland, Maurice. *Grammaire de la langue potêvatémie*. ms. NA 20 (Box X) Box 2 in Jesuit Missouri Province Archives, St. Louis, MO, 1868.

Ganiódaío' (John Arthur Gibson). *Concerning the League: The Iroquois League Tradition as Dictated in Onondaga*. Translated by Hanni Woodbury, Reg Henry, and Harry Webster from the manuscript of A. A. Goldenweiser. Algonquian and Iroquoian Linguistics, Memoir 9. Hull, Quebec: Canadian Museum of Civilization, 1992.

Gansworth, Eric. "My Hair was Shorter Then." In *Nickel Eclipse: Iroquois Moon*. Lansing, MI: Michigan State University Press, 2000.

Gawasowaneh (Arthur C. Parker). "The Seven Star Dancers." In *Seneca Myths and Folk Tales*. Buffalo, NY: Buffalo Historical Society, 1923.

Gegwédjiwébĭnûñ. "The Sky Clears. . . ." In *Chippewa Music*, by Frances Densmore. Smithsonian Institution Bureau of American Ethnology Bulletin 45. Washington, DC: Government Printing Office, 1910.

Hágaga (Sam Blowsnake/Carley). *The Autobiography of a Winnebago Indian*, by Paul Radin. University of California Publications in American Archaeology and Ethnology, 16:7 (April 15, 1920).

_____. "Teachings." In *The Winnebago Tribe* by Paul Radin. Thirty-Seventh Annual Report of the Bureau of American Ethnology of the Smithsonian Institution. Washington, DC: Government Printing Office, 1923.

_____. "Red Horn." In *Winnebago Hero Cycles: A Study in Aboriginal Literature*, by Paul Radin. Baltimore, MD: Waverly Press, 1948.

_____. *The Trickster*, by Paul Radin. New York, NY: Schocken Books, 1956.

Häh-shēh´träh (George Wright). "The Origin of the World." In *Wyandot Folklore*, by W. E. Connelley. Topeka, KS: Crane and Company, 1899.

Halftown, Truman, John Armstrong, and Henry Stevens. "The Origin of White Corn"; "The Bean Woman (A Fragment)." In *Seneca Fiction, Legends, and Myths; Part 1 and 2*, by Jeremiah Curtain and J. N. B. Hewitt. Thirty-Second Annual Report of the Bureau of American Ethnology of the Smithsonian Institution. Washington, DC: Government Printing Office, 1918.

Hall, Robert L. *An Archaeology of the Soul: North American Indian Belief and Ritual.* Urbana, IL: University of Illinois Press, 1997.

Halsey, John R. Personal Communication, 2009.

Handbook of North American Indians. William C. Sturtevant, General Editor. Washington, D.C. : Smithsonian Institution, 1978—present.

Hen´toh (B. N. O. Walker). "The Origin of the World." In *Huron-Wyandot Mythology*, by C. M. Barbeau. Canada Department of Mines Geological Survey Memoir 80, Anthropological Series, no.11. Ottawa, ON: Government Printing Bureau, 1915.

Hilger, Sister M. Inez. "Chippewa Child Life and its Cultural Background." Smithsonian Institution. *Bureau of American Ethnology Bulletin* 146. Washington, DC: Government Printing Office, 1951

Hinook Mahiwi Kilinaka (Angel DeCora). "The Sick Child." *Harper's New Monthly Magazine* 98 (February 1899): 446-448.

Hudaju (John Kayrahoo). "The Small Deer Charm"; "An Old Hunter's Reminiscences." In *Huron-Wyandot Mythology*, by C. M. Barbeau. Canada Department of Mines Geological Survey Memoir 80, Anthropological Series, no.11. Ottawa, ON: Government Printing Bureau, 1915.

Isaac, John. "Long Trail to the East." *Journal of American Folklore* 46 (October-December, 1933): 416.

Jameson, Anna. *Winter Studies and Summer Rambles in Canada.* 3 vols. London: Saunders and Otley, 1838.

Jiles, Paulette. *North Spirit: Travels Among the Cree and Ojibway Nations and Their Star Maps.* Toronto: Doubleday Canada, 1995.

Johnson, Elias. "Legendary." In *Legends, Traditions, and Laws of the Iroquois or Six Nations, and History of the Tuscarora Indians.* Lockpart, NY: Union Printing, 1881.

Johnston, Basil. "Personal Manitous and the Vision Quest"; "The Nature of Animals." *Ojibway Heritage.* Toronto, ON: McClelland and Stewart, 1976.

_____. "Weendigo"; "Personal Manitous." *The Manitous.* New York, NY: Harper Collins, 1995.

Josette, Shunien. "The Origin of Maple Sap"; "Stories of the Sky" In *The Menomini Indians*, by Walter Hoffman, M.D. Fourteenth Annual Report of the Bureau of Ethnology of the Smithsonian Institution. Washington, DC: Government Printing Office, 1896.

Jung, Patrick J. "Forge, Destroy, and Preserve the Bonds of Empire: Euro-Americans, Native Americans, and Métis on the Wisconsin Frontier, 1634-1856." MA thesis, Marquette University, 1997.

Kāgigē Pinase (John Penesi). "Now Great-Lynx." In *Ojibwa Texts*, by William Jones and Truman Michelson. 2 vols. Publications of the American Ethnological Society 7. New York: E. J. Brill, 1917, 1919.

Kah-Ge-Ga-Gah-Bowh (George Copway). *The Life, History, and Travels of Kah-Ge-Ga-Gah-Bowh.* Albany, NY: Privately printed, 1847.

Kaluskap the Master. "Song of the Stars." In *Algonquian Legends*, by Charles Leland. 1884. Reprint. New York, NY: Dover, 1992.

Kapahpwah (Clarence Godfroy). "Snowshoe Dance." In *Miami Indian Stories*, by Martha Una McClurg. Winona Lake, IN: L. W. Schultz, 1950.

Kéhachiwinga (Mountain Wolf Woman). "Livelihood." In *Mountain Wolf Woman.* Ann Arbor, MI: University of Michigan Press, 1961.

Keller, Robert H. "An Economic History of Indian Treaties in the great lakes Region." *American Indian Journal* 4 (February 1978): 2-20.

Ki´tcimak´wa. "Song for Securing a Good Supply of Maple Sugar." In *Chippewa Music*, by Frances Densmore. Smithsonian Institution Bureau of American Ethnology Bulletin 45. Washington, DC: Government Printing Office, 1910.

Kūgigēpināsi'kwä (Marie Syrette). "A Moose and His Offspring." In *Ojibwa Texts*, by William Jones and Truman Michelson. 2 vols. Publications of the American Ethnological Society 7. New York, NY: E. J. Brill, 1917, 1919.

LaDuke, Winona. "Under the Wild Rice Moon." In *The Winona LaDuke Reader*. Stillwater, MN: Voyageur Press, 2002.

Laidler, George. "A Huron Christmas Carole. Notes on Hymn 745 in the Anglican Book of Common Praise." Archives, Hamilton Public Library, Hamilton, ON. Undated typescript.

Lankford, George. *Reachable Stars: Patterns in the Ethnoastronomy of Eastern North America*. Tuscaloosa, AL: University of Alabama Press, 2007.

Le Gros. "Monaatoowaukēē—The Thunder Spirits." C. C. Trowbridge Manuscripts, Burton Historical Collections, Detroit Public Library, Detroit, Michigan. Reprint. *Meeārmeear Traditions*, edited by Vernon Kinietz. Ann Arbor, MI: University of Michigan Press, 1938.

Leland, Charles. "Song of the Stars." *Algonquian Legends*. 1884. Reprint. New York, NY: Dover 1992.

Lewis, G. Malcolm. "Geological Interpretation of Red Sky's Migration Chart," "The Indigenous Maps and Mapping of North American Indians," *The Map Collector* 9 (December 1979): 27.

Lone Wolf. "The Seventh Fire." In *Ritual and Myth in Odawa Revitalization*, by Melissa A. Pflüg. Norman, OK: University of Oklahoma Press, 1998.

Lyons, Oren. "Sovereignty and the Natural World Economy." In *Justice for Natives: Searching for Common Ground*, edited by Andrea Morrison. Montreal, QC: McGill-Queen's University Press, 1997.

Majigikwewis (Rose Mary Shingobe Barstow). "Who Was Really the Savage?" Minneapolis, MN: Minneapolis Public Schools, 1979.

Ma-ka-tai-me-she-kia-kiak (Black Hawk). *Life of Ma-ka-tai-me-she-kia-kiak or Black Hawk*. 1834. Reprint. New York, NY: Dover, 1994.

Mandarong (Joseph White and Mrs. White). "The Legend of the Thunderers." *Journal of American Folklore* 4:15 (October-December, 1891): 289-294.

Maracle, David Kanatawakhon. *One Thousand Useful Mohawk Words*. Guilford, CT: Audio-Forum, 1992

Martin, Pete. "The Underwater Lion." In *Wisconsin Chippewa Myths and Tales and Their Relation to Chippewa Life*, by Victor Barnouw. Madison, WI: University of Wisconsin Press, 1977.

Martin, Susan. *Wonderful Power*. Detroit, MI: Wayne State University Press, 1999.

Maskwawā´nahkwatōk (Louise Dutchman). "Getting Bounty from the English"; "The Origin of the Dream-Dance"; "The Women of the Eastern Sky." In *Menomini Texts*, by Leonard Bloomfield. Publications of the American Ethnological Society, vol. 12. New York, NY: G. E. Stechert, 1928.

McDougall, Mike. "Wolf." In *Angwamas Minosewag Anishinabeg—Time of the Indian*. Minnesota Chippewa Tribe: St. Paul, MN: COMPAS, 1977.

Mec´kawigábau. "He is Gone." In *Chippewa Music II*, by Frances Densmore. Smithsonian Institution Bureau of American Ethnology Bulletin 53. Washington, DC: Government Printing Office, 1913.

Michelson, Truman. "Fox miscellany." Smithsonian Institution. *Bureau of American Ethnology Bulletin* 114. Washington, DC: Government Printing Office, 1937

Midāsuganj. "Nänabushu and the Mallard." In *Ojibwa Texts*, by William Jones and Truman Michelson. 2 vols. Publications of the American Ethnological Society 7. New York, NY: E. J. Brill, 1917, 1919.

Miller, Aurelia Jones. "The Stone Giants"; "The Coming of Spring." In *Seneca Myths and Folk Tales*, by Arthur C. Parker. Buffalo, NY: Buffalo Historical Society, 1923.

Miller, Dorcas S. *Stars of the First People.* Boulder, CO: Pruett Publishing Company, 1977.

Mononcue. "Speech." *The Indian and the White Man; or, the Indian in Self-Defense*, by D. W. Risher. Indianapolis: Carlon & Hollenbeck, 1880.

Nabinoi. "Addik Kum Maig." In *Algic Researches, Comprising Inquiries Respecting the Mental Characteristics of the North American Indians*, by Henry Rowe Schoolcraft. 2 vols. 1839. Reprint. New York: Garland, 1979.

Nabunwa. "The Magician of Lake Huron." In *Oneota, or the Red Race of America*, by Henry Schoolcraft. NewYork, NY: [n.p.], 1847.

Näkuti. "Origin of the Menominee." In Anthropological Papers of the American Museum of Natural History. vol.13, pt.1, by Alanson Skinner. New York: Trustees of the American Museum of Natural History, 1913.

Náwajíbigókwe. "The Origin of the Midé." In *Chippewa Music I*, by Frances Densmore. Smithsonian Institution Bureau of American Ethnology Bulletin 45. Washington, DC: Government Printing Office, 1913.

Nehtsī'wihtuk (Charles Dutchman). "The Birth of Menapus." In *Menomini Texts*, by Leonard Bloomfield. Publications of the American Ethnological Society, vol 12. New York, NY: G. E. Stechert, 1928.

Nichols, John D. "'Chant to the Firefly': A Philological Problem in Ojibwe." In *Linguistic Studies Presented to John L. Finlay*, edited by H. C. Wolfart. *Algonquian and Iroquoian Linguistics Memoir* 8 (1991): 113-126.

Northrup, Jim. "Barbed Thoughts"; "Jabbing and Jabbering." In *Walking the Rez Road.* Minneapolis, MN: Voyager Press, 1995.

Oshcabewis (Paul DeMain). "Chai Vang and Relationships in the Wisconsin Northwoods." *News From Indian Country*, September 28, 2005.

Oshkosh, Niopet. "The Origin of Maple Sap"; "Mashenomak, the Great Fish." In *The Menomini Indians*, by Walter Hoffman, M.D. Fourteenth Annual Report of the Bureau of American Ethnology of the Smithsonian Institution. Washington, DC: Government Printing Office, 1896.

Parker, Ely S. "Maple Feast." In *Iroquois Folk Lore: Gathered from the Six Nations of New York*, by W. M. Beauchamp. Syracuse, NY: Dehler, 1922.

Pä-skin´. "The Bear Maiden." In *The Wild Rice Gatherers of the Upper Lakes*, by Albert Jenks. Nineteenth Annual Report of the Bureau of American Ethnology of the Smithsonian Institution. Washington, DC: Government Printing Office, 1897-1898.

Pokagon, Chief Simon. *O-Gi-Maw-Kwe Mit-i-Gwa-Ki: (Queen of the Woods).* Hartford, MI: C. H. Engle, Publisher, 1901.

Pontiac. Speech, May 5, 1763; Speech, July 1, 1763. The Navarre Journals. Burton Historical Collections, Detroit Public Library, Detroit, MI.

Power, Susan. "Lake of Dreams." *The Utne Reader* 79 (January-February 1997): 82-111.

Ramsey, Jarold. *Coyote Was Going There: Indian Literature of the Oregon Country.* Seattle, WA: University of Washington Press, 1977.

Rave, John, Warudjáxega (Terrible Thunder-Crash, Jasper Blowsnake), Hágaga (Big Winnebago, Sam Blowsnake/Carley). "Teachings." In *The Winnebago Tribe* by Paul Radin. Thirty-Seventh Annual Report of the Bureau of American Ethnology of the Smithsonian Institution. Washington, DC: Government Printing Office, 1923.

Rockwell, David. *Giving Voice to Bear.* Lanham, MD: Roberts Rinehart, 1991.

Rolo, Mark Anthony. "We Are Still Here." Madison, WI: Progressive Media Project, 2000.

Schoolcraft, Henry Rowe. "Chant to the Firefly." In *Oneota, or the Red Race of America.* New York, NY: [n.p.], 1847.

Sioui, Christine. "The Diaspora." Manuscript, 2004.

Sioui, Linda. "Danse Sacréé." Manuscript, 2005.

Skanawati (John Buck). "The Origin of the World." In *Iroquoian Cosmology, First Part,* by J. N. B. Hewitt. Twenty-First Annual Report of the Bureau of American Ethnology of the Smithsonian Institution. Washington, DC: Government Printing Office, 1903.

_____. "Dead Feasts." In *Iroquois Folk Lore: Gathered from the Six Nations of New York,* by W. M. Beauchamp. Syracuse, NY: Dehler, 1922.

Skinner, Alason. Alanson Skinner. "Social Life and Ceremonial Bundles of the Menomini Indians." Anthropological Papers of the American Museum of Natural History, vol. 13, pt 1. New York, NY: Museum of Natural History, 1913.

_____. "Lacrosse." In *Folklore of the Menomini Indians.* Anthropological Papers of The American Museum of Natural History, vol.13, pt 3. New York, NY: Museum of Natural History, 1915.

Smith, David Lee. "The Evening Star"; "The Legend of Hopoekaw"; "How Graywolf Became Guardian of the World." In *Folklore of the Winnebago Tribe,* by David Lee Smith. Norman, OK: University of Oklahoma Press, 1997.

Sosondowa (Edward Cornplanter). *The Code of Handsome Lake, the Seneca Prophet,* edited and transcribed by Arthur C. Parker. Albany, NY: New York State Museum, 1913.

_____. "The False Face Society." In *Seneca Myths and Folk Tales,* by Arthur C. Parker. Albany, NY: New York State Museum, 1913.

Steckley, John. "The Huron Carol." Unpublished manuscript.

Stevens, Henry, Truman Halftown, and John Armstrong. "The Origin of White Corn"; "The Bean Woman (A Fragment)." In *Seneca Fiction, Legends, and Myths; Part 1 and 2,* by Jeremiah Curtain and J. N. B. Hewitt. Thirty-Second Annual Report of the Bureau of American Ethnology of the Smithsonian Institution. Washington, DC: Government Printing Office, 1918.

Stevens, James Aronhiotas Thomas. "*Iah Enoinkwatewennahton´se´* : We Will Not Lose Our Words." In *Genocide of the Mind: New Native American Writing,* edited by MariJo Moore. New York, NY: Thunder's Mouth Press, 2003.

Sweet, Denise. "Dancing the Rice." In *Returning the Gift,* edited by Joseph Bruchac. Tuscon, AZ: University of Arizona Press, 1994.

Tecumseh. "Speech at Vincennes," August 15, 1810. Draper Series YY, the Tecumseh Papers, Draper Manuscripts. Wisconsin Historical Society, Madison, Wisconsin.

Tekahionwake (E. Pauline Johnson). "The Corn Husker." In *Canadian Born.* Toronto, ON: George Morang, 1903.

Tenskwatawa. "Meskwaunkwāātar"; "Pukeelāūwau." Trowbridge Manuscripts. Wisconsin Historical Society, Madison, Wisconsin.

Thunderbird Clan. "Warfare." In *The Winnebago Tribe* by Paul Radin. Thirty-Seventh Annual Report of the Bureau of American Ethnology of the Smithsonian Institution. Washington, DC: Government Printing Office, 1923.

Tremblay, Gail. "Sehià:rak." In *New Voices from the Longhouse,* edited by Joseph Bruchac. Greenfield Center, NY: Greenfield Review Press, 1989.

Treuer, David. *The Hiawatha.* New York: Picador, 1999.

Trigger, Bruce. *The Children of Aataentsic.* Montreal, QE: McGill-Queen's University Press, 1976.

Unidentified Anishinabe. "The Red Swan." In *Algic Researches, Comprising Inquiries Respecting the Mental Characteristics of the North American Indians,* by Henry Rowe Schoolcraft. 2 vols. 1839. Reprint. New York, NY: Garland, 1979.

Unidentified Haudenosaunee. "The Pole Star." In *Myths of the Iroquois,* by Erminnie A. Smith. Second Annual Report of the Bureau of American Ethnology for the Years 1880-1881. Washington, DC: Government Printing Office, 1883.

Unidentified Menominee. "Manabus Frightened by the Birds"; "Lacrosse"; "The Boy Who Caught the Sun"; "Origin of the Dipper." In *Folklore of the Menomini Indians*, by Alanson Skinner and John Satterlee. Anthropological Papers of The American Museum of Natural History, vol.13, pt 3. New York, NY: Museum of Natural History, 1915.

Unidentified Meskwaki. "The Coming of Death." In "Episodes in the Culture-Hero Myth of the Sauks and Foxes," by William Jones. *Journal of American Folklore* 14 (October-December 1901): 225-238.

_____. "How Turtle Lost His Place Among the Great Manitous." In *Ethnography of the Fox Indians*, by William Jones and Margaret Welpley Fisher. Smithsonian Institution Bureau of American Ethnology Bulletin 125. Washington, DC: US Government Printing Office, 1939.

_____. "They That Chase After the Bear." In *Fox Texts*, by William Jones. Leyden: E. J. Brill, 1907.

Unidentified Odawa. "Peeta Kway." In *Algic Researches, Comprising Inquiries Respecting the Mental Characteristics of the North American Indians*, by Henry Rowe Schoolcraft. 2 vols. 1839. Reprint. New York, NY: Garland, 1979.

Unidentified Ojibwe. "The Lone Lightning." In *The Red Race*, by Henry Rowe Schoolcraft. New York, NY: [n.p.], 1847.

Unidentified Potawatomi. "The Enchanted Bears." In *The Mascoutens or Prairie Potawatomi Indians: Part III—Mythology and Folklore*, by Alanson Skinner. Bulletin of the Public Museum of the City of Milwaukee 6:3 (January 22, 1927): 327-411.

Unidentified Seneca. "The Chestnut Tree Guarded by the Seven Sisters." In *Seneca Fiction, Legends, and Myths, Part 2*, by Jeremiah Curtain and J. N. B. Hewitt. Thirty-Second Annual Report of the Bureau of American Ethnology of the Smithsonian Institution. Washington, DC: Government Printing Office, 1918.

Unidentified Wendat. "How The Wyandot Obtained the Tobacco Plant." In *Wyandot Folklore*, by W. E. Connelley. Topeka, KS: Crane & Company, 1899.

Vizenor, Gerald. "I Know What You Mean, Erdupps MacChurbbs: Autobiographical Myths and Metaphors." In *Growing Up in Minnesota: Ten Writers Remember Their Childhoods*, edited by Chester Anderson. Minneapolis, MN: University of Minnesota Press, 1976.

Warren, William. "Ending of the French Supremacy." In *History of the Ojibway People*. 1885. Reprint. St. Paul, MN: Minnesota Historical Society, 1984.

Warudjáxega (Terrible Thunder-Crash, Jasper Blowsnake), Hágaga (Big Winnebago, Sam Blowsnake/ Carley), and John Rave. "Teachings." In *The Winnebago Tribe* by Paul Radin. Thirty-Seventh Annual Report of the Bureau of American Ethnology of the Smithsonian Institution. Washington, DC: Government Printing Office, 1923.

Wāsāgunäckank. "Nänabushu and the Wolves"; "The Death of Nänabushu's Nephew"; "Nänabushu Slays Toadwoman, Healer of the Manitous'; "Star of the Fisher." In *Ojibwa Texts*, by William Jones and Truman Michelson. 2 vols. Publications of the American Ethnological Society 7. New York, NY: E. J. Brill, 1917, 1919.

White, Richard. *The Middle Ground*. New York, NY: Cambridge University Press, 1991.

Williams, Ted. C. "The Reservoir." In *The Reservation*. Syracuse, NY: Syracuse University Press, 1976.

Wyman, Walker D. *The Chippewa: A History of the Great Lakes Woodland Tribe Over Three Centuries*. River Falls, WI: University of Wisconsin-River Falls Press, 1993.

Yäh-rohn-yäh-äh-wih (Deer is Sailing in the Sky, Catherine Coon Johnson). "The Origin of the Sun-Shower"; "A War Adventure." In *Huron-Wyandot Traditional Narratives*, by Marius Barbeau. National Museum of Canada Bulletin 165, series 47. Canada: Department of Northern Affairs and National Resources, 1960.

Young Bear, Ray A. "The Significance of a Water Animal"; "The Language of Weather." *Tamaqua* 2:2 (Winter/Spring 1991): 30-31.

ACKNOWLEDGMENTS
▼▼▼▼▼▼▼▼▼▼▼▼▼▼▼▼

Water Spirit, 1972, by Norval Morrisseau (1932-2007), his name in modified Cree syllabic letters for Ojibwe *Osâwâbikobinesi*, or Copper Thunderbird, courtesy Gabe Vadas and the Canadian Museum of Civilization; *The Diaspora*, courtesy Claudine Sioui; GREAT LAKES NATIVE LITERATURES: "When Beaver Was Very Great," permission Midwest Tradition Books; giant beaver skeleton by Dominique Dufour, permission of Canadian Museum of Nature, Ottawa; Paleo-Indian points by G. Gillette for Vol. 15, p. 21, in *Handbook of North American Indians*, Smithsonian Institution; Old Copper Culture tools, courtesy George Stuber; "The Legend of Manitou Island and Sleeping Bear Point," by Fred Ettawageshik, courtesy American Philosophical Society Library. WINTER: John Buck, courtesy National Anthropological Archives, Smithsonian Institution; "Indian Graves at the Mouth of the St. Peters," courtesy Minnesota Historical Society; B. N. O. Walker, courtesy of Research Division, Oklahoma Historical Society; *The Significance of a Water Animal*, courtesy Parkland College; *Trailing You*, courtesy Greenfield Review Press; Sam Blowsnake, courtesy Wisconsin Historical Society; Otter skin medicine bag, courtesy Detroit Institute of Arts; *Ball Play on the Ice*, courtesy The Minnesota Historical Society; John Gibson and Edward Cornplanter, courtesy National Museum of the American Indian, Smithsonian Institution; "Thatótáho," courtesy Iroquois Indian Museum; "The Seventh Fire," courtesy University of Oklahoma Press; "The Dancing Stars," courtesy Penumbra Press; *Danse Sacrée*, courtesy Linda Sioui; "Weendigo," courtesy HarperCollins; Hinook Mahiwi Kilinaka (Angel De Cora), courtesy Cumberland County Historical Society. SPRING: *Indian Sugar Camp, Dacota Village, Midé Lodge*, courtesy Clarke Library, Central Michigan University; Kéhachiwinga (Mountain Wolf Woman), courtesy Wisconsin Historical Society; "Walking the Rez Road," courtesy Voyageur Press; *Fishing by Torchlight*, courtesy Royal Ontario Museum; *Removal of the Indiana Pottawatomi in 1838*, courtesy Tippecanoe County Historical Association; *Tenskwatawa*, courtesy Smithsonian American Art Museum; *I'm Making You Up*, courtesy Chrystos; from *Night Flying Woman*, courtesy Minnesota Historical Society; from *The Hiawatha*, David Treuer, courtesy Macmillan/Picador; *I Know What You Mean, Erdupps MacChurbbs*, courtesy University of Minnesota Press. SUMMER: "The Underwater Lion," courtesy University of Wisconsin Press; *Canoe of Indians*, courtesy St. Louis County Historical Society; *Fishing by Torchlight*, courtesy Royal Ontario Museum; "The Evening Star," courtesy University of Oklahoma Press; *George Copway*, courtesy Coburg Public Library; Drum (or Dream) Dance drum, courtesy Milwaukee Public Museum; *Mononcue*, courtesy Sallie Cotter Andrews; "Personal Manitous and the Vision Quest," "Getting Nowhere Fast," courtesy HarperCollins; *Guarding the Corn-fields*, courtesy Clarke Library, Central Michigan University; *Dancing the Rice*, courtesy Denise Sweet. FALL: From *Mountain Wolf Woman*, courtesy University of Michigan Press; "Who Was Really the Savage?" courtesy Minneapolis Public Schools; *Sehià:rak*, courtesy Calyx Press; *My Hair Was Shorter Then*, courtesy Michigan State University Press; *Black Hawk*, courtesy Smithsonian American Art Museum; from *The Reservation*, courtesy Syracuse University Press; "Sovereignty and the Natural World Economy," courtesy McGill-Queen's University Press; "The Nature of Animals," courtesy McClelland & Stewart; "One, Two, Three," courtesy Penumbra Press; "How Graywolf Became Guardian of the

World," courtesy University of Oklahoma Press; *Snowshoe Dance at the First Snowfall*, courtesy Smithsonian American Art Museum; "Chai Vang and Relationships in the Wisconsin Northwoods," courtesy Paul DeMain; *Wolf*, courtesy Mike McDougall; "Ghost Suppers" and photos of Fred and Frank Ettawageshik, courtesy Frank Ettawageshik; "We Are Still Here," courtesy *The Progressive*.

WITH GRATEFUL THANKS

This book began with a fellowship from the National Endowment for the Humanities, which gave me a year free from teaching to begin the decade-long process of learning about Great Lakes indigenous literatures. Unfortunately I failed to obtain the names of many librarians in the USA and Canada who helped me, but I wish to thank particularly reference librarians who generously gave their time and expertise at the University of Toronto, the Ontario Archives, the Hamilton, Ontario, Public Library, the Wisconsin Historical Collections, the Minnesota Historical Society, the Bentley Historical Library at the University of Michigan, the Burton Historical Collections of the Detroit Public Library, the Clarke Historical Library at Central Michigan University, Calvin College, the Western Reserve Historical Collections, the American Philosophical Society, and the Library of Congress. Two research assistants, Stacey and Jeanne, organized me. John Halsey, State of Michigan archaeologist, patiently kept me from making grievous mistakes. John Steckley, a contemporary scholar of Huron, was always generous with his time and answers to questions. Jean Moon of the Wyandot Mission Committee of the John Stewart United Methodist Church in Upper Sandusky, Ohio, and Sallie Cotter Andrews were helpful with Huron-Wendat materials. Dominique Dufour was kind enough to take a photo of a giant beaver skeleton in the Canadian Museum of Nature, including conscripting his family to pose. John Newman of Kinsman-Robinson Galleries in Toronto made it possible for me to obtain rights to reproduce the Norval Morrisseu painting on the cover. Linda Sioui, of the Wendake Writers Group, remained patient and helpful as the years passed, providing me with information, contacts, and support whenever I asked.

The manuscript was sent to Native readers from Great Lakes nations who were willing to designate a reader. For their unfailing generosity and devoted attentiveness, I would like to thank Frank Ettawageshik of the Odawa, Tom Topash of the Potawatomi, Joyce King of the Haudenosaunee, David Grignon of the Menominee, Linda Sioui of the Huron-Wendat, Paul DeMain of the Oneida, and Basil Johnston of the Anishinâbe. Algonquianist Ives Goddard, now retired from the Smithsonian Institution, provided essential leads to experts and some etymologies. Ethnologist Nicholas Smith and linguist Conor McDonough Quinn, having worked with Penobscot and other Algonquian languages, provided some background to the poem "The Song of the Stars." Other linguists, such as Richard Rhodes, John D. Nichols, J. Randy Valentine, John E. Koontz, and Johannes Helmbrecht, gave valuable help without hesitation.

My greatest thanks, however, must go to Loretta Crum, Esq. of the Boreal Press and Carl Masthay, linguist and Algonquianist of St. Louis, Missouri, who came to this book at a critical juncture and, working for small pay and strawberry jam, helped bring it to completion. Without their gifts of time and their advice on etymologies and factual matters, this book would not be. Any remaining mistakes are the editor's.

Of the many others who helped by listening sympathetically during the twelve years it took to complete this book, Sharon Dean, John Haskin, and Diana VanAntwerp deserve especial thanks. And lastly, my gratitude to Dancer, Carlo, Bella, and BlackJack, who waited patiently.

EDITING NOTES

Terms Used for Native Peoples: As everyone learns in grade school, "Indian" was the name Columbus used to refer to the indigenous or (always-capitalized) Native peoples of North America when he met them in 1492 because he mistakenly believed that he had landed on the coast of India. The indigenous peoples of this continent had nothing linguistically or culturally in common with the residents of India, but as the old "Indian" joke tells it, "Be thankful for small favors. At least Columbus didn't land in Turkey."

There are several words used to refer to the indigenous peoples of North America. Since no term is acceptable to everyone, I have used "Native" when possible, with the exception of "Native American," which has come to mean a Native person from the USA. The term "indigenous" is actually the most accurate. Except for modernizing Native languages and updating punctuation, the texts have been left as they were originally published; many use the term "Indian." Persons whose ancestors were Euro-American as well as Native are usually referred to as Métis (/may-TEE/) in Canada and as mixed-blood or mixed descent in the USA. Because "mixed-blood" is a derogatory term coined by slave owners in the US South, I have used Métis for all Euro-Native peoples though it is seldom used in the USA. Most persons with some Native heritage refer to themselves with a Native nation designation, and I have respected that whenever possible.

The blend word "Amerindian" arose in the late 1800s in Smithsonian Institution publications by Americanists. The word also appears in Quebec French as "*amérindien/enne*" rather frequently, far more than in USA publications. The term "Amerind" is strictly linguistic and restricted to use by "lumpers" in language classification, but it has spread to recent genetic studies as if there were only four or five Amerindian groups since the last ice age. "Amerind" should not be used in culture studies.

Artists in this book are listed by their Native names whenever possible; not all writers have Native names or were willing to share them. Native people might have several personal names during one lifetime. Names can be changed at initiation ceremonies, as part of a healing ceremony to fool evil spirits, or to mark an accomplishment. English names are listed after Native ones in the Bibliography to facilitate using other sources where Native names are missing or difficult to find.

Indigenous-language Words: Words in indigenous languages have been left as they were first printed unless more accurate spellings or meanings could be supplied. This may be confusing for several reasons. Different nations from different language families used different words for the same creatures or concepts. Fashions in writing Native languages, which were not written until after Contact, have changed through time, and so early texts sometimes have words syllabifically divided by hyphens (instead of by morpheme, or sense unit); later ones have diacritic marks often following a word style now left behind. Some writers left out pronunciation guides entirely. Spelling differs in the USA and Canada. When possible the editors have listed the original spelling first, followed by the more accurate term and any translations with or without parentheses. Long translations and commentary on meanings have been put in the endnotes.

Birth and Death Dates: The editor has endeavored to give birth and death dates for all contributors. Some lack dates for one or more of the following reasons: no dates were ever recorded; the records are sealed to persons who are not enrolled band or nation members; finding dates would require extensive research on the part of band or nation archivists and no personnel could be made available.

LITERATURE INDEX
▼▼▼▼▼▼▼▼▼▼▼▼▼▼▼

BY GENRE
STORY

PERSONAL NARRATIVE

POETRY AND SONG

INDEX

For literature listed by nation and genre, please see Literature Index